EUROPEAN ENCOUNTERS

ALBERT LOVETT

First published 2003 by
UNIVERSITY COLLEGE DUBLIN PRESS
Newman House, 86 St Stephen's Green
Dublin 2, Ireland
www.ucdpress.ie

© the editors and contributors, 2003

ISBN 1-900621-87-8

All rights reserved. No part of this publication
may be reproduced, stored in a retrieval
system, or transmitted in any form or by any means,
electronic, photocopying, recording
or otherwise without the prior
permission of the publisher.

Cataloguing in Publication data available from the British Library

Typeset in Ireland in Plantin and Fournier
by Elaine Shiels, Bantry, Co. Cork

Text design by Lyn Davies

Index by Helen Litton

Printed on acid-free paper in England by

MPG Books, Bodmin, Cornwall

European Encounters

Essays in Memory of Albert Lovett

edited by
JUDITH DEVLIN
and
HOWARD B. CLARKE

UNIVERSITY COLLEGE DUBLIN PRESS
PREAS CHOLÁISTE OLLSCOILE
BHAILE ÁTHA CLIATH

Et las tres artes del triuio como dixiemos ensenna a omne seer bien razonado, et las quatro del quadruuio le fazen sabio, et estos otros tres saberes, con aquellos, le fazen complido e acabado en bondad e le aduzen a aquella bien auenturança empos la que non a otra.

King Alfonso X, *General Estoria* Parte Iª, Libro VII, Capítulo XXXIX

Vive en este volumen el que yace
en aquel mármol, colega glorioso;
sus cenizas allí tienen reposo,
y dellas hoy él mismo aquí renace.

Luis de Góngora y Argote, 1614 (adapted)

Contents

Illustrations		ix
Contributors to this volume		xi
Acknowledgements		xiii
Introduction		1

1 Albert Lovett (1944–2000): *An Appreciation* — 5
HUGH GOUGH

HISTORIOGRAPHY

2 1066, 1169 and All That: *The Tyranny of Historical Turning Points* — 11
HOWARD B. CLARKE

3 The Reputation of a King: *Edward II from Chronicle and Written Record to Compact Disc and Internet* — 37
SEYMOUR PHILLIPS

4 The Lombard League: *History and Myth* — 55
EDWARD COLEMAN

5 A Typical Anomaly? *The Success of the Irish Counter-Reformation* — 78
TADHG Ó hANNRACHÁIN

POLITICS AND DIPLOMACY

6 Irish–European Integration: *The Legacy of Charles V* — 97
DECLAN M. DOWNEY

7 A Lawyer in Politics: *The Career of Sir Richard Nagle c.1636–1699* — 118
JAMES MCGUIRE

8 Ireland and Colonial America: *The Viewer and the Viewed* — 132
MAURICE J. BRIC

9 Towards Democracy: *Irish-born Elites in Canada and the United States 1820–1920* — 155
DAVID DOYLE

Contents

10 The Anglo-American Alliance and the Irish Question *185*
in the Twentieth Century
RONAN FANNING

11 Britain's Second EEC Application: *The Irish Dynamic* *221*
JANE TOOMEY

CULTURE

12 A Sailor on the Seas of Faith: *The Individual and the Church in* *239*
'The Voyage of Máel Dúin'
ELVA JOHNSTON

13 Medical Men and Learned Societies in Ireland, 1680–1785 *253*
EAMON O'FLAHERTY

14 'Precedent Covenants': *Daniel Maclise's 'Marriage of Strongbow* *270*
and Aoife' and the Writers of Irish History
JOHN MCCAFFERTY

15 Newman's Dream Realised: *Elgar, Gerontius and the Catholic* *282*
Origins of Modern Englishness
RICHARD ALDOUS

16 'La Révolution Introuvable': *Raymond Aron, May 1968 and* *299*
Symbolic Violence in the French Revolutionary Tradition
DAVID KERR

17 Nature and Nationalism in Modern Ireland *316*
MARY E. DALY

18 The *Wehrmacht* Exhibition and the Politics of History *336*
in Germany
WILLIAM MULLIGAN

19 The City as Symbol: *Architecture and Ideology* *363*
in Post-Soviet Moscow
JUDITH DEVLIN

Index *405*

Illustrations

Frontispiece: Albert Lovett

Between pp. 274 and 275

1. Guinness advertisement of 1966 commemorating the nine hundredth anniversary of the battle of Hastings.
2. Daniel Maclise, *The Marriage of Strongbow and Aoife*.
3. and 4   Details from Maclise's *Marriage of Strongbow and Aoife*: Strongbow, the reluctant Aoife and her father, Diarmait Mac Murchada, and Strongbow's followers.
5. and 6   Microscopic drawings by Edward Barry and an anonymous archaeological drawing which together illustrate the wide range of activities of Irish learned societies of the mid-eighteenth century.
7. Eugène Delacroix, *Liberty Guiding the People* (1830).
8. Dembour and Gangel, *February 1848*.
9. Barricades before the attack. Rue St Maur, 25 June 1848.
10. J. L. E. Meissonier, *The Barricade: Memory of Civil War* (1849).
11. and 12   Alfred Rethel, *The Dance of Death of the Year 1849*.
13. Soviet prisoner of war, Heidelager, Oerbke, 1941.
14. The *Wehrmacht* and genocide in Tarnopol.
15. 'Not war in the conventional sense'. Photo of the second exhibition, Berlin, 2001–2.
16. Paul Henry, *The Potato Diggers*.
17. Paul Henry, *In the West of Ireland*.
18. Falconet's monument to Peter the Great in St Petersburg.
19. Zurab Tsereteli, Peter the Great, Moscow.
20. The removal of the Dzerzhinsky monument, Moscow, August 1991.
21. Dzerzhinsky in the Garden of Sculptures of the Era of Totalitarianism.
22. Head of Lenin, Ulan Ude, still in place in 1996.
23. V. Klykov, Monument to Marshal Zhukov at the entrance to Red Square.
24. Poklonnaya Gora, indicating the scale of the memorial.
25. Zurab Tsereteli, St George, Victory Monument.
26. The rebuilt Kazan Cathedral on Red Square.

Illustrations

27 The rebuilt Cathedral of Christ the Saviour.
28 St Sergei Radonezh blessing St Dmitri Donskoi on the eve of the battle of Kulikovo field, Cathedral of Christ the Saviour.
29 Popular shrine at the site of the Ipatiev House, Yekaterinburg.

Contributors to this volume

DR RICHARD ALDOUS teaches modern British history. He has written extensively on British politics and culture, most recently in *Tunes of glory: the life of Malcolm Sargent*. He is currently working on a study of political rivalry in the age of Gladstone and Disraeli.

DR MAURICE J. BRIC, MRIA, is a graduate of University College Cork and the Johns Hopkins University. He has published on the history and culture of eighteenth-century Ireland and America, and his *Ireland and America: the economy of an emigration, 1760–1800* will be published later this year.

DR HOWARD B. CLARKE has worked mainly on the local history of the county of Provence, the English west midlands, and Dublin and its hinterland in the Middle Ages. His Irish Historic Towns Atlas fascicle *Dublin, part I, to 1610* was published recently.

DR EDWARD COLEMAN is a specialist in the history of the Italian city communes in the twelfth and thirteenth centuries. He has published recently on communal historiography, relations between the communes and the papacy, and the concept of civic identity. He is currently preparing a study of Cremona.

PROFESSOR MARY E. DALY, MRIA, has published extensively on her research areas: the Great Famine, the urban history of Ireland in the nineteenth and twentieth centuries, economic and social history and public policy in twentieth-century Ireland, and women and work both in Ireland and elsewhere in modern Europe.

DR JUDITH DEVLIN has written on nineteenth-century French popular culture and on contemporary Russian history. Her most recent publication is *Slavophiles and commissars: the enemies of democracy in contemporary Russia* (1999). She is currently working on a study of the Stalin cult.

DR DECLAN M. DOWNEY lectures in modern European and Asian history. His specialist interests lie in the Irish émigré elite in the Habsburg Netherlands, Spain and Austria, and in Japanese-European relations. He is co-director of the Database Project on Irishmen in the Spanish and Austrian Military Service.

DR DAVID DOYLE, a Dubliner, has taught American history at University College Dublin since his return from the United States in 1973. His publications include *Ireland, Irishmen and revolutionary America, 1760–1820* (1981) and, with others, *Irish immigrants in the land of Canaan* (2003).

PROFESSOR RONAN FANNING, MRIA, head of the Department of Modern History, is a specialist in the fields of British-Irish relations and Irish foreign policy. He is a co-editor of the Royal Irish Academy's *Documents on Irish foreign policy* (three volumes to date).

Contributors to this volume

PROFESSOR HUGH GOUGH teaches courses in the history of modern Europe and of twentieth-century France in particular. His main research area is the French Revolution and one of his major publications is *The newspaper press in the French Revolution* (1988).

DR ELVA JOHNSTON lectures in early medieval Irish history. Her research interests include church history, the history of sexuality, literacy in early medieval Ireland, and medieval travel literature. She has published on sexuality and sanctity, and is currently completing a monograph on literacy.

DR DAVID KERR is currently writing a cultural history of revolution in nineteenth-century France. He has previously published *Caricature and French political culture 1830–1848* (2000). His research interests also include the history of Paris and of nineteenth-century popular theatre.

DR JOHN MCCAFFERTY's research interests include the late medieval church in Ireland and the Church of Ireland in the sixteenth and seventeenth centuries. He is the director of the Micheál Ó Cléirigh Institute for the Study of Irish History and Civilisation at University College Dublin.

MR JAMES MCGUIRE is an early modernist, with a special interest in the history of Irish politics and of Anglo-Irish relations in the later seventeenth century. He is currently managing editor of the Royal Irish Academy's *Dictionary of Irish biography*.

DR WILLIAM MULLIGAN has published extensively on civil-military relations in the Weimar Republic. He is currently writing a biography of General Walther Reinhardt, the first head of Army Command in Weimar Germany. His research also extends more broadly into international relations in the modern period.

DR EAMON O'FLAHERTY specialises in early modern continental history, with particular reference to French intellectual history in the seventeenth and eighteenth centuries and to the social history of ideas. He is also interested in eighteenth-century Ireland and in the history of his native Limerick.

DR TADHG Ó HANNRACHÁIN teaches in the fields of early modern Ireland and the history of the Middle East. His current research area is the European Counter-Reformation. His monograph *Catholic reformation in Ireland: the mission of Rinuccini 1645–1649* was published recently.

PROFESSOR SEYMOUR PHILLIPS, MRIA, acting head of the Department of Medieval History, is also the current chairman of the Combined Departments of History. His research interests are thirteenth- and fourteenth-century Britain and Ireland, war and society in medieval Europe, and relations between medieval Europe and the wider world.

DR JANE TOOMEY has published on the question of Ireland and Britain's second application to join the European Economic Community. Her research interests include British foreign policy in the twentieth century, Britain and European integration, and European integration since 1945.

Acknowledgements

The editors and publisher are grateful to the following for financial assistance towards the realisation of this project: the Department of Medieval History, University College Dublin; the trustees of the T. P. MacDonnell Memorial Fund; the Academic Publications Committee of University College Dublin; and the Publications Committee of the National University of Ireland.

The photograph that constitutes the frontispiece was kindly supplied by Mary Kelleher. For responding so cheerfully and effectively to their request for suitable *Leitmotive* in Albert Lovett's mother-tongue, the editors thank their learned colleague, Martin Cunningham of the Department of Spanish, for suggesting two apposite passages – the one medieval and the other early modern. Finally the editors wish to place on record their deeply felt appreciation of the enormous contribution made by the executive editor of the University College Dublin Press. Barbara Mennell's own editorial labours far exceeded the call of duty in the circumstances and it is true to say that the benefits of her advice and expertise are apparent on every page of this book.

Introduction

This volume is dedicated by his colleagues to the memory of Albert Lovett: an accomplished scholar and linguist, passionate and widely read in music, art, literature and politics – which he discussed with a wit, irreverence and rapidity that disguised his serious purpose – an entertaining lecturer, dedicated teacher and an amusing, and sometimes scurrilous, commentator on academic life and politics. The History Department has been a tamer and duller place since his departure.

As Alfonso the Wise, king of Castile and Léon, observed in the thirteenth century, the three arts of the trivium (grammar, rhetoric and logic) teach a person to be well reasoned, while the four arts of the quadrivium (arithmetic, geometry, astronomy and music) make him wise. Together they render him complete and bring him to a state of incomparable good fortune. These were Albert Lovett's values too. In a later age that Albert himself chronicled with distinction, Luis de Góngora y Argote's epigraph in sonnet form to a history of the reign of Philip II (*rey siempre glorioso*) posits the thought that a man, while yet lying in the tomb, may be reborn and may live on in a volume of historical recreativity. This process we have endeavoured to emulate.

Prodded at last into collective productive activity with this project (a notion of mass endeavour that, like a Five Year Plan, might have excited his mirth), we have produced a book that reflects not only the variety of our fields of research, but also, we hope, some of Albert's concerns. From his mother, a refugee from the Spanish Civil War, he derived his interest not only in Spain but also in Europe and the wider world beyond the secure harbour in the south of England in which he grew up. An inveterate traveller, he was not content with imaginary journeys, or with the travelling in time of the good historian. At the end of term, he set off for fields more exotic than those afforded by Belfield, visiting Mexico, the wide open spaces of Kansas ('take the money and run') and, over a decade before the fall of the Berlin Wall, venturing through the German Democratic Republic and Czechoslovakia by car, with a tent in the back, confounding bureaucrats' attempts to frustrate such manifestations of the free spirit. Albert was caught between the worlds in which he grew up and worked, which were peripheral to the European continent he loved, and the heart of Europe, which his imagination inhabited, and the wider world he enjoyed exploring. The title of the volume and its subject matter, to some extent, reflect these concerns.

Travel is thus one of the themes that runs through the book, and indeed, through Albert's life. Elva Johnston explores imaginary travel literature: examining an early medieval example of the genre, she shows that it was not a purely frivolous exercise, but a pretext for polemical discussion of political and religious questions. Several contributors discuss an aspect of one-way travel – migration. Declan M. Downey looks at the fortunes of the Wild Geese, who left Ireland for continental Europe in the seventeenth and eighteenth centuries, to find fame and fortune there. Maurice J. Bric examines the cultural and economic roots of Irish migration to North America in the seventeenth and eighteenth centuries. David Doyle pursues this story, discussing Irish elites in Canada and the USA in the late nineteenth and early twentieth centuries.

Ireland's links with and place within the wider world are a recurring theme in several contributions. Tadhg Ó hAnnracháin, comparing the progress of the Counter-Reformation in Ireland and Hungary, argues that Ireland did not fit the general pattern of the Counter-Reformation in Europe and that, exceptionally, it was able to resist state-sponsored Reformation. This he ascribes to both the weakness of the state and the vitality of the resisting culture, which drew strength from a continentally educated elite of clergymen. James McGuire outlines the career of Richard Nagle, who rose to high office under James II, but who risked and lost all in the Williamite wars, ending his days in the not wholly uncongenial setting of James's court-in-exile outside Paris. Ronan Fanning discusses how American policy towards Ireland evolved over the twentieth century, developing from a surprisingly tepid initial friendship to strained relations during the Second World War and the initial phases of the Cold War (despite Ireland's fundamentally anti-Soviet stance) to close co-operation at the end of the century. Part of the explanation for this surprisingly fraught story was the Irish authorities' insular attitude to world affairs, which they insisted on seeing through the prism of partition. Hence, the strategic concerns of the early Cold War were expected to take second place to Ireland's nationalist preoccupations. What shifted these attitudes, as Jane Toomey demonstrates, was the need to engage with Europe. When Britain decided to apply for membership of the European Economic Community, Ireland was obliged to follow suit, joining (or rejoining, as Declan M. Downey would observe) the new Europe, with results that Albert approved. A fervent European, Albert wholeheartedly approved Irish enthusiasm for the European enterprise: recent mishaps in this relationship would have provoked irreverent quips.

If attitudes to the outside world are a theme that recurs in the book, so too is that of attitudes to nature. Elva Johnston touches on it in her piece. Eamon O'Flaherty discusses the new scientific culture of the seventeenth and eighteenth centuries and its view of nature as something to be studied, mastered, exploited and improved upon. Coinciding with the rise of the new English culture and the reinvention of English identity, the inquiries of the scientific revolution and Enlightenment in Ireland tended to be pursued as part of the great Protestant enterprise: progress was understood to be implicit in the endeavour. Mary E. Daly examines the place of nature within twentieth-century Irish official nationalism. Landscape, she argues, was a site of controversy and confusion, as it reflected history and culture. Hence, the manufactured, 'improved' landscapes of the great demesnes of Enlightenment Ireland (which in the nineteenth century degenerated into the more resonant image of Castle Rackrent) were rejected by the new authorities in the twentieth century in favour of the idealised peasant rusticity depicted by Paul Henry. Possessed by the myth of an imagined Gaelic Ireland, whose authenticity was measured by the degree of its isolation from other, especially English, influences, the official culture struggled to reconcile its proclaimed values with its more practical and ambivalent impulses towards the complex landscape of reality.

The gap between perception and reality, and history as a means of understanding complexity (or of offering an acceptable account of these complexities) are the subject of several essays. Public memory and historical consciousness are thus major themes of the book. Seymour Phillips examines the historical reputation of the controversial Edward II from contemporary accounts to the present, revealing how the historical figure has been obscured by an enduring, but largely illusory image. Howard B. Clarke demonstrates how cultural preoccupations have shaped major historical accounts of the past. The influence of error and preconception, and even prejudice, once attributed to our benighted predecessors in previous centuries, is shown to be by no means confined to the misty past, as he invites us to reconsider the significance ascribed to the coming of the Normans to England in the eleventh century and of the Anglo-Normans to Ireland in the twelfth century. John McCafferty takes up the theme of the Anglo-Norman invasion of Ireland from a different angle, analysing Maclise's famous painting of *The marriage of Aoife and Strongbow*. He is interested not so much in the historical 'mistakes' of the painting, as in the way in which it reflects historical readings of the past, seeing Maclise's work as a painting less of a (largely imagined) event than of an evolving historical consciousness. Edward Coleman tackles the problem of historical consciousness from a different perspective, showing how the same event has been reinterpreted and redeployed for different purposes. Examining the Lombard League (a largely misrepresented episode in twelfth-century Italian history and an emblem, during the Risorgimento, of Italy's struggle for independence), he reviews how, from Sigonio to Verdi and the contemporary Northern League, it has entered the arsenal of Italian politics and how historians have contributed to this process. David Kerr also investigates how understandings or misunderstandings of the past influence later events, discussing continuity and change in French political culture. Challenging Aron's view that 1968 was a farcical re-enactment of the revolutionary tradition of the nineteenth century, he suggests that there was greater continuity than Aron was ready to concede – a continuity obscured by the tendency to mythologise nineteenth-century revolutions and to ascribe to them an heroic military purposefulness they did not have. William Mulligan takes up the problem of the public understanding of history and the resistance of public memory to the history of historians. He examines the reaction to the *Wehrmacht* exhibition of the mid-1990s, which challenged one of the Federal Republic of Germany's cherished myths – that of the 'unsullied *Wehrmacht*'. Richard Aldous, like John McCafferty, analyses a particular work of art – Elgar's *Dream of Gerontius* – offering an historical reading of its changing reception and significance in a society challenged and changed by war and modernity. Finally, Judith Devlin discusses how historical images and consciousness have been manipulated by the authorities, in the reshaping of post-Soviet Moscow, to consolidate their legitimacy.

Covering a wide range of time and place, these essays would, perhaps, have offered Albert some entertainment, as they reflect his own extensive interests. Conservative but iconoclastic, reserved yet vocal, cautious yet imbued with a black and bawdy wit, Albert brought a gale of fresh air through the corridors of the History Department. His sudden death from heart failure on 12 April 2000 at the age of fifty-five not only constituted a personal tragedy but also deprived the History Department in University College Dublin of one of its most outstanding historians.

The editors
September 2002

CHAPTER I

Albert Lovett (1944–2000)

An Appreciation

Hugh Gough

Albert Lovett's sudden death on 12 April 2000 came as a profound shock to his family and to his friends in England, Ireland and continental Europe. A person of vibrant energy, whether in the corridors of Belfield, in the lecture theatre or on the squash court, he was at the height of his powers as a historian and in the advanced stages of a carefully researched history of the European Coal and Steel Community.

Albert Lovett came to University College Dublin in the autumn of 1970. He was later promoted to statutory lecturer and in 1995 became Jean Monnet Professor of the History of the European Union. Born in London in 1944, he read history at Sidney Sussex College, Cambridge, and completed his PhD under the direction of the distinguished Spanish historian, John Elliott. He was awarded a Spanish Ministry of Foreign Affairs research scholarship in 1968 and, in the year before coming to Dublin, a Sir James Knott Research Fellowship at the University of Newcastle. His energy and ability were immediately apparent on his arrival in University College Dublin. Conversations were fast moving affairs, driven by his mental curiosity, his broad interests and his rapid diction. Yet they were always informative and challenging because of his wide reading, and unfailingly humorous because of his scepticism and his dislike of sloth and complacency. He kept relentlessly abreast of the latest publications in a variety of areas, as well as his own, and although history was his consuming passion, it was closely rivalled by politics, current affairs, art and music. He frequently returned from research trips abroad, laden with pictures for use in lectures, or with posters to line the walls of the History Department office. These were often preceded by postcards from cities such as Madrid, Burgos, Salamanca, Florence, Paris or Brussels, sent to a wide range of friends and colleagues, carrying comments on colleagues or the skulduggery of university politics.

His teaching contribution to University College Dublin will be remembered by many generations of students. He preferred lectures to seminars or tutorials, and made them into dramatic performances, delivered from a carefully crafted text with speed, passion and cynical wit. Since his death, many students have recalled the indelible impression that his lectures left on them. He had a great respect for students, whatever their ability, as long as they showed interest, and they in turn admired him for his commitment, his erudition and his eccentricity. For years he taught magisterial survey courses on the history of Europe and Britain in the early modern period, covering topics as diverse as religion and witchcraft, demography and print, politics and economics. More recently he switched to the twentieth century with courses on modern Germany, twentieth-century Europe and the history of the European Community. His range was impressive in an age of increasing specialisation, but he liked the breadth and radiated in his courses what he termed, in the preface to one of his books, his 'admiration and awe of French scholarship' encountered during his research into early modern Europe. This admiration dated back to the mid-1960s when, arriving as a research student unannounced and dishevelled at the Casa de Velasquez one afternoon, looking for a bed, he was welcomed by the Director and ushered into the library which contained the works of great French historians such as Fernand Braudel and Emmanuel Le Roy Ladurie. He never looked back and the experience underpinned his strong commitment to the UCD library. He often advised students that universities had no need of administrators, lecturers and buildings, as long as they had a quality library. Constantly frustrated by inadequate funding, he nevertheless worked with the history librarian, Máirín Cassidy, to build up an impressive collection of secondary printed works on modern European history – and especially that of Spain – which will be one of his major legacies.

Research and writing were central to his academic career and he had an impressive publications record. In 1977 he published a monograph on Mateo Vasquez de Leca and the administration of late sixteenth-century Spain.[1] In 1978 there followed a general history of early modern Europe that became a standard text for Leaving Certificate students.[2] In 1986 he published a history of sixteenth-century Spain, and meanwhile a steady stream of detailed articles appeared in major international journals.[3] Then, having completed the academic hat trick of monograph, national history and European survey, he turned to the twentieth century and the origins of the European Community. This abrupt change of direction was prompted by a fear that early modern historians would become dispensable dinosaurs in the gloomy atmosphere of the debt-ridden 1980s and by a total lack of adequate funding in Ireland at that time for historical research outside the country. The switch was courageous, but facilitated by his linguistic ability. He was bilingual in English and Spanish, fluent in French, learnt German in the 1980s and could read Italian without difficulty. His monograph on the origins of the European Coal and Steel Community was unfinished at the time of his death but he had already produced several important articles. Typically, the research took him to archives around Europe and the United States of America, largely at his own expense. His last article, for example, contained references to archives in Bonn, Koblenz, Florence, Paris and London and to newspapers in Paris, New York, Düsseldorf and London. He was an active member of the Board of European Studies in University College Dublin and of the Institute of European Affairs.

There was a certain symmetry in Albert Lovett's professional career. He began as an historian of multinational empire (the Habsburg) and ended it as an historian of a contemporary confederation (the European Union). One of his earliest articles was on financial corruption under Philip II, and the European Union – to which he was passionately committed – was enmeshed in corruption in the years before he died. He had a combative personality, laced with a strong sense of ironic humour and a commitment to equity, honesty and quality. He disliked chauvinism and complacency, and detested the insular mediocrity of university politics and promotion procedures. His death cut short a career when it was approaching its peak, yet something of his wry humour and commitment to a broad vision of history is reflected in words that he wrote, in a review article on the great French historian Fernand Braudel.

> At a time when many English historians have taken refuge in narrative history, the style which takes the thinking out of writing, Braudel has returned to a richer and more optimistic tradition. His boundless curiosity and his generous spirit, qualities hard to find in academic circles, have produced a synthesis which stands unequalled in modern times.

Albert Lovett shared Braudel's boundless curiosity for continental European history with several generations of UCD students. His books and articles, along with their memories, bear witness to that. So, too, do the students who learnt from him.

Notes

1 A. W. Lovett, *Philip II and Mateo Vásquez de Leca: the government of Spain (1517–1592)* (Geneva, 1977).
2 A. W. Lovett, *Europe 1453–1610* (Dublin, 1978).
3 A. W. Lovett, *Early Habsburg Spain, 1517–1598* (Oxford, 1986).

HISTORIOGRAPHY

CHAPTER 2

1066, 1169, and All That

The Tyranny of Historical Turning Points

Howard B. Clarke

'O what A brave world do wee Live in!'[1] Thus mused the petty constable of the parish of Leamington Hastings, Warwickshire, over three centuries ago. His brave new world of Restoration England was different from Aldous Huxley's. For one thing, religious affiliation still mattered, for a few years later we are informed that 'whereas John Over was chosen Cunstable as aforesd. and hee being a papist was not thought fitt to Serve therefore wee doe choose Richard Cleber to Serve as Constable for this yeare ensuing 1684'.[2] It was different again from the world of eleventh-century monks, whose consciousness of an expanding and progressive environment was tinged by reflections, anticipatory and retrospective, of the passing of the first millennium AD. Not long after the year 1000 a monk of Evesham or Worcester was moved to address his contemporaries as 'we who have progressed through the last part of the millennium and beyond'.[3] As in our own time, one's passage through a millennial boundary was something of a trial and its successful completion was at least a minor source of personal satisfaction.

1066 AND ALL THAT

Even more of a trial, or so it often appears, is the 'anniversarianism' that afflicts our time-conscious world. The commemoration of great events in the past is a perfectly legitimate exercise in itself and some of the less obvious examples have led to genuine advances in our understanding of the past. To take a single instance from recent Irish historiography, attention was focused in 1997 on the Dublin parliament that had met seven centuries earlier. The outcome was an improved edition of the surviving account of its deliberations, together with a series of interpretative essays containing many new insights.[4] It has sometimes (though not invariably) been quite otherwise with the very greatest events – the so-called turning points of history – partly because old controversies tend to resurface in varying degrees of disguise. By way of illustration I propose to examine first one of the many anniversarial productions of the late 1960s relating to that perennially controversial topic in the historiography of these islands, the Norman Conquest of England (Plate 1). It will be my contention that, if 1066 is one of the best-known dates in English history, it is also one of the least understood.[5]

Round full circle, 1895–1969

In 1895 J. H. Round published his collection of essays under the title of *Feudal England: historical studies on the eleventh and twelfth centuries*. With due regard to opportunistic timing, it was reprinted in 1964.[6] Some of this material had first been published shortly before in *English Historical Review* and elsewhere, but it is fair to regard this collection as the true historiographical landmark. As such, it shares with F. W. Maitland's *Domesday Book and beyond* (1897) joint honours for the most brilliant contribution by nineteenth-century scholarship to the late Anglo-Saxon and Norman periods. Round, a native of the county of Essex, was nothing if not forthright, and not infrequently demonic, as when he demolished E. A. Freeman's Senlac, palisade and reputation in the study entitled 'Mr Freeman and the battle of Hastings'.[7] Something of Round's forthright approach comes out in the following passage from the famous essay on the introduction of knight service:

> I am anxious to make absolutely clear the point that between the accepted view [Freeman's] and the view which I advance, no compromise is possible. The two are radically opposed. As against the theory that the military obligation of the Anglo-Norman tenant-in-chief was determined by the assessment of his holding [in hides or carucates] ... I ... hold that his military service was in no way derived or developed from that of the Anglo-Saxons, but was arbitrarily fixed by the king, from whom he received his fief, irrespectively both of its size and of all pre-existent arrangements.[8]

Round eschewed 'the anticataclysmic tendencies of modern thought',[9] an approach that was clearly echoed in R. A. Brown's *The Normans and the Norman Conquest* (1969). One of the minor ironies in the background to the whole controversy is that Brown was brought up and schooled just over the Essex border, at Ipswich in Suffolk. His debt to Round is obvious:

> The great thesis of John Horace Round, reinforced by Frank Merry Stenton, remains untouched though not unchallenged: at the top level of the feudal hierarchy, the quotas, the *servitia debita*, of knight service, known from unimpeachable evidence to have been owed by tenants-in-chief to the crown in the later twelfth

century when written records are comparatively plentiful, can be traced back to the reign of William the Conqueror but no further, and in no case, not even in that of the bishopric of Worcester, does the quota of knight service demanded from a magnate's honour correspond in any way to the previous assessment of the same land for military service in the pre-Conquest fyrd. . . . By his enfeoffments King William obtained from his vassals the obligation of some five thousand knights [Round's own estimate], and between this, the so-called feudal host of historians, and the pre-Conquest military system of the fyrd there is no continuity.[10]

For Brown, the well-attested fact that Anglo-Saxon hide units survived as knights' fees 'is literally one of mere antiquarian interest and of no further significance', since 'the process and method of subinfeudation was [sic] a matter for the tenant-in-chief or other tenant and of no necessary concern to the king or other superior lord'.[11]

Just to reinforce the historiographical continuity here, reference should be made to Brown's treatment of a crucial piece of original evidence, to which we shall return later:

A surviving writ of William the Conqueror from as early as 1072, upon which Round rightly placed great reliance as 'the [recte a] climax of [recte to] [his] argument', summons Ethelwig abbot of Evesham to come to the king at Clarendon with the five knights owed in respect of his abbey, and it is known from twelfth-century evidence that the quota of Evesham Abbey was five knights.[12]

Thus the controversy between the continuists descended from Freeman and the discontinuists descended from Round seemed to have come full circle and the historiographical period from 1895 to 1969 may fairly be described as 'the Round era'.

On the surface of, and more especially in the background to, the Round era of historical interpretation, one can identify a number of characteristic assumptions and attitudes. One of these is superficial in the sense of being open and on the surface. In their treatment of the introduction of feudalism into England, both Round and Brown chose the quotas of military service as the core of their argument. The argument is basically this. In about 1070 King William made a series of bargains with most of the great tenants-in-chief, lay and ecclesiastical, as to how many knights their fiefs should provide for the royal army. Most of the quotas are five or a multiple thereof, with sixty as the normal maximum, and the regularity has led these writers to see the firm hand of the Conqueror behind this scheme. In this way, some five thousand knights would be supplied for the 'feudal army'. The emphasis is therefore placed on the obligations of between one hundred and two hundred tenants-in-chief to their feudal superior, the king. To quote Round:

> The essential feature we have to keep in view when examining the growth of knight service is the *servitium debitum*, or quota of knight service due to the crown from each fief. . . . The whole question turns upon the point whether or not the tenants-in-chief received their fiefs to hold of the crown by a quota of military service, or not. . . . What we have to consider is not the relation between the tenant-in-chief and his undertenant, but that between the king and his tenants-in-chief: for *this was the primary relation that determined all below it.*[13]

In other words, once this point is proven, it is also proven that 'feudalism' was introduced into England with the Norman Conquest.

Behind this particular choice of battlefield by Round and Brown, it is possible to detect four underlying attitudes. The first of these arises from the final words of the previous quotation, which reflect an element of what one might call 'aristocratic determinism'. Round castigated his opponents because it seemed to him that they preferred 'to ignore, or at least to minimize the importance of the tenant-in-chief, the "middleman" of the feudal system'.[14] For Brown, too, 'feudal society in its upper levels was essentially a military society – and *it is the upper levels which are the test of feudalism*, itself an affair of lordship, tenurial lordship, of lords and would-be lords and the relationships between them'.[15] Before coming to England, knights in Normandy were men 'undertaking a variety of gentlemanly employments'.[16] Having arrived, the same author's 'new, virile and militant aristocracy' are described, along with 'clattering and jingling contingents of mounted knights, with gonfanons and shields displayed', who 'must have been a familiar sight in rural England as they rode upon the business of their lords, and lorded it over the countryside. . . . The hand-picked quality of the new Norman aristocracy who followed William the Conqueror to England was characteristic of the age'.[17] According to Brown, 'the hard training, technical achievements, common attitudes and growing cult of knighthood gave a new degree of cohesion to the largest [!] and most dominant class of lay society'.[18] One might be tempted to conclude that, for Brown, the peasantry who formed over eighty per cent of the total population had no part whatsoever to play in lay 'society'. It would be wrong, however, to imagine that Brown had never heard of peasants, for the very word occurs further down the same page and merits seven references and one cross-reference in his index. But reading Round and his latter-day disciple, we can only suppose that they dwelt in a world of antediluvian Torydom, as descendants of East Saxons and East Angles living towards the close of the second millennium AD. Round's outlook also reflects that of late Victorian England, when too much 'liberalism' and growing German might were liable to be the country's undoing. For Round, Hastings was lost because of an almost anarchical excess of liberty, the want of a strong centralized system, the absorption in party strife, the belief that politics are statesmanship, and that oratory will save a people. . . . like Poland, England fell, in large measure, from the want of a strong rule, and from excess of liberty. . . . the voice of 'a sovereign people' . . . availed about as much to check the Norman Conquest as the fetish of an African savage, or the yells of Asiatic hordes. What was the Empire, what was India . . . to one whose ideal, it would seem, of statesmanship, was that of an orator in Hyde Park? [Here Round is attacking Freeman's admiration for W. E. Gladstone] . . . Forts and soldiers, not tongues, are England's want now as then. . . . When the Franco-German war had made us look to our harness, he [Freeman] set himself at once, with superb blindness, to sneer at what he termed 'the panic', to suggest the application of democracy to the army, and to express his characteristic aversion to the thought of 'an officer and a gentleman'. How could such a writer teach the lesson of the Norman Conquest?[19]

Closely related to aristocratic determinism is a second underlying attitude that was characteristic of the Round era, namely, an innate feeling that the Normans were a Good Thing. For Round,

> the land was ripe for the invader, and a saviour of Society was at hand. While our fathers [the Anglo-Saxons] were playing at democracy, watching the strife of rival houses, as men might now watch the contest of rival parties, the terrible duke of the Normans was girding himself for war.[20]

Round enjoyed 'an instinctive feeling that in England our consecutive political history does, in a sense, begin with the Norman Conquest'.[21] He chided the Freeman school for failing to 'bring themselves to adopt the feudal standpoint or to enter into the feudal spirit'.[22] For Brown, as for Jordan Fantosme,

> the Normans are good conquerors. . . . It is probable that the aristocratic preference for country life stems in this country only from the Norman Conquest, for the Old English nobility frequently had town houses. In the broadest sense, to set down the results of the Norman Conquest is to write the rest of English history down to the present day, and to add the histories of all those countries who [sic] were to feel the impact or the influence of post-Conquest England.[23]

Could he have had Ireland in mind? At any rate, 'by 1087 the principal actors of future English history are already in their places or waiting in the wings'.[24] The corollary of this view is that the losing side in this aristocratic competition must have been effete and degenerate, and Brown quotes with evident relish Thomas Carlyle's surrealistic and high-blown depiction of pre-Conquest England:

A gluttonous race of Jutes and Angles, capable of no great combinations; lumbering about in pot-bellied equanimity; not dreaming of heroic toil and silence and endurance, such as leads to the high places of the Universe and the golden mountain-tops where dwell the spirits of the dawn.[25]

We are not so far removed, after all, from the classic caricature of English historical mythology: 'The Norman Conquest was a Good Thing, as from this time onwards England stopped being conquered and thus was able to become top nation' (Figure 1).[26] And aristocratic determinism naturally demands that one identifies with the winning side.

Figure 1 A typical illustration by John Reynolds for W. C. Sellar and R. J. Yeatman, *1066 and all that*. The story that Duke William had an accidental fall on the sandy beach at Pevensey, Sussex, which was circulating in the following century, was allegedly interpreted by a knight standing nearby as a favourable omen, the future king 'holding' England in his hands.

The third underlying attitude is associated with what constitutes an extraordinary irony concerning the Round era of interpretation. In their anxiety to stress the fact that 'feudalism' was Norman and therefore of continental origin, Round's disciples have failed to face up to a true intellectual challenge. Stenton is known to have left England only once in his lifetime and neither Round nor Brown gives one the impression of ever having ventured far outside the frontiers of the former Anglo-Norman state. The battlefield for all of them is limited to that particular part of western Europe. Yet it is a well-established part of modern scholarship that feudal institutions, howsoever defined, had their origins in the area between the Loire and the Rhine valleys, in Carolingian Austrasia and Neustria, and were diffused from there through much of western Europe. When we examine the writings of scholars based on evidence from this region, however, an enormous gulf opens up between their concepts of feudalism and those of the Round era. Is it any wonder that undergraduates in these islands who first acquaint themselves with 'feudalism' by reading Round, Stenton or Brown should find themselves completely flummoxed when confronted by any of these continental writers? Even F. L. Ganshof's book *Feudalism* (1944), representing intentionally a relatively narrow continental approach, reads a little strangely beside his contemporary Stenton. But what is our poor undergraduate to make of G. Duby's assertion that the fief was not the most essential ingredient of western European feudal society? How odd, therefore, that the Round school, so much at pains to prove that feudalism was continental in origin, should take so little notice of what continental historians have to say about it. Of northern France in the ninth and tenth centuries, Brown commented: 'there the outlines of a new and feudal society were being hammered out upon the anvil of incessant war'.[27] There is no question here of any *servitia debita* ('services owed'), yet the latter attain god-like proportions once the scene shifts to England after 1066.

The fourth underlying attitude of the Round school follows on directly from this point. Round liked to keep his history simplistic by keeping it aristocratic. The argument that 'feudalism' came with the Norman Conquest is established by concentrating selectively on the new royal family, on the upper levels of the new aristocracy and on the quota system worked out between them. This simplistic outlook was nurtured and sustained by means of a conservative overemphasis on what is royal, noble and militaristic. All else is conveniently set aside, be it English or continental. As Round himself knew,

> If my own conclusions be accepted, they . . . will restore, *in its simplicity*, a theory which removes all difficulties, and which paves the way to a reconsideration of other kindred problems, and to the study of that aspect of Anglo-Norman institutions in which they represent the feudal spirit developed on feudal lines.[28]

It is difficult to be sure precisely what he had in mind in the latter half of this sentence but, ironically enough, Round may have been more perceptive than he realised, as will be suggested below.

The overt characteristic of the Round era that has already been referred to is the technical one of placing heavy emphasis on the *servitia debita*. Its underlying attitudes, it has been suggested, are aristocratic, pro-Norman, narrow and simplistic. A sixth and final characteristic is again superficial and applies to 'extremists' on both wings of the continuist versus discontinuist debate.

That characteristic is venom. The gentry controversy set in the period 1540–1640 is another notable example of how certain issues seem to transmogrify historians into Player Kings, displaying all the emotions of which they are capable and occasionally, it would seem, all at once. Much of Round's venom, as is well known, was reserved for Freeman. In the index to *Feudal England*, the entry for 'Freeman' extends over 23 cm, whereas William the Conqueror himself earns only 4.5 cm. The 'qualities' of Round's then deceased opponent to which he adverts include the following:

> confuses individuals, his assumptions, his pedantry, misconstrues his Latin, imagines facts, his supposed accuracy, his guesses, his confused views, his dramatic tendency, evades difficulties, his special weakness, his Domesday errors and confusion, his wild dream.

Easily the most notorious blackguards on the other wing were H. G. Richardson and G. O. Sayles, who described Round as 'amateurish and undisciplined. Often hasty and muddled', they asserted, 'he fouled the wells of truth as much as any of his fellows who were made to feel the lash of his criticism'.[29] Round's chief fault, however, was to have been a pupil and admirer of Bishop Stubbs, for whom Richardson and Sayles reserved their choicest language as the original sinner beyond the Round era. 'It is, indeed, evident', they claimed, 'that he had little capacity for thinking clearly about the nature of historical truth and of its attainment; ... Stubbs was disabled by the weakness he had for approaching a problem with the solution already in his mind; ... the first eight chapters of the *Constitutional history*, which take the story from the dim beginnings to the Norman Conquest, are worse than worthless to the uninstructed'.[30] Richardson and Sayles did discover some 'wheat among the chaff. But in the mountain of chaff the wheat is now of little account, and the chaff is fit only to be thrown away'.[31]

Military quotas and the Evesham writ

The primary sources on which the Round era relied for its confident assertions about the introduction of regular quotas of military service for the great tenants-in-chief may be divided into three basic categories. The first of these consists of chronicles written during the twelfth and thirteenth centuries. The Abingdon chronicle suggests that after the disturbances following upon the Conquest had died down, it was noted *in annalibus* by the king's command what knights should be demanded from bishoprics and abbacies for the defence of the realm when need arose.[32] In the context of *c.*1071 Orderic Vitalis says that the king gave out the lands of England among his followers to command the service of 60,000 knights.[33] The Ely chronicle claims that in 1072, for the Scottish campaign, King William demanded knight service from the bishops and abbots, which thenceforth became a perpetual right.[34] Matthew Paris intimates that in 1070 the king imposed military service on bishops and abbots holding baronies.[35] When evaluating this evidence, points to bear in mind are that none of these chronicle sources is contemporary with the events; all but Orderic mention bishops and abbots only among the tenants-in-chief; none of them mentions the term *servitia debita*, although the mid-twelfth-century Ely chronicle does have the words *debita militie obsequia* ('due services of a body of knights'); and all agree in placing the imposition of knight service around 1070 x 1072. Orderic's 60,000 knights are nonsense, of course, but it has been shown that he employs this particular number regularly to signify 'a great many'.

The second body of evidence comprises the *cartae baronum* ('barons' charters') of 1166, that is, very nearly a century after the event. These *cartae* are not records of the *servitia debita* as such, but they do provide information which enabled Round to determine what the quotas must have been *in that year*. One of the questions asked of the tenants-in-chief in 1166 was how many knights had their predecessors enfeoffed up to the year 1135. Certain replies hint that this was sometimes difficult to determine, but many tenants-in-chief do appear to have known the answer to this question, suggesting that written records dating from at least as far back as Henry I's reign still survived in 1166. But 1070 was at least a whole generation earlier.

The third piece of evidence has already been referred to, namely, the writ of military summons addressed by the Conqueror to Æthelwig, abbot of Evesham. What this little document says is as follows:

> William, king of the English, to Æthelwig, abbot of Evesham, greeting. I command you to summon all those who are under your administration and jurisdiction to bring before me on the octave of Pentecost at Clarendon all the knights that they owe me, properly equipped. You also, on that day, shall come to me and bring with you, properly equipped, those five knights which you owe me from your abbey. Witness Eudo the steward. At Winchester.[36]

This writ is the only surviving scrap of record evidence to suggest that *servitia debita* were established early in the Conqueror's reign and, even so, it is a twelfth-century cartulary copy of a lost original. It therefore has been made to bear an enormous burden of proof for the so-called introduction of 'feudalism' into England. The chaotic Evesham Abbey cartulary in which it survives has never been published and the Latin text which most historians appear to have used is that produced by Round in 1895. In the five-and-a-half lines it occupies in the 1964 reprint of *Feudal England*, Round succeeded in introducing not only 'feudalism' but also no fewer than twenty-five errors and misimpressions in his transcript. Furthermore, he refers the reader in a footnote to the wrong manuscript, although he does at least get the folio number right. Yet countless people have blithely relied on this 'amateurish and undisciplined' text. This is not to suggest, however, that the essential meaning of this writ has therefore been distorted, but persistent resort to a shoddy transcript does symbolise that equally persistent desire for simple answers to complex problems.

In his discussion of the Evesham writ, Round found 'the vigour of its language' convincing.[37] Most historians have accepted it at face value and only Richardson and Sayles appear to have had any qualms about it:

> We do not, in sober fact, know the purpose of the writ of summons; we do not know who were summoned or their numbers; we are not even certain of the year of the summons. The only certain fact, beyond those in the writ itself, is that it was issued before Æthelwig's death in 1077 [*recte* 1078]. . . . And if, instead of surmising with Round that the date of the writ is 1072, we surmise that its date lies between 1067 and 1070, which seems equally possible, how then do we interpret it and what becomes of Round's thesis? We cannot build upon such flimsy foundations.[38]

What is clear at this point is how absolutely critical becomes the interpretation of this Evesham writ. It is, after all, 'our only feudal summons from the entire Anglo-Norman age'.[39] That being so, one obvious question we have to ask ourselves is how justified are we in constructing any theory on the basis of one document, applying to one abbey, at one moment in time. The time factor is more important when we remember that Evesham Abbey's quota, if such it be, did not always stand at five but for a good part of the twelfth century remained at four-and-a-half knights, thanks to a favour from Henry I.[40] In other words, this quota, even if established in the early 1070s, cannot correctly be said to have been permanently 'fixed'. Then again, three other texts accompany the writ on the same folio of the cartulary and at least two of them are open to suspicion. Moreover, the whole lot are written over a partially erased pre-Conquest charter in favour of Hereford Cathedral, which by the early twelfth century was proving to be an embarrassment to the monks of Evesham in connection with a complicated squabble they were enjoying with the monks of Crowland.

In short, a good deal of uncertainty surrounds this vital witness to the introduction of 'feudalism'. But as Round himself wrote, there was nothing 'to be gained by forging a document which admits, by placing on record, the abbey's full liability'.[41] It is true that, in the Norman period, Evesham monks entered upon their heroic age of forgery, but the abbey's inmates seem to have been just as prone to bungle the job as they were to attempt it in the first place. The writ still stands as an authentic document, but the argument that is customarily based so firmly on its testimony should be regarded as nothing more than an hypothesis. The danger is that Round's 'theory' (a word he quite frequently used himself) has been too readily lifted into the realm of hard fact, for the reasons outlined above. According to Brown, 'institutional studies miss half the point and all the fun of history, which is why "Administrative History", the characteristic product of our century, is generally so dull'.[42] It may well be tremendous fun to construct confident and sweeping theories on the basis of slipshod nineteenth-century scholarship and aristocratic prejudices, and to serve them up as 'history' to undergraduates and the general reader (the intended audience of *The Normans and the Norman Conquest*). More positively there were already refreshing signs to the contrary around 1970, when the problem began to be seen as a social one as well as a technical one and the social fundamentals suggested different and more rewarding approaches.[43]

Hides, carucates and military service

Without entering into enormous detail here, I should like to propose another approach of this kind. In the Middle Ages, as in the present day, the cost of fielding a fully equipped and trained army was considerable. From the crown's point of view, the cost was charged directly to the military elite. That any medieval English king, pre-Conquest or post-Conquest, held strong theoretical opinions about the raising of royal armies is unlikely. Most of them were probably more interested in techniques of fighting and of organising troops on the battlefield. The deployment of an army was a supremely practical matter and, throughout the medieval period, methods and details were changed to suit contemporary conditions. If we were to examine how the task was accomplished in, say, the eighth, the tenth and the twelfth centuries, we should find similarities and dissimilarities in each period. If we here ask ourselves about the impact of the Norman Conquest on methods of raising royal armies, it is not really a question of looking for one method before 1066 and another method after 1066, despite the cataclysmists' tendency to polarise the issue.[44] In order to test this assertion, the fundamental features of army recruitment in the generations before and after 1066 will now be summarised.

In the England of King Edward the Confessor the military elite consisted of an unknown number of housecarls and thegns, together with members of the great dynastic families that provided most of the earls. These men held varying amounts of land, ranging from one or two hides to several hundred of them. The county was in principle the unit of service, for we hear of shire levies being called out. Within each shire the land was divided into five-hide or six-carucate units, which were expected to supply one professional and fully equipped warrior for a period of up to sixty days per annum. These warriors constituted what has been termed the 'select fyrd'; in addition there was a general obligation on the part of all able-bodied free men to defend the homeland.⁴⁵ A similar system had been operated in Carolingian Francia, where four *manses* constituted the territorial support for one soldier. In England the scheme went back presumably to the formation of shires and hundreds or wapentakes north of the Thames in the first half of the tenth century. In those days it may have worked along fairly uniform lines, whereas a century later seigneurial interests were gaining strength. Jurisdictional privileges had been granted to favoured churches, giving them certain powers over one or more hundreds, while the practice of appointing earls as governors of groups of counties enabled a few families to rise into political prominence.⁴⁶ One result was that, by the Confessor's reign, military recruitment had been partially seigneurialised. Thus Eadric the steersman appears to have acted as commander of the bishop of Worcester's contingent from the 300 hides of Oswaldslow Hundred, a function performed by the local earl outside such ecclesiastical 'immunities'. When it was a question of national defence, as in the autumn of 1066, the system worked well enough. The military defeats at Fulford and at Hastings, and the victory at Stamford Bridge, should not be allowed to influence unduly our view of army recruitment in this period. When, however, a dispute arose between king and earl, as in 1051, the loyalty of many thegns must have been placed under severe strain. Surveying the late Anglo-Saxon military scene, we receive a general impression that the territorial system of recruitment to the royal army had been complicated and compromised by the powers of private lords. It is surely no accident that Edward the Confessor and Harold II continued to rely on household troops (housecarls), who might be given land, but who were essentially paid mercenaries. These apart, hidated or carucated land, cultivated by slaves, unfree and free peasants, provided for the maintenance and sustenance of professional warriors.

In the early Norman period the military elite comprised an unknown number of English thegns and French knights, along with a smaller class of magnates. These men, as in pre-Conquest times, held varying amounts of land, ranging from one or two hides to several hundred. Military recruitment was complicated by the option open to the first Norman kings of using *two* methods of raising an army. One was to call out the traditional fyrd, probably in a supporting role.⁴⁷ The other method was to strike a series of bargains with tenants-in-chief as to how many knights each should contribute to the royal army, again for a period of up to sixty days per annum. Despite the paucity of contemporary evidence, we may reasonably suppose that many lay and ecclesiastical landholders found themselves obligated to supply an agreed number of professional warriors, usually five or a multiple thereof. Some of these warriors were in turn granted land with which to support themselves, though many were retained as household troops in the uncertain years of political consolidation. For the native warriors the unit of service remained the shire; for the foreigners it became the lordship or 'honour' of their masters. When it was a question of national defence, as in 1085, the two systems were found wanting, hence the panic measures for the quartering of soldiers brought over from the Continent and the laying waste of the east coast.[48] When, as in 1075, a rebellious earl attempted to force a crossing of the River Severn, he was thwarted by troops headed by Sheriff Urse, Bishop Wulfstan, Abbot Æthelwig and Walter de Lacy.[49] These and other incidents during the first post-Conquest generation demonstrate what we should expect to have been the case: that a period of uncertainty and of trial and error followed upon the Norman victory at Hastings. Again it is surely no accident that mercenary troops were commonly employed in Anglo-Norman England and let it not be forgotten that the victorious army at Hastings was itself composed mostly of mercenaries. At the same time barons and those knights who were given so many hides or carucates of land were supported in their military role by the labour of slaves (in declining numbers), unfree and free peasants.

Stripped to their essentials and devoid of theories about military quotas and tenurial legalities, for which there is virtually no contemporary evidence, the methods of raising a royal army in the generations before and after 1066 were different from one another, but not fundamentally different. How could they have been fundamentally different when the principal means of supporting a military elite, the labour of peasant masses, remained precisely the same? The differences are therefore primarily administrative. The establishment of quotas of knight service was *administratively* quite distinct from reliance on shire levies: that is why the two procedures could coexist in the first post-Conquest generation. This is also why any attempt to prove that one procedure was derived from the other breaks down.[50] But to claim that military quotas represent some kind of social revolution is totally unjustifiable. Socially late Anglo-Saxon and early Norman England were strikingly similar. What happened to the system of military recruitment foreshadowed what would happen in King Stephen's reign to the system of direct taxation: the degree of seigneurialisation was carried a stage further. Another parallel is the seigneurialisation of more hundreds and wapentakes after the Conquest.[51] In England, as on the Continent, the growth of seigneurial power was an evolutionary, not a revolutionary, process. The compactness of the island kingdom enabled most late Anglo-Scandinavian, Anglo-Norman and Angevin rulers to resist seigneurial encroachments on their powers and rights far more successfully than their continental counterparts, which gave English feudalism its distinctive character. Thus the first three Norman kings were able to insist on the pre-Conquest sixty-day annual term of military service, rather than the continental custom of forty days.[52] The latter became customary only in the reign of Stephen, that heyday of seigneurial encroachment. Even such vigorous kings as Stephen's predecessors had made some concessions to the new territorial aristocracy, witness the construction of limited numbers of private castles: not to have done so would have been impolitic. But the essence of the Norman Conquest is seen in the continuance of strong, orderly, centralised government down to the late 1130s.[53]

For all these reasons, the so-called 'feudal army' of the cataclysmic school of historians proves to be a shadowy force. As it happened, large royal armies were rarely necessary in Anglo-Norman England, where most warfare took the form of sieges and skirmishes. Before and after 1106 the need for professional soldiers was felt more on the Continent than in England, which made it impractical to rely principally on any sort of army raised on the island. William Rufus and Henry I resorted frequently to the use of mercenary troops, who were more or less institutionalised under Stephen.[54] The first reference to scutage occurs in 1100 and the first certain money fief was granted in 1103.[55] After the customary term of service, whether sixty or forty days, knights were converted at will into paid troops.[56] The early pipe rolls of Henry II's reign show that England was being defended by mercenaries who were paid with money raised by the mechanism of scutage.[57] *Milites solidarii* ('hired knights') are first documented in 1162, the last year when danegeld is known to have been collected.[58] In other words, knight service had rapidly evolved into a financial system intended to supply not warriors but cash.[59] The peculiar needs of the old Anglo-Norman state and of the new Angevin Empire made a home-produced feudal army an unnecessary attribute of English feudalism.

In effect the knight's fee became a unit of taxation, just as the hide and the carucate had long since been. Scutage, initially restricted to Church lands, is only the most obvious aspect of this development, for 'by the opening years of the twelfth century, and perhaps even earlier, scutage was beginning to overshadow knights' service as the central feudal military obligation'.[60] In the reign of Henry I the rate was thirty shillings a fee; in 1156 twenty shillings; in 1159 and 1161 two marks.[61] Over-enfeoffed tenants-in-chief were compensated by retaining the scutage collected from excess fees and, of course, the burden of this tax was ultimately shouldered by the peasants who paid customary dues. In the Evesham Abbey manorial extents of c.1190 the tax is referred to as *servitium regis* ('king's service'), a term that has to be understood in this context not as military services performed by knights, but as money payments paid by peasants. Similarly the occasional taxes, *auxilium* ('aid') and *donum* ('gift'), were assessed on knights' fees and appear under the same names in manorial surveys. Thus, down to 1162, the fee joined the hide, the carucate and the sulung (in Kent) as a taxable unit, just as in the Conqueror's reign the quota system coexisted with the territorial system as a method of raising a royal army. Practicality rather than theory would have determined which unit was chosen. In 1110 an aid for the marriage of Henry I's daughter to the German emperor – a standard feudal obligation – was levied in England at the rate of three shillings a hide.[62] This levy may be compared with the customary arrangement of the bishops of Chichester, whereby reliefs were paid not on the knight's fee, but at the rate of one mark a hide.[63] These are apt illustrations of the fusion of feudal and non-feudal elements so characteristic of Anglo-Norman England. And with so many taxes being demanded from above and passed on below, it is hardly surprising that private lists of subtenants, military and non-military, have survived.[64]

1169 AND ALL THAT

Many historians of medieval Ireland have drawn a contrast between the Norman Conquest of England in and after 1066 and that of Ireland in and after 1169. The one was brief and thorough; the other long-drawn-out and superficial. So thorough was the Norman conquest of England that the modern descendants of those distant protagonists, with the obvious exception of supersensitive historians, tend to view with what Charles Haughey might call 'bovine equanimity' this major turning point in their long history. On the other hand, the incomplete nature of the conquest of Ireland leads nationalists in particular to regard the year 1169 as the beginning of eight hundred years of English misrule, perpetuated by the political partition of the island in the early twentieth century. In 1966 the battle of Hastings was celebrated as well as commemorated in the town of Battle in Sussex by the publication of a special edition of *The Hastings Observer* and by jousting on the site below the abbey's ruins (Figure 2).[65] In 1969 the arrival of the Anglo-French contingents was greeted by official silence and by the rapid destruction of a stone tablet erected at Baginbun. These and other differences are important, but they conceal as much as they reveal of underlying attitudes to these distant events.

Lineal descendants

The most obvious parallel with John Horace Round is his near contemporary, Goddard Henry Orpen. The first volume of Orpen's seminal work, *Ireland under the Normans, 1169–1333*, was published in 1911, sixteen years after *Feudal England*. Just like Round, Orpen identified with the winning side. Ireland in 1169, he alleged, was still in a tribal state, with no adequate legal machinery for enforcing the observation of rights and the performance of duties. A body of primitive Aryan custom had remained almost unchanged and the Vikings had made matters worse by reinforcing a natural 'tribal' propensity towards anarchy and turmoil. Until the coming of the Anglo-French,

Howard B. Clarke

An 'Observer' Look at the Invaders

HOW SHALL WE FARE UNDER NORMAN RULE?

FOR the last 50 years England has been the most peaceful country in the world. We have had our troubles, of course.

Between the death of Canute in 1035 and the accession of King Edward in 1042 there was contention for the throne, but we got over it without any serious bloodshed or disturbance of our way of life. We trembled on the brink of civil war in 1051 when Earl Godwin and King Edward quarrelled, and again a year later when Earl Godwin returned in force from his short exile. There has been fighting on the Welsh border and unrest in Northumbria. But since 1016 until a year ago Kings Canute and Edward have given the country as a whole more enjoyment of peaceful living than any of our neighbours can boast.

We have prospered in our peaceful years. Our systems of law and local government have become established and respected. We have had no need of a Truce of God to limit murder, robbery and rape to Tuesdays and Wednesdays as has been tried on the Continent. We have kept them under a decent control for seven days in the week.

Envy of Europe

Trade has flourished. With a population of over 10,000, London is in the top 10 of the commercial centres of the world and has left Normandy's Rouen well behind. Our coinage is the envy of Europe, and our taxes are better collected and more cheerfully paid than in most other countries. We can be said never to have had it so good.

What can we expect now? William the Bastard has long had the reputation of being utterly ruthless in the achievement of his ambitions. We can be certain that all opposition will be mercilessly quelled. He has threatened death, fire and bondage for all who stand against him, and he will keep his word. He has not hesitated to devastate his own country when he thought turning it into a wilderness was the best way of overcoming his enemies.

A Cut-Throat Army

If we don't resist, if we accept and collaborate? William is not a Hun, a Mongol, a Turk. He has not invaded England to destroy it. He will be as anxious as no doubt many of us are to preserve the good living we have been enjoying. He wants to have England as a jewel in his diadem, not a barren cinder.

But let us not deceive ourselves. We have not voluntarily accepted him as our king. We have required him to recruit and employ an army of adventurers and cut-throats. If they seek our co-operation at all, it will only be after they have killed, plundered and enslaved enough of us to give them what they want of land, loot and power. William is a stern disciplinarian. We can probably rely on him to hold their worst excesses in check and to impress on them that if they want to make good in England they must leave enough of it and of us too. So some of us may save our lives by collaborating with the Normans. It is doubtful if we shall save much else.

We may count on it that all who hold land of any importance will be dispossessed. Other kinds of wealth will be confiscated. The heaviest possible taxes will be imposed. There will be exactions of food and labour. They will do as they will with our women, and it will be death to say them nay. It will be a long time before Englishmen again hold any high offices of Church or State. The oppression will continue until Normans are born and grow up in security in an England which they feel to be theirs and all Englishmen who remember a free England are dead.

England's End?

Is it the end of England? We have been an island people. The Danes nearly drew us into Scandinavia, but we made Englishmen out of those who settled among us. We may do the same with the Normans in time, but we shall never again be the easy-going insular English we are now. These Normans have become wholly Latins and Europeans. They are also highly efficient, brilliant organisers. We shall be Latinised and organised.

It may not all be one-way traffic, though. The Normans have not been slow to take over other people's institutions if they worked. By the grace of God they may find something workable in ours.

Figure 2 Extracts from '*The Hastings Observer*, 16 October 1066'. The prognosis for England in 1066, as conceived by C. H. Dand in 1966.

26

Ireland had never felt the direct influence of a race more advanced than herself. Irish fighters stood no chance against the arrows, lances and military skill of the foreigners, who gave the Hiberno-Norse inhabitants of Wexford a rude shock by presenting them with a serious alternative to 'a horde of naked Irish kerns'.[66] Just like Round, too, Orpen evinced an interest in the early history of castles and contributed a number of articles on the subject.[67] So influential was his work that for much of the twentieth century the new foreigners in Ireland were to be called 'Normans', reverting to 'English' or becoming hybrid 'Anglo-Normans' or 'Cambro-Normans' only towards the end of that century.

Orpen was not alone in holding such views; rather they were typical of the Anglo-Irish ascendancy of his time. Let us consider, by way of example, some of the richer offerings of The Revd E. A. D'Alton, whose *History of Ireland from the earliest times to the present day* appeared in a second edition in 1910. 'If the Irish were wronged and robbed, and if they lost their liberties', he asked in his preface, 'were they not themselves largely to blame?' Citing Froude with apparent approval, D'Alton averred that 'if [the Irish] had . . . any real genuine national spirit they would have pushed "the pitiful handful of English into the sea". But they did not. . . . It was not, therefore, the strength of England, but rather the weakness and folly of Ireland, which led to the loss of her liberty.'[68] Back in 1910, of course, the age-old problem was still a current reality and D'Alton could assert with chilling topicality that

> In the vast majority of the Irish of the present day we can still trace the faults and the virtues of the original Celtic race. The want of initiative in the mass of the people, their utter helplessness without capable leadership, their reluctance to combine for any purpose, their want of foresight, their inability to take pains, their instability and infirmness of purpose – have not these characteristics appeared in the twentieth century as well as in the twelfth? . . . It would be as well for Irishmen to ask is there not something amiss with themselves . . . .[69]

To all appearances, the Irish suffered from a similar set of defects to those of the Anglo-Saxons before 1066. In both contexts, conquerors are superior beings by virtue of being conquerors. True to form,

> these Normans . . . were as brave and daring as their kinsmen on the Continent, loved change and adventure, and were ready to embark on any enterprise which promised the excitement of war and conquest. Their arms, their armour, their method of fighting were the same. . . . But the term [knight] had been extended, and, in England especially, had received a new significance, and was applied to those vassals who, in accordance with the system established by William the Conqueror, held their lands by military tenure. They were bound to aid their

master in his wars, to equip and maintain for his service a certain number of horsemen fully armed, and to service him in the field as a knight.[70]

In other words, these knights abided by the quota system that was central to Round's argument. It goes without saying, of course, that 'these men-at-arms or knights who came to Ireland were all of good birth'.[71]

It is possible to trace a line of lineal descent across the political divide of 1921–2, especially in the hallowed halls of Trinity College, Dublin, though not exclusively so. To start with, the major figure was Edmund Curtis, for whom 'the Normans were a race made to conquer'.[72] It may surprise many readers to learn that 'the conquest of Ulster makes the finest story in the Conquest after that of Leinster. John de Courcy['s] . . . onslaught was worthy of the Norman race at its best'.[73] From Curtis the line descended to Jocelyn Otway-Ruthven, whose book published in 1968 was dedicated to his memory.[74] Though called *A history of medieval Ireland*, the story starts in earnest only in 1169 and is preceded by an introductory chapter by Kathleen Hughes devoted to the benighted Celts, who otherwise receive only occasional cursory and disapproving glances from the book's principal author. One of the glaring characteristics of this school of historians is to exaggerate the geographical extent of the Anglo-French colony in Ireland. Time and again one reads that 'three-quarters of the land of Ireland had been occupied and brought under the control of the government in Dublin', or 'the gradual expansion of the English colony in Ireland until it reached its greatest point when something like three-quarters of the island had been feudalized', or 'the Normans controlling about two-thirds of the island', or 'almost two-thirds of the country was occupied and divided up. . . . Military conquest was promptly followed by the establishment of effective administration within a new framework of manors, baronies and shires', or 'in the thirteenth century, the greater part of the country came under English rule'.[75]

As I have pointed out elsewhere, there has been a parallel tendency to exaggerate the number and size of real towns in medieval Ireland.[76] Again let us consider the following statements: 'One result of the Anglo-Norman invasion was that towns and markets sprang up everywhere', or 'the growth of towns which took place throughout the greater part of Ireland during the early [sic] medieval period was almost entirely due to Norman influence', or 'it was the Anglo-Normans who effectively planted a proper network of towns and cities throughout all of Ireland, except for the western fringes which remained under Irish control during the period'.[77] Yet a proper analysis, coupled with a careful distinction between town and market settlement (the so-called rural borough), shows that only about one-fifth of the entire island was serviced by cities, towns and the bigger market settlements at the colony's zenith (Figure 3). Partly because of consistent misrepresentation of

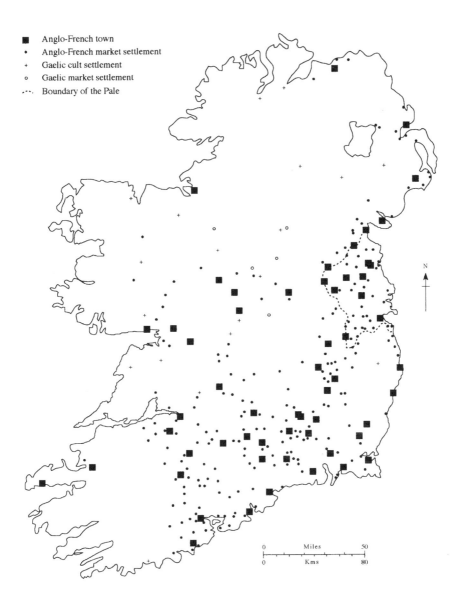

Figure 3 The distribution of cities, towns and market settlements in Ireland c.1270.

the urban evidence, historians have equally consistently been misled into portraying a bigger and a stronger colony than is likely to have existed in actuality. Similarly there has been a widespread failure to distinguish the lordship of Ireland from the colony of Ireland. The medieval colony, with its manors, market settlements, towns and a few cities, was always significantly smaller in size than the medieval lordship.[78] Anglo-French lordship in Ireland naturally and rapidly adapted to Gaelic circumstances and to Gaelic traditions. The rural and urban colonists put up a measure of resistance, but most of them were let down by 'those who defaulted on the responsibilities of lordship'.[79]

Competing nationalisms

Being a land of competing nationalisms in the twentieth century, Ireland produced a parallel tendency to all of this. Orpen and his Anglo-Irish ascendancy viewpoint were naturally and understandably assailed by the scholar-revolutionary, Eoin MacNeill. Thus 'Mr Orpen's history' is dismissed as 'largely a laboured attempt to prove that the backward state of Ireland was the cause and justification of the invasion'.[80] What is termed 'popular history' is 'the product of a peculiar obsession of mind, that makes Ireland appear a sort of hotel, in which the important people are always distinguished visitors, and the permanent residents, when they are not under orders, are occupied with quarrelling children and other household worries in the garret or the basement'.[81] MacNeill had a feisty ally in the person of the redoubtable Alice Stopford Green. Like her contemporary D'Alton, she was acutely aware of present-day circumstances, though from the opposite perspective. In 1908 she observed:

> The Irish of today have themselves suffered by the calumny of the dead. They, alone among the nations, have been taunted with ancestors sunk in primitive disorders, incapable of development in the land they wasted. A picture of unrelieved barbarism 'hateful to God' served to justify to strangers the English extirpation of Irish society. . . . For their birthright – they have been told – they have inherited the failings of their race, and by the verdict of the ages have been proclaimed incapable of success in their own land, or of building up there an ordered society, trade, or culture . . . .[82]

For her later work, *History of the Irish state to 1014* (1925), she adopted MacNeill as her leading guide.[83]

Some of MacNeill's observations were directed towards feudalism and its analogues. According to him, 'Mr Orpen is obsessed with the notion that the Irish order and the feudal order were as poles apart', for 'when Norman feudalism came to Ireland, it was just emerging from a condition similar to what it found in Ireland'.[84] MacNeill's 'feudal system' was characterised by centralisation and, in the circumstances of 1919, this could only be regarded as a Bad Thing.[85] His lineal descendants, however, appear to have toyed with the idea that feudalism could be a Good Thing, provided that it occurred in Ireland and before 1169. In a much-quoted article published in 1978, Donnchadh Ó Corráin, citing MacNeill, declared that 'the type of society that was emerging in Ireland in the eleventh and twelfth centuries was one that was moving rapidly in the direction of feudalism'.[86] Here feudalism is equated with local hereditary lordship and a narrower, more powerful and exclusive lordly class. Something similar can be found in one sentence in F. J. Byrne's contribution to the second volume of *A new history of Ireland*: 'further evidence of the feudalisation of Irish society is seen in the fact that the over-kings were now acting as *domini terrae* ["lords of the land"]'.[87] Still more recently, Charles Doherty, referring to evidence for peasant revolts, the transition from round to rectangular houses, the abandonment of raths, and the use of heavier ploughs, boldly asserts that 'there is no longer any reason why Ireland should remain outside the "feudal" debate'.[88]

Historians belonging to this broad-based tradition of Irish nationalism treat of feudalism in a particular way. They never offer any kind of precise definition, partly because their sources give very little help in that direction. Secondly, they do not write about the period after 1169, when feudal institutions, howsoever defined, can be identified and described in some detail. Thirdly and rather strangely, they appear to regard it as a Good Thing. One possible gloss on that is that feudalism is being equated with ongoing modernisation in a twelfth-century context. In order to suggest that Ireland was not so backward as the Orpen school would have it, features that more properly represent a more forceful and sophisticated kind of kingship are labelled 'feudal'. Ironically, therefore, both of the competing nationalisms in Ireland, like English nationalism across the water, have tended to use 'feudalism', defined and undefined, as a yardstick of the advancement of society. The prevailing conservatism of Irish society of all shades and opinions may have something to do with this, for even neo-Marxist Brian Graham has allowed himself to be seduced by its charms.[89]

In conclusion, I do not wish to claim that the events surrounding the years 1066 and 1169 were not historical turning points in England and in Ireland; the long-term consequences of both were enormous. What I do wish to emphasise is the amount of historical distortion that is to be associated with the interpretation of these events. Some of these distortions are serious, even outlandish. There is a strong tendency, for example, to periodise English and Irish history in such a way that the Middle Ages are thought to begin in 1066 and 1169 respectively. This mode of thinking has been enshrined in no less a work than *A new history of Ireland*, whose second volume is entitled *Medieval Ireland, 1169–1534*. Most archaeologists, not to be outshone by their peers in the rival discipline, go one better, by one year, by having 'Viking Ireland' give way to 'medieval Ireland' in 1170, when Hiberno-Norse Dublin and Waterford were captured by the Anglo-French conquerors. In the year marking the dawn of the third millennium AD a truly dreadful book, at least in its brief medieval section, called *A history of Ireland* was published.[90] It belongs to a series billed as 'compact, readable and informative national histories'. This book, too, starts essentially in 1170, with a few token pages devoted to the preceding period back to Mesolithic times. National histories, it would seem, are still a fertile breeding ground for historical untruths, and historical turning points the beginning and end of many of them. In its striking of attitudes and in its system of thought, the 'tyranny' has regrettably 'progressed through the last part of the millennium and beyond' as yet another Bad Thing.

Notes

I am grateful to the Ulster Society for Irish Historical Studies for inviting me to air this theme on 29 November 2001. I wish also to thank Sarah Gearty of the Irish Historic Towns Atlas for her improved version of Figure 3.

1 Warwick County Record Office, DRO 43a/173, *s.a.* 1677.
2 Ibid., 6 Jan. 1684.
3 [J. A.] Giles (ed.), *Vita quorundum Anglo-Saxonum: original lives of Anglo-Saxons and others who lived before the Conquest* (London, 1854), p. 387: 'nos ... qui in ultima millenarii sumus parte et ultra progressi'. The text is the earliest Life of St Ecgwine, the founder of Evesham Abbey who was also a bishop of Worcester. For other references to millennial writings see G. Duby, *L'an mil* (Paris, 1967).
4 J. Lydon (ed.), *Law and disorder in thirteenth-century Ireland: the Dublin parliament of 1297* (Dublin, 1997).
5 Since the outbreak of anniversarianism in the 1960s, more sober judgements and new insights have been published. Notable among these advancements are the following monographs: M. T. Clanchy, *England and its rulers, 1066–1272: foreign lordship and national identity* (Oxford, 1983; 2nd edn, enlarged, 1998); M. Chibnall, *Anglo-Norman England 1066–1166* (Oxford and New York, 1986); A. Williams, *The English and the Norman Conquest* (Woodbridge, 1995); R. Bartlett, *England under the Norman and Angevin kings, 1075–1225* (Oxford, 2000).
6 References are to the reprint, in which the text was reset. Both the original and the reprint were published in London.
7 Round, *Feudal England*, pp. 258–305.
8 Ibid., p. 208.
9 Ibid., p. 182.
10 R. A. Brown, *The Normans and the Norman Conquest* (London, 1969), pp. 219–21.
11 Ibid., p. 221.
12 Ibid., p. 224.

13 Round, *Feudal England*, p. 197 (italics mine).
14 Ibid., p. 198.
15 Brown, *Norman Conquest*, p. 43.
16 Ibid., p. 48.
17 Ibid., pp. 230, 242, 262.
18 Ibid., p. 240, quoting Stenton.
19 Round, *Feudal England*, pp. 302–4. Cf. A. Briggs, *Saxons, Normans and Victorians* (Bexhill-on-Sea, 1966), pp. 20–2.
20 Round, *Feudal England*, p. 305.
21 Ibid., p. 247.
22 Ibid., p. 198.
23 Brown, *Norman Conquest*, pp. 49, 100 (n. 179), 203.
24 Ibid., p. 211.
25 Ibid., p. 5, n. 11; T. Carlyle, *History of Friedrich II of Prussia, called Frederick the Great*, 6 vols (London, 1858–65), I, p. 415. On Carlyle see also Briggs, *Saxons, Normans and Victorians*, pp. 3–4.
26 W. C. Sellar and R. J. Yeatman, *1066 and all that* (London, 1930; reprinted Harmondsworth, 1960), p. 25. There is an almost inevitable Irish imitation, even down to the style of the illustrations: E. J. Delaney and J. M. Feehan, *The comic history of Ireland* (Cork, 1964). This is a shortened version of the two-volume work published in 1951.
27 Brown, *Norman Conquest*, p. 10.
28 Round, *Feudal England*, p. 208 (italics mine).
29 H. G. Richardson and G. O. Sayles, *The governance of mediaeval England from the Conquest to Magna Carta* (Edinburgh, 1963), p. 20.
30 Ibid., pp. 5, 6, 22.
31 Ibid., p. 21. Cf. Briggs, *Saxons, Normans and Victorians*, pp. 16–18.
32 *Chronicon monasterii de Abingdon*, J. Stephenson (ed.), 2 vols (London, 1858), II, p. 3.
33 *The Ecclesiastical history of Orderic Vitalis*, M. Chibnall (ed.), 6 vols (Oxford, 1969–80), II, pp. 266–7 and n. 7.
34 *Liber Eliensis*, E. O. Blake (ed.) (London, 1962), p. 216.
35 *Matthaei Parisiensis Historia Anglorum sive . . . historia minor*, F. Madden (ed.), 3 vols (London, 1866–9), I, p. 13.
36 British Library, Cotton Vespasian B XXIV, f. 18.
37 Round, *Feudal England*, p. 238.
38 Richardson and Sayles, *Governance of mediaeval England*, pp. 64–5. For the correct date of Æthelwig's death see H. B. Clarke, 'The early surveys of Evesham Abbey: an investigation into the problem of continuity in Anglo-Norman England' (PhD thesis, University of Birmingham, 1977), pp. 32–3.
39 C. W. Hollister, *The military organization of Norman England* (Oxford, 1965), p. 117.
40 C. Johnson and H. A. Cronne (ed.), *Regesta regum Anglo-Normannorum 1066–1154*, II, *Regesta Henrici primi 1100–1135* (Oxford, 1956), p. 69, no. 831.
41 Round, *Feudal England*, p. 238.

42 Brown, *Norman Conquest*, p. 57.

43 E. King, 'The Peterborough "Descriptio militum" (Henry I)', *English Historical Review* LXXXIV (1969), 84–101; E. King, 'Large and small landowners in thirteenth-century England', *Past and Present*, 47 (1970), 26–50; S. Harvey, 'The knight and the knight's fee in England', *Past and Present* 49 (1970), 3–43.

44 Cf. the remarks of E. John, 'English feudalism and the structure of Anglo-Saxon society' in *Orbis Britanniae and other studies* (Leicester, 1966), pp. 152–3.

45 C. W. Hollister, *Anglo-Saxon military institutions on the eve of the Norman Conquest* (Oxford, 1962), p. 26.

46 It has been suggested that by the formative reign of Æthelstan (924–39), when the kingdom of England was 'united' for the first time, there were six earls south of the River Humber, each earldom containing 12,000 hides of land: H. M. Chadwick, *Studies on Anglo-Saxon institutions* (London, 1905), pp. 216–18.

47 The continuing use of the fyrd was stressed, perhaps overstressed, in Hollister, *Military organization*, pp. 216–60.

48 *Two of the Saxon chronicles parallel...*, C. Plummer (ed.), 2 vols (Oxford, 1892–9), I, pp. 215–16.

49 *Florentii Wigorniensis monachi Chronicon ex chronicis*, B. Thorpe (ed.), 2 vols (London, 1848–9), II, p. 11.

50 E. John, *Land tenure in early England: a discussion of some problems* (Leicester, 1964), pp. 140–61.

51 H. M. Cam, *Liberties and communities in medieval England: collected studies in local administration and topography* (London, 1963), pp. 59–60, 64–90, 124–8.

52 Hollister, *Military organization*, pp. 89–100, 286–8.

53 It is necessary to draw a distinction between the institution of kingship and the governmental machinery that underpinned it, on the one hand, and the personalities of individual kings and the dynastic situations in which they found themselves, on the other hand. Dynastically the Norman kings were always insecure, partly because, despite the welter of progaganda in the Norman chronicles, the Bayeux Tapestry and Domesday Book, their legitimacy was derived from nothing better than the outcome of a particular battle.

54 J. O. Prestwich, 'War and finance in the Anglo-Norman state', *Transactions of the Royal Historical Society* 5th ser., IV (1954), 19–43; J. Schlight, *Monarchs and mercenaries: a reappraisal of the importance of knight service in Norman and early Angevin England* (Bridgeport, Conn., 1968), pp. 34–52.

55 W. A. Morris, 'A mention of scutage in the year 1100', *English Historical Review* XXXVI (1921), 45–6; B. D. Lyon, *From fief to indenture: the transition from feudal to non-feudal contract in western Europe* (Cambridge, Mass., 1957), p. 34 and n. 85. The earliest money fief may have been that described by William of Malmesbury referring to 1066 itself: ibid., pp. 33–4.

56 Schlight, *Monarchs and mercenaries*, pp. 20–1.

57 Ibid., pp. 55–6.

58 Ibid., p. 66.

59 Ibid., p. 75. The reduction of the Evesham Abbey quota to four-and-a-half knights by 1107 is an early indication of this process.

60 Hollister, *Military organization*, p. 204.

61 Ibid., pp. 191–215 for a full discussion of the evidence.

62 Ibid., p. 194. It may have represented the danegeld of that year.

63 J. H. Round, 'The knight service of Malmesbury Abbey', *English Historical Review* XXXII (1917), p. 252.

64 Clarke, 'Early surveys of Evesham Abbey', pp. 334–9.

65 The eight hundredth anniversary in 1866 passed by with very little fanfare: Briggs, *Saxons, Normans and Victorians*, pp. 13–15.

66 G. H. Orpen, *Ireland under the Normans, 1169–1333*, 4 vols (Oxford, 1911–20; reprinted 1968), I, p. 152.

67 G. H. Orpen, 'Motes and Norman castles in Ireland', *Journal of the Royal Society of Antiquaries of Ireland* XXXVII (1907), 123–52; G. H. Orpen, 'Motes and Norman castles in County Louth', *Journal of the Royal Society of Antiquaries of Ireland* XXXVIII (1908), 241–69; G. H. Orpen, The origin of Irish motes', *Journal of the County Louth Archaeological Society* II (1908–11), 50–6; G. H. Orpen, 'Motes and Norman castles in Ossory', *Journal of the Royal Society of Antiquaries of Ireland* XXXIX (1909), 313–42; G. H. Orpen, 'Croghans and Norman motes', *Journal of the Royal Society of Antiquaries of Ireland* XLI (1911), 267–76.

68 E. A. D'Alton, *History of Ireland from the earliest times to the present day*, 2 vols, 2nd edn (London, 1910), I, pp. vii–viii.

69 Ibid., pp. viii–ix.

70 Ibid., p. 222.

71 Ibid.

72 E. Curtis, *A history of Ireland*, 6th edn (London and New York, 1950), p. 49.

73 Ibid., pp. 61–2.

74 A. J. Otway-Ruthven, *A history of medieval Ireland* (London, 1968). A second edition appeared in 1980.

75 Respectively M. D. O'Sullivan, *Italian merchant bankers in Ireland in the thirteenth century* (Dublin, 1962), p. 135; J. F. Lydon, *The lordship of Ireland in the Middle Ages* (Dublin, 1972), p. 80; B. J. Graham, 'The towns of medieval Ireland' in R. A. Butlin (ed.), *The development of the Irish town* (London, 1977), p. 49; F. H. A. Aalen, *Man and the landscape in Ireland* (London, 1978), p. 111; A. Cosgrove, *Late medieval Ireland, 1370–1541* (Dublin, 1981), p. 1.

76 H. B. Clarke, 'Decolonization and the dynamics of urban decline in Ireland, 1300–1550' in T. R. Slater (ed.), *Towns in decline, A.D. 100–1600* (Aldershot and Burlington, Vermont, 2000), pp. 161–8.

77 Respectively J. Lydon, *Ireland in the later Middle Ages* (Dublin and London, 1973), p. 14; Graham, 'Towns of medieval Ireland', p. 29; T. B. Barry, *The archaeology of medieval Ireland* (London, 1987), p. 118.

78 Cf. Clarke, 'Decolonization', pp. 168–9.

79 R. R. Davies, 'Lordship or colony' in J. Lydon (ed.), *The English in medieval Ireland* (Dublin, 1984), p. 146.

80 E. MacNeill, *Phases of Irish history* (Dublin, 1919; reprinted 1968), p. 303.

81 Ibid., p. 349.

82 A. S. Green, *The making of Ireland and its undoing 1200–1600* (London, 1908), pp. x–xi.

83 A. S. Green, *History of the Irish state to 1014* (London, 1925), p. vii: '. . . endeavouring to divest myself of prejudice and ignorance'. On her place in Irish historiography see R. F. Foster, 'History and the Irish question', *Transactions of the Royal Historical Society* 5th ser., XXXIII (1983), 169–92; reprinted in C. Brady (ed.), *Interpreting Irish history: the debate on historical revisionism 1938–1994* (Dublin and Portland, Oregon, 1994), here at pp. 137–9.

84 MacNeill, *Phases of Irish history*, pp. 297, 301.

85 Ibid., p. 302.

86 D. Ó Corráin, 'Nationality and kingship in pre-Norman Ireland' in T. W. Moody (ed.), *Nationality and the pursuit of national independence* (Belfast, 1978), p. 32.

87 F. J. Byrne, 'The trembling sod: Ireland in 1169' in A. Cosgrove (ed.), *A new history of Ireland*, II, *Medieval Ireland, 1169–1534* (Oxford, 1987), p. 12. Cf. D. Ó Cróinín, *Early medieval Ireland 400–1200* (London and New York, 1995), pp. 291–2, a section entitled 'Feudalization in Ireland, c.1000'.

88 C. Doherty, 'The Vikings in Ireland: a review' in H. B. Clarke, M. Ní Mhaonaigh and R. Ó Floinn (eds), *Ireland and Scandinavia in the early Viking Age* (Dublin, 1998), pp. 323–4.

89 B. Graham, 'Anglo-Norman colonization and the size and spread of the colonial town in medieval Ireland' in H. B. Clarke and A. Simms (eds), *The comparative history of urban origins in non-Roman Europe: Ireland, Wales, Denmark, Germany, Poland and Russia from the ninth to the thirteenth century*, 2 parts (Oxford, 1985), pp. 355–71.

90 M. Cronin, *A history of Ireland* (Basingstoke and New York, 2001). It naturally comes as no surprise to be informed that 'by the middle of the thirteenth century, English influence . . . stretched across three-quarters of Ireland . . . by the beginning of the fourteenth century, two-thirds of the island of Ireland was under English control': ibid., p. 22.

CHAPTER 3

The Reputation of a King

Edward II from Chronicle and Written Record
to Compact Disc and Internet

Seymour Phillips

The general opinion of Edward II from his own day to the present has been that he was a failure: that as a king he was incompetent and neglectful of his duties, leaving the business of government to ill-chosen and self-serving councillors; and that as a man he had a fatal ability to create enemies through his attachment (possibly homosexual in nature) to favourites, through his hostility to the English magnates, and finally through his alienation of Isabella, his wife and queen. In combination, these failings were to prove disastrous to the peace and stability of his kingdom and ultimately fatal to Edward II himself.[1]

Part of Edward II's problem, both with his contemporaries and with posterity, was the very fact that he succeeded a powerful and, by contemporary standards, highly successful king. The *Commendatio lamentabilis*, a lengthy eulogy of Edward I composed by John of London at the time of Edward's funeral in 1307, claimed that

> [o]nce with Alexander, king of Macedon, we defeated the kings of the Medes and the Persians and subdued the provinces of the East. Now, at the end of time, with great King Edward, we have borne a ten-year war with Philip, famous king of France; we have won back Gascony, taken by guile, with force of arms; we have got Wales by slaughter; we have invaded Scotland and cut down her tyrants at the point of the sword.[2]

Edward I's powerful treasurer, Walter Langton, bishop of Coventry and Lichfield, with whom the future Edward II quarrelled bitterly in 1305 and who was to be dismissed and put on trial for peculation early in the new reign, had scenes from the life and campaigns of his royal patron painted on the walls of his magnificent new episcopal palace, which was itself designed as a smaller version of Caernarfon Castle. Whoever followed Edward I on the English throne would be hard put to match up to the glowing opinions and martial reputation of his predecessor, all the more so since these opinions conveniently glossed over the many problems Edward I had bequeathed to his son. To take but two: although a peace treaty was made with France in 1303, Edward I had, whatever John of London might say, effectively been defeated by the French in the long war over Gascony; while in 1307 Edward was farther than ever from achieving his ambition to conquer the Scots.

Edward II also suffered because he was so different in character both from his more readily understood and infinitely more successful father and from his own son and successor, Edward III. As the fourteenth-century chronicler, Jean le Bel of Liège, an admirer of the English crown, who had first-hand knowledge of England and who wrote after the victories of Edward III, was to remark, 'it was commonly believed in England, and had often happened since the time of King Arthur, that a less able king would often come between two valiant monarchs'.[3] Thus, according to Le Bel, Edward I, who was wise, a man of prowess, bold and enterprising and fortunate in war, and who conquered the Scots three or four times, was succeeded by Edward II, who did not resemble him either in wisdom or in prowess, who governed savagely and with the advice of others, and who was defeated in 1314 with all his barons by King Robert of Scotland at the battle of Bannockburn.

Another factor contributing to Edward II's reputation was that, unlike France, where the *Grandes chroniques* provided a carefully structured and lavishly illustrated account of French history which was intended to reflect and to embellish the glory of the monarchy, there was no tradition in early fourteenth-century England of official history writing. The nearest to such a work in Edward II's time was the continuation down to the year 1306 by a monk at Westminster of Matthew Paris's St Alban's chronicle, the *Flores historiarum*. This praised Edward I and was possibly intended for presentation to Edward II at his coronation in 1308.

However, despite the fact that Westminster abbey 'in some respects stood in a similar relation to the English kings as St Denis did to the French ones', since 'its patron was the king, it was the scene of coronations, a royal mausoleum, and situated close to the scene of government',[4] it was not to be the source of historical writing favourable to the crown. This is all the more remarkable given the attention lavished by the crown on the abbey church and on the shrine of the royal saint, Edward the Confessor, since the reign of Henry III. On the contrary, Edward II appears to have been on bad terms with the monks of Westminster for much of his reign. This situation was reflected in, and perhaps caused by, such royal actions as Edward's occupation of the manor of Eye, covering the area of the modern Pimlico and Mayfair, from 1316 until the end of his reign, and in his retention from 1320 of a cottage and large garden within the precincts known as 'Burgoyne'. More seriously for his posthumous reputation, the bad relationship was also reflected in the further continuation, from 1306 to 1327, of the *Flores historiarum* by the Westminster monk, Robert of Reading, who probably wrote to justify the seizure of power by Isabella and Mortimer in 1326 and was unsparing in his vilification of Edward II, accusing him of being paralysed by sloth, of cowardice in battle, of failing to keep his word, of rapacity and avarice, and of stupidity and tyranny. When describing Isabella's mission to France in 1325, for example, Robert denounced Edward's cruelty to his queen:

> Oh! The insane stupidity of the king of the English, condemned by God and men, who should not love his own infamy and illicit bed, full of sin, and should never have removed from his side his noble consort and her gentle wifely embraces, in contempt of her noble birth.[5]

On another occasion the author poured scorn on the fact that in early September 1315 Edward II was nearly drowned when a boat overturned while he was rowing in Cambridgeshire, to which he had gone with 'a great company of simple people'. Writing of Edward II's deposition, the author was at pains to make it appear, contrary to most other evidence, that the king resigned the throne of his own free will. Edward is represented as saying:

> I greatly lament that I have so utterly failed my people, but I could not be other than I am; I am pleased that my son who has been thus accepted by all the people should succeed me on the throne.[6]

It is also possible that the hostility which had grown up between Westminster Abbey and the crown during the reign of Edward II was one reason why Edward III refused the monks' request that his father should be buried there, and instead chose St Peter's Abbey, Gloucester, which was then endowed with a magnificent royal tomb and with other patronage.

There was no shortage of comment and criticism among other contemporary or near-contemporary writers in England. In a memorable passage of his *Polychronicon*, probably begun in or soon after 1327, Ranulf Higden, a monk at St Werburgh's Abbey in Chester, produced a description of the personality and character of Edward which was to be quoted by several other fourteenth-century chroniclers and which has strongly influenced subsequent opinion:

> King Edward was a man handsome in body and of outstanding strength, but, if common opinion is to be believed, most inconsistent in behaviour. For, shunning the company of the nobles, he sought the society of jesters, singers, actors, carriage

drivers, diggers, oarsmen, sailors, and the practitioners of other kinds of mechanical arts. He indulged in drink, betrayed confidences lightly, struck out at those standing near him for little reason and followed the counsel of others rather than his own. He was extravagant in his gifts, splendid in entertainment, ready in speech, but inconsistent in action. He was unlucky against his enemies, violent with members of his household, and ardently attached to one of his familiars, whom he sustained above all, enriched, preferred, and honoured. From this obsession opprobrium came upon the lover and obloquy to the loved one; scandal was brought upon the people and the kingdom was damaged. He also promoted unworthy and incapable men to office in the church, and in his days there was a dearth of grain and a constant mortality among farm animals, such as had scarcely been seen before.[7]

Thomas of Otterbourne, the probable author of the chronicle of the Franciscan house at Lanercost in Cumberland, who became lector of the Franciscans at Oxford some time before 1350, supplied a graphic account of Edward II's rustic activities:

From his youth he devoted himself in private to the art of rowing and driving carts, of digging ditches and thatching houses, as was commonly said, and also with his companions at night to various works of ingenuity and skill, and other pointless and trivial occupations unsuitable for the son of a king.[8]

The anonymous *Brut* chronicle quotes some verses, mocking Edward II's love of rowing, which were allegedly sung by Scottish maidens after his defeat by the Scots in 1314. The occasion of the lines was the discomfiture of Sir Edmund Mauley, the steward of the royal household, who

for drede went and drenchede him-self in a fresshe ryver that is callede Bannokesbourn; therefore the Scottes saide, in reprofe and in despite of Kyng Edward, foralsemiche as he lovede forto go by waters, and also for he was descomfitede at Bannokesbor(n)e, therfore maidenes made a songe therof, in that contre, of Kyng Edward of Engeland, and in this manner thai songe:

> Maidens of England, sore may you mourn,
> For you have lost your men at Bannockburn with
>   'Heavalow'.
> What, would the king of England have won Scotland with
>   'Rumbalow'?.[9]

This is, however, only a small part of the information and the opinion contained in the *Brut*, which survives in many manuscripts: in a short version that ended in 1333 and in a long version ending in 1377; and also in three different languages, French, English and Latin. Although the identity of the author or authors is unknown, the account of the reign of Edward II shows a definite bias towards the side of Edward's first cousin and inveterate opponent, Thomas earl of Lancaster; the author described the cult which sprang up after the execution of Lancaster in 1322; and in his account of the deposition of Edward II he also went to great lengths to demonstrate that the disasters of Edward II's reign were the fulfilment of the prophecies of Merlin.

At least three chroniclers wrote works devoted in whole or in part to Edward II's life. The well informed and extremely perceptive author of the *Vita Edwardi secundi*, who appears to have written at intervals during the reign and to have finished his work shortly before the disasters of 1326-7, described Edward II at his accession as 'a robust young man' who 'did not achieve the ambition that his father had set before himself, but directed his plans to other objects', most notably his favourite, Piers Gaveston, who lorded it over the English magnates 'like a second king, to whom all were subject and none equal'.

> If he had habituated himself to the use of arms, he would have exceeded the prowess of King Richard. Physically this would have been inevitable, for he was tall and strong, a fine figure of a handsome man. But why linger over this description? If only he had given to arms the labour that he expended on rustic pursuits, he would have raised England aloft; his name would have resounded through the land. What hopes he raised as Prince of Wales! How they were dashed when he became King![10]

Another apparent attempt at a biography is the *Vita et mors Edwardi secundi*, traditionally attributed to the Oxfordshire knight, Sir Thomas (Laurence) de la More, a nephew of John Stratford, archbishop of Canterbury, who was a witness to many of the dramatic events attending the deposition of Edward II in 1327. The *Vita et mors* is actually an abbreviated version of the *Chronicon* written by Geoffrey le Baker of Swinbrook in Oxfordshire, who probably obtained much of his information from More but did not begin writing until after 1341. Although unsparing in their criticism of the royal favourites, Piers Gaveston and the Despensers, these two works are sympathetic to Edward II, especially in the predicament he faced after his deposition, and are the source of the tales of Edward's ill-treatment while a prisoner and of his brutal murder at Berkeley castle. Le Baker's gruesome story of the murder of Edward II, allegedly by the insertion of a red-hot iron into his bowels, has coloured all subsequent accounts of the reign, both literary and historical.

The remaining work, the *Gesta Edwardi de Carnarvon*, was 'written in its present form towards the end of Edward III's reign'[11] by a canon of the

Augustinian priory at Bridlington in Yorkshire. It was, however, derived from a lost chronicle begun late in Edward II's reign. Part of the chronicle's interest lies in the prophetic writings, drawn from the works of John of Bridlington, which are inserted at intervals in the text. The prophetic verses about Edward II, which were included at the end of the account of his reign, were intended (like the *Brut* author's use of the prophecies of Merlin) to show that the disasters he experienced had been foretold, and were immediately preceded by a character sketch of Edward II derived from, but not identical to, the passage in the *Polychronicon* of Ranulf Higden that has already been cited.

The chronicles are not, however, the only sources of comment on Edward II. Criticism came even from within the royal circle. The exchequer memoranda roll for 1315–16, for example, records that in July 1314 Robert of Newington in Kent, a messenger in the royal household, remarked that Edward could not be expected to win battles (he had been defeated by the Scots at Bannockburn the month before) if he spent the time when he should have been hearing Mass in 'idling and applying himself to making ditches and digging and other improper occupations'.[12] A more public form of protest against Edward II's behaviour took place at Pentecost, 22 May 1317, when a woman dressed as a theatrical player rode into Westminster Hall while Edward was feasting with his magnates and presented a letter to the king. Under questioning she revealed that she had been induced to do this by one of Edward II's own household knights 'who were annoyed that the king was neglecting knights, who had served his father and himself in battle' and was promoting others 'who had not borne the heat of the day'.[13] This episode almost certainly relates to the marriages in late April of Roger Damory and Hugh Audley the younger to Elizabeth and Margaret de Clare, two of the three heiresses to the valuable lands of the earldom of Gloucester, and to the politically sensitive partition of their inheritance which had been ordered on 17 April.

Sermons were another device for expressing criticism of or outright opposition to Edward II and his regime. In late December 1314, the chancellor of Oxford University, Master Henry de Harclay, preached a sermon to commemorate the murder in December 1170 of Archbishop Thomas Becket at the hands of Henry II's knights and implied that final punishment for Becket's death might be visited upon the fourth generation, apparently referring to Edward II. Although Edward II had been on bad terms with Archbishop Robert Winchelsey until the latter's death in 1313, there had never been any question of a violent resolution as in 1170. It is likely that Harclay was more concerned by the controversial appointment by the pope in October 1313 and the impending consecration on 14 January 1314 of Walter Reynolds, the royal chancellor and an ally of Edward since he had been Prince of Wales, in place of the renowned scholar, Thomas Cobham, who was the choice of the monks of Canterbury.

At the very end of Edward II's reign the sermons delivered by three of the leading clergy before the session of parliament assembled at Westminster in January 1327 apparently formed a carefully graduated progression, preparing the way for the actual deposition of the king, who was then imprisoned at Kenilworth. According to the Lanercost chronicler, on 13 January Adam Orleton, the bishop of Winchester, preached on the theme 'A foolish king destroys his people'; on 14 January John Stratford, bishop of London, used the text 'My head is sick'; and finally on 15 January Walter Reynolds, the archbishop of Canterbury and a former close ally of the king, began by stating that 'the voice of the people is the voice of God'.[14]

Less well known are the sermons in which itinerant preachers in Scotland in 1307 foretold that after the coming death of Edward I, *le roy coveytous*, the Scots and the Welsh would join together in an alliance against the English; a similar pattern of events occurred around 1315 at the time of Edward Bruce's invasion of Ireland, when Irish Franciscans preached against English rule. There is no way of judging the impact of such sermons in arousing opposition to English rule in Scotland and Ireland, but the English authorities in both countries were sufficiently concerned to report them to their superiors in Westminster. Ironically, in about 1310 another Irish Franciscan, named Malachy, had apparently even preached before Edward II, his court, and the bishops, and had strongly condemned the vices of the age.

Another ecclesiastical protest, this time in the form of a letter addressed by 'a certain regular of admitted authority' to the king's confessor is recorded by the author of the *Vita Edwardi secundi* under the year 1316:

> Since a king is so styled from the fact of ruling, as one who should rule his people with laws, and defend them with his sword from their enemies, he is fittingly called king while he rules well, but when he despoils his people he is rather adjudged a tyrant. Indeed our king as he passes through the country takes men's goods and pays little or nothing or badly. Those to whom anything is due from such a cause, to save themselves trouble, often make an agreement to remit a percentage, in order that the balance may be paid quicker. Formerly, indeed, the inhabitants used to rejoice to see the face of the king when he came, but now, because the king's approach ruins the people, his departure gives them great pleasure and as he goes off they pray that he may never return. The king, moreover too often visits religious houses . . .[15]

A further category of comment is the literary genre often referred to as 'political songs', many of which survive in English, French or Latin texts from the thirteenth and fourteenth centuries and relate to various reigns and political situations. One of them, the *Poem on the evil times of Edward II*, was written in the 1320s. While the author is critical of what he sees as the oppressive government of Edward II, he also bemoans the state of society in general:

> The Church, from pope and cardinals to parish priest, is corrupt. Money rules in the ecclesiastical courts, the parson has a mistress, abbots and priors ride to hounds, friars fight for the corpses of the rich and leave the poor unburied. Chivalry is in decay; instead of going on crusade, earls, barons and knights war among themselves. Justices, sheriffs, and those who raise taxes for the king are all bribable, so that the poor are taxed while the rich escape. Physicians charge too much, lawyers and traders cheat their clients. The poor are perennial victims.[16]

Other poems of the period include two celebrating the death of Gaveston in 1312, which are composed as parodies of familiar Church hymns, and another marking the death of the courageous young earl of Gloucester, allegedly betrayed by one of his knights, named Bartholomew, at the battle of Bannockburn in 1314. Another poem on the battle was composed by the English Carmelite friar, Robert Baston, who had been taken along by Edward II to mark the expected English triumph over the Scots and was instead taken prisoner and required to write verses in praise of the Scottish victory. The fifteenth-century Scottish chronicler, Walter Bower, gave them an honoured place in his *Scotichronicon*, since 'in view of their excellence these verses are certainly not to be hidden under a bushel, but should be set forth on a candlestick'.[17] The execution of the earl of Lancaster in 1322 was followed by the composition of an office of 'St' Thomas of Lancaster, which was intended to demean the authority of the king who had executed him as much as to extol the merits of the martyred earl. Such poems were probably far more influential than the occasional attempts made by the royal administration at counter-propaganda: in 1316–17, for example, at the time of the great famine, Edward II was presented 'as the wise king, dealing with the famine with aplomb and rectitude, like the pharaoh who had put Joseph in charge of the granaries of Egypt in the time of the patriarchs'.[18]

Poems of social protest are usually anonymous, but it has been suggested that, although they often purport to represent the voice of the 'common people', they were the work of educated writers, probably including clerics of the calibre of the distinguished Oxford scholars Master Ralph Acton and the Dominican friar, William of Pagula. The author of the *Vita Edwardi secundi* also falls to some extent into the same category. While unsparing in his criticism of the personal failings of Edward II and the inadequacies of his government, he is also at pains to describe the failings of others, such as Edward's cousin and long-time opponent, Thomas of Lancaster, as well as the papal curia.

The charges that were laid against Edward II at the time of his deposition in January 1327 were broadly in line with the comments of chroniclers and other critics. He was accused, among other things, of being personally incapable of governing, of allowing himself to be led and governed by others, who advised him badly; of devoting himself to unsuitable work and occupations, while neglecting the government of his kingdom; of exhibiting pride, covetousness and cruelty; and of putting to death, imprisoning, exiling and disinheriting the great men of his kingdom; of failing to observe his coronation oath through the influence of his evil councillors; of abandoning his kingdom and doing all in his power to cause the loss both of it and of his people; and of being incorrigible and without hope of improvement.

One of the most serious and embarrassing forms of protest that could be experienced by a medieval king was the appearance of an impostor claiming a close family relationship or even calling his legitimacy as ruler into question. In the case of Edward II's reign, this appears to have occurred on two or three occasions. On 22 May 1313, when Edward II and Isabella were on the point of crossing to France for a state visit to Paris, a certain Richard de Neueby, described as a yeoman from Gascony, came to the royal court at Eltham in Kent, claiming that he was the king's brother. Rather than throwing him into prison or worse, Edward II gave him thirteen pounds, after which nothing more is heard of him. In 1316 a clerk named Thomas de Tynwelle was accused of saying publicly in Oxford that Edward II was not his father's son. It is not clear whether Thomas meant this to be taken literally or whether he was in effect remarking that Edward II 'was not the man his father was', which was after all a common opinion. There is also the possibility that the episode represents something of a town versus gown dispute within Oxford. After a number of hearings in 1316 Thomas was eventually acquitted.

The best known and the most serious of these episodes was the humiliating occasion in late June 1318, when a certain John of Powderham, from Exeter, appeared at Oxford, claiming that Edward II was an impostor and that he was the rightful king. John was taken to Northampton where he was brought before the king, who was at first inclined towards leniency. After being advised very strongly that such a public challenge to his royal status could not go unpunished, John was summarily tried and executed on about 20 July. Ironically, although the incident took place at a very delicate stage in the negotiations between Edward II and Thomas of Lancaster, which resulted in the Treaty of Leake in early August 1318, it does not appear to have had any political context. John of Powderham was probably just a deranged individual acting for reasons of his own. In the 1330s this incident was referred to by the Dominican scholar Robert Holcot in his lectures on the *Book of wisdom* and was to be quoted from that source by Walter Bower, the author of the *Scotichronicon*, in the 1440s when he was writing about James I of Scotland.

Virtually all the evidence cited so far is critical, sometimes venomously so, of Edward II both as a person and as a king. This was not, however, the whole story, since there were also counter-opinions. One of the elements was the cult of the royal saint, Edward the Confessor (canonised in 1162 during the reign of Henry II), which had been consciously developed by the English monarchy in the years before 1307, and which was given significant emphasis in Edward II's coronation in 1308. Just as Edward himself was very conscious that his name bore the connotations of sanctity, so too were those who tried to promote Edward II's own claims to sanctity and even to canonisation after 1327. The cult of Edward the Confessor also helped to inspire the otherwise unknown Adam Davy to write his English poem, *Five dreams of Edward II*, at about the time of Edward II's coronation in March 1308, and with the apparent intention of presenting the poem to the new king. In the poem Edward II is depicted variously as a knight standing before the shrine of St Edward (a conscious echo of the ceremony of Edward's knighting in 1306); as a pilgrim entering Rome upon an ass (as Christ had entered Jerusalem before the Crucifixion); as a crusader accompanied on crusade by Christ himself; and, finally, standing before the high altar at Canterbury, clad all in red, a colour suggestive of martyrdom.

An even more extraordinary prophecy is contained in a work known as the *Verses of Gildas*, which was composed by an unidentified author, apparently writing around the middle of the reign of Edward II. Although the subject of the prophecy is described only as *Rex noster nunc regnans*, it is clearly intended to refer to Edward II. The prophecy begins, not with a great achievement in the Holy Land, but with Ireland, to which the king will go in 1320 after a certain grave crisis. Once in Ireland, Edward will bring about peace between the English and the Irish, who will then all live together under one English law. From Ireland, Edward will then go to Scotland, in company with the English, Irish and Welsh, and there defeat the Scottish rebels and put Robert Bruce to flight. *Rex noster* will then go to Gascony and kill all the French found there, after which the son and heir of the king of England by his French queen, *quae nunc est*, will become king of Scotland and reign there for the lifetime of his father. On his return from Scotland, the king will honour the magnates of England who come to seek his grace, and will exile all the greatest rebels. As if these prophecies were not fantastic enough, Edward II will then conquer France, pass through Spain, defeat the rulers of Africa, receive the submission of Egypt, and advance to Babylon in Persia. After reconquering the Holy Land, the pope will three times offer him the crown of the world, which he will finally graciously accept. Edward's career will then culminate in the defeat of the emperor of Constantinople, the conquest of the world, the subjection of the pope and cardinals, who will be forced to live by the apostolic rule, and the abolition of the very name of pope.

Neither Adam Davy nor the author of the *Verses of Gildas* is known to have had any direct contact with Edward II, and the prophecies embodied in their writings may be regarded as the triumph of hope over experience. However, between 1317 and 1319 there was the strange episode of the holy oil of St Thomas of Canterbury, allegedly given to Thomas Becket by the Virgin Mary, while Becket was in exile in France after 1164. According to an accompanying legend, the fifth king of England after the reigning king (that is Henry II) would be a good man and a champion of the Church, and by virtue of the holy oil he would succeed in recovering the Holy Land from the infidel. Edward II became personally involved in this after he was persuaded that he was the prophesied king and that the oil would be the answer to his political troubles, if he were to be anointed with it. Edward's efforts to persuade the pope to allow this were firmly rejected by John XXII, and the incident resulted only in Edward II's embarrassment, and in the arrest and subsequent flight from captivity of the apparent instigator of the whole idea, an English Dominican, Nicholas of Wisbech, who had earlier been the confessor of Edward II's sister, Margaret, the duchess of Brabant. As Edward himself remarked in 1319, in a very frank letter to the pope, which is revealing both of the king's piety and of his gullibility in religious matters, he had through his own 'imbecility' allowed the unscrupulous friar to take advantage of his 'dovelike simplicity'.

Edward II's reputation for holiness developed further after his death, in part no doubt as a way of counteracting the political effects of the cult which had already developed around the name of Edward's first cousin, Thomas of Lancaster, after the latter's execution in 1322. Ranulf Higden, the author of the *Polychronicon*, remarked, after telling the red-hot iron story, that some people thought that Edward II should be placed among the saints. Higden countered this view with an account of Edward's vices and the failure of his government, but also made a very interesting choice of religious imagery in referring to Edward's promotion of unworthy churchmen, whom he described as 'a beam in his eyes and a lance in his side'.[19]

In contrast, Geoffrey le Baker's account of Edward II's death seems positively designed to prepare the way for a cult of royal sanctity. The literary device of the bishop of Hereford's ambiguous message to Edward II's gaolers is followed by the terrible details of Edward's murder, by a comparison of his sufferings with those of Christ and a description of him as a glorious martyr. Le Baker also asserted that at the time of his deposition Edward was prepared to end his life for Christ, knowing that a good shepherd should place his soul at the service of his sheep. At an earlier stage in his chronicle Le Baker had claimed that Edward had escaped from the disaster at Bannockburn in 1314 through the intervention of the Mother of God.

Geoffrey le Baker was writing in the 1340s, by which time a movement to present Edward II as a holy figure and even to have him canonised may have been gathering strength. The famous letter written to Edward III by the Genoese cleric, Manuel Fieschi, some time in the late 1330s, in which he claimed to have met the former Edward II and to have heard his confession, presents Edward as a holy figure, who had taken the guise of a hermit after escaping from Berkeley castle in 1327. In the course of extensive travels 'Edward' had allegedly visited Pope John XXII at Avignon, had been to the shrine of the Three Kings at Cologne 'for the purposes of devotion'; and had finally gone to northern Italy where he entered a hermitage belonging to the castle of Melazzo before moving to another hermitage near Cecima in the diocese of Pavia, in Lombardy, where he was 'always the recluse, doing penance', and praying to God for Edward III and other sinners.

Another example is that of the Dominican scholar, Thomas Ringstead (a pupil of Robert Holcot), who was bishop of Bangor between 1357 and 1366, but who was teaching in Cambridge in the 1340s. In her study of Ringstead's lectures on the *Book of proverbs*, Dr Beryl Smalley found an intriguing story about Prince Edward of Caernarfon and his father Edward I, which must have its roots in their famous quarrel in 1305: Edward I

> had cast him off under the influence of evil counsellors. He bore the injury patiently and came to his father's help on a winter's night, when the king was riding along a muddy, dangerous road. Fearing for his safety, Prince Edward took the horse's bridle and walked beside him until the danger was over. The king did not know who had come to his rescue.

And so, according to Ringstead, *Talis filius fuit Christus*.[20] At the end of the fourteenth century a writer at St Albans Abbey also expressed the opinion that Edward was especially blessed by God and deserved to be numbered among the saints.

The magnificent tomb erected in memory of Edward II in his burial place in Gloucester Abbey showed Edward as a figure of great nobility, in contrast to the tragedy and humiliation with which he met his end. The tomb attracted a steady flow of pilgrims whose offerings paid for the remodelling of the south transept between 1331 and 1336 and of the choir between 1337 and about 1355. Royal patronage, by Edward III, Queen Philippa, and the Black Prince, encouraged the growth of Gloucester Abbey as a pilgrimage centre with a special royal connection. There is however no clear evidence of a systematic attempt, whether by Dominican enthusiasts or by royal authority, to start a formal process for the canonisation of Edward II as a saint until the reign of Richard II, who had his own dynastic and political reasons for wanting a royal saint in the family. In 1385 Richard sent a delegation to the curia to press Urban VI for his great-grandfather's canonisation. Richard's work bore fruit on 4 December 1389 when the newly consecrated Pope Boniface IX ordered the archbishop of Canterbury to enquire into the life, merits and miracles of Edward II. The resulting book of miracles was delivered to the pope in Florence early in 1395. Despite further English diplomatic pressure, nothing had come of the attempted canonisation when Richard II was deposed in 1399, after which no further action is known. Unfortunately the book of miracles, which might have thrown a great deal of light both on contemporary opinions on Edward II and on popular piety, is no longer extant.

However much Richard II and other enthusiasts may have tried to enhance the memory and reputation of Edward II, others were working against them. Ironically the cult of Edward II's first cousin and opponent, Thomas of Lancaster, continued to flourish until the Reformation. The St Albans chronicler, Thomas Walsingham, even recorded erroneously that Lancaster had been canonised in 1389; wishful thinking perhaps, but possibly influenced by Richard II's attempts to have Edward II canonised at the very same time. Several of the chroniclers writing shortly before or during the reign of Richard II, such as the Bridlington author of the *Gesta Edwardi de Carnarvon*, Henry Knighton in Leicester, and Thomas Burton at Meaux in Yorkshire, quoted Ranulf Higden's unflattering portrait of Edward II, while Burton also expressed a sharply critical opinion of Edward II's morals in his remark that Edward delighted greatly in the vice of sodomy. Those involved in politics at the highest level were also conscious that Edward II's deposition had created a precedent for future action. In 1387, during the 'Wonderful Parliament', Richard II's opponents pointedly reminded him of his great-grandfather's fate. When Richard II was eventually deprived of his throne in 1399, the dramatic events of 1327, and probably also the likely fate of a deposed king, were very much in the minds of everyone involved.

Although the cult of Edward II as a prospective saint does not appear to have survived the fourteenth century, in later centuries an extensive literary tradition developed around him, variously expressed by historians, playwrights, poets, and political commentators, and deriving its energy from the adverse opinions of the chroniclers as well as from the precedents for political action set by Edward II's deposition and death. Most writers concentrated on the relations between Edward and his favourites, especially Gaveston, who even played a role in French political controversy when in 1588 Jean Boucher drew a parallel between Gaveston and another Gascon gentleman, the Duc d'Epernon, the favourite of the French king Henry III.

In sixteenth-century English publications, Holinshed's *Chronicles*, for example, were distinguished by their author's critical but also sympathetic and balanced judgement of Edward, and by his understanding of the implications of Edward's overthrow for the future of English politics. Holinshed also thought that there had been a sexual relationship between Edward II and Gaveston, but it was only in Christopher Marlowe's famous play, *Edward II*, written in about 1592, that such a relationship was made explicit. More frequently, its nature was hinted at cautiously or cited as a dreadful example and warning of the fate that had befallen kings who allowed themselves to be influenced by favourites and so estranged themselves from their subjects.

In 1596 the poet Michael Drayton published his *Mortimeriados; the lamentable civil wars of Edward the Second and the barons*, which he revised and republished in 1603 under its more familiar title, *The barons' wars*. In the seventeenth century a number of works on Edward II (whose career was often treated in parallel with that of Richard II) were published at times of political excitement. A tortuous poem of 4060 lines by Sir Francis Hubert, *The deplorable life and death of Edward II*, was published in 1628, at about the time of the murder of Charles I's favourite, the Duke of Buckingham. An anonymous pamphlet of 1648, *The people informed of their oppressors and oppressions*, compared the power of Gaveston under Edward II with that of Buckingham, and justified the deposition of Edward II and by implication that of Charles I as well.

The history of the most unfortunate prince King Edward II was written in 1627, either by Henry Cary, Viscount Falkland and lord deputy of Ireland, or, according to recent opinion, by his wife Elizabeth Cary. The work was apparently not published until the time of the Exclusion Crisis in 1680 (with a thoughtful introduction by Sir Winston Churchill, father of the future duke of Marlborough, displaying sympathy for Edward II) and then again in 1689, after the deposition of James II. In the same year there also appeared Sir Robert Howard's *Historical observations upon the reigns of Edward I, II, III, and Richard II*, in which the virtues and achievements of Edward I and Edward III are treated in parallel and contrasted with the errors and failings of Edward II and Richard II. Howard also had something to do with a work published in 1713, *The history of the life and reign of Edward II* while a further reminder of Edward and Gaveston was provided in an anonymous pamphlet, published in London in 1720, *The prime minister and king*.

A significant contrast to the general condemnation of Edward II is *The History of Edward III*, by Joshua Barnes, which was published early in 1688 and dedicated to James II, and which is also distinguished by the amount of original research undertaken by its author. Having argued that Edward II was, at the last, truly repentant of 'all his former vanities', he noted the worthy things which Edward II had done in his lifetime, 'and might have done more, had he not been so miserably interrupted',[21] such as the foundation of Oriel College and St Mary's Hall at Oxford, the house of Carmelite friars at Oxford and the Dominican house at King's Langley in Hertfordshire.

The fascination with Edward II and his fate lived on into the nineteenth century when it became part of an increasingly public debate on the nature of male sexuality, fuelled by such episodes as Marcus Stone's painting of Edward II and Gaveston, which was exhibited at the Royal Academy in 1872, and the trial of Oscar Wilde in 1895. In 1887 Havelock Ellis had published the first modern unexpurgated edition of Marlowe's play, *Edward II*, which drew attention, although in a somewhat defensive way, to the sexual implications of the text. Despite a growing interest in the play among literary societies from the 1880s, it remained unperformed until 1903; and as late as 1908 the Board of Education 'advised that in school history lessons the story of Edward II "be passed over in discreet silence"'.[22]

Serious academic study of the reign of Edward II had, however, already begun and continued into the early decades of the twentieth century. Influenced by the increasing availability of both administrative records and chronicle narratives, by the growth of history as an academic discipline, and by the progress of political reform, this research tended to concentrate on the implications of Edward II's reign for the constitutional development of England. Over and above the constant political crises and the chaos and bitterness of civil war, the reign was seen by historians such as Bishop William Stubbs, T. F. Tout and J. C. Davies as exhibiting a struggle between the king and the magnates on issues of constitutional principle, with the king seeking in the last resort to build up the power of his household as an inner bastion of government secure from baronial control and with attempts by the magnates to reform the royal administration and to manage royal policy in the interests of some greater ideal of constitutional liberty. The importance of Parliament was also seen as being greatly enhanced by its role in the operation of the Ordinances of 1311, in the Statute of York of 1322, and in the final deposition of Edward II. Edward's very ineffectiveness was seen by Tout almost as a blessing: 'A strong successor to Edward I might have made England a despotism; his weak and feckless son secured the permanence of Edwardian constitutionalism'. The 'constitutional' view of the reign held sway until the 1970s when it was challenged by J. R. Maddicott and J. R. S. Phillips in detailed studies of two of the leading magnates, Thomas earl of Lancaster, Edward II's first cousin and his most bitter opponent, and of Aymer de Valence earl of Pembroke, who was also a cousin of Edward II and generally a loyal ally. These and other studies have shown the complexity of the politics of this period, and the importance of understanding individual behaviour and motivations. As a result many of the earlier certainties have largely dissolved.

Edward II has not, however, been the subject only of recent specialised research monographs. The range of interest in and of reference to him is extraordinary. A number of writers have produced accounts of the reign for a general audience and there have been some notable historical novels on the period, especially those by the French writer Maurice Druon. In Italy there are plaques to commemorate Edward II's alleged presence at the castle of Melazzo, near Acqui Terme north of Genoa, and another near Cecima at the former Benedictine abbey of Sant' Alberto di Butrio, marking the supposed tomb of Edward II. These claims are also presented as established facts in the tourist information contained in guidebooks and in local websites. Indeed a general search of the Internet will reveal a great many references to Edward II at all levels of sophistication and accuracy.

Edward II has been made the subject of medical analysis, one early twentieth-century medical author going so far as to argue that the incompetence and peculiarities of behaviour of Edward II were the result of a physical degeneration of the brain. There has been particular interest in Christopher Marlowe's play, *Edward II*, which has been staged many times both in its original form and also in Bertolt Brecht's adaptation made in 1922–3. Sidney Lumet's 1966 film of a John le Carré spy novel set in London, *The deadly affair*, reached its climax during a Royal Shakespeare Company production of *Edward II*. The sexual connotations of the play have made it the focus of numerous doctoral theses and of much other critical writing, and were emphasised in Derek Jarman's very explicit 1992 film version of the play. More recently, the depiction of Edward and of Gaveston in Mel Gibson's 1995 film *Braveheart* has brought the story of Marlowe's play to an even wider audience. In the late 1980s the English composer Peter Tranchell (1922–93) even projected an opera on Edward II. This never came to fruition, but in 1995 a ballet based on the plot of Marlowe's play, with music by John McCabe and choreography by David Bintley, was premiered by the Stuttgart Ballet and successfully revived by the Birmingham Royal Ballet in 1997. Edward's musical associations also extend to a 'folk/reggae' band, named *Edward II* and active since the late 1980s: one of their recorded albums has the evocative title of *Edward the second and the red hot polkas*. It is not too much to say that Edward II and his reputation became a significant part of the sexual politics of the late twentieth century.

Part of the problem of Edward II, and therefore also a major problem for any modern biographer, is that his reputation has in a sense been in the 'possession' of so many people both in his own day and down to the present time. Edward II is one of the few English kings (together with 'bad' King John and Henry VIII and his six wives) about whom nearly everyone still 'knows' something: in Edward's case that he was homosexual and that he was murdered with a red-hot iron. Whether either piece of information is necessarily true and whether it is possible for the historian faced with so many centuries of received opinion and prejudice to reach a more balanced conclusion on Edward II and his reign is another matter entirely.

Notes

1 This essay is based on a longer and fully annotated chapter forming part of a study of the reign of Edward II, which will appear as part of the English Monarchs Series published by the Yale University Press.

2 Beryl Smalley, *English friars and antiquity in the early fourteenth century* (Oxford, 1960), p. 9 (the translation is taken from her ch. 1, 'The English public'); the full Latin text of the *Commendatio* is in the *Chronicles of the reign of Edward I and Edward II*, W. Stubbs (ed.), 2 vols, Rolls series (London, 1883), II, pp. 3–21. The passage cited is in ibid., p. 14.

3 *Chronique de Jean le Bel*, J. Viard and E. Deprez (eds), 2 vols, Société de l'Histoire de France (Paris, 1904), I, p. 4.

4 Antonia Gransden, 'The uses made of history by the kings of medieval England', *Collection de l'Ecole de Rome*, LXXXII (1985), 469. The role played in the affairs of the English monarchy by Westminster Abbey was even greater than that played by St Denis in France, since in the latter case coronations took place in the cathedral of Reims.

5 Antonia Gransden, *Historical writing in England*. II *c.1307 to the early sixteenth century* (London, 1982), p. 21, citing *Flores historiarum*, H. R. Luard (ed.), 3 vols, Rolls series (London, 1890), III, p. 229.

6 *Flores historiarum*, III, p. 235; the translation is that of Gransden, *Historical writing in England*, II, p. 17.

7 *Polychronicon Ranulphi Higden*, J. R. Lumby (ed.), 8 vols, Rolls series (London, 1882), VIII, pp. 298–300. The translation is my own.

8 *Chronicon de Lanercost*, J. Stevenson (ed.) (Edinburgh, 1839), p. 236; the translation is that of Gransden, *Historical writing in England*, II, p. 13.

9 *The Brut*, F. W. D. Brie (ed.) (London, 1906), p. 208. The original text is: 'Maydenes of Engelande, sare may ye morne,/ For tynt ye have [lost] youre lemmans at Bannokesborn with heavalogh./ What wnde the Kyng of Engeland have ygete Scotlande with Rombylogh.' The verses are cited in Michael Prestwich, *The three Edwards: war and state in England, 1272–1377* (London, 1980), p. 81. 'Heavalow' and 'rumbalow' were expressions used by oarsmen.

10 *Vita*, pp. 1, 40; the latter forms part of an assessment of Edward II in the year 1313. The current edition of the *Vita Edwardi secundi* is that by N. Denholm-Young (London, 1957). The translation is that of the editor. A new edition of the Vita is in preparation by Dr Wendy Childs of the University of Leeds.

11 Gransden, *Historical writing in England*, II, p. 13.

12 Hilda Johnstone, 'The eccentricities of Edward II', *English Historical Review* XLVIII (1933), 264–7, citing the memoranda roll for 1315–16, PRO E.368/86, m.32d. A modern observer might have commented that Edward should have been training for war rather than saying his prayers.

13 *Johannis de Trokelowe et Henrici de Blaneforde, chronica et annales*, H. T. Riley (ed.), Rolls series (London, 1866), pp. 98–9.

14 See R.M. Haines, *Archbishop John Stratford: political revolutionary and champion of the liberties of the English church, ca.1275/80–1348* (Toronto, 1986), using the evidence of the Lanercost chronicler. The Canterbury chronicle, Trinity College, Cambridge, MS R5.41, has a slightly different version of the texts employed: Haines, *Archbishop John Stratford*, pp. 185–6.

15 *Vita Edwardi secundi*, p. 75 and p. xvii (editor's translation). The text breaks off at this point. There is nothing to indicate the identity of the 'regular' (that is, a member of a religious order), but since the king's confessor was always a Dominican friar and had an easy and intimate access to the king, it is worth speculating that the 'regular' was a member of the same order. The letter refers to issues such as the purveyance of goods for the king's household, which had been a source of political tension since the time of Edward I.

16 This summary of the poem is in the words of Dr J. R. Madicott in his important paper 'Poems of social protest in early fourteenth-century England' in W. M. Ormrod (ed.), *England in the fourteenth century* (Woodbridge, Suffolk and Dover, NH, 1986), pp. 132–3.

17 *Scotichronicon by Walter Bower*, D. E. R. Watt (ed.), 8 vols (Aberdeen, 1991), VI, p. 367. The Latin text of the poem, with a facing translation, is published in ibid., pp. 366–59.

18 William Chester Jordan, *The great famine: northern Europe in the early fourteenth century* (Princeton, 1996), pp. 177, 258 n. 4 (citing Kathryn Smith, 'History, typology and homily: the Joseph cycle in the Queen Mary Psalter', *Gesta* XXXII (1993), 147–59.

19 *Polychronicon*, VIII, p. 300.

20 Smalley, *English friars and antiquity*, pp. 211–15, 219, 338. As Dr Smalley points out, the story must be apocryphal, since, although Edward did follow his father around in 1305, their quarrel and final reconciliation took place in the summer and autumn and not in winter.

21 Joshua Barnes, *The history of that most victorious monarch Edward III, king of England and France, and lord of Ireland, and first founder of the most noble Order of the Garter, etc., etc.* (Cambridge, 1688), pp. 3, 18–23.

22 Peter Horne, 'The besotted king and his Adonis: representations of Edward II and Gaveston in late nineteenth-century England', *History Workshop Journal* LXVII (1999), 32.

CHAPTER 4

The Lombard League

History and Myth

Edward Coleman

Italy experienced momentous political change during the 1990s. The two main parties of left and right, the Socialist Party (PSI) and the Christian Democrats (DC), which had dominated the Italian politics since 1945, suddenly and dramatically collapsed, whilst entirely new groups emerged as players on the political stage. The demise of the old guard was due, in part, to events taking place outside Italy – specifically the fall of the Berlin Wall and the collapse of Communism – which removed the ideological certainties which had defined left and right in post-war Italy, as in several other west European countries. But there were also trends closer to home which combined to hasten the passing of the old and the coming of the new. In particular, widespread public discontent with the entire political system (*partitocrazia*) began to surface, perhaps liberated by the winds of change elsewhere. Government was portrayed as an over-centralised, bloated bureaucracy, paralysed by corruption and croneyism, totally incapable of delivering adequate public services. Politicians too found themselves subject to criticism and soon also in several cases to criminal prosecution. A series of trials held in Milan exposed illegal collusion on the part of politicians, financiers and industrialists (*tangentopoli*) and, in so doing, destroyed the careers of a number of hitherto prominent figures – notably the former prime minister and leader of the PSI, Bettino Craxi, who fled the country, and the former foreign minister, Gianni de Michelis (DC), who served a jail term. Broadcast on TV, the *tangentopoli* hearings became a national soap opera; the chief state prosecutor, Antonio di Pietro, became something of a national folk-hero.[1]

Despite the apparently seismic nature of the change in the political landscape, the forces of left and right soon regrouped. Indeed both effected speedy returns to government, albeit under new names (*Partito Democratico della Sinistra* and *Forza Italia*) and with the help of new coalition partners: not quite a case of *plus ça change, plus la même chose*, but close. The decline and fall of the two main parties turned out in the end to be less significant than it first appeared. But the emergence of a 'protest vote' and new parties still seems, a decade later, to represent a watershed, particularly so with regard to rise of the movement known as the Lombard league.

The Lombard league has never been a conventional political party. In fact it began as an 'anti-party', a protest against *partitocrazia* and all that the term represented. There is no doubt that it was the principal beneficiary of the wave of contempt for old-style politics that swept Italy in the early 1990s. *Tangentopoli* too played into its hands.[2] The league made a virtue of being outside the loop of mainstream politics, even though participation in two coalition governments and ministerial chairs for prominent *leghisti* have since rather undermined its 'outsider' status.[3] The leadership of the party too has always been unconventional, not to say controversial, none more so than the flamboyant and mercurial Umberto Bossi, whose popularity amongst his supporters remains undimmed despite his manifest eccentricities and lack of political correctness. But it is above all its policy of independence for northern Italy that marks the league out as a radically different. Although initially less extremist, it has come to favour the break up of the Italian state and the establishment of a separate republic in the north, or *Padania* as it has been christened.[4]

This ambitious – some would say unrealisable – project is grounded in the belief that reform of existing state institutions (which the other parties advocate endlessly) is not only impossible, but not even worth attempting. Instead, the league argues that the economically vibrant, fiscally compliant, law-abiding north should be allowed to go it alone, throwing the centre and south back on their own resources. It is thus, stripped to its basics, a policy that appears to be a variation on the theme of 'two Italies' (north and south), which has long been a common political and cultural construct, particularly since the Unification of the peninsula in 1860. Yet, although commentators are generally agreed that Italy as a nation has suffered a perennial 'identity crisis' since Unification, the actual break-up of the state did not feature on any party political agenda until the arrival of the league.[5]

Interestingly, although the league revels in its mould-breaking image and its rejection of the past, it has reached far back into Italian history for its inspiration and its very name.[6] The modern *leghisti* consciously style themselves as heirs of the first Lombard league, an alliance of Lombard city communes formed in 1167 against the German emperor Frederick I. The league holds its rallies at Pontida, in the foothills of the Alps near Bergamo, where representatives of the medieval communes supposedly swore allegiance to their league. Its badge depicts the figure of a knight holding aloft a sword, an image based on a statue erected at Legnano, site of the famous battle won by the medieval league in 1176. The party itself has been nicknamed *il carroccio*, a reference to the war chariot of the city communes, which was pulled by oxen, and served as a standard and rallying-point in battle.[7]

Besides these superficial borrowings, the acquisition of a historical precursor clearly gives resonance to the political programme of the modern league. The medieval communes took on a monolithic centralised state – just as the modern league is attempting to do – and they prevailed. United in their league, the communes may also be portrayed as an embryonic *Padania*, a Lombard 'nation' struggling for rights and autonomy. The medieval league therefore both serves as an encouraging example to the modern *leghisti* and as a historical legitimisation of what the party is trying to do. It might be added that it has the additional advantage of cloaking the less savoury companions of modern separatism – intolerance, xenophobia, racism – in a heroic and romantic hue.

At another level, the adoption of the medieval league also works on the grounds that the best policy for radicals is to appear to be traditional. There are few episodes in medieval history better known to Italians generally than that of the Lombard league and, thanks to the continuing influence of nineteenth-century interpretations of the topic (which will be further discussed below), its outcome is still viewed very positively. There is, however, one problem with all this, and it is a problem rich with irony. A little over a century before the present Lombard league, the story of its medieval 'predecessor', with all the attendant symbols just discussed, was adopted by Italian patriots during the *Risorgimento* and used to justify the unification of Italy. In other words, two political movements pursuing diametrically opposed programmes – the creation of the Italian nation state and its destruction – and separated by a relatively by short period of time, have drawn on precisely the same historical traditions.[8]

The Lombard league therefore raises questions of interest for political scientists, modern historians and medievalists alike. Why did this story of military and diplomatic conflict in the mid-twelfth century continue (or begin?) to exercise a fascination many centuries later? Why did contradictory versions of events emerge, and which version is more historically accurate? Why did the league attract so many myths, and what do the myths tell us about the assumptions and aspirations of the society that invented them? On the whole, medieval historians have been less active in these debates than their colleagues in modern history and the political sciences, and for this reason the discussion which follows will be framed from an avowedly medieval perspective. Given this premise it is appropriate to begin at the beginning with an examination of the medieval sources concerning the Lombard league.[9]

MEDIEVAL SOURCES

It is perhaps surprising to discover, given the number of myths and misconceptions surrounding the Lombard league, that the surviving primary sources relating to it are relatively rich. Certainly in comparison with what is available for the first half of the twelfth century, there is a veritable explosion of source material in the years between the formation of the league in 1167 and the peace settlement made between the cities and Frederick Barbarossa at Constance in 1183.

On the documentary side there is a considerable amount of material that emanated from the league itself.[10] The majority of these documents are records of the formal adherence of cities to the league, or of mutual pledges, agreements and alliances between the various member cities. The key recurring terms which appear in these documents are 'pact/treaty' (*pactum*), 'oath/pledge' (*giuramentum*), peace/agreement (*pax et concordia*). Representatives from two or more cities bound themselves solemnly to aid and assist one another against common enemies. Clauses covering economic co-operation were also frequently included.[11]

These documents give an impression of the shifting and fluid nature of the Lombard league. Beginning in 1167 with five founder members – Milan, Cremona, Bergamo, Brescia and Mantua – by 1183 its adherents numbered seventeen. It had gradually drawn in, willingly or unwillingly, most of the important cities of Lombardy; but it is important to remember that some cities had left in the meantime and some never joined at all. It was therefore neither a spontaneous nor an all-embracing alliance: cities joined or left when they thought it opportune. Nor was it unprecedented. Cities had been concluding pacts of this kind since the early twelfth century, always with an eye to extract maximum advantage in respect of local struggles for power and territory with their neighbours and rivals. It could be said that the Lombard league was different only in that it ultimately became larger than any previous inter-city alliance.[12] It is also true that, unlike earlier alliances, the league was formed with the specific purpose of frustrating the plans of the German emperor in Italy. But it would be an over-simplification to characterise it baldly as 'anti-imperial'. In fact, the terms and conditions of most of the pacts associating cities with the league envisage them giving aid against mutual enemies who, when identified, are not (as one might expect) the emperor, but other cities. The conflict of c.1158–76 was thus as much about local politics and war in northern Italy as about Frederick's attempts to impose imperial rule there.

A similar impression comes across from reading the terms of the great peace treaty of Constance that formally ended hostilities in 1183.[13] Although the preamble to the treaty refers to the 'cities and persons who are in the

Lombard league' (*civitates et persone que sunt in societate lonbardie*) as if these represented all Lombards, elsewhere in the text care is taken to distinguish the cities adhering to the league from those that did not. The fact that the latter group (which included important cities such as Pavia, Cremona, Como and Genoa) were, in the words of the text, 'on our side' (*que sunt et fuerunt in parte nostra*), that is, on the imperial side, underlines once again that Lombardy was by no means united against the emperor.

Turning to narrative sources, the only chronicler who appears to see the conflict as one between 'nations' is Frederick Barbarossa's uncle, Otto, bishop of Freising. Otto's *Deeds of Frederick Barbarossa* (*Gesta Frederici I imperatoris*), written in 1157, contains a brief but famous account of northern Italy as it appeared to this German prelate. Otto was highly intelligent and well educated, and his observations are consequently thought provoking. He discusses the 'the situation of the land and the customs of the nation' (*de ipsius terre situ nationisque ritu*), the 'nation' being for the bishop, in his classicising fashion, 'Italy', though he was well aware that 'Italy' did not exist as a polity.[14] It is noteworthy that he uses exclusively social and cultural criteria to define 'nation', alluding to factors such as the survival of written Roman law, the cultivation of Latin letters and rhetoric, the habit of living in cities. In other words, Otto does not suggest that Italian national identity was forged by war against a foreign invader, as so many other commentators have done since.[15]

No contemporary Italian chronicler writes of Italy or Lombardy as a 'nation'. The many chronicles that describe Frederick Barbarossa's campaigns do so exclusively from the view point of single cities.[16] Naturally enough there are several hostile accounts from Milan which was in the eye of the Fredrician storm.[17] But one of the fullest and most illuminating narrative sources comes from the nearby city of Lodi. This was written by Otto and Acerbo Morena, father and son, between 1164 and 1168 and was then continued by an anonymous author.[18] Otto and Acerbo were natives of Lodi: Acerbo became *podestà* of the city in 1162. In their day Lodi was one of the cities allied with Frederick Barbarossa and their chronicle gives a detailed pro-imperial account of Frederick's wars. But it does so in the wholly local context of Lodi's attempt to remain independent of its powerful neighbour Milan. As one historian has recently noted, the unequivocal support expressed for Frederick in the Morena's chronicle is simply because 'he loves Lodi and hates Milan'.[19]

Similarly limited horizons are typical of other annals of neighbouring cities.[20] The overall picture is of Frederick Barbarossa blundering around in Lombardy, intervening in local wars which started before he arrived and which continued long after he was gone. Each city tried to take advantage of his presence to steal a march over its neighbours and rivals. 'Lombard' versus

'German' does not apply; the notion of 'national' struggle never arises. Whilst it is clear that the Lombard league stimulated a great deal of interest amongst contemporaries, the primary sources give very little comfort to the idea that a national identity (whether Italian or Lombard) was born as a consequence of the conflict.

LATE MEDIEVAL AND EARLY MODERN WRITING ON THE LEAGUE

The Lombard league continued to be written about throughout the Middle Ages. Its memory remained strong in those cities that had been members, above all in Milan. Amongst late medieval Milanese chronicles the works of Galvano Fiamma (1283–1344) are particularly important.[21] Fiamma was very interested in the use of the *carroccio* and his extensive *excursus* on the subject was paraphrased so often in later literature that it became established as a stock description, a prototype for all *carrocci* – Milanese, Lombard, Italian. However, some of the details of Fiamma's description of the *carroccio* are of doubtful historical veracity. He writes, for example, that special troops were detailed to guard the *carroccio* with their lives in battle, and names their leader as a certain Alberto da Giussano.[22] The notion of this so-called 'company of death' caught the imagination of later writers and was to become one of the most pervasive and enduring of all myths attached to the Lombard league.[23] The figure of the knight from the statue at Legnano, which appears on the modern league's badge, is widely assumed to be Alberto da Giussano.[24] Yet it seems virtually certain that the company of death and Alberto da Giussano were figments of Galvano Fiamma's imagination. Fiamma was writing around a century and a half after the time of the original league, and in general known as a somewhat unreliable witness.[25] Neither Alberto da Giussano nor the company of death are mentioned by any source contemporary with the league; nor do they feature in Bonvesin della Riva's *De magnalibus urbis mediolani* (c.1288), the late thirteenth-century Milanese chronicle from which Fiamma derived the rest of his description of the *carroccio*.[26]

Another incident in the history of the league which was to become an integral one in later accounts – the congress of Pontida – is probably also mythical, or at best a greatly elaborated version of a real event. At this meeting oaths were supposedly sworn by representatives from the five founder cities of the league at the monastery of S.Giacomo Maggiore, Pontida, in April 1167.[27] It is an inherently plausible event. Chronicles, including the Morena chronicle, mention a congress of cities held around this time, though not specifically at Pontida; two acts of association involving the same five cities, enacted in unspecified locations in late February and early March of

1167, also survive.[28] But the first source to locate the congress at Pontida is Bernadino Corio's (1459–1513/19) *Storia di Milano*, which is too late to be considered wholly reliable.[29] Later writers, especially in the nineteenth century, were to further embellish the story with picturesque details.

It is highly significant also that the myths surrounding the *carroccio*, the company of death and the oaths of Pontida found their way into the discussion of the Lombard league contained in Carlo Sigonio's *Historiae de regno Italiae* (1574).[30] The impressively wide scope and authoritativeness of Sigonio's history led it to be considered the *capolavoro* of Renaissance historiography, and an indispensable manual for the history of Italy for subsequent generations. So although its account of the league included fictional as well as factual elements, these were accepted and repeated by later authors on the basis of their respect for Sigonio as an 'authority'. Furthermore, the incorporation of the episode into this first erudite history of Italy lifted the league out of the Milanese context within which it had been confined in the historical literature of the later Middle Ages, and placed it on a wider, one might say, 'national' stage.

The Sigonian tradition of the history of Italy, in which the Lombard league had its acknowledged place, was maintained by other scholars in the seventeenth and eighteenth centuries. But a new level of sophistication and professionalism was attained by Lodovico Antonio Muratori (1672–1750), 'founding father' of modern Italian historical scholarship and a luminary of the European Enlightenment. Muratori dealt with the league in two of his works, the *Annali d'Italia*, his history of Italy, and the *Antiquitates Italicae*.[31] He was sceptical about some of the late medieval accretions to the story, such as the Pontida oaths, preferring to rely on the testimony of twelfth-century sources.[32] He considered the battle of Legnano (1176) important and the Peace of Constance (1183) crucial but, as one would expect from the librarian of the Estense court in Modena, one of the last surviving city states in Italy in the eighteenth century, he saw the principal cause of the wars of 1158–76 as the rivalry between cities. For Muratori the Lombard league was an atypical and inevitably temporary arrangement. As Sigonio before him in the sixteenth century (and for that matter Otto of Freising in the twelfth century), Muratori had no difficulty with the notion of 'Italy' as a cultural entity. But he would have considered it inconceivable as a political 'nation'.

THE NINETEENTH CENTURY: THE MYTHS PROLIFERATE

The consensus of erudite historiography in the seventeenth and eighteenth centuries was, then, that the importance of the Lombard league lay largely in its effect on relations between the various city communes – a view, incidentally, shared by many modern scholars (as we shall see). However, this consensus was widely rejected in the nineteenth century owing to the impact of new ideas of republicanism and nationalism on historical writing.

Undoubtedly the pioneering work here was Jean-Charles Léonard Sismonde de Sismondi's *Histoire des républiques italiennes* first published in 1807.[33] A Swiss, Sismondi was deeply imbued with both the ideas of Swiss federalism and the social and political doctrines of Revolutionary France. The sub-title of the work – 'The origin, progress and fall of Italian freedom' – speaks volumes about its didactic intent: 'history has no importance', Sismondi writes in the introduction, 'but as it contains a moral lesson'.[34] Sismondi began his history of Italy in the last years of Roman Empire, shortly before the invasion of the Ostrogoths, but the greater part of the work is devoted to the period 1100–1500. As he sought to link past events to his own time he brings the story up to Napoleon's invasion of Italy in 1796, which is praised as a liberation, and the subsequent period of Austrian domination, which is viewed with abhorrence. The work concludes with what amounts to a rallying cry:

> Italy is crushed. But her heart still beats with love of liberty, virtue and glory; she is chained and covered with blood; but she still knows the strength of her future destiny: she is insulted by those for whom she has opened the way for every improvement; but she feels she is formed to take the lead again; and Europe will know no repose till the nation, which, in the Dark Ages, lighted forth the torch of civilisation with that of liberty, shall be enabled herself to enjoy the light which she created.[35]

Naturally the Lombard league was a key episode for Sismondi. He believed that the league's conflict with Frederick I was a medieval precursor of the struggles against monarchy, tyranny and oppression in western Europe during his lifetime. 'Harsh and haughty' Frederick and his 'barbarian' army were his villains of the piece: the emperor's first expedition into Italy in 1154, for example, 'spread havoc and desolation; the line by which he marched through Milanese territory was marked by fire'. The Milanese, on the other hand, were portrayed by Sismondi as a heroic people ready to make any sacrifice to preserve their liberty. They donated all their wealth to the common war treasury, and 'contented themselves with black bread'. Indeed, in placing Milan in the vanguard of Italian resistance, Sismondi comes close to *equating* Milan with Italy – 'they [the Milanese] saw clearly that they must perish; but it would be for the honour and liberty of *Italy*' [my emphasis].[36]

Sismondi was unabashed that his nascent Italian 'nation' was far from unified, and curiously makes no attempt to downplay the existence of pro- and anti-Milanese (and hence pro- and anti-Frederick) alliances of cities. But if Milan stood for 'Italy', where did that leave her enemies Pavia, Cremona, Como and Lodi? Sismondi knew his medieval Italian history well enough to be aware that it would be absurd to label these cities 'pro-German', but by avoiding the issue, he seriously undermines his 'war between nations' model.

Clearly, Sismondi's *Histoire des républiques italiennes* is a political polemic rather than a work of history. Inspired by hatred of imperial monarchy, centralised bureaucracy and admiration for small liberal states such as his native Swiss confederation, Sismondi unashamedly sought to use the example of the Lombard league's struggles against the empire in the twelfth century to illustrate an early nineteenth-century political agenda. He would not be the last to do so. Despite, or perhaps because of, its overt political message, the book enjoyed widespread and enduring popularity in the nineteenth century, being translated into Italian and English, abridged and frequently reprinted. Its influence is discernible in a number of later works.

Heavily politicised writing on medieval Italy is a feature of the period up to 1848.[37] During this time a noticeably anti-German tone emerges, particularly amongst members of the so-called *scuola cattolico-liberale*, such as Manzoni (1785–1873), Troya (1784–1858), Balbo (1789–1853) and Cantù (1804–95), whose perspective on Italy's past was strongly conditioned by the rising clamour in northern Italy for independence from Austria.[38] The struggle between Frederick Barbarossa and the league suited their purpose in this respect. Firstly the enemy was 'Germanic' – indeed Barbarossa's army is depicted as just another in a long line of invading German armies, stretching back to the barbarian invaders of the Roman empire; other historical invasions of Italy, for example by the French in 1265 or 1494, were less applicable. Secondly, again in contrast to 1265 and 1494, in 1176 the Lombards successfully repelled the invader and secured their independence. Thirdly, as the cities were allied in a league, they could be thought of in a sense as a 'proto-nation'; Legnano thus could be adopted as a 'proto-national' victory.[39]

Politically speaking, these historians were neo-guelphs, and thus they attributed a prominent historical role to the papacy, portraying the popes as protectors of the Italian people throughout the centuries.[40] Here too, the Lombard league was a useful model, owing to the alliance forged against Barbarossa by Pope Alexander III (1159–81) and the communes. Encapsulating these trends, one of the architects of neo-guelphism, Vicenzo Gioberti (1801–52), claimed the victory of the league was: 'the first national act of newborn Christian Italy emerging from the shell of barbarism'.[41] Luigi Tosti (1811–97), a monk at Monte Cassino, whose *La lega lombarda* was published in 1846, also tells the story with flagrant pro-papal and anti-German bias. Moreover, Tosti's liking for colourful anecdotes led him to dwell on precisely those incidents, such as the oaths of Pontida, which have little or no corroboration in medieval sources.[42] Crudely expressed, the neo-guelph view of the twelfth century ranged, on the one side, the pope, Christian civilisation, the Latin people and republican liberty against, on the other, tyrannical power, schism, Germanic barbarism and feudal 'anarchy'.[43] In the climate of the times, it was natural that the neo-guelphs should see the events of 1162–76 reflected in those of 1848–59, the Austrian Empire as Barbarossa's German Empire, Pius IX as Alexander III, and the Italian patriots as the Milanese and the other citizens of the league.[44] There was an opposing neo-ghibelline historical school, spear headed by figures such as Niccolini, Ranieri, Vanucci and La Farina. These writers significantly downplayed the role of the papacy, but their influence was less pervasive than that of the neo-guelphs.[45]

It should be stressed that the reinterpretation of the Lombard league in nationalist terms was far from being confined to academic circles in the mid-nineteenth century. It is equally evident in the spheres of literature, art and music. And poets, artists and musicians were, of course, far more cavalier in their attention to historical accuracy than were historians. Amongst the earliest poetic muses on the theme of the Lombard league, Cesare Cantù's *L'algiso o la lega lombarda* (1828) and Giovanni Berchet's *Fantasie* (1829), stand out.[46] In Cantù's work, the love story of its chief protagonists, Algiso and Ildegarda, is set against the backdrop of the siege and destruction of Milan by Frederick Barbarossa in 1162. Cantù, a fervent nationalist, equated the struggle between the communes and Frederick with a struggle between 'Latin' and 'Germanic' culture and values. His work exhibits the tendency, noted earlier, to equate Italy with Milan in the medieval context, not least in Frederick Barbarossa's lines pronounced on the final capitulation of the Lombard capital – 'Oggi l'Italia è serva'. Indeed Barbarossa is the chief target of Cantù's venom: he depicts the emperor as wantonly cruel and pitiless. For Berchet too, writing his *Fantasie* in political exile in London, Barbarossa was: 'arrogant and coarse as Cain, a devil who swoops again and again on Italy with his hangmen, oppressing above all Lombardy with the high-handedness of his fearsome will, and with all the habits of those who come here to dominate us and steal that which is ours'.[47] Berchet dwells particularly on the battle of Legnano, from which he depicts the emperor fleeing humiliated and in disguise. His powerful prose consolidated the notion that 'the German' was Italy's perennial adversary, in an unbroken line from the barbarians who invaded on the Roman empire, through Barbarossa in the Middle Ages, to the Austrians of the nineteenth century.[48]

Another to take up the this theme was Terenzio Mamiani. A political exile, like Berchet (in his case in Paris), Mamiani wrote his *A Dio, in commemorazione della lega lombarda* in 1842.[49] The plot is similar to Berchet's *Fantasie*, and the condemnation of Barbarossa as a foreign tyrant equally strong. But Mamiani also stresses the religious angle, emphasising that the struggle of the league received the support, indeed the symbolic blessing, of the pope. So to just cause and indomitable spirit is added that ultimate ineffable guarantee of success – divine favour.

If the medieval league was evoked with particular intensity during the heady years of the 1830s and 1840s, it did not disappear as *leitmotif* of Italy's new nationhood after 1860. Giosuè Carducci's *Canzone di Legnano*, a poem inspired by the seven hundredth anniversary of the battle of Legnano (1876), appeared in 1879.[50] In a set of eleven poems entitled *Canzone del carroccio*, Carducci's pupil and his successor in the chair of Italian literature at the University of Bologna, Giovanni Pascoli (1855–1912), evoked a similarly nationalist and patriotic message. The work was dedicated to Milan, but also involved Bologna, thus showing the cross-city, 'quasi-national' unity engendered by medieval league, symbolised by the *carroccio*, whilst the battle of Legnano is explicitly compared here to the *Cinque giornate* of Milan (18–22 March 1848).[51]

As in literature, so in painting the league became a favourite subject. A recent survey counted thirty major nineteenth-century Italian paintings on the theme of the Lombard league, of which six depict the oaths of Pontida, and ten the battle of Legnano.[52] Amongst the most important are those by Francesco Hayez (1791–1882)[53] and Massimo D'Azeglio (1798–1866). D'Azeglio, painter, writer, publicist, patriot, man of action, and later prime minister of Piedmont (1850–2), even built and decorated a replica *carroccio* that was carried with the troops of the Italian general Giovanni Durando (1804–69) on campaign against the Austrians in the Veneto in the spring of 1848.[54] In the later nineteenth century the *carroccio* became a kind of all-purpose symbol, reproduced on a wide range of publications from scholarly journals to popular magazines, and on objects such as shields, coins medals and mementos; it could stand for Milan, or Lombardy, or Italy, according to preference.[55]

In music, the lyrics of Goffredo Mameli's *Fratelli d'Italia*, subsequently adopted as the national anthem of Italy, subtly juxtapose several local and regional patriotic images from different parts of Italy to create a sense of a nationwide journey (*cammino*) towards independence and statehood. The contribution of the north to this profile was, naturally, the league, and the lyric touchstone was Legnano, though it could just as easily have been Pontida or the *carroccio*, as the various elements of the myth were becoming interchangeable by this stage.[56] However, undoubtedly the most interesting fusion of history, nationalism and music in this period occurs in Verdi's opera, *La battaglia di Legnano*. The opera house in mid-nineteenth century Italy was, of course, a meeting-place not only of the powerful and the influential, but also of intellectuals and radicals, and, as such, acted as much as a political forum as an artistic venue. Verdi, of all composers, was acutely aware of this and exploited its possibilities in his earlier patriotic operas

Nabucco (1842) and *I lombardi alla prima crociata* (1843). He wrote *La battaglia di Legnano* during the fervid year of 1848 and it was given its first performance in Rome on 27 January 1849, two months after Pius IX and the cardinals had fled the city, and two weeks before the proclamation of the Roman republic. In these circumstances, and given the overtly nationalistic treatment of the theme, it is hardly surprising that reaction was explosive.[57] It also goes without saying that outrageous liberties were taken with historical facts. The main plot centres on Arrigo, a thinly disguised Alberto da Giussano, and his love for Lida, who believing him killed in battle marries his comrade-in-arms, Rolando. Other by now familiar myths and legends concerning the Lombard league duly make their appearance: Arrigo, for example, joins the company of death, though Verdi's librettist, Cammarano (for obvious political reasons), shifts the setting for the oath-swearing from Pontida to Milan. As in contemporary literature, Frederick Barbarossa is stereotyped as a monstrous foreign tyrant. The battle of Legnano itself occurs off-stage, but we learn from the troops returning to Milan that Arrigo has slain Frederick Barbarossa and been mortally wounded in the process.

The interest of all this in the context of the present discussion is, of course, that it provides a further illustration of how the local and civic impulses, which were the real motors of the original Lombard league, were subsumed, obliterated and ultimately forgotten as the story was pressed into the service of *Risorgimento* ideology. The introductory chorus of the opera, for example, which begins 'Long live *Italy*/A holy pact binds all her sons together/ At last it has made of so many/a single people of heroes', was greeted by a deluge of applause at the opening performance. Significant too the last words of the dying Arrigo – '*Italy* is saved/I die . . . and I bless heaven'[my emphasis]. It is unsurprising that the librettist should distort historical facts and motives: most librettists did. But the nature of the distortions in this case was unquestionably conditioned by representations of the Lombard league in other artistic media and, ultimately, in contemporary historical writing.

The years 1848–9 were, in fact, the high watermark of interest in the league as a vehicle for the expression of nationalist sentiment. Following the Unification of Italy in 1860 circumstances changed, and its appeal seems to have waned somewhat in this respect. In part, this was probably the result of disillusionment with the achievements of the *Risorgimento*. Enthusiastic parallels with the medieval league may have begun to seem somewhat misplaced and overly idealistic. Cesare Vignati's *Storia diplomatica della lega lombarda*, which was published in 1867, marked a shift towards a more sober approach, rooted in the study of the twelfth-century sources, even though Vignati himself was far from free from *Risorgimento* influences.[58] It was even possible for another historian, Francesco Bertolini, to write in 1876 that the battle of Legnano was unnecessary as Frederick was ready to negotiate the year before, that the victory of the league in the battle was due simply to massive numerical superiority, and that the delay in negotiations until 1183 (preceded by a separate settlement between pope and emperor in 1177) actually meant the communes ultimately gained less than they might have done. Such a deconstruction of the near-mythical importance of Legnano would have been unthinkable thirty years earlier.[59] The celebrations surrounding the seven hundredth anniversary of the battle of Legnano in 1876 were the last gasp of the *Risorgimento* love affair with the Lombard league. A ceremony was held at Legnano to unveil a statue commemorating the victory of the league over Barbarossa. In the event only the base was complete, and another twenty-five years were to pass before Enrico Butti's statue was finally put in place. By a curious irony the generation for which the statue would have had resonance had by then passed away and it remained largely forgotten until it was taken up again a century later by the modern league, and invested with an altogether different meaning. Whereas in the late nineteenth century it was a symbol of Unification, today it has become a symbol of separatism.

THE TWENTIETH CENTURY: HISTORICAL SCHOLARSHIP AND SEPARATIST POLITICS

Very little was written about the Lombard league in the first half of the twentieth century. The republican, nationalist, *Risorgimento* paradigm was at a dead end by the 1870s. It would be fair to say also, without labouring the point, that during the fascist era in Italy, in terms of the 'politicised past', attention shifted from the Middle Ages to the Ancient world. But it was probably also simply a matter of the cyclical nature of historiographical fashion. There were flickerings of a revival of interest in the post-war period, and in the last quarter century or so the league has returned as a major theme, both *per se*, and – as in this discussion – with regard to its complex and unusual historiography.

Modern writing on the league takes its cue from two seminal articles published in the 1960s by the distinguished Bolognese medievalist, Gina Fasoli. Fasoli argued that the events of *c*.1158–76 were the result of an inevitable conflict between two diametrically opposed political systems, but definitely not a 'national' struggle.[60] A number of other scholars have since revisited the theme: the major contributions of Franco Cardini and Ernst Voltmer, who have been particularly attentive to historiographical issues, will be evident from the references attached to the preceding discussion. But the important work of Renato Bordone,[61] Alfred Haverkamp[62] and Pierre Racine,[63] amongst others,[64] should not go unmentioned. The consensus which has emerged amongst these historians is that, in order to be properly understood, the league has to be first cleansed of the myths and legends which became accreted around the theme, particularly in the nineteenth century. The important questions to be asked – how and why did the city communes come to create the league in the first place, and what impact did the league have on contemporary north Italian politics and society? – seem deceptively simple. But, until relatively recently, the fog of myth and legend continued to obscure scholarly enquiry.

Beyond this fundamental premise, stress has been laid on the divisions within the league, the inequalities of its membership and the fact that each city was out for its own ends. The league functioned effectively as a military alliance under the pressures of war, but it was unable to hold together in peacetime, as its collapse in the immediate aftermath of the Peace of Constance demonstrates. So, on two counts, the 'nationalist' (Italian or Lombard) interpretation of the league has to be rejected: firstly, because the unity of its members was a front which was always subject to severe strains and ensured that the league dissolved immediately after the Peace of Constance in 1183. Secondly, even the superficially more persuasive argument that the league was edging towards being an embryonic state with its common officials, common treasury, common judicial process and common army, is invalidated by lack of will on the part of the cities to retain them.[65]

If there was at all a contemporary sense of 'national' struggle, of Italian against German, Latin against Teuton, curiously enough it is to be found not in sources emanating from the league but from the league's ally, the papacy. Several historians have drawn attention to the increasingly 'nationalistic' and anti-German tone of papal letters from the pontificate of Adrian IV onwards, even though today most would consider too extreme the view expressed by Michele Maccarone that this trend culminated in Pope Innocent III envisaging a united Italy under a kind of papal protectorate.[66] There is little doubt, however, that successive Popes thought of the Lombard communes as the first and crucial line of *Italian* defence against German interference in Rome and the Papal States. The city communes, on the other hand, despite the creation of the Lombard league, remained resolutely local in what Fasoli termed their 'aspirations'.

Given that mainstream modern historiography has emphasised the lack of evidence to suggest that the twelfth-century communes saw themselves as representing Lombardy or Italy, it might be wondered where this leaves the modern league's claim to be 'descended' from a medieval 'predecessor'. Certainly its utilisation of the bank of images and symbols associated with the medieval league (all to a greater or lesser extent mythologised, as we have seen) exposes it as unoriginal, in that this had all been done before during the *Risorgimento*. But there are other ways in which the modern league's evocation of its medieval namesake are particularly problematic.

One might consider, for example, the main enemy of the modern league – Rome, the capital of Italy, the centre of state bureaucracy and institutions, 'Roma padrona' (the Roman 'landlady' who is always asking for more rent, in the parlance of the league). Yet, in the twelfth century, there was no stauncher ally of the Lombard league than Rome, the papacy and Pope Alexander III. The league even named the new town it founded to block Barbarossa's passage over the Appennine mountains Alessandria in the pope's honour. Had it not been for the efforts of Alexander III and, later, those of his thirteenth-century successors, Gregory IX, Urban IV and Innocent IV, who supported the second Lombard league against Barbarossa's grandson, Frederick II, and his heirs, the city communes might well have succumbed to imperial domination.[67]

Secondly, there are no real grounds for believing the medieval league was 'secessionist' or 'separatist' in the style of the modern league: the communes were not campaigning to set up a separate Lombard state. On the contrary, the cities explicitly recognised their membership of the larger body politic, which was the German Empire, when they included a 'saving fealty to the emperor' (*salva fidelitate imperatoris Federici*) clause in the terms of pacts between them, including adherence to the Lombard league, as they often did. Certainly, at one level, these pacts can be read as declarations of defiance against the empire, but in part they were also attempts to safeguard of the rights and interests of cities *within* the empire.[68] The communes sought, and by the Peace of Constance ultimately obtained, recognition of their 'liberties', or customs, within the pre-existing constitutional framework of the Italian kingdom, ruled by the German emperors.

The notion of a nascent twelfth-century Lombard 'nation' disintegrates further when one looks at the military campaigns of Barbarossa in Italy. One of the main reasons the emperor was able to sustain the war for nearly two decades (1158–76) was the lack of unity amongst the Lombard cities. Despite the existence of the league, the constant changing of sides and settling of local scores, which was typical of all cities, enabled the emperor to play one off against the other. The destruction of Milan in 1162, to take the most emblematic example, was ordered by Frederick but carried out by Milan's enemies – Cremona, Como, Lodi and Pavia. Yet the same cities helped refound and rebuild Milan a few short years later and joined the league against Barbarossa.

As it happens, quite a strong case can be made for northern Italy having a high degree of economic or cultural unity in the twelfth century (as astute contemporaries such as Otto of Freising were quick to realise). Outside Italy too, in other parts of Europe, 'Lombards' were recognised as a homogeneous group.[69] But in political terms the only cohesive force was the kingdom, and it was the *strengthening* of royal powers by the emperor Frederick that the cities opposed and formed their league to resist. Even the very name *Padania*, which the modern league uses to underwrite its sense of a historically legitimate and geographically coherent state, is a misnomer in medieval terms. Although the Romans called the area north of the river Po *Trans-Padania*, the term was unknown in the twelfth century, the era of the league, when the whole region was commonly referred to as Lombardy.[70]

It therefore must be concluded that there is absolutely no historical case whatsoever to support linkage between the modern league and the league of the twelfth century and that claims to the contrary are baseless political rhetoric. Whilst there certainly are parallels between the methods of the modern league and the *Risorgimento* patriots (albeit directed towards opposite ends), today's *leghisti* appear shallow and superficial even in a straight comparison with their nineteenth-century predecessors. This is particularly the case, when one recalls that many of the historians, writers, intellectuals and artists who evoked the Lombard league in the cause of Italian unity were, as has been mentioned, quite literally 'at the barricades'. The same could not be said today. On the contrary, the anachronistic interpretation of the medieval league, which is the foundation of the propaganda of the modern league, is seriously out of step with modern professional historical opinion. Today's medievalists are not flocking to join Umberto Bossi on the platform at Pontida. It also seems unlikely that the modern league will be able to obtain widespread popular support for its view of history in the way that occurred during the *Risorgimento*, not least because, ironically, of the residual traces of the *Risorgimento* interpretation of the conflict between the communes and Barbarossa which linger still in older school text books. Ultimately, neither the *Risorgimento* nationalist nor *Padanian* separatist reading of the medieval league is sustainable. But both are interesting examples of how – surprisingly perhaps – medieval history has been, and continues to be, manipulated in the service of modern political programmes.

Notes

It gives me great pleasure to contribute this essay on Italian history to the volume in memory Albert Lovett. Albert was a frequent visitor to Italy where he consulted the EU archives in Fiesole. He travelled extensively in the country and, knowing my research interests, often sent me postcards from the places he visited. These postcards and their messages remain an enduring personal reminder for me of his ebullience, wit and innate feeling for history of all periods.

1   Bettino Craxi was prime minister of Italy between 1983 and 1987. He died in Morocco in 2000. Gianni de Michelis was foreign minister between 1989 and 1992. After his release from prison he rebuilt his political career in his home city of Venice in the late 1990s, standing a candidate for mayor of the city and becoming secretary of the rump PSI in 1997. The former leader of the DC

and seven times prime minister, Giuliano Andreotti, was cleared of collusion with the Mafia in 1999 after an investigation and trial lasting four years. Italy's prime minister at the time of writing, media tycoon Silvio Berlusconi, received an *avviso di garanzia* (notification that he was under investigation) in 1994 which has not as yet led to a trial. Antonio di Pietro founded his own party (*Lista di Pietro*) in May 2000 and was elected to both the Italian senate and the European parliament. On contemporary politics in Italy see R. O'Daly and C. Jenkins, *Italy to 2000: forging the second republic* (London, 1995), and M. Frei, *Italy: the unfinished revolution* (London, 1996).

2   The league first made a major impact at a national level in the elections of 1992 when it obtained 8.7 per cent of the vote, and this rose to a high point of 10.8 per cent in 1996. In retrospect, it now appears as if the mid-1990s may have been the moment of the league's greatest success, symbolised by the declaration of a 'Republic of the North' or *Padania* on 15 September 1996. In the most recent general election in 2001, however, the party's vote slumped to 3.9 per cent.

3   Umberto Bossi, the party leader, is, at the time of writing (July 2002), minister without portfolio for institutional reform and devolution in the Berlusconi government.

4   The devolution of power to regions is in itself not unusual in Italy, indeed it is enshrined in the national constitution drawn up in 1945. Since then Sicily, Sardinia, Valle d'Aosta, Trentino-Alto-Adige and Venezia-Friuli-Giulia have all been granted special status. One of the problems with *Padania* is that is not a recognised region of the Italian state, but an invention of the league to designate the north of the peninsula, or roughly speaking the Po valley. Another is that, unlike the other regions mentioned, it does not have a significant minority that speak a language other than Italian, or a strong historical tradition of separatism.

5   On the 'two Italys' and the 'southern question', amongst many works see A. Lepre, *Italia addio? Unità e disunità dal 1860 a oggi* (Milan, 1994); L. Cafagna, *Nord e Sud. Non fare a pezzi l'unità d'Italia* (Venice, 1994); J. Schneider (ed.), *Italy's 'Southern question': orientalism in one country* (Oxford, 1998), and G. Bellardelli, 'Le due Italie', in G. Bellardelli, L. Cafagna, E. Galli della Loggia, G. Sabbatucci (eds), *Miti e storia dell'Italia unita* (Bologna, 1999), pp. 53–62, where it is correctly pointed out that the north–south divide is only one of several deep 'cleavages' in post-Unification Italy. I would like to thank Giulia Cecere for discussing this issue with me and for generously giving me a copy of her *Nord e sud nella storia d'Italia. Le radici della questione meridionale* (Florence, 2000).

6   The movement is now known as *Lega Nord*, but this is the outcome of a merger of several like-minded organisations in 1991 including the *Lega Lombarda* (founded 1984). Until the mid-1990s the party badge displayed the words *Lega Lombarda* inset beneath the larger title of *Lega Nord*.

7   The knight has remained a central symbol of the party since its foundation, even though other symbols such as the red cross of St George on a white background and, more recently, a six-leaved, star-shaped plant set within a green circle (representing the fertility of the Po plain?) have also been adopted. On the medieval *carroccio*, see further below, notes 9 and 22.

8   On the origins and development of the party see: D. Vimercati, *Lombardi alla nuova crociata. Il 'fenomeno lega' dall' esordio al trionfo. Cronaca di un miracolo politico* (Milan, 1990); R. Biorcio et al., *La lega lombarda* (Milan, 1991); I. Diamanti, *La lega. Geografia, storia e sociologia di un nuovo soggetto politico* (Rome, 1993).

9   Medievalists are becoming increasingly interested in the issues of 'nation' and 'national identity' in the Middle Ages and in the accompanying historiographical problems. See, for example, A. Smyth (ed.), *Medieval Europeans: studies in ethnic identity and national perspectives in medieval Europe* (Basingstoke, 1998) and P. Geary, *The myth of nations: the medieval origins of Europe* (Princeton and Oxford, 2002). The series 'Peoples of Europe', currently being published by Blackwell, should also be mentioned. However, to the best of my knowledge, the only medievalist who has seriously considered the Lombard league in this context is the Ernst Voltmer in his *Il carroccio* (Turin, 1994), a stimulating work which will be cited frequently in the discussion that follows (see esp. pp. 24–31). Some of the ideas that I develop in this article were first aired in my 'Italy's first Lombard league?', *History Today* XLVI, 10 (1996), 6–8. As was said, much more work has been done on these topics at the modern end of the spectrum, although with inevitable backward glances to Early Modern and Medieval Italy. The classic starting point remains F. Chabod, *L'idea di nazione* (Rome and Bari, 1961). The now very extensive modern literature can be accessed through works such as R. Romano, *Paese Italia. Venti secoli d'identità* (Rome, 1994), which contains a strong attack on the ideology of the modern league in the introduction; A. Schiavone, *Italiani senza Italia. Storia e identità* (Turin, 1998); E. Galli della Loggia, *L'identità italiana* (Bologna, 1998); Bellardelli et al., *Miti e storia*; A. Russell Ascoli and K. von Henneberg (eds), *Making and remaking Italy: the cultivation of national identity around the Risorgimento* (Oxford and New York, 2001), in which see, in particular, S. Patriarca, 'National identity or national character? New vocabularies and old paradigms', pp. 299–319. I thank my colleague David Kerr for providing me with these references.

10 Mostly collected and published in C. Vignati, *Storia diplomatica della lega lombarda* (Turin, 1867), republished with an introduction by R. Manselli (Turin, 1966). This edition and its accompanying historical commentary remain an obligatory reference point for the study of the Lombard league even today. On Vignati see below, note 58.

11 A good example, including all the cited terms, is the pact made in March 1167 between Cremona, Milan, Mantua, Bergamo and Brescia which in effect founds the Lombard league. See Vignati, *Storia diplomatica*, pp.109–11.

12 G.Fasoli, 'La lega lombarda. Antecedenti, formazione, struttura', in F. Bocchi, A. Carile and A. I. Pini (eds), *Scritti di storia medievale* (Bologna, 1974), pp. 257–78.

13 The treaty of Constance survives in numerous copies and has been much studied, particularly on the occasion of its 800th anniversary in 1983. Convenient modern editions of the text can be found in *Studi sulla pace di Costanza* (Milan, 1984), pp. 73–104, and in *Die Urkunden Friedrichs I*, H.Appelt (ed.), Monumenta Germaniae historica [henceforth MGH], Diplomata regum et imperatorum Germaniae, X, part 4 (Hanover, 1990), n. 848. Further discussion of this most important document can be found in *La pace di Costanza, 1183. Un difficile equilibrio di poteri fra società italiana ed impero* (Bologna, 1984).

14 Otto of Freising, *Gesta Friderici I imperatoris*, B. de Simson (ed.), MGH, Scriptores rerum germanicarum in usum scholarum XLVI (Hanover and Leipzig, 1912), repr. (Hanover, 1978) Book 2, ch. 14. English translation by C. C. Mierow, *The deeds of Frederick Barbarossa* (New York, 1953).

15 The implications of Otto's concept of 'nation' are discussed in R. Bordone, *La società cittadina del regno d'Italia. Formazione e sviluppo delle caratteristiche urbane nei secoli XI e XII* (Turin, 1987), pp. 9–18.

16 L. Capo, 'Federico Barbarossa nelle cronache italiane contemporanee', *Bollettino dell'Istituto Storico Italiano per Il Medio Evo* XCVI (1990), 303–45.

17 In particular the strongly anti-imperial *Gesta Frederici imperatoris in Lombardia auctore cive mediolanensis (annales mediolanenses maiores)*, O. Holder-Egger (ed.), MGH Scriptores rer. ger. in us. schol., XXVII (Hanover, 1892); Capo, 'Federico Barbarossa', pp. 320–2.

18 Otto and Acerbo Morena, *Historia Frederici I*, F.Güterbock (ed), MGH, Scriptores rer. ger. in us. schol., N.S. VII (Berlin, 1930); Capo, 'Federico Barbarossa', pp. 327–30.

19 C. Wickham, 'The sense of the past in Italian communal narratives', in C. Wickham, *Land and power: studies in Italian and European social history, 400–1200* (London, 1994), pp. 295–312, esp. p. 304.

20 Wickham, 'The sense of the past', p. 307; a number of the most important city chronicles are collected in *MGH, Scriptores*, XVIII, XIX.

21 Galvano Fiamma, *Manipulus florum sive historia mediolanensis*, L.A. Muratori (ed.), Rerum Italicarum Scriptores, XI (Milan, 1727), coll. 619 ff. See also Galvano Fiamma, *Manipulus florum, cronica milanese del trecento, capitoli clxxiii–ccxxi: Federico Barbarossa e Milano*, R. Figerio (ed. and trans.) (Milan, 1993), dealing specifically with Frederick I and Milan; Voltmer, *Il carroccio*, pp. 44–5. *Chronicon extravagans, Chronicon maius*, A. Ceruti (ed.), *Miscellanea di storia italiana* (Turin, 1869), VII, pp. 439–784.

22 'Tunc (1176) fuit facta in Mediolano una societas que dicta fuit societas militum de la morte . . . et fuit eorum capitaneus Albertus de Gluxiano, habens vexillum communitatis', Fiamma, *Chronicon maius*, p. 718. On the *carroccio*, apart from the essential work of Voltmer, see also H. Zug-Tucci, 'Il *carroccio* nella vita comunale italiana', *Quellen und Forschungen aus italienischen Archiven und Bibliotheken* LXV (1988), 1–104.

23 M. Carpinello, *Alberto da Giussano: tra mito e storia* (Milan, 1993).

24 Voltmer, *Il carroccio*, p. 20, n. 37.

25 E. Cochrane, *Historians and historiography in the Italian Renaissance* (London and Chicago, 1981), p. 109

26 Bonvesin de la Riva, *De magnalibus urbis mediolani*, P. Chiesa (ed.) (Milan, 1998); earlier edn F. Novati (ed.) in *Bullettino dell'Istituto storico Italiano per il Medio Evo e Archivio Muratoriano*, XX (1898), 61–176. Italian translation, G. Pontiggia (ed.), *Le meraviglie di Milano* (Milan, 1974). English translation, T. Dean (ed.), *The towns of Italy in the later Middle Ages* (Manchester, 2000), pp. 11–16. On Bonvesin see B. Sasse-Tateo, *Tradition und Pragmatik in Bonvesins 'De magnalibus mediolani'. Studien zur Arbeitstechnik und zum Selbstverständnis eines Mailänder Schriftstellers aus dem späten 13 Jahrhundert* (Frankfurt, Bern and New York, 1991). Although Bonvesin does not mention Alberto da Giussano he does mention a 'chief official' or 'foreman' of the *carroccio* (*magister*), a term which itself does not appear in earlier sources. Fiamma's Alberto da Giussano may be an elaboration of this reference: Voltmer, *Il carroccio*, pp. 43–4.

27 The monastery was founded in the eleventh century, destroyed by Bernabò Visconti in 1373 and rebuilt in the 1480s. It is substantially intact today.

28 Vignati, *Storia della lega lombarda*, pp. 103–13.

29 Bernadino Corio, *Storia di Milano*, A. Morisi Guerra (ed.) (Turin, 1978); on Corio see *Dizionario biografico degli italiani*, XXIX, pp. 75–8, and *Lexikon des Mittlealters* (Munich and Zurich, 1984), III, coll. 236 ff.

30 Carlo Sigonio, *Historiae de regno Italiae libri quindecim ab anno DLXX usque ad MCC continent* (Venice, 1574); G. Tabacco, *The struggle for power in medieval Italy* (Cambridge, 1989), pp. 8–10; Voltmer, *Il carroccio*, pp. 147–50; Cochrane, *Historians and historiography*, pp. 309–14.

31 L. A. Muratori, *Antiquitates Italicae medii aevi*, 6 vols (Milan, 1738–42); Muratori, *Annali d'Italia dal principio dell'era volgare fino all'anno MDCCL*, 12 vols (Rome, 1752–4). See also G. Falco and F. Forti, *Opere di L. A. Muratori* (Milan and Naples, 1964), pp. 579–772, 1017–1501.

32 Muratori considered the Lombard league and Frederick I in Dissertation CDVIII of the *Antiquitates*; see F. Cardini, 'Federico Barbarossa e il romanticismo italiano', in Cardini, *Dal medieovo alla medievistica* (Genoa, 1989), pp. 177–224, esp. p. 180.

33 J. C. L. Sismonde de Sismondi, *Histoire des républiques italiennes. De la Renaissance de la liberté en Italie, de ses progrès, de sa décadence et de sa chute*, 7 vols (Paris, 1808–17); abridged and translated into English as *Italian republics or the origin, progress and fall of Italian freedom* (Paris and Florence, 1841). The page references in the following notes are from this English edition. See the comments of A. Lyttleton, 'Creating a national past: history, myth and image in the *Risorgimento*', in Ascoli and Von Henneberg (eds), *Making and remaking Italy*, pp. 27–74, esp. pp. 42–6; Cardini, 'Federico Barbarossa', pp. 184–5.

34 Sismondi, *Italian republics*, p. 1.

35 Ibid., p. 270.

36 Ibid., pp. 27, 28, 30.

37 G. Fasoli, 'Problemi medievali nella storiografia risorgimentale', in F. Bocchi et al. (eds), *Scritti di storia medievale*, pp. 645–62; I. Porciani, 'Il medioevo nella costruzione dell'Italia unita: la proposta di un mito' in R. Elze and P. Schiera (eds), *Il medioevo nell'ottocento in Italia e in Germania* (Bologna, 1988), pp. 163–91.

38 B. Croce, *Storia della storiografia italiana nel secolo decimo nono* (Bari, 1921), pp. 128–43. Cantù's *Storia universale*, published in 1838, which depicts Frederick I as the enemy of the league and the tyrant who destroyed Milan in 1167, was used as a textbook in schools and became very influential. Lyttleton, 'Creating a national past', pp. 46–50; Cardini, 'Federico Barbarossa', pp. 187–91.

39 Cardini, 'Federico Barbarossa', p. 186.

40 In essence the idea of the 'neo-guelphs' was to imitate the Guelph party of medieval Italy by forging an alliance with Papacy and negotiating with Austrian Empire for formation of an independent Italian confederation of principalities. Its champions were Vincenzo Gioberti and Cesare Balbo. Their position appeared initially strengthened by election of Giovanni Maria Mastai Ferretti, who had reputation as a liberal, as Pope Pius IX in 1846. But ultimately Pius IX opposed Italian nationalism. P. Herde, *Guelfen und Neoguelfen. Zur Geschichte einer nationalem Ideologie von Mittelalter zum Risorgimento* (Wiesbaden, 1986).

41 'Il primo atto nazionale dell'Italia cristiana e neonata, schiusa appena dal guscio delle barbarie', quoted in Cardini, *Federico Barbarossa*, p. 197, from Gioberti's treatise, *The moral primacy of the Italians (Primato morale e civile degli italiani)*, published in 1843.

42 L. Tosti, 'Storia della lega lombarda' in Tosti, *Opere complete* (Rome, 1866), VI; Croce, *Storia della storiografia*, pp. 145–7.

43 Cardini, 'Federico Barbarossa', p. 198.

44 F. Cardini, *La vera storia della lega lombarda* (Milan, 1991), p. 133.

45 Croce, *Storia della storiografia*, p. 167 ff.

46 Amongst others who tried their hand at literary evocation of the Lombard league in the early nineteenth century was Cesare Balbo, who later turned to the writing of history. Similarly, Cantù, as we have seen, wrote history as well as verse. The cross-fertilisation between history and literature is very marked in this period: Cardini, 'Federico Barbarossa', pp. 187–9.

47 'Superbo e ruvido come Caino, seccafistole per eccellenza, calato e ricalato in Italia co'suoi manigoldi, angariò principalmente la Lombardia colla prepotenza d'una volontà feroce, con quei soliti bei modi di chi scende di là padroneggiarci, a raspar quel che è nostro', quoted in Cardini, *Federico Barbarossa*, p. 189. See F. Cardini, *Il Barbarossa, vita, trionfi e illusioni di Federico I imperatore* (Milan, 1992), for further discussion of Frederick and Italy. O. Engels, 'Federico I Barbarossa e l'Italia nella storiografia più recente', *Bollettino dell'Istituto Storico Italiano per il Medio Evo* XCVI (1990), 39–60, covers the evolution of Frederick's image in post-*Risorgimento* Italian historiography.

48 Berchet (1783–1851) drew heavily on Galvano Fiamma's chronicle for his information. Consequently he includes the legend of the company of death, and another legend according to which three white doves representing the Milanese martyr-saints Martirion, Sisinnius and Alessander flew from their tombs in the church of S. Simpliciano to alight on the banner of the *carroccio* on the battlefield of Legnano, much to the consternation of Barbarossa and his army: Voltmer, *Il carroccio*, p. 15.

49 Cardini, 'Federico Barbarossa', pp. 195–6.

50 G. Carducci, *Canzone di Legnano. Il parlamento*, in Carducci, *Poesie*, R. Siri (ed.) (Naples, 1969), pp. 557–670. The great popular success of this poem had the effect of further enhancing the reputation of the legendary Alberto da Giussano, who is given a prominent role: Voltmer, *Il carroccio*, pp. 19–20.

51 G. Pascoli, *Le canzoni di re Enrico. I La canzone del carroccio*, cited in Voltmer, *Il carroccio*, p. 20.

52 Voltmer, *Il carroccio*, p. 14, nn. 20, 21.

53 Hayez is discussed in Lyttleton, 'Creating a national past', pp. 34–42.

54 D'Azeglio wrote an order of the day to Italian troops on this campaign, appealing explicitly to the spirit of Legnano and the alliance between Pope Alexander III and Lombard league. He sought to depict the war as a struggle against enemies of God and Italy; a sort of crusade. Durando's forces surrendered to the Austrians near Vicenza on 10 June. D'Azeglio was wounded and taken prisoner: Voltmer, *Il carroccio*, p. 17.

55 Voltmer, *Il carroccio*, p. 21.

56 M. Fubini, 'La lega lombarda nella letteratura dell'ottocento', in *Popolo e stato in Italia nell'età di Federico Barbarossa* (see below note 64), pp. 399–420; P. Brunello, 'Pontida', in M. Isenghi (ed.), *I luoghi della memoria: simboli e miti dell'Italia unita* (Bari, 1996), pp. 15–28; G. Martini, 'La battaglia di Legnano: la realtà e il mito', *Nuova Antologia* CXI (1976): 357–71;

E. Sestan, 'Legnano nella storia romantica', in G. Pinto (ed.), *Storiografia dell' otto e novecento* (Florence, 1991), pp. 221–40.

57   After the first performance the entire last act had to be encored, after the second performance Verdi and the cast were cheered through the streets as they toured Rome in a carriage. See J. Budden, *The operas of Verdi*, revised edn, 2 vols (Oxford, 1992), I, pp. 387–415 (my thanks to Michael O'Neill for providing me with this reference). See also M. A. Smart, 'Liberty on (and off) the barricades: Verdi's *Risorgimento* fantasies', in Ascoli and Von Henneberg (eds), *Making and remaking Italy*, pp. 109–18, esp. pp. 112–13; Cardini, 'Federico Barbarossa', pp. 205–8.

58   Vignati was politically active in the cause of Italian independence in 1848. Following the Austrian restoration he lost his job as a teacher and was under police surveillance until Italian independence in 1860: *Storia diplomatica della lega lombarda*, pp. vi–vii. The concluding sentence of his *Storia diplomatica della lega lombarda*, pp. 401–2, shows that he had lost none of his patriotic fervour: 'Seven centuries later we remembered the blood gloriously shed by the Italian cities for their individual independence, we remembered "the first and most noble war fought by the modern peoples of Europe against tyranny" [Sismondi], and we rose up as an independent nation'. ('Noi dopo sette secoli ricordammo efficacemente il primo sangue che le città italiane gloriosamente versararono per la loro individuale independenza, ricordammo "la prima e la più nobile guerra che i popoli moderni d'Europa combatterono contro la tirannide", e sorgemmo nazione independente').

59   F. Bertolini, *La battaglia di Legnano* (Naples, 1876); Cardini, 'Federico Barbarossa', pp. 210–11.

60   G. Fasoli, 'Federico Barbarossa e le città lombarde', and 'La lega lombarda. Antecededenti, formazione, struttura', both reprinted in Bocchi et al. (eds), *Scritti di storia medievale*, pp. 229–55, 257–78. Fasoli restated her views on the subject, virtually unchanged, in a later article: 'Aspirazioni cittadine e volontà imperiale', in R. Manselli and J. Riedmann (eds), *Federico Barbarossa nel dibattito storiografico in Italia* (Bologna, 1982), pp. 131–56.

61   R. Bordone, 'I comuni italiani nella prima lega lombarda: confronto di modelli istituzionali in un'esperienza politico-diplomatica', *Komunale Bündnisse Oberitaliens und Oberdeustchlands im Vergleich*, special issue of *Vorträge und Forschungen* XXIII (1987), 45–58; Bordone, 'L'influenza culturale e istituzionale nel regno d'Italia', *Friedrich Barbarossa. Handlungsspielraüme und Wirkungsweise des staufischen Kaisers*, special issue of *Vorträge und Forschungen* XL (1992), 147–68; Bordone, 'La lombardia nell'età di Federico Barbarossa' in G. Andenna, R. Bordone, F. Somaini and M. Vallerani (eds), *Comuni e signorie nell'Italia settentrionale: la Lombardia* (Turin, 1998), pp. 327–84 [VI of G. Galasso (ed.), *Storia d'Italia*, 24 vols (Turin, 1978–98)].

62   A. Haverkamp, *Herrschaftsformen der Frühstaufer in Reichsitalien*, 2 vols (Stuttgart, 1970); Haverkamp, 'La lega lombarda sotto la guida di Milano (1175–83)', in *La pace di Costanza, 1183*, pp. 159–77.

63   P. Racine, 'La paix de Constance dans l'histoire italienne: l'autonomie des communes lombardes', in *Studi sulla pace di Costanza*, pp. 223–48.

64   Many other contributions are to be found in *Popolo e stato in Italia nell'età di Federico Barbarossa. Alessandria e la lega lombarda* (Turin, 1970), the proceedings of a conference, held

two years earlier, which marked the return of the Lombard league as a major theme amongst Italian medievalists.

65   Fasoli, 'La lega lombarda', pp. 274–6.

66   M. Maccarone, *Chiesa e stato nella dottrina di papa Innocenzo III*, Lateranum, N.S. VI, 3–4 (Rome, 1940), esp. pp. 148–51; cf. B. Bolton, 'Except the lord keep the city . . . : towns in the papal states at the turn of the twelfth century', in Bolton, *Innocent III: studies on papal authority and pastoral care* (Aldershot, 1995), pp. 199–218.

67   M. Vallerani, 'Le città lombarde tra impero e papato (1226–36)', in *Comuni e signorie nell'Italia settentrionale*, pp. 455–82; P. Racine, 'Résurrection de la ligue lombarde' in Racine, *L'occident au XIII siècle. Destins du saint empire et de l'Italie* (Paris, 1994), pp. 183–202.

68   See examples in Vignati, *Storia della lega lombarda*; Fasoli, 'La lega lombarda', pp. 267–8.

69   R. Bordone, 'I "lombardi" in Europa. Primi risultati e prospettive di ricerca', *Società e Storia* XVII, 64 (1994), 1–17.

70   G. Andenna, 'Il concetto geografico-politico di Lombardia nel Medioevo', in *Comuni e signorie nell'Italia settentrionale*, pp. 3–19; D. Zacani, 'The notion of "Lombard" and "Lombardy" in the Middle Ages', in *Medieval Europeans*, pp. 217–32.

CHAPTER 5

A Typical Anomaly?

The Success of the Irish Counter-Reformation

Tadhg Ó hAnnracháin

The fate of the Reformation in Ireland has been a much-debated topic in the historiography of the early modern period. By contrast, the development of the Catholic church in the late sixteenth and seventeenth centuries has been the subject of remarkably little scholarly disagreement.[1] This essay attempts to revisit the reasons for the remarkable success of Catholic reform in the island, in the process addressing itself to one of the central assumptions concerning the Irish Counter-Reformation, namely that Ireland's experience was anomalous in European terms on the grounds that it represented the only area where Catholic reform succeeded in opposition to the state. This issue is of topical importance because the parallel debate concerning the Reformation has recently witnessed a marked impatience on the part of two non-Irish historians with what they characterise as an insular preoccupation with *Sonderweg*, the notion that the Irish experience was unique.[2] Was the success of the Catholic church in Ireland truly a European anomaly or was it in fact merely a variation on a broader theme?

On the last day of August 1619, a Croatian Jesuit, Marino de Bonis, committed to paper one of a series of reports concerning his missionary endeavours in the southern part of the kingdom of Hungary, almost a century after that area had fallen under Turkish domination. Writing from Belgrade, to which he had returned after months of journeying, his assessment of the region was couched in bleak terms:

> From here I do not know how to write other than concerning miseries, travails, sufferings, and continual dangers to life, in which we find ourselves in the cultivation of this desolate and savage vineyard of the Lord. The more one journeys in these districts, the greater miseries are made apparent. Lately I have been in a new world, as I call the province of Carascevo, where I have found new Indies, and I

lived there about three months. I believe that perhaps for one hundred years there has not been a Catholic priest there.³

The chief danger to the Jesuit was not from the Turks who were broadly tolerant of Christian clergy, and indeed often welcomed their presence because of their crowd-drawing capacity which resulted in taxable markets, but from bandits who filled him with a lively and probably justified terror. As he recalled in a somewhat self-dramatising vein:

> fifteen or twenty times a day I recommended my soul to God the Creator and Redeemer for whose glory I exposed myself to such sufferings and risks of my life, considering how he gave his life for the salvation of all, so also I was exposing mine for these his creatures redeemed with his own blood.⁴

This tendency on the part of the author to emphasise the nature of his difficulties and also of his achievements should perhaps be borne in mind when analysing the other aspects of his correspondence, but even so his testimony remains of considerable interest to a student of the Irish Counter-Reformation. Marino de Bonis was clearly shocked by the level of ignorance which he encountered. He reported the stupefaction of many to whom he preached 'that our souls are immortal, and that God has created all things, and that he sees, knows, punishes and rewards everyone, according to their merits or demerits'.⁵ Yet in the midst of, and often in tandem with, profound ignorance of Catholic dogma, the Jesuit continually encountered a surprisingly tenacious allegiance to the Roman faith. In the village of Secase, for instance, he recorded the assembly of an enormous crowd curious to see a priest celebrating mass for the first time. Despite their lack of familiarity with the spectacle, the local population defiantly informed him that their faith was that of the pope in Rome. Included in this general conviction were a number of people who did not apparently believe in God.⁶ Other so-called Catholics were unable to make the sign of the cross.⁷ In the larger town of Carascevo he was met with even greater enthusiasm, the inhabitants insisting

> that although you see us in this desolate country, we are Romans and our ancestors have always maintained the Roman faith, which we also profess. But because we have had nobody who would teach us either faith or law, we have all become savage men.⁸

Not surprisingly, in the light of such sentiments, the local Catholic population was extremely insistent that the Jesuit 'should not abandon them' again. ⁹ The neighbouring town of Sebise, however, was equally determined to acquire his services and eventually he won the consent of the inhabitants of Carascevo that he could depart for a short space of time, provided that he returned to celebrate the feast of St John the Baptist in the town. As it transpired, this promise became a source of great disappointment to the people of Sebise who 'desired infinitely to have a priest'[10] and who provided him with an escort back to Carascevo, which refused to leave his company until they too had extorted a promise that he would favour their town with a return visit.

Intermingled with the avowedly Catholic population in the region, Marino de Bonis also commonly encountered 'enemies of the faith, that is heretics and schismatics'.[11] This was particularly the case in the smaller villages where the number of Catholics had dwindled to a mere handful. Yet although the Reformation had left its mark, the quality of religious observance and education of the reformed population was little different from that of their Catholic neighbours and they were similarly dissatisfied with their lack of competent pastors. In many cases they showed themselves equally willing to listen to the Jesuit and he reported that a great number of the Protestant population whom he encountered 'said to me that they would all be of the Roman faith, which I was teaching, if I wished often to come among them'.[12] Two years previously he had encountered a similar reaction when with some colleagues he had preached in an area near the river Drina containing 'many thousands of heretical Calvinists . . . who said that they would have embraced the Roman faith, which we were preaching, if we wished to leave some priest who would instruct them in the faith'.[13] By early 1620, Marino de Bonis was convinced of the truth of this possibility, writing to Rome: 'If here there were workers, great good would be accomplished. Wherever I go they say to me, if you stay with us, we will all be of your religion. And what can I alone do?'[14]

In light of the general assumption that language represented a considerable barrier to the progress of the Reformation in Ireland, it is of considerable interest that linguistic difficulties seem to have caused only minor difficulties to the Jesuit in his mission of conversion and confirmation. Although he bitterly regretted his own inability to speak Romanian, he did not confine his attention to Slavonic and Hungarian speakers but through means of interpreters reached out also to the numerous population of Romanian descent and language whom he encountered. This extended even to hearing confessions by interpretation.

It seems probable that Marino de Bonis's influence on the religious culture of this area was less than he wished to believe. At times in his correspondence, amid the praises to God for the souls he has redeemed, brief indications of frustration also surface. Yet, even if this is true, then it seems clear that the Jesuit still managed a very notable impact. What were the factors which allowed him to do so?

One can surmise that the most important factors were first, the fact that the Turkish authorities offered no threat either to his person or to those who hosted him and second, the lack of educated competition. Marino de Bonis appears to have been the only university educated cleric to have entered this region in decades. Consequently he encountered nobody with the expertise to challenge or confront him in debate. Not only was he dealing with a religiously unsophisticated population but also with a highly receptive one. While one would not wish to minimise the extent to which the agents of both Reformation and Counter-Reformation strove to impose the values and practices of an educated elite on the general populace, the level of popular anxiety in early modern Europe concerning issues of salvation must be acknowledged. A genuine hunger for clergy competent in terms of both education and personal morality to mediate between the people and God was a critical element of the religious revolution of this era in Europe. In an area like Turkish Hungary, challenged psychologically as well as materially by the fact of non-Christian conquest, the need to establish a secure interface with the Almighty was probably particularly acute. In this regard, the attractions of a missionary such as Marino de Bonis for the reformed and Orthodox population were almost as great as for those who continued to consider themselves Catholics.

This is not to deny that, as a specifically Catholic missionary, the Jesuit may have enjoyed a number of secondary advantages. Among these was his ability to portray himself as an authentic representative of the population's own ancestral tradition. This notion of a shared religion – and in terms of much of what he encountered it can have been little more than a notion – provided an important bridge between the product of a new and elite conception of Catholicism and the religious practices of an isolated and almost entirely uneducated population.[15] The ritual of the Catholic sacraments also provided a concrete focus for the religiosity of a fairly credulous community. Marino de Bonis reported several apparently miraculous cures which followed the celebration of mass and baptism. The occasional distribution of an *Agnus Dei* too was a highly effective strategy since these were venerated as objects of sacred power and rapidly gained currency as potential sources of divine and miraculous intercession. The Jesuit's determined insistence that he required no payment for his religious services also helped to create a positive impression. This appears to have carried great weight particularly among those who did not consider themselves Catholics. As he reported:

> They could not then marvel enough that I had come to visit them in those places so hidden and savage without any interest, not wishing to take from them any payment or remuneration whatsoever, except a little to eat . . .[16]

When viewed from an Irish perspective, Marino de Bonis's reports are of considerable comparative interest. Twenty-five years later in 1645 a group of Italian clerics, including the future secretary of the congregation of *Propaganda*

Fide, Dionysio Massari, arrived in a similarly isolated and peripheral part of Europe, also a century removed from the direct jurisdiction of a Catholic power, namely Kenmare Bay in south Kerry. He and his companions were impressed by the distance which they had travelled to what the head of the party referred to as 'barren and unknown parts in which an Apostolic minister had never set foot'.[17] The ethnographic detail in their reports to Rome concerning the strange dress, customs and food of the Irish, including classical stereotypes such as the extraordinary fecundity of Irish women, bear abundant witness to the exoticism which they perceived in their new environment.[18] Yet the reaction of Massari and his companions to the population of this desolate area was entirely different from that of Marino de Bonis in Hungary. With astonishment he reported that despite the persecution of their heretical enemies 'amidst mountains and barren places, I found the knowledge of the holy Catholic faith flourishing' and that he did not encounter a single child who could not recite the 'Our Father' and the 'Hail Mary'.[19] Over the course of two lengthy sojourns in the island during the next four years, Massari's opinion of the firm hold which Catholicism enjoyed over the Gaelic population of Ireland was rather confirmed than diminished.

As noted above, it has become something of a truism in the historiography of the Irish Counter-Reformation that Ireland represents a European anomaly as a unique area of the continent where Catholic reform succeeded against the wishes of the state. At first glance, Massari's testimony would appear to indicate that the Irish case did represent something dramatically different from an area like Turkish Hungary. Yet a more careful sifting of evidence suggests that what Massari encountered in Kenmare simply represented a different point on a spectrum of Catholic evangelisation. To some extent, the joint diocese of Ardfert and Aghadoe could be portrayed as a fulfilment of Marino de Bonis's prophecy of what could be accomplished in the peripheral areas of Europe if trained clergy were at hand to administer to the population's hunger for educated spiritual guidance. Had an Italian of Massari's stamp entered this area at the beginning of the century rather than in 1645, then it seems probable that his comments would have borne a closer resemblance to those of the Croatian Jesuit in the wreckage of the kingdom of Hungary. But the Catholic diocese of Ardfert had been transformed in the decades prior to Massari's arrival by a prolonged influx of continentally educated clerical exiles. By the 1630s there was a pool of perhaps fifty seminary-educated priests in the diocese who included among their numbers at least six doctors of theology (Richard O'Connell, Maurice O'Connell, Donncha Falvy, Florence O'Mahony, James Pierce and John O'Connor and three doctors of canon law, Edmund Pierce, Malachy O'Connell and another unnamed individual).[20] The administration of the joint bishopric was in the hands of one of these highly educated figures, Richard O'Connell, who was also an extraordinarily experienced and hardworking pastor. A further testimony to the impact which O'Connell and his priests had made was provided in the wake of the rebellion of 1641, when the bishop was sufficiently confident of his capacity to sway the local population that he offered to guarantee the lives and property of Protestants who had sought refuge in Tralee if they were prepared to convert to Catholicism.[21]

The factors which allowed the Catholic clergy of the diocese of Ardfert to establish themselves as the local experts on spiritual matters probably resembled in many respects those which facilitated Marino de Bonis's evangelisation in Turkish Hungary. They too were able to present themselves as authoritative intermediaries with the Almighty, and offered in combination the added attractions of their local provenance, dependence on voluntary contributions, linguistic ability and claim to represent ancestral tradition. Most critical of all, however, was the fact that they found it possible to discharge their functions without an undue degree of danger either to themselves or to those who hosted them. While the attitude of the state in Ireland was not so broadly tolerant as that of the Turkish rulers of Hungary, in practical terms it offered even less menace to the resident Catholic clergy than the bandits who aroused such a lively terror in Marino de Bonis. Without the support of an effective coercive apparatus, the Protestant state church was thrown on the defensive because it seems probable that in terms of both numbers and quality of personnel it was competing at a disadvantage. Indeed, the penalties which did exist against Catholic practice may have acted as a disadvantage to the official church, because they were not sufficient to curtail the evangelical and pastoral activity of the Catholic clergy, but were productive of resentment and popular appreciation of the hardship which Rome's agents were forced to endure.

This point alone does not of course explain the religious complexion of seventeenth-century Ireland, but its critical importance should not be ignored. The historiographical debate concerning the failure of the Reformation in Ireland has provoked surprisingly little concrete research on the mechanics of Catholic success, even by those scholars who see the advance of the Counter-Reformation as an integral aspect of Protestant failure. There has been a distinct underestimation of the manner in which Catholic reform in the localities was organised by seminary educated bishops, making use of cadres of continentally trained clergy, not only in a direct pastoral role but also in a supervisory capacity overseeing other clerical personnel who had not been educated abroad. This was typically accomplished by dividing a diocese into a number of deaneries. In the case of Ossory, which may have acted as a model for other sees, eight such units were established, each with a continentally educated vicar foran who was responsible for convening the priests of the deanery at monthly intervals for discussion, examination and study.²² Because the quality of Catholic organisation has been underestimated, its potential vulnerability to determined state harassment has not been considered in detail, despite the views expressed in this regard both by officials of the state and by the clergy of the Catholic church themselves. When a genuine attempt was made during the 1650s to destroy the organisation of Rome's shadow church in the island, considerable negative success was achieved. Synodal evidence indicates that not until the 1690s was the institutional damage of the Cromwellian period made good.²³

There is no compelling evidence that the setbacks endured by the Counter-Reformation in the 1650s led to a distinct weakening of the population's identification with the church of Rome. As Marino de Bonis experienced in Hungary, religious identity and affiliation did not necessarily depend on any sure grasp of doctrine. The bitter resentments of the Cromwellian era may in fact have served to confirm notions of loyalty to Rome, while simultaneously reducing the effectiveness of the Catholic reform movement. Nevertheless, the response of the Calvinists of Turkish Hungary to the Jesuit missions indicate that Christian populations without access to educated clergy were prepared to consider clerical services from alternative confessions. Educated clergy acted as the nut on the bolt of popular belief. In the long run Irish receptivity to Protestant evangelisation would almost certainly have been enhanced if the Catholic church had been unable to rebuild the structures destroyed during the Cromwellian interregnum.

The purpose of the present essay, however, is not to investigate the politics of why the Catholic clergy escaped sustained persecution in the later seventeenth century. As a number of scholars have pointed out, the problem of whether religious allegiance in Ireland had taken on a definitive form by 1650 differs intrinsically from the question of how the Catholic church had taken a decisive advantage by that date.²⁴ In that latter regard, the freedom of the Catholic clergy to conduct their church building project in Ireland, which I have identified as both vitally significant and considerably underestimated, none the less merely represented the culminating phase of a longer process, during which a state-imposed Reformation had failed to establish itself as the religion of the indigenous population.

The most recent contribution to the long-running debate on the failure of the Irish Reformation has laid the stress firmly on the fatal coincidence during the sixteenth century of the Tudor programme of state building with the attempted introduction of an entirely external Reformation.²⁵ The deployment of evidence from Scotland, Wales, Germany and Norway to support this thesis has introduced a very useful comparative dimension to the topic. In the process, traditional assumptions concerning the role of language have been challenged and the provocative notion put forward that the Irish experience of Reformation can be seen as typical rather than anomalous. It has been argued that the failure of the state-sponsored church in Ireland has parallels with the inability of certain German rulers to impose a second Calvinist Reformation on an already Lutheranised population, thus bringing to the attention of Irish historians a different continental experience from that of the commonly mentioned but superficially investigated case of Bohemia.[26]

The thesis that the state-sponsored confessionalisation of a population which had already experienced a form of early modern religious reform was at best a chancy enterprise coexists comfortably with the contention expressed above that the success of the Counter-Reformation depended to a large extent on the failure of the state's repressive apparatus. Yet, particularly if the point of departure taken is that of Catholic success rather than Protestant failure, the question concerning the original impulses towards Catholic reform remains problematic. How did a country which showed little or no inclination towards a popular Reformation subsequently generate an indigenous movement of Catholic reform and was this an exceptional development in contemporary European terms?

If, as a test case for these questions, attention is focused once again on Ardfert, then it becomes clear that four conditions were necessary to allow the diocese to reach the point of religious development which so impressed Massari and his companions. Firstly, a plentiful number of young men from the diocese, including members of elite local families, had been willing to journey abroad to seek a Catholic education. Secondly, they had been able to enrol as students in a variety of third-level continental establishments. Thirdly, having completed a course of study they had been prepared and able to return. Finally, on their re-entry into the island they had found it possible to function relatively freely despite their status as agents of an illegal confession.

These conditions are best considered in reverse order since the fourth appears the least problematic, rooted as it is in the political history of Stuart Ireland. For a variety of reasons, including most importantly the personal conviction of the monarchs, the lack of local elite support, and the fear of provoking rebellion by pursuing unpopular policies too hastily, the state chose not to engage in an all-out assault on the Catholic clergy, except during the 1650s.

Point three, namely the return of seminary-educated clergy to Ireland, raises a number of considerations. First the geographical location of Ireland and the existence of a multitude of trading links with the Catholic continent, while probably most important in allowing the original outflow of students, certainly also facilitated the re-entry of clerical exiles. The trip back was not without its dangers: it is unlikely that the apprehensions experienced in 1625 by Thomas Walsh, the Catholic archbishop of Cashel, as he prepared to take ship for Ireland were unique,[27] but the constant flow of mercantile traffic between the southern Irish ports and the continent was a major advantage to the clerical diaspora. Was Norway, a country where – in contrast to Ireland – an external state-sponsored Reformation without popular support *did* prove successful, in such easy contact with the Counter-Reformation heartland? Secondly, in comparison to other expatriate clerical communities, was there a high rate of return of Irish clerical exiles to the locality whence they originated and where they operated most effectively as agents of the Counter-Reformation? The pattern which Christopher Haigh has noted for northern England, according to which many priests failed to return to their native areas, where real evangelical work awaited them, but opted instead for the less favourable south, does not, on the basis of admittedly impressionistic evidence, appear to hold true for Ireland.[28] The surnames of the continentally educated priests of Ardfert point compellingly to their local origin.[29] On a national level, the twenty-seven resident bishops appointed in the island between 1618 and 1646, for instance, overwhelmingly held sees in their province of origin and most actually returned to their native diocese or to one immediately adjacent.[30] The bishops themselves also emphasised to Rome the necessity of appointing local clergy because these could expect to be supported by the population.[31]

There has been no systematic investigation of why so many continentally trained Irish clergy proved willing to return to the island, but this is surely a question worth posing. The oath to go back to Ireland on mission, which the continental colleges required of students, is hardly sufficient to explain this phenomenon on its own, although it was probably important in ensuring that Irish foundations were not subsumed into the support network of the permanent exile community. That Spain was already a society over-supplied with priests may have helped ensure that students trained in the Iberian peninsula ultimately made priestly careers in their country of origin rather than that of the educational host. This question assumes particular significance when consideration is taken of the materially unenticing life which awaited the products of the continental colleges in Ireland. Much has been made in the past of how unattractive Irish benefices were to Protestant university graduates from England and Scotland, but the same factors of course existed in a more intense form with regard to the Catholic clergy. The correspondence of Irish clerics to Rome in the period before 1641 is full of discontent concerning the miserable existence which they were forced to eke out. These complaints were particularly acute on the part of the bishops, a group largely recruited from the elite stratum of Irish society, who were well aware of the discrepancy between their income and that of even their most beggarly European counterparts, and who complained bitterly that their episcopal duties demanded standards which they lacked the financial resources to support.[32]

In terms of point two, namely the provision of education to Irish students, the network of Irish continental colleges which had developed since the late sixteenth century was clearly critical in supplying the recruits to the Catholic Church, which helped to transform it in the decades prior to 1641 and provide an interesting parallel with the development of the established church. By the fifth decade of the seventeenth century, no fewer than eighteen different establishments had come into existence.[33] As production centres of clerical personnel, these foundations out-performed the state's institution at Trinity College. This can rightly be seen as a remarkable achievement but it is one which has attracted relatively little research.[34] It has often been noted that in Ireland the church by law established was allocated inadequate resources by the temporal power. However, the shadow church which produced the continental colleges was entirely dependent on charitable contributions. The web of resources which sustained these European foundations was complex. Of crucial importance was certainly the good will and intermittent financial support of the host governments. Nevertheless, it seems impossible that the monetary contributions of essentially disinterested powers could actually bear comparison with the resources allocated by the island's monarch to the educational apparatus of the official church. Support from the ecclesiastical establishment in France, Spain and Rome did, it is true, act as an additional resource: Cardinal de Sourdis, for instance, played a vital role in helping the college at Bordeaux to establish itself while the papacy provided a variety of supplementary scholarships. Assistance from the Irish exile and mercantile community, particularly in Spain, provided a third stream of support.[35] However, the critical factor in maintaining the colleges, which were frequently on the brink of bankruptcy, was the determination of their founders and administrators to keep them in being and the equal determination of students to endure economic hardship in pursuit of their education. In essence, the colleges succeeded as clerical production lines despite the resources available rather than because of them.

The contrast with the performance of the established church in this regard is pronounced, but were the Irish colleges also exceptional in contemporary continental terms? Comparative research is unfortunately almost non-existent, yet the Hungarian experience of figures such as Marino de Bonis indicates that nothing similar to the Irish network of colleges existed for south central Europe and the northern Balkans. Perhaps the most salient feature which strikes an Irish reader of the reports of the Jesuit missions in Turkish Hungary and Transylvania is the sheer paucity of seminary trained Catholic priests. A portion of the kingdom of Hungary was still under Christian control but, despite the willingness of the Turkish authorities to allow Catholic missionaries operate without restriction, only a tiny number seem to have been directed south. In Ireland, by contrast, although nowhere in the island offered itself as a secure site for a seminary, a steady stream of trained clergy entered the island from abroad. That Spanish Habsburg concern for the Catholicism of the Irish exceeded Austrian Habsburg interest in Hungary is unlikely. The contemporaneous conquest of Bohemia may have been a factor in diverting clerical personnel to the north, but the critical difference was probably the number of Irish who came to the continent to seek a seminary education. Almost certainly, it was Irish demand which created the continental college movement, not the colleges which created Irish demand.

But how did that demand originate? In this context the question of the success of the Irish Counter-Reformation coils back on itself to the first point raised with regard to the diocese of Ardfert, namely what disposed the community to produce so many young men eager to journey to the continent for education as priests. As in the debate on the failure of the Reformation it would appear that the original impulse towards the maintenance of Catholicism remains the point of maximum importance, without which all other factors would have been rendered essentially irrelevant.

That Gaelic-Irish disenchantment with the Reformation can be located in the experience of the expansion of the Tudor state in the sixteenth century seems certain. The argument put forward by Bottigheimer and Lotz-Heumann that the alienation of political and ecclesiastical elites was particularly significant in this context makes compelling sense.[36] Their additional contention that the attempt to create a genuine Protestant church was compromised by the fact that it was launched in a confessional age of harder religious certitude is also worthy of serious attention. Historians of the Irish Catholic Church may consider the notion that the late sixteenth and early seventeenth centuries witnessed a resurgent Catholicism 'disposed and well able to exploit every weakness in the official [c]hurch' somewhat exaggerated.[37] None the less, the contemporary religious divisions in Europe almost certainly did exert influence on Irish affairs. In particular, the representation by Gaelic and Gaelicised magnates of their resistance to the Tudor monarchy as religiously motivated reflected the fact that this was the most convenient way to render their struggle meritorious and comprehensible to continental observers. As early as the 1550s, figures who had given evidence of conformity under Surrender and Regrant were appealing to France for protection from what they portrayed as heretical aggression. Similar overtures to the continent were replicated for the rest of the century, reaching an unlikely culmination in the religious rhetoric of Hugh O'Neill in the 1590s. Yet although practical politics may have dictated the initial recourse to the religious card, once in play its effects multiplied in different directions. For those displaced by Tudor centralisation, to conceptualise themselves as the victims of a heretical assault on a Catholic people provided a reassuring psychological explanation for the trauma which had occurred. It was certainly far more acceptable than the contemporary English notion that a barbarous people had been subdued by a superior civilisation and it rendered their plight comprehensible within the dominant intellectual paradigm of continental Europe to which many fled for refuge. The elaboration of this notion in texts such as Philip O'Sullivan Beare's *Historiae Catholicae Iberniae compendium* helped to perpetuate this historical mythology for future generations. It is striking, for example, that even John Lynch, the moderate and anti-nuncioist polemicist of the 1650s and 1660s, accepted the basic narrative position of O'Sullivan Beare with little evidence of difficulty.[38]

Religion offered the opponents of the expansion of the Tudor state a mental framework which both dignified their actions and allowed them to appeal to continental powers for practical support. To a culture undergoing a series of massive changes, Catholicism offered a foothold in modernity which did not necessitate an acceptance of past barbarity. In the early seventeenth century it may also have provided the psychological ballast which allowed modernising elements of the Gaelic elite, for example such as the MacCarthys of Muskerry in south-west Munster, to embrace other aspects of anglicisation with greater speed.

The existence of a recusant Old English community facilitated this process, although to conceptualise the spread of the Counter-Reformation in Gaelic Ireland as another example of the diffusion of Old English culture is probably mistaken. The agents of counter reform in Gaelic Ireland were almost always of Gaelic stock and a variety of continental controversies indicated their prickly rejection of the notion that the Old English of Ireland represented their spiritual guides.[39] Rather the simultaneous spread of the Counter-Reformation in both communities appears to reflect a parallel if connected development. As in the case of Gaelic Ireland, Old English Catholicism benefited as the century progressed from the widespread alienation of the established colonial community from a state structure increasingly perceived as oppressive and unreceptive to their needs. The range of exactions demanded by the state, summarised by the local community under the umbrella term 'cess', undoubtedly contributed to the conditions under which the Old English of Ireland were prepared to abandon conformity to the church by law established.[40] The degree of control exerted by local gentry over ecclesiastical resources of finance and patronage provided the material underpinning for this process.[41] Nevertheless, as has been noted in the past, there are obvious dangers in establishing a simple causal relationship between economic discontent and religious dissidence. Nor does the latest attempt to compare the Old English experience to the rejection by established Lutheran communities in Germany of a second 'Calvinist' Reformation appear to offer a solution.[42] For while there are evidently structural similarities, the essential difference remains as to why the Old English embraced the Counter-Reformation in the first place. The popular acceptance by Lemgo or Brandenburg of the initial Lutheran Reformation can be assumed to have been governed by the same range of factors which facilitated its success in other parts of Germany. Once in place, this brand of reformed religion understandably proved difficult to displace. But the central question with regard to the Old English remains not why that community resisted the Jacobean state's attempt to inculcate the Reformation, but why it imported the Counter-Reformation in the latter decades of the sixteenth century. From unlikely beginnings, a genuinely popular movement of Catholic reform quickly spread through the Pale community and the urban oligarchies of the colonial towns.

Together with resentment of cess, the pre-existing identity of those who began to define themselves as 'Old English' c.1580 may have facilitated the process whereby religion was to become a principal vehicle of expression for communal resistance to the impositions of the state. In this regard, Jim Murray's exploration of the politico-cultural dimension of Old English attachment to Catholicism is extraordinarily suggestive. At the core of the identity of the clerical leadership of the colonial community was a proud belief that the historical justification of the English presence in Ireland derived from their mission to extend the canon law of the western church to Gaelic Ireland and thereby to civilise it. The leap from tax discontent to recusancy becomes immediately more comprehensible if influential clerical figures were already disposed to consider the traditional religion of their community in ideological and defensive terms. That early sixteenth-century concern about slippage towards Gaelic laxity could easily translate into hostility towards Protestant innovation seems eminently plausible.[43] The marked sense of superiority evinced by early seventeenth-century Old English recusants towards the Catholicism of the Gaelic Irish indicates the tenacity with which older conceptions of the religious relationship between the two peoples survived.[44]

If such processes were at work, and the hypothetical nature of these arguments must be borne in mind, then should they be considered exceptional in contemporary European terms? On one level they clearly should not. The intertwining of communal and religious identity in post-Reformation Europe was hardly unique to Ireland. The receptivity of the Irish population to the preachers of the Counter-Reformation also had analogues elsewhere in the continent. In Turkish Hungary, Marino de Bonis aroused a similar fervour to his Irish counterparts despite labouring under even greater handicaps in an area where a previously Catholic identity had either lapsed or was in the process of collapse. Yet the peculiar status of the Irish kingdom/colony, which saw one colonial elite displaced by another in the course of the expansion of the Tudor state into Gaelic Ireland, meant that the island acquired a decidedly unusual religious complexion and as a result genuinely anomalous structures emerged. As Patrick Corish has noted, the resident proscribed post-Tridentine episcopate of the seventeenth century represented one particularly significant example of this process.[45] The manner in which a Counter-Reformation church without property was forced to embrace the domestic household has also been cited in the past as an aberrant and highly influential aspect of Irish Catholicism.[46] There is a possibility that this unique feature has been overestimated in terms of its impact: in the long run it seems probable that the vitality of Irish Catholicism owed more to tribalism than to domestic practice, yet it is undeniable that the Irish pattern was different in this respect from the continental norm. Although they have attracted less scholarly attention, in terms of ubiquity, numbers and success, the Irish continental colleges should also be seen as genuinely remarkable. For two hundred years, the dominant ecclesiastical institutions of the island were located outside its boundaries. At present, I am unaware of any precise parallel to this development in any other part of Europe. Consequently, it is possible to sustain the position that what happened in Ireland was structurally unique without subscribing to the notion that a predominantly Catholic community evolved because this was 'the natural or elemental faith of the people',[47] and without rejecting the need to refer Irish experience to a wider context. On the contrary, further comparative investigation of how the island's experience both differed from and resembled that of other parts of the continent offer the greatest potential for an enriched understanding of the 'typical anomaly' which the Irish Counter-Reformation represented.

Notes

1 This despite excellent work undertaken from a number of different perspectives: see for example Patrick Corish, *The Catholic community in the seventeenth and eighteenth centuries* (Dublin, 1981) and Corish, *The Irish Catholic experience* (Dublin, 1985); Donal Cregan 'The social and cultural background of a Counter-Reformation episcopate, 1618–60' in A. Cosgrove and D. McCartney (eds), *Studies in Irish history presented to R. Dudley Edwards* (Dublin, 1979), pp. 85–117; Colm Lennon, *The lords of Dublin in the age of Reformation* (Dublin, 1989); Raymond Gillespie, *Devoted people: belief and religion in early modern Ireland* (Manchester, 1997).

2 Karl Bottigheimer and Ute Lotz-Heumann, 'The Irish Reformation in European perspective', *Archive for Reformation History* 89 (1998), 352.

3 'Di quà io non vi so scriver altro che di miserie, travagli, patimenti, et continovi pericoli della vita, ne' quali ci troviamo coltivando questa inculta et insalvatichita vigna del Signore. Quanto più si va per questi contorni, tanto maggiori miserie si trovano. Ultimamente son stato in un mondo nuovo, dico nella provincia di Carascevo, dove ho trovato Indie nuove, et ho dimorato quivi circa tre mesi. Credo che forse da più di cento anni non mai vi è capitato alcun sacerdote cattolico':

Report of Marino de Bonis to Marino Gondolán, 31 Aug. 1619 in Balázs Mihály, Fricsy Ádám, Lukács László and Monok István (eds), *Erdélyi és hódoltsági jezsuita missziók 1–2 1617–1625* (Szeged, 1990), p. 366.

4   'Quindeci e vinte volet il dí raccommandavo lo spirito a Dio Creatore e Redentore, per la cui gloria mi mettevo a tanti patimenti e risichi della vita, considerando come egli haveva data la sua vita per la salute di tutti, così anco io esponevo la mia per quelle sue creature redente col suo proprio sangue': de Bonis to Gondolan, in ibid., pp. 366–7.

5   'L'anime nostre sono immortali, e che Iddio ha creato ogni c osa, e che egli vede, sa, punisce e premia ciascuno, conforme alli meriti e demeriti': de Bonis to Gondolan, 1 Jan. 1620, in ibid., p. 377.

6   De Bonis to Gondolan, 31 Aug. 1619, in ibid., p. 368.

7   De Bonis to Gondolan, 5 Aug. 1619, in ibid., pp. 350–1.

8   'Se bene [. . .] ci vedete in questo paese deserto, noi siamo Romani e li nostri antichi hanno sempre tenuta la fede Romana, la quale anche noi professsiamo. Ma perchè non havemo havuto chi ce insegnasse né la fede, né la legge, siamo fatti tutti huomini selvatichi': de Bonis to Gondolan, 31 Aug. 1619, in ibid, p. 367.

9   'Che io non li abbandonasse': de Bonis to Gondolan, 31 Aug. 1619, in ibid., p. 367.

10 '[D]esiderano infinitamente havere qualche sacerdote': de Bonis to Gondolan, 31 Aug. 1619, in ibid., p. 368.

11 'Nemici della fede, cioè heretici e scismatici': de Bonis to Gondolan, 31 Aug. 1619, in ibid., p. 369.

12 '[M]i dicevano, che tutti sariano della fede Romana, che io insegnaavo, se spesso volessi venire tra di loro': de Bonis to Gondolan, 31 Aug. 1619, in ibid., p. 369.

13 'Brief relation of the state of the Christians subjected to the Great Turk by Marino de Bonis, 1617', in ibid., p. 299.

14 'Se qua ci fussero operarii, gran bene si faria. Dovunque vado mi dicono, se voi starete con noi, tutti saremo della vostra fede. E che cosa posso far io solo?': Report, de Bonis to Gondalán, 1 Jan. 1620, in ibid., p. 378.

15 A bridge of more importance in other parts of Europe, namely the mass, does not seem to have been a factor of similar importance because in many parts of the region mass had not been celebrated for decades.

16 'Non potevano poi abbastanza meravigliarsi che io ero venuto a visitarli in quei luoghi tanto ascosi e selvatici senza alcun mio interesse, non volendo pigliar da essi cosa alcun di pagmento o remuneratione, se non qualche poco di mangiare': Marino de Bonis to Marino Gondalán, 31 Aug, 1619, in ibid., p. 369.

17 '[T]ractus steriles et incognitos quo minister Apostolicus nunquam excensionem in terram fecerit': GianBattista Rinuccini to Cardinal Pamfili, 25 Oct. 1645 in Stanislaus Kavanagh (ed.), *Commentarius Rinuccianus, de sedis apostolicae legatione ad foederatos Hiberniae Catholicos per annos 1645–9*, 6 vols (Dublin, 1932–49), II, p. 5.

18 Ibid., pp. 12–13; Rinuccini to Alessandro Celli, undated and unpaginated, Archivio Arcivescovile di Fermo, III c/10.

19 Kavanagh (ed.), *Commentarius Rinuccianus*, II, p. 13; Archivio di Propaganda Fide [hereafter APF]: 'Miscell. Varie', 9, p. 56.

20 Brendan Jennings, 'Miscellaneous documents. II 1625-40' in *Archivium Hibernicum* XIV, 9 (1949); APF, 'S.O.C.G.', 140, ff. 69r-77r.

21 Kavanagh (ed.), *Commentarius Rinuccianus*, I, p. 311.

22 See David Rothes 'Relatio status' in 'Miscellanea Vatico-Hibernica' in *Archivium Hibernicum* III (1914), 88; Catholic diocesan organisation is treated in much greater detail in Tadhg Ó hAnnracháin, *Catholic Reformation and the war of the three kingdoms in Ireland* (Oxford, 2002).

23 Alison Forrestal, *Catholic synods in Ireland, 1600–1690* (Dublin, 1998), p. 193.

24 See in particular Karl Bottigheimer, 'The failure of the Reformation in Ireland: une question bien posée', *Journal of Ecclesiastical History* XXXVI (1985), 197-200.

25 Bottigheimer and Lotz-Heumann, 'Irish Reformation', 313-53; this article also offers a succinct summary of the previous debate on this topic

26 Ibid., 322-52.

27 Thomas Walsh to Luke Wadding, 1 Sept. 1628 in Brendan Jennings (ed.), *Wadding papers* (Dublin, 1953), pp. 269-73.

28 Christopher Haigh, 'From monopoly to minority: Catholicism in early modern England', *Transactions of the Royal Historical Society* 5th series, XXXIII (1981), 129-47.

29 Jennings, 'Miscellaneous documents', no. 9.

30 Cregan, 'Social and cultural background of a Counter-Reformation episcopate', pp. 85-117.

31 Michael Olden (ed.), 'Episcopal comments on the 'Decreta pro Recta Regimine', *Archivium Hibernicum* XXVII (1964), 6.

32 See for example APF, 'S.O.C.G.', 140, ff. 34r-35v, 79rv.

33 T. J. Walsh, *The Irish continental college movement: the colleges at Bordeaux, Toulouse, and Lille* (Dublin and Cork, 1973), map 1.

34 Helga Hammerstein, 'The continental education of Irish students', *Historical Studies* VIII (1971), 139-53 and Walsh, *Irish continental college movement*, provide an introduction to the topic.

35 Walsh, *Irish continental college movement*, pp. 60-1, 91-2.

36 Bottigheimer and Lotz-Heumann, 'Irish Reformation', p. 331.

37 Ibid., p. 336.

38 Tadhg Ó hAnnracháin, 'Though hereticks and politicians should misinterpret their good zeale: political ideology and Catholicism in early modern Ireland' in Jane Ohlmeyer (ed.), *Political thought in seventeenth century Ireland: kingdom or colony* (Cambridge, 2000), pp. 158-9.

39 See for example Jennings, *Wadding papers*, pp. 125-36.

40 Ciaran Brady, *The chief governors: the rise and fall of reform government in Tudor Ireland, 1536–1588* (Cambridge, 1994), pp. 209-44.

41 Lennon, *Lords of Dublin, passim*; Lennon, 'Mass in the manor house: the Counter-Reformation in Dublin, 1560-1630' in James Kelly and Daire Keogh (eds), *History of the Catholic diocese of Dublin* (Dublin, 2000), pp. 112-26; S. G. Ellis, 'Economic problems of the church: why the Reformation failed in Ireland', *Journal of Ecclesiastical History* LXI (1990), 239-65.

42 Bottigheimer and Lotz-Heumann, 'Irish Reformation', 338-50.

43 James Murray, 'The diocese of Dublin in the sixteenth century: clerical opposition and the failure of the Reformation' in Kelly and Keogh, *History of the Catholic diocese of Dublin*, pp. 92–111; ideological alienation of the Old English is also discussed by Nicholas Canny, *The formation of the Old English elite in Ireland* (O'Donnell Lecture, Dublin, 1975) and by Brendan Bradshaw, 'The beginnings of modern Ireland' in Brian Farrell (ed.), *The Irish parliamentary tradition* (Dublin, 1973), pp. 68–76.

44 See for example John Roche's comments on his Gaelic episcopal colleagues in P. Corish (ed.), 'Two reports on the Catholic church in Ireland in the early seventeenth century', in *Archivium Hibernicum* XXII (1959), 146; see also Aidan Clarke, 'Colonial identity in early seventeenth century Ireland' in T. W. Moody (ed.), *Nationality and the pursuit of national independence, Historical Studies* XI (Belfast, 1978), 57–71.

45 Corish, *Irish Catholic experience*, pp. 96–122.

46 A point originally raised by John Bossy, 'The Counter-Reformation and the people of Catholic Ireland, 1596-1641' in T. D. Williams (ed.), *Historical Studies* VIII (1971), 155–69.

47 Bottigheimer and Lotz-Heumann, 'Irish Reformation', p. 352, have suggested that this conviction is still cherished by Irish historians.

POLITICS AND DIPLOMACY

CHAPTER 6

Irish-European Integration

The Legacy of Charles V

Declan M. Downey

When the Irish people voted overwhelmingly in favour of the Maastricht Treaty, the view was expressed in *The Spectator* that the Irish had voted for that treaty for the same reasons that cats might vote for tin openers. Such remarks have found some resonance in the equally condescending rhetoric of insularists, isolationists, and ironically in that of some of the self-styled 'liberal-progressives' and 'left-wing intellectuals' in Ireland who have, only in the very recent past, welcomed Ireland's embrace of European Union as what they term 'her discovery of European values' and thus her 'attainment of maturity'. These attitudes not only do an injustice to Ireland's membership of (and role within), the European Union; they are also founded on ignorance of an historical process of Irish cultural, economic, political and social integration in Europe, notably in the Habsburg lands and in France. This process of early modern Irish integration in Europe began over 440 years before Ireland's entry into the EEC. It was inaugurated with a formal treaty signed in 1529 between James FitzGerald, eleventh earl of Desmond, and the German emperor and king of Spain, Charles V.

Such was the extent of Irish *émigré* integration with their continental host societies that statesmen of Irish birth and of Irish descent attained the highest political office. In the late seventeenth century the Kerry-born Dominic O'Daly played a significant role as chief adviser, personal ambassador-plenipotentiary and ultimately as chief minister of Joao de Braganza, king of Portugal. Meanwhile, Francis Taaffe of Ballymote, County Sligo, became prime minister of the Duchy of Lorraine in 1697. Ricardo Wall (of Limerick origin) was the great reforming prime minister of Spain during the reigns of Ferdinand VI and Charles III in the late eighteenth century. In late nineteenth-century Spain, Leopoldo O'Donnell (of Sligo–Donegal origin) was not only a distinguished military hero but was also a great reformer and liberal prime minister under Isabella II. Around the same time Eduard Taaffe (of Sligo–Louth origin) gave distinguished service as prime minister of the *Cislethanian*, the Austrian part of the Austro-Hungarian Empire under Emperor Franz-Josef while Marshal Edme Patrice Maurice MacMahon (of Clare origin), duke of Magenta, became president of the Third Republic. More recently in the twentieth century, another great French president and international statesman of Irish ancestry was General Charles de Gaulle.[1] These European statesmen of Irish origin are emblematic of the many Irish 'Wild Geese' who integrated with and served their host societies as academics, administrators, bankers, diplomats, ecclesiastics, merchants, military and naval officers, scientists and statesmen from the sixteenth to the twentieth centuries.[2] Of the Irish in eighteenth-century Europe, the English historian Macaulay observed:

> they were to be found everywhere . . . at Versailles and at Saint Ildefonso, in the armies of Frederick [the Great] and in the armies of Maria Theresa . . . Scattered all over Europe were to be found brave Irish generals, dexterous Irish diplomatists, Irish Counts, Irish Barons, Irish Knights of Saint Lewis [*sic*] and of Saint Leopold, of the White Eagle and of the Golden Fleece, who if they had remained in the house of bondage [Ireland under the penal laws], could not have been ensigns of marching regiments or freemen of petty corporations. [3]

Significantly, Macaulay draws attention to the chivalric honours obtained by the Irish through their own abilities and merit. Micheline Kerney-Walsh, a distinguished authority on Irish *émigrés* on the continent, also noted the admittance of Irishmen or men of Irish origin into the prestigious Spanish orders of Santiago, Calatrava and Alcántara as being indicative of their successful assimilation. Kerney-Walsh has identified 200 knights of Irish origin in the principal Spanish order, that of Santiago.[4] Such honours signified their recognition in their host society. The most prestigious honour of all was that of the Order of the Golden Fleece, founded in 1430 by Philip the Good, duke of Burgundy. Between 1690 and 1920, seven knights of Irish origin were invested in the Austrian branch of the Order while three knights of Irish origin were invested in the Spanish branch of the Order.[5] Irish membership of the Order is both socially and politically significant in that its membership was the most exclusive in Europe.

While much has been published on the Irish in France,[6] this essay is concerned with Irish *émigrés* in Habsburg Europe – principally the Spanish *Monarquía* and the Austrian *Hausmacht*.[7] Successful integration may be judged by the immigrant's ability to absorb the host society's culture and to contribute to its cultural, professional, economic and political life. Between 1580 and 1900, Irish *émigrés* collectively known as 'The Wild Geese' in Spain, Flanders and Austria met these criteria for successful integration.[8] Through the mechanism of military, diplomatic and administrative service, the Irish were integrated within Habsburg Spain, Flanders and Austria. As the military historian, Harman Murtagh, observed of the Austrian *Hausmacht*, 'the Habsburg monarchy was the principal employer of the Irish in central Europe. Its multinational character was particularly favourable to the advancement of gifted foreigners – over 100 Irishmen were Austrian field-marshals, generals or admirals, with correspondingly greater numbers in the lower commissioned ranks'.[9] Through their personal merits and professional achievements, they became distinguished and ennobled. In John Silke's memorable words, these Irish *émigrés* and their descendants 'continued, generation after generation, to win honour in their adopted countries, in church, court, and camp'.[10]

Principally, it was through military service that the Irish interacted and integrated with their host societies on the Continent. Brendan Jennings, Micheline Kerney-Walsh, Christopher Duffy, Gráinne Henry and Robert Stradling have studied the development of the Irish military communities in Habsburg Europe.[11] However, Louis Cullen, Augustín Guimera and Maria Begoña Villar Garcia have shown how integration and assimilation were also achieved by Irish mercantile communities (many of whom were long established since the Middle Ages).[12] In this respect the role of the Irish scholarly and ecclesiastical foundations on the continent should neither be underestimated nor forgotten.[13] Many of the Irish *émigrés* who achieved wealth and/or distinction intermarried among the great aristocratic and princely families of the Spain, Flanders, Austria, Bohemia and Hungary. By this means they became part of what Thomas Barker identified as the 'strategic elite'.[14]

By way of illustration, some notable representatives of this elite are worth mentioning. For example, Philip IV's treasury council minister, Count Dermot O'Sullivan-Beare, married Doña Mariana de Cordóba y Aragón, an heiress of the ducal House of Sessa and descendant of 'El Gran Capitan' Gonzalo de Cordóba, hero of the *Réconquista*.[15] In the Austrian *Hausmacht*, General Count Henry O'Donnell von Castlebar married the Wallachian Princess Leopoldine Cantacuzène, descendant of the Byzantine emperor Ioannes VI Kantakuzènos. Indeed other Irish families in the *Hausmacht* such as the Walsh family made similar strategic marriage alliances with the princely Liechtenstein, Colloredo and Kinsky dynasties, while the Taaffe von Carlingford family intermarried with princely houses of Haugwitz and Lindenau.[16]

The foundation of Irish colleges and seminaries also contributed greatly towards the process of Irish integration in Europe. These establishments played a vital role not only in providing Irish Catholics with educational opportunities denied them at home but also in preserving so much of Irish civilisation which would otherwise have been lost. Consciousness of ethnic and religious fellowship influenced patronage of these colleges among the Irish *émigrés*. However, such empathy extended beyond them among their host societies.

When Philip II transferred the Irish hostel in Valladolid to Salamanca on 3 August 1592, it was incorporated in the university as a distinct Irish college. It received royal collegial status, support, protection and privilege. Later in 1610, these privileges were reaffirmed by Philip III who bestowed the title of Collegio Real de San Patricio de los Nobles Irlandeses, Salamanca.[17] Within a short time of this foundation other Irish hostels were reconstituted as royal colleges in the Spanish Habsburg *Monarquía*: Alcalá, Evora and Lisbon (1593), Douai (1594), Antwerp (1600), Santiago de Compostela (1605), Leuven (1606), Lille (1610), Seville (1611), Nieupoort (1627) and Madrid (1629). Considering the Spanish Crown's interest in educating Irishmen and thereby forming the first generation of the Irish Counter-Reformation, it is also significant that Spanish ecclesiastics and nobles were equally benevolent. The Irish college at Alcalá was founded by Count Jorge de Paz y Silveira whose mother was a MacDonnell from Antrim. The Irish college at Seville was founded by the Archdeacon Don Félix de Guzman and Count Jeronímo de Medina Farragut.[18] Interestingly, the Irish Franciscan college in Prague, founded in 1629 under the protection of Emperor Ferdinand II, received patronage not only from Irish-Austro-Bohemian families such as the Bourkes, Butlers, Kavanaghs, Taaffes and Walshes, but also from some of the indigenous nobility. For instance, the college library was endowed by the Austro-Bohemian magnate, Count Wenzel Adalbert von Sternberg.[19] In this respect, the host societies of Irish *émigrés*, particularly in Habsburg Europe, facilitated and sponsored the survival of Ireland's national patrimony.

Significantly the first ten Irish colleges on the continent were established in the Spanish *Monarquía* under royal supervision and protection between 1592 and 1611. By 1629 that number had increased to twelve while another Irish college had been founded in the Austrian Habsburg *Hausmacht*. It was not until 1625 and 1627 that the Franciscan and pastoral Irish colleges were finally established in Rome.[20] In the meantime the character of the first generation of the Irish Counter-Reformation had a Castilian and regalist formation.

As Daniel Szechi has noted, the shared experience of a Latin-based culture through classical education and Catholicism and of a universal code of patrician hospitality emphasised values which were common to the Irish *émigrés* and their hosts. This sense of empathy and the network provided by the pre-existing Irish émigré communities and the Irish colleges eased the integration of their newly arrived compatriots by hospitality, help and introduction to the local élites and authorities.[21]

The royal and the imperial status accorded to the Irish colleges by the Spanish and the Austrian Habsburg monarchies respectively is quite unique in that colleges established in these territories for the education of English and Scots Catholics, while receiving patronage and protection, did not receive crown status and privilege. Furthermore, within the Spanish *Monarquía*, Irish *émigrés* and exiles enjoyed full rights of citizenship. This is in itself quite significant and unique, since the *Monarquía* at that time was very suspicious of non-nationals to whom its social, political and economic institutions were closed. Provided the Irish met the meritocratic and/or nobiliary requirements for admission to academies and offices, or for promotion, decoration or elevation and for investiture in chivalric orders, their Irish nationality or descent was not a disqualification.[22] As Charles II observed in 1680: 'The Irish have always enjoyed in the Spanish dominions the same rights as Spaniards in respect of the obtaining of offices or employments. No obstacle has ever been placed in their way of their obtaining political or military appointments.'[23]

Apart from the rights and privileges evidently enjoyed by Irish *émigrés*, the facility with which they, especially the Gaelic, entered Spanish society and its institutions may be explained by their identification with Spain's culture and people. During the early modern period there was widespread belief in the Milesian origin-legend that the Gaelic-Irish descended from northern Spain. The obvious advantages of this origin-legend were certainly exploited to full potential by the Irish for advancing their political objectives, careers and social ambitions in Spain. From 1529 to 1630 the Irish appeals to the Spanish Crown for political and military support invoked their common racial and religious heritage.[24] *A brief relation on Irish affairs*, presented by the pro-Spanish Archbishop Florence Conry of Tuam to Philip III in 1618, provides a good example of Gaelic hispanophilism:

> And therefore the Auncient Irish [Gaelic], as these that are descended from the Spanyards desire allwayes to be governed by the Kings of Spayne and their successors, and bear greate affection and love to the Spanish nation. Contrarywise greate hate and enmity to their enemies, and are in sharpness of wit and valour in warr, altogether like unto the Spanyard . . .[25]

Conry's observations and sentiments reveal a sense of identity among the Gaelic Irish which transcended the geographical distance between them and Spain – a 'pan-Iberianism'. Indeed the fact that they received such privileges and sympathy reveals reciprocal fellow feeling from their hosts. In Spain the Irish were regarded as 'northern Spaniards' – *Nos hermanos irlandeses, los españoles del norte*.[26] The accommodation of the Irish in Spain may be further explained by reference to the concept of the 'Old Ordered Society'. Both Gaelic and Spanish aristocracies maintained similarly strict hierarchical structures and codes of etiquette. The hereditary professional nobilities of both elites uniquely differed from the norms of contemporary European social structures which were then in transition from feudal to early-modern systems.[27] Hence there was an easy flow of Irish priests, scholars, professionals and military officers into important positions in Spain from the sixteenth to the eighteenth centuries.[28]

Underpinning the ease of access and integration that the Irish enjoyed in Habsburg (and later, Bourbon) Spain, and their rights and privileges, was a formal legal and constitutional foundation: the Treaty of Dingle (28 April 1529). This treaty between James FitzGerald, eleventh earl of Desmond and the Holy Roman Emperor of the German nation and king of Spain, Charles V, inaugurated the early modern Irish integration in Europe by granting the Irish the rights and privileges of citizenship within the Habsburg monarchy.

The Treaty of Dingle (1529) was the culmination of a diplomatic process initiated by the great Geraldine potentate, James, eleventh earl of Desmond (1520–9). Geraldine diplomacy had been active on the Continent since the late fifteenth century. During this period the Geraldines concentrated on securing the borders of their palatinate, strengthening their local economy and consolidating their political power in the south of Ireland. James FitzGerald, ninth earl (1468–87), and Maurice, tenth earl (1487–1520), cultivated political and diplomatic contacts with the duchy of Burgundy and the kingdom of France through their trading links with Bruges and Bordeaux. Rogier van Maerlant, a Bruges merchant, acted as resident-agent for Desmond at the Burgundian Court during the 1470s and the 1490s.[29] In the light of contemporary European diplomacy, Desmond's maintenance of a resident-agent at the Burgundian court was quite advanced. It was the age when the various Italian states were engaged in the development of diplomatic procedure and protocol, the age of the Renaissance which gave rise to modern diplomacy. In 1470 the senate of the Venetian Republic accredited a resident ambassador to Burgundy. The duchy of Milan followed suit in 1475. It would seem that the house of Desmond was well aware of contemporary European political and diplomatic practice, and of the importance of being represented at the court of Charles the Bold.[30] This was even more relevant when the emerging Tudor state and its policy of centralisation represented a threat to the seigneurialism of the autonomous aristocracy of Ireland.[31] By June 1523, Desmond had entered a treaty of alliance with Valois France against Tudor England at a time when Henry VIII was trying to enhance his international position.[32] Following the defeat of the French by imperial forces and the capture of Francis I at Pavia in 1525, Desmond sought to preserve his own dynastic interests by a more significant diplomatic manoeuvre – the negotiation of an alliance with the greatest power in Christendom, the Holy Roman Emperor, Charles V.

On 16 October 1528, Desmond's envoy, Sherek, arrived at San Sebastian and proceeded to the court in Toledo, bearing gifts of Irish hawks and wolfhounds and a letter of entreaty for the emperor. The presentation of falcons to Charles V has its own significance. Fealty and goodwill to the emperor were traditionally expressed in the presentation of prize-falcons to the emperor, having received from him some special privilege or favour. A famous example was that annual tribute of Maltese falcons by the Knights Hospitaller of St John, to whom Charles V had given Malta as their headquarters following their expulsion from Rhodes by the Ottoman Turks in 1530. That Desmond observed this protocol is in itself indicative of his diplomatic sophistication. It is also significant in that the export of the highly prized Irish hawk to the continent was forbidden under English law. Desmond's envoy was well received, accredited due honour and succeeded in gaining the emperor's interest in the proposal.[33] Desmond offered himself as a subject and his palatinate as a dominion of the emperor in return for recognition of his title, trading privileges in the empire, and military assistance against Henry VIII.[34] This was the first formal submission of a Hiberno-Norman magnate to the external authority of the emperor. It set a precedent which later Irish nobles would follow.

Of the Desmond–imperial correspondence of 1528–9 preserved in Brussels, there is a passing reference to the reception of the Geraldine envoys at Toledo in a letter from the duke of Béjar, a member of the council of state, to his duchess in November 1528.[35] He also mentions that they were accompanied to court by a *caballero* (knight) from Galicia. Perhaps this was one of the two Spaniards mentioned in an English intelligence report on 5 November.[36] Considering the centuries-old commercial contacts between northern Spain and south-western Ireland,[37] it is possible that this Galician nobleman was an agent or liaison officer for Desmond's interests in Galicia, Asturias, Cantabria or the Basque provinces.

Unfortunately very little documentary material survives from the palatine court of Desmond. However, the crucially astute timing of Desmond's proposed submission to Charles V in 1528 and the language employed in his correspondence indicates that James, his counsellors or his secretary were well informed of the current continental politico-military situation: the strain in Anglo-Imperial relations over Henry VIII's divorce proceedings against Catherine of Aragon and the inherent threat these matters posed for Charles's foreign policy. The Habsburg–Valois struggle for supremacy in Europe was in progress and by early 1528 the English had allied with the French. Informed calculation rather than mere opportunism was behind the Geraldine–imperial alliance.[38] The imperial grand chancellor, Mercurino de Gattinara, who directed Charles's foreign policy between 1522 and 1529, advised that the two conditions necessary for the successful achievement of the imperial ideal were domination of Italy and alliance with the papacy. To this end, France had to be contained, not only on her eastern and southern borders, but also to her north and north-west by an alliance with England. Since the English had allied with the French, the prospect of an alliance with an Irish potentate such as Desmond had a certain strategic attraction.[39]

On 24 February 1529, Charles V appointed his personal chaplain and confessor, Don Gonzalo Fernández, ambassador extraordinary to Desmond.

The commission of one of the emperor's closest confidants in this matter is indicative of the importance and confidentiality that Charles attached to his intrigue with Desmond. Fernández was given letters of credence and instructed to obtain categorical information concerning Desmond's motives; military resources and proposed strategies; to assure Desmond of imperial benevolence and of inclusion in a possible Anglo-Imperial treaty; and to explain to Desmond the fundamental concerns of imperial policy towards England:

> You may tell him that we have always desired . . . the friendship of England, not only for his [Henry's], own sake but also on account of our close relationship and the affectionate friendship which the Kings of Spain, my predecessors, have entertained for him. That we have also done everything in our power to maintain the said alliance and friendship but that lately the King has declared for the King of France, and sent us a challenge [sic] and what is still worse led away by false and wicked persuasions is now trying to get a divorce from our aunt, the Queen of England his legitimate wife, and give the Kingdom of Ireland to his bastard son [the duke of Richmond] . . .
>
> These are things which we can nowise tolerate, as they might be the source of much scandal among Christian princes, very detrimental to England itself, and besides injurious to the Queen and the illustrious Princess Mary, her only daughter and heir in that kingdom. Things having come to such a pass, we intend preventing the aforesaid evils as much as we can, and waging war on the King of England. We therefore accept the count's services, and hope he will employ his forces and means against the common enemy, promising that we will sign no treaty of peace with England unless he [Desmond] is comprised of it with all his friends and vassals . . . [40]

The sentiments expressed in this Instruction encapsulate the personal and dynastic interests of Charles V concerning the necessity of an imperial ally in the North Atlantic. While the emperor valued an alliance with Desmond, at the same time he did not explicitly assume the overlordship of Desmond lest it prejudice the rights of his cousin, Mary Tudor. Nevertheless he allowed himself room for manoeuvre in this matter. It would be advantageous to have a foothold in the Desmond palatinate in the event of reconciliation with England. In this regard Desmond would be accommodated in an Anglo-Imperial treaty. Even so, by accepting Desmond's offer of allegiance and alliance and by extending imperial protection to him, Charles implicitly accepted the overlordship of Desmond given the terms which the earl had made.

The imperial envoy left Toledo for the Desmond palatinate on 3 March 1529. He had petitioned Charles for a payment of 120 ducats for his travel expenses and received 400 ducats instead.[41] The council of Castile had devised a ruse to distract the Tudor government from the real nature of Fernández' mission. It was alleged that he had gone to England to collect some debts owed to the emperor.[42] However, suspicions were soon aroused in the English embassy at Valladolid and its secretary Edward Lee's warning to Cardinal Wolsey to interview Fernández arrived too late.[43] Interestingly, English suspicions did not concern intrigue with Desmond but focused on some important letters concerning Queen Catherine's marriage to the late Prince Arthur, and her second espousal to Henry VIII.[44] Such correspondence would have been important in the current divorce proceedings since they were concerned with the papal licence for Catherine to marry Henry despite the canonical impediment of consanguinity. By the time that Lee wrote to Wolsey on 19 April, Fernández had already departed for Ireland. On the same day when Lee wrote to Wolsey, Charles V wrote to his ambassador in London, Don Iñigo de Mendoza: 'It is necessary to preserve the Queen's rights'.[45] The emperor made no reference to his chaplain's mission in this brief.

Fernández sailed to Berehaven, the seat of the O'Sullivan-Beare family who were later prominent in the pro-Spanish Habsburg cause of the 1590s and 1600s.[46] From there he wrote to Desmond and he received a reply within four days addressed to him as 'Chaplain to our Sovereign Lord, the Emperor'.[47] The manner of address indicates that the earl now considered himself as an imperial feudatory. On 21 April 1529, Fernández was received with full honours by Earl James, his council, and the corporation and inhabitants of Dingle.[48] Apart from its convenient geographical location on the south-west coast of Ireland, Dingle was also significant as a venue for an imperial reception. It had been since early medieval times a port of embarkation for Irish pilgrims going to the great shrine of Santiago de Compostela, the patron saint of Spain and of the *Réconquista*. Dingle was also a major trading port with northern Spain and was inhabited by a sizeable number of Spanish merchants and fishermen. The medieval parish church was built, like many of the houses, in a Spanish style, and was dedicated to St James.[49] Medieval Dingle, like Galway further north on the west coast of Ireland, was under considerable Hispanic influence.[50]

Imperial–Geraldine negotiations continued for almost a week until a treaty was signed on 28 April 1529. It was framed in the form of a *Supplicatio*, that of a lesser prince to a greater. In the first part of the document, Desmond gives a detailed report on the history of his Cambro-Norman and Gaelic lineage, the reasons for his enmity towards the Tudor regime and the strength of the forces at his disposal.[51] While simultaneously tracing his descent from the ancient royal house of Wales,[52] and from Spain through his Gaelic ancestry, Desmond provided a classic *apologia* for seigneurialism. The second part of the document is a formal statement of submission to imperial authority.

It reflected the ideology of the *Reichsidee* or universal monarchy as professed by Gattinara, Alfonso de Valdés, Charles's Latin secretary, and other Spanish humanists,[53] in which the emperor was regarded as the ultimate arbiter of justice and protector of Christian civilisation:

> I the aforesaid count, beg and entreat that in consideration of the above stated facts, of the wrongs and injuries inflicted upon me and mine by the Kings of England, His most invincible, sacred and august majesty, the Emperor be pleased to provide opportune redress . . . I faithfully place myself with all my estates, vassals, relatives and adherents under the protection of the mighty prince, chosen and appointed by God and men to be supreme Lord of the World, and to redress the wrongs of mankind . . . I promise under my Faith duly to observe all the commands and orders of Your Imperial Majesty . . . like a true and loyal subject. Should I ever do or attempt to do anything displeasing to Your Majesty, I place myself beforehand under correction and punishment, in the presence of Gonzalo Fernández, Master Dionisio [Dennis] Mitdonle [sic], Dennis Cather [sic], Doctor of Arts and Medicine and Maurice Herly Dean of Ardfert.[54]

It is probable that the last three dignitaries who witnessed the Treaty of Dingle had contributed to the negotiations and to the draft of this document. Even Fernández may have made some suggestions. The qualifications held by the Geraldine dignitaries indicate that they were well learned and may have studied in a continental university. Perhaps they were also acquainted with the *Reichsidee*. Very little is known about the four Geraldine envoys who went to Toledo the previous year. One of them was a priest, described as a chaplain of the earl of Desmond. It seems that this ecclesiastic accompanied the imperial envoy to Desmond in spring 1529 and returned with him to Toledo.[55] It is highly probable that the earl's chaplain was also the treaty-witness Maurice Herly, dean of Ardfert (in whose ecclesiastical jurisdiction Dingle is located).[56] The ease and frequency with which Desmond's chaplain travelled back and forth to Spain suggests a certain familiarity on his part with Spanish ways.

On the day before the conclusion of the Treaty of Dingle, Desmond, in a letter to Charles V, gave an account of Fernández' reception and made a personal submission of himself, his property and his followers to imperial suzerainty and protection. This letter, which accompanies the more formal treaty, serves to emphasise his seriousness concerning the alliance. It also accentuates the gravity of the earl's decision.[57] Another matter of great significance in the Geraldine–Habsburg negotiations in Dingle was the presentation of a golden cup by Fernández on behalf of the emperor to Desmond. In imperial tradition a golden *Liebenkelch* or loving-cup would be presented by the emperor to a vassal-lord or city council in recognition of their loyal services to the empire. Such cups bore the arms of the Holy Roman Empire, the personal arms and a medallion-portrait of the reigning emperor. The ceremony of the loving-cup traditionally follows a great banquet in honour of a monarch, or in reaffirmation of a fellowship, confraternity or an alliance. It was also part of the etiquette in sealing a solemn treaty.[58]

Some time in May 1529, the imperial envoy returned to Spain. It seems that it was only then that the English embassy in Valladolid discovered the true nature of Fernández' activities, even though English intelligence had been aware of Geraldine–Habsburg communication.[59] On 31 May, the secretary of the English embassy in Valladolid, Edward Lee, wrote to Henry VIII that he had received a letter the previous day from an English agent, Thomas Batcock, at Renteria (near San Sebastian), who informed him that Fernández, of whom he had earlier informed Cardinal Wolsey had gone to England, was in fact sent by the emperor to Desmond and had just returned to Spain with a chaplain of the earl.[60] Also on 31 May, the English ambassador, Bishop Ghinucci of Worcester and Lee, wrote to Wolsey about their discovery of Fernández' dealings with Desmond. Interesting details emerge from this letter:

> on 17 May John Gwyn of Balaskelaye or St Michael's in Ireland [Ballinskelligs, County Kerry] arrived at San Sebastian . . . The courier who was sent by the Emperor to the Earl told him [Batcock] that he [Gwyn] conducted Gonzalo Fernández, the Emperor's chaplain to Dingwell [Dingle]. mariners say he [Gwyn], comes to get 4,000 men to teach the Irishe warfare. He [Gwyn], denies this but he is suspect as he does much service to the Earl and conveyed his [Desmond's] chaplain to the Court [Toledo], and the Emperor's chaplain to him [Desmond], and now conveys both of them to the Court.[61]

Significantly, the Venetian ambassador to Spain reported to the senate of the Serene Republic that he had difficulty in obtaining information about the Geraldine–Imperial negotiations and the emperor's plans for visiting Italy in the spring of 1529.[62] That the Venetians should be interested in Desmond's intrigues with Charles V, just as the English were alarmed, reveals that there was concern among European powers at the prospect of an imperial ally in Ireland. This concern should be considered in the context of the current politico-military situation in Italy. Venice, the papacy and France had formed the anti-imperial league of Cognac in May 1526. After its defeat and the sack of Rome by imperial forces in 1527, England allied with France early in 1528. The Aragon divorce was proceeding in England while the pope, Clement VII, was the emperor's captive. In this context and in the wake of the Genoese fleet's defection to the emperor and the defeat of the French, Desmond seized his opportunity to negotiate a Geraldine–Imperial alliance.[63]

It is important to note that in his negotiations with Charles V, Desmond did not pretend to be a national leader, nor indeed did he offer the overlordship of Ireland to the emperor. As befitting his position and title as *comes palatinii Desmondiae* or count palatine (in English style an earl), he represented only his jurisdiction and offered its overlordship and allegiance to the emperor. Under the terms of Pope Adrian IV's bull *Laudabiliter*, the papal fiefdom of Ireland was entrusted to the overlordship and protection of Henry II and his successors, the kings of England. This provided the constitutional and legal basis for the English claim to Ireland. Indeed the claims of the Hiberno-Norman and the Old English communities rested ultimately on the authority of *Laudabiliter*. (This point may also help to explain their adherence to Catholicism after the English Reformations and their disdain for the Protestant New English as well as their suspicion of their Gaelic coreligionists.) The bull decreed that this trust was given on the conditions that the rights of the Catholic church in Ireland be preserved, that it would observe Roman discipline, and that justice would be maintained by the English monarchy in Ireland.

It was on the grounds that justice was not being administered by the Tudor regime, in Desmond's opinion, that his seigneurial rights were being threatened, and that Henry VIII was at this point in time a *de facto* schismatic, that he appealed to the secular vicar of Christ, the Holy Roman Emperor, for protection. In this respect Desmond maintained that Henry VIII had forfeited his right of overlordship under the terms of *Laudabiliter*. Therefore Desmond was claiming his feudal right of transferring his allegiance to another liege-lord. It was an act of *translatio imperii* – transfer of overlordship or authority. Significantly, in Desmond's correspondence with Charles V no mention was made for obtaining papal approval or confirmation. This may suggest that he was aware of the sack of Rome in 1527 and that Clement VII was *in manu imperatoris*. The pope was not in a position to argue with Charles or Desmond. The Geraldine move into the imperial camp at this point in time not only indicates well-informed calculation on their part, but also suggests a good understanding of European *Realpolitik*.[64]

On his return to Spain Fernández reported to the emperor on his conference with Desmond; he was positive but cautious. While he was satisfied with the good faith and goodwill of Desmond, he was nevertheless unimpressed by the military standards of the Geraldine forces and was wary of Desmond's feud with his neighbours (the Butlers of Ormond, his uncle, Thomas FitzThomas-FitzGerald and the MacCarthys of Muskerry). Apart from these deficiencies, especially in the military as assessed by continental standards, Fernández recognised the potential and talent; all that was required was modern discipline and training. The fearsome courage (even if foolhardy) and the skilled horsemanship of the Geraldine cavalry particularly impressed the imperial ambassador extraordinaire.[65]

Obviously the Geraldine alliance was advantageous, but if it were to be really effective it would cost Charles V great expense in order to bring the Desmond forces up to contemporary European standards. Military training, discipline, armour, modern weaponry and artillery would have to be provided, not to mention an enlargement of the Atlantic fleet. As matters stood in 1529, Charles was already militarily overstretched especially in the Mediterranean and Italy. While he had effective land forces, it was at sea that he was vulnerable. It just happened to be his good fortune that Andrea Doria had led the Genoese fleet into alliance with him in July the previous year.[66]

In June 1529 the French forces in Italy were decisively defeated by the imperial army at Landriano. Charles was once again master of Italy and the Anglo-French alliance of 1528 was in disarray. However, it was time for some form of settlement in Christendom since the Ottoman Turks were almost at the gates of Vienna. With the Geraldine alliance concluded in April, and now with Italy under his control, Charles concluded the Treaty of Barcelona with Pope Clement VII in July 1529. The pontiff finally agreed to receive Charles in Italy and crown him Holy Roman Emperor. The treaty also obliged him to align the Holy See to the interests of the empire. This process outmanoeuvred the designs of Francis I and exasperated Henry VIII. The French king was forced to come to terms with Charles, and the Treaty of Cambrai was signed on the 3 August 1529. Francis renounced his claims over Artois and Flanders and his interests in Italy. Charles abandoned (temporarily), his claims to the old duchy-lands of Burgundy around Dijon. The treaty was sealed symbolically the following year by the marriage of the emperor's sister, Eleanor, to the French king. Shortly after the treaty was signed, Francesco Sforza was recognised as duke of Milan and imperial feudatory.[67]

At Barcelona in July 1529, Charles wrote to the earl of Desmond informing him that he received his letters, Fernández' report and of his ratification of the Treaty of Dingle. He thanked the earl for his goodwill, his submission and alliance. The emperor also granted Desmond's request for favoured status and trading privileges for Geraldine merchants and subjects in the lands of the empire. He gave his personal assurance that, if at any time Desmond or his adherents should require imperial assistance, they would be welcomed, favoured and well treated in all the dominions of the *Monarquía*. This letter was apparently written after the Treaty of Barcelona, since as Charles concludes that he is on the eve of departure for his coronation in Italy and remarks that Desmond's courier may have witnessed these preparations. Once settled in Italy Charles promised to write to Desmond 'according to time and requirement' and hoped that the earl would do likewise.[68] It is possible that Charles thought that given the opportunity at some future date, he could devote some of his resources to improving the military prowess of Desmond and establish a secure imperial base on the south-west coast of Ireland.

At that time the very fact of a Geraldine–Imperial alliance, and the fear and uncertainty it would arouse in England and France, helped serve Charles's interests in keeping pressure on Henry VIII and keeping the French out of Flanders. The Treaty of Cambrai left French allies such as England and Venice in a weak position. By the end of 1529 Venice surrendered all her possessions in Apulia to the Aragonese kingdom of Naples. This *paix des dames*, so called because it was negotiated by the French queen-mother and Archduchess Margaret of Austria, heralded the downfall of Thomas, Cardinal Wolsey. Among other considerations, his continental policies were now ruined.[69]

By the time that Charles's letter of assurance and ratification reached the Geraldine palatinate, Earl James had been assassinated, though it is not known for certain if this was owing to Tudor design or internecine intrigue in the house of Desmond. Most probably it was the latter, though there may have been some Henrician connivance. Earl James was succeeded by his uncle and rival, Thomas FitzThomas-FitzGerald. He had sought and was granted recognition by Henry VIII. For the time being Desmond was reconciled with the Tudor regime, and the prospect of an imperial bridgehead in Ireland diminished. As events unfolded in England and Ireland during the early 1530s, the uneasy peace ended with the Kildare–Geraldine rebellion of 1534–5. Before his death in December 1534 the twelfth earl, Thomas of Desmond had sent envoys to renew the alliance of 1529 with Emperor Charles V. Geraldine–Imperial intrigue against Henry VIII was resumed.[70]

The significance of the Treaty of Dingle (1529) may best be appreciated by its legacy in both political and socio-economic terms. Politically, it set the precedent and model for future Hispano-Irish alliances for the realisation of Irish incorporation within the Spanish Habsburg *Monarquía* – in 1534–5, 1569–70, 1579–80, 1596 and 1601–2.[71] In this respect we may appreciate Henry VIII's legislation to raise Ireland to the status of a kingdom (1541) and to declare himself and his successors as kings of Ireland and thereby remove the constitutional claims of the papacy or the claims of Irish magnates to *translatio imperii*. However, this legislation was revised under the Catholic Queen Mary I and her consort Philip II, and from a traditionalist and papal perspective, *regularised* by Pope Paul IV in 1555.[72] By 1596, Philip II accorded the rights and privileges of being subjects of the *Monarquía* to *all* Irish Catholics who supported the campaign against Elizabeth I led by Hugh O'Neill and Red Hugh O'Donnell.[73] This was reconfirmed by the dying king in 1598[74] and by his heir Philip III.[75] These privileges were enjoyed by the subsequent waves of Irish emigrants to the *Monarquía* from 1601 onwards. Even with the change of ruling dynasty in Spain, the first Bourbon king, Philip V, decreed in 1701 that 'the privileges and graces of the Irish' would continue. These privileges included the rights 'to live, trade and acquire property in the Spanish dominions' whether 'domiciled or resident'. It was not until April that year that similar rights were accorded to English Catholics in Spanish territories.[76]

Notes

1 For O'Daly see M. MacCurtain, 'Dominic O'Daly' in A. M. Brady and B. Cleeve (eds), *A biographical dictionary of Irish writers* (Mullingar, 1985), pp. 340-1. See too T. S. Flynn, *The Irish Dominicans 1536-1641* (Dublin, 1993), pp. 120-2, 155, 187, 195-9, 225, 280-5, 309-10; M. McCurtain, 'An Irish agent of the Counter Reformation, Dominic O'Daly', *Irish Historical Studies* XV, 60 (1967), 391-406. For Wall see M. Walsh 'Lieut. General Ricardo Wall (1694–1778)', *Irish Sword* II (1954–6), 88–93; for O'Donnell see R. S. Ó Cochláin, 'Leopold O'Donnell and the Spanish–Moroccan campaign, 1859–60', *Irish Sword* VII (1965–6), 181–95. For Taaffe see A. J. P. Taylor, *The Habsburg monarchy, 1809–1918* (London, 1948), pp. 154–7, 169–89, 211, 213, 228, 256, and D. M. Downey, 'Wild geese and the double-headed eagle: Irish integration in Austria c.1630–c.1918', in E. Sagarra and P. Leifer (eds), *Austro-Irish links thorugh the centuries* (Vienna, 2002), pp. 41, 45–6, 55–6. For McMahon see R. Shepherd, *Ireland's fate: the Boyne and after* (London, 1990), p. 198; for De Gaulle see P. Joannon, *De Gaulle and Ireland* (Dublin, 1991), pp. ix, 5-7. De Gaulle's maternal ancestors were from County Down.

2 See J. J. Silke, 'The Irish abroad', in T. W. Moody, F. X. Martin and F. J. Byrne (eds), *A new history of Ireland*, 5 vols to date (Oxford, 1976), III pp. 587–653, and J. G. Simms, 'The Irish on the continent, 1691–1800', in ibid., pp. 587–653; H. Murtagh, 'Irish soldiers abroad, 1600–1800', in T. Bartlett and K. Jeffrey (eds), *A Military history of Ireland* (Cambridge, 1995), pp. 294-314; L. Cullen, *Irish brandy houses in eighteenth century France* (Dublin, 2000); B. Jennings, *Wild geese in Spanish Flanders, 1582–1700* (Dublin, 1964); M. K. Walsh, 'The wild goose tradition', *Irish Sword* XVII (1987–90), 4–17; T. O'Connor (ed.), *The Irish in Europe, 1580–1815* (Dublin, 2001); D. M. Downey, 'La Paz de Westfalia: vista desde Irlanda' in B. García García and F. Villaverde (eds), *350 Años de la Paz de Westfalia 1648–1998, Del antagonismo a la integración en Europa* (Madrid, 1999), pp. 203–16, 403–14.

3 Quoted in Shepherd, *Ireland's fate*, pp. 195–6.

4 Silke 'The Irish abroad', pp. 605–6; M. Kerney-Walsh, *Spanish knights of Irish origin*, 4 vols (Dublin, 1965), I, introduction, vi.

5 Downey, 'Wild geese', pp. 42–3. See P. van Damme, C. Terlinden, C. van Renynghe de Voxvrie and H. Pauwels, *La toison d'or. Cinq siècles d'art et d'histoire* (Bruges, 1962). Knights of Irish origin in both branches of the Order are listed in pp. 46–70.

6 On the Irish in France see, for example, J. C. O'Callaghan, *The Irish brigades in the service of France* (Glasgow, 1870); Cullen, *Irish brandy houses*; H. Gough and D. Dickson (eds), *Ireland and the French Revolution* (Blackrock, 1990).

7 The *Monarquía* refers to the possessions of the Spanish Crown, the *Hausmacht* refers to the hereditary possessions of the Austrian Habsburg dynasty, that is Austria, Bohemia and Hungary. From 1477 until 1555 the Burgundian Netherlands were an Habsburg hereditary possession.

After the abdication of Charles V they were attached to the Spanish Crown from 1555 until 1714. From 1714 until 1804 they were part of the Austrian Habsburg *Hausmacht*.

8   Silke, 'The Irish abroad', pp. 587–635.
9   Murtagh, 'Irish soldiers abroad', p. 300.
10 Silke, 'The Irish abroad', pp. 593, 605–6.
11 See B. Jennings, *Wild Geese, passim*; M. K. Walsh, 'The wild goose tradition', pp. 4–17; C. Duffy, 'Some Irishmen in the Imperial Service', *The Irish Sword* V (1961–2), 75–80; G. Henry, *The Irish military community in Spanish Flanders 1586-1621* (Dublin, 1992); R. Stradling, *The Spanish monarchy and Irish mercenaries: the wild geese in Spain 1618-1668* (Dublin, 1994); Downey, 'Wild geese'.
12 Cullen, *Irish brandy houses*; A. Guimera Ravina, *Burghesía extranjera y comercio atlantico. La empresa comercial irlandesa en Canarias (1703–1771)* (Santa Cruz de Tenerife, 1985); M. B. Villar Garcia (ed.), *La emigracion irlandesa en el siglo XVIII* (Malaga, 2000).
13 J. Brady, 'The Irish colleges in Europe and the Counter-Reformation', *Proceedings of the Irish Catholic Historical Committee* (1957), 1–8; C. Giblin, 'The contribution of the Irish Franciscans on the continent in the seventeenth century', in M. Maher (ed.), *Irish spirituality* (Dublin, 1981), pp. 88–103; D. M. Downey, 'Agostiniani e scotisti. Il contributo irlandese nella Contrariforma en Europa' in L. Vaccaro, C. M. Pelizzi (eds), *Storia religiosa dell' Irlanda* (Milan, 2001), pp. 159–94.
14 T. H. Barker, *Army, aristocracy, monarchy: essays on war, society and government in Austria, 1618–1780* (New York, 1982), p. 31.
15 Silke, 'The Irish abroad', p. 606.
16 For more detailed discussion on Irish familial alliances with the princely and major noble houses of the Austrian Habsburg *Hausmacht* see Downey, 'Wild geese', pp. 44–7, 48–52.
17 T. Corcoran, 'Early Irish Jesuit educators', *Studies* XXIX (1940), 546; and J. Corboy, 'The Irish College at Salamanca', *Irish Eccclesiastical Record* LXIII (1944), 248–9.
18 For the foundation at Alcalá see Silke, 'The Irish abroad', p. 627. For the foundation at Seville, see St Patrick's College Maynooth, Salamanca Archives [hereafter Sal. Arch.], legajo 40, no. 1, f. 1n., and f. 7n. u. Theological chairs at the Irish College in Lisbon were endowed by Count Antonio Fernando Ximénez: see Irish Jesuit Archives Dublin, MacErlean Transcripts: Rectores Coll. Hib. Hispalensis; British Library [hereafter BL] Lansdowne MS, vol. 71, no. 49; and P. F. Moran, *Spicilegium ossoriense; being a collection of original letters and papers illustrative of the history of the Irish Church from the Reformation to the year 1800* 3 vols (Dublin, 1874–84) [hereafter *Spicil. Ossor.*], 1, 82. Santiago and Salamanca were foremost among the Spanish cities to offer shelter and education to Irish students.
19 Giblin, 'Irish exiles in Catholic Europe', pp. 5 and 15. Francis Taaffe was founding patron of the Irish Franciscan friary and college at Boulay, Lorraine in 1697–1700. Interestingly, its clergy were required to be competent in both German and French so that they could minister effectively in the locality; also B. Jennings, 'Irish Franciscans in Prague', *Studies* XXVIII (1939), 210–22; also see H. Helga Robinson-Hammerstein, 'The university, the common good and Irish medical students as refugees in early eighteenth-century Prague' in H. Robinson-Hammerstein (ed.), *Migrating scholars: lines of contact between Ireland and Bohemia* (Dublin, 1998), pp. 44–61. A collection of scholarly articles on the variety of Irish émigré experience and

an updated historiography concerning this period is provided in T. O'Connor (ed.), *The Irish in Europe, 1580–1815* (Dublin, 2001).

20 In 1625 the Irish Franciscan College of St Isidore was founded in Rome. In 1627 the Irish Pastoral College of St Patrick was founded in Rome. The Pastoral College was entrusted to Jesuit supervision.

21 D. Szechi, *The Jacobites: Britain and Europe 1668–1788* (Manchester and New York, 1994), pp. 127–8; Simms, 'The Irish on the continent', pp. 629–56; Robinson-Hammerstein, 'The university, the common good', pp. 44–61.

22 Kerney-Walsh, *Spanish knights*, I, pp. i–iv.

23 See J. MacErlean, 'Ireland and world contact', *Studies*, VIII, 3, pt I (1919), 307–9; A. J. Loomie, 'Religion and Elizabethan Commerce with Spain', *Catholic History Review* LX (1964), 46–8; *Calendar of State Papers Ireland, 1586–1588* [hereafter *Cal. S. P. Ireland*], p. 400: entry 21 Aug. 1587.

24 See D. M. Downey, 'Culture and diplomacy: the Spanish-Habsburg dimension in the Irish Counter Reformation movement, *c*.1529–*c*.1629' (PhD thesis, University of Cambridge, 1994), passim.

25 TCD Abbott's Catalogue 580, MS. E 3. 8, ff. 49–52: 'A brief relation of Ireland and the diversitie of Irish in the Same', a copy of an account of Irish affairs presented to Philip III in 1618 by Florence Conry, OFM. A note on the top left-hand corner of the document, in Archbishop James Ussher's handwriting states 'Presented to the Court of Spayne *c*.an. 1618 by Florence the pretended Archbishop of Tuam and thought penned by Philip O'Sullevan-Beare'.

26 Archivo Historico Nacional, Madrid, B. 1217: Count Caracena, Governor of Galicia, to Philip III, Aug. 1602.

27 On the concept of 'Old Ordered Society' and educational institutions see R. L. Kagan, *Students and society in early modern Spain* (Baltimore and London, 1974); R. Trevor-Davies, *The golden century of Spain, 1507–1621* (London, 1967), pp. 280 ff.; and for Irish professional-aristocratic structures see L. Bieler, 'The island of scholars', *Revue du Moyen Age Latin* VIII, 3 (1952), 213; K. Nicholls, *Gaelic and Gaelicised Ireland in the Middle Ages* (Dublin, 1972).

28 See MacErlean, 'Ireland and world contact', 307–9; A. J. Loomie, 'Religion and Elizabethan commerce with Spain', *Catholic History Review* LX (1964), 46–8; and *Cal. S. P. Ireland, 1586–1588*, p. 400: entry 21 Aug. 1587.

29 StadsArchief Brugge, Comercieël-Handels Afdeling West Vlaanderen, MS. V 128: 'De Hoogwaardig en Hoogwelgebohrnen Heer Rogier van Maerlant te Brugge, vertegenwoordiger in het Grootertogdom [Burgondië – Burgundy] voor de Graaf d'Esmont in Ierlandt, is naar de Hof in Brussel gegaan... Maart 1474'. Another reference to him as Desmond's agent appears in the year 1490. Between *c*.1383 and 1590 there had been an 'hotel' or consulate of the 'Irish nation' in Bruges and one in Antwerp after 1500.

30 G. Mattingly, *Renaissance diplomacy*, repr. ed. (New York, 1988), p. 84.

31 D. B. Quinn, 'Aristocratic autonomy, 1460–1494', in T. W. Moody et al. (eds), *A new history of Ireland*, 5 vols (Oxford, 1987), II, pp. 591–4. For a more detailed study of the background to Geraldine politics and diplomacy and intrigues with the French and later the Habsburg monarchy see Downey, 'Culture and diplomacy, pp. 1–32.

32 On the Desmond–Valois Treaty of Askeaton 20 June 1523 and its ratification at St Germain-en-Laye later that year see Downey, 'Culture and diplomacy', pp. 5–634. For a history of the presentation of falcons to the Spanish crown by the Knights of St John see J. Sire, *The Knights of Malta* (New Haven and London, 2000), pp. 59–63.

33 *Letters and papers, foreign and domestic of the reign of Henry VIII, 1509-1547*, 21 vols (London, 1862–1932) [hereafter *L & P, Hen. VIII*], IV, ii, 1529–1530, 4878: 26 Oct. 1528 Thos. Batcock to ?. BL Cotton Vespasian MSS C. iv. 264 [hereafter BL Vesp. MSS]. For the prohibition on exporting Irish hawks to the Continent see: T. O'Neill, *Merchants and mariners in Medieval Ireland* (Dublin, 1987), pp. 102–3. On imperial falconry see: L. von Späth, *Geschichte der Reichsfalknereiskunde in Österreich* (Innsbruck, 1903).

34 *L & P, Hen. VIII*, IV, ii, 1529–1530, no. 4878: 26 Oct. 1528, Thomas Batcock to ?; also BL Vesp. MSS C. iv. 264.

35 Archivo Historico Nacional, Madrid, Archivo de la Casa de los Duques de Béjar, MS 311, fo. 71, b.

36 *L & P, Hen. VIII*, IV, ii, 4911, Sylvester Darius, English agent in Bayonne to Brian Tuke, Wolsey's protégé, 5 Nov. 1528.

37 T. O'Neill, Merchants and mariners, pp. 84–5; P. Macinêira, Bares, puerto hispánico de la primitiva navegación occidental (Santiago de Compostela, 1947).

38 Downey, 'Culture and diplomacy', pp. 4–23.

39 Ibid. pp. 9–14; B. Beinert, 'El testamento politico de Carlos V de 1548. Estudio critico', in *Carlos V (1500–1558). Homenaje de la universidad de Grenada* (Madrid, 1958), pp. 401–8.

40 BL Add. MSS 28, 578, f 47: Emperor Charles V's instruction to his chaplain and personal envoy, Gonzalo Fernández, dated Toledo, 24 Feb. 1529; see also *L & P Hen. VIII*, IV, iii (1529–30), no. 5322. BL Add. MSS 28, 578, f 24: for Fernández' letter of credence, same date. It is interesting to note that when Charles V gave this Instruction to Fernández, he was aware, as stated in this document, that Henry VIII planned to appoint his illegitimate ten-year-old son, Henry FitzRoy, duke of Richmond, as nominal lord lieutenant of Ireland. The appointment actually took place in June 1529. See L. McCorristine, *The revolt of Silken Thomas* (Dublin, 1987), p. 43. It was thought that Richmond would play a major role in the future administration of Ireland. See D. B. Quinn, 'Henry FitzRoy, duke of Richmond, and his connection with Ireland, 1529–30', *Bulletin of the Institute of Historical Research* XII (1934–5), 175–7.

41 BL Add. MSS. 28, 173: Fernández' petition to the emperor, 24 Feb. 1529, to order the payment to him of 120 Ducats for his travel expenses to Ireland. He left Toledo on 3 March 1529 with an allowance of 400 Ducats. See also *L & P Hen. VIII*, IV, iii, no. 5323.

42 BL Vesp. C. iv. 299: Ghinucci and Lee to Wolsey, dated Zaragoza, 5 Apr. 1529. '[T]he Emperor asked Monseigneur Pernott [Nicholas Perrenot, Seigneur de Granvelle, a Burgundian nobleman appointed to the Council of State in 1529, after a diplomatic career; after Gattinara's death in 1530 Granvelle became Charles's Secretary for Imperial and Foreign Affairs], to convey to His Majesty's servant (Ghinucci) the Emperor's concern over His Majesty's great matter (the Aragon Divorce) and . . . the Emperor was sorry that anything should happen to interfere with the ancient amities between England, Spain and Burgundy, and he took heavily the intended divorce between the King and Queen.' The emperor threatened to appeal to a General Council in order

to defend his aunt's case. At the end of the letter, they report that Fernández has gone to England to recover some debts owed to Charles. He is a nephew of Marcus, otherwise Dr de Puebla, who negotiated the Queen's first marriage, and probably had some letters concerning her second. Lee recollects that Fernández once told him that he had some papers of his uncle relating to these marriages and he (Lee) had intended to ask him for them.) See also *L &P Hen. VIII*, IV, iii, no. 5423.

43   BL Vesp. MSS. C. iv, 296: Lee to Wolsey, dated Zaragoza, 19 Apr. 1529. He advises the Cardinal to interview Fernández: if he was sent to England to recover debts, then he should have been sent to His Eminence (Wolsey) with a commission to do so, and with one from the Archbishop of Toledo and the Bishop of Palencia for redemption of their pensions. Lee thinks that Fernández and his brother gave all their uncle's papers concerning the Queen's marriages to the emperor. Both Lee and Ghinucci would have spoken with Fernández but he had departed when they arrived at the Court in Zaragoza. See also *L & P Hen. VIII*, IV, iii, no. 5469.

44   *L & P Hen. VIII*, IV, iii, no. 5469.

45   BL Add. MSS. 28, 578, 160: Charles V to Yñigo de Mendoza, dated Zaragoza, 19 Apr. 1529. See also *L &P Hen. VIII*, IV, iii, no. 5468.

46   J. J. Silke, *Kinsale* (Liverpool, 1970), for O'Sullivan Beare and Dunboy.

47   BL Add. MSS. 28, 579, 329: 'Capellan del Emperador Nuestro Soberano Señor', inscription on Desmond's letter to Fernández. See also *L &P Hen.* VIII, IV. iii, no. 5501. See R. Bagwell, *Ireland under the Tudors* 3 vols (London, 1885–90), I, p. 185; his account of Fernández' mission is detailed though somewhat biased against the earl of Desmond.

48   See R. Bagwell, *Ireland under the Tudors*, 3 vols (London, 1885–90), I, p. 185.

49   For Spanish influence in medieval Dingle see: C. Smith, *Antient and present state of the county of Kerry* (London, 1756), pp. 175–7; and also J. MacKenna, *Dingle* (Killarney, 1985), pp. 21–2, and illustrations on p. 26.

50   See J. Hardiman, *History of the town and county of Galway* (Dublin, 1820), p. 204.

51   BL Add. MSS. 28, 578, 194: Desmond to Charles V, dated 28 Apr. 1529. Another original copy, probably that made for the emperor, is kept in Archives Générales du Royaume de Belgique, *Négociations d'Angleterre* [hereafter Arch. Gén. Roy. Belg. , Négoc. d'Angl.],I, 25, 71, 90.

52   Arch. Gén. Roy. Belg., Négoc. d'Angl., I, 25, 71, 90; See B. FitzGerald, *The Geraldines: an experiment in Irish government 1169–1601* (London, 1951).

53   J. Lynch, *Spain under the Habsburgs*, 2 vols, 2nd edn (Oxford, 1981), I, pp. 74–6; also P. von Rassow, *Die Kaiser-Idée Karls V* (Berlin, 1932); J. M. Doussinague, *La politica internacional de Fernando el catolico* (Madrid, 1944); M. Bataillon, *Erasme et l'Espagne: recherches sur l'histoire spirituelle du XVIe siècle* (Paris, 1937), pp. 243–53; J. Sanchez Montes, 'Actitudes del español en la epoca de Carlos V', *Estudios Americanos*, III (Sevilla, 1951), pp. 169–99. See also R. Menéndez Pidal, *Idea imperial de Carlos V* (Madrid, 1945), and J. A. Maravall, *Carlos V y el pensamiento politico del renacimiento* (Madrid, 1960).

54   Arch. Gén. Roy. Belg., Négoc. d'Angl. I, 25, 71, 90: original copy probably made for Charles V dated 28 Apr. 1529. BL Add. MSS. 28, 578, 194: for another original copy, probably that made for Desmond in the also dated 28 Apr. 1529.

55   BL Vespasian MSS C. iv. 324; *L &P Hen. VIII*, VI, iii, nos. 5619, 5620.

56 During this period of diplomatic history it was common for ecclesiastical dignitaries to be entrusted with diplomatic missions, and some high-ranking clerics, such as deans or archdeacons, without episcopal dignity, acted as chaplains to the higher aristocracy, and performed as personal envoys on behalf of their noble charges.

57 This personal letter is addressed: 'Invictissimo ac Sacratissimo Domino Karolo Dei Gratia, et Augusto Domino Nostro, cedula cum summa reverentia et subjectione se tradi jubet.' Dated 'apud villam nostram de Firma [Ventry or Fermoyle?], die XXVII Luce Aprilis [Sunday], Anno Domini Mo. VC. XXIX', and signed 'Vester humilis et fidelis servus et subditus Jacobus, Comes Desmondiae, Dominus Desie et Ogonill, ac libertatis Kyerrigie etc.' BL Add. MSS 28, 578, 194; Arch. Gén. Roy. Belg. , Négoc. d'Angl. I, 25, 71, 90.

58 R. Bagwell, *Ireland under the Tudors*, I, p. 184. Examples of the imperial golden 'Liebenkelchen' may be seen in the Stadtsmuseum of Vienna, and in several other former Imperial cities.

59 See Downey, 'Culture and diplomacy', pp. 15–20.

60 *L &P Hen. VIII*, IV, iii no. 5619: Lee to Henry VIII, Valladolid, 31 May 1529.

61 *L &P Hen. VIII*, IV, iii no. 5620; Ghinucci and Lee to Wolsey, Valladolid, 31 May 1529, and BL Vesp. MSS. C. iv. 324.

62 Archivio di stato di Venezia, Sen. Sec. XI, fo. 10. 31. 62: Venetian resident at Barcelona to the senate, 13 Dec. 1528. 'It is said that the Emperor is in secret conference with the Count of Ismond [Desmond] in Ireland, but it is difficult to know what is the purpose. There is some talk at Court of His Majesty's [Charles V] plans to go to Genova [Genoa] very soon.' Archivo General de Simancas, secretaria de estado, 331, negociaciones de Venezia, Legajo 6391: a copy of an intercepted dispatch from a Venetian agent in Toledo to the resident in Barcelona: 'The English Ambassador [at Valladolid], is unable to know what business the Emperor has with the delegation from the Count of Ismond [Desmond] for his servant here is now in prison . . .'.

63 Downey, 'Culture and diplomacy', pp. 13–20.

64 Ibid., pp. 1–6, 16–17, 20–21.

65 BL Add. MSS 28, 579, 329: Fernández' account of his arrival at Dingle, and his parley with Desmond dated 28 Apr. 1529.

66 J. Lynch, *Spain under the Habsburgs*, pp. 88–9. R. Lockyer, *Habsburg and Bourbon Europe 1470-1720* rep. edn (New York, 1989), pp. 226–7.

67 J. Lynch, *Spain under the Habsburgs*, pp. 88–9. R. Lockyer, *Habsburg and Bourbon Europe 1470-1720* rep. edn (New York, 1989), pp. 226–7

68 BL Add. MSS 28. 579, 330: 'Pour la response au Comte de Wismont en Irlande de par l'Empereur': Charles V to the earl of Desmond, dated July 1529; also BL Add. MSS 28 173,13; *Arch. Gén. Roy. Belg. Negoc. d'Angl.* I. 25, 71, 90. *Cal. S. P. Spanish, 1529–1530*, no. 84.

69 J. J. Norwich, *A History of Venice* (London, 1982), pp. 441–2; Wolsey's failure to secure the king's desired divorce of Catherine, the failure of the Anglo-French alliance, the victory of Charles V over the pope and his allies, and the revocation of the Legatine Court to Rome in response to Catherine's appeal, and the humiliating summons of Henry to appear before the Papal Court in person or by proxy, led to Wolsey's dismissal from the office of Lord Chancellor in late 1529. See too H. M. Smith, *Henry VIII and the Reformation* (London, 1948).

70 During the Geraldine Revolt of Silken Thomas, Lord Offaly, 1534-5, contacts were resumed with the Imperial Court. In June 1534, Eric Godscalke, an Imperial chaplain, was sent by Charles V to Earl Thomas of Desmond, at Dingle. See McCorristine, *Revolt of Silken Thomas*, pp. 74-94.

71 Downey, 'Culture and diplomacy', pp. 41-58, 66-88, 91, 94-105.

72 Ibid. pp. 56-8, 63-4; S. Ellis, *Tudor Ireland: crown, community and the conflict of cultures 1470-1603* (London, 1985), pp. 210, 232-3.

73 Ellis, *Tudor Ireland*, pp. 100-5. Archivo General de Simancas, secretaria de estado, legajo 2604: Philip II to the Irish Catholic nobles in the confederacy led by Hugh O'Neill, earl of Tyrone and Red Hugh O'Donnell, earl of Tyrconnell, 14 Aug. 1596.

74 Archivo General de Simancas, secretaria de estado, legajo 839: Philip II to O'Neill O'Donnell, Sept. 1598.

75 Archivo General de Simancas, seccion de guerra antigua, legajos 539 & 3143; Ibid., secretaria de estado, legajos 839 & 840, f. 4; legajo 2511: *consulta* of the council of state, 1 July 1600; legajo 187: Philip III to the adelantado mayor of Castile, Madrid, 10 July 1600; Silke, *Kinsale*, pp. 69-73; Downey, 'Culture and diplomacy', pp. 113-36.

76 See MacErlean, 'Ireland and world contact', 307-9; A. J. Loomie, 'Religion and Elizabethan commerce with Spain', *Catholic History Review* LX (1964), 46-8; and *Cal. S. P. Ireland, 1586-1588*, p. 400: entry 21 Aug. 1587.

CHAPTER 7

A Lawyer in Politics

The Career of Sir Richard Nagle c.1636–1699

James McGuire

If the seventeenth-century House of Commons was overwhelmingly representative of the landed elite, it was the lawyers in the House of Commons who could articulate the concerns and grievances of rustic gentlemen. It was the lawyers in particular who offered plausible legal or constitutional solutions and gave form and content to the aspirations and demands of parliament. Not all parliamentarians appreciated this role and after the failure of the 1692 parliament, Bishop William King of Derry could blame the members of the House of Commons for 'minding the harangues of lawyers too much who could not forget their being for clients and so colouring the sense of their party'.[1] It has only recently become possible to quantify the extent to which members of the Irish parliament in the seventeenth and eighteenth centuries were either practising lawyers or at least the recipients of a legal education.[2] But it has long been clear that lawyers played a significant, often leading, role in parliament in the seventeenth century. Each of the seventeenth-century speakers of the Irish House of Commons was a lawyer, at a time when the holder of that office enjoyed a political significance perhaps comparable, however anachronistically, with a modern speaker of the United States House of Representatives.[3] Three of these seventeenth-century speakers were serjeants at law: Sir Nathaniel Catelyn in 1634, Sir Maurice Eustace in 1640 and Sir Audley Mervyn in 1661. Sir Richard Levinge in 1692 was solicitor general. Three were attorneys general: Sir John Davies in 1613, Sir Richard Nagle in 1689 and Robert Rochfort in 1695.[4] Of these lawyers in politics, Nagle is one of the less well known, his obscurity perhaps having more to do with the extent to which success determines posthumous fame, than with the relative importance of the role he actually played. This essay seeks to reconstruct Richard Nagle's career to the extent that the sources allow and attempts an evaluation of its significance for later seventeenth-century Ireland.

A Lawyer in Politics: Sir Richard Nagle

Richard Nagle was born c.1636 into a prominent County Cork family, whose surname is sometimes given as Nangle and occasionally Neagle. The Nagles were an Old English Catholic family, whose forebears had lived in the Blackwater valley in north County Cork since the early fourteenth century. Richard was the second of at least five sons of James Nagle of Clenor and his wife Honora, one of the Nugents of Aghanagh, also in County Cork.[5] By the time Richard was born, Old English families such as the Nagles had, to their great resentment, lost to the Protestant New English those places of 'honour, profit and trust'[6] which they regarded as their birthright. They were still in the 1630s substantial landowners, though that too was soon to change in the aftermath of the confederate wars. James Nagle, Richard's father, forfeited his estate under the Commonwealth, though after the Restoration he was again living in County Cork, this time at Annakissy.

A second son, Richard grew to adulthood at an unpropitious time for the Catholic gentry. He was said to have been educated by the Jesuits, and may have been intended for the priesthood,[7] but there are no career details for the 1650s. Three years after the restoration of the monarchy, he turned to the law, seemingly the first member of his family to do so in the seventeenth century, and in 1663, at the comparatively late age of twenty-seven, he was admitted to Gray's Inn which, before the upheavals of the 1640s and 1650s, had traditionally attracted Irish and recusant applicants.[8] Five years later he was called by King's Inns to the Irish bar.[9] In 1669 he married Joan Kearney of Fethard, County Tipperary, whose sister would later marry his elder brother Pierce.[10] They lived at Carrigacunna, a Nagle property in County Cork, and from 1684 in Dublin. As a barrister he appeared for both Protestant and Catholic clients, and clearly built up a reputation which later hostile pamphleteers willingly conceded: 'a cunning Irish lawyer . . . he was a man of great parts, educated among the Jesuits and therefore very inveterate'.[11] Bishop William King would later write that Nagle studied law to 'a good perfection' and appeared for many Protestants 'so that he knew the weak part of their titles'.[12] Sporadic glimpses of his legal practice can be seen in contemporary correspondence.[13] As it expanded he acquired more land in north Cork and Waterford and the extent of his earned wealth is evident from substantial loans which he had the funds to make, in 1683 (£1,800) and 1686 (£2,000), and which are recorded in the Dublin statute staple.[14] In 1686 he could tell the lord lieutenant that no chief justice's place 'would equal his present gains which he must consider because of his great charge of children', which now amounted to seven sons and six daughters.[15]

Nagle's involvement in politics began in 1686, a year after James II's accession. Initially he appeared as a reluctant participant. At least that was how it seemed to the hapless viceroy, the second earl of Clarendon, whose correspondence during 1686 provides the most frequent references to Nagle's growing involvement in public affairs, an involvement which invariably rests on his role as legal adviser for dispossessed Catholic landowners. After their first meeting in February, when Nagle had brought him a petition for reversal of outlawries from Lord Gormanston and other Catholic petitioners, Clarendon wrote of him with comparative warmth: 'a Roman Catholic, and a man of the best repute for learning as well as honesty amongst that people'.[16] That initial impression remained for some months, and was not even shaken by Nagle's nomination at Whitehall to the Irish privy council along with ten others, mostly Catholics, whose appointment required dispensation from taking the oath of supremacy.[17] More telling perhaps, though Clarendon does not seem to have adverted to it in his correspondence, was the fact that Nagle's nomination can only have come from advice tendered by Richard Talbot, earl of Tyrconnell, and that his nomination suggested that Nagle was to be part of Tyrconnell's emerging plans to replace Protestants with Catholics in positions of both civil and military significance. Clarendon, however, found more professional reasons for disapproval, which he expressed to the earl of Sunderland, the secretary of state at Whitehall:

> he is a very learned and honest man, but I beg leave to observe to your lordship that he is a practising lawyer and I doubt will think it hard to quit his profession for that which brings no advantage, though it will be a great honour, for it will not look well that a man who has the honour to be of the king's privy council should be crowding at the bar of the chief justice bare-headed and his bag in his hand ... but I will speak with Mr Nagle tomorrow and let him know the king's gracious intentions towards him.[18]

To Clarendon's manifest approval Nagle turned down the offer of a seat on the privy council, making it clear that it was not a position for which he had lobbied. As Clarendon reported to Sunderland: 'he [Nagle] was extremely surprised and wonders his friends will move in his behalf without first consulting himself; he tells me to leave his practice will be his ruin, and to appear at the bar after he is a councillor will be very indecent, even for the king's service'.[19] He asked, however, that he might keep the formal letter of appointment 'as a mark of the king's grace and favour'.[20]

Nagle's refusal of a seat on the privy council came just days before Tyrconnell's arrival in early June with a commission to be commander-in-chief of the army in Ireland (a humiliating snub for Clarendon, who was being deprived of one of the traditional viceregal functions). And soon Nagle's growing political engagement with Tyrconnell became apparent even to the trusting and beleaguered Clarendon. If Tyrconnell's formal commission was to reform the army (which meant purging Protestants and appointing Catholics), he was quick to raise the cause of the dispossessed Catholic proprietors, with which he had been associated since the 1660s. Both Sunderland at Whitehall and Clarendon in Dublin Castle had recognised that, with a Catholic king on the throne and Tyrconnell's political power in the ascendant, Catholic expectations would inevitably focus on a significant modification of the Restoration land acts, with all the consequences that would entail for the Protestant political nation which had emerged over the preceding thirty years. To head off the inevitable Catholic demands for amending legislation in a new Irish parliament, they sought instead a commission of grace under which Catholic proprietors, or ex-proprietors, who had fared badly under the 1660s settlement would be financially compensated from a fund to which Protestant proprietors would contribute in return for confirmation of their land titles.[21]

Tyrconnell was clearly determined to thwart this stratagem. He saw it as imperative to preserve his freedom of action so that, on his return to Whitehall in the autumn, he might press for the summoning of an Irish parliament to pass amending legislation. The disadvantaged Catholic proprietors wanted land, not monetary compensation.

As the summer advanced, Nagle's role as Tyrconnell's adviser became increasingly apparent. In late July it was noted in Dublin Castle that he had been present at a three-hour meeting between Tyrconnell and the Catholic primate, Archbishop Dominic Maguire.[22] When Tyrconnell went to see Clarendon to arrange a consultation on what Clarendon called 'our great affair', he asked that Nagle should be present, along with Major-General Justin MacCarthy, Lord Chief Justice Keating and the solicitor general.[23] Soon after, Clarendon invited both Nagle and Lord Chancellor Porter to dinner, after which Nagle, somewhat disingenuously, told Clarendon that Tyrconnell had told him 'something' of Clarendon's plans for a commission of grace, and had asked him to prepare something on it in writing. But in the conversation which followed, Nagle left the viceroy in no doubt about what his opinion would be:

> he could not believe a commission would be useful, or that it would bring in any money considerable; that whatever should be thought fit to be done, either for confirming the present settlements, or for the relief of such of the old proprietors as ought to be relieved, would be done best by parliament; but that he thought it was yet too soon to think of calling a parliament; that many things were necessary first to be done, and even the acts ought first to be prepared and agreed on; which he owned would take up very much time, for the several interests ought to be first felt [?] and discoursed with, that is, some of the most considerable of them; and till he had done that and fully weighed things (for there were many difficulties in the way) he could not put anything into writing tho' my Lord Tyrconnell was in great haste.[24]

This passage has been quoted at length as it shows the extent to which Nagle, the well-briefed Catholic barrister, had become not only a legal adviser but a political strategist for Tyrconnell and the Catholic interest. The strategy he unfolded was the strategy that Tyrconnell and he would follow over the coming twelve months. Any doubts about Nagle's political commitment that Clarendon may have had before this after-dinner conversation were now unsustainable. In the light of what he had just heard, he told his brother Rochester that the forthcoming conference with Tyrconnell would allow him to see 'what these people drive at', though he could hardly have been in much doubt. He added, rather lamely: 'I will keep them to the point; that is, that Mr Nagle and his people shall set down what they would have, and what they would think fit for the king to do.'[25]

The weakness of Clarendon's position was made humiliatingly clear a week later on 7 August, the day arranged for the conference on the land question. It was to have started at 10 a.m., but only the lord chancellor, Sir Charles Porter, and the solicitor general, Sir John Temple, showed up. Tyrconnell arrived three hours late and full of excuses, but without Nagle. When asked where he was, he replied: 'Faith, my lord, it is very late: we cannot talk much now. Mr Nangle, I believe, is not so ready as he will be a few days hence'. Asked by Clarendon to propose a day when Nagle would be ready Tyrconnell suggested the following Friday.[26] When the plenary meeting eventually took place, Nagle admitted that he had drawn up nothing, and that 'many things were to be considered of before matters could be put into writing'. But he did tell them that both he and Chief Baron Rice were of the opinion that a commission would do nothing, bring in a very small sum of money, if any, and confirm those estates which ought not to be confirmed. At this point both Tyrconnell and MacCarthy 'closed with that [Nagle's] opinion with much vehemence'.[27] Looking back at these events a month later, Clarendon chose to represent Nagle's reluctance to engage with contrary opinions as a sign of weakness: 'with all his learning and skill he could not confute the reasons of those who differed with him, by any other arguments, than the single saying he was of another opinion'.[28] But clearly Nagle and Tyrconnell were keeping their arguments for Whitehall, where ultimate power lay. There was no advantage to be gained by revealing their position to an increasingly enfeebled Dublin Castle administration which they hoped soon to replace.

Nagle's commitment to the Tyrconnell enterprise, and the centrality of his role in it, were underlined soon after the Dublin Castle conference when he accompanied Tyrconnell on his return to Whitehall. Before setting out he told Clarendon, whose political talents he could not be accused of overestimating, that he was going to England purely for heath reasons.[29] Ineffective Clarendon may have been, but he had had no doubt about Nagle's purpose.

He was quick to warn those with an interest in Irish land of the news that Nagle would be accompanying Tyrconnell to court and of its likely import. As he told his brother Rochester: he 'is a very able man and therefore more to be watched'.[30]

Nagle's increasingly pivotal role heightened the already anxious political atmosphere among the Protestant interest in Ireland. Lord Longford told the duke of Ormond: 'The English are much alarmed at my Lord Tyrconnell's carrying over Mr Nagle with him, which they conjecture, and will not be persuaded out of it, his lordship has done with a design to prevail upon his Majesty to call a parliament here in order to the breaking of the Acts of Settlement and Explanation.'[31] And why, Sir Robert Southwell asked rhetorically of Sir William Petty, was 'Mr Nagle, the great surveyor of Ireland' in London?[32]

But opinion at Whitehall was not so easily convinced that it was either possible or desirable to modify the land settlement by means of a new act of parliament. And there was open scepticism about Tyrconnell's unconcealed ambition to be viceroy in place of Clarendon. In this climate Nagle seems at first to have been cold shouldered and, if an admittedly hostile pamphleteer is to be believed, had to wait 'some time e'er [he] could gain admittance to kiss the king's hand', spending the meantime with Fr Petre and 'the rest of that furious cabal'.[33] The prevailing view at Whitehall, argued by Sunderland, the Secretary of State, was that a declaration confirming the acts of settlement and explanation would be needed should Tyrconnell prevail on the king to appoint him viceroy. This of course would tie Tyrconnell's hands.[34] The means devised by Tyrconnell and Nagle to thwart Sunderland's plan was the Coventry letter.

The Coventry letter was in effect a manuscript pamphlet written by Nagle in which he argued robustly, though anonymously, against any royal declaration confirming the existing settlement.[35] What was needed, ran the argument, was a new Irish land act, which would restore many 'innocent' Catholics whose cases had not been heard by the court of claims in the 1660s. For Catholics in Ireland the unique opportunity offered by a co-religionist on the throne must not be lost. Nothing could support the Catholic religion in that kingdom but to make Catholics there considerable in their fortunes, which was an argument clearly designed to prick the conscience of the pious James II.

Ostensibly written by Nagle on 26 October, during an insomniac night in Coventry on his return journey to Ireland, the letter had all the appearances of having been carefully drafted while Nagle was still in London. Indeed it is likely that its origins lay in Nagle's undisclosed ruminations in the summer, though the device of a letter from Coventry may have been suggested by the political situation Tyrconnell and Nagle found at Whitehall.

Among Protestants, as word got out about its contents and manuscript copies were gradually passed around, it became notorious and added to that sense of uncertainty which the beneficiaries of the Restoration settlement increasingly felt. Indeed Sir William Petty immediately wrote a ten-page reply, which was never published. In the short term the Coventry letter achieved its immediate objective and put paid to Sunderland's plans for a royal declaration to accompany the announcement of Tyrconnell's appointment as viceroy. But despite this significant, if limited success, Nagle found it politic to disown authorship, letting it be known on his return to Dublin that 'he would arrest any man in an action of ten thousand pound, who should father it on him', a threat which very likely explains Petty's sardonic comment to Southwell: 'Here is an answer of 10 sheets to the "Coventry letter" – we must not say Mr Nagle's'.[36]

With Tyrconnell's formal appointment as lord deputy in January 1687, Nagle moved from being an influential strategist for the Catholic interest to being part of the new viceroy's administration. Two days after being sworn in, Tyrconnell appointed him attorney general in succession to Sir William Domville, who had held the post since 1661.[37] In becoming attorney general, Nagle was taking a position which, in the latter half of the seventeenth century, had superseded in importance, if not in precedence, the post of prime serjeant. Besides giving legal advice the attorney general by the 1680s was responsible for instituting and pursuing proceedings on behalf of the crown.[38] The implications for Protestant Ireland of Nagle's being attorney general were anticipated with anxiety and glee, the latter most triumphantly in Dáibhidh Ó Bruadair's 'Caithréim an dara Séamuis' (The triumph of King James).[39]

From the beginning of the new viceroyalty Nagle was a member of what Thomas Sheridan, Tyrconnell's somewhat semi-detached chief secretary, called the lord deputy's 'cabinet'.[40] Given a knighthood on his appointment as attorney general, he lost no time in implementing the strategy outlined to Clarendon the previous summer.[41] On 12 February, the day Tyrconnell was sworn in, he lodged an information against the city of Dublin concerning their claims to certain liberties and franchises.[42] It was an early indication of what would occupy his attention in the coming months, reforming borough charters. The *quo warranto* challenges, which Nagle as attorney general orchestrated throughout Ireland, where necessary taking recalcitrant boroughs to court, were designed to restore local government to the previously ousted Catholic elite while at the same time ensuring that borough representation in the anticipated parliament would be predominantly Catholic.[43] Closely linked with these proceedings was the appointment of Catholic sheriffs, which Nagle, along with Thomas Nugent and Stephen Rice, both recent appointees to the bench, strongly urged and with success.[44]

The main purpose of the anticipated parliament, the substantial modification of **the Restor**ation land acts, was never in doubt. Policy and its implementation in the first six months of Tyrconnell's government were clearly the means to that end, though the lord deputy could not openly announce his intentions. While the catholicisation of the army, the boroughs, the judiciary and other civil offices was perfected, the land question as such remained off the agenda, at least until Tyrconnell travelled to Chester in August 1687 to meet the king. Nagle accompanied him to what was apparently intended as a meeting to discuss the state of the Irish revenue and its administration. What emerged was far more significant: the sidelining of Thomas Sheridan, Tyrconnell's secretary and first commissioner of the revenue, in which Nagle had some role, and secondly, and more fundamentally, permission to consider and recommend substantial amendments to the Restoration land settlement.[45] Tyrconnell and Nagle returned to Dublin with James's permission to have alternative bills prepared to modify the restoration land acts.

The extent of Nagle's involvement in the subsequent drafting of these bills can be inferred from the office he now held and the role he had played in 1686 in providing the intellectual justification for new legislation. But it is important to stress that the far-reaching repeal legislation, enacted in very changed circumstances in the Jacobite parliament two years later, bore little resemblance to the bills drafted in Dublin over the winter of 1687–8. One of these drafts provided for claims of innocence not heard by the original court of claims to be reopened, with monetary compensation for any Cromwellian settlers who lost out in the process. The other draft, apparently favoured by Tyrconnell, provided that all estates in contention should be divided equally between old and new proprietors, with the latter allowed to retain all improvements made since the 1650s.[46] Either of these bills, if enacted, would have met the expectations of the old proprietors while leaving intact a substantial amount of land in Protestant ownership.

When the draft bills were taken to London in March 1688, Nagle did not travel with them. That was left to Sir Stephen Rice and Chief Justice Nugent, though both Nagle and Rice were alleged to have advised against the unimpressive Nugent's appointment as emissary. According to the well-informed anonymous author of *The secret consults of the Romish party in Ireland*, either Nagle or Rice told the author that Nugent 'was good for nothing but to spoil a business'.[47] Whatever fears there may have been about Nugent's suitability for the task, the delegation seem to have convinced Whitehall by May that a bill should be prepared on the lines of the compromise enshrined in the Tyrconnell draft.

The whole enterprise came a sudden halt in the summer of 1688 with the crisis of James's monarchy. After the king had gone into exile, Nagle was alleged to have been involved in 'a jesuitical stratagem' to have a delegation sent to the exiled court seeking James II's permission for terms to be made with Prince William of Orange.[48] Certainly there were brief contacts but they may have had no more significance than a desire by Tyrconnell to play for time sufficient to assess the prospects for a Jacobite stand in Dublin.

When James II came to Ireland the following spring, Nagle was at the height of his power and influence. He was continued in office as attorney general.[49] The parliament which met in May was returned on the basis of Nagle's handiwork in remodelling the borough charters, and Nagle was himself returned for County Cork (of which his brother Pierce was sheriff); at the same time his younger brother David became member for Mallow.[50] Another brother, James, was appointed sergeant-at-arms to the Commons (and later clerk and engrosser of chancery writs).[51] On 7 May, the day parliament assembled, Richard was elected to the speakership, effectively a government appointment if seventeenth-century precedents in both England and Ireland are taken into account.[52]

Nagle's role as Speaker is difficult to reconstruct. The parliamentary journals were burned by the common hangman in 1695 and the accounts of the parliament that survive deal mostly with proceedings in the House of Lords. Glimpses of the proceedings can be gleaned from other sources, such as the reports of the French ambassador, comte d'Avaux. One of his despatches described how Nagle successfully headed off an attempt by MPs to have the House send its thanks to Louis XIV for his military support, arguing that this was a matter for James II, not the Commons.[53] Williamite accounts quite reasonably blamed Nagle for legislation which, in repealing the Restoration land acts and attainting over 2,000 substantial Protestants, went much further than anything Nagle had actually planned or envisaged in 1687–8. He was after all both chief law officer of the crown (even if the prime serjeant technically took precedence) and the author of the Coventry letter. The proviso in the Act of Attainder putting it 'out of the king's power' to pardon Protestants was apparently attributed to Nagle's 'malice and jesuitical principles', though Conor Cruise O'Brien has quite ingeniously seen it as evidence of the conditional character of Catholic loyalty to the crown, suggesting that in 1689 the Catholic MPs were the 'true whigs'.[54]

With the prorogation of parliament in July, Nagle's role in the Jacobite administration became increasingly significant. In August, when the earl of Melfort was effectively forced to resign as secretary for war, the French ambassador, D'Avaux, was astonished that Melfort should be replaced by the militarily inexperienced Nagle, 'un habile homme pour les affaires de droit, mais qui est si neuf dans celle de la guerre qu'il n'en a pas les premiers éléments'.[55] The king weakly defended himself to the ambassador on the grounds that he could not withstand the continual importuning of the Irish.[56] As might be expected the clever and adaptable Nagle threw himself with enthusiasm into his new duties, preparing army lists and equipping the Jacobite forces for now imminent war.[57] And even the sceptical D'Avaux seems to have been won around, writing to Louis XIV the following February of 'une grande union entre le duc de Tirconnel, le chevalier Negle et moy'.[58]

Despite defeat at the Boyne and James II's hasty departure for France, the war was not yet over, as William III's subsequent failure at the first siege of Limerick showed. In September 1690, when Tyrconnell travelled to France for consultations with both James and the French government, Nagle either accompanied him or followed on soon after. They returned to Ireland together in January 1691, landing at Galway, and with a meagre £8,000 from Louis XIV travelled on to Limerick.[59] Nagle resumed his duties as secretary of state for war and attorney general, but little is discernible of his role or influence over the succeeding months when Jacobite politics in Ireland was deeply divided over seeking peace or continuing the war between the followers of Patrick Sarsfield and Tyrconnell. As the unsympathetic Charles O'Kelly put it in his allegorical account of the war, Tyrconnell had 'returned to Ireland better prepared to manage a treaty than to continue the war; for the chief Cyprian [Irish] gownmen [lawyers] who fled into Syria [France] after the battle of Lapithus [the Boyne] were now returned with their patron'.[60] On Tyrconnell's death in August 1691, which Nagle described as 'a fatal stroke to this poor country in this nick of time', a sealed commission from James II came into effect, appointing Nagle, Alexander Fitton, the Jacobite lord chancellor, and Francis Plowden, commissioner of the revenue, as lords justices.[61] They seem, however, to have had no significant part in the treaty negotiations of late September and early October. The senior law officer on the Jacobite side was in fact James II's solicitor general for Ireland, Sir Theobald (Toby) Butler. By November Nagle was on his way into permanent exile in France. Outlawed since October 1689 by the court of King's Bench in London, Nagle forfeited his estate when County Cork was taken by the Williamite army and it was subsequently granted to Viscount Sydney, William III's lord lieutenant of Ireland.[62]

Throughout the 1690s, Nagle remained in James II's service at St Germain. He is referred to in court correspondence as secretary for war and attorney general for Ireland up to his death in 1699, though it is clear from the Stuart papers that his duties were not confined to Irish business.[63] He was inevitably drawn into disputes at the exiled court, in particular with Thomas Sheridan, over the strategy to be adopted for a Jacobite restoration.[64] He continued, none the less, to enjoy the king's confidence to the extent that James appointed him a commissioner of the royal household in 1698 and nominated him in his will as a member of a council to advise the queen on the guardianship of the prince of Wales.[65] In fact, Nagle predeceased the king by two years, dying at St Germain-en-Laye on 4 April 1699.[66]

Nagle's is one of those careers that faded into obscurity at an early stage. Indeed it was only in the 1930s that his death date was discovered by Richard Hayes, his entry in the *Dictionary of National Biography* having assigned him only *floruit* dates. Yet, in his day, his role was of central importance to the revival of the Catholic interest. Without its revival, made possible through the accident of a Catholic monarch, he might have lived out his days as an able and increasingly wealthy counsel at the Irish bar. But he could not resist the allure of politics. In that respect he resembles and is comparable with another seventeenth-century lawyer, Sir Audley Mervyn, the eloquent defender of the Protestant interest.[67] Both were senior law officers of the crown, one as prime serjeant under Charles II, the other as attorney general under James. Both were speakers of the House of Commons. For his part Nagle may have had more practical experience as a practising counsel than had Mervyn, but both of them used their positions under the crown to serve the interest out of which they came. Both their careers ended in relative obscurity, though Mervyn at least enjoyed his estates.[68]

Notes

1 Trinity College Dublin (hereafter TCD), Lyons MSS 264 A.

2 For further information on lawyers in parliament and politics in the seventeenth century see D. F. Cregan, 'Irish recusant lawyers in politics in the reign of James I', *Irish Jurist* V (1970), 306–20; Jane Ohlmeyer, 'Irish recusant lawyers during the reign of Charles I' and Brid McGrath, 'Parliament men and the confederate association', both in M. Ó Siochrú, *Kingdoms in crisis* (Dublin, 2001). For invaluable biographical information on MPs, lawyers *inter alia*, see Brid McGrath, 'The membership of the Irish House of Commons, 1613–15' (MLitt thesis, University of Dublin, 1986) and 'A biographical dictionary of the membership of the House of Commons, 1640–1641' (PhD thesis, University of Dublin, 1997); Aidan Clarke, *Prelude to Restoration in Ireland* (Cambridge, 1999), ch. 6 of which contains a biographical account of all members of the 1660 convention, many of whom went on to sit in the 1661–6 parliament. For lawyer MPs from the 1690s (some of whom sat in the 1661–6 parliament), see the magisterial E. M. Johnston-Liik (ed.), *History of the Irish parliament*, 6 vols (Belfast, 2002).

3 In England the situation was largely similar: twenty of the speakers who served from the beginning of the seventeenth century to the 1689 convention were lawyers by profession, another had attended at the Middle Temple, and only two appear to have had no legal education. See David L. Smith, *The Stuart parliaments 1603–1689* (London, 1999), pp. 243–4.

4 For a list of Speakers of the Irish House of Commons see T. W. Moody et al. (eds), *A new history of Ireland* 5 vols (1984), IX, p. 537.

5 Basil O'Connell, 'The Nagles of Garnavilla', *Irish Genealogist* III, 1 (1956), 17–24; 'The Nagles of Mount Nagle', *Irish Genealogist* II, 12 (1955), 377–89; 'The Nagles of Annakissy', *Irish Genealogist* II, 11 (1954), 337–48.

6 D. F. Cregan, 'The confederate Catholics of Ireland: the personnel of the confederation, 1642–9', *Irish Historical Studies* XXIX (1994–5), 508.

7 [William King], *The state of the Protestants of Ireland under the late King James's government* (London, 1691), p. 83.

8 *The register of admissions to Gray's Inn, 1521–1889* (London, 1889); D. F. Cregan, 'Irish Catholic admissions to the English Inns of Court 1558–1625', *Irish Jurist* V (1970), 95–114.

9 E. Keane et al. (eds), *King's Inns admission papers* (Dublin, 1982), p. 360.

10 *Irish Genealogist*, II, 11 (1954), p. 348.

11 *A full and impartial account of all the secret consults . . . of the Romish party in Ireland* (London, 1690), p. 55.

12 *State of the Protestants*, p. 83.

13 British Library (hereafter BL) Add. MSS 46958, ff. 17–20: correspondence between Richard Nagle, 'counsellor at law' and Sir J. Perceval of County Cork, 1681; National Library of Ireland (hereafter NLI), Orrery papers on microfilm: Richard Nagle's opinion on the will of the late earl of Orrery.

14 Jane Ohlmeyer and Éamonn Ó Ciardha (eds), *The Irish statute staple books, 1596–1687* (Dublin, 1998), p. 127.

15 *Calendar of State Papers domestic, 1686–7* (hereafter *Cal. S.P.*), p. 153; *Irish Genealogist* II, 11 (1954), 337.

16 Clarendon to earl of Rochester, 27 Feb. 1686, in S. W. Singer (ed.), *The correspondence of Henry Hyde, earl of Clarendon, and of his brother, Laurence Hyde, earl of Rochester, with the diary of Lord Clarendon from 1687 to 1690* 2 vols (London, 1828), I, p. 273; (hereafter cited as *Clarendon corresp.*).

17 *Cal. S.P. domestic, 1686–7*, pp. 117–18; Historical Manuscripts Commission (hereafter Hist. MSS Comm.), Ormonde MSS, new series, VII, 423.

18 *Cal. S.P. domestic, 1686–7*, p. 147.

19 Ibid., p. 153.

20 *Clarendon corresp.*, I, p. 445.

21 R. Bagwell, *Ireland under the Stuarts*, 3 vols (London, 1909–16), III, pp. 169–70.

22 Clarendon to Rochester, 31 July 1686: *Clarendon corresp.*, I, p. 514.

23 Ibid.

24 Ibid., pp. 515–16.

25 Ibid., p. 516.

26 Clarendon to Rochester, 7 Aug. 1686: *Clarendon corresp.*, I, pp. 524–6.

27 Clarendon to Sunderland, 14 Aug. 1686: *Clarendon corresp.*, I, pp. 537–9.

28 Hist. MSS Comm.: Ormonde MSS, VII, 461: Clarendon to the duke of Ormond.

29 Hist. MSS Comm.: Ormonde MSS, VII, 449: Clarendon to the duke of Ormond, 28 Aug. 1686.

30 *Clarendon corresp.*, I, p. 555.

31 Hist. MSS Comm.: Ormonde MSS, VII, 449–50.

32 Marquis of Lansdowne (ed.), *Petty–Southwell correspondence* repr. edn (New York, 1967), p. 233.

33 *A full and impartial account . . . of the Romish party*, p. 54.

34 J. G. Simms, *Jacobite Ireland 1685–91* (London, 1969), p. 31.

35 Hist. MSS Comm.: Ormonde MSS, VII, 464–7; J. T. Gilbert (ed.), *A Jacobite narrative of the war in Ireland* (Dublin, 1892), appendix, pp. 193–201.

36 *A full and impartial account of all the secret consults . . .*, p. 55; *Petty-Southwell correspondence*, p. 271.

37 James L. Hughes (ed.), *Patentee officers in Ireland 1173–1826* (Dublin, 1960), p. 95; Nagle's patent was dated 15 February 1687.

38 A. R. Hart, *History of the king's serjeants* (Dublin, 2000), pp. 51–2.

39 John C. Mac Erlean (ed.), *Duanaire Dháibhidh Uí Bhruadair. The poems of David Ó Bruadair*, pt III (London, 1917), pp. 88–9; see Éamonn Ó Ciardha, *Ireland and the Jacobite cause, 1685–1766: a fatal attachment* (Dublin, 2002), p. 77.

40 Hist. MSS Comm.: Stuart papers, VI, 18.

41 Hist. MSS Comm.: Ormonde MSS, VIII, 349.

42 *Calendar of the Clarendon state papers* (Oxford, 1970), V, p. 672.

43 *A full and impartial account of all the secret consults*, pp. 79, 85; *Clarendon state papers*, V, 678; Jacqueline Hill, *From patriots to unionists: Dublin civic politics and Irish Protestant patriotism 1660–1840* (Oxford, 1997), pp. 59–60; Simms, *Jacobite Ireland*, pp. 35–6; A. R. Hart, *History of prime serjeants*, p. 52.

44 Hist. MSS Comm.: *Stuart papers*, VI, 18.

45 Hist. MSS Comm.: *Stuart papers*, VI, 28, 36; Bagwell, *Stuarts*, III, 172; John Miller, 'Thomas Sheridan (1646–1712) and his "Narrative"', *Irish Historical Studies* XX, 78 (1976), 120–1; John Miller, 'The earl of Tyrconnell and James II's Irish policy, 1685–1688', *Historical Journal* XX (1977), 803–23.

46 Simms, *Jacobite Ireland*, pp. 40–1.

47 *The secret consults of the Romish party in Ireland*, p. 115.

48 Ibid., p. 146.

49 Hist. MSS Comm.: *Stuart papers*, I, 40.

50 A list of members returned to the House of Commons is printed in *An exact list of the lords spiritual and temporal who sat in the pretended parliament at Dublin* (London, 1689); see J. G. Simms, *The Jacobite parliament of 1689* (Dundalk, 1966), appendix.

51 Hist. MSS Comm.: *Stuart papers*, I, 42, 45.

52 David L. Smith, *The Stuart parliaments 1603–1689*, p. 79. The exception to the rule in Ireland was the election of Sir Audley Mervin in 1661, when Dublin Castle had made known its preference for Sir William Domville, the attorney general.

53 Bagwell, *Stuarts*, III, 224.

54 Conor Cruise O'Brien, *The great melody: a thematic biography of Edmund Burke* (London, 1992), pp. 16–17.

55 James Hogan (ed.), *Négociations de M. le comte d'Avaux en Irlande, 1689–90* (Dublin, 1934), p. 445.

56 Ibid., pp. 429–30.

57 John D'Alton, *Illustrations, historical and genealogical, of King James's Irish army list (1689)* (Limerick and Kansas City, 1997), pp. 893–4; Simms, *Jacobite Ireland*, p. 133.

58 *Négociations de M. le comte d'Avaux en Irlande, 1689–90*, p. 623.

59 T. Crofton Croker (ed.), *Narratives illustrative of the contests in Ireland in 1641 and 1690* (London, 1841), p. 132.

60 Charles O'Kelly, 'Macariae excidium or the destruction of Cyprus' in T. Crofton Croker (ed.), *Narratives illustrative of the contests in Ireland in 1641 and 1690*, p. 74.

61 Philip W. Sergeant, *Little Jennings and fighting Dick Talbot: A life of the duke and duchess of Tyrconnell*, 2 vols (London, 1913), I, p. 561; Simms, *Jacobite Ireland*, p. 242.

62 J. G. Simms, *The Williamite confiscation in Ireland 1690–1703*, pp. 32–3; *Cal. S.P. domestic, 1693*, pp. 2–3.

63 Hist. MSS Comm.: *Stuart papers*, I, 68, 109, 110, 127–8; II, 88.

64 Vincent Geoghegan, 'Thomas Sheridan: toleration and royalism' in D. George Boyce et al. (eds), *Political discourse in seventeenth- and eighteenth-century Ireland* (Basingstoke and New York, 2001), p. 46.

65 Hist. MSS Comm.: *Stuart papers*, I, 127–8.

66 R. Hayes, 'Biographical dictionary of Irishmen in France', *Studies* XXXIV (1945), 109.

67 A. R. Hart, 'Audley Mervin: lawyer or politician' in W. N. Osborough (ed.), *Explorations in law and history* (Dublin, 1995), pp. 83–105.

68 I am very grateful to Professor Jane Ohlmeyer for her helpful advice in the preparation of this chapter.

CHAPTER 8

Ireland and Colonial America

The Viewer and the Viewed

Maurice J. Bric

For Britain and Ireland, the westward voyages of the early modern period promoted a new age of 'enterprise and empire'. For Ireland and the British Americas, they also reflected a special and shared relationship with the imperial metropolis in London which was reinforced by a myriad of political, commercial and personal networks. These connections did not develop in a consistent way on either side of the Atlantic. Moreover, as colonial society evolved during the course of the eighteenth century, they became less driven by their Old World historical legacies than by the challenge to establish viable societies and economies in America. In this essay, I examine some of the ways in which the different outposts of the empire viewed one another over time and space.[1]

During the early modern period, most saw America as part of the emerging world of the First British Empire, the foundations of which had been laid in Tudor Ireland. During the sixteenth and early seventeenth centuries, the hallmarks of British expansion in Ireland were the various plantations. These were intended to establish 'the Englishry' in contemporary Ireland although, at times, many planters also saw themselves as more than the mere exponents of a new imperial system. In the words of Sir Thomas Smith (1513–77), they should emulate 'Rome, Carthage, and all others whither *any notable beginning* hath been', by promoting 'English laws and civility' in Ireland. However, the island became more turbulent with the passage of the century and, by 1573, Smith admitted that the 'hopes of . . . reforming the Irish were too lightly grounded', or even a 'pretence', as the vice-president of Munster, Sir William Herbert (d. 1593) put it in 1588. The 'continual rebellions' of the 'wild Irishry' posed a military as well as a cultural challenge which, by 1580, many saw as intractable. As a result, the more benevolent aspects of plantation were abandoned, as well as the possibility that 'a mixed plantation of British and Irish . . . might grow up together in one nation'.[2]

After 1610, this change of direction was clearly seen in Ulster, when revised *Orders and conditions* were presented for the six counties which had been escheated there three years earlier. In effect, the plantation of Ulster abandoned a policy of anglicising Ulster's native Irish in favour of settling the region with Lowland Scots and English. The plantation designated three types of participant. The first two, the *undertakers* and *servitors*, were to be of Scottish or English origin, although the second also included 'deserving' corporations such as Trinity College, Dublin, the City of London, and the Established Church. For these, the 'adventure' of the plantation was clearly stated: to nurture 'civility' and the 'true religion' as well as to ensure that the 'flight of the earls' had closed the book on Irish opposition to imperial expansion. These aims had little appeal for the majority of the third group, the *native Irish*, especially after the Irish attorney general, Sir John Davies (1606–19), argued that plantation was a strategy to enable the Irish 'in tongue and heart, and every way else, [to] become English'. Thus, the fate of the Ulster Irish depended, at best, on the scheme's failure and, at worst, on its modification.[3]

During the 1560s, a similar experiment in Munster had also sought to develop a reformed society whose leaders of 'eminence or nobility' might curb the 'servile nature' of the native majority there. Until the 1640s, this plantation was neither as effective nor as organised as the Ulster scheme, although, as a matter of expediency, some of the native Irish did adapt to the new order. Whether successful or not, however, plantation was regarded by the native Irish as 'alien', not in the sense that it was 'foreign', as in that it did not seek to involve them. It represented 'a war of two civilisations' which, especially during the Cromwellian period, was intensified by the ways in which other colonisation schemes were outlined and developed. As such, the native Irish did not consider themselves to be, nor were they perceived to be, part of the 'promise' of plantation, at least as this was promoted from Dublin Castle.[4]

In Ulster, the majority of those who identified with the new agenda were of Scottish-Presbyterian origin. Although the plantation there was upset by the civil war of the 1640s and 1650s, it was subsequently relaunched. As before 1640, the connection with Scotland is clear. Such was the movement of 'reliable' and 'elite' Scottish tenants to Ireland that, in 1636, the Scottish privy council had resolved that tenants could emigrate only with their landlords' permission, while by 1660 all but one of Ireland's sixty-eight Presbyterian ministers were located in Ulster. These links with Scotland were reinforced by a continuous flow of immigrants which for the twenty-five-year period between 1690 and 1715, was estimated by Archbishop Edward Synge of Tuam (1716–41) at 50,000 Scottish *families*. Although there were important differences between the later and earlier Scottish immigrations, both combined to give much of contemporary Ulster an ethno-cultural physiognomy which distinguished it from other areas of the island.[5] This heritage also influenced the ways in which the province interacted with British America during the course of the seventeenth and eighteenth centuries.

The elitism of plantation was also reflected in the penal laws, the earliest of which were passed against the backdrop of reformation and civil war. However, after the Williamite settlement had more or less decided the land question in Ireland, the laws that were passed between 1695 and 1710 sought to ensure that the political and military energies of the Jacobites, which had been sapped at the battles of the Boyne and Aughrim, would not be recharged through other channels to threaten the legacy of the 'Glorious Revolution'. Religious tests were attached to holding the franchise and public office, to the ownership and inheritance of land, to access to education and the professions, and to the organisation and practice of religion. As Synge put it in 1731, 'the design of these laws is, so to lessen their [Catholic] number or break their power, that they may be no longer formidable to those whom they are justly suspected to have good inclination to destroy'.[6] As such, the passage of the penal laws elaborated on plantation theory and initiated the 'age of the Protestant ascendancy' in which the religious, political and cultural distinctions of earlier years were now, at the dawn of the eighteenth century, legally reinforced.

In seventeenth-century America, a similar association between 'civility' and a restricted polity was inherited from the ideology of plantation in Ireland.[7] In 1637, John Winthrop (1588–1649) suggested that if Massachusetts was 'bound to keep off whatsoever appears to tend to our ruin or damage, then we may lawfully refuse to receive such whose dispositions suite not with ours and whose society will be hurtful to us'. For the colony's General Court, this meant excluding certain types of Irish immigrant and in 1654,

> considering the cruel and malignant spirit that has from time to time been manifest in the Irish nation against this English nation, . . . [it] hereby declare[d] their prohibition of bringing any Irish men, women or children, into this jurisdiction.

In other colonies, Winthrop's concern for 'peaceability' was echoed in policies that discouraged the immigration of nonconformists and outlined various measures 'to prevent the Growth of Popery'. As in its better-known Irish equivalent, passed in 1704, the latter legislation imposed penalties on 'any Popish bishop, priest or Jesuit' who exercised sacerdotal functions or who, in the words of the Maryland Act, would 'endeavour to persuade any of her majesty's liege people to embrace and be reconciled to the Church of Rome'. Also in 1704, Maryland imposed a duty of twenty shillings on each incoming Irish Catholic servant 'to prevent the importing [of] too great a Number of Irish Papists into this Province', while in New York, the connection between the penal laws of the Old and New Worlds was explicitly made when Thomas Dongan, the Irish Catholic governor of New York under James II (1683–8), argued that the English laws which disabled Catholics from holding land did not apply in the colonies, a case he subsequently lost. Over fifty years earlier, Cecilius Calvert had anticipated at least the spirit of this decision when he suggested that colonial law should not be 'repugnant or contrary, but, as neare as conveniently may bee, agreeable to the laws of England'. Reinforcing this after the accession of William and Mary, Maryland's governor John Seymour (1703–9) stated that the 'declared Enemys of our Church and State' would not be indulged, wherever they lived, and this was reflected in legal schedules that were Atlantic in design, scope and impact.[8]

In any event, such laws also reflected a commitment to the single-interest polity. This concept was central to the development of colonial America, although in part it had its roots in an English Whig tradition which, in Edmund Burke's words, united 'a body of men . . . for promoting by their *joint endeavours*, the *national interest* upon some particular principle in which they were all *agreed*'. The Puritans' religious 'ideal of a pure church' had also promoted this notion in colonial New England, while in Pennsylvania the Quakers' 'cause and reputation of truth' gave it a similar currency there. Thus, even among the 'mixed multitudes' of provincial Pennsylvania, the Quaker leaders supposed that society had but one 'morally superior' interest group which could legitimately claim to represent the welfare of the colony as a whole. This assumption continued even after the Quakers lost their numerical majority in the colony and the idea that 'the interest of [their] one part of society' was 'the object of the whole polity', endured as an article of political faith in America until the end of the eighteenth century.[9]

Against this background, it could be argued that the penal laws sought a particular definition of the single-interest polity and to have this accepted by the community as a whole. As such, the laws were most keenly implemented when this polity was understood to be under threat, from either inside or outside that community. For example, when Massachusetts proscribed the Jesuits in 1647, the General Court had assumed that the order would ally with Nova Scotia and French Canada 'to engage the Indians to subdue New England'. Even Maryland's pioneering Toleration Act (1649) was suspended during periods of war with France so 'that none who professed the Popish Religion', and thus, France's presumed allies, 'would be protected' in law. However, as the colonial elite struck deeper roots during the course of the eighteenth century and the traditional condescension and political fear of the Catholic abated, the penal laws were, more often than not, as dead as the papers on which they were written. This does not mean that the penal laws were totally ignored because as John Bowes, the lord chancellor of Ireland (1757–67) noted in 1759, the reality was that the penal laws 'did not presume a Papist to exist in the kingdom'. The inference was that, despite their neglect, the laws could always be invoked not only to secure the polity from military danger, but to ensure a due deference to the constituted establishment of church and state. As a result, the Carrolls and other leading Catholic families in Maryland, for example, had no *formal* political power between 1690 and the American Revolution.[10]

During a visit to London in 1708, even William Penn (1644–1718) experienced the partisan potential of the laws at first hand after a 'complaint' had been made that Mass was being celebrated in Philadelphia by Jesuits from Maryland. As he wrote to his Ulster-born provincial secretary, James Logan, 'ill use is [being] made of it against us here', despite the declared toleration of Pennsylvania's *Frame of government* (1682) and *Charter of liberties* (1701). A more rigorous application of the 'anti-Popery' laws followed. This did not last long and in 1741, Fr Henry Neale reported that his communicants in Philadelphia had again 'all [the] liberty imaginable in the exercise of our business'. However, although the penal laws were thus often relaxed and, in some cases, totally ignored, Neale knew that Catholic worship was not *legally* permitted (and indeed, it remained so until after the American Revolution) and that he should not adopt a misplaced status for either himself or his church in contemporary Philadelphia. In a similar way, the *de facto* extension of the franchise during the course of the eighteenth century did not necessarily mean that the single-interest polity was being jettisoned. As Gary Nash has observed of colonial New York, rank and status had to be 'carefully preserved and social roles differentiated if society was to retain its equilibrium', while New England evolved into nothing more than a 'democracy without democrats'.[11] Therefore, the urge to promote a single-interest polity continued during the colonial period and whether this was expressed in subtle or obvious ways, it was seldom such as to encourage Catholic Ireland to identify with the grander designs of the First British Empire in Ireland or, with the exception of the West Indies and Newfoundland, the British colonies in America.[12]

Aside from the ideology of plantation and the single-interest polity, seventeenth-century colonists were also influenced by another Old World view, that America was 'an outlet to so many idle, wretched people as they have in England', as the Spanish ambassador to London put it in 1611. Most of them resented this perception and in any event, they did not want convicts and servants from Britain and Ireland to become charges on their own fledgling communities, especially after such people were excluded from the second Navigation Act (1663). They resisted the portrayal of the New World as a dumping ground for the 'rogues and vagabonds' of the Old, all the more so because in James MacSparran's words, 'though some of these Felons do reform, yet they are so few, that their Malversation has a bad Effect upon the Morals of the lower Class of Inhabitants'. Such attitudes greatly influenced the evolution of colonial law on European immigration, although, in many cases, immigrants were associated with 'paupers' and convicts who were considered to be particularly undesirable. In 1700, for example, Massachusetts forbade the admission of anybody who was 'likely to be a charge to the place' and obliged ship captains, 'under penalty of £5 for every name that was omitted', to provide the local custom house with the name, description and 'circumstances so far as he knows', of their passengers. In 1722, a year after 6,000 people had been infected by a fever which many associated with recent arrivals from Ireland, Boston's selectmen also announced that they would take bonds from Irish immigrants 'to save the town harmless from all charges' and, if necessary, deport any who were being 'maintained *at the cost of the province*'. These laws were not mere formalities. In 1755, for example, the selectmen spent £14 to return an Irishman who had become a charge on the colony.[13] Such actions, and the attitudes which they reflect, reinforced the supposed inhospitality of New England as a whole and helped to ensure that the region did not become a prominent destination for Irish emigrants during the colonial period.

Unlike New England, the southern colonies were more concerned about incoming European convicts rather than poor white immigrants. While convicts might not have been unwelcome earlier in the seventeenth century, by 1671, Virginia's General Court had become so uneasy with the 'great nombres of felons and otheyr dessperate villaines sent hither' that it prohibited the 'landing of any [further] jail birds' within the colony. Thereafter, many of these 'wicked villaines' were diverted to the West Indies, where in the words of Massachusetts' agent, 'it is well known that they will be willingly entertained'. In 1717, however, the Transportation Act widened the list of transportable crimes to include a number of non-capital offences such as vagrancy and indeed, between 1735 and 1743, the only period for which authoritative Irish figures are available, over half the convicts who were shipped from Ireland were, in fact, vagrants. In Virginia, these immigrants were no more welcome than they had been before 1671 and many colonists believed that the broader definition of 'transport' would renew the immigration of a type of settler whom they had spent the previous forty years trying to keep out. As a result, they drew up a schedule of fines which proved to be so prohibitive that they constituted, in the words of Richard West, lord chancellor of Ireland (1725–6), 'a virtual prohibition of convicts' from Britain and Ireland. These duties also affected Ireland's *servant* trade with Virginia in that some merchants were involved in the transportation of convicts as well as servants.[14] After Virginia effectively withdrew the financial comfort of the convict trade, these merchants looked to Maryland which had accepted the Transportation Act without protest. As a result, one merchant observed in 1746 that 'convicts and servants sell better [there] & may be imported without any risque'.[15] Thus the fate of both types of immigrant was often associated in the public mind, and among Irish emigrants the image of Maryland as a harsh station endured for much of the eighteenth century.

In the middle colonies, the regulation of immigration was also influenced by a view that convicts and other poor European immigrants could destabilise the community. After its protests against the Transportation Act went unheeded, Pennsylvania passed its own Convict Act in 1722. This act demanded 'a true and just account' of all those who entered the colony but by imposing a duty of £5 on each convict, as well as a bond of £50 'for the good behaviour of such convict persons for the space of one year', it also sought to circumvent the Transportation Act by *provincial* regulation. Seven years later, the Irish Servant Act extended similar measures to servants amid fears that the rising tide of German and Irish immigrants might become 'a heavy burden and charge upon the inhabitants of this province'. Both pieces of legislation had potentially serious implications for Irish emigration to the Delaware, although in some ways they were self-defeating. For example, there were no provisions for checking the accuracy and truth of passenger lists; this was left to the discretion of the ship captain. The captain was required merely to return his lists to the local customs official and he, in turn, was obliged only to collect them. Moreover, the laws could be evaded by landing passengers at the Delaware ports of Newcastle and Wilmington. In any event, they were amended in the Duty Act of 1730, and in 1742 the privy council revoked them as being incompatible with the Navigation Acts.[16]

In New York, ship captains were asked to furnish lists of passengers within twenty-four hours of arrival and to return to their port of origin those who had come without property, 'manuall craft or occupaceon', or security 'for their well demeanor'. The colony's revised 'duke's laws' (1683) also included immigrants within the ambit of its poor laws although, by 1701, it had repealed many of these laws as being 'inconvenient and burthensome'. Moreover, its law 'to prevent vagrant and idle persons from being a charge and expense' on the colony (1721) was not specifically associated with immigrants, while the requirement to file passenger lists was largely ignored. One of the city's newspapers, the *Independent Reflector*, later challenged such official apathy on 'the importation of mendicant foreigners' and warned that 'that which is virtuous in Theory, becomes vicious in Practice'. However, such protests were half-hearted and in any event, the colony did not consider poverty to be an acute social problem until well into the eighteenth century. Thus, both New York and Pennsylvania were less inclined to use their respective laws governing the poor and the marginal to regulate European immigration. This was especially so during the eighteenth century when, together with other aspects of their Old World heritage, they applied their laws in a pragmatic way which would not discourage Irish emigrants from considering the real opportunities which America offered.[17]

A number of books and pamphlets also encouraged potential emigrants to look beyond colonial charters and laws, whatever their background and focus. Most of these writings described the topography and potential of the American colonies which, in the words of one, 'sagacious industry and long acquaintance will discover'. The pamphlets which were written and sponsored by William Penn also offered religious toleration as well as practical information on a range of subjects, from the organisation and management of the Atlantic voyage to the acquisition, seeding and stocking of land in America. As with private letters, such published accounts were circulated beyond the walls of those who bought them and were publicised by colonial representatives who were appointed for that purpose. In 1669, for example, the Carolina proprietors sent an agent to Ireland to advertise their colony, while Penn appointed factors in a number of European cities, including Dublin, soon after his patent was confirmed in 1681. However, it was not until the early decades of the eighteenth century – when the application of the penal laws was at its most rigorous in Ireland, New England was fading as an option for Irish settlers, and James Logan was appointed as Penn's provincial secretary – that Penn's promise of civil and religious freedom struck a more responsive chord in Ireland. Thus Logan noted that the Irish immigrants who came to Pennsylvania during the 1720s 'say the Proprietor [had] invited People to come & settle his Countrey, [and that] they are come for that end'.[18]

These publications also sought to answer some of the more negative characterisations of life in America. For example, George Alsop's widely circulated *Character of the province of Maryland* (1666) forcefully rejected the 'abusive exclamations' that had 'stigmatiz'd' Maryland servants 'for slaves' and rather like the Irish immigrant Job Johnson in 1767, he saw in his detractors 'the clappermouth jaws of the vulgar' who would thoughtlessly and ignorantly deny the 'poor and industrious' of the Old World an opportunity for betterment in the New. Intending servants were also reminded that their indentures usually provided an important protection in colonial law. In New York, for example, the colonial courts invariably awarded servants their freedom if a master was held to be in breach of contract, while in Pennsylvania a law of 1700 stipulated:

> That no servant, bound to serve his or her time in this province, or counties annexed, shall be sold or disposed of to any person residing in any other province or government, without the consent of the said servant, and two justices of the peace of the county wherein he lives or is sold.

The law could also be invoked to prevent 'Barbarous usage', to keep a servant's family together, to improve 'a miserable Condition', or to ensure the payment of freedom dues. For many aspiring Irish emigrants, such a benign code confirmed Pennsylvania as 'a good poor man's country where there are no oppressions of any kind whatsoever'. It also suggested that servitude in Pennsylvania was not necessarily an invidious path towards the 'promise' of the New World. Thus Johnson spoke for many when he recalled that his 'only encouragement' to go to Pennsylvania

> was because Many Go to America worth nothing yet some of them servants and hear or see them Come back again, in two or three years worth more than they would have been by staying at home while they lived and yet they would Not Content themselves at home, but went back again which was sufficient to Convince any one that the Country was Good.[19]

Servitude gave more than access to America. It was also central to broader strategies to attract settlers to British North America. Some of these promotions were peculiar to the earlier phases of colonial development. Between 1636 and 1683, for example, Lord Baltimore's *Conditions of plantation* linked the distribution of the more substantial land allotments in Maryland to the importation of servants. As such, his promotions were intended to attract settlement as well as investment. In June 1680, George Talbot of County Roscommon was awarded 32,000 acres 'for transporting 640 persons within twelve years', while in Pennsylvania the London Society of Free Traders was given 20,000 acres on the understanding that imported servants would develop the fishing and fur trades within its ambit. Most colonies also offered servants 'headrights' of between fifty and eighty acres when their indentures expired, although during the eighteenth century, these arrangements were, more often than not, used to settle the more outlying and frontier areas and so secure the British presence in North America. During the 1720s, Logan justified giving frontier land in Pennsylvania to Ulster Presbyterian immigrants because they had already 'proven' their 'bravery' when Derry and Enniskillen were defended against the approaching Jacobites in 1689. With such settlers, he argued that the colony would be secure against 'any disturbance' in the future.[20]

During the course of the eighteenth century, a number of southern colonies promoted other schemes to encourage emigration from Ireland. In 1731, South Carolina embarked on a programme of assisted emigration and township settlement that included land grants, exemptions from taxation, and the supply of provisions and tools to sow a farm or to develop a trade in the colony. On 31 January 1734, and following application to the legislature, a number of Ulster Presbyterians who had recently arrived in Williamsburgh were given eight hogsheads of corn, two of peas, two of salt, and eighteen barrels of beef. By 1761, however, some argued that the concessions were not having 'the desired Effect' and in 1766, 1767 and 1768 (during which the importation of black slaves was also prohibited) a second promotion promised exemption from taxes for ten years, one hundred acres for each immigrant head of household, and fifty for each family member, as well as payment of passage money. These 'projects' appealed to pre-arranged groups rather than to the immigration of individuals and, as such, they had a seventeenth-century ring to them. Moreover, the fact that they were restricted to Protestant settlers and effectively focused on Ulster suggested that the confessional undertones of the earlier Irish plantations were being applied to the development of the Anglo-American south. Protestant clergymen took a conspicuous role in organising their communicants to take advantage of the concessions. However, the expected surge in the number of Irish servants did not happen and in June 1768 one of Carolina's leading political and commercial personalities, Henry Laurens, concluded that he would have to make 'an end of the account of the [Irish] servants by giving them away to save great expense'.[21]

Such promotions were complemented by emigrants' letters and published 'letters of advice' which usually pitted the socio-economic troubles of Ireland against the opportunities of contemporary America. At various times during the course of the eighteenth century, the enclosure of common lands, the reorganisation of the tithe system, increasing prices and rents, and the greater expectations, 'vigorous methods' and percentage demands of tithe agents, encouraged a number of popular protest movements to seek 'justice for the poor'. Some of these protests, especially those directed against increased rents and high renewal fines, coincided with periods of high emigration. In Ulster, for example, many of the twenty-one-year and thirty-one-year leases which had been set under the terms of the Williamite settlement expired during the late 1710s and 1720s and the renegotiated leases were set at higher rates. Against this background, emigration was 'a practical alternative' to life in Ireland and, in Thomas Wyndham's opinion, the emigration of the 1720s was particularly high because of those 'who make merit of raising rents as high as possible, setting them by cant to the highest bidder, without regard to the true value of the lands, or the goodness of the [existing] tenant.' The *Belfast News-Letter* outlined the contrast:

> It would swell the advertisement too great a length to enumerate all the blessings those people enjoy who have already removed from this country . . . from tenants they are become landlords, from working for others they now work for themselves, and enjoy the fruits of their own industry.

Thus, as Henry Johnston wrote in 1773, Irish emigrants could come 'out of a Land of Slavery [and go] into A Land of Liberty and freedom'.[22] In such circumstances, America became less an 'adventure' than an escape.

Only a small number of emigrants' letters survive from the colonial period and most of these were written from the middle colonies. Even some of these are of dubious authenticity, including John Murray's often-cited letter to the Revd Baptist Boyd, minister at Aughnacloy, County Tyrone. However, Boyd's letter was widely circulated in contemporary Ireland and included the central themes of most of the *genre*, whether intended for private reading or public recitation. In 1737, Murray described the flora, fauna and produce of the 'very strong Lan [sic] [and] rich Ground' of New York and listed not only his own wages for keeping 'a Skulle for wee Weans', but also those for labourers (4s. 6d. a day), spinners (4s. 6d. a week) and tailors (20s. per suit of clothes). The price of land in his vicinity was given as '£10 a Hundred Acres for ever, and Ten Years Time tell ye get the Money, before they wull ask ye for it'. It was indeed 'a bonny Country'.[23]

Nearly thirty years later, William and Job Johnson wrote that their brother in Derry would

> make Well out at Making of Broomes [to] sweep Houses with [in Pennsylvania], their Being a Great Call for Such Tradesmen [at] sixpence per Broom . . . He Might Make Easily six of them Each Day Besides [having] Meat and Drink as Slatabogie [two miles east of Maghera, Co. Derry] Never can Afford.

David Lindsey was convinced that he also should set sail for 'Pennsilvena'. Writing to his cousin in 1758, he remarked that the 'good Bargains of your lands in that Country Doe greatly encourage me to pluck up my spirits and make Redie for the Journey.' Thirty years earlier the Westmeath Quaker, James Wansbrough, suggested to his cousin in New Jersey that 'if you or your sons Doe write unto me and give me good Encouragement I will transport mysellf and family and soninlaw . . . but pray tell me what is ye best Comodyty to teake into yt Contrey.' Thus it is clear that private letters from America were not without influence and it was with this in mind that Murray's letter had been 'printed and dispers'd in Ireland' in the first place. 'Tell aw the poor Folk of your Place', it had asked Boyd, 'that God has open'd a Door for their Deliverance'. In 1725, the Quaker, Robert Parke, promoted Chester County, Pennsylvania in a similar fashion and added that although his was 'as full an Account as Possible', he knew that 'other Letters might Suffice' if it fell short.[24]

Some alleged that such 'advices' were too one-sided and that unflattering accounts of America were often censored by the ship captains and merchants who managed Ireland's passenger trade. As one observer put it in 1729,

> I believe the people are imposed on and deceived by the accounts they receive from their relations and correspondents . . . and by the indirect practices and

insinuations of masters of ships . . . [who] go about and send their factors and agents round the country, tempting and ensnaring them.

Four years later, another writer charged that while 'the richer sort' were being assured that 'their posterity will be for ever happy,' 'the poorer sort' were being deceived by the accounts of the 'great wages given there [in America] to labouring men.' Thus, although one servant, Daniel Kent, sent favourable reports back to Limerick, his father observed that 'some of the People' who had sailed with his son had met 'since their arrival in America with the severest cruelty and hardship'. In 1767, Job Johnson addressed such conflicting accounts and ascribed the 'Desire to hear ill' of Pennsylvania, for example, to those who 'would keep their friends there [in Ireland] with them in Bondage and Slavery', while Parke wrote that 'talk [that] went back to Ireland that we were not Satisfied in coming here' was 'false'.[25] Thus potential Irish emigrants did not lack advice on life in America, negative as well as positive, legal as well as personal, and were also aware that circumstances varied from colony to colony. Their reactions were also influenced by their own cultural heritage and circumstances in Ireland as well as by the 'pull' and 'push' of economic factors and networks.

This was particularly true of Ulster's Presbyterians. Because they did not belong to the established Church of Ireland, Presbyterians were excluded from civil office, obliged to pay tithes to the established ministry and, as Alexander Crawford wrote from Donegal in 1736, 'as Bound Slevs to Bishop [and] minestor By thire hurying yus into Bis[h]ops Corts'. As a result, they were, in the words of their memorial of 1728, 'put on a level with the Papists', a situation which they greatly resented. Against this background, many prepared to join their cousins in America to enjoy what 'is denied them in their own country'. In choosing to do so, they were often influenced by their ministers, as Ezekiel Stewart of Fortstewart, County Donegal, noted in 1729:

> The Presbiteirien Ministers have taken their shear of pains to seduce their poor ignorant heare[r]s by bellowing from their pulpits against ye landlords and y^e [Episcopal] clargey, calling them rackers of rents and screwers of tythes, with other reflections of this nature which they know is pleasing to their people; at ye same time telling them that God had appoynted a country for them to dwell in (nameing New England) and desires them to depart thence, where they will be freed from the bondage of Egipt and to ye land of Canaan etc.

Many Irish Presbyterians responded to such appeals without diffidence. Their view of colonisation and settlement was Atlantic in its scope and, as such, it was, relative to other types of emigrant at least, easy to make the second step to permanent settlement in America.[26]

The same was true of Ireland's Quakers, for whom Pennsylvania was a natural magnet. Most of their emigrants left Ireland during the first quarter of the eighteenth century, when the penal laws were implemented with a particular rigour. Some were people of substance, some not, although in total it has been estimated that they did not exceed 2,500 in number. However, because all emigrated within wide Quaker networks, with letters of identification and introduction (the so-called certificates of removal), and with the reinforcement of community structures that were only geographically split by the Atlantic ocean, emigration was perceived by them in positive terms.[27] As such, they were closer to the Atlanticism of the Ulster Presbyterian than to the European focus of the Irish Catholic.

Relative to Ireland's Presbyterians and Quakers, the continental colonies were not important to the Irish Catholic world, at least until the middle of the eighteenth century. Instead, as J. G. Simms has observed, it was on the European rather than on the American mainland that 'the real history' of contemporary Irish Catholicism was being traced. This is not to suggest that the Americas were ignored by Irish Catholics although, at times, there was a sense in which, as part of the wider British world, the colonies had the liberty to limit ambition and success. Thus, since Irish Catholics were 'very desirous to do better', as the Dublin-trained Anglican minister, Charles Woodmason noted of Carolina in the 1760s, there were 'many concealed Papists' and Protestant converts among the colony's population who drifted from their old religion in order to do so. In Maryland, the fifth Lord Baltimore converted to Anglicanism in order to recover his proprietorship, while his cousin served in the Maryland Assembly for seventeen years after he did likewise in 1738. Writing to his son in Eton in 1739, this assemblyman advised:

> In point of Religion, [to] be not too much attached to any [opinions] grown up with you [for] Bigotry and superstition in Religion is a grand Error [and t]he Church of England as by Law Established is worthy of your consideration.

Such attitudes were little different from those of the 'crypto-Catholics' of contemporary Ireland who sought 'refuge' in the 'convert rolls' when their position, estates or prospects seemed to be under threat. Accordingly, potential Catholic emigrants to the continental Americas were aware that they were trading one 'fragment of empire' for another, where the penal laws were applied unevenly over time and place, and where, as the more general laws on immigration and settlement suggested, Old World prejudices were never far away.[28]

However the colonies were perceived and understood in Ireland, as they began to evolve from the more ideologically driven utopias of the seventeenth century to the more commercially driven cultures of the eighteenth, attitudes to emigration changed, especially in the middle colonies of America and the northern parts of Ireland. What linked these two parts of the Atlantic world were the commercial structures of the flaxseed and linen industries.

In Ireland, the linen industry was encouraged by the Linen Board (founded in 1711) as well as by export bounties that were introduced in a series of supportive laws. Of particular importance was the Linen Act of 1705, which permitted the direct shipment of Irish white and brown linens to the British Americas, while the Bounty Acts of 1743 and 1745 subsidised their export through English ports. As the linen industry consequently grew in most areas of the island, Ireland also became a major market for American flaxseed. This was especially so after 1733, when bounties were introduced to subsidise the trade. Two years earlier, the Navigation Acts had been amended to allow direct importation from America to Ireland. As a result, Irish purchases of American flaxseed had risen eight-fold by 1740 and continued to grow thereafter, while, in America, the *per capita* consumption of Irish linens also increased, doubling between 1751 and 1771. These developments had a particular impact on Ulster where both products were central to the provincial economy. As Robert Stephenson concluded in 1757,

> if the whole account of all of the linen manufactures promoted by the Linen Board in Leinster, Munster and Connaught, and a considerable part of Ulster, were valued ... they would not equal the returns made by one of the northern districts, where the manufacture was generally established.

Most of the one and a quarter million pounds that were allocated to support the industry between 1700 and 1775 was spent in Ulster and, by 1770, the province was producing more than 80 per cent of Ireland's total linen output and buying most of America's flaxseed export to Ireland.[29]

In the colonies, Philadelphia and New York soon emerged as major importers of Irish linen, and by 1766–7 as much as 96 per cent of Ireland's import of American flaxseed also originated in the two ports. It was a lucrative business which also helped to redress an unfavourable balance of trade with Britain and Ireland 'especially', as Jared Elliot noticed in 1760, 'when we consider how difficult it is for us to make Returns to Europe'. Consignments of flaxseed could be paid for in bills of exchange in Ireland and these could then be used to purchase and ship goods through ports in Britain. Alternatively, the holds of the returning vessels could be filled with servants as well as linen for *direct* transportation back to America. Shipping servants was a cash business and, as such, 'an advantageous returning freight', as one house put it in 1774, 'and is *all paid ready down at Shipping*'. Given that merchants normally received between ten to twenty pounds for each servant, at a time when the cost of passage was about four to five pounds, the profit was not insignificant.

Servitude thus evolved a commercial importance that was crucial to the success of America's developing flaxseed trade with Ireland. Yet its importance was not the same everywhere.[30]

Every year, considerable quantities of linen were shipped to America from all the major ports of Ireland. In Dublin, however, and to a lesser extent in Cork, because available cargo space could be filled from a broader commercial inventory, without resorting to passengers, the servant trade was not as vital to Irish-American business as it was in Ulster. After 1745, these ports also shipped increasing consignments of linen indirectly to America through English ports. The export bounties that were paid by this diversion were, in the words of Benjamin Fuller, one of Philadelphia's leading merchants in the trade, 'a considerable thing and will more than pay all Charges in getting them [Irish linens] to this Market'. As a result, leading American houses in Dublin and Cork also looked at America through British ports, while they acted as commission agents on behalf of principals in Britain, the West Indies, and North America, in addition to managing their own interests. In Ulster, however, the flaxseed/passenger roundabout had a different and more crucial importance which was highlighted by a constant flow of vessels to colonial America, especially to the middle colonies. This trade was all the more systematic because it was managed by families and mercantile interests that spanned the Atlantic. It was more self-contained than it was in the rest of Ireland and this, together with the tendency to sail directly to America, gave a special impetus to the passenger trade between Ulster and America.[31]

Next to linen, Ireland's other staple industry was provisions, the export of which was particularly important in the southern and eastern parts of the island. Consignments to America peaked during the 1760s and early 1770s, encouraged by the repeal of the Cattle Acts in 1759 and increased orders during the Seven Years War. By 1770, Cork was the major source of beef entering colonial New York and Philadelphia. During the seventeenth century, the city had already developed a valuable trade with the Caribbean and shipped many of its accounts either on its own vessels or on the several hundred others that weighed anchor there *en route* to the West Indies from British and other European ports. As a result, pastoral farming was a profitable business in the regional hinterlands of Dublin, Cork, Limerick and Waterford, although, at a time of rising population, some found the increased rents for the remaining arable land hard to bear. It was no coincidence that Munster and Leinster were the epicentres of the Whiteboy movement during the 1760s and 1770s, or that in 1753 thirty-five emigrant vessels left Cork for America when there was a reputed 'want of tillage' in the region.[32] In a sense, however, these departures were an aberration because in Munster, economic hardship, however acute, rarely produced the same impulse to emigrate as in Ulster. In part, this is because seasonal labour, both within Ireland and to places such as Newfoundland, provided alternative outlets that were a familiar and established part of the regional culture. Moreover, those who were involved in the Irish provisions trade operated in a world where the servant trade was incidental to commercial interests, at least until the 1750s or so, when the trade assumed a greater importance in the ledgers of non-Ulster as well as Ulster merchants.

While Irish emigrants were not uninfluenced by their perceptions of particular colonies, however they had been formed, commercial, mercantile and personal networks thus ensured that at least during the eighteenth century, the majority sailed for either the Delaware or the Hudson. On 25 November 1727, Logan informed his proprietor that 'we have from the North of Ireland, great numbers yearly, 8 or 9 shiops this last ffal [sic] discharged at Newcastle . . . [they] say there will be twice the number next year.' Later, as some 1,865 entered Philadelphia in 1729, he paused to remark that 'it looks as if Irel^d is to send all its inhabitants hither, for last week not less than six ships arrived'. However, Irish traffic to the Delaware dipped during the 1730s although it soon recovered and steadily grew until the outbreak of the American Revolution, especially from Ulster ports. Between 1750 and 1775, over half of the American-bound vessels which advertised for 'passengers and freight' in the *Belfast News-Letter* gave the Delaware as their destination. Ulster's passenger traffic also rose during this period and between 1771 and 1775, at least 16,000 left Ulster for the Delaware ports of Newcastle, Wilmington and Philadelphia while an estimated 8,000 also entered from other ports in Ireland. Of these, at least half made the onward journey all the way upriver to Philadelphia. Some of the remainder went on to New York. However, the Hudson was a secondary attraction for Irish emigrants, perhaps partly because the majority of its Irish entrances were from Dublin and Cork, where the passenger flow was more irregular and casually organised than was the case in Ulster. In any event, during the last peak of Irish emigration prior to the American Revolution (1771–5), New York was a third-choice destination after Philadelphia and Maryland and may have attracted as few as 3,000 from both parts of the island.[33]

Further to the south, the Chesapeake also attracted Irish immigrants, although it had never been an appealing destination for them. From the middle of the eighteenth century, however, the diversification of Maryland's economy, together with the shift to slave labour, offered new opportunities. There was a demand for all types of labourer and craftsmen to build everything from houses to hogsheads, as well as process and ship the region's tobacco staple. In 1729, the foundation of Baltimore at the head of the tidewater on Chesapeake Bay placed the port in an ideal situation to satisfy the growing labour needs of the back-country and in December 1774 one of the town's leading houses, Woolsey & Salmon, noted that 'within these two years, there has been 6000 servants sold in this Town from England *and Ireland*'. For most of the colonial period, however, Annapolis was the major port of Maryland and its port books reveal that whereas only 972 Irish arrived there between 1764 and 1769, 4,896 did so during the following six years. Moreover, 5,104 of these came from non-Ulster ports as opposed to 764 who landed from Ulster. Thus, Annapolis's late-colonial records confirm that most of Maryland's Irish immigration came from outside Ulster and that the passenger flow surged from the late 1760s.[34]

Unlike Maryland, Charleston drew most of its emigrants from Ulster, especially from the port of Larne. This traffic owed a lot to the promotions of the 1760s which, during that decade, made the port the second most attractive American destination for vessels of Ulster origin. During 1767 and 1768, 1,453 and 1,089 Irish settlers availed themselves of South Carolina's programmes of assisted emigration while others settled in Georgia under similar initiatives. Although these schemes were cancelled in 1768, the link between Charleston and Larne endured and, with the exception of the years of the revolutionary war, four to five vessels sailed the route every year until the end of the century, each carrying about 200 passengers. Many of these people travelled as members of families and were organised by Presbyterian ministers such as William Martin and William Beatty who acted as local agents for the American trade. Relative to Philadelphia and New York, however, Charleston was, in the words of Jacob Price, more a 'shipping point' than a 'commercial centre' or '*general entrepôt*'. As such, many of its Irish immigrants passed through the port *en route* to the back-country of the Carolinas and Georgia, where their presence put a particular cultural stamp on the region that has lasted to the present day.[35]

These emigrants had at least one thing in common with those who had sailed from Ulster to New England during the first wave of Irish emigration fifty years earlier. Most were Presbyterians who, in the words of one of the earlier emigrants, the Revd James McGregor, sought in America 'the opportunity of worshipping God according to the dictates of conscience and the rules of His inspired Word'. In 1718 alone, five vessels landed six ministers and 750 people in Boston, of whom the majority were, in Cotton Mather's words, 'of so desirable a character . . . [and] from the north of Ireland'. However, the congenial welcome that these emigrants expected from their co-religionists was soon replaced by conflict and friction, since many Bostonians regarded the new arrivals as 'foreigners' and 'not good Subjects'. As a result, New England lost its appeal for intending Irish emigrants and Governor Jonathan Belcher (1730–41) later reported that there were 'but few Irish' in his colony 'and indeed, the people of this country seem to have such an aversion to them, so they find but little encouragement' to go there.[36]

The fate of these early-eighteenth-century Irish Presbyterians is a reminder of how the narrower sense of 'mission' of a particular colony characterised attitudes to immigration. Massachusetts was not unique in this respect and, in various ways, the emigration policies of colonial Carolina and Maryland also reflected their respective cultures and, from Ireland, were seen to do so. The middle colonies had been founded as more pluralist societies and this too determined the attitude of both the viewer and the viewed to the peopling of Pennsylvania and New York. In each of these regions, however, economic and commercial connections with Ireland added a new dimension to the ways in which they would be seen during the eighteenth century. Moreover, they also provided an access that was not available a century earlier. To this extent, the ideological inheritance of the Old World planter was slowly superseded by the pragmatism of the New World entrepreneur as a society of accommodation evolved from one of exclusiveness. Irish emigrants recognised that this was especially true of the middle colonies and, although more traditional appeals attracted some to others of the continental colonies, it was in Pennsylvania and to a lesser extent in Maryland and New York, that a new Irish community would be invented after the American Revolution.[37]

Notes

The author wishes to thank Nicholas Canny, Kevin Kenny and Kerby Miller for comments on an earlier draft of this article.

1 Theodore K. Raab, *Enterprise and empire: merchant and gentry involvement in the expansion of England, 1575–1630* (Cambridge, Mass., 1967). For the political connections between colonial America and contemporary Ireland, see Thomas Bartlett, '"This famous island set in a Virginian sea": Ireland in the British Empire, 1690–1801' in P. J. Marshall (ed.), *The Oxford history of the British empire*, 5 vols (Oxford, 1998), II, pp. 253–75, and Maurice J. Bric, 'Ireland, America and the reassessment of a special relationship, 1760–1783', *Eighteenth-century Ireland* XI (1996), 88–119.

2 Smith is quoted in Nicholas P. Canny, 'Changing views on Gaelic Ireland', *Topic: 24* XII (1972), 23, and in David B. Quinn, 'Sir Thomas Smith (1513–1577) and the beginnings of English colonial theory', *Proceedings of the American Philosophical Society* LXXXVII, 4 (1945), 553. Herbert is quoted in Karl S. Bottigheimer, *English money and Irish land* (Oxford, 1971), p. 13. The final quotation is from Sir John Davies, as quoted in ibid., p. 9. The most recent introduction to early modern Ireland is Nicholas Canny, *Making Ireland British* (Oxford, 2001). See also the articles by Jane Ohlmeyer and T. C. Barnard in Nicholas Canny (ed.), *Oxford history*, I, pp. 124–47 and 309–27. The two approaches to plantation in early-seventeenth-century Ireland are discussed in Eugene Flanagan, 'The anatomy of Jacobean Ireland: Captain Barnaby Rich, Sir John Davies and the failure of reform' in Hiram Morgan (ed.), *Political ideology in Ireland, 1541–1641* (Dublin, 1999), pp. 158–80.

3   Davies is quoted in Flanagan, 'Anatomy of Jacobean Ireland', p. 173. For Davies and the colonisation of seventeenth-century Ireland, see Hans S. Pawlisch, *Sir John Davies and the conquest of Ireland: a study in legal imperialism* (Cambridge, 1985), and Hiram Morgan, 'The colonial venture of Sir Thomas Smith in Ulster, 1571–1575', *Historical Journal* XXVIII (1985), 261–78.

4   Nicholas P. Canny, 'Dominant minorities: English settlers in Ireland and Virginia, 1550–1650' in A.C. Hepburn (ed.), *Minorities in history* (London, 1978), p. 53, and G. A. Hayes-McCoy, 'Gaelic society in the late sixteenth century', *Historical Studies* IV (1963), 61. For the Munster plantation, see Michael MacCarthy-Morrough, *The plantation of Munster: English migration to Southern Ireland, 1583–1641* (Oxford, 1986). The ideology and organisation of plantation are also analysed in Ciaran Brady and Raymond Gillespie (eds), *Natives and newcomers: essays on the making of Irish colonial society, 1534–1641* (Dublin, 1986). For the native Irish and plantation, see Hiram Morgan, 'The end of Gaelic Ulster: a thematic interpretation of events between 1534 and 1634', *Irish Historical Studies* XXVI (1988), 8–32, and Canny, *Making Ireland British*, pp. 432–55, *et passim*.

5   Raymond Gillespie, *Colonial Ulster: the settlement of east Ulster, 1600–1641* (Cork, 1985), p. 30; Guy S. Klett, *Presbyterians in colonial Pennsylvania* (Philadelphia, 1937), p. 12, and Toby C. Barnard, 'Identities, ethnicity and tradition among Irish Dissenters, *c.*1650–1750' in Kevin Herlihy (ed.), *The Irish dissenting tradition 1650–1750* (Dublin, 1995), pp. 2–4. Synge is quoted in Charles A. Hanna, *The Scotch-Irish, or the Scot in north Britain, north Ireland and North America*, 2 vols (New York, 1902), I, p. 614. For the demographic make-up of early-seventeenth-century Ulster, see Gillespie, *Colonial Ulster*, pp. 50–63.

6   For the penal laws, see S. J. Connolly, *Religion, law and power: the making of Protestant Ireland, 1660–1760* (Oxford, 1992), and Thomas Bartlett, *The fall and rise of the Irish nation: the Catholic question, 1690–1830* (Dublin, 1992). Synge is quoted in T. W. Moody et al. (eds), *A new history of Ireland* (hereafter, *NHI*), 5 vols to date (Oxford, 1976), VI, p. 106.

7   For the Irish background to the settlement of America, see K. R. Andrews et al. (eds), *The Westward enterprise: English activities in Ireland, the Atlantic, and America, 1480–1650* (Baltimore, 1988), and Nicholas Canny, *Kingdom and colony: Ireland in the Atlantic World, 1560–1800* (Baltimore, 1988) and 'Fashioning a British Atlantic world' in Nicholas Canny et al. (eds), *Empire, society, and labor: essays in honor of Richard S. Dunn*, special supplement to *Pennsylvania History* (hereafter, *PH*), LXIX (1997), 6–45, and *Oxford History*, I.

8   R. C. Winthrop (ed.), *Life and letters of John Winthrop*, 2 vols (Boston, 1869), I, p. 182; J. D. Butler, 'British convicts shipped to American colonies', *American Historical Review* II (1896), 20; William H. Brown et al. (eds), *Archives of Maryland*, 72 vols (Baltimore, 1883–1972), XXVI (1704), pp. 340–1, 349–50; Audrey Lockhart, *Some aspects of emigration from Ireland to the North American colonies between 1660 and 1775* (New York, 1976), pp. 137–8, 135, and David W. Jordan, *Foundations of representative government in Maryland, 1632–1715* (Cambridge, 1987), pp. 4, 166. The phrase 'peaceability' is taken from Michael Zuckerman, *Peaceable kingdoms: Massachusetts towns in the eighteenth century* (Cambridge, Mass., 1970).

9   Edmund Burke, 'Thoughts on the present discontents' (London, 1770) in *The Works of Edmund Burke*, 8 vols (London, 1852), III, p. 170 (italics mine); Perry Miller, *The New England mind: from colony to province* (Cambridge, Mass., 1953); Richard Bauman, *For the reputation of*

truth: politics, religion, and conflict among the Pennsylvania Germans, 1750–1800 (Baltimore, 1981), and Sally Swartz, *'A mixed multitude': the struggle for toleration in colonial Pennsylvania* (New York and London, 1987). For the continued currency of this notion after the American Revolution, see Richard A. Ryerson, 'Republican theory and partisan reality in revolutionary Pennsylvania' in Roland Hoffman and Peter J. Albert (eds), *Sovereign states in an age of uncertainty* (Charlottesville, 1981), pp. 104–5, 114.

10 Emberson Edward Proper, 'Colonial immigration laws: a study of the regulation of immigration by the English colonies in America', *Columbia University Studies* (hereafter, *CU St*) XII, 2 (New York, 1900), 27, 58 *et passim*, and Richard J. Purcell, 'Irish colonists in Colonial Maryland', *Studies* XXIII (1934), 288. Bowes is quoted in W. E. H. Lecky, *A History of Ireland in the eighteenth century*, 5 vols (London, 1892), I, p. 470. For a discussion of how the penal laws affected Maryland's Catholics, see Ronald Hoffman, *Princes of Ireland, planters of Maryland: a Carroll saga, 1500–1782* (Chapel Hill and London, 1996).

11 William Robert Shepherd, 'History of proprietary government in Pennsylvania', *CU St*, VI (New York, 1896), 369; John Tracy Ellis, *Catholics in colonial America* (Baltimore, 1965), pp. 373–4; Gary Nash, *The urban crucible: social change, political consciousness, and the origins of the American revolution* (Cambridge, Mass., 1979), p. 7, and Michael Zuckerman, 'The social context of democracy in Massachusetts', *William and Mary Quarterly* (hereafter, *WMQ*), 3rd ser., XXV (1968), 523, 535.

12 For the West Indies, see Sean O'Callaghan, *To hell or Barbados* (Dingle, 2000), and Hilary McD. Beckles, 'A "riotous and unruly lot": Irish indentured servants and freemen in the English West Indies, 1644–1713', *WMQ* XLVII (1990), 503–22. For Newfoundland, see Cyril Byrne, 'The Waterford colony in Newfoundland, 1700–1850' in William Nolan and Thomas P. Power (eds), *Waterford: history and society* (Dublin, 1992), pp. 351–72.

13 Marcus Wilson Jernegan, *Laboring and dependent classes in colonial America, 1607–1783* (Chicago, 1931), pp. 177, 192, 195; Mildred Campbell, '"Of people either too few or too many": the conflict of opinion on population and its relation to emigration' in William Appleton Aiken and Basil Duke Hennington (eds), *Conflict in Stuart England: essays in honour of Wallace Notestein* (London, 1980), p. 188; *Acts and resolves, public and private, of the province of Massachusetts Bay*, 21 vols (Boston, 1869–1922) I (1700–1), pp. 451–2, *c*.XXIII, II (1722–3), p. 244, c.V, and Stephen Wiberley, 'Four cities: public poor relief in urban America, 1700–1775', (PhD thesis, Yale University, 1975), p. 49. McSparran is quoted from the forthcoming work by Kirby Miller and David Doyle, *'To ye land of Canaan': letters, memoirs, and other writings by Irish immigrants to colonial and revolutionary America, 1675–1814* (Oxford, 2003). I am grateful to both authors for allowing me to quote from the unpublished script of this important work.

14 J. C. Ballagh, 'White servitude in the colony of Virginia', *Johns Hopkins University Studies* (hereafter, *JHU St*), 13th ser., VI–VII (Baltimore, 1895), 36; Samuel McKee, *Labor in colonial New York, 1664–1776* (New York, 1935), p. 92; David Noel Doyle, *Ireland, Irishmen and revolutionary America* (Dublin, 1981), p. 64; and Lockhart, *Aspects of emigration*, ch. 6. West is quoted in Eugene Irving McCormac, 'White servitude in Maryland, 1634–1820', *JHU St* XXII, 3–4 (Baltimore, 1904), 102. For British attitudes to transportation, the most authoritative study is A. Roger Ekirch, *Bound for America: the transportation of British convicts to the colonies, 1718–1775* (Oxford, 1987).

15 Library of Congress (hereafter, LC), Davey and Carson Letterbook (1745–50), letter to Robert Travers, Dublin, 5 June 1746. For estimates of the number of convicts who were sent to the colony, see Kenneth Morgan, 'The organization of the convict trade to Maryland: Stevenson, Randolph & Cheston, 1768–1775', *WMQ*, XLII (1985), 202.

16 James T. Mitchell and Henry Flanders, comps, *The statutes at large of Pennsylvania from 1682 to 1801*, 16 vols (Harrisburg, 1896–1911), III, 264–8, c.CCXLVIII, IV, 135–40, c.CCCVII and *ibid*., 164–71, c.CCCXIV, and Thomas M. Truxes, *Irish-American trade, 1660–1783* (New York, 1988), p. 128. For an excellent analysis of these laws, see Swartz, *Mixed multitude*, ch. 4 *et passim*.

17 *The colonial laws of New York*, 5 vols (Albany, 1894–6) I, 132, and Steven J. Ross, '"Objects of charity": poor relief, poverty, and the rise of the almshouse in early-eighteenth-century New York City' in William Pencak and Conrad Edick Wright (eds), *Authority and resistance in early New York* (New York, 1988), pp. 140–1. The *Reflector* (1753) is quoted in Michael Kammen, *Colonial New York: a history* (New York, 1965), pp. 297–8 and the 1721 law in Samuel McKee, 'Indentured servitude in colonial New York', *New York History* XXXI (1931), 153–4. For more general analysis of the city's attitudes to the poor and poverty, see Robert E. Cray, *Paupers and poor relief in New York City and its rural environs, 1700–1830* (Philadelphia, 1988).

18 Andrew White, *A relation of the colony of the Lord Baron of Baltimore* (London, 1633), as in Richard Walsh (ed), *The mind and spirit of early America: sources in American history, 1607–1789* (New York, 1969), p. 2; Abbott E. Smith, *Colonists in bondage: white servitude and convict labor in America, 1607–1776* (Chapel Hill, 1947), p. 59; Marcus Wilson Jernegan, *The American colonies, 1492–1750* (New York, 1929, repr. 1965), p. 306, and William H. Engle and John B. Linn (eds), *Pennsylvania Archives*, 2nd ser., 19 vols (Harrisburg, 1876–93), X, 97, Logan to John Penn, 25 Nov. 1727. See also Albert Cook Myers (ed.), *Narratives of early Pennsylvania, West New Jersey and Delaware* (New York, 1912) and Nicholas Canny, 'The Irish background to Penn's Experiment' in Richard S. Dunn and Mary Maples Dunn (eds), *The world of William Penn* (Philadelphia, 1986), pp. 139–56.

19 G. Alsop, *A character of the province of Maryland* (London, 1666) in *Fund Publications of the Maryland Historical Society*, XV (Baltimore, 1880), pp. 57, 94; Alun C. Davies (ed.), '"As good a country as any man needs to dwell in": letters from a Scotch–Irish immigrant in Pennsylvania, 1766, 1767, and 1784', *PH*, L (1983), p. 320; John Bioren, publ., *Laws of Pennsylvania* (Philadelphia, 1810) I, 10, c.XLIX; Robert O. Heavner, 'Economic aspects of indentured servitude in colonial Philadelphia' (PhD thesis, Stanford University, 1976), pp. 9–10, Miller and Doyle, *Land of Canaan*, Smith, *Colonists in Bondage*, p. 22, and Public Record Office of Northern Ireland (hereafter, PRONI), D2092/1/3 and T3700/1.

20 McCormac, 'White servitude in Maryland', pp. 21, 12–13; Gary B. Nash, 'The free society of traders and the early politics of Pennsylvania', *Pennsylvania Magazine of History and Biography* LXXIX (1965), 147–73, and James Leyburn, *The Scotch-Irish: a social history* (Chapel Hill, 1962), p. 191. See also 'White servants as a measure of defence' in Warren B. Smith, *White servitude in colonial South Carolina* (Columbia, S.C., 1961), pp. 27–37.

21 Smith, *Servitude in colonial South Carolina*, pp. 54–5, 64–5, 42–3, and Jean Stephenson, *Scotch-Irish migration to South Carolina, 1772* (Strasburg, Va, 1971), p. 7. See also Erna Risch, 'Encouragement of immigration as revealed in colonial legislation', *Virginia Magazine of History*

and Biography XLV (1937), 1–10; Robert L. Meriwether, *The expansion of South Carolina, 1729–1765* (Philadelphia, 1964), and E. R. R. Green, 'Scotch-Irish emigration: an imperial problem', *Western Pennsylvania Historical Magazine* XXXV (1952), 193–209, and 'Queensborough Township: Scotch-Irish emigration and the expansion of Georgia, 1763–1776', *WMQ* XVII (1960), 183–99.

22 Lecky, *Ireland in the eighteenth century*, II, p. 7, n.1; Maurice J. Bric, 'Priests, parsons, and politics: the Rightboy protest in County Cork, 1785–1788', *Past and Present* 100 (1983), 117; Dickson, *Ulster Emigration*, pp. 24, 40–5; PRONI, T659, Pelham Correspondence, Wyndham to unknown, 11 Jan. 1728–9, *Belfast News-Letter*, 3 June 1766, and PRONI, 3578, Johnston to Moses Johnston, dated 28 Mar. 1773. In the (Dublin) *Freeman's Journal*, 13 Jan. 1774, Wyndham's suggestion was echoed as an explanation for the high emigration of the early 1770s: 'his [Lord Donegall] estate was parcell'd out, and set I may say by auction, to the highest rent and fines.' For the popular movements, see Maurice J. Bric, 'The Whiteboys, 1760–1780' in William Nolan (ed.), *Tipperary: history and society* (Dublin, 1985), pp. 248–84, and James S. Donnelly, 'Hearts of oak, hearts of steel', *Studia Hibernica* XXI (1981), 7–73.

23 Earl Gregg Swem (ed.), 'Letter of James Murray of New York to Rev. Baptist Boyd of County Tyrone, Ireland' (Metuchen, N.J., 1925), 1. Murray's letter was originally published in the (Philadelphia) *Pennsylvania Gazette*, 27 Oct. 1737. In 'On the trail of early Ulster emigrant letters' in Patrick Fitzgerald and Steve Ickringill (eds), *Atlantic crossings* (Newtownards, 2001), pp. 13–26, Michael Montgomery shows that the Murray's supposed letter was most likely intended to be read in public rather than in private and that as such, it is of dubious authenticity and a 'pseudo-letter'. In more general terms, the poor survival rate of actual emigrants' letters is all the more remarkable in view of the number which were written. On 2 Mar. 1766, the Johnsons wrote to their brother in Maghera, County Derry, 'this being the ninth [time] that we have sent home this year', Davies, 'As good a country', p. 317. For more general comment on these letters, see Trevor Parkhill, 'Philadelphia Here I come: a study of the letters of Ulster emigrants in Pennsylvania, 1750–1875' in H. Tyler Blethen and Curtis W. Wood (eds), *Ulster and North America* (Tuscaloosa, 1997), pp. 118–33. As already cited, the major work on emigrants' letters by Kirby Miller and David Doyle will be published shortly.

24 Davies, 'As good a country', 318, PRONI T2493, David Lindsey to Thomas Fleming, 19 Mar. 1758, and Swem, 'Letter of James Murray', 1–2. Parke is quoted from Albert Cook Myers, *Immigration of the Irish Quakers into Pennsylvania, 1682–1750* (Swarthmore, 1902), p. 78, and Wansbrough from Miller and Doyle, *Land of Canaan*.

25 Green, 'The "strange humours" that drove the Scotch-Irish to America, 1729', *WMQ* XII (1991), 118; 'Roscommon', *To the Author of Those Intelligencers Printed at Dublin* (New York, 1733), p. 2; Miller and Doyle, *Land of Canaan*, p. 201, Davies, 'As good a country', p. 320, and Myers, *Immigration of the Quakers*, p. 71.

26 Miller and Doyle, *Land of Canaan*; Green, 'Scotch-Irish Emigration', p. 198, and PRONI, Castleward letters, book 3, D2092/1/3/141, Ezekiel Stewart to Michael Ward, 25 Mar. 1729. For the background to the memorial of 1728, see J. C. Beckett, *Protestant Dissent in Ireland, 1687–1780* (London, 1948).

27 Myers, *Immigration of the Irish Quakers*, pp. 81–2, and Richard S. Harrison, 'The evolution of the Irish Quakers' in Kevin Herlihy (ed.), *The religion of Irish dissent 1650–1800* (Dublin, 1996), pp. 69–75.

28 *NHI* IV, 643, and Miller and Doyle, *Land of Canaan*. Woodmason is quoted in Leroy V. Eid, 'Irish, Scotch and Scotch-Irish, a reconsideration', *Journal of Presbyterian History* CX (1986), 219, 222. For conversions from Catholicism to Anglicanism in connection with promotion and office, see Kerby Miller, *Emigrants and exiles: Ireland and the Irish exodus to North America* (New York, 1985), pp. 150–1. For 'crypto-Catholicism' in contemporary Ireland, see Bric, 'Whiteboy movement', 248–51, and T. P. Power, 'Coverts' in T. P. Power and Kevin Whelan (eds), *Endurance and emergence: Catholics in Ireland in the eighteenth century* (Dublin, 1990), pp. 101–27.

29 Truxes, *Irish-American trade*, pp. 176–7, 33–6, 193–200, 284 and ch. 9; W. H. Crawford, *Domestic industry in Ireland: the experience of the linen industry* (Dublin, 1972), pp. 3–5, and Dickson, *Ulster emigration*, p. 8. Stephenson is quoted from John J. Horner, *The linen trade of Europe* (Belfast, 1920), p. 98. For the Linen Board, see 'The Irish linen board, 1711–1828' in Louis M. Cullen and T. C. Smout (eds), *Comparative aspects of Scottish and Irish economic and social history* (Edinburgh, 1977), pp. 77–87.

30 Truxes, *Irish-American trade*, p. 199; LC: Blair McClenachan papers, 15 Aug. 1774 and Davey and Carson Letterbook (1745–50), 28 Oct. 1748, 21 Nov. 1749. Elliot is quoted in Thomas M. Truxes, 'Connecticut in the Irish-American Flaxseed Trade, 1750–1775', *Eire-Ireland* XII (1977), 37.

31 Truxes, *Irish-American trade*, pp. 184–5, 74–8, 46–55. Fuller is quoted in ibid., p. 179. For the development of commission agencies, see K. G. Davies, 'The origins of the commission system in the West Indies trade', *Transactions of the Royal Historical Society* LII (1952), 89–107.

32 Truxes, *Irish-American trade*, pp. 147, 154, and Lockhart, *Aspects of emigration*, p. 50. See also R.C. Nash, 'Irish Atlantic trade in the seventeenth and eighteenth centuries', *WMQ* XLVII (1985), 229–56 and Francis G. James, *Ireland in the Empire, 1688–1770* (Cambridge, Mass., 1973).

33 Dickson, *Ulster emigration*, pp. 224–5, appendix E. Logan is quoted in Karl Geiser, *Redemptioners and indentured servants in the colony of the commonwealth of Pennsylvania* (New Haven, 1901), p. 37 and in Historical Society of Pennsylvania, Logan papers, Letterbooks III, p. 302. For the figures for the Delaware and Hudson, see my *Ireland and America: the economy of emigration, 1760–1800* (forthcoming). Much lower figures for Philadelphia are given in Marianne Wokeck, *Trade in strangers: the beginnings of mass migration to North America* (University Park, Pa., 1999).

34 Woolsey and Salmon are quoted in Paul Kent Walker, 'The Baltimore community and the American Revolution' (PhD thesis, University of North Carolina, 1973), p. 37 and Annapolis's records from see Eid, 'No freight paid so well'. See also Russell R. Menard, 'From servants to slaves: the transformation of the Chesapeake labour system', *Southern Studies* XVI (1977), 355–90.

35 Smith, *White servitude in Colonial Carolina*, pp. 65–6 (Dublin); *Sleator's Public Gazetteer*, 21 May 1765. Price is quoted in John J. McCusker and Russell R. Menard (eds), *The economy of British America, 1607–1789* (Chapel Hill and London, 1985), p. 185.

36 Klett, *Presbyterians in colonial Pennsylvania*, p.19, Charles K. Bolton, *Scotch-Irish pioneers in Ulster and America* (Boston, 1910), p.109, and Miller and Doyle, *Land of Canaan*. McGregor is quoted in Miller and Doyle, *Land of Canaan* and Belcher in Truxes, *Irish-American Trade*, p. 363, n.119.

37 For Irish immigration after the American Revolution, see Maurice J. Bric, 'Patterns of Irish emigration to America, 1783–1800', *Eire-Ireland* XXXVI (2001), 10–28.

CHAPTER 9

Towards Democracy

Irish-born Elites in Canada and the United States
1820–1920

David Doyle

Albert Lovett required by his very presence a constant critical self-inquiry into one's research life, teaching and ideas. Thus this broadest of men, who held sharp views on the enforced conformities which, centuries ago, had damaged his beloved Spain, managed to evoke a free self-inquisition in those who did not attain his standards of scholarship, output and energy. His ideas and interests varied. But one constant was his conviction that justice required efficiency, whether in the Habsburg possessions of old, or the nascent European institutions of the 1950s, and even in today's history departments. He saw that petty or tired discriminations prevent this everywhere. He thus anticipated economists' recent findings that jobbery, connection and all bloc prejudice are dysfunctional because they ensure the misallocation of talent and capacity. In a very English term, he held that a university must be a 'broad church' to encompass the factual, investigative, archival, imaginative and critical talents rarely found in single individuals but which in interplay are central to all humane disciples. The ideal society itself would merge liberality and efficiency: 'Europe is diversity' as he said to me in mellower years. This helps explain why he could shift from governmental history within narrow time-frames to fascination with Fernand Braudel's notions of the *longue durée* and the full horizon – that is with those cultural landscapes, spread out in space and depth, which were the milieu of the creative administrators he admired. True, he never fully reconciled the democratic values and processes which he cherished with these themes, but therein was he not typical of a whole generation of informed New Europeans?

His ideas may be applied to the Irish diaspora. In a Braudelian long view, the Irish can be seen as a creative irritant in the anglophone North Atlantic world (as in its dependencies in Australasia) starting from *c.*1600 until 1922 and beyond, constantly pressing that world towards a more inclusive efficiency of ever more just ends, removed from the coteries of privilege which long warped its liberties, franchises, assemblies, legislation and administrations. Overseas, even at home, most Irish after 1775 realised that their own social and political progress was inseparable from liberal and, later, democratic change (a process complicated but not reversed by the initial ruthless secularism of the French Revolution). Indeed they saw that their social advancement and political empowerment were inseparable (if not at all the same thing) as for many the need for escape from subordination often led to a slow, even reluctant, education in political reform. Those too advanced for their time, notably the United Irish exiles of the 1790s and both socialist progressives and Catholic social reformers of 1910–20, were often derided by the immigrant mainstream, and found their feet only when they attached themselves to more gradualist, indigenous patterns of change, the former in Jeffersonian Republicanism,[1] the latter among the New Deal Democrats.[2] In Canada, the same rooting in gradualist reform took place for their few Irish radicals, even when, like Edmund Bailey O'Callaghan, they fled south to settle down. Their democratic liberalism was often thus the result of their conservative participation in new ways. Indeed recent studies emphasise this realism of local immersion[3] outside the great metropolises of New York, Philadelphia and Chicago. The extent of such liberalising change seems the more remarkable, apart from the creative turbulence of the revolutionary, Jeffersonian and Civil War eras and becomes something of a mystery. Strangely, it may not be separable from the very conformities of Ireland itself, the 'this is it' fatalism of a tightly articulated society for whose members any gains were normally incremental. Liberalism abroad may partly have represented an adjustment to how things were done, though grand ideas and advanced movements periodically invigorated or coloured such change.

The homeward feedback which all this entailed remains sadly unexplored (not least given that some emigrants returned, if but few in number). This may be because the linkage of constitutional change with social promotion was itself a pervasive theme in the United Kingdom and Ireland also in these years. However, by embedding democratic advance in a nexus of licit, very Victorian, self-improvements, both American and Canadian models spiked the arguments of those for whom such change in Ireland, and indeed its nationalist outcomes, were threats to Great Britain's stability and prosperity.

A whole world of scholarship for the Irish in six anglophone countries abroad illuminates this central liberal theme, but usually without such sharp focus.[4] Indeed, much present scholarship obscures it. Certainly the more recent work of Donald Akenson does so, as does the multi-volume Irish World Wide series.[5] So too do most recent works on the Scots Irish.[6] Other scholars are more attuned to the theme, although their focus is often lost in the need to take on board the real gains in this post-political, largely value-free 'social adjustment' history. They are also often somewhat cramped by an understandable need to play down past conflicts.[7]

For a direct access to this theme, we may examine the Irish-born elites in their host societies. They lived in changing societies. They were beneficiaries of a process of political and constitutional reform. Slowly they came to press for it themselves. By insisting on their own self-definitions within these liberal societies, they in turn extended the limits of liberty. At all times, as outsiders to a greater or lesser degree, their 'political' had to be *politic*, their social aspiration to be calculated, their class and group relations to be diplomatic, their religious convictions premised on laws of voluntary adherence. Such constraints themselves helped to purge these Irish-born elites of residual Jacobite or Williamite outlooks: outward liberal agenda matched internal renewal. Begun in the antecedents of the American Revolution, full success was attained earliest, even by the 1850s, in Australia and California and certainly last, if not least, in Scotland, where it came in 1918 and more fully after 1945. As all major destinations had changing colonial, provincial, and state jurisdictions, each regionally distinctive, the pattern could vary greatly, perhaps most notably in Canada; even Great Britain contained three nations and politically distinct regions within England itself. Yet the thrust towards equality and representation was everywhere under way by the 1820s and 1830s. As a rule, it proved earlier more fruitful for Irish Protestants than for Irish Catholics;[8] this was quite apart from differences in the usual timing of their group migrations and overseas re-education, because there were major divides even amongst *contemporary* emigrants of both broad groups (and of the sub-groups within them).

Here I examine two 'receiver' nations, Canada and the United States, as locales of Irish elite achievement. Between them they made up the great mass of overseas emigrants.[9] They also contained the great majority of *all* Irish-born living abroad, even including those living nearby in Great Britain.[10] I focus on those who merit scholarly coverage in the dictionaries of national biography of those countries. The pitfalls of this approach are obvious, but the merits are also plain. Are the Irish-born memorialised therein representative of their own group experience? Is their selection not filtered by the very prejudices the Irish once encountered? Yes, but it is also true that modern historical scholarship has been systematically generous in recording all real contributions to national life, especially since 1920, more so since about 1960. The three Canadian and American works reflect these emphases and notably so for the Irish. Such recorded lives often highlight the themes we seek. They do so more clearly than those monographs on the Irish overseas that are often narrowly focused on their experience in the cities and towns of the mid-Victorian or American Civil War era, from 1850 to 1880.

Were Canada and the USA comparable? In size and resources then the world's second and third largest nations,[11] both were effectively, if not wholly, of English legal culture and language, were interdependent in trade and economy (certainly after 1849) and each was independent of Great Britain, the one since 1776, the other more or less domestically since 1867 (if not *de jure* until 1931). But their differences also impress. If both had federal polities over vast areas (after 1790 and 1867 respectively), Canada enjoyed a structured bi-culturalism, the United States a less formal melting-pot multi-culturalism. In 1870–1, Canada had a population of four million and federal revenues of only twenty million dollars; its southern neighbour had forty million people and federal revenues of over four hundred million dollars. Federal income was in both very low at $5 and $10 respectively per capita, so that in both liberalism was strongly rooted in the realities of a minimalist degree of centralism.[12] Higher population and revenues underline the fact that more established and diverse trade, politically independent development, and better soil and resources had given the somewhat smaller USA considerably greater wealth, attraction and muscle. The two countries' capacity to absorb immigrants was thus quite different. Indeed Canada from 1871 to 1900 attracted only about one million migrants (including just 82,000 from Ireland), and lost many of these southwards. Crucially, it also additionally lost around one million Canadian-born to the United States, many of Irish-born parentage.[13]

This development gap remained until 1900, with the American population doubling from 1865 until then, whilst Canada's grew from 3.5 to only 5.5 million. Yet even in 1870, huge areas of both countries were either quite unsettled or largely undeveloped, not merely their deserts, plains, mountain, glacial 'shield', taiga and tundra regions, but lands almost everywhere. Four fifths of the land of the late Confederacy were uncleared and unfarmed. Canada did not finally begin to replicate both America's prairie and urban growth until after 1900, when Irish mass migration was ending. Prominent in pre-1840 settlement of Ontario and the Maritime provinces, Irish immigrants played little or no part in settlement of the prairie provinces. Contrary to the recent impression in Irish diaspora studies, rural and urban populations in both countries finally equalised rather late and around the same time, by the 1920–1 censuses.

Partly because the overall wealth and urban centres of Canada were much less absorptive, many of Canada's Irish immigrants originally went to the land,[14] as later to the United States. America's urban growth rates were remarkable. In *both* societies, the 'new Irish' from about 1840 onwards clearly preferred town jobs, a pre-Famine adjustment to Irish rural crisis and the newer British model of urban commercial-industrial prosperity. Their preference was reinforced by a changed economics of things, as adoption of free trade in England in 1849 caused Canadian businessmen to depend upon American markets (a process not reversed by imperial preference in the

1890s). All this – quite apart from the contrast in political culture – directed the great majority of Irish emigrants to North America towards the United States. Even most Irish newcomers to Canada thenceforth went south.

Yet in Canada, relatively smaller numbers of Irish arrivals had already ensured a larger demographic and social impact, especially for the period between 1830 and 1880. In the United States, up to five million Irish arrivals between 1800 and 1920 could never match the country's overall population growth. During the Revolutionary era, perhaps one fifth of the population was of Irish birth or ancestry, whereas by 1900 only one thirteenth was of Irish birth or parentage. In short, imperial connection (longer-lasting in Canada) gave the Irish a privileged access to North America, which later became more competitive. The 'imperial' phase of migration initially saw a numerical and social predominance of Irish Protestant (including Presbyterian) immigrants, with shifts towards a preponderance of Catholics (at first gradual, then overwhelming) from around 1800 in the American case and roughly twenty years later in the Canadian. The changing structure of Irish-born elites in both societies reflects these trends closely, with a significant 'delay factor'. The Irish-born or descended political elite of America's revolutionary and early national era (from the 1770s until 1820) was largely Protestant and republican. The equivalent elite in Canada, divided between Tories and reformers (in a kaleidoscope of parties), was likewise largely Protestant, but it was imperial in outlook even after Confederation in 1867. We shall later suggest why this was so. It was certainly not a mere reaction to Irish Catholic nationalism (as cruder Tories then maintained), since almost all Irish Catholic immigrants to Canada were also loyal to the imperial order; nor was it simply the natural affinity of Irish Protestants in diaspora to British culture abroad, since to the south these Protestants were midwives first to American independence and then to advanced democracy. There, they changed somewhat with the revivalist Second Great Awakening of the 1820s and the rise of the Whig party from 1834 but they were never to shed their original anti-imperial republicanism.

Were the Irish rewarded for their choice of either country, by representation in the elites of those societies? And if so, to what extent? Can their appearance therein be used as a measure or standard of the liberal credentials and broadening opportunities of these new societies? Overall, their numbers in the 'national biography' compilations may seem tiny compared to the received inflows from Ireland. The *Dictionary of American Biography*, planned in the 1920s, contains 326 Irish-born entries, or 2.4 per cent of the whole.[15] The new *American National Biography*,[16] a product of the 1980s and 1990s (as updated by July 2002), contains 281 or 1.6 per cent. The *Dictionary of Canadian Biography*[17] contains 480 Irish-born for the years 1771–1920, or 7.9 per cent of all entries for those years. In the Canadian work, and to an extent in the first American one, the *Dictionary of American Biography*, numbers are fairly proportionate to the Irish-born elements in both countries between 1800 and 1920. They are not reasonably so in the second, the *American National Biography*. Table 1 illustrates the pattern for both countries, with the caveat that the American data in it are taken from the newer work, which is much less full on the Irish.

Table 1

Irish-born in the Dictionary of Canadian Biography and the American National Biography, by decade of death

	Canada			United States		
Decade	Total entries	Irish entries	Percentage Irish	Total entries	Irish entries	Percentage Irish
1771–1800	504	23	4.6	550	28	5.1
1801–20	502	26	5.2	547	31	5.7
1821–35	479	31	6.5	471	20	4.2
1836–50	538	42	7.8	532	13	2.4
1851–60	521	50	9.6	438	8	1.8
1861–70	524	57	10.9	658	17	2.6
1871–80	574	51	8.8	672	17	2.5
1881–90	586	62	10.6	814	16	2.0
1891–1900	597	61	10.2	969	22	2.3
1901–10	648	49	7.6	881	22	2.5
1911–20	622	29	4.7	1102	17	1.5

Source: Compiled from *Dictionary of Canadian Biography* and *American National Biography*, ANB on-line to July 2002.

This decline from the first to the second American works mirrors both the absolute decline in numbers of the Irish-born in the twentieth century and the proportionate decline in the numbers of 'ever-lived' Irish in the United States as the total population grew from 76 million in 1900 to 275 million in 2000. Irish-born apart, the 1900 population included high cumulations of Irish-Americans (including 'Ulster Americans'), still largely married amongst themselves. By contrast, by 2000 most Irish-Americans had multi-ethnic ancestry,[18] while the country's population included the myriad descendants of approximately 15 million continental European *permanent* migrants to the United States between 1871 and 1920, and of an increasing flow of Asian and Latin-American immigrants after 1963. Such dictionaries thus reflect not merely changing composition of national populations. With a definite time lag, they also reflect the host society's recognition, however slow, of the component sub-elites within Americanising population stocks. The Johnson-Malone *Dictionary of American Biography* reflected the readiness, first of scholars, then of contemporary New Deal America, to take some measure of 'ordinary' Irish America (belatedly 'arrived' under Franklin Roosevelt). In a creative overlap, it also embodied the diversities and autonomies of a still very state-centred America of the half-century before that and of the regional and ethnic memories linked to this reality: thus the 'Scots-Irish' from the revolutionary to the civil war era and beyond figure very considerably (if more so in the second and third generation). John Garraty's 1999 *American National Biography* by contrast reflects not merely a changed demography. His bent is towards the new progressive and gendered social and political history, especially for 1880–1980; older ethnic and religious subcultures are less well served, as are political and military figures of regional import. It is thus not just a hundred eminent nineteenth-century Irish he drops; consistently he also sheds scores of America's other Protestant religious leaders, civil war officers and state politicians. Another factor is also involved. His generation has seen the 'melting' of Irish America through systematic intermarriage (as that of Malone and Johnson's parents had seen the final, decisive exogamy of the Scots-Irish). Some scholars thus even doubted by the 1990s that Irish America was still a useful concept.[19] For all these reasons, one cannot say Johnson and Malone were 'right' or that Garraty is 'wrong'. Given space constraints, they reflect their separate times' diminishing, but equally well-grounded, concerns with the Irish-born. And between them they preserve a most scholarly data bank of 429 Irish, of whom 178 have newly benefited from a second research essay sixty years after the first.

The Canadian *Dictionary* is distinctive. Of roughly the same size as the American works, yet serving a much smaller population base, it is organised by periods. Together these approaches make for a fuller cross-section of Irish achievements in any decade.[20] Local and provincial biographies are much better served because fully national ones are fewer in number. The early twentieth-century emphasis (found in Malone and Johnson) on office-holders, politicians, entrepreneurs, military, and major ethnic, educational and religious leaders, for both nation and region, is complemented by the new social history's concern with labour, community, reform and local figures. A growing recognition of stage, screen and sport, as of the arts, serves the Irish well in the Canadian, as in the new American work.

These distinctions are important when we move from general to particularised careers in the two countries. We may examine lives in North America both in time and by careers. I have used the Canadian occupational groupings to aid comparability, with some modifications and additions. Chronological comparison (again using the Canadian periodisation), is more straightforward. The 'bunching' of groups and knots of Irish tells us a great deal.

Chronologically, there is no direct relation between the numbers of Irish in these national samples and the numbers of Irish-born of different censuses. Since (following Canadian practice) we examine the latter by their death (not birth) cohorts, there should be some relation of these to the Irish-born populations of around fifteen to twenty years before, when their careers were at full flow. However, immigrants often take somewhat longer to find their feet and establish themselves, especially if short on education or connections, so the samples should have a clearer relation to the numbers of Irish-born of twenty-five to forty years before. It is hard to perceive any such outcome, except perhaps in regard to Irish-born judges in Canada, deceased in the period 1881–90.[21] We may also be seeing a process of filtration, of a slowness to discern upward mobility among the Irish in the host societies.[22]

From 1771 to 1820, from 4.6 per cent to 5.7 per cent of all those in both the *American National Biography* and the *Dictionary of Canadian Biography* are of Irish birth. The full Irish-born population, uncounted in the USA until 1850, cannot in 1790 have surpassed about 5.5 per cent of all Americans but thereafter was 5.1 per cent in 1860, 4.7 per cent in 1870 and only 2.1 per cent in 1900. Those of them recorded in the *American National Biography* in fact dropped from 3.0 per cent of the notables studied by it who died between 1841 and 1850, falling to 1.8 per cent of its subjects among those dying in the period 1851–60. This rises to between 2.0 per cent and 2.6 per cent in each of the following five decades between 1861 and 1910, as mid-century immigrants matured or found their feet, before dropping again to 1.5 per cent for the period 1911–20. There is thus little relationship to preceding decadal population shifts amongst the Irish-born. Indeed it has little real relation to studies of other elements in the Irish-born middle classes, at any point from 1800 to 1900, despite the fact that the Irish middle class by 1900 had near-parity with its native-born American counterpart, even it were not in the national 'power elite' or on the very heights of finance and of the new corporations and cartels (then still untypical of the US economy).[23]

For reasons already noted, the Canadian biographies offer fuller material. They are more proportionate to the Irish-born there by decade, if less so to their variable social salience and denominational patterns. Such immigrants were fewer by comparison with America's but they were a larger fraction of the country's people as a whole. In 1851–2, they ranged from 18 per cent in Ontario (the peak year there), to 6 per cent in Quebec and in Newfoundland.[24] By 1871, less than a quarter of a million Irish-born accounted for only six per cent of the new Confederation's people and by 1901, 123,000 constituted three per cent.[25] Despite such falling numbers, one would expect higher numbers of elite entrants, as education available to immigrants – whether before departure or after arrival – increased significantly from the 1860s onwards. But this alone cannot explain the better elites-to-population ratio in Canada.

For the years 1881 to 1900, from ten per cent to eleven per cent of *Dictionary of Canadian Biography* entries are of Irish-born. Their careers were principally established in the 1860s and 1870s. From 1821 until 1850, the range had been between six to eight per cent. On balance there must remain some suggestion that filters, both at the time itself and in subsequent scholarship, have affected the picture, if less so than in the American case.

Never afraid of common sense, the late Dennis Clark noted in 1985 that the configurations in Irish communities would match the changing structures of the North-American economy.[26] Their elites should likewise. Occupational analysis of the national biographical samples bears this out, but only partly. It works better for Canada, where moderate improvement came early outside the cities.[27] In the case of the US, there is a time-lag, under-representation and even skewing from what occupational data should lead us to expect. In other words, put simply, the recorded or 'famous' Irish-born industrialists, financiers and commercial men never quite match their known counterparts in the rising, even wealthy middle classes. It is possible there were both internal and external boundaries to constant high-level achievement, but the middling-sort character of most business- and white-collar gains, their modest roots, also underpinned such fame.[28]

Prominent clergy, journalists and soldiers are more common, at least in the older *Dictionary of American Biography*. They are not so in the newer *American National Biography*. Likewise, whilst Scots Irish politicians are fairly well represented down to 1900, at least in the *Dictionary of American Biography*, their numerous ordinary Irish counterparts are not. An exception is that Fenian leaders are recalled in the earlier *Dictionary of American Biography*. To get some better measure of things, the entries in both the *Dictionary of American Biography* and the later *American National Biography* have been combined to create a fuller sample (tables 2 and 3). Plainly for the Irish the worlds of religion, of words, of rebellion and of war still loom too singularly in these American records. Granted that at the time the Irish may have found specialised market niches in these, yet both American census data and the Canadian samples suggest their activities in these were not *markedly* unbalanced from the bread-and-butter eminences which Clark's thesis should lead us to expect.

A good place to begin to grasp the contrasts is with Canada's eighteenth-century origins, from the conquest of Quebec in 1763.[29] The first Canadian-Irish elites were military and official, primarily Anglicans. This partly reflected a transfer of America's imperial frontier patterns, as Canada was reconstructed from its Quebec foundation in the wake of American independence. It also meant the reinforcement of a pattern established in Nova Scotia and the Great Lakes region after the Seven Years' War. Half of all noted Irish-born of Canadian service or settlement, who died between 1801 and 1820, were, or had been, officials; one third had served in the British armed forces (table 2); some others had operated as traders and explorers under official licence. Anglican church presence between the 1760s and 1830s, strongly Irish, was also quasi-official. This pattern set the trend of high proportions of officials, still marked amongst the Irish-born elite who died between 1881 and 1900. This Irish-Canadian pattern differs radically from American patterns, even pre-revolutionary ones. It qualified the demand for responsible government and set some Irish on the more conservative side of the debate, even after the Durham report; but it also created a tradition of fairly efficient public service that was conserved after Union (of Upper and Lower Canada) in 1841 and later after Confederation in 1867. Irish penetration and part creation of this system depended on army connections, on Irish friendships and kinship, and on patronage. Three special nodules merit notice. In Nova Scotia, the Dublin-born administrator, Richard Bulkeley, an old army friend of Lord Cornwallis, assisted thirteen provincial governors and lieutenant-governors between 1769 and 1798, and with fellow Dubliner, John Parr, governor from 1782 to 1791, provided for American loyalist settlers. One of the latter was Charles Inglis, the loyalist rector of New York City from 1777 to 1783 who later became Anglican bishop in Halifax.[30] A second web was organised by the Carleton brothers, successive governors in Canada proper. Guy Carleton's work for the liberal Quebec Act and in defence of the province from American invasion was followed by his brother Thomas's efforts to consolidate his work and to ensure post-revolutionary control of Indian trade and relations from posts at Vincennes, Kaskasia and Detroit before final abandonment of the region to the USA in 1796.[31] This last goal used a third Irish group. For, while adding other Irish officials, Thomas moved in much of Sir William Johnson's old regime for superintendency of Indian affairs from upstate New York[32] to run the system, notably his kinsman Guy Johnson and the longer serving Matthew Elliott. After 1796, these and other Anglo-Irish officials such as Peter Russell (a former aide to Dubliner Sir Henry Clinton in the Carolinas' campaign) began the settlement of contiguous lands in Ontario.[33] No easy generalities about Anglo-Irish preferences in Canada for 'a ruling class, an established church and a controlled parliament' (W. G. Godfrey)[34] do justice to the protean effects of these ginger groups. In Nova Scotia, Bulkeley defended Acadian expulsion, sent black America loyalists off to Sierra Leone and provided background to the extraordinary effort at setting up landlordship in Île St Jean (Prince Edward Island), after its conquest, which bedevilled human relations there for a century.[35] His strict governance, added to climate and underdevelopment, meant that many Americans left his province within a decade of arrival. But his tight rein on public spending also led to local demands for an assembly. One might contrast his regime with that of the Carletons, Guy setting the foundations of the Quebec *habitans'* adjustment to imperial rule, his brother Thomas helping ensure that loyalist settlers in the Lakes region were contented and that Indian allies also found havens. Yet, as Thomas Carleton aged, his inefficiencies (like Bulkeley's) also triggered reform demands, voiced by Joseph Willcocks from Cork, even though once a scion of the Peter Russell connection. Can it be that even the most conservative Anglo-Irish brought with them a culture tending to creative polarity? – the dilution of royal *dirigisme* by representation.

Yet the Canadian Irish service elite's habitual acceptance of appointed, rather than elected, position lasted long. If the odd incompetent found preferment,[36] it enabled others to carry public service traditions into the Canada of representative government and of provincial and federal autonomy. This helped ensure that Canada had more structured educational, legal, financial and police services than was the case in much of the United States. It also shaped their future: the role of Irish officials in British Columbia was unusual and perhaps prepared it for four Irish-born Prime Ministers.[37] It may explain the irony whereby Catholic churchmen (whether immigrants, or French- or English-speaking Canadians) seemed comfortable with the ordered, if often condescending, place granted them by the country's well-articulated and contested societies. Guy Carleton and his contemporaries had early protected the very principle of authority against what pioneer Meath priest James Jones called the 'levelling democratic spirit' in his years in Nova Scotia (1785–1800).[38] The good side of this shared mistrust lasted. Even amongst the mid-to-late Victorian cohort of Irish-born, who died by 1900, the public service ethos, and a tendency towards social inclusion, remained linked, despite much tension over how expressly Catholicism might be accommodated outside Quebec. And every immigrant Orange leader determined to reign in popery[39] was balanced by liberal and 'conservative-liberal' Anglo-Irish immigrants determined to structure cohesion and to mirror in Ontario Quebec's liberalism towards *its* religious minority. Indeed the determination of reformer Francis Hincks not to follow the 'Clear Grit' faction down the path to social radicalism probably owed much to the Anglo-Irish concern for cohesion and religion.[40]

The contrast with post-independence America was striking. Partly this was because the dominant Irish culture there ran on a spectrum from Presbyterian to evangelical, to enlightened (well into the 1820s), each element distinctively Americanised, so much so that some more recent immigrants had fled it, such as George Gillmore, a well-educated Covenanter from County Antrim.[41] The widespread shift to short-term elective offices, even magistracies; the further loosening of commercial life and farm settlement; competitive republican parties and the boldness of opinion and its permitted expressions; and the slow, cumulative impact of democratic equality prior to its political fulfilment, all these invigorated and vagariated the Irish elite there. Its revolution-era cohort that died between 1801 and 1820 included only a handful of appointed officials as opposed to a score of elected ones and a robust group of very politicised journalists.[42] These were but fragments of a much wider upsurge, especially in the second generation. Many of these Irish politicians had been officers in the revolutionary war, both in militias and formal units. Such connections did not harden, as in Canada in that era, into a self-serving, if able, civilian elite. The interplay of elective office and localised polities and pressures, prompted even the naturally conservative to embrace the representative principle. To be sure, if there was room for the in-migration and social ascent of Catholics, secular and evangelical currents diminished their impact on the upper reaches of society for generations. An exception was the federal navy, the one area of national life found free of structural prejudice by a papal delegate, Archbishop Bedini, as late as 1853. He was right: its officer corps varied from 150 to less than 1000 between 1789 and 1844, and thereafter from 1000 to under 1900 until 1904, yet it had the single most observable group of senior Irish-born figures in American life, churches apart.[43] Elsewhere, the very nature of the new society was inimical to cohesive elites. For the Irish-born the only possible exception was the shipping and merchandising empire established at that very time by the Brown brothers of Baltimore (and originally of Ballymena), a triumph of Ulster family discipline over the fissiparous ambitions released by republican society. Other attempts, such as that of the Crocketts in Tennessee, did not prove successful in the longer run.[44]

After mid-century, Irish elites in both countries reflected the economic long-cycle booms of 1842–57 and of 1858–77 and the mature industrialism thereafter. Canada was slower than the USA to develop railways, partly because of a belated Anglo-Irish preference for canals over railroads, especially on the part of Hamilton Killaly, who was in charge of Canada's public works from the late 1830s to the early 1860s.[45] It was also slower to industrialise. In New York and Philadelphia, there were Irish manufacturers, such as the innovative locomotive builders Matthew Baird and Isaac Dripps, or the streetcar and electric tram-maker John Stephenson.[46] Indeed by 1900, there were eight thousand Irish-born manufacturers and industrial executives in the United States involved in small- to the largest-scale industries, such as rubber manufacturer Joseph Banigan, or meatpackers Michael Ryan and Michael Cudahy.[47] Unlike their Protestant counterparts, Catholic industrialists had usually been taken to America as children, come as untrained youths, or had had some prior training in Dublin or Britain. The exceptions were those in the clothing trades from Ulster or those in western mining and its spin-offs.[48] Montreal, Quebec City, Toronto and Halifax had equivalents of all this including the shipbuilders Henry Dinning and William Lawrence, locomotive builder James Good, and large-scale furniture maker George Armstrong.[49] But Canada's frontier offered no fast fortunes unlike America's: despite disorganised Irish rushes for the gold of the Fraser River in 1858 and the Klondike in 1898, Canada's real mineral wealth, like that of Colorado, required high capitalisation, and so there would be no Canadian versions of James Fair and John Mackay.

Perhaps more unique to Canada was the marked Irish Protestant role in finance and insurance, strongest in Montreal.[50] As in America, prior success in commerce after youthful arrival was the usual origin of this. But in the United States, by contrast, there was less a pattern than occasional breakthrough, such as that of the Browns of Baltimore. Nonetheless the growth of prudent calculation over demagogic rhetoric was early marked there by William J. Duane's reluctance, as secretary of the treasury, to stand over Andrew Jackson's theory that available credit and national finances were rigged by a Philadelphia in-group. It was marked too by the later economic sobriety of men like E. L. Godkin and R. E. Thompson. 'Populist' versus 'established' currents thus continued in the nineteenth-century Ulster American diaspora as in its late eighteenth-century antecedents. The fragmentary if real degree to which both currents crowded rising Irish Catholic interest in these areas, and ascribed exclusion to incapacity, in Pennsylvania no less than in Montreal and Toronto, must remain conjectural. But by 1900, major financiers such as William Grace, Marcus Daly, Richard Kerens, Denis Sheedy and Eugene Kelly had broken every mould.[51] It is striking that banking and brokerage were the only prestigious occupations that saw a decline rather than a rise in numbers of their active members in the USA between immigrants and American-born Irish.[51] Was their initial success too singular, and (apart from the Grace clan) were the Irish financiers largely unable to institutionalise their knowledge, or to hedge, diversify and transmit their holdings? Was the success of the Irish Emigrant Savings Bank directors in New York uncharacteristic? Why then were those in Toronto and Montreal successful?

The natural engrossment of political position by such men took place in both countries. In Canada, 1851–1900, up to two thirds of all Irish active in big and multiple businesses also sought political office; around half of those with one major business, or one or several lesser ones, sought elective office. Less than a third sought no office whatever. 'Big' businessmen who failed to do so, such as St Catherine's Peter Larkin, were a rarity. The pattern was true of both Protestant and Catholic Irish, of St John's and Halifax as of Toronto and Montreal.[52] In the United States, certainly from the 1870s, there were many similar cases. But much national, even big city, politics tended to be left to professionals, if the business-minded Republicans were more careful to direct their politicians and journalists (and much less likely to underline whether their *protégés* were Irish-born). The Democrats, by contrast, powerful in cities – if from 1860 until 1912 usually powerless outside them in the north – made too much of the 'Irish' element in things, promoting a wide variety of

Table 2

	Canada		United States	
	1801–20	1881–1900	1801–20	1881–1900
Armed Forces	9	13	11	10
Business	[7]	[54]	[15]	[17]
—finance	–	11	1	4
—commerce	6	29	8	8
—manufactures	–	18	2	4
—other	2	41	5	16
Office holding[1]	8	34	5	6
Politics				
—federal	9	23	9	4
—provincial	6	29	N/R	N/R
—state	N/R	N/R	12	1
—local, other	—	14	2	4

Source: Compiled from *Dictionary of Canadian Biography* and *American National Biography*, ANB on-line to July 2002, with DAB data added. Multiple careers may overlap. Bracketed figures alone refer to individuals. N/R: not relevant.

1 Refers to appointive offices only

talent, little of it now recalled.[53] Often petty office holding due to patronage was not part of a directive hierarchy of legal office, nor even of a national politics. All three types of business–politics linkage, designed to co-opt or to neutralise administrative power, have been derided by radicals then and since; but both had merits. Each ensured more Irish upward mobility than our formal stories show. Each surely *also* neutralised the anti-democratic biases common to much European, even Irish whiggish, business elites in Europe, whether in Canada or the USA.

There was also another side. In Canada the old public-service elite, when unchallenged, had clogged up the country's infrastructural needs. In America, Jacksonian anti-governmentalism – partly demagogic, partly genuinely competitive, partly rurally simplistic – had, by contrast, wrecked sound financial order for a decade and vetoed state and federal aid to such improvement (whilst 'covering' slavery). Yet in both countries, whether in office, or influencing it, the more impressive mid-century businessmen cleared many paths, whilst looking after their own interests. My impression, and I am not a historian of Canada, is that in that country's smaller contexts this proved more restrictive, so that whilst a 'coterie Irish' did very well there, it was often to block opportunities for later immigrants. In the United States, by contrast, widespread decentralisation and large-scale growth meant opportunities for newer, lesser Irish inclined to 'break in'. Most of these and, more strangely, the several score Irish-born federal congressmen and senators of the years 1880–1920 are lost to the full record, where their Canadian Irish equivalents are not so. In both countries, such men, in interaction, despite their short-take horizons, yet ensured that democratic process informed the rise of politicised large business, and quickened the drive to a 'progressive' response in the second generation which they helped form. There was a debit side. Such interplays so curbed the recognition given Irish-born labour leaders that few are recalled in the national dictionaries, despite the many recorded in specialised compilations.[54]

Journalism became the nervous system of the continent's emergent democracy. Contrary to myths about a people of the pen, the Irish in America produced no authors systematically concerned with the rise of liberal and democratic society there, either amongst immigrants or even visitors from home. The evidence suggests that culture shock was partly to blame; it was easier to come to terms with the country in bits and pieces.[55] Perhaps, too, contrasts were painful.[56] Instead they poured all their insights into journalism, the world of democracy on the hoof, sometimes even on the run. Here the Irish role was extraordinary, drawing on the vigorous and critical press of Belfast, Dublin and Cork since 1760. Between 1770 and the 1820s, Irish immigrants actively fostered American independence and then legitimated (if vociferously) the partisanship central to America's party system from Matthew Carey, J. D. Burk, Samuel Loudon and William J. Duane in the east, to Joseph Charless in the new west (at St Louis).[57] They saw the connection between the new politics and an older Irish craft. If less well known and more muted, the same link between immigrant reform journalism and a politics seeking responsible and popular government emerged in every Canadian province. Its adepts were usually Protestant and liberal in Ontario, Catholic in the Maritime provinces and Newfoundland, diverse in Quebec. Francis Collins from Newry secured freedom of the press in 1829 in Upper Canada.[58] Pre-Confederation politicians such as Joseph Willcocks, Francis Hincks, Edward Whelan, John Talbot, Bernard Devlin, and Timothy W. Anglin, quite apart from D'Arcy Magee, launched varyingly liberal-to-radical papers in the critical Collins mould.[59] Conservative journalists, like James Shaw, and Orange leader, Ogle Gowan, were not silent either.[60] And some, such as John McCoubrey from Waterford, disturbed by the polarisation, simply tried to create a standard of non-partisanship. As Confederation gained momentum, more established figures founded, bought or ran presses, such as Samuel Watson, George Perry, and John Riordon.[61] The last, the Limerick-born pioneer of mass-produced paper in Canada, acquired control of the *Toronto Mail*, for defaulted debt, in 1870. Even the tiny minority of Irish immigrants who looked to annexation to America to fulfil the dream of radical equality, whether during the 1837 revolts in the east, or the 1867–71 excitements in the West, produced journalists, quite apart from the Fenians. Like the latter, they may be charitably seen as politically naive, or more critically as dangerous to the interests of the Irish and their liberal maturity in both new countries.[62] They may be set beside those who were too immature to know when their pro-reform journals should dampen down and cease faction.[63] Both types suggest that word-mastery could create groundless or unmerited demands even upon democratic power.

As popular government developed in both countries, there was a shift towards a weekly Irish Catholic, and/or Irish nationalist, press to differentiate their distinctive positions from those shared with their neighbours.[64] Usually the titles were edited by immigrants. As late as the 1880s and 1890s, there were well over a hundred such papers in the United States. But as secular dailies became a staple in cities, with rotary machinery, the Irish bought these too, and their journalists edited or reported for many of them.[65] The same men often shifted between roles in the two forms of intelligence, as the cases of John Devoy, J. I. C. Clarke and Patrick Ford show.[66] To counteract some of the illiberal and anti-abolition parochialism of their fellow immigrants, Thomas Kinsella edited the Brooklyn *Daily Eagle* and John Savage a pro-Stephen Douglas organ, whilst others such as John Nugent, combated nativism on their own account, Nugent in his own San Francisco *Herald*.[67] By contrast J. McLeod Keating, John Maginnis and others lent their talents to the south and the Confederacy.[68]

Such men were responsible for many innovations: Dublin-born J. Russell Young pioneered war journalism at First Bull Run and J. B. Mc Cullagh ('Mack') developed the 'interview' during Reconstruction.[69] David Croly, John Hall, William Erigena Robinson, and R. Ellis Thompson developed a styles that enabled weighty, complex issues to be crisply canvassed in the new dailies. As party and business pressures sought homogenisation of opinion, Irish journalists developed a conscious *esprit* to prioritise human interests and moral principle - for them inseparable – in their stories.[70] They were quite aware of this, and of its links to their own sub-culture's free press. Major magazine founders Patrick Donahoe, E. L. Godkin, Peter Collier, and Samuel McClure found ways to make reform issues sit easy on the sideboards of the 'fruit dish' Irish and others and thereby nudged stand-pat political machines toward social reform.[71]

Elites in journalism and law were linked. Irish concerns could acquire assured permanency only through the legal and judicial process, since before the 1930s political reform was filtered very closely by judicial fiat. There is evidence that the Irish fully grasped this. Yet despite a real flowering of legal history in recent decades, the role of Irish-born and second-generation lawyers and lawyer politicians (1850–1920) awaits study in both countries, and for America has progressed little beyond Wittke's insights a generation ago, except in studies of individual states of the progressive era.[72] This may be partly because the post-Reconstruction years, and state law then, arenas of their chief impact, are amongst the least studied areas of this new legal history.[73] Many Irish-born lawyers were cautious; they were very few. There were but 1300 of them in 1900, in their total male workforce of almost three quarters of a million. These were just over one per cent of the country's lawyers.[74] Unsurprisingly their leaders, such as Patrick Collins and Bourke Cockran, took up safe reform only.[75] Most understood that minorities cannot be indifferent to special protections. The growth of law schools then so characteristic of 'Irish diaspora' universities is surely a key marker and the debates within them gave a rationale to the causes of the journalists and offered the chief route whereby forensic skill could be turned to elite status. The real change in reform-mindedness (conventional from 1900 until 1920) came in the American-born generation, which saw a fivefold increase in the number of lawyers in their generation.[76] The apparently better integration of Irish lawyers in Canada into the judiciary, magistracy, politics and society may have disinclined them to an activist mindset, but this also had to do with distinct legal traditions, the then absence of a bill of rights and a theory of popular sovereignty, and the cost of risking a high profile.

Table 3

Nineteenth-century Irish-born careers in DCB, ANB and DAB: Services

	Canada		United States	
	1801–20	1881–1900	1801–20	1881–1900
Arts, stage	1	3	2	8
Authors	1	19	4	6
Educators	4	22	1	7
Journalists	1	9	5	15
Law	1	11	4	2
Medicine	1	2	4	4
Religious	9	23	6	26
Science etc.[1]	1	8	1	4
Engineers etc.[2]	2	12	3	3
Labour etc.[3]	–	8	1	15

Source: Compiled from *Dictionary of Canadian Biography* and *American National Biography*, ANB on-line to July 2002, with DAB data added.

1 Includes inventors.
2 Includes architects and surveyors.
3 Includes community leaders and social reformers.

One may wonder whether such articulate freedoms of mind could have developed outside the religious cultures which had nurtured such men in Ireland. Unsurprisingly, many of them defended the transfer to North America of various models of religious education. Indeed, in New York, Boston, Montreal, and Toronto, they broke with each other, very noisily as such men do, on how *exactly* to do this. I believe much of this stemmed from the aforesaid reluctance to think through liberal society and its promise and from their disagreements over how far to reconcile church demands (often glibly put by converts like J. B. McMaster and Orestes Brownson) and the political realities (outside Quebec).

Yet the close association, almost identity, of religion and education has been persuasively reasserted for the Irish in both the United States and Canada and for both Catholic and Protestant. They helped to define the patterns of schooling, state and voluntary, in both countries. Yet a caveat must be added to the usual heroic versions: virtually no immigrant Irishmen became or remained teachers in the later nineteenth century. The contrast with women's achievements could not have been greater.[77] Much religious leadership was either simultaneously or consecutively active as to both types of schooling. Protestants of all sorts exemplified this as much as Catholics; that they rarely sought separate schooling may disguise this somewhat.[78] Such schooling had dual functions: parents wished the best for their offspring in changing and highly competitive conditions, and also wished the transmission of their beliefs. Both goals ensured community improvement and cohesion between generations. The expense of private provision of religious schooling inclined both Catholics and Anglicans to seek state support for it, fully forthcoming only in Ontario, Quebec and Newfoundland, but *not* throughout the United States, nor usually in the rest of Canada. Irish Presbyterians and Methodists, by contrast, trusted to the vaguer inter-denominational Christianity of public or common schools then usual in both countries; in Ontario and the upper mid-west, they were prominent in creating this pattern, which influenced other areas. From the Civil War, a secular emphasis spread within and thence from the education systems of the larger American cities. Together with the growth of knowledge and economic life, this led to greater demands for secondary and tertiary religious education also, and for more universal church schooling for Catholics, on the basis that poverty obliged more than half Irish immigrants' children to attend public schools.

Despised in colonial times in America, indeed even in Ontario and rural America into the 1820s (and hence often left to the Irish), the upgrading of education at every level fostered their most singular elite, which we may almost term a single one, a religio-educational one. From Toronto to Louisiana, Christianity had rested on a seamless process of group formation, of which schooling was one component.[79] The new priorities of an age of improvement prompted the Irish to focus this tradition into the niche of schooling, as they sensed that its other supports were dwindling. This set up real tensions in every state and province, for schooling was everywhere a very public preoccupation. This is perhaps what the foundress of the Loreto sisters in Ontario, Ellen Dease, meant when she expressed it: 'Education here is carried to excess'. Yet the evidence shows that this new emphasis had much to do with the retention, indeed expansion, of religious practice amongst North American Irish between 1880 and 1920, if regionally this varied. [80]

'The captains and the kings depart.' Amongst those of Irish birth, almost half of those detailed for the American Council of Learned Societies for 1935 disappear from the national biography volumes designed for it for the twenty-first century. The military officers of the wars first to establish America, and then to re-unite it, fade away, whether they were Scots Irish or not, whether denominationally active or profane, whether career officers, volunteer adopted patriots, or soldiers of fortune. So too do nearly half their politicians of the same era and, later, makers of urban democratic republicanism. If those who were movers and shakers survive, removed are the linkmen, fixers and operators no less central to the republic's design. Many men of business, most characteristic of all democratic types in Tocqueville's famous view, disappear too, both the traders and manufacturers of smaller early cities and localised markets, as well as the great entrepreneurs and financiers like shipbuilder John Roach or railroad magnate Richard Kerens of the boom capitalism of the later nineteenth century. Once-innovative editors and combative journalists disappear, as do community-oriented spokesmen and writers. Founder pastors, whether bishops or evangelisers, of every faith, are now left to more specialised denominational encyclopaedias. [81]

Oddly, this great revision has occurred as more detailed study has demonstrated the existence of much larger Irish elites and middle classes from the 1780s to 1900, considerably before the supposed twentieth-century breakthrough. In a country of pell-mell achievement, replacement and replication within an ethnic kaleidoscope, short-takes and shorter memory must winnow even scholarly consensus by generation. For many it is impossible to take the measure of the human patterns even of one's own time. A Braudelian completeness becomes a chimera, but imposes the duty to sketch its outline. This requires a reconstruction of changing socio-ethnic and economic orders, and the choice of a representative sample from *amongst* multiple elites to vivify and humanise the results. Democracy must be seen in its own human actualities. Over-confident and incestuous coteries that sought to contribute to its vast diversities (sometimes for unimaginative advantage) must be set both into and against that picture. The 'little elites' amongst the Scots-Irish of yesteryear and the Irish America of a later time intuitively grasped all this.

If Canada's more conservative memory now recalls a better cross-section of such people, in Victorian times its structured and more hierarchical polities made free Irish activity then difficult.[82] Whereas in America prejudice was activated as a local instrument of faction, in Canada it occasionally became a virtual instrument of party and elites, however covertly, partly because elements of 'English' Canada came to see Quebec as potentially disunionist, fearing its convergence with strong Catholic elements (among the Irish, Quebec out-migrants, Scots highlanders, and some west and south Germans) in Ontario and the Maritime provinces.[83] Once Protestant animus became allied, in some circles, with a proscriptive secular nationalism, the latter could cut two ways, and offered escape both towards, and away from, the inclusion of creeds and ethnicities as such. Its protagonists thus split on the rights of denominational schools. Oddly the idea was partly borrowed from Thomas D'Arcy Magee, for whom (in Canada as in Ireland) authentic nationality must *provide* for pluralism of conviction. In the individualist United States, by contrast, generations of Irish partly made themselves, whereas in Canada some believed they should accept assigned roles. This may help explain (granted the primary economic difference) why most Irish chose the USA after an initial pre-famine preference for Ontario and the Maritime provinces. Unfortunately this collective decision then survived after Confederation, and even Canada's successful acceleration and liberalisation from *c.*1900.

According to A. R. M. Lower, a scholar of the early twentieth century, people in North America 'as a rule preferred' and rewarded 'the ordinary politicians . . . the railroad builders, lumber kings, mining magnates', men on the 'driving, ambitious, accomplishing' side of things. He understood that 'some basic contrast in attitude to life' set these people, so crucial to national structure, apart from the equally vital, the humble and less ambitious, the *habitans*, the Catholic Irish of Ontario's 'holylands', or the Protestant Irish patriarchs who attempted rural bloc settlements.[84] But most Irish in America, like many Canadian migrants to the United States, were drawn to the buzz of the driving, accomplishing style whilst attempting to keep the essentials of their faith and its 'acquiescence, acceptance, harmony with life'.[85] Their own chosen forms of eminence show well this ambivalence.

Strangely, once the sustaining root of vast post-immigrant communities had receded, many of their nineteenth-century leaders of all sorts seem now quaint and only a few arrest the mind. Alice Lalor from Kilkenny fought Philadelphia's yellow fever when that city was first federal capital. She then personally set up her Visitation order successively in Washington, Mobile, St Louis and Baltimore. Ellen Dease from Naas, educated in Dublin and Paris, brought the Loreto tradition of polished schooling to Ontario in 1847 (of all years), and spread it through a hub of thirteen houses. She bravely adjusted to the Ontario requirement of state accreditation and training from 1874, and of a more practical curriculum – eliminating her previous emphasis on French.[86]

Albert Lovett was not a believer but he studied Catholicism closely as central to his Spanish, Habsburg and early modern interests. He rightly saw Peter Canisius as pivotal and regretted the loss of the essentials of his catechesis in contemporary Irish schools, if only because his students increasingly made poorer sense of Europe's past. Catholicism, he once remarked to me (*à propos* of Europe and Latin-America), was 'an extraordinary living museum of everything'. It is also its own Braudelian world, congruent with many historical worlds. In that world, two Mother Teresas (for so Miss Lalor and Miss Dease were known in life) could by their energetic courses reconcile much in the divided mindsets which Arthur Lower saw as inseparable from North America's democratic life. These foundresses were themselves governors of institutions compliant to just state authority. Close to their Irish-born and Irish-descended communities, the two women also sketched out continuities and integrities on the path to the humane democratisation of both uprooted peasants and of forceful Irishmen on the make. They may be set beside Catherine Hume Blake, surely one of the founders of home education, whose Anglican 'low church' seriousness and broad learning created a dynasty of transatlantic liberal democracy in her sons.[87] Such Irishwomen did not theorise Tocqueville's interconnection of democracy, education, public spirit, voluntary service and religious faith: they brought it forth.

It is perhaps not surprising that James Little, one of the first to alert Canada to its prodigal wasting of natural resources and the need for conservation, was nurtured in such Irish Christian culture; nor that his Iowa-born American counterpart, W. J. McGee, the son of an immigrant miner and farmer, had experienced its assumptions, however transplanted and rudimentary. The methods they adopted, of research, publicity, political connection and service commissions, had been furthered by the open procedures of their emergent democracies.[88]

Notes

As used here, elites will be multiple, and refer to sustained achievement in diverse endeavours. No one pattern of elites, their relations, or structure of society is assumed.

1   Michael Durey, *Transatlantic radicals and the early American republic* (Lawrence, KA, 1997); David A. Wilson, *United Irishmen, United States* (Dublin, 1998); Maurice J. Bric, 'The American Society of United Irishmen', *Irish Journal of American Studies* VII (1997), 163–77; Walter J. Walsh, in Ronald H. Bayor and Timothy J. Meagher (eds), *The New York Irish* (Baltimore and London,

1996), pp. 48–69; McCurtin, McArthur, T. A. Emmet and Caldwell letters and commentaries in Kerby Miller, Bruce Boling, David Doyle and Arnold Schrier (eds), *Irish immigrants in the land of Canaan* (New York, 2002), pp. 780 ff.

2   L. A. O'Donnell, *Irish Voice and organized labor in America* (Westport, CT, 1997), pp. 99–216; David Doyle 'The Irish and American labour, 1880–1920', *Saothar* 1 (1975), 42–53; David Montgomery, 'The Irish and the American labour movement' in D. N. Doyle and O. D. Edwards, *America and Ireland, 1776–1976* (Westport, CT, 1980), pp. 205–18; Emmet Larkin, *James Larkin* (London, 1968), pp. 166–227; Kenneth J. Heineman, *A Catholic New Deal* (University Park, PA, 2000); J. McShane, *'Sufficiently progressive': catholicism, progressivism and the bishops' program of 1919* (Washington, 1986); Deidre M. Maloney, *American Catholic lay groups and transatlantic social reform in the progressive era* (Chapel Hill, NC, 2002).

3   David T. Gleeson, *The Irish in the South, 1815–1877* (Chapel Hill, NC, 2001); Timothy J. Meagher, *Inventing Irish America: generation, class and ethnic identity in a New England city, 1880–1928* (Notre Dame, IND, 2001).

4   The United States, Great Britain, Canada, Australia, New Zealand, and South Africa. There is no composite bibliography, though the USA, New York city and state, the UK and Canada have fairly complete ones, by Patrick Blessing (1992), Marion Casey (1995), Maureen Hickman (1986) and Seamus Metress, the last on the USA overall (1981), on Canada (1988, with Wm. M. Baker), and on the states and regions of the USA (1986). For newer titles by subject see Michael Glazier (ed.), *Encyclopedia of the Irish in America* (Notre Dame, IND, 1999).

5   D. H. Akenson, *Being had* (Port Credit, Ontario, 1985); D. H. Akenson, *Small differences* (Montreal, 1988); D. H. Akenson, *The Irish diaspora* (Belfast, 1993 and 1996); a fine exception is his *The Irish in Ontario* (Montreal, 1984), a valid if somewhat too civic an exploration of intra-Irish relations in one township; A. Bielenberg (ed.), *The Irish diaspora* (London and New York, 2000) [except pp. 43–44 on Scotland by R. B. McCready]; Patrick O' Sullivan (ed.), *The Irish world wide: history, heritage, identity*, 6 vols (London and Leicester, 1992–7) including I, *Patterns of migration* (1992); II, *The Irish in the new communities* (1992); III, *The creative migrant* (1994); IV, *Irish women and Irish migration* (1995); V, *Religion and identity* (1996); VI, *The Meaning of the famine* (1997).

6   Patrick Fitzpatrick and Steve Ickringill (eds), *Atlantic crossroads* (Newtownards, County Down, 2001); H. Tyler Blethen and Curtis W. Wood, jr (eds), *Ulster and North America: transatlantic perspectives on the Scotch-Irish* (Tuscaloosa and London, 1997); Patrick Griffin, *The people with no name: Ireland's Ulster Scots, America's Scots Irish and the creation of a British Atlantic world, 1689–1764* (Princeton, 2001), ends as their real politicisation (in our terms) just begins.

7   Notably, David Carroll Cochran, 'Ethnic diversity and democratic stability: the case of Irish Americans', *Political Science Quarterly* CX (1996), 587–604; Kevin Kenny, *The American Irish: a history* (London and New York, 2000); Kerby A. Miller, *Emigrants and exiles* (New York, 1985); Thomas H. O'Connor, *The Boston Irish: a political history* (Boston, 1995); Ronald H. Bayor and Timothy J. Meagher (eds), *The New York Irish* (Baltimore and London, 1996), pp. 222–3, 337–56, 374–94; George E. Reedy, *From the ward to the White House* (New York, 1991); Stephen Erie, *Rainbow's End* (Berkeley, 1988); Lawrence J. McCaffrey, *The Irish diaspora in America*, rev. ed.

(Washington DC, 1984); David N. Doyle, 'The Scots Irish' in Glazier (ed.), *Encyclopedia*, pp. 842–51 and Leroy Eid, 'Scotch-Irish and American Politics', ibid., pp. 839–42; T. P. Power (ed.), *The Irish in Atlantic Canada, 1780–1900* (Fredericton, 1988); Terence Murphy and G. Stortz (eds), *Creed and culture . . . in Canadian society* (Montreal, 1993); Brian Clarke, *Piety and nationalism . . . in Toronto, 1850–1895* (Montreal, 1993); Colm Kiernan (ed.), *Australia and Ireland, 1788–1988* (Dublin, 1986); Patrick O' Farrell, *The Irish in Australia* (Kensington, NSW, 1987). A solid history of the Irish in English politics from the 1880s to the 1970s is needed, and a study of its bases equivalent to Michael Funchion (ed.), *Irish American voluntary organisations* (Westport, 1983). See Alan O'Day 'Irish diaspora politics in perspective: the United Irish Leagues of Great Britain and America, 1900–1914' in Donald MacRaild (ed.), *The great famine and beyond* (Dublin, 2000), pp. 214–39.

8 Of course the situation of Quebec between 1774 and 1841, of Franco-Spanish Louisiana before 1803, and of Argentina, amongst regions of real Irish immigration, were non-comparable, so that Newfoundland is the major exception, its Irish population almost wholly Catholic, and briefly the island's majority in the 1830s and 1840s. Its population is not included in Canada's until 1950. Its major figures since its foundation are included in the *Dictionary of Canadian Biography*, although it joined Canada only in 1949. Briefly, see C. W. Doody, in Robert O' Driscoll and Lorna Reynolds, *The untold story: the Irish in Canada*, 2 vols (Toronto, 1988), I, pp. 195–201.

9 When calculated with emigrants to Australasia, they made up: 1815–45, 570,000 to Canada (54 per cent) and 420,000 to the USA (40 per cent); from 1846 to 1870, 390,000 to Canada (13 per cent) and 2,380,000 (80 per cent) to the USA; 1871–1921, 155,000 to Canada (6 per cent) and 2,114,000 (87 per cent) to the USA. D. N. Doyle, 'The Irish in Australia and the United States: some comparisons, 1800–1939', *Irish Economic and Social History* XVI (1989), 79. Discrepancies with other calculations (e.g., D. H. Akenson, *Small differences*, Appendix I, p. 193) are usually because outflow figures gathered by donor countries rarely coincide with inflow data recorded overseas: cf. Walter Nugent, *Crossings: the great transatlantic migrations, 1870–1914* (Bloomington, 1992), table 14, p. 65 for a capsule German example. I prefer 'receiver' data where available, Akenson the 'sender' figures, which tend to be smaller.

10 In 1881, as between the four major locales: the United States 61 per cent, Great Britain 26 per cent, Australia 7 per cent and Canada 6 per cent. After Akenson, *Irish diaspora*, table 10, p. 54.

11 America *after* the acquisition of Alaska (1867).

12 United States, *Historical statistics*, Series A 1–2, Y 335; B. R. Mitchell, *International historical statistics: the Americas*, 2nd ed. (London, 1993), ser. A 1 and G 6, pp. 1 and 670. Additionally, in 1874, Newfoundland's population was 161,000, and by 1901, still but 217,000. Ibid., p. 3.

13 Nugent, *Crossings*, pp. 138–41; J. A. King, 'Genealogy, history and Irish immigration', *Canadian Journal of Irish Studies* X (1984), 41–50. Operative also from Newfoundland, these processes cut the Irish stock there to less than one third.

14 For this early phase, see Akenson, *Irish in Ontario*; C. J. Houston and Wm. Smyth, *Irish emigration and Canadian settlement* (Toronto, 1990); Donald MacKay, *Flight from famine: the coming of the Irish to Canada* (Toronto, 1990), the famine being lesser ones of the 1820s; and the articles by Brendan O'Grady, Terence Punch, P. M. Toner and D. Aidan McQuillan in O' Driscoll and Reynolds, *Untold story*, I, pp. 203–13, 215–29, 231–5, 263–70.

15 Allen Johnson and Dumas Malone (eds), *Dictionary of American biography* 20 vols (New York, 1928–37) [hereafter cited as DAB; volume herein references are to those of this first edition]. Lists in its earlier editions of its Irish-born entries omit some of these and include some American-born Irish, such as Charles Daly.

16 Edited by John A. Garraty in 24 volumes (New York and Oxford, 1999), cited ANB. Like its predecessor, it was sponsored by the American Council of Learned Societies. Its list of its Irish-born entries, in vol. 24, pp. 672–3, is also defective.

17 *Dictionary of Canadian biography* (Toronto, 1966–98), 14 vols, to XIV: 1911–1920 [hereafter cited as DCB with Roman numerals for volume references].

18 This was plainly understated to census takers in 1980: Patrick Blessing, *The Irish in America: A guide to the literature* (Washington DC, 1992), table 18, pp. 309–10, as shown in detailed fieldwork by Reginald Byron, *Irish America* (Oxford, 1999), pp. 142–59. He reports over three-quarters of his 'Irish' sample to be of multiple ancestry in Albany, where the Irish were long the dominant ethnicity; by contrast, just over half the entire state's self-denoting Irish in 1980 claimed single ancestry.

19 Ibid., 286–99 and *passim*; Richard Alba, *Ethnic America: the transformation of white America* (New Haven, 1990); Richard Alba, 'Social assimilation among American Catholic national origin groups', *American Sociological Review* XLI (1978), 1030–46; Stanley Lieberson, *From many strands: ethnic and racial groups in contemporary America* (New York, 1988); Michael Hout and Joshua R. Goldstein, 'How 4.5 million Irish immigrants became 40 million Irish Americans', *American Sociological Review* LIX (1994), 64–82, their first figure being out by at least one million.

20 Contrary to the Irish impression today, whilst around two-thirds of these entries concern Irish Protestants, these are preponderantly of Church of Ireland and dissenting backgrounds from the area of the present Republic of Ireland, as the dictionary's own nativity tables (where provided) would suggest. Ulster Presbyterians, whilst present, were always a minority. Over sixty per cent of Canada's Irish-born were Protestant in 1871. Cf., C. J. and W. J. Smyth, *Irish emigration and Canadian settlement* (Toronto, 1990), pp. 226–35.

21 Lewis Drummond (Quebec), Andrew Elliott (British Columbia), Joseph Curran Morrison (Ontario) and Sir Bryan Robinson (Newfoundland): DCB, XI: 281–83, 299–301, 617–19 and 760–62 respectively.

22 I think this has been demonstrated for Halifax, 1838–71: Terrence Punch, 'Anti-Irish prejudice in nineteenth-century Nova Scotia: the literary and statistical evidence' in T. P. Power (ed.), *The Irish in Atlantic Canada, 1780–1900* (Fredericton, N.B., 1991), pp. 13–22, amplified by A. J. B. Johnston, 'Nativism in Nova Scota', ibid., pp. 23–9.

23 David N. Doyle, *Irish America: native rights and national empires* (New York, 1976), pp. 38–90; Dale Light, 'The role of Irish-American organisations' in P. J. Drudy (ed.), *The Irish in America: emigration, assimilation and impact* (Cambridge, 1985), pp. 117–23, 127–33; D. G. Hackett, 'The social origins of nationalism: Albany, New York, 1754–1835', *Journal of Social History* XXI (1988), 659–81; Marion Casey, 'New York's Irish middle class, 1850–1870' (unpublished MA thesis, New York University, 1986). Meagher, *Inventing Irish America*, pp. 45–6, and Stephan Thernstrom, *The other Bostonians* (Cambridge, 1973) confirm that in New England the rise was a second generation one only.

24 On the eve of the Famine, they were sixteen per cent in Ontario, although dropping with recession and out-migration, and six per cent in Quebec. Akenson, *Being had*, table 4, p. 83.
25 Calculated from data in Akenson, *Small differences*, p. 182 and in Mitchell, *International historical statistics*, ser. A1.
26 D. J. Clark, 'The Irish in the American economy,' in Drudy (ed.), *Irish in America*, pp. 231–51.
27 A. G. Darroch and M. D. Ornstein, 'Ethnicity and occupational structure in Canada in 1871', *Canadian Historical Review* LXI (1980), 305–33.
28 Sources cited in note 19 above; almost all regional monographs for 1850 to 1900 show modest but real rise for a fifth of the Irish born by the 1880s, and somewhat earlier for Canada, America's mid-west and California. For New York, city and state, which had a quarter of Irish America's middle classes by 1900, the process itself has been documented: Cormac Ó Gráda, 'The famine, the New York Irish and their bank' in A. E. Murphy and R. Prendergast (eds), *Contributions to economic thought: essays in honour of R. D. C. Black* (London, 2000), pp. 227–48.
29 Canada originally referred only to the Quebec province and its claimed interior; Upper Canada was separated from Quebec in 1791 redefined as Lower Canada. The two were combined by Act of Union in 1840, and known as Canada West and Canada East until Confederation in 1867. New Brunswick and Nova Scotia joined at its inception, newly created Manitoba in 1870, British Columbia the next year, Prince Edward Island in 1873, the two new prairie provinces in 1905, and Newfoundland not until 1949. The DCB assume the whole as a unit of study throughout, and modern usage has largely abandoned the distinct pre-1867 'two Canadas' terminology.
30 DCB, IV, 109–12 (Bulkeley); IV: 603–5 (Parr); and V: 444–5 (Inglis). Veterans Gilfred Studholm and Winckworth Tonge (DCB, IV, 723–4 and 736–8) were lesser satellites, whereas Henry D. Denson, though a land grantee and agent for New England immigration, distanced the Halifax 'gang': DCB, IV: 208–9.
31 DCB, V: 141–55 (Guy) and 155–62 (Thomas) and references therein. Guy Carleton's successor as Lieut. Gov. in Quebec, Hector Cramahé (1771 ff.), a Dubliner of Huguenot parentage, was less sympathetic to the Quebecois than his former commander: DCB, IV, 787–93.
32 DCB, IV: 395–8; J. T. Flexner, *Lord of the Mohawks* (Boston, 1979); M. W. Hamilton, *Sir William Johnson, colonial American* (New York, 1976); Henry Hamilton, sent directly to Detroit in 1775, had not been part of the Johnson regime: DCB, IV: 321–5.
33 DCB, IV: 393–4 (Guy Johnson); V: 301–2 (Elliott); V: 729–32 (Russell). Also Reginald Horsman, *Matthew Elliott: British Indian agent* (Detroit, 1964); and D. H. Plaunt, 'The Honourable Peter Russell administrator of Upper Canada', *Canadian Historical Review* XX (1939), 258–74; Sir John Johnson, Sir William's colonial-born son, took over the superintendency in 1783, and later settled at Kingston, providing continuity to a newer stream of Irish officials and veterans.
34 Speaking of Thomas Carleton, DCB, IV: 156.
35 Irish-born officials and military prominent in this process included Walter Patterson and Thomas Busby (DCB, IV: 115–16, 605–11); see G. F. O' Dwyer, 'Irish soldiers at the siege of Louisburg, Nova Scotia', *Journal of the American-Irish Historical Society* XXVII (1928), 278–84; A. H. Clark, *Three Centuries and the island* (Toronto, 1959); Rusty Bitterman, 'Agrarian protest

and cultural transfer: Irish immigrants' in Power (ed.), *Irish in Atlantic Canada*, 96–106; Brendan O'Grady, 'A people set apart: the County Monaghan settlers in Prince Edward Island', *Clogher Record* XII (1985), 41–4.

36 DCB, IX: 295, on John Gaggin, a hunting, fishing Cork soldier finding roost as a British Columbia magistrate; cf., D.B. Smith, '"Poor Gaggin": Irish misfit in the colonial service', *British Columbia Studies* XXXII (1976/7), 41–63.

37 J. A. Lavin, 'The Irish in British Columbia', in O'Driscoll and Reynolds (eds), *Untold story*, I, pp. 431–7, 441.

38 DCB, V, 358–9.

39 DCB, X, 262–3 (George Duggan), 309–14 (Ogle Gowan), 360 (Arthur Hopper), 503–4 (F. H. Medcalf), none of them from Ulster.

40 For example, J. Willoughby Crawford and John Ross (DCB, X, 200–1, 631–3), quite apart from the liberal Hincks, Baldwin and Willcocks families.

41 DCB, V, 343–5. Longer stay dissident Presbyterians in the same upstate New York, happily went with the United States: see Miller et al. (eds), *Irish immigrants*, Margaret Wright letter and essay.

42 Documents are contained in Miller et al. (eds), *Irish Immigrants*, parts four to seven.

43 US *Historical Statistics*, Ser. Y912; Bedini's report is in *Historical Records and Studies*, 23 (1933), 262–436; for Irish-born officers, DAB, III: 572–3 (John L. Cathcart, 1767–1843) and V: 390 (Thomas Dornin, 1800-74). ANB, II: 250–2 (John Barry, 1745–1803), II: 929–30 (Johnston Blakely, 1781–1814), V: 368 (Gustavus Conyngham, 1747–1819), XV: 171–2 (Hector McNeill, 1728–85), XIX: 5–6 (S. Clegg Rowan, 1808–90) and XIX, 743–4 (John Shaw, 1774–1823). The pattern pre-dated Robert Smith, of Strabane parentage and from Baltimore's Irish mercantile community, who became Secretary of the Navy in 1801. But the regular army officer corps did not usually admit Irish Catholics until the Civil War: Kevin Stanton, 'American West and Irish soldiers', in Glazier, *Encyclopedia*, pp. 23–5.

44 D. N. Doyle and K. M. Miller, ' Ulster migrants in an age of rebellion: the Crocketts of Raphoe', *Irish Economic and Social History* XXII (1995), 77–87.

45 DCB, X, 402–6. His father had helped build Ireland's Grand Canal, and was a contemporary of Christopher Colles, who envisioned the Erie Canal. His scheme, of canals left vulnerable to US control of the Great Lakes, was lambasted by military men, helped trigger Confederation to aid defense, yet oddly anticipated the 1958 St Lawrence Seaway.

46 DAB, I: 511; V: 458; XVII: 583–4.

47 US Immigration Commission, *Reports*, 1910, 41 vols, XXVIII, *Occupations of first and second generations of immigrants* (Washington DC, 1911), pp. 75, 140, 163, 166–7 and 223, gives 7903 Irish-born as against 9591 English- and Welsh-born in these categories. There were also 12, 160 second generation Irish Americans in these.

48 DAB, XV: 639–40 (shipbuilder John Roach); William E. Devlin, 'Shrewd Irishmen: Irish entrepreneurs and artisans in New York's clothing industry, 1830–1880' in Bayor and Meagher, (eds), *New York Irish*, pp. 169–92; David Emmons, *The Butte Irish* (Urbana and Chicago, 1989); R. M. James, 'Nevada', in Glazier (ed.), *Encyclopedia*, pp. 660–3.

49 DCB, XI: 30–1 (Armstrong), 264 (Dinning), 357–8 (Good) and 501–2 (Lawrence).

50 Apart from Sir Francis Hincks, notably Matthew Gault, the Workman brothers, and William McMaster, DCB, X, 717–18 and XI, 335–6, 406–16, 574–8, 936–7.

51 DAB V: 45–6 (Daly); X: 353–4 (Kerens); XII: 75–6 (Mackay) and XVII: 57–8 (Sheedy); ANB, VII: 671–2 (Fair); IX: 362–4 (Grace) and XII: 517–18 (Kelly). US Immigration Commission, *Reports*, XXVIII, *Occupations*, pp. 223, 642-3, 678-9. In 1900, 3.2 per cent of 73,000 bankers and brokers were Irish-born, and 3.1 per cent were second generation; contrast manufacturers (data cited n. 47) and lawyers (data cited n. 74).

52 I base these proportions on close analysis of the sample of businessmen and politicians provided in DCB XII (1891–1900), *passim*. For Larkin, ibid., 529–30. Catholic immigrants co-pioneered this pattern, e.g., Patrick Power (1815–1881) in Halifax and Thomas Ryan (1804–89) in Montreal, whilst no Orange leaders did (DCB, XI: 709–10, 780–2).

53 In Worcester, no less than 42 per cent of all Irish-born and American Irish Catholics listed in 1919 in a town survey had held governmental or political office; Meagher, *Inventing Irish America*, p. 111.

54 Contrast David Montgomery, 'Labor', in Glazier, *Encyclopedia*, pp. 525–31 and Gary M. Fink (ed.), *Biographical dictionary of American labor* (Westport, CT, 1974), with DAB, XII: 154–5 (F. J. McNulty), XX: 581 (J. Lendrew Wright); ANB, VIII: 61 (John Fitzpatrick) and XII: 230–1 (Mother Jones, born Mary Harris); DCB, XI: 504–5 (Richard Leahey) and 637–9 (Samuel Myers); XIII: 23–5 (John Armstrong) and 778–81 (D. T. O'Donoghue); XIV: 488 (John Hewitt) and 788–9 (M. J. O'Brien); for Canadian context, Gregory Kealy, *Toronto workers 1867–1892* (Toronto, 1980).

55 *A selection of books from the Stephen Griffin collection presented to the National Library of Ireland, 1999-2000* (Dublin, 2000); J. Cummins, *Catalogue of the Stephen Griffin collection* (Dublin, 2002, on NLI website); Joseph Skelly, 'Is there a Hibernian de Tocqueville? Irish travellers' impressions of America, 1730–1880' (unpublished MA thesis, UCD, 1986).

56 In 1891, up to half of all Irish-born *adults* aged 25–60 were living abroad. Next nearest were Scotland and Norway, with *c.* 25 per cent so domiciled: age cohort corrections to Akenson, *Irish diaspora*, p. 54. Almost a third of the remaining Irish population was either freely or involuntarily constrained, in schools and institutions (including staffs), in the security services, as farm servants and in religious orders. *Census of Ireland, 1891. Summaries of tables in county books*, p. v, and tables 9, p. 5, and 36, pp. 56–7. A very large minority of mature adults were unmarried.

57 DAB, IV: 23 (Charless); V: 468–9 (Duane); XI: 536 (Loudon); David A. Wilson, *United Irishmen, United States* (Dublin, 1998).

58 John Ward, 'Francis Collins' in O' Driscoll and Reynolds, *Untold story*, II, pp. 609–17.

59 DCB, V: 854–9 (J. Willcocks); IX: 489–94 (D'Arcy Magee); 828–35 (Whelan); 618–19 (Thomas Parke); X: 45–6 (Robert Bell); 229–30 (Devlin); 671–2 (Talbot); XI: 406–16 (Hincks); XII: 23–8 (Anglin).

60 DCB, X: 650–1 (Shaw). Such men could trim to Sir James Macdonald's conservative overtures to their Irish Catholic rivals.

61 DCB, X: 456 (McCoubrey) and XI: 645 (Perry), 753–4 (Riordon) and 911–2 (Watson).

62 Edmund B. O'Callaghan in DCB, X: 554–60 and DAB, XIV: 613; John Talbot in DCB, X: 671–2, and Leonard McClure in DCB, IX: 478–80.

63 To Bernard Devlin and Edward Whelan, one might add M. Hamilton Foley, James Hogg and others: DCB, IX: 267–8 and 391–3.

64 DCB, VIII: 228–31 (Charles Donlevy); Curtis Fahey, 'Irish Catholics and the political culture of Upper Canada: the case of the *Toronto Mirror*, 1837–1865' in O'Driscoll and Reynolds, *Untold Story*, II, pp. 811–27; Robert F. Hueston, *The Catholic press and nativism, 1840–1860* (New York, 1976), 14–15, 28–30, 32 ff., simplifies the origins as anti-nativist, and puts them too late; contrast William L. Joyce, *Editors and ethnicity: the formative years of the Irish American press, 1848–1883* (New York, 1976), pp. 49–73 ; Mary A. Frawley, *Patrick Donahoe* (Washington, 1946); Eugene Willging and Herta Hatzfeld, *Catholic serials of the nineteenth century in the United States*, 2nd series, 15 vols (Washington, D.C., 1959–68), with remarkable detective work (the first series was on smaller states, which had later titles).

65 'Sketches of Boston journalists' in J. B. Cullen, *Story of the Irish in Boston* (Boston, 1889), pp. 311–35 is a primary source on this process.

66 DAB, V: 264–5 (Devoy); VI:, 518 (Ford) and Clarke in the ANB; for John Devoy, *Recollections of an Irish rebel* (New York, 1928); Terry Golway, *Irish rebel* (New York, 1998); J. I. C. Clarke, *My life and memories* (New York, 1925); James P. Rodechko, *Patrick Ford and his search for America* (New York, 1976). Clarke and Ford were recipients of Rockefeller and Republican Party support in later journalism years, pressures of which Thomas Cummins would have been aware (n. 70 infra).

67 DAB, X: 420–1(Kinsella); XVI: 388–9 (Savage); DCB, X: 522–3 (Nugent, who served in Canada on the Fraser River commission for President James Buchanan, whom he had known in his days as a Washington correspondent for the *New York Herald*).

68 DAB, X: 274–5; Gleeson, *The Irish in the south*, pp. 116–18, 168–9 (Maginnis) and 62–3, 98–100, 116–17 (J. C. Prendergast). John Mitchel's *Southern citizen* was an influential brief foray, pp. 70–1.

69 DAB, XII: 5 (McCullagh) and XX: 630–1 (Young).

70 Thomas J. Cummins, *My Irish colleagues of New York: Reminiscences and experiences of a journalist, 1861–1901* (New York, 1901). Cummins had worked on the *New York Herald*, with J. I. C. Clarke, J. Devoy, J. J. O'Kelly, Thomas Kinsella, John Nugent and others; its Scottish owner-editor, J. Gordon Bennett (1795–1872), thus ran a school of Irish journalism for a quarter of a century. A Democrat and an inactive east Highlands Catholic long at odds the New York archdiocese, he had an agenda of creating an Irish opinion independent of the Church to which he finally returned.

71 DAB, V: 361–2 and ANB, VI: 714–15 (Donahoe); ANB, IX: 152–4 (Godkin); V: 240–1 (Collier) and XIV: 887–9 (McClure). Files of the 1890s and 1900s *Donahoe's Magazine, Collier's*, and *McClure's Magazine* are in the New York Public Library; Godkin's *Nation* is widely available.

72 Carl Wittke, *The Irish in America* (Baton Rouge, 1956), pp. 233–5; J. D. Buenker (ed.), *Historical dictionary of the progressive era, 1890–1920* (London, 1989).

73 But see for example Timothy W. Gleason, *The origins of the watchdog concept of the press* (Ann Arbor, 1986).

74 Immigration Commission, *Reports*, XXVIII, *Occupations*, pp. 223, 642–3, 678–9; J. B. Cullen, *Story of the Irish in Boston*, a survey, listed only fifteen Irish-born lawyers against thirty-eight listed, all but one of whom had been educated from childhood in the USA.

75 DAB, IV: 309–10 (Collins); ANB, V: 126–7(Cockran); James McGurrin, *Bourke Cockran* (New York, 1948).
76 To 6750; women lawyers also increased fivefold, if only from ten to fifty-six, between the two Irish generations, Immigration Commission, *Reports*, XXVIII, *Occupations*, as cited n. 74, with pp. 241, 690 and 697 for women. G. P. Curtis, *American Catholic who's who* (St Louis); *The book of Chicagoans* (Chicago, 1905); and *Who's who in New England* (Chicago, 1909) list considerable numbers of Irish-American lawyers; Meagher, *Inventing Irish America*, p. 108 shows how the profession dominated the Irish in Worcester, Mass., a second generation one.
77 Daniel Murphy, *A history of Irish emigrant and missionary education* (Dublin, 2000), pp. 169–318; Mary J. Oates, 'Educating immigrants: a Boston case study'; Janet Nolan 'Education: Irish-American teachers in public schools, 1880–1920'; Timothy Walch, 'Education, parochial' and Philip Gleason, 'Education, higher' all in Glazier (ed.), *Encyclopedia*, pp. 234–6, 236–9, 239–43, 243–5. On numbers, Immigration Commission, *Reports*, XXVIII, *Occupations*, pp. 223 and 241, shows just 979 Irish-born men as teachers, not a tenth of one per cent of male immigrants, increasing to but three tenths of one per cent of the second generation male workforce. By contrast, Irish women teachers were 1.5 per cent of Irish working women in America, and among second generation Irish-American women were 8.1 per cent of their cohort at work, an extraordinary 9.6 per cent of all women teachers in the country.
78 For example in the USA, John Hall (1829–1898) from Armagh, chancellor of the City University, New York; Thomas McAuley (1778–1862), from Coleraine, of Transylvania University; William A. Rogers (1832–98), from Waterford, scientist at Alfred University; and R. Ellis Thompson (1824–1924), from Lurgan, economist at the University of Pennsylvania, had strong religious motivation in their careers. See DAB, VIII: 137–8; XI: 554; XVI: 114 and XVIII: 469–70. For Canada, examples (all in DCB) include textbook pioneers Alexander Davidson and Robert Murray in VIII: 202–4 and 651–2; university and department founders Hugh Bell, VIII: 73-5, Michael Boomer, John Mc Caul, and William McMaster, in XI: 89–90, 540–2 and 574–8; and those who sought religious access for pupils, such as Andrew Henderson in IX: 388–9 and Matthew Richey in XI: 733–5. There were also Irish-born secularisers, notably Thomas J. Robertson, former chief inspector of Irish National Schools, brought in to head the Normal School, Toronto, in 1847: IX: 667–8.
79 Murray W. Nicolson, 'The education of a minority: the Irish family urbanized', in O'Driscoll and Reynolds, *Untold story*, II, pp. 759–84; Ann Taves, *The household of faith* (Notre Dame, 1986); Colleen McDannell, *The Christian home in Victorian America* (Bloomington, Ind., 1986).
80 David Noel Doyle, 'Irish Catholicism in the diaspora: the case of the United States' in Brendan Bradshaw and Dáire Keogh (eds), *Christianity in Ireland* (Blackrock, Dublin: 2002), pp. 231–48 and table 2, p. 239 and citations. Meagher, *Inventing Irish America*, pp. 103–4, 155–6, 158–62, 203–5, 223–6, 262–3, localises these themes.
81 Joseph B. Code, *Dictionary of the American hierarchy*, 2nd ed. (New York, 1964); J. F. Woolverton, *Colonial Anglicanism in North America* (Detroit, 1984); R. Balmer and J. R. Fitzmier, *The Presbyterians* (Westport, CT, 1993) and Russell E. Hall, 'American Presbyterian churches – a genealogy, 1706–1982', *Journal of Presbyterian History* LX (1982), 95–128,

offer guides to them, each with its separate biographical source publications. More Irish Presbyterian clergy and educators went to America and Canada after 1800 than before, contrary to stereotype.

82 Terence Murphy and Gerald Stortz (eds), *Creed and culture: the place of English-speaking Catholics in Canadian society, 1750–1930* (Montreal, 1993); Brian Clarke, *Piety and nationalism in Toronto, 1850–1895* (Montreal, 1993); and Cecil J. Houston and W. J. Smyth, *The sash Canada wore* (Toronto, 1980).

83 Demographically the fear was not groundless, but politically (as Sir John Macdonald understood) it was, since not only did the feared groups – with distinct ethnic and provincial interests – never converge *en bloc*, but many Catholic bishops, and some lay leaders, could not accept the liberal politics many in these groups believed necessary to their advancement and a good in itself. A humorous instance was when Quebec's Bishop J. P. F. La Force excommunicated Fermanagh-born Judge John Maguire for condemning Bonaventure County priests for misuse of their authority in an election . . . only to have the penalty lifted at the behest of his brother-in-law, Bishop John Horan of Kingston (see DCB, X, 487–8). A more serious one was Cardinal Taschereau's prohibition of the Knights of Labor, overruled by Leo XIII on Irish-American episcopal intervention.

84 Catherine A. Wilson, 'The Scotch-Irish and immigrant culture on Amherst Island, Ontario' in H. Tyler Blethen and C. W. Wood, jr (eds), *Ulster and North America*, pp. 134–45; Bruce Elliott, *Irish migrants in the Canadas* (Kingston and Montreal, 1988); Edward Jackman, 'The Irish Holylands of Ontario' in O' Driscoll and Reynolds, *The untold story*, II, pp. 739–52 .

85 A. R. M. Lower, *Colony to nation*, 3rd ed. (Toronto and New York, 1957), pp. 69, 243; A. R. M. Lower, 'Two ways of life', in the Canadian Historical Association, *Annual report of the Canadian Historical Association* (1943), pp. 5–19.

86 DAB, XVII: 376 (Lalor); DCB, XI: 240–1 (Dease).

87 DCB, XI: 434; some of her writings are edited in the *Canadian Historical Review* XV (1934), 283–8 and LVI (1975), 45–58.

88 One of the 'lumber kings', Little (1803–83) was born in Londonderry, came to Ontario in 1823, published conservation tracts in the 1870s, and won the Montreal conservation conference of 1882 before his death: DCB, XI, 521–3; on McGee, Whitney R. Cross, 'W. J. McGee and the idea of conservation', *The Historian* XV (1952–3), 148–62; for his influence, James Penick, jr, *Progressive politics and conservation* (Chicago, 1968) and Harold Pinkett, *Gifford Pinchot: private and public forester* (Urbana, 1970).

CHAPTER 10

The Anglo-American Alliance and the Irish Question in the Twentieth Century

Ronan Fanning

When the twentieth century began, the United States, preoccupied throughout the nineteenth century with territorial expansion and with civil war and its aftermath, was largely isolated from an international system in which Britain's status as a great imperial power was unquestioned. In 1901 Theodore Roosevelt became 'the first president to insist that it was America's duty to make its influence felt globally, and to relate America to the world in terms of a concept of national interest'.[1] Ireland was still embedded in the century-old United Kingdom of Great Britain and Ireland, and the devolution of domestic government known as Home Rule remained the horizon of nationalist aspirations.

If the nineteenth century was the heyday of British imperial power, the twentieth was the American century. By the year 2000 victories in both world wars had been crowned by victory in the Cold War and the collapse of the Soviet Union had set the seal on American supremacy. The British had meanwhile lost their empire, were still agonising about their uneasy relationship with the European Union and were grappling with the problems of the peace process which seemed to mark the end of thirty years' guerrilla war in Northern Ireland. Ireland – albeit only the larger part of the partitioned Ireland which had achieved independence under the terms of the Anglo-Irish Treaty of 1921 – had by then enjoyed the status of a wholly independent sovereign republic outside the British Commonwealth for half a century and had been a fully committed member of the European Union for over a quarter of a century.

These developments refashioned the Irish question in mid-century. Between 1919 and 1949 (when the coming into effect of the Republic of Ireland Act resolved all ambiguity about Irish sovereignty), the Irish question was about independence: Irish and British governments wrestled to convert the United States government to their respective views of how Irish independence could legitimately be achieved, limited or exercised. The field of struggle shifted, although the terms of engagement stayed much the same, when the Irish question became, in effect, the governance of Northern Ireland question; although that question remained moot until the first phase of the contemporary crisis culminated in the abolition of the parliament and government of Northern Ireland in 1972-3.

This essay argues that the relationship between the United States and the United Kingdom dictated the American response to the Irish question throughout the twentieth century. Changes in American policy towards Ireland were likewise determined by shifts in Anglo-American relations and the most significant of those shifts were triggered by the three great international crises of the twentieth century: the First World War, the Second World War and the Cold War.

THE IMPACT OF THE FIRST WORLD WAR

The early years of the First World War demonstrated that Britain alone could no longer tilt the balance of power in Europe and an Anglo-American alliance became the primary objective of British foreign policy that it has since remained. British ministers were persuaded as never before of the need to eliminate causes of friction with the United States and the first among these was the Irish question.

In the aftermath of the Easter Rising of 1916, Lord Aberdeen, the Liberal government's viceroy in Ireland from 1906 until 1915, warned from New York that the executions of the revolutionary leaders had severely shocked not only Irish-Americans 'who previously had little or no sympathy with the Sinn Féiners' but also 'a number of Americans, whose attitude towards England has hitherto been entirely friendly, especially in relation to the War'. The Irish vote would be influential in the 1916 presidential election, advised Aberdeen, and he urged an Irish settlement 'that will deter the mass of opinion ... from moving in the pro-German direction'.[2] The British ambassador in Washington, Cecil Spring-Rice, also reported that American attitudes had 'changed for the worse ... They have blood in their eyes when they look our way'.[3]

'It is in America that the real motive for this policy is to be found', complained one Unionist critic of Lloyd George's efforts at conciliation in Ireland and another threatened to resign rather than defer to the necessity 'to avoid American complications'.[4] But Unionist bluster could not disguise the constraints imposed by new geostrategic realities and the British government under both Asquith and Lloyd George remained determined to sanitise Irish policy for American consumption, as their campaign of character assassination against the homosexual Sir Roger Casement in July 1916 so grotesquely demonstrated.

Casement had been convicted of high treason on 29 June 1916 and American pleas for leniency had begun even before the trial. The British ambassador to France acidly encapsulated the prevailing wisdom in Whitehall: 'hang him and chance public opinion in the States'. Ministers and officials set about vindicating his execution by circulating photographed excerpts of graphic descriptions of homosexual acts allegedly drawn from Casement's diary; they pursued this campaign through the British embassy in Washington (which targeted members of the Roman Catholic hierarchy as well as Congressional leaders), the American ambassador in London and hand-picked American journalists.[5] Asquith himself delivered the *coup de grâce* at a luncheon on 1 August with the American ambassador, Walter H. Page. The prime minister, noted the ambassador in a memorandum for President Woodrow Wilson,

> showed a very eager interest in the Presidential campaign, and he confessed that he felt some anxiety about the anti-British feeling in the United States. . . . *He spoke of the unmentionable Casement diary, which shows a degree of perversion and depravity without parallel in modern times.* 'In all good conscience to my country and to my responsibilities I cannot interfere.'[6]

When Casement was hanged at Pentonville jail less than forty-eight hours later most American critics had been effectively silenced although, in order to make assurance doubly sure, the British naval attaché in Washington, Captain Guy Gaunt, went on peddling the choicer extracts from the diaries for another three weeks.[7]

But neither Casement's death nor President Woodrow Wilson's re-election had exorcised the American factor from Irish policy when Lloyd George became prime minister in December 1916. The need for 'a settlement of the Irish question' for the 'maintenance of good relations with the United States' loomed large in a memorandum considered at the inaugural meeting of his new war cabinet [8] and Lloyd George hammered home the point in his very first speech as prime minister.[9] In March 1917, when the foreign secretary, Arthur Balfour, shortly before his departure on a diplomatic mission to Washington, asked Walter Page why the British were so unpopular in the United States, the response was brutally direct. 'It is the organised Irish. Then it's the effect of the very fact that the Irish question is not settled. You've had that problem at your very door for 300 years. What's the matter that you don't solve it?'[10] Cecil Spring Rice, Page's counterpart in Washington, concurred.

The question is one which is at the root of most of our troubles with the United States. The fact that the Irish question is still unsettled is continually quoted against us . . . The President is by descent an Orangeman and by education a Presbyterian. But he is the leader of the Democratic party in which the Irish play a prominent part, and he is bound in every way to give consideration to their demands.[11]

On 10 April, only four days after the United States had entered the war, President Wilson personally typed a confidential message to his secretary of state, Robert Lansing, instructing Ambassador Page to tell the prime minister unofficially and most confidentially that 'the failure so far to find a satisfactory method of self-government for Ireland' alone stood in the way of 'absolutely cordial' Anglo-American co-operation.[12] Lloyd George welcomed the intervention, as well he might given that he had sent Wilson a secret message through Page soliciting just such a presidential request 'that the Irish question should be settled' which he could use to persuade Edward Carson, the leader of the Ulster Unionists, to accept the establishment of the Irish Convention.[13]

The Irish Convention, which first assembled in July 1917, likewise exemplified Lloyd George's anxiety to placate American opinion. Although it ultimately collapsed in failure in April 1918, the Convention provided a deliberative public forum for all Irish political groupings, which was consonant with the Wilsonian commitment to self-determination, and it bought Lloyd George's government eight months' breathing space when they could claim to be attempting to solve the Irish question when they had in fact shelved it.

With Carson on the point of resignation to pre-empt the prospect that the war cabinet might implement a proposed report by the Convention which was unacceptable to the Ulster Unionists, it was the American dimension which again preoccupied the prime minister:

> if the Government refused to act under these circumstances, everyone in Great Britain and throughout the world – notably in AMERICA – would say we were sacrificing the interests of the War to that of a small political section. In fact they would say we were doing it merely because Carson was in the Government. . . .
>
> The Irish in AMERICA would be more rampageous than ever, and Wilson's position, embarrassing enough as it is now with Germans and Irishmen on his flank, would become untenable. The Irish are now paralysing the War activities of AMERICA. . . . If AMERICA goes wrong we are lost. I wish Ulster would fully realise what that means. I am afraid they don't.[14]

Carson's resignation and the collapse of the Convention was followed by the conscription crisis of the spring of 1918 – when the last great German offensive on the western front persuaded the war cabinet that they must extend conscription to Ireland, contrary to the advice of their officials in

Dublin Castle who warned that it would outrage all shades of nationalist opinion. 'The effect in America would be very bad', advised the new British ambassador, Lord Reading,[15] and yet again the need to mollify Washington shaped policy. The British sought to vindicate their shift from conciliation to coercion by alleging that Sinn Féin were plotting with Germany, although the evidence was too flimsy even to convince the war cabinet.[16] But the strategy was for Washington's consumption: 'although it may be insufficient for a jury it will be sufficient for America', observed Austen Chamberlain[17] and a frenetic exchange of telegrams between Whitehall and Washington record Reading's vain efforts to persuade President Wilson that evidence of the alleged plot should first be published in the United States.[18]

The entry of the United States into the war quickly persuaded American naval chiefs of 'Ireland's geopolitical utility'.[19] The first six American destroyers had arrived at Queenstown on 4 May 1917 and by August the US navy had thirty-five destroyers and two tenders based there – the British never had more than four destroyers at Queenstown during this critical phase of the battle of the Atlantic and only eleven by the end of the war. By August 1918, sixty-nine US ships were based at Queenstown and such was the influx of American naval personnel – nearly 7000 at its peak – that parents were warned in a sermon at the Catholic cathedral 'to look out for their young daughters especially since there had lately arrived on our shores hundreds of vultures, yea I might say thousands of them, who were preying upon the purity of our daughters of Queenstown'.[20] There were also seven American submarines and three Dreadnought battleships based at Berehaven and four US naval air stations were also established: at Queenstown, Whiddy Island in Bantry Bay, Lough Foyle and Wexford. Admiral Bayly, the commander-in-chief of the western approaches, when asked what difference the arrival of American ships had made to his command, replied, 'All the difference'.[21] The recollection of the geostrategic advantages of being able to deploy American naval and air forces in Irish bases was an enduring legacy of the First World War.

Sustaining the Anglo-American alliance remained a guiding principle of British policy throughout the Paris peace conference of 1919. With Jews, Poles, Egyptians and many others joining the Irish in clamouring to participate, President Wilson had to soft-pedal on self-determination; he was unwilling 'to imperil the work of the entire conference or Anglo-American co-operation in order to force an Irish settlement'.[22] But the British realised that they could not long postpone applying some form of self-determination to Ireland and Lord Edward Grey, the former foreign secretary, only agreed to accept a temporary appointment as ambassador in Washington on the understanding that the government would launch a new Irish initiative.[23] 'In Anglo-American relations one comes on Irish difficulty everywhere', proclaimed one of Grey's telegrams from Washington. 'It poisons atmosphere . . . a statement of Irish policy on self-government is now very desirable' and the Foreign Office circulated the Cabinet with a survey of American opinion to the same effect.[24]

By the autumn of 1919 a review of Irish policy had become imperative because the Home Rule Act of 1914 was due to come into effect once the last of the peace treaties was ratified. On 7 October, Lloyd George appointed a Cabinet committee on Ireland and its first report, on 4 November 1919, marked the most significant shift in British policy since the first Home Rule Bill of 1886 and provided the blueprint for the Government of Ireland Act of 1920. Again and again it referred to the importance of American opinion and to the necessity, 'now that the war is over, and that the Peace Conference has dealt with so many analogous questions in Europe' of making 'a sincere attempt to deal with the Irish question once and for all'. That Ulster, too, should govern itself – the main recommendation was that there should be two devolved parliaments in Ireland (a southern parliament for nationalist Ireland and a northern parliament for unionist Ireland) – was necessary to heal the bitter feud between Ireland and Britain

> which is now seriously imperilling the relations of Great Britain both with the rest of the Empire and with the United States of America . . . It follows all American and Imperial precedents . . . by withdrawing British rule once and for all from Ireland in Ireland's local affairs it takes away the reproach of coercion which is the principal ingredient in Irish hostility to Great Britain, and in American and Dominion suspicion of British policy.[25]

Ulster Unionists protested in vain at the destructive impact of the Anglo-American alliance on their preference to remain an integral part of the United Kingdom. 'It is high time that America – or those who pretend to speak for America but are not real Americans – should learn to understand that we are still a great power and that we are not subordinate to America or to any other power',[26] raged Carson in the debate on the 1920 bill. But Arthur Balfour (the former Conservative prime minister and Unionist champion whose efforts to contain the damage done by the Irish question to Anglo-American relations went back to 1890 when he was Irish chief secretary[27] and who later led the British delegation at the Washington naval conference of 1921–2) voiced the new realism. The significance of the 1920 act, he argued, was 'not that Ireland is going to be better governed but that we've made our Irish policy on all fours with our European policy of self-determination, and which no American can say is unfair'.[28]

The 1920 act coupled with the Anglo-Irish Treaty of 1921 achieved that purpose and, for more than fifty years, Britain's Irish policy remained essentially uninhibited by American criticism.

THE IMPACT OF THE SECOND WORLD WAR

The Irish Free State 'was the first country in the British Commonwealth, aside from the United Kingdom, to receive recognition from the United States. Accredited by the King of England, a minister of the Irish Free State [Timothy Smiddy], presented his credentials on October 7, 1924. A minister of the United States [Frederick Sterling], accredited to the governor-general, was appointed on February 19, 1927.'[29] The delay of over three and a half years in the appointment of an American minister testifies to the insignificance of Ireland in the larger American scheme of things and it impinged little upon Anglo-American relations between the wars. British influence in the United States was immense, reported Smiddy, who had

> observed the increasing sympathy of Americans, especially those from whom the governing classes are derived, with Great Britain. In the leading universities the vast majority of the teaching staff are strongly pro-British, both politically and socially, and very active in their endeavours to promote the entry of the USA into the League of Nations. These remarks apply to the influential press, except the Hearst, and even the latter quite recently remarked that Great Britain gave a moral lesson to the world by the way in which she honoured her bond. Great Britain is regarded by them as the power on which the stability of Europe depends, and there is the feeling, which is freely expressed, that an 'entente cordiale' – though informal – between the peoples of the USA and Great Britain is the best guarantor of world peace.[30]

In the long term, Smiddy's remarks serve as an overture to what became a constant refrain of Irish diplomats reporting from Washington for the rest of the century; in the short term, they illustrate the improbability of the United States government identifying with the Irish government's anti-partitionism. When the establishment of the Boundary Commission in 1924 highlighted differences between the British and Irish governments on partition, the State Department instructed the American ambassador in London to do nothing which 'might imply adherence to the point of view of either of the interested governments'.[31] After the Boundary Commission culminated in the tripartite agreement between Britain, the Irish Free State and Northern Ireland on 3 December 1925 (which copper-fastened the border between independent Ireland and Northern Ireland), American neutrality on Irish partition remained the order of the day. Since all Irish governments aspired to end partition and all British governments to uphold the status quo, the non-interventionist impulse underpinning American neutrality effectively endorsed the British position.

There was no further statement of American policy on partition until 1938 when John Cudahy, the American minister at Dublin, raised the issue with President Roosevelt in the context of the Anglo-Irish negotiations then taking place in London. Eamon de Valera, reported Cudahy, had made no progress in trying to persuade his British prime ministerial counterpart, Neville Chamberlain, to address the issue. Cudahy urged Roosevelt to invite the British ambassador at Washington to the White House to express his interest 'in the settlement of Anglo-Irish differences' and so break the logjam in the negotiations; otherwise 'the opportunity for co-operation between these two neighbouring islands, which means so much for the peace of the world, will be lost for a generation, at least'.[32]

Cudahy was the least anglophile American minister appointed to Dublin since independence but his entreaties fell on deaf ears in the State Department. The reply there drafted for the president argued that

> a final solution of Anglo-Irish relations, and of the Irish internal problem, would be an immeasurable gain from every point of view, but I am not convinced that any intervention – no matter how indirect – on our part would be wise or for that matter accomplish the effect we had in mind. In the long run considerations of national defence may well lead England voluntarily to take the action you now urge us to advocate . . . but I feel it would be a healthier solution, even if a slower one, if her decision were reached voluntarily, and on the basis of her own self-interest, then as a result of representations from a third power.[33]

In June 1939 John D. Hickerson, the acting chief of the State Department's division of European Affairs, likewise resisted Irish-American protestations to the president 'against the arbitrary and immoral division of Ireland' by insisting that the matter was 'the exclusive concern of the British and Irish Governments'; so, too, did Secretary of State Cordell Hull, who declared in March 1940 that the partition of Ireland was 'a matter in which the United States Government could not properly intervene'.[34]

The American policy of doing nothing to offend the British on Irish issues in effect offered the British government a veto on American responses to Irish importunities. Hence the reaction to an Irish arms-purchasing mission headed by Colonel Michael J. Costello in May 1939 when the State Department advised the British embassy in Washington of their hesitation 'to facilitate the purchase of arms – artillery in particular – in this country without definite assurance that such purchases would be agreeable to the British government'.[35] British assurances duly paved the way for some arms sales to the Irish government but this came to an end with the outbreak of the Second World War when the State Department 'changed its arms policy in view of Ireland's neutrality and took the position that all military and naval matériel not required by the United States rearmament program must be made available to the United Kingdom and to other nations resisting aggression'.[36]

The outbreak of war also shifted attention away from partition to renewed consideration of the geostrategic significance of Irish bases which had preoccupied the Anglo-American alliance in 1917–18. This shift was accelerated by the return of Winston Churchill from the political wilderness to serve as first lord of the Admiralty in Chamberlain's war cabinet. Churchill had always vehemently opposed the Anglo-Irish defence agreement of April 1938 which had relinquished the ports – Cobh (Queenstown), Berehaven and Lough Swilly – retained by the British under the defence annex to the 1921 treaty and which facilitated the policy of neutrality pursued by de Valera's government throughout the war.

Fears of hostile American reaction to Churchill's wanting 'to seize the ports' inhibited his colleagues from supporting him during a cabinet confrontation in October 1939. 'And what would USA say?', expostulated the dominions secretary, Anthony Eden.[37] But once Churchill became prime minister in May 1940, his belligerence was tempered by similar inhibitions, especially when the fall of France exposed Britain's dependence on the United States for its very survival. When the war cabinet considered a proposal from the South African prime minister, Jan Christian Smuts, that Britain should immediately occupy the Irish ports to prevent their suffering the fate of the Norwegian ports which had been seized by the Germans, Churchill demurred: while they should not shrink from seizing the ports as a 'last resort', it would be 'unwise at this moment to take any action that might compromise our position with the USA'. Neville Chamberlain was even more adamant in his opposition to the Admiralty's ambitions to seize the ports because of the 'possibly unfavourable reaction which would be caused in the USA by any forcible measure against Ireland'.[38]

The importance which Churchill attached to nurturing Britain's 'special relationship' with the United States and his own close personal relationship with Roosevelt softened Churchill's policy towards neutral Ireland throughout the war: hence the re-drafting of the passages relating to Ireland in Churchill's letter of 8 December 1940, asking Roosevelt for the aid which became known as Lend Lease and which Churchill described as one of the most important letters he ever wrote. The aggression of the first draft (which referred to the use of Ireland as an essential base for British defensive operations and to the desirability of the United States government inducing de Valera to give the required naval and air facilities) was diluted in the final draft, largely because of intervention of the British ambassador at Washington, Lord Lothian, who warned against offending the Irish-American lobby and embarrassing Roosevelt in an election year.[39]

American antagonism towards Irish neutrality was sedulously fostered by David Gray, who had succeeded John Cudahy as US minister in Dublin in April 1940. Gray, whose wife was an aunt of Eleanor Roosevelt, enjoyed direct access to the White House and shared none of Cudahy's admiration for de Valera. Working in close co-operation with John Maffey, the United Kingdom representative to Ireland, Gray inspired what Maffey described as the 'educational' mission of Frank Aiken, the minister for the co-ordination of defensive measures, to the United States to seek ships and military supplies in the spring of 1941. Aiken's 'education' took the form of a disastrous interview with Roosevelt who was so enraged by Aiken's insistence that Ireland feared British aggression as well as German aggression that he pulled off the tablecloth with all the silver and delph laid for lunch on the presidential desk. The US president and government, noted the head of the dominions intelligence department in the Foreign Office, 'seem to be dealing with Mr Aiken as we desire'; five weeks later, on 13 May 1941, the foreign secretary, Anthony Eden, reassured the American ambassador in London that Washington would be advised in advance in the unlikely event of the British deciding to occupy the Irish ports.[40]

The odds against any such British action became astronomical when the United States entered the war: 'by the end of 1941 the matter was dead as far as we were concerned', wrote Admiral Godfrey, the director of British Naval Intelligence.[41] American recognition of the geostrategic implications of Irish neutrality first found expression in March 1941, more than eight months before Pearl Harbour, when the American chief of Naval Operations, acting on the assumption that the United States was on the verge of war, approved secret plans to build two naval bases in Northern Ireland. Work began on the more important base, in Derry (the second was on Lough Erne), in June 1941 and it was operational by February 1942 – by April 1943, it was much the largest escort base in the United Kingdom The strategic significance of Northern Ireland was reaffirmed during the Anglo-American naval staff discussions on 27 March 1941 when the protection of shipping in the north western approaches of the United Kingdom was identified as the principal task of American naval forces in the Atlantic.[42]

On 23 December 1941, at his first wartime summit with Churchill, Roosevelt proposed that the United States should take over the defence of Northern Ireland, 'thus freeing British troops for employment elsewhere' and the first American troops sent to the United Kingdom duly disembarked in Belfast on 26 January 1942. By May 1942, there were 32,000 Americans stationed in Northern Ireland and the number peaked at 120,000 in 1944. De Valera's protests against their presence fell on such deaf ears that when the Irish minister at Washington protested to the State Department that 'his Government and people (believed) that these American troops were going to be used to attack the Irish forces', Roosevelt's caustic private response 'was "that he only wished they would"'. Official antipathy to Irish neutrality in a Washington now at war found powerful expression in the *Pocket guide to Northern Ireland* issued to GIs in 1942.

Eire's neutrality is a real danger to the Allied cause. There, just across the Channel from embattled England, and not too far from your own billets in Ulster, the Axis nations maintain large legations and staffs. These Axis agents send out weather reports, find out by espionage what is going on in Ulster. The Ulster border is 600 miles long and hard to patrol. Axis spies sift back and forth across the border constantly.

The southern Irish, reported the intelligence officer to the US First Armored Division in similar vein, 'are the most treacherous people on earth'.[43]

The Irish government's inability to comprehend the extent to which the American government had identified with the British perspective on partition and on Irish neutrality is largely explicable in terms of the mutual repugnance that bedevilled their relationship with David Gray. Hence the extraordinary indictment of Gray drawn up at the end of the war by Joe Walshe, the secretary of the Department of External Affairs:

He has never missed an opportunity of showing his anti-Irish spleen and of encouraging anti-Irish elements in this country to take an attitude hostile to the State. This applies, not merely to our neutrality, but to the whole ambit of our relations with Great Britain, including . . . especially partition . . . [He passes] at least four days out of every seven with a group of effete [Anglo-Irish] nobles who are more violently anti-Irish than the worst John Bull in Britain. He is a toady of the very worst type, and the ordinary man-in-the-street is of the opinion that the Irish section in the State Department has gone completely daft or has deliberately set out to make America detested in Ireland. . . . It would not matter very much if David Gray confined himself to his Notes and diplomatic splutters addressed to our Minister (to many of which we send no reply), but his all-consuming hatred for the country is unfortunately known to the great majority of the population.

What particularly infuriated Walshe was the British enjoyment of Gray's 'campaign against this country' and Maffey's admissions 'in moments of excessive frankness that Gray was doing his [Maffey's job] better than he himself'.[44]

Maffey's assessment of Gray was indeed a mirror image of Walshe's and he waxed eloquent in his recognition of 'how great a debt' Britain owed him:

He came to Dublin in April, 1940, and was there during the dark days when France fell, when we stood alone and when Dublin opinion formed a very low estimate of our chances of survival. Although America was still neutral (and it was Mr de Valera's declared belief that this neutrality was unshakeable) Mr David Gray was outspoken in his condemnation of the Axis aggressors, in his support of Britain's stand for liberty and in his criticism of the unhelpful attitude of the de

Valera Government to our cause. The American representative in Dublin has a unique importance. . . . Practically every Irish family has relations in America. It is a constant surprise to me to find how many of the ordinary people in Eire have spent time in America. For these very reasons the American minister is expected to say comfortable things. Mr Gray did not. . . .

It would be difficult to estimate the importance of the help which the Legation gave the British cause here during those difficult days. His association with me was overt and significant. It had a profound effect on Irish opinion at a critical stage of the war. Though it may escape the notice of the historian, Mr David Gray's arrival in Dublin was a milestone in Irish history, and Irish history means a great deal more than the history of Ireland. An American Minister had the temerity to make it plain to Irish Nationalists that they were no longer the darling Playboy of the Western World, and to point out that the audience were bored. This rang down a curtain and raised a new one. We have been able to co-ordinate our policies with Mr Gray in every way. Our association has shown us that if this co-ordination of American and British policy in Eire is raised to the highest plane it cannot fail to have decisive consequences in laying the Anglo-Irish spectre.[45]

Maffey's encomium serves as a monument to David Gray as the personification of Britain's 'special relationship' with America, just as Walshe's diatribe is a monument to Dublin's personification of Gray as the source of American antagonism. Many of the charges against Gray were well founded: he *was* anti-Irish, anti-Catholic, personally hostile to de Valera and a snob who preferred the society of the Anglo-Irish.[46] But the virulence of their antipathy towards Gray blinded Irish ministers and officials from recognising that, for the most part, he faithfully reflected the sentiments of his superiors in Washington.

On 4 March 1945, for example, the State Department advised Gray that Ireland would not be among the countries invited to the inaugural conference of the United Nations in San Francisco because Irish neutrality was 'inconsistent with historic bonds of blood and friendship with this and other United Nations'. Indeed the State Department sometimes took an even harder line than Gray, as when they rejected his request for the appointment of a press attaché to the Dublin legation on the grounds that 'Ireland has "missed the boat" and our present policy is to leave Ireland severely alone' and that they saw no point in sending an officer to Dublin 'for the specific purpose of either ascertaining or attempting to influence public opinion'.[47]

The impact of Irish neutrality on American policy was spelt out in the State Department's briefing manual for Harry Truman when he succeeded to the presidency on Roosevelt's death on 12 April 1945.

Policy towards Ireland is currently directed towards ensuring that Irish neutrality does not in any way hamper the prosecution of the war in Europe or prevent Axis war criminals being brought to justice after the war. At this late stage of the war, Ireland is neither being asked to abandon its neutrality nor being supported in its efforts to become a participant in the peace settlement. The partition question is one in which the United States cannot become involved.[48]

A month later, the United States' relations with Ireland reached their nadir when de Valera called upon the German minister on 2 May to offer his condolences on Hitler's death. Secretary of State Stettinius sent instructions from San Francisco that the president should be specially advised of de Valera's action and the State Department even entertained a proposal floated by Maffey to Gray for 'the joint withdrawal of all United Nations' diplomatic representatives' from Dublin for the duration of de Valera's term in office.[49] Although the State Department advised the president against severing diplomatic relations with Ireland – citing de Valera's adjourning the Dáil and sending messages of sympathy to the White House, to the State Department and to his widow when Roosevelt died as reflecting greater grief than in the case of Hitler [50] – this is one of only two references to Ireland in the massive president's secretary's file in the Truman papers.[51]

On 10 May 1945, two days after the end of the war in Europe, an intelligence report prepared for the American joint chiefs of staff on 'British Capabilities and Intentions' revealed how the Anglo-American alliance constrained Washington's post-war Irish policy:

Ireland. There is no reason for believing that Ireland's policy of strict neutrality and independence will change in the post-war period, in spite of the fact that Ireland is completely dependent upon Great Britain for its foreign trade and physical protection.

Great Britain's policy toward Ireland will also remain the same – that is, resignation, non-interference in Irish domestic affairs, friendly commercial relations, maintenance of the status quo as regards Northern Ireland, and concern over Ireland's strategic position as a possible base of enemy operations against Britain.[52]

American determination to do nothing in regard to Ireland which might put British noses out of joint and the post-war legacy of resentment in Washington at Ireland's neutrality were equally reflected in the State Department's advice to President Truman against sending a message of congratulations to Seán T. O'Kelly when he was elected president of Ireland in June 1945, notwithstanding their admission that this constituted a departure from 'normal procedure' with a 'friendly nation'. But they argued that a presidential message could be interpreted as American recognition 'that Ireland is completely dissociated from the British Commonwealth' and Truman was further advised that it was 'general policy that Ireland has "missed the boat" during the war and that we should "do the minimum" toward her'.[53]

Truman never questioned the State Department line on Ireland. Politically, the new president was trapped in what the Irish legation in Washington ruefully recognised as 'President Roosevelt's shadow' when Eleanor Roosevelt's personal representations to Truman thwarted their renewed efforts in 1946 to have David Gray withdrawn from Dublin.[54] Personally, moreover, Truman identified with the views 'on the whole subject of Mr de Valera and the Irish' expressed in Gray's valedictory letter of resignation in April 1947 and instructed that it be brought to the attention of the new minister in Dublin, George Garrett. Gray's deep resentment at 'the attempt to stir up a religious issue in America [by highlighting the grievances of the Catholic minority in Northern Ireland] to serve the ends of a foreign politician' may also have touched a chord with Truman who held 'deep-seated convictions . . . on Franco and Catholic obscurantism in Spain'.[55]

Clement Attlee's ousting Churchill from Downing Street in the British election of July 1945 had no more impact upon the Anglo-American perspective on Ireland than Truman succeeding Roosevelt. 'No change in policy towards Eire is anticipated', reported Gray after Maffey (now ennobled as Lord Rugby) had told him of his first meeting with the new Dominions Secretary, Lord Addison.[56] Nor did the 1948 election in Ireland (when the first Inter-Party government took office under John A. Costello as Taoiseach and Sean MacBride as Minister for External Affairs) inaugurate a change of policy on partition or neutrality as the Cold War dawned.

THE IMPACT OF THE COLD WAR

To 'do the minimum' towards Ireland remained the recurrent theme of American policy towards Ireland for the first twenty-five years of the Cold War. That policy was set fast in 1948–9 when the enactment of the Republic of Ireland Act and the final breach with the Commonwealth coincided with the new Irish government's rejection of the invitation to join the newly established North Atlantic Treaty Organisation (NATO).

The 'special relationship' was exceptionally important to the United States at the outset of the Cold War when they looked to an enfeebled Britain as the lynch-pin of their anti-communist alliance. The British had already ended financial aid to Greece and Turkey – so giving birth to the Truman Doctrine – and in June 1947 Secretary of State George C. Marshall had launched the programme of economic aid for Europe which became known as the Marshall Plan. A global review presented by the Central Intelligence Agency (CIA) to the inaugural meeting of the National Security Council (NSC) identified 'the possibility of economic collapse in Western Europe and the consequent accession to power of Communist elements' as the greatest threat to American security and it placed Britain within the critical area.

> The United Kingdom, supported by the British Commonwealth and Empire, was formerly a major stabilising influence in the world economy and the balance of power but its capabilities are now greatly reduced. In view of its critical economic position, it must curtail drastically its overseas commitments, with a consequent reduction of its power and influence abroad. Existing British overseas commitments are so extensive and important that their precipitate liquidation would create conditions prejudicial to security interests of the United States.[57]

'The British public and Government seem to be feeling the sensitiveness of a proud people faced with diminishing prestige and forced to seek favours', concluded a State Department assessment.[58] In such a climate American policy-makers inevitably continued to cut the coat of Irish policy from British cloth. Hence the State Department's advice to President Truman before de Valera's courtesy call during his unofficial 1948 visit to the United States to stick rigidly to the pre-war line. If de Valera raised the subject of partition, he should 'be informed that this Government considers the matter as the concern of the Irish and United Kingdom Governments, and one in which this Government should not intrude'.[59]

The so-called 'British School' in the State Department had reigned supreme since the Roosevelt years when 'the "purists", in the sense of "co-ordination" of British and American policies and correlation of the State Department to the Foreign Office, went unchallenged'.[60] The most effective anglophile was Dean Acheson, under-secretary of state from August 1945 until June 1947 and secretary of state from January 1949 until 1953. The British embassy in Washington had identified the ardour of Acheson's anglophilia even before the Second World War[61] and, throughout his four years as secretary of state during Truman's second term as president, he nourished an extraordinarily close relationship with the British ambassador, Oliver Franks.[62]

It was Franks who first addressed 'the particular problem of Ireland' during the working group's exploratory talks on security in Washington which led to the establishment of NATO. He suggested it would be easier for Ireland 'to join an arrangement to which countries on the west side of the Atlantic were also party rather than one which was limited to the United Kingdom and other European countries alone'.[63] Ireland was 'important strategically and could provide manpower and military facilities', argued Frederick Hoyer Millar, the British delegate, at a meeting of the working group on 26 July 1948; it 'would probably be willing to join any association of which the United States was a member'.[64]

But the tone of the debate on Ireland's place in the new security arrangements changed after the taoiseach, John A. Costello, dropped his diplomatic bombshell in Ottawa on 7 September, setting in train the events leading to the Republic of Ireland Act and the severance of Ireland's last link with the Commonwealth. When, two days later, the Washington working group reviewed a paper on the territorial scope of the proposed security arrangements, Hoyer Millar backed a 'change in language' diluting the desirability of Irish membership.[65] The British calculated that 'Northern Ireland's strategic reliability was not worth bartering for an end to Eire's military neutrality and that Eire, if included in NATO, would . . . raise the embarrassing issue of Partition within the forum of NATO'.[66]

Such suspicions were confirmed in Washington when the American legation reported on a conversation with Costello on the night of 27 October which revealed a 'curiously truculent bitterness' towards the British. 'He declared unequivocally that he was determined to go down the line . . . to make the settlement of Partition a condition precedent' to Ireland's joining the Pact; an invitation to join 'would be rejected under existing conditions'.[67]

The formula finally agreed by the working group was that 'Iceland, Norway, Denmark, Ireland and Portugal should be invited to join the Pact *if they are willing* (author's italics)'. It was also agreed that the United States would be responsible for extending the invitations.[68] But a British caveat, indicating that 'their Government would have comments to make on the timing and method of any approach, whether formal or informal, to Eire', reflected their determination to control Irish policy albeit through the Americans as agents.[69] The report of a working party of British officials under the chairmanship of the cabinet secretary, Sir Norman Brook, spelt out the strategic significance of Ireland's breach with the Commonwealth:

> now that Eire will shortly cease to owe any allegiance to the Crown, it has become a matter of first-class strategic importance to this country that the north should continue to form part of His Majesty's dominions. So far as can be foreseen, it will never be to Great Britain's advantage that Northern Ireland should form part of a territory outside His Majesty's jurisdiction. Indeed it seems unlikely that Great Britain would ever be able to agree to this even if the people of Northern Ireland desired it.[70]

Three days later, on 4 January 1949, the terms of the 'informal and oral' invitation to be communicated by the American minister in Dublin, George Garrett, to Irish Minister for External Affairs, Seán MacBride, were dispatched from the State Department. They concluded by requesting as soon as possible any views the Irish government might wish to express informally concerning the form and timing of an official approach.[71]

It was a question expecting the answer 'No', as the further instructions dispatched from the State Department to Garrett on 10 January demonstrate: if the Irish government raised partition, 'you should make clear that we consider two questions totally unrelated and that we take their action in raising partition question to mean they are not seriously interested in Atlantic Pact and will accordingly not consult them further'. Garrett was also instructed to keep his British counterpart in Dublin, who had already been told of the substance of the despatch of 4 January, fully informed.[72]

Years later, Ted Achilles, the State Department official who drafted the instructions of 4 and 10 January, summed up their significance in less diplomatic language.

> We did invite Ireland to join the pact as an important stepping stone in antisubmarine warfare. We doubted that they would accept. They replied that they would be delighted to join provided we could get the British to give them back the six Northern counties. We simply replied, in effect, that 'it's been nice knowing you' and that was that.[73]

Patrick Gordon Walker, the parliamentary under-secretary at the Commonwealth Relations Office, put things even more succinctly in informal discussions with the American embassy in London. The British government was 'anxious to have North[ern] Ireland available in case of war . . . and US interests equally require this'.[74]

Seán MacBride's belated attempt to create room for manoeuvre by suggesting that the Irish government might accept a military commitment in the Pact on condition that they 'controlled arms' for the entire island was doomed to failure. Dean Acheson, by now ensconced as secretary of state, pronounced such terms 'obviously unacceptable' and slammed the door on all ambiguity. Even in the unlikely event of the Irish government accepting an invitation *without* mentioning the partition issue, 'they should be told purpose of Pact is security and not settlement of such problems'.[75]

When George Garrett finally received the Irish government's *aide mémoire* from Seán MacBride on 8 February 1949, citing partition as the reason why Ireland could not join the Pact, he already knew that the State Department would 'consider that by this decision the Irish have pretty well washed themselves out of the picture'.[76] And out of the picture Ireland remained, notwithstanding the attempts to persuade Acheson that the British would welcome American mediation on partition made by Seán Nunan, the Irish minister in Washington, and by Senator J. C. O'Mahoney.[77] Armed with the assurance of the American ambassador in London that 'Attlee himself formulated the British policy on partition and that there is no difference of opinion within the Cabinet',[78] Acheson clung limpet-like to the traditional State Department position that 'partition was a matter for settlement between Eire and the British, . . . and we, as old and good friends of each, did not want to get into the dispute'.[79] Acheson responded similarly to Seán MacBride's plea for American mediation on partition at their meeting in Washington on 11 April: involvement in 'a matter which was not an American concern . . . would be resented in England and . . . would cause far more harm than it could possibly do good'.[80]

American anxiety to ensure that their Irish policy never caused resentment in England is, perhaps, best exemplified by their agonising over sending a message of congratulations to the Irish government on the inauguration of the republic (on 18 April 1949). George Garrett had sought the advice of the president's special counsel, Clark Clifford, on 2 April[81] and Acheson asked the American ambassador in London to seek British approval. The Foreign Office, doubtless delighted by such a striking demonstration of American deference to their wishes, responded with magnanimity; they had not the 'slightest objection' to the United States government sending such a message, but would consider it 'perfectly natural and normal'.[82] The State Department likewise resisted Congressional pressure immediately to elevate the status of their legation in Dublin to an embassy on the grounds that it could be construed 'as an indication of . . . approval of Irish government policies'.[83]

The naivety of Irish expectations that they could use American leverage on the British over partition must be set in the context of mounting concern in Washington about what Ambassador Douglas had identified in August 1948 as a rising tide of anti-American feeling in post-war Britain

> both in and out of the government. . . . At times their attitude towards [the] US borders on the pathological, and there have been moments when the feeling here almost resembles an anxiety neurosis. . . . Britain accepts our assumption of world leadership in face of Russian aggression, and Anglo-American unity today is more firmly established than ever before in peacetime. But Britain has never before been in a position where her national security and economic fate are so completely dependent on and at the mercy of another country's decisions. Almost every day brings new evidence of her weakness and dependence on [the] US. This is a bitter pill for a country accustomed to full control of her national destiny. . . . They are at [the] mercy of forces beyond their control and must rely at every critical turn on US decisions. They are therefore extremely sensitive to any US action or inaction.

The causes of British anxiety in 1948 listed by Douglas were legion: the Berlin crisis, American criticism of British tardiness with regard to economic integration in western Europe, American delay in giving military guarantees to western Europe, American unwillingness to accept explicit responsibilities in the Middle East, American hostility to the sterling area and reluctance to make concessions in respect of the British economic crisis. Nevertheless, concluded Douglas, 'the British appreciate the imperative need for the closest US–UK relationship and on the whole to accommodate their views to ours'.[84] A year later Douglas was still urging the need for 'great self-restraint and . . . real sympathy for the British difficulties'; he warned, too, of the dangers of provoking Attlee's government into standing 'on a strong anti-American platform' in the 1950 election.[85]

Ireland was an area where the Americans could readily do the accommodating without in any way jeopardising their own interests. A 'Review of the world situation' prepared by the CIA in April 1949 (which attempted to draw up a balance sheet of the relative security positions of the United States and of the Soviet Union) exposed the dimensions of American indifference to Ireland's not joining NATO. It identified the inclusion of Norway, Denmark, Portugal and Italy as strengths and the absence of Sweden and exclusion of Spain and Austria as weaknesses; but of Ireland it made no mention whatsoever.[86]

The geostrategic reality was that Ireland's participation in NATO was unnecessary for NATO's success because Northern Ireland (as part of the United Kingdom) was in NATO and effectively provided for what the State Department's Policy Statement on Ireland in August 1950 described as 'the strategic unity of the British Isles'.[87] Ireland's 'military potential was by no means an element essential' to NATO's success because Irish bases would merely be 'complementary to those already available through the adherence to North Atlantic Treaty of Great Britain and Northern Ireland. The denial of Ireland to enemy forces is already encompassed in existing NAT commitments', concluded NSC 83/1, the key document for an assessment of American strategic interests in Ireland during the Cold War.[88]

NSC 83/1 ('The Position of the United States Regarding Irish Membership in NATO and Military Assistance to Ireland under a Bilateral Arrangement'), was prompted by Seán MacBride's attempts in 1950–1 to negotiate a bilateral defence treaty with the United States.[89] It recognised that Ireland could make 'a valuable contribution' to NATO and that 'its unqualified adherence would be both logical and desirable'; but it also noted that the Irish government's refusal 'to separate the question of adherence to NATO from the partition issue . . . puts a price on its adherence'. NSC 83/1 reaffirmed Washington's unwillingness to pay that price and advised against doing anything 'to strengthen an apparently developing Irish belief that the United States is susceptible to an approach for bilateral arrangements'. Such arrangements 'would create friction and resentment among the NAT signatories who have assumed collective mutual assistance obligations'. Worst of all was the danger of gratuitously adding to the burden of British resentment.

The recommendations in NSC 83/1 – that the United States should, first, 'continue its policy of 'readiness to welcome Ireland' as a member of NATO, while 'leaving the initiative to Ireland' and, second, should 'avoid discussion of bilateral arrangements' outside NATO – were adopted by the National Security Council on 2 November 1950 and approved by President Truman next day. Ten years later – in the same month, coincidentally, when John Fitzgerald Kennedy was elected president – the National Security Council Planning Board reviewed NSC 83/1 and concluded that 'it remains valid and does not require updating'.[90]

Kennedy's affinity with the British prime minister, Harold Macmillan, and his careful cultivation of the 'special relationship' belied his Irish Catholic ancestry. Kennedy was 'British inclined and . . . makes no secret of his firm attachment to Britain', reported Dr T. J. Kiernan, the Irish ambassador in Washington, only three months before the ill-fated president's euphoric visit to Ireland. Kiernan also advised that Kennedy would want to avoid raising the subject of partition 'when Britain has so many pressing problems to solve'.[91]

Nor did things change under the Johnson administration. The State Department countered one of the periodic protests from the Irish-American lobby that 'a state of occupation' existed in Northern Ireland with arguments that 'the government of Northern Ireland is a freely elected one which represents the majority's views in a society where the right to dissent is protected by law', that it was not United States policy 'to intervene in the domestic affairs of sovereign states', that the department considered 'the relations between the British authorities and Northern Ireland to be just such an internal matter' and that they valued the continued use of the naval base at Londonderry 'because of its usefulness in meeting US security requirements'.[92] Such security considerations continued to colour American attitudes throughout the Nixon years as one Irish ambassador, William Warnock, discovered when paying his farewells in 1973. His comment on the closeness of the relationship between Ireland and the United States notwithstanding 'Ireland's decision not to join NATO' prompted an acid rejoinder from the secretary of state which spoke volumes for the enduring American resentment at Irish neutrality: 'that in this way Ireland could enjoy the benefits of the Alliance without any of the headaches'.[93]

The Nixon administration remained essentially unmoved by Irish-American Congressional pressure throughout the first and most violent phase of the Northern Ireland crisis. Although a bipartisan initiative in June 1969 by Congressmen Tip O'Neill and the Republican Philip Burton of California attracted 102 signatories to a letter to President Nixon protesting against anti-Catholic discrimination in Northern Ireland, the State Department's response was as succinct as it was dismissive: '(1) the U.S. has no basis to intervene in internal controversies in other sovereign countries; (2) Northern Ireland is an internally self-governing region of the UK; (3) the problems of Northern Ireland can best be resolved by those directly concerned; (4) HMG and the Government of Northern Ireland are aware of the concerns of Americans as expressed by Congressmen O'Neill and Burton'.[94] Such was the Irish government's inability to counter the British stranglehold in Washington during these years that the admittedly ultra-conservative Irish ambassador, William Fay – a 'good friend and golfing partner' of Secretary of State Rogers – advised that it would be imprudent 'to become involved in any Congressional activity on this subject'.[95]

The eruption of violence in Northern Ireland, in August 1969, starkly exposed the Irish government's inability to counter the 'special relationship'. When Hugh McCann, the secretary of the Department of External Affairs, sought the support of American ambassador, John Moore, for Irish efforts to inscribe the crisis on the agenda of the UN's Security Council, Moore replied 'that, because of United States alliances etc., the attitude of the State Department would be negative'. Although Moore was personally sympathetic – he took the trouble to make a flying visit to the American embassy in London on 19 August to telephone Secretary of State William Rogers and a contact in the White House because 'he was satisfied that any telephone call to the United States which he made from (Dublin) would be "tapped" by the British' – his analysis proved correct.[96]

The State Department's note[97] in response to the *démarche* presented by the Irish *chargé d'affaires* at Washington, Seán Ó hEideáin, disingenuously declared that the United States government had 'no appropriate basis to intervene with regard to the domestic political situation or civil disturbances in other sovereign countries' and that they believed 'that the problem concerning Northern Ireland can best be resolved by those who are directly concerned'. In effect, observed Ó hEideáin, this accepted 'the British contention that the situation is an internal British matter'; he concluded that the 'traditional State Department assumption that Ireland by geography and history belongs within the British sphere of influence ... will take a lot of changing'.[98]

A bilateral meeting between Secretary of State Rogers and Irish minister for external affairs, Patrick Hillery, during the UN General Assembly in September 1969 confirmed these geo-political realities. Hillery's explanation that his purpose in bringing the Northern Ireland question to the UN was 'to keep trying to get the British to talk on this matter', evoked the time-honoured State Department response from Rogers ('that we did not wish to interfere in problems between our good friends') and he fobbed Hillery off with the suggestion that, if there were any specific matters he wished to raise with the US government, he should feel free to get in touch with Ambassador Moore.

After expressing hope that the time might come when Rogers 'could give "a little encouragement" to the British on working out a solution in Northern Ireland and appreciation that he had been given a hearing, Hillery concluded on a note of resigned pathos: "I have got all from you that I could have asked"'.[99] Resignation likewise characterised Hillery's brief meeting with Rogers during Nixon's visit to Ireland a year later when, while expressing 'his government's concern over the situation in Northern Ireland', he obviously regarded it as pointless to press even for minimal American intervention.[100]

The Nixon administration were sustained in their non-interventionism by their ambassador in London, Walter Annenberg, whose telegrams reveal how Foreign Office officials kept their American counterparts well informed about just how far they were willing to go in sustaining Jack Lynch's beleaguered government. Hillery's periodic visits to London, reported Annenberg, were 'only of importance as reassurance of good UK-Irish relations despite Ulster problem. For domestic political reasons, Irish officials must be seen as active, and HMG [is] perfectly prepared to cooperate by accepting routine visits on roughly semi-annual schedule.'[101] As Rogers advised Nixon before Jack Lynch's St Patrick's Day visit to Washington in 1971, the United States continued 'to consider that problems in Northern Ireland are the domestic responsibility of the United Kingdom, of which Northern Ireland is a part'.[102]

Nor did the events of Bloody Sunday in Derry, on 30 January 1972, make a significant impact on American attitudes despite the advice of the American embassy in Dublin that Irish sensitivities about Northern Ireland had 'risen to a very high degree'. It reported on the 'resentment' and 'bitterness' arising from American unwillingness to support Irish efforts to have the issue of Northern Ireland inscribed on the UN Security Council and General Assembly agendas in 1969, and to the American 'refusal to intervene with [the] British' after the introduction of internment in August 1971. When Hillery called upon Secretary of State Rogers on 3 February, they predicted that he would 'not be satisfied by polite expressions of sympathy' and would 'expect at least a US commitment to approach [the] British and ask them to take steps to relieve tensions'. The advice from the Dublin embassy was that the 'US should be forthcoming on this issue' on the grounds that the 'cost to US relations with Ireland of not doing anything' considerably outweighed the 'possibility that US relations with Britain will suffer very much if we approach HMG'.[103] Hillery's representations were

> likely to be emotionally charged. We do not believe, however, that our response to the Irish government should be based primarily upon concerns for Ireland's problems, although these cannot be totally ignored. We believe that our response should be based upon our own interests . . . It is in our national interest to show as much responsiveness as possible to Dr Hillery's appeal. We believe that we could

at least agree to tell the British about his approach, to repeat to them his concerns, and to tell them something about our own. We do not believe that the expression of concern amounts to the abandonment of a basically neutral position.[104]

The Dublin embassy's divergence from the traditional hard line in the aftermath of Bloody Sunday got short shrift in Washington. Although the secretary of state acknowledged that Hillery had not asked the US 'to "intervene" in the Irish situation in any formal sense' or to 'adopt a hostile attitude towards Great Britain', he had suggested that they approach 'the British and advise them in a friendly fashion that they should change their policy towards Northern Ireland'. The response was unyielding: Rogers 'did not believe it would be useful for us to make judgements in this situation and therefore we could not go to the British and tell them that their policy is wrong and that they should change it. Such an approach to the British would be taking sides.'[105]

The restrictions upon the Irish government's room for manoeuvre again emerged at a meeting in the White House between Hillery and President Nixon in October 1972. Although Nixon stressed that the US was 'not in a position to openly or publicly intervene in Northern Ireland', he expressed his appreciation of the Lynch government's 'constructive attitude in cooperating with the British to find a peaceful solution'. Hillery replied with what had become his stock response: that 'his government did not seek open or public declarations by the United States government' but hoped that they would make their views known in their 'private discussions with the British'.[106]

THE CARTER INITIATIVE

Although the paucity of archival material released under the thirty-year rule makes it more difficult to trace the evolution of policy from 1972, Irish pressure in Washington for a relaxation of the hawkish rigidity of the Cold War began to build after the change of government in Dublin in 1973. John Hume was by then 'already successfully ploughing his parallel furrow in Washington, gaining the support of Ted Kennedy for the SDLP/Irish State stance against violence in the North', which assumed added significance after the collapse of Northern Ireland's power-sharing executive in 1974. Irish diplomats sent to Washington by the new minister for foreign affairs, Garret FitzGerald, notably Michael Lillis and Seán Donlon, 'brought together as leaders of Irish-American opinion what soon became known as the Four Horsemen: Speaker Tip O'Neill, Senators Ted Kennedy and Pat Moynihan, and Governor Hugh Carey'.[107]

Lillis (a press officer in the consulate in New York who was promoted as counsellor to the Washington embassy in 1976) and Donlon (as the head of the Anglo-Irish division of the Department of Foreign Affairs) sought 'to use Washington to persuade the British government' to reaffirm their commitment to power-sharing in order to strengthen moderate Catholic nationalists. 'Lillis won the confidence and respect of Tip O'Neill' and welded the Four Horsemen 'into a club with which to beat NORAID [the Irish Northern Aid Committee] and [Irish National] Caucus supporters' of the IRA.[108]

The Four Horsemen rode into the ascendant when a Democratic president, Jimmy Carter, entered the White House and when Tip O'Neill became Speaker of the House in January 1977. Michael Lillis, who 'had established a relationship with the political leaders on Capitol Hill that had no parallel among other EC missions (and that) was of major importance in relation to Northern Ireland', laid the groundwork for the initiative. He brought the Irish government's 'contacts with the Irish Congressional leadership to a stage of intimacy never hitherto achieved, the results of which were demonstrated in the joint statement of the "Four Horsemen" on St Patrick's Day 1977, which launched the Friends of Ireland movement in Congress'.[109] Tip O'Neill's influence was decisive in persuading the new president 'to drop the "hands-off" US policy towards Northern Ireland'. Although O'Neill acknowledged, in a confidential note on behalf of the Four Horsemen to Secretary of State Cyrus Vance, that 'it would be simplistic to expect early dramatic developments', he urged that the United States 'should take whatever helpful initiatives . . . lie within its power'.[110]

The upshot was the Carter initiative which took the form of a seven-paragraph statement on Ireland issued from the White House on 30 August 1977. It appealed to Irish-Americans not to support violence in Ireland and committed the Carter administration to the establishment in Northern Ireland of a form of government commanding broad support in both communities there. It also stated that, in the event of a peaceful settlement, the United States would be prepared with others to provide aid for investment in new employment.[111]

What Carter's statement said was less significant than what it symbolised. None understood its significance better than the British who thwarted the initial intention of launching the initiative on St Patrick's Day and who, 'having at first tried to discourage any initiative at all, then tried to detach the promise of aid from the search for an acceptable solution'.[112] Indeed Seán Donlon, who as ambassador to Washington in 1978–81 took every advantage of 'the spectacular opening that Michael Lillis had achieved',[113] has acknowledged

> British influence and the skills of British diplomacy in exploiting to the full the special relationship between London and Washington. It took six months of patient

and, at times, painful and bruising Irish diplomatic activity to overcome the many obstacles created by the British and to nudge the Carter administration into its new position.[114]

The substance of the initiative fell on fallow ground. Although James Callaghan's Labour government murmured a ritual welcome, it was increasingly dependent on the votes of the eleven Ulster Unionist MPs for its parliamentary majority at Westminster. But the symbolism was immense. The United States government's policy had been governed by the principle of non-intervention for over seventy years, ever since the Anglo-Irish settlements of 1920-2 had partitioned Ireland. President Carter had broken that principle beyond repair and had taken 'an important first step in undermining the British government's position, notwithstanding the mild nature of the actual content'.[115] His initiative 'was the first direct presidential expression of a legitimate US interest. It conflicted directly with the wishes of the British Foreign Office, and set in motion a bout of international activity, which bore fruit in the Anglo-Irish Agreement in 1985.'[116]

After the election of a Republican president, Ronald Reagan, in November 1980, 'the US foreign policy establishment reverted to its traditional stance: that the United States should not anger Great Britain, its closest Cold War ally, by meddling in its internal affairs'.[117] In Britain, too, power had shifted to the right when Margaret Thatcher led the Conservative Party to victory in the general election of 1979. With 'the relationship between prime minister and president . . . about to enter a phase of almost delirious mutual admiration',[118] Tip O'Neill and Ted Kennedy got nowhere when they asked Reagan to press Thatcher to negotiate an end to the hunger-strike in which ten IRA prisoners died in 1981. Reagan's national security adviser, Richard V. Allen, saw '"little to be gained by such a meeting" [and] was more upset at the verbal "harassment" that Irish-American demonstrators were giving British diplomats in the United States. . . . "It is intolerable that the representatives of our staunchest ally in the world are subjected to this sort of treatment".'[119] Reagan again 'rebuffed O'Neill's requests to add Ireland to the agenda' for his Washington meeting with Thatcher in 1983 and efforts to enlist support for the Report of the New Ireland Forum in 1984 likewise came to nothing. The National Security Council agreed with the State Department 'that it would be inappropriate to draw the White House into the middle of this complex, historical problem' and argued that they should not allow themselves 'to be used by the Irish; particularly since the Irish have not been especially supportive of (United States) interests on such issues as Central America'.[120]

But, thanks to Seán Donlon, the Irish government had an ally in 'the key player on Irish matters in the US administration in the first half of the 1980s':

former Californian Supreme Court judge, William Clarke, who became national security adviser in 1981. Bill Clarke was a personal friend of Donlon (now the secretary of the Department of Foreign Affairs) and his efforts, together with Tip O'Neill's, 'ensured that there was in Washington a bipartisan network capable of responding to Irish needs'.[121] Clarke visited Donlon in Ireland five times between 1981 and 1985. 'Any time Thatcher was due to meet Reagan, Donlon set up a meeting with Clark to discuss Northern Ireland and how the administration might let Thatcher know of its continuing concern.'[122]

The Clarke–O'Neill axis was instrumental in persuading 'Reagan – fresh off a sentimental trip to his ancestral home of Ballyporeen in Ireland in the summer of 1984 – . . . to overcome the pro-British leanings of the US State Department'. Relations between Margaret Thatcher and Garret FitzGerald had sunk to their lowest ebb as a result of her pre-emptory 'Out! Out! Out!' dismissal of the three options in the New Ireland Forum Report in her press conference after their Chequers summit on 19 November 1984. O'Neill's representations, in urging Reagan to persuade Thatcher to soften her stance at their Camp David summit on 22 December, were crucial.[123] Although Reagan's intervention was not entirely altruistic – 'his Administration was irritated both with O'Neill and with the Irish government' for their leftist stands on Nicaragua and, as one National Security Council official put it, they hoped to use it 'as a lever against Tip in order to get Contra aid moving'[124] – it was decisive in setting the Thatcher–FitzGerald negotiations back on track. This culminated in their signing the Anglo-Irish Agreement at Hillsborough on 15 November 1985.

Thatcher's sensitivity to American pressure – she had been criticised by the *New York Times* and the *Washington Post* – surfaced at her Camp David press conference (when she denied that there had been a breach with the Irish government) as well as in her address to a joint session of Congress in February 1985 (when she stressed that negotiations with the Irish government were continuing).[125] Margaret Thatcher's autobiography makes no mention of Northern Ireland in either her account of the Camp David summit or of her address to Congress.[126] But, in the dark days after she had been forced to resign as prime minister in 1990, when asked privately by a puzzled supporter why she had signed the Anglo-Irish Agreement, she confessed: 'It was the pressure from the Americans which made me sign that Agreement'.[127]

AFTER THE COLD WAR

The last decade of the twentieth century, like the first, was atypical. The end of the Cold War drained the substance out of Anglo-American strategic imperatives as the key determinant of Irish policy. In December 1990, a year after the fall of the Berlin Wall and weeks after the reunification of Germany, the last remaining NATO military installation in Northern Ireland (the RAF radar station at Bishop's Court) was shut down. The circumstances described as unforeseen in the 1949 statement of British strategic interests[128] had come to pass. The political significance of the shift found expression in the celebrated declaration by the then secretary of state for Northern Ireland, Peter Brooke, on 1 November 1990, that 'the British government has no selfish strategic or economic interest in Northern Ireland'. That formulation was reiterated by Prime Minister John Major in the Downing Street Declaration in December 1993 and it also found a place in the New Framework for Agreement in Northern Ireland in February 1995. Ending the protracted guerrilla war with the IRA now took precedence and, in the words of an Irish government official, the strategic argument was ditched 'to reassure Sinn Féin who had always assumed that this was the reason why Britain was still in Ireland'.[129]

The unprecedented collapse of British influence in Washington in the mid-nineties was also atypical. In 1988–92, when 'the Bush administration had followed a cautious, State Department line',[130] the 'special relationship' had remained special, particularly when 'the Gulf War was a stunning political success for Major and Bush [which] sealed their friendship'. Indeed the American ambassador in London, Raymond Seitz, concluded that, 'if anything, the President and Prime Minister were too close' during the final phase of 'twelve cosy years [when] Republicans in Washington and Conservatives in London had grown accustomed to each other'. Hence the otherwise inexplicable and crassly partisan behaviour of British ministers and officials during the 1992 American presidential election between Bush and Clinton. Foreign Secretary Douglas Hurd 'momentarily set aside his diplomatic discretion and sent [Secretary of State] Jim Baker a good-hunting message' which was leaked. The Conservative Central Office sent two of its officials to the United States 'to advise Bush's campaign managers on how to pull a rabbit from an electoral hat . . . and they were too obvious and too smug in doing so'.[131] But what particularly infuriated the Clinton camp was the Home Office trawl through its passport files, at the request of someone in the Bush administration, looking for 'anything that would indicate Clinton had sought to change his nationality in order to avoid the Vietnam draft' during his time in Oxford; this, too, was leaked to the media.[132]

When Bush was defeated, these Tory efforts 'to dig up dirt on Mr Clinton to assist the Republican cause' had the effect of 'curdling . . . Anglo-American relations for the next four years'.[133] Clinton understandably felt 'he owed little to the British and nothing to the Conservatives'. The end of the Cold War, moreover, meant that 'the transatlantic relationship had lost the sobering structure and rehearsed vocabulary which two generations of presidents had inherited with the job'[134] and made it easier for the Clinton administration to settle the score. Relations between London and Washington sank to their nadir in January 1994 when, to John Major's self-confessed 'astonishment and annoyance',[135] the White House issued a visa to Sinn Féin president, Gerry Adams. A prolonged anti-Clinton campaign in the British press culminated in a front-page story in *The Times* in August 1996 which described American links with Britain as at their lowest ebb since the American Revolution.[136] Clinton's decision overruled the opposition not only of the British government but also of the secretary of state, the attorney general, the director of the FBI and the American ambassador in London. 'It was the first time the United States had ever gone against Britain on an issue relating to Northern Ireland', claimed the National Security Council's Nancy Soderberg, one of Clinton's key advisers on Northern Ireland. 'It was an extraordinary decision, one based on the president's personal preference, and . . . responding to the aspirations of a section of the American population, rather than the national security interests of the United States.'[137] Although, as Michael Cox has pointed out, 'Clinton later rebuilt his bridges with the British government, there is little doubting the fact that because of his intervention on Ireland, damage was done to a relationship once considered (by some at least) to be special.'[138]

Many in the American establishment, most notably in the State Department, concurred. A number of career diplomats in the American embassy in Dublin formally dissented from the hibernophile Ambassador Jean Kennedy Smith's advice that Adams be granted a visa and accused her of being 'more attuned to Irish rather than US interests'.[139] Raymond Seitz, the first career diplomat ever to be awarded the plum of the American ambassadorship to the Court of St James, who likewise saw Jean Kennedy Smith as 'a promotion agent for Adams', believed the episode

> demonstrated that British interests – on a matter of deep importance to Her Majesty's Government and minor importance to the United States – did not weigh heavily in the political scales of the Clinton White House. Whether this was an aberration in the post-war pattern of close co-operation or a signal that the nature of the relationship itself had shifted fundamentally with the end of the Cold War was a question left hanging in the air.[140]

That question was not left hanging for long. That, only a month before he authorised the Adams visa, Clinton had himself insisted that, as long as he was president, 'the United States' relationship with the United Kingdom will indeed be special' and that it was based on 'a common strategic world vision and a commitment to acting on common values', favoured the aberrant interpretation.[141] So did the improvement in relations between London and Washington after the election of Tony Blair's Labour government and the strength of the personal relationship established between Blair and Clinton, not least in regard to advancing the peace process in Northern Ireland. So, above all, did the election of George W. Bush as president of the United States and the subsequent restoration of the 'special relationship' between Blair's Britain and Bush's America in the aftermath of the attack on New York on 11 September 2001. By the end of the first year of the twenty-first century it was abundantly apparent that the Clinton years were indeed the exception that proved the rule that had governed the triangular relationship between Britain, the United States and Ireland throughout most of the twentieth century: that ties of history and kinship between Ireland and America counted for little when cast into the balance against the strategic significance of Britain's role as America's most important ally at moments of international crisis.

Notes

1 Henry Kissinger, *Diplomacy* (London, 1994), p. 38.

2 House of Lords Record Office [hereafter HLRO] Lloyd George papers (hereafter LGP), D/14/3/8 Aberdeen to Lloyd George, n. d. (received on 16 June 1916).

3 Spring Rice to Sir Edward Grey, 16 June 1916 cited in Alan J. Ward, *Ireland and Anglo-American relations 1899–1921* (London, 1969), p. 112. Spring-Rice's advice fell on deaf ears in the Foreign Office where his views were suspect because of his Irish, albeit Protestant, birth and because, after two terms in Washington, formerly as an embassy secretary and, since 1913, as ambassador, he was thought to have gone native. Many senior Foreign Office officials, moreover, were fervent Unionists; none more so than the permanent under-secretary until June 1916, Arthur Nicolson, who 'believed that the Liberal Government had cynically resurrected Home Rule for party gain and had thereby provoked righteous resistance'. Spring-Rice 'found himself in the unenviable position of seeming to [President] Wilson a mere British chauvinist, while in Britain he was regarded by the more traditionally-minded realists of the Foreign Office as too pro-American': D. C. Watt, *Personalities and policies: studies in the formulation of British foreign policy in the twentieth century* (London, 1965), p. 31 and Stephen Hartley, *The Irish question as a problem in British foreign policy, 1914–18* (London, 1987), p. 7. Only months before Britain declared war on Germany, Nicolson had gloated to the British ambassador in Berlin about the UVF's Larne gunrunning: 'I hope you were amused by this "coup" . . . so wonderfully organised and so beautifully carried out'. Ibid., p. 10.

4 British Library (hereafter BL) Add MS 49758 f. 307: Balfour papers, Lord Salisbury to Arthur Balfour, 13 June 1916; 49777 ff. 175–8: Walter Long to Arthur Balfour, 15 June 1916.

5 Hartley, *Irish question*, pp. 79–95.

6 Ward, *Ireland and Anglo-American relations*, p. 123. The italicised sentence was silently excised when the memorandum was first published in Burton J. Hendrick, *The life and letters of Walter H. Page*, 3 vols (London, 1930 edn), II, p. 169.

7 Ward, *Ireland and Anglo-American relations*, p. 123.

8 Stephen Roskill, *Hankey – man of secrets*, 3 vols (London, 1970), I, pp. 335–7, 8 Dec. 1916.

9 Catherine B. Shannon, *Arthur J. Balfour and Ireland 1874–1922* (Washington DC, 1988), p. 225.

10 Hendrick, *Walter H. Page*, II, p. 251.

11 Ward, *Ireland and Anglo-American relations*, p. 132.

12 Ibid., pp. 146–7.

13 A. J. P. Taylor (ed.), *Lloyd George: a diary by Frances Stevenson* (London, 1971), p. 155, 25 Apr. 1917.

14 HLRO LGP F/82/8/4: Lloyd George to Bonar Law, 12 Jan. 1918.

15 Public Record Office, London (hereafter PRO) CAB 23/14/16–17.

16 PRO CAB 23/14/94–100: War cabinet minutes, 22 May 1918.

17 HLRO LGP F/7/2/11: Austen Chamberlain to Lloyd George, 3 May 1918.

18 BL Add MSS 49741/178–95: Balfour papers.

19 G. R. Sloan, *The Geopolitics of Anglo-Irish relations in the twentieth century* (London and Washington, 1997), p. 143 *et seq*.

20 Ibid., p. 160, n. 40.

21 Ibid., p. 147.

22 Francis M. Carroll, *American opinion and the Irish question 1910–23* (Dublin, 1978), p. 123.

23 Keith Robbins, *Sir Edward Grey* (London, 1971), pp. 351–3.

24 PRO CAB 27/69, C.I. 1 and 2.

25 PRO CAB 27/68/4–10: 'First report of the Cabinet committee on the Irish question', 4 Nov. 1919 (C. P. 56).

26 Hansard 123 H. C. Deb.5. s. 1272.

27 Shannon, *Balfour and Ireland*, p. 215.

28 Balfour was speaking at the Cabinet meeting of 12 May 1921 which decided that the elections provided for under the 1920 Act should proceed. Keith Middlemas (ed.), *Thomas Jones Whitehall diary – Ireland 1918–25*, 3 vols (Oxford, 1971), III, p. 65.

29 Canada followed suit in 1927, South Africa in 1929, Australia in 1940 and New Zealand in 1942. 'American Policy on Establishment of Relations with Foreign Countries', Division of Historical Policy Research, Department of State, March 1947, Decimal File of the Department of State, 711.00/5–747, National Archives, Washington DC. All subsequent references from the National Archives in Washington (hereafter cited as NAW) are to the Decimal File of the Department of State unless otherwise indicated .

30 Smiddy to the Minister for External Affairs, Desmond FitzGerald, 4 Feb. 1926, in Ronan Fanning, Michael Kennedy, Dermot Keogh and Eunan O'Halpin (eds), *Documents on Irish foreign policy. II 1923–26* (Dublin, 2000), p. 541.

31 Phillips to Kellogg, 18 Mar. 1924 (841d.00/676), cited in NAW 841.d.00/8–2448: 'United States policy on the Irish partition question', Division of Historical Policy Research, Department of State, Research Project No. 73, July 1948.
32 John Bowman, *De Valera and the Ulster question 1917–1973* (Oxford, 1982), pp. 168–9.
33 Roosevelt to Cuddahy, 9 Feb. 1938, 'United States policy on the Irish partition question', p. 7.
34 'United States policy on the Irish partition question', p. 8.
35 Seán Cronin, *Washington's Irish policy 1916–1986* (Dublin, 1987), pp. 66–9.
36 'United States policy on the Irish partition question', pp. 8–9.
37 Paul Canning, *British policy towards Ireland 1921–1941* (Oxford, 1985), p. 255.
38 War cabinet minutes, 16 and 20 June 1940, quoted in Canning, *British policy*, pp. 275, 279.
39 See Warren F. Kimball, *Churchill and Roosevelt: the complete correspondence. 1 Alliance emerging* (Princeton, 1984), pp. 89–107.
40 Joseph T. Carroll, *Ireland in the war years* (Newton Abbot, 1975), pp. 101–4.
41 Quoted in Deirdre McMahon, *Republicans and imperialists: Anglo-Irish relations in the 1930s* (New Haven and London, 1984), p. 234.
42 Sloan, *Geopolitics of Anglo-Irish relations*, pp. 211, 215, 219–22.
43 David Reynolds, *Rich relations: the American occupation of Britain, 1942–45* (London, 1995), pp. 14, 90, 109, 118–19.
44 National Archives of Ireland, Department of Foreign Affairs (hereafter NAI DFA) P 48: Secret and hand-delivered letter from Joe Walshe to the Irish minister in Washington, Robert Brennan, 11 June 1945.
45 Copy of a letter from Maffey to Sir Eric Machtig of the Dominions Office, 25 Feb. 1943 – the extract was forwarded by the British ambassador in Washington, Lord Halifax, to secretary of state, Cordell Hull: Roosevelt Presidential Library, Hyde Park, New York, Gray papers. 'I heartily subscribe "to thim sentiments"', added Roosevelt in his covering letter to Maude Gray, 27 May 1943: T. Ryle Dwyer, *Strained relations: Ireland at peace and the USA at war 1941–45* (Dublin, 1988), p. 18.
46 For a fuller analysis, see Ronan Fanning, 'The Anglo-American alliance and the Irish application for membership of the United Nations', *Irish Studies in International Affairs*, II (1986), 35–61.
47 NAW 124.4d/2–1345: Joseph Grew to David Gray, 29 March 1945.
48 Truman Presidential Library, Independence, Missouri: Truman papers: President's secretary's file (PSF): 'The foreign policy of the United States', sent to President Truman by Secretary of State Stettinius on 16 Apr. 1945, p. 46.
49 NAW 711.41 d/5–545: Gray to Grew, 5 May 1945.
50 NAW 711.41 d/5–545: Joseph Grew to President Truman, 7 May 1945.
51 The other reference concerns Truman's meeting with Irish Minister for External Affairs, Sean MacBride, on 22 Mar. 1951 – see below, p. 203.
52 NAW R. G. 218 JCS 000.1 Great Britain (5–10–45), appendix D, p. 29. This passage was included *in toto* in an amended version of the report dated 5 Dec. 1945 (JIS 161/4) and in a more elaborate version of the report dated 28 Dec. 1945 (JIS 161/8). This noted that Ireland, 'being only loosely associated with the British Commonwealth, will employ its army only in its own

defense' and predicted that, because of Ireland's 'proximity . . . and its potential use as a stepping-stone for invading forces', Britain would 'lend all possible aid' if Ireland were attacked. See also JIS 340/1, 3 Feb. 1946.

53 NAW 841d.00/6–1845.
54 See Fanning, 'Anglo-American alliance', 43–4, for a fuller account.
55 David Gray to President Truman, 16 Apr.1947 and Dean Acheson's minute of 5 May 1947 noting that 'Mr. Clifford at the White House tells me that the President was very much impressed by Gray's letter', NAW 123 Gray, David (1945–9); Dean Acheson, *Present at the creation* (New York, 1969), p. 169. Truman was a Mason and correspondence with his Masonic friends concerning the ill-treatment of Masons in Spain occasioned a vitriolic memorandum to Acheson: 'I've never been happy about sending an ambassador to Spain, and am not happy about it now and unless Franco changes in his treatment of citizens who do not agree with him religiously I'll be sorely tempted to break off all communications with him in spite of the defense of Europe'. Truman to Acheson, 2 Aug. 1951, Truman Presidential Library: Acheson papers, box 66: memoranda of conversations, Aug. 1951.
56 NAW 741.41d/8–2945, 29 Aug. 1945.
57 Truman Presidential Library: CIA 1, 26 Sept. 1947, PSF (NSC meetings), box 203.
58 NAW R. G. 59: secretary of state's weekly summary, 22 Sept. 1947.
59 NAW 032/–948: Marshall to Truman, 9 Mar. 1948.
60 Truman Presidential Library: secretary of state, folder 2: box 159: PSF Subject File: Unsigned memorandum, 9 Nov. 1948, marked 'Secret and Confidential to the President only – Personal State Dept.'
61 In a review of some 250 'leading personalities in the US' Acheson was singled out as 'well known to this Embassy, with whom (sic) he has always been on friendly terms. . . . He readily appreciates the British point of view in matters affecting Anglo-American relations', PRO FO 371/22834 – I owe this reference to Professor Ted Wilson of the University of Kansas.
62 The two men regularly met alone in their homes, before or after dinner and Acheson described Franks as 'one of the most able – and also most delightful – men it has ever been my good fortune to know and work with. . . . We talk regularly, and in complete personal confidence, about any international problems we saw arising. Neither would report or quote the other unless, thinking it would be useful in promoting action, he got the other's consent and agreement. . . . No one was informed even of the fact of the meeting': Acheson, *Present at the creation*, p. 323. Franks spoke in similarly fulsome terms about Acheson as 'quite the most remarkable man I have known intimately. . . . He has a quite astounding loyalty to friends. . . . I have been close to Dean and heard him say more things frankly than . . . other . . . people': Truman Library: Transcript of European Recovery Programme interview with Lord Franks, 27 June 1964, pp. 10–11.
63 NAW 840.20/7–948 TSF: memo of working group meeting, 9 July 1948.
64 NAW 840.20/2–349.
65 The original draft – that 'it would be desirable to have Norway, Denmark, Portugal, Iceland and Ireland as full members' – was amended to read 'it might well be desirable'. Hoyer Miller also stressed that Britain still wanted Norway and Portugal in the Pact. NAW 840.20/2–349 mm 15: memo of meeting of 9 Sept. 1948.

66 Ian McCabe, *A diplomatic history of Ireland, 1948–49* (Dublin, 1991), p. 106.
67 NAW 741.41d/10–2848.
68 Portugal, which was to receive a joint Anglo-American approach, was an exception.
69 NAW 840.20/12–2448: Washington security talks – report of the working group to the ambassador's committee, 24 Dec. 1948, Annex D, p. 2.
70 1 Jan. 1949, quoted in Sloan, *Geopolitics of Anglo-Irish relations*, pp. 249–50.
71 NAW 840.20/1–449: Under-Secretary of State Lovett to American legation in Dublin 4 Jan. 1949.
72 NAW 840.20/1–849: Under-Secretary of State Lovett to American legation in Dublin 10 Jan. 1949.
73 Truman Library: Transcript of Oral History Interview with Theodore Achilles, 13 Nov. 1972, p. 62.
74 NAW 841d.00/1–1449: London to secretary of state (tel. 175), 14 Jan. 1949.
75 See Dublin to secretary of state (tel. 26), 29 Jan. 1949 and secretary of state to Dublin (tel. 23), 4 Feb. 1949, NAW 840.20/1–2949.
76 NAW 840.20/2–1149: Garrett to Hickerson, 11 Feb. 1949.
77 See memo from Hickerson to Acheson, 5 Apr. 1949 (NAW 841d.00/4–549) and O'Mahoney to Acheson, 19 Feb. 1949. O'Mahoney 'was of a good-humoured opinion . . . that a great number of State Department officials were more in sympathy with the Whigs and Tories than the Irish on any question affecting the Irish people' – a comment which attracted the pencilled gloss 'Whig Ranney!' on the report in question from an anonymous State Department colleague. Hugh McCann, then a counsellor in the Irish embassy, recalled F. G. Ranney (then the Irish desk officer in the State Department) telling him that one of his principal pleasures in life was reading the court circular in *The Times*: interview with Hugh McCann, 10 Sept. 1985.
78 NAW 841d.00/3–1549: Lewis Douglas to Dean Acheson, 15 Mar. 1949. One member of the Cabinet (Frank Pakenham, then the minister for Civil Aviation) in fact dissented from the guarantee of Northern Ireland's territorial integrity embodied in the Ireland Act of 1949: see Ronan Fanning, 'The response of the London and Belfast Governments to the declaration of the Republic of Ireland Act, 1948–9', *International Affairs* (winter 1981–2), 110–11.
79 NAW 841d.00/3–449: Acheson to Lewis Douglas, 4 Mar. 1949.
80 NAW 840.20/4/1149: Acheson's memorandum of conversation with MacBride, 11 Apr. 1949. MacBride, who asked to meet Acheson alone, 'said that Ireland was strongly in favour of the Atlantic Pact and would like to join in signing it but that no Irish Government could have lasted two months which had done this as long as the partition question remained unsettled'.
81 NAW 841d.00/4–949. MacBride later complained to Garrett that the British, who had been unable to resist the temptation to tell him about the American inquiry when he was in London, 'appeared "jubilant" over the fact that the U.S. had asked British "permission" before sending the U.S. message': NAW 841d.00/5–2449.
82 NAW 841d.01/4–1149: Ambassador Lewis Douglas to secretary of state (tel. 1464), 11 April 1949.
83 See Jack Hickerson's minute to Acheson, 6 May 1949 and the correspondence between Acheson and Senator Saltonsall, NAW 121.41d/4–1349. The State Department ultimately

bowed to Congressional pressure and promoted George Garrett to ambassadorial rank in March 1950

84 NAW 711.41/8–1148: Lewis Douglas to the State Department (tel. 3625), 11 Aug. 1948.

85 Truman Library: Acheson papers, box 64: Douglas to Acheson, 15 Aug. 1949.

86 Truman Library: PSF, NSC meetings, box 206, CIA 4–49.

87 NAW 611.40a/8–1550.

88 Truman Library: Truman papers: PSF box 209.

89 See Ronan Fanning, 'The United States and Irish participation in NATO: the debate of 1950', *Irish Studies in International Affairs* I (1985), 38–48, for more extensive quotations from NSC 83/1.

90 Memorandum from James S. Lay Jr (executive secretary to the NSC) to the NSC, 10 Nov. 1960 – attached to the copy of NAW NSC 83/1.

91 Richard Aldous, 'Perfect peace? Macmillan and Ireland', in Richard Aldous and Sabine Lee (eds), *Harold Macmillan: aspects of a political life* (London, 1999), p. 141.

92 NAW POL 32–3 IRE: William B, Macomber, Jr. (assistant secretary for congressional relations) to Congressman William F. Ryan, 2 June 1967.

93 NAW POL 15–5 IRE–US: Memorandum of conversation between the secretary of state and the Irish ambassador, 2 Aug. 1973.

94 NAW POL IRE–US 1969: Memorandum for Henry A. Kissinger on the letter to the president of 24 June 1969 from Congressmen O'Neill and Burton et al., 27 June 1969 – a copy of the O'Neill–Burton letter and the list of 102 signatories is appended. Cf. John Dumbrell, 'The United States and the Northern Ireland conflict 1969–94: from indifference to intervention', *Irish Studies in International Affairs* VI (1995), 115.

95 NAI DFA 2000/14/465. Rogers so described Fay after his sudden death while on leave in Dublin on 7 Sept. 1969 in conversation with Irish minister for External Affairs, Patrick Hillery, on 22 Sept. 1969, NAW POL IRE–US 1969. See also Ronan Fanning, 'Playing it cool: the response of the British and Irish governments to the crisis in Northern Ireland, 1968–69', *Irish Studies in International Affairs* XXII (2001), 57–85.

96 NAI DT 2000/6/658: Hugh McCann's minute of conversations with John Moore on 19 August 1969, 20 Aug. 1969.

97 NAI DFA 2000/14/465: 26 Aug. 1969.

98 NAI DT 2000/6/659: 'Northern Ireland: State Department Reaction', Seán Ó hEideáin to Department of External Affairs, 28 Aug. 1969.

99 NAW POL IRE–US 1969: Memorandum on secretary of state's bilateral talk with minister for External Affairs Hillery, 22 Sept. 1969.

100 NAW 952/10–8–70: Telegram from the American embassy in Dublin to the secretary of state, summarising the discussions between Rogers and Hillery at Dublin Castle on 5 Oct. 1970.

101 NAW London – 1715, 2–26–71: Annenberg to secretary of state, 26 Feb. 1971.

102 NAW POL–IRE 1971: Memorandum to the president on the Lynch visit, 12 Mar. 1971.

103 NAW Dublin 128/2–2–72: Telegram from American embassy in Dublin to secretary of state, 2 Feb. 1972.

104 NAW Dublin 139/2–3–72: Telegram from American embassy in Dublin to secretary of state.

105 NAW POL IRE–US 083918: State Department to embassy in Dublin, 7 Mar. 1972, briefing material on 'semantic difficulties re Hillery visit' for 'use as necessary'.

106 NAW POL 7 IRE 1972: Memorandum of conversation between the president and the Irish foreign minister, 6 Oct. 1972.

107 See Garret FitzGerald's appreciation on the death of Tip O'Neill, 'The most helpful ally Ireland ever had in Washington', *The Irish Times*, 8 Jan. 1994.

108 Jack Holland, *The American connection: US guns, money and influence in Northern Ireland* (New York, 1987), pp. 122–3.

109 Garret FitzGerald, *All in a life: an autobiography* (Dublin, 1991), pp. 330, 348.

110 John A. Farrell, *Tip O'Neill* (Boston and New York, 2001), pp. 512–13.

111 See Holland, *American connection*, pp. 127–8, for the full text of the Carter initiative.

112 Holland, *American connection*, p. 126.

113 FitzGerald, *Autobiography*, p. 331.

114 Seán Donlon, 'Bringing Irish diplomatic and political influence to bear on Washington', *The Irish Times*, 25 Jan. 1993.

115 Adrian Guelke, *Northern Ireland: the international perspective* (Dublin, 1988), ch. 7, p. 139.

116 Dumbrell, 'The United States and the Northern Ireland conflict', 116.

117 John Aloysius Farrell, 'Reagan, O'Neill aided North Ireland peace – Thatcher heard appeals, files show', *Boston Globe*, 30 June 2000. This article, based on documents released under the US Freedom of Information Act by the Reagan Presidential Library, contains material not included in the author's biography of Tip O'Neill.

118 Raymond Seitz, *Over here* (London, 1998), p. 318.

119 Allen to Ed Meese, 27 Aug. 1981, quoted in Farrell, 'Reagan, O'Neill'.

120 Ibid. Peter Sommer to National Security Adviser Robert C. McFarlane, ? May 1984.

121 Donlon, 'Bringing Irish diplomatic and political influence'.

122 Holland, *American connection*, p. 143.

123 Farrell, *Tip O'Neill*, 623–4 – see especially O'Neill to Reagan, 13 Dec. 1984 ('The best hope for a peaceful, lawful and constitutional resolution to the tragedy of Northern Ireland may be in serious jeopardy as a result of Mrs Thatcher's public statements.') and Reagan to O'Neill, 9 Jan. 1985 ('I made a special effort to bring your letter to her personal attention and to convey your message of concern. I also personally emphasized the need for progress in resolving the complex situation in Northern Ireland, and the desirability for flexibility on the part of all the involved parties.')

124 Farrell, *Tip O'Neill*, p. 624.

125 Guelke, 'The American connection', p. 147.

126 Margaret Thatcher, *The Downing Street years* (London, 1993), pp. 466–9.

127 Alistair McAlpine, *Once a jolly bagman – memoirs* (London, 1998), p. 272.

128 See p.200.

129 Sloan, *Geopolitics of Anglo-Irish relations*, pp. 265–6.

130 Dumbrell, 'The United States and the Northern Ireland conflict', 121.

131 Seitz, *Over here*, pp. 320–1.

132 Conor O'Clery, *The greening of the White House* (Dublin, 1996), p. 25.

133 Alan Watkins, 'Enoch saw the future when he shook Bill Haley's hand', *Independent on Sunday*, 6 Aug. 2000, p. 21.

134 Seitz, *Over here*, pp. 321–2.

135 John Major, *The autobiography* (London, 1999), p. 456.

136 Cited in Michael Cox, 'Northern Ireland: the war that came in from the cold', *Irish Studies in International Affairs* IX (1998), 80.

137 O'Clery, *Greening of the White House*, pp. 106, 133.

138 Michael Cox, 'Thinking "globally" about peace in Northern Ireland', *Politics* XVIII, 1 (1998), 63. I owe this reference to Adrian Guelke who kindly provided me with a pre-publication copy of 'The international system and the Northern Ireland peace process', a paper which he delivered to the Institute for British–Irish Studies conference on 'Renovation or revolution? New territorial politics in Ireland and the United Kingdom' at University College Dublin on 3 April 2002.

139 See O'Clery, *Greening of the White House*, pp. 82–8.

140 Seitz, *Over here*, pp. 289, 292.

141 O'Clery, *Greening of the White House*, pp. 123–5.

CHAPTER 11

Britain's Second EEC Application

The Irish Dynamic

Jane Toomey

Douglas Hurd, in an address to the Institute of European Affairs on 21 March 1994, clearly illustrated the extent to which joining the European Economic Community (EEC) was a watershed in British and Irish history:

> Britain and Ireland joined the Community together because of a sense of our place in history. For the British it was about finding a new place in the world after two centuries of imperial experience. . . . For the Irish, membership in 1972 was about Ireland's place in history, confirming Ireland's position in Europe as a modern state . . . and its decisive shift away from the embrace of Britain.[1]

If one takes a closer look at this declaration, it is also possible to ascertain one of the subtle but at the same time crucial variables in any discussion relating to Britain and Ireland's second applications to join the Community. The word 'together' is indicative of the entire relationship between the two countries when it came to the bid for membership, but is symptomatic of the way in which the Irish application has been eclipsed by the British one. While this is inevitable, it is at the same time regrettable, for the Irish case is of significant interest to our understanding of the broader process and dynamics of European integration.

This article argues that, in order to understand Harold Wilson's application to the EEC more fully, greater attention needs to be paid to Ireland's approach to European unity in the 1960s. For the predicament facing both London and Dublin in the 1960s was identical: 'they did not want to knock on some doors and had already knocked on others that were not open'.[2] Instead of being seen as a mere appendage to Britain's application, the Irish approach can indeed be incorporated into a framework for comparative analysis. Only then can one begin to answer such key questions as: what were the motivating factors that impelled Ireland to seek membership during the Wilson era? Was

Britain's case unique or did in fact other countries exhibit any similarities in terms of their approach to the EEC? What was the impact of Ireland's policy on Wilson's attempt and exactly how much did Irish concerns impinge on Whitehall thinking when it came to their European policy?

IRELAND'S APPROACH TO EUROPEAN UNITY

A member of the Irish delegation's verdict on how the negotiations were proceeding, as a result of the third application to join the EEC, could easily be applied to the first and second bids for membership: 'We're riding along on the backs of the British.'[3] Had it not been for the British decision to seek entry, it is highly unlikely that the Irish would have contemplated exploring the option at the time. 'Une île derrière une île',[4] sheltered behind Britain, it is no wonder that Ireland maintained such an insular attitude until the beginning of 1960s. Believing that what happened in Europe was largely irrelevant, statements such as 'we are outside the whirlpool of European politics, we are largely untouched by the intrigues of European diplomacy',[5] voiced in 1934 by John Costello, later the taoiseach, further reinforced this view. The advent of war in 1939 did nothing to alter the consensus, for 'it was as if an entire people had been condemned to live in Plato's cave, with their back to the fire of life'.[6] Ireland, refusing to be drawn into the theatre of war, chose instead to remain neutral. In this context, it is not surprising that Ireland exhibited little enthusiasm for the process of European integration that began after the Second World War. Participation in the Marshall Plan and membership of the Council of Europe and the Organisation for European Economic Co-operation (OEEC) were as far as the Irish were prepared to travel down the European path. Both the 'neutrality' card and the 'partition' card were employed to explain why Ireland refused to join the North Atlantic Treaty Organisation (NATO). 'In essence', observes Gary Murphy, 'the parameters of Irish foreign policy at this time continued to be defined by the relationship with Britain'.[7] Calls for a 'United States of Europe' fell on deaf ears as Dublin showed no interest in signing the Treaty of Rome.

Thus, 'up to 1957, Ireland had only one foot rather gingerly placed on the path towards European integration'.[8] What would lead to a change of heart for Ireland to begin to turn towards the nascent EEC? The main driver was economics – a growing acknowledgement of the limits and failings of protectionism. With Seán Lemass as taoiseach, often referred to as a 'mould breaker' and a 'mould maker',[9] and Thomas Whitaker navigating the economic course as secretary of the Department of Finance, it is not surprising that the merits of free trade were about to be embraced, shifting Ireland from an inward looking to an outward looking economy seeking new markets. In October 1956, a decision was taken by the secretaries of the Departments of External Affairs, Industry and Commerce, Agriculture, Finance and the Taoiseach to scrutinise the viability of Irish association with other OEEC countries in a free trade area.[10] This was partly a response to the unveiling of Whitaker's report entitled 'Economic Development', which not only drew attention to the multiple weaknesses of the Irish economy but also pointed the way towards remedying them. Old approaches would fast be abandoned in favour of new innovative measures; there was a growing understanding, he argued, of 'the need to introduce a little stick as well as carrot'.[11] Just as Frank Lee's report had proved the catalyst in speeding up London's recognition of the merits of joining the EEC in 1961,[12] politicians in Ireland were finally coming to the stark realisation that the Irish could not keep hiding in the 'Plato-like' cave any longer.

Hand in hand with the proposal to open up the Irish economy went fear of the consequences of Britain joining the EEC without Ireland:

> We have applied for membership of the EEC because it would be economic disaster for us to be outside the Community if Britain is in it. We cannot afford to have our advantageous position in the British market turned into one of exclusion by a tariff wall, particularly as our chief competitors would be inside this wall.[13]

One only has to look at these words from Lemass to ascertain the degree to which Britain's decision to seek membership necessitated similar action on the part of the Irish. It was largely inevitable that, if Britain joined, Ireland would quickly follow suit, for in simple terms to do otherwise would have been akin to economic suicide. It was sheer economic necessity which impelled the Irish to knock on the door of Europe, for instead they might well not have been referred to as 'an island behind an island', but the 'bankrupt island behind Britain'. Besides, the question of sovereignty did not pose a serious threat either to eliciting or maintaining support for an application to the EEC. Ireland, owing to a combination of historical and geographical factors, had not exercised the level of autonomy thought to be at the disposal of British policymakers. Joining the EEC was seen by many as a way of increasing as opposed to diminishing her independence. Furthermore, as T. K. Whitaker has observed, when it came to the decision: 'No farmer was going to say no to protected prices of the Community on the grounds of sovereignty, it just did not weigh in the scales.'[14]

It was these factors – the changing domestic economic agenda and the external influence emanating from Britain – that led to the publication in June 1961 of a White Paper on the EEC and the formal application for membership two weeks before Britain, on 31 July 1961. The path from this point on, however, was not so smooth, and as a result Ireland never even reached the negotiating table. Reservations about Irish membership were aired by members of the Six and the Commission on both economic and political grounds. Determined to rid the Six of any doubts about Ireland's capacity to join and her so-called 'special problems', the taoiseach not only invited European journalists to a detailed session of questions in Dublin, but also set out to visit the capitals of the Six in October 1962.[15] Whitaker recalled Lemass telling him gloomily after his meeting with de Gaulle: 'We have to work hard, he thinks association is good enough for us'.[16] 'Work hard' they did, actively expressing their desire to join the EEC at every turn. At the end of the month the Council of Ministers decided to allow Ireland to enter into negotiations but had yet to set a date. However, it was of little consequence because the French President Charles de Gaulle's *non* to Britain on 14 January 1963 temporarily put an end to all the applicants' hopes of joining the Community.[17] Hence, Britain was not the only country to be seen as 'awkward' in the eyes of the continentals. Ireland, too, was subject to a rigorous screening for suitability and came very close to being disqualified. Furthermore, while Britain might have considered that it had no alternative to joining the EEC, the real meaning of 'no alternative' could truly be understood only by the Irish.

Desmond Williams has contended that 'the foreign policy of states is of course determined by a number of factors, by economic interest, geographical location and military power, also by their past history and by present events'.[18] Pragmatic economic reassessment, the intensity of Ireland's relationship with Britain and the changed international landscape ensured that Ireland had to apply for membership of the EEC at the beginning of the 1960s. Very similar motivations guided the second bid for membership.

'BRITAIN FIRST, THE REST LATER'

When de Gaulle vetoed British membership of the Community in 1963, the Irish were automatically barred from joining too. As one Whitehall official put it at the time: 'When our negotiations were suspended in January 1963, the Irish did not pursue the matter further.'[19] Both countries had reached an impasse and it would be another four years before any concrete attempt was made to launch another application process. On 1 May 1967, Wilson met with the taoiseach, now Jack Lynch, to discuss the prospect of British membership of the EEC. It was confirmed that 'if we decided to negotiate for entry into the community, the Irish would undoubtedly renew their application'.[20] Within a matter of days, both countries had again declared their intent to seek membership of the EEC.

The signing of the Anglo-Irish Agreement in 1965 necessitated even deeper economic meetings between the two countries. For example on 8 and 9

November 1967, a meeting of the Anglo-Irish Economic Committee took place. The meeting was regarded as 'the first opportunity, since our applications were made, for officials from both capitals to sit around a table and review progress'.[21] This illustrates the extent to which economics and foreign policy continually overlapped and also the way in which both countries prioritised the economic over political dimensions of integration.

In the second place, referring to the meeting between Wilson and Lynch in February 1968, the *Cork Examiner* highlighted the significance of personal diplomacy: 'The terse, uninformative terms of the official communiqué must not be allowed to disguise the fact that meetings between Mr Lynch and Britain's Mr Wilson are very important in the context of the bid for membership of the European Community.'[22] Lynch was classified as 'a firm believer in eventual Irish entry into the Common Market',[23] and it is easy to see how at times his unswerving belief in the inevitability of admission to some extent assuaged Wilson's despair. Speaking about Ireland's hopes of entry, 'Mr Lynch asserted that while he would not like to speculate on how long it would take "it will certainly happen in a matter of years". The same feeling inspires and encourages Mr Wilson.'[24] Thus, against the high wall de Gaulle had erected around Europe, it was helpful that, in Lynch, Wilson had a firm advocate not only of Irish but also of British entry to the EEC. The British had on their side a staunch ally to defend their economic policies and European credentials. On numerous occasions the Irish were keen to portray the British in the best possible light – after the visit to Paris in November 1967, Hugh McCann, Secretary of the Department of External Affairs,'reports the Irish as having defended our position on the sterling balance on orthodox lines'.[25]

Finally, through the Irish, the British managed to gain further insights into the attitudes of the French and the so-called 'friendly five'. For example, Axel Herbst, Director General for External Relations of the Commission, confirmed to Britain's ambassador to Ireland, Andrew Gilchrist, other equally pessimistic assessments of Britain's prospects. He was reported as leaving Ireland 'with the distinct impression that, notwithstanding Mr Wilson's determination to bring British negotiations to a successful close, it will be a very, very long drawn-out affair, that there is in fact little hope whilst the General is in the saddle'.[26]

Considerable tension was to arise, however, over the tactics of the application process, when it became clear that Britain might join without Ireland. Just as it was automatically assumed that Ireland would apply for membership of the EEC if Britain did, it was taken for granted that the two countries would naturally negotiate at the same time. It was not something that was questioned or debated until the British foreign secretary, George Brown, delivered his Western European Union speech on 4 July 1967. The speech was indicative of British thinking at the time, that Britain's ultimate goal was to join the Community quickly; anything that might delay progress was to be cast aside as excess baggage. Granted, Britain would more than likely make efforts to reclaim that baggage, but only when its destination had been reached. On 7 July 1967, Francis Gallagher (head of the western economic department 1965-7, and head of the common market department 1967-8) alerted the Irish to an approach then being mooted in the Council of Ministers: 'Britain first, the rest later'.[27]

> We naturally hoped that the Irish would be able to join the community at the same time as ourselves. But this might not prove possible in the event and we were certainly not committed to holding back until Ireland or any other country was ready.[28]

Lynch, who consistently held the view that the Ireland and Britain should join the EEC at the same time, responded three days later:

> Our purpose in seeking parallel negotiations is to ensure the adoption of procedure which will afford the Irish government an opportunity of representing their views when any issue of direct concern to Ireland arises in the course of the British negotiations and, of course, vice versa. Our anxiety on this score is naturally greater than that of other countries, since the terms on which Britain joins the community will have a far greater impact on Ireland than on other new entrants.[29]

The growing tension over tactics was captured by one commentator, Wesley Boyd, who, writing in the *The Irish Times* a month later, remarked:

> Mr Wilson seems determined to get Britain into the Common Market. He will have enough troubles of his own without adding those of other countries to his shoulders. There can be no doubt that he is favourably disposed towards Ireland's application and would like to see us a member of the EEC along with Britain. However, if he sees an opportunity of taking Britain in without Ireland he can hardly be expected to let it pass. He could well argue that British membership is the best guarantee of Irish membership.[30]

Boyd's empathetic approach to London's negotiating stance was, it appears, in the minority. Elsewhere, Brown's statement led to bafflement and bemusement. In reaction to the speech, headlines such as 'George Brown bombshell shocks Irish EEC hopes' were not uncommon,[31] and such cynicism amongst the Irish ultimately led the taoiseach personally to seek a clarification from the prime minister. The drama which accompanied the speech was largely due to the way it was interpreted. Taken in isolation it signalled a lack of interest in other applicant countries, yet what Brown was trying to address was a worst-case scenario. As Wilson emphasised, in response to a letter from Lynch, 'a situation could conceivably arise in which the processes of negotiation and ratification of our entry had been completed but yours had not'. He went on to point out that 'the proposed year's standstill was intended as a safeguard for the trade relationship between our two countries'.[32] Not content to leave the matter to rest, Lynch reiterated the point when he wrote to Wilson to inform him of the results of his own 'probe' of EEC capitals.[33] He stated that he had 'received not only a warm welcome and assurances of support for our application for membership, but also acceptance of our view as to the importance of parallel negotiations and simultaneous entry to the Community for both our countries'.[34]

The overriding concern on the part of the Irish was that the two countries would march in unison towards Europe, not one behind the other. Constant reference to 'simultaneous negotiations' and 'simultaneous accession' were heard as a result of Brown's speech. The Irish had been woken from their complacency. No longer able to take a back seat and allow Britain to drive them towards Europe, they now had to forge their own way. Ironically, Brown's speech served as a timely reminder of the need to adopt a more proactive approach to formulating an Irish European policy. As Boyd pointed out in *The Irish Times*:

> As far as simultaneous negotiations and accession is concerned, Mr Brown has sounded the warning note – Britain cannot de depended upon to support this Irish policy. Ireland must press its own case vigorously. The Taoiseach and Mr [Charles] Haughey have been doing this and the measure of their success is that the governments of the Five and the European Commission do not regard simultaneous negotiation and accession as a problem.[35]

What impact did such concerns have on the Wilson administration? Did it ignore Ireland's fears? The answer to these pertinent questions is a resounding 'no'. The Wilson administration consistently wrestled with the problem of how to assuage Ireland's doubts. This was mainly because the British needed the Irish to form a united front, thus preventing de Gaulle from exploiting differences between the applicant states. It is to closer analysis of the impact of Ireland's policy on Whitehall decision making that this article now turns.

'ASSOCIATION' OR 'UN ARRANGEMENT INTERMÉDIARE'?

'Sympathy but impossibility' is how Whitaker summed up de Gaulle's attitude towards Britain and Ireland's aspiration to full membership when the Irish went over to meet with the general in November 1967.[36] With this in mind, it is hardly surprising that the Irish were asked if they had ever contemplated associate membership. The taoiseach stated that:

> the President had then gone on to refer to the fact that some of the difficulties attached to the British application created difficulties for Ireland also. He then said that in the event of British negotiations and ultimate membership being delayed for a considerable period we would have French support and goodwill for securing an interim arrangement which would eventually lead to full membership.[37]

On a similar note, the *Irish Press* pointed out that Lynch was keen to emphasise that any such 'associate' arrangement 'would require long and detailed negotiations within the context of the Treaty of Rome, the Anglo-Irish Free Trade Agreement and the GATT [General Agreement on Tariffs and Trade] countries'.[38] Initially, then, the reaction to de Gaulle's suggestions was generally not favoured. As McCann pointed out, even consideration of 'interim' arrangements might weaken the momentum towards membership; 'nevertheless they would have to take a look at it, if only because of the publicity in Paris which would lead to questions in the Dáil'.[39] As for the mention of the need for another Lynch–Wilson meeting, 'McCann thought this would be a natural development but at a later stage when last week's talks had been fully studied; in any case the Irish did not want to appear to be running to mother.'[40]

The idea of association was not, however, taken off the French agenda. When Bernard Ledwidge met with the Irish ambassador in Paris, Mr Commins, he reported that 'the French had left the Irish with the impression that as far as France was concerned, association as a stepping-stone to full membership was available, at least to Ireland'.[41] To the British, '[v]ague French talk about association was a red herring'.[42] Ledwidge, for instance, worried that:

> [I]t looks as if the General turned his redoubtable charm on the Irish to some effect. He has sent them away with the idea that their application is not necessarily linked with Britain's in his eyes and might have a different fate, if that prospect interested the Irish Government. Apparently he has also interested them at least a little in the possibilities of association as a sort of delayed membership, if the answer to their present application proves to be negative.[43]

'At least a little' was certainly the operative phrase now, as what was earlier dismissed outright was now attracting an increasing amount of attention. The 'red herring' was brought up at the Anglo-Irish Economic Committee which met in Dublin on 8 and 9 November 1967. Upon probing from Sir Arthur Snelling, Whitaker believed that the term 'association' had been implied for all the applicants. 'A war of nerves' was how Snelling described the confrontation with the French,[44] as the general raised obstacle after obstacle in order to prevent the British making any progress towards membership of the EEC. Anything less than full membership, he pointed out, was insufficient. 'Association, even if it were available to us, would not meet this fundamental requirement.'[45] His sentiments were echoed by Anthony Galsworthy at the British Embassy in Paris who was told that 'the general feeling in the Prime Minister's entourage was that de Gaulle's remarks either amounted to no more than a gesture of goodwill or else represented an attempt "to turn the British flank"'. He concluded that 'the French, of course, have an obvious interest in popularising at the moment the concept of association as a kind of purgatory for applicants'.[46]

De Gaulle's second veto of British entry to the EEC, delivered on 28 November 1967, destabilised Anglo-Irish relations still further. Gilchrist contended that while the Irish had initially dismissed the General's suggestions, the devaluation of sterling and the second *non* to Britain had prompted the Irish to have second thoughts and he concluded that 'they are very far from endorsing our own reiteration of "nothing but full membership"'.[47] He went on to cite part of Lynch's speech to the Annual Conference of Fianna Fáil (21 November 1967):

> It will be necessary to examine carefully other possibilities open to us for entering into an interim arrangement with the Community on the clear understanding that any arrangement that might be negotiable would be a step towards membership and not a substitute for membership.[48]

What exacerbated the picture of an Irish government considering an alternative entry strategy were statements from those such as the minister for finance, Charles Haughey, to the effect that 'it would not be impossible for this country to become a member of the Common Market without Britain'.[49]

With Irish observers stressing the extent of de Gaulle's determination to deter the British from entering the EEC, it was becoming even more pertinent that the British did not lose momentum at this stage. London took seriously the prospect of a possible rupture with Ireland in the wake of the second veto, indicating that it wanted to know the extent to which 'the Taoiseach is interested in pursuing the offer of association or an "interim arrangement" which President de Gaulle put to Mr Lynch when they met in Paris earlier this month'.[50] The problem facing the British was that they could clearly not afford to probe the matter too deeply with the Irish; to do so would have been to put themselves in a more vulnerable position than they were already in. The French, in particular, might use a watering down of Britain's demands for full membership as a way of verifying the doubts de Gaulle had expressed in his continued opposition to British membership. A cautionary warning was sounded by Derek Day, who stated that while it certainly would be interesting to have an inside view of Irish intentions with regard to exploring alternatives to full membership:

> it is not suggested that this idea should be put to Mr Lynch or to the Irish government. As you know, the Prime Minister has come out strongly against association. This is the policy of Her Majesty's Government. We don't want to look as if we were weakening in any degree. If we say anything to the Irish, it might leak.[51]

THE END OF THE 'RED HERRING'

But the alarm in London that Ireland might acquire some form of associate membership while Britain remained outside the EEC was relatively short-lived. A consensus began to emerge in official circles at the turn of 1967–8 that, although on the surface the alternatives open to Ireland were certainly present, they were little more than deviations that led nowhere. As Norman Statham put it: 'the fact is that, whatever the French might mean by interim arrangement . . . I cannot see the Five going alone with anything like this if, as would be evident, it would be unwelcome to us.'[52] Paradoxically, however, while acknowledging that the vague suggestions put forward by the general amounted to nothing more than tactical manoeuvres designed to further confuse and thwart the British, officials in London observed that there was still a tendency on the Irish side 'to flirt with this possibility'.[53]

By the end of January 1968, London had less cause for concern, because the Irish, upon exploring these alternatives, found little or no substance behind them. McCann, for example, entered into discussions with officials in Paris and Brussels in order to ascertain the seriousness of the French offers. The discussions, it was reported to London, persuaded the Irish government that 'the French hint was not serious, but was probably dropped for tactical reasons', a way of dividing the applicants.[54] Britain was consequently keen to reiterate the importance of the four applicants remaining in unison, and strongly believed that all attempts to hinder the momentum towards full membership should be resisted. The Wilson administration had already begun to entertain thoughts of co-operation with the Benelux countries and was keen to show the Irish that Europe was not just represented by France although, ironically, the second veto had for all intents and purposes shown that, while de Gaulle was ensconced in the Elysée, it was.

A meeting between Wilson and Lynch in February 1968 provided just the forum in which to press the Irish 'to encourage the Taoiseach to maintain solidarity with the other applicants for membership by not giving away to pressure'.⁵⁵ London was at pains to emphasise the undesirability of anything less than full membership, which 'could only be a second best'. It was also adamant that any such offer amounted to nothing more than 'a red herring whose purpose is to divert attention from our applications for full membership'. It went on to warn that the French would never offer something without expecting something in return. Hence, if the Irish entertained the General's suggestions they would ultimately have to choose between the EEC and the Anglo-Irish Free Trade Area Agreement.⁵⁶

By this stage, however, it is clear that Britain was preaching to the converted. Emerging from the talks, Lynch's comments confirmed that the Irish were in full agreement with their British counterparts on what course of action to take next. When asked about the possibility of meeting with the 'friendly five', he volunteered that while obviously they would prefer French involvement, if this did not prove possible they 'would be willing' to meet in their absence. This was, Whitaker suggested

> the firmest statement which Mr Lynch has made about circumventing the French Veto. Up to now, as British officials have suggested more than once to me, Mr Lynch has been hedging his bets, refusing to say whether or not he was on the side of the angels. Angels, of course, are British.⁵⁷

So why had the Irish briefly toyed with de Gaulle's ambiguous offers? Furthermore, to what extent was it under British pressure that the Irish gave up on these suggestions? The most likely answer to the first question lies in the radical evolution that had taken place in Irish politics over the previous decade. Ireland was not so vulnerable and ignorant as was sometimes made out, and key policy-makers were well aware that de Gaulle probably viewed Dublin as no more than a pawn on his European chessboard. Yet, to dismiss such offers outright would have been detrimental in Ireland's position. Under pressure from party, polity and public, Lynch had to persevere, and be seen to be exploring all possible options. With increasing pressure to move away from the smothering embrace of Britain, it is no wonder that Irish officials went through the diplomatic motions. The majority of course knew what the outcome might be, but at the same time had to be seen to try.

In answer to the second question, British pressure to adhere to the policy of 'all or nothing' did not instigate but, more likely, reinforced Ireland's ultimate rejection of de Gaulle's proposals. Between the nebulous nature of the alternatives and the stark economic realities, it is no wonder that Ireland soon retreated back to Britain's original tactics. Careful pragmatic thinking permeated Irish opinion to a degree often overlooked, as an editorial in *The Irish Times* at the time demonstrates:

It would be unworthy to suppose that in his suggestions to the Taoiseach, the General was merely baiting the British, but no man in his position speaks merely for the benefit of his immediate audience. His remarks are meant to ricochet – and will already be bouncing off chambers in London and Washington as well as Brussels. . . .The French have no word for 'blarney' – no equally expressive word, at any rate. Diplomatic occasions resound with prose about the historic links between the participating countries. Let us, above all, make sure that we do not read too much into the politeness and consideration with which our delegation was received; the General's great-grandmother will not weigh one ounce in the scales when our entry chances come to be evaluated.[58]

This is telling, when one considers that it was penned not upon careful coaching from anyone but back at the beginning of November 1967.

CONCLUSION

To look at Britain's second application to the EEC in isolation is to ignore the interaction and communication that took place between the other applicants which ultimately shaped the entire process. Having examined the Irish case and the exchanges that took place between London and Dublin, one can draw four conclusions. The first relates to the motivating factors of applicant countries. Britain was not the only country slow to develop any sense of what might be termed 'European spirit'. Unlike the 'founding fathers', Ireland and Britain had little reason before 1960 to display any genuine interest in the formal process of European integration. Psychologically as well as physically, they were cut off from mainland Europe and had a different experience in war, so while Jean Monnet and Robert Schuman were drawing a blueprint for the future of Europe, Eamon de Valera, John Costello, Winston Churchill and Anthony Eden felt no such enthusiasm for the supranational approach to European integration undertaken on the continent. It was only the lack of viable alternatives that finally led them to seek admittance to the club that Monnet and Schuman had created. Having explored other options, notably the European Free Trade Association (EFTA), the British came to the realisation that the only possible course of action was to immerse themselves in the EEC. The Irish, even newer to the scene of contemplative reassessment, were quick to follow suit. Fundamentally, it was these differences that set the two islands apart from the Six, leading them to be classified as 'different', 'unsuitable' and even 'awkward'.

The second conclusion is that the Wilson administration – even if slow to commit to the idea of membership for complex reasons – once decided on membership, adhered rigidly to a policy of 'all or nothing'. 'Full' membership was sought; no half measures or watered down proposals such as 'association' would be entertained. A careful examination of the Irish application to join the EEC illustrates this. Time and time again, the Irish were cajoled into leaving behind their temptation to explore de Gaulle's alternatives. The British were adamant that 'interim arrangements' would not satisfy their requirements and therefore could be dismissed immediately. It is only through looking at Anglo-Irish diplomatic exchanges that one can fully understand British rejection of alternatives to full membership. It was neither a rash nor a regretted decision, but one taken after much deliberation.

Indeed, the third conclusion is that it was this rigid adherence to an 'all or nothing' policy that succeeded in the long term in securing a place for Britain in Europe. While it certainly did not reap any rewards for Wilson, it paved the way for Edward Heath to maintain that Britain was 'fully European' and had only ever been interested in 'full membership'. Had Wilson abandoned the notion of 'full membership' and been content to explore alternatives, it might well have been used as ammunition to paint Britain in a less than 'European' light in years to come. In this respect, Wilson's application to join the EEC can be classified a 'successful failure'.

The final conclusion is that Britain and Ireland were both committed to a policy of entering 'together, if at all possible'. At first one might think this just an Irish plea, but the British were similarly keen on this entry strategy. There were visible signs of apprehension at times over Ireland's flirtation with de Gaulle's offer of 'association' and 'interim arrangement'. Thus, Whitehall released a steady flow of reasons why the Irish should refrain from entertaining such thoughts. On both sides of the sea, at different times and for sometimes very different reasons, Ireland and Britain feared that one but not the other would gain entry to the EEC. It is this dimension more than any other that not only dominated, but also defined and shaped Anglo-Irish policy towards Europe during the Wilson era. As Robin O'Neill, private secretary to both George Thomson and Fred Mulley (ministers responsible for EEC affairs during the 1960s), points out, 'each country was indeed afraid that the other might get in first: but the real fear surely was the first in might then spoil the chances of the other, either deliberately or unintentionally'.[59]

Notes

1 Douglas Hurd, address to the Institute of European Affairs, 21 Mar. 1994, quoted in P. Gillespie (ed.), *Britain's European question: the issues for Ireland* (Dublin, 1996), p. 7.

2 Interview with Thomas Whitaker (Secretary to the Department of Finance, 1956–1969), 19 Feb. 2001.

3 Public Record Office (hereafter PRO): FCO 75/1, Sir Con O'Neill's report on the negotiations for entry into the European Community, June 1970–Jan. 1972, sent to Sir Alec Douglas Home.

4   J. Blanchard quoted in B. Chubb, *The government and politics of Ireland* (London, 1992), p. 6.
5   *Dáil Éireann Parliamentary Debates* (1934) vol. 53, col. 62.
6   F. S. L. Lyons, *Ireland since the famine* (London, 1971), pp. 557–8.
7   G. Murphy, 'Ireland's view of Western Europe in the 1950s' in M. Kennedy and J. Morrison Skelly (eds), *Irish foreign policy 1919–66* (Dublin, 2000), p. 250.
8   P. Keatinge, 'Ireland and the world, 1957–82', in F. Litton (ed.), *Unequal achievement* (Dublin, 1982), pp. 225–40 (p. 228).
9   *The Irish Times*, 12 May 1971.
10 National Archives Ireland: Department of the Taoiseach (hereafter NAI DT), S 15281–D, interim report of the Committee of Secretaries, 18 Jan. 1957.
11 Interview with Whitaker.
12 See, for example, N. Beloff, *The general says no: Britain's exclusion from Europe* (Harmondsworth, 1963).
13 Lemass quoted in D. Keogh, *Ireland and Europe 1919–1989: a diplomatic and political history* (Cork, 1990), pp. 232–3.
14 Interview with Whitaker.
15 NAI: DT S 16877/Q/61.
16 Interview with Whitaker.
17 Between July 1961 and April 1962, Ireland, the United Kingdom, Denmark and Norway had applied to join the EEC.
18 T. D. Williams, 'Irish foreign policy 1949–1969', in J. J. Lee, *Ireland* (Dublin, 1979), p. 136.
19 PRO: FCO 30/230, MEK 4/1/4, Part A, Background Brief sent by Gallagher to Ratford, 27 Apr. 1967.
20 Ibid.
21 PRO: FCO 30/230, MEK 4/1/4, Part B, speaking notes for use by Snelling, sent by Smith to Cambridge, 30 Oct. 1967.
22 *Cork Examiner*, 15 Feb. 1968
23 PRO: FCO 30/231, MEK 4/1/4, Part B, biographical note on Jack Lynch.
24 *Cork Examiner*, 15 Feb. 1968
25 PRO: FCO 30/230, MEK 4/1/4, Part A, telegram number 97, Gilchrist to Commonwealth Office, 6 Nov. 1967.
26 PRO: FCO 30/230, MEK 4/1/4, Part A, telegram number 38 Gilchrist to Commonwealth Office, 18 Oct. 1967.
27 Quoted in *The Irish Times*, 14 Aug. 1967
28 PRO: FCO 30/230, MEK 4/1/4, Gallagher to Snelling, 7 July 1967.
29 PRO: FCO 30/230, MEK 5/1/4, Part A, Lynch to Wilson, 10 July 1967.
30 *The Irish Times*, 14 Aug. 1967
31 *Sunday Independent*, 9 July 1967
32 PRO: FCO 30/230, MEK 4/1/4, Part A, Wilson to Lynch, 29 July 1967.
33 Wilson had, at the turn of 1967, undertaken a 'probe' of capitals with Brown, to ascertain 'whether or not to activate arrangements for entry'. See H. Wilson, *The Labour government 1964–1967: a personal record* (London, 1971), pp. 327–44 (p. 328).

34 PRO: FCO 30/230, MEK 4/1/4, Part A, Lynch to Wilson, 17 Aug. 1967.
35 *The Irish Times*, 14 Aug. 1967
36 Interview with Whitaker.
37 Statement by the taoiseach to *The Irish Times*, 6 Nov. 1967.
38 *Irish Press*, 6 Nov. 1967
39 PRO: FCO 30/230, MEK 4/1/4 Part A, telegram number 97, Gilchrist to the Commonwealth Office, 6 Nov. 1967.
40 Ibid.
41 PRO: FCO 30/230, MEK 4/1/4, Part A, telegram number 1107, Ledwidge to Foreign Office, 7 Nov. 1967.
42 Ibid.
43 Ibid.
44 PRO: FCO 30/230, MEK 4/1/4, Part A, speaking notes prepared for Snelling at the meeting of the Anglo-Irish Economic Committee on 9 and 10 Nov. 1967.
45 Ibid.
46 PRO: FCO 30/230, PMEK 4/1/4, Part A, Galsworthy to Statham, 10 Nov. 1967.
47 PRO: FCO 30/230, MEK 4/1/4, Part A, Gilchrist to Thompson, 12 Dec. 1967.
48 PRO: FCO 30/230, MEK 4/1/4 Part A, Lynch quoted in Gilchrist's letter to Thompson, 12 Dec. 1967.
49 Quoted in *The Irish Times*, 27 July 1967
50 PRO: FCO 30/230, MEK 4/1/4, Part A, Williams to Andrews, 29 Nov. 1967.
51 PRO: FCO 30/230, MEK 4/1/4, Part A, Day to Williams, 30 Nov. 1967.
52 PRO: FCO 30/231, MEK 4/1/4, Part B, Statham to Audland, 28 Dec. 1967.
53 PRO: FCO 30/231, MEK 4/1/4, Part B, Jordan-Moss to Audland, 8 Jan. 1968.
54 PRO: FCO 30/231, MEK 4/1/4, Part B, Overton to Statham, 31 Jan. 1968.
55 PRO: FCO 30/231, MEK 4/1/4, Part B, background notes to the Wilson and Lynch meeting 14 Feb. 1968, sent by Smith to Cambridge
56 PRO: FCO 30/231, MEK 4/1/4, Part B, Brief by the Commonwealth Office – taoiseach's visit 14 Feb. 1968, Smith to Cambridge.
57 Quoted in *The Irish Times*, 15 Feb. 1968
58 *The Irish Times*, 6 Nov. 1967
59 Author's correspondence with Robin O'Neill, 31 May 2001

CULTURE

CHAPTER 12

A Sailor on the Seas of Faith

The Individual and the Church in
The Voyage of Máel Dúin

Elva Johnston

The early medieval Irish imagined a landscape that came into being through names, names that formed an historical palimpsest.¹ Throughout the island ecclesiastical names coexisted, overlaid and sometimes replaced those of the pre-Christian past.² But naming the land was not enough for, obviously, the island was surrounded by an ocean, one that was only partly known and whose limits receded far and away. Ireland lay at the gates of the unknown. The familiar world of classical geography, the globe made up of the three continents of Europe, Asia and Africa, was enclosed by uncharted waters and Ireland lay on their boundaries.³ These boundaries were open to exploration and Irish Christians assiduously set out to know and to name the seascape surrounding their island. Knowledge and naming went hand in hand.

They did so in at least two separate but interconnecting ways: one empirical, the other imaginary. Thus, Irish clerics physically explored the north Atlantic. For example, the ninth-century Irish geographer Dicuill gives an important insight into the motivations and accomplishments of Irish clerical voyagers in his *Liber de mensura orbis terrae*.⁴ In a famous and memorable passage, he depicts Irish monks on a scientific expedition to the then unsettled Iceland closely observing what they regarded as unusual physical and astronomical data.⁵ These and similar empirical observations fed into intellectual speculations and into explorations that took place in the imaginations of writers. Such writers constructed narratives that transmuted real events and actual maritime experiences. They wove actuality together with urgent religious and social concerns. These included, very broadly, the organisation of Irish society, the role of the church within it and the duties of individuals and their kindreds towards the secular and ecclesiastical.

From as early as the seventh century, tales known as *immrama*, literally 'rowings-about', began to be developed in response to these concerns.

Immrama, unlike many other Irish tale types, are of patently Christian origin and the exploits of their heroes are set in the Christian era.[6] The *immram* genre it draws on a variety of influences. Thus, the literary geography of the overseas paradise is influenced to some degree by Christian apocrypha,[7] and, in a very general way, by classical examples such as the *Aeneid* and, less directly, the *Odyssey*,[8] as well as by native Irish otherworld tales known as *echtrai*.[9] In the *immram* the intrepid monastic voyager, not the pagan warrior, is usually the hero. The outlines of the *immram* genre can be clearly seen in Adomnán's tale of the cleric and voyager, Cormac, in the late seventh-century *Vita Columbae*.[10] Cormac's quest for a *terra secreta* on the ocean is a deft blend of the believable and miraculous. Similarly, full-scale *immrama* drew creatively on the known and the imagined, albeit in very individual measures. The voyagers of these tales, starting from Ireland, 'row about' several islands before, generally, returning once again to Ireland. The structure is usually circular, the voyage bound in by a shared point of departure and arrival.

While most of the extant voyage tales are written in Irish, the single most influential example is the Latin *Nauigatio Sancti Brendani Abbatis*.[11] This polished narrative was probably written in Ireland during the second half of the eighth century, or at the latest towards the beginning of the ninth.[12] The *Nauigatio* is a *speculum monachorum*, a mirror for the ideal monastic life. Brendan visits islands that explore the best way for an abbot to create, and a monk to live in, the ideal monastic community. The saint's journey is measured by the canonical hours and the paschal cycle. The text is structurally unified but appears to draw on a rich tradition. Beneath the apparently naïve surface, the *Nauigatio* treats land and ocean as allegorical and as essentially religious in nature: the voyagers' adventures point towards religious ideals and states.[13] This treatment of land and sea is a common feature of the voyage tale genre. Over time, the seemingly realistic element, which is prominent in the *Nauigatio*, was largely replaced by the fantastic and the obviously symbolic. The *Nauigatio*'s masterful mix of the real with the imaginary was replaced by one where the latter became dominant. Different islands came to stand in for differing social and/or religious experiences in ways that were clearer but not subtler. Through their idealised utopias or extreme dystopias, the writers of the *immrama* were able to express their ideologies and set up mirrors to the ordering of contemporary society. Islands were states of mind and cultural statements. They could also exist at the borders of this known world and other worlds. They faced at once towards earth, and towards heaven and hell.

Immram Curaig Maíle Dúin, or 'The Voyage of Máel Dúin' uses its ocean and ocean islands as a social laboratory.[14] As its title suggests, *Immram Maíle Dúin*[15] is written in Irish. It more than likely dates from towards the end of the ninth century or the first part of the tenth.[16] Like other typical examples of its genre, *Immram Maíle Dúin* draws on a variety of sources. The allusions to earlier tales within its narrative are often skilful and suggest a target audience that was familiar with the tales that generated these allusions. Its author was clearly steeped in Christian texts, knew at least some classical literature and was very familiar with vernacular tales. *Immram Maíle Dúin* contains references to the Old Testament, the Gospels, the Psalms, as well as the *Aeneid*, *Nauigatio Sancti Brendani* and the Irish tale *Immram Brain mac Febail*. These references range from the integral to the superficial. The central role of borrowing and allusion combined with the episodic nature of the tale, something implicit in its very genre, may lead to a dismissal of the narrative as a hodgepodge. This is misleading, for *Immram Maíle Dúin* is well worked out and thematically consistent. Despite verbal and thematic echoes of other works, it manages to avoid being merely slavish.[17] The narrative is profoundly textual and, in many ways, demonstrates the maturity of the genre. The author is confident enough to play with its *topoi* and he frequently subverts the expectations of his audience. Within its episodic framework, Máel Dúin's adventure is cleverly structured. This revolves around a series of opposing categories, usually expressed as different islands, very much in the structuralist mode. For instance, warfare is opposed to peace and virginity to sexual licence.

The tale takes its eponymous hero through many otherworld islands that vary from the fairly unremarkable to the outright fantastic. These disparate scenes are united by the intention of the author. This voyage tale articulates different ways of organising society, with Ireland as the always implied point of comparison. Thus, it is no surprise that the narrative covers many aspects of early medieval Irish life, for this is a text that is pre-eminently concerned with society and the correct ordering of the communities within it. These aspects include the role of women, the relationship of the warrior to those in authority, and the place of the church. Its otherworld islands are not, in the main, places of mystical experience, but are the sites of social experiment. They exist on the borders between the real and the otherworldly; text and context are not collapsed but brought into a form of dialogue. This dialogue is externalised into an otherworldly island landscape.

The tale itself is long as well as episodic. It is not repetitious, for its conservative, almost certainly clerical, author had a large number of concerns. It is hardly surprising then that Máel Dúin visits an almost Polynesian number of islands during his adventures. The theme that holds the tale together, however, is the role of the church in Irish society and here the author shows himself to be both highly critical and deeply idealistic. It is useful to summarise the main points of the tale before looking in greater depth at the author's treatment of this theme.

Its hero, Máel Dúin, is the son of a nun raped by Ailill, a member of Eóganacht Ninussa. The latter were a branch of the ruling dynasty of Munster and were associated with the Aran Islands.[18] Ailill is eventually killed in battle, fulfilling the dictum that those who live by the sword die by it. The nun is, however, a friend of the wife of the king of Munster. The queen takes the child and raises him as one of her own children. A typical Irish hero, the young Máel Dúin outdoes the other young men at the royal court in prowess and appearance during his youth. In jealousy, one of his companions accuses the hero of not knowing his father, highlighting the importance of paternity in an agnatic society. Máel Dúin confronts the queen and she eventually tells him the name of his true father. But an ideal foster-mother, she regards Máel Dúin as one of her own children. Nevertheless, Máel Dúin travels to the territory of Eóganacht Ninussa and discovers that his father has been killed by marauders from over the sea. Máel Dúin is incited to seek vengeance by a cleric and with the help of a druid plans a murderous voyage. The druid hedges in this journey with a taboo: Máel Dúin must take only a certain number of companions with him to complete his mission of vengeance. However, three of Máel Dúin's foster-brothers accompany him against his will. As a result he is driven into the ocean by a storm. On the ocean he visits many islands – some horrifying, others paradisial and some inhabited by clerics. It is an adventure of spiritual growth, in which Máel Dúin must escape, among other things, the pleasures of a land of women. Eventually, he meets a hermit, originally from Tory Island, who tells him that he must learn to forgive his enemies. Máel Dúin returns to Ireland and he and his enemies forgive each other. Thus, Máel Dúin reverses the violence and sins of his father and rejects the values of the blood feud. Overall, Máel Dúin's voyage is almost a *Bildungsroman* with the hero experiencing a spiritual growth. Ultimately, he accepts that his martial exploits must be dictated by the needs of forgiveness and peace.

A great deal of the narrative's organisation depends on the framing tale. This is made up of a long prologue, which tells of Máel Dúin's conception, youth and attempt at revenge, and a shorter epilogue that acts as a brief but telling closure. The frame-tale bears a particularly important relationship to the rest of the narrative because the themes elaborated and developed throughout the text are first indicated in the prologue and brought to their highly ideological conclusions in the epilogue. For instance, in the prologue, Máel Dúin's special status as a hero is expressed through his parentage. His father is a violent warrior, whose epithet is *ochar agha* 'edge of battle'. Yet he is also a *tigerna* 'lord' and loyal vassal of the king of Munster. His non-violent mother is a *banairchinnech*, the female superior of a community of nuns.[19] Máel Dúin, unlike the typical *immram* hero is a layman but his parentage sets him apart from his fellows. Already, at his very conception, there is a hint at the oppositions between secular and ecclesiastical that Máel Dúin will eventually mediate and transcend through his adoption of a Christian ethic of living. The forced act of sex between his parents is a botched foreshadowing of this and Máel Dúin's father, Ailill, is perilously close to being labelled a *díbergach* 'bandit'. *Díbergaig*, described as 'sons of death', preyed off settled communities and are roundly condemned in ecclesiastical documents.[20] Ironically, the *díbergach*-like Ailill, who rapes a nun in a church, is himself killed by actual *díbergaig* in a church. Lay society, as such, is not openly condemned, but the chaos resulting from an improper relationship between the warrior and the church brings about the tragedy of rape and violent death. Much of *Immram Maíle Dúin* is concerned with strategies for avoiding this tragedy. The author seems to suggest that only people living life together in a truly Christian community provide the solution.

The nature of these Christian communities is of crucial importance within the tale. The old, long-established, churches are shown to be as much in moral decline as lay society. Decline is a major concern of this tale, for its pessimistic author views Irish society as violent, venal and chaotic. The church, rather than acting against these trends, is seen as contributing to them. Significantly, it is a member of a church community who sets in motion the action of the narrative. He is named Briccne, and is described as *nemthengthach*, 'poison-tongued'. The name Briccne is reminiscent of the very similar Bricriu. Here is an obvious echo of Bricriu *Nemthenga*, the pagan 'poison tongue' who serves as a catalyst for conflict in several incidents associated with the Ulster Cycle, especially in *Fled Bricrend*.[21] The similarity of the name and epithet of both characters is too close to be coincidental. In fact, Bricriu is sometimes known as Briccne.[22] Furthermore, they share the same function: they incite action. Briccne, contrary to the Christian ethic of forgiveness, provokes Máel Dúin to avenge his father's violent death in the following scene:

> I n-araile aimsir iar sin ro batar lín oclach i relic chille Dubcluana i cor liac. Arsised iarum a cos Maíle Duin for folaig n-athloisce na hecailsi 7 ba tairrsi no leicedh an licc. Alaile fer nemthengthach do muindtir na cille, Briccne a ainm, asbertsidhi fri Male Duin, bad ferr ol se bad a digail dognethea inn fir ro loiscedh sund inas cor liac tara cnamaib loma loistighi.[23]

[At another time, after that, a group of warriors was in the graveyard of the church of Dubchluain, casting stones. Then Máel Dúin's foot was planted on the burnt ruin of the church and it was over it that he threw the stone. A certain poison-tongued man of the community of the church, named Briccne, said to Máel Dúin: 'It would be better', he said, 'if you were to revenge the man who was burnt there in place of throwing stones over his bare burnt bones'.]

These bones belong to Máel Dúin's father. The burnt church's very name, Dubchluain, can be translated as black meadow. *Cluain* is a common element in church names. Clonmacnoise and Clondalkin are examples and there are many more.[24] This suggests that Dubchluain could be interpreted as 'Black church'. Briccne seems to inhabit an anti-church rather than a church and its name seems to function as the outward sign of Briccne's inner moral blackness. It is also possible to identify the Dubchluain of *Immram Maíle Dúin* with an actual place within the ambit of Eóganacht Ninussa.[25] In fact, the presence of a real church of Dubchluain would strengthen the dichotomy between appearance and reality implicit in the entire episode. Dubchluain seems to be an ordinary west Munster church, but is really the locale for a moral vacuum. Dubchluain is both an actual and a spiritual wasteland. It is the opposite of the bare desert-like place, the *deserta/dísert* where the holy man or woman seeks God.

In effect Dubchluain fails to fulfil the legal requirements of a church of good standing, for it is ruined and its community, if much of it is left, does not seem to be engaging in pastoral duties.[26] Briccne's preaching is hardly of the sort envisaged in the vernacular legal material. He suggests that vengeance would be the proper course for Máel Dúin to follow. There is no hint, here, of a Christian ethic of forgiveness. Briccne is not without motivation, however. His church was destroyed by *díbergaig* from over the sea, and his inciting of violence between lay warriors may represent the universalisation of his feud with lay society. The cycle of feud is an important theme in *Immram Maíle Dúin*. Instead of attempting to end violence, Briccne tries to create more mayhem. The church's ruin dramatically highlights the results of *díbergach* violence, a violence that lies outside the social control of kingdom and kindred. Additional implications swirl around Dubchluain. There is another word, *cluain*, which has the meaning of deception, falsehood, and trickery.[27] This is mainly attested much later in the history of Irish, especially from the seventeenth century, but there is a possible example in *Acallam na Senórach* and Carey has plausibly argued for its use in *Tochmarc Becfhola*.[28] Briccne is a member of the church of 'Black Trickery'. The name of the church may have evoked a whole range of implications for the audience of the tale. The Devil is the Father of Lies (Jn 8:44) and Dubchluain follows a devilish ethic of feud. It could be argued that the failed cleric Briccne tricks Máel Dúin, through a false moral authority, into following an ungodly quest for revenge. Máel Dúin's *immram* follows its course from the ruins of a spiritually sterile underworld into a limitless and liminal ocean back to the gateways of Ireland. The hero's quest begins in an echo of hell on earth.

Significantly, Máel Dúin's next visit is to a physical wasteland, the rocky and remote Burren in Corco Mruad. The Irish word *bairenn/boirenn* refers literally to a rock district. There, Máel Dúin seeks the advice of a druid, Nuca. Oskamp has argued that Nuca is simply a representative of the international type of the wise man.[29] On the surface, he does seem to fulfil this type for he is described as a *sénaire* 'seer',[30] but this is undercut in the narrative. Nuca attempts to help Máel Dúin's quest for revenge, thus following the example of Briccne. The druid and the poison-tongued cleric are equated and it is insinuated that the Christian Briccne is in reality no different from the pagan druid. There are further possible interpretations. If the church of Dubchluain is a centre of 'Black Trickery', the druid's action in helping Máel Dúin might imply that he is following the work of the Devil. The Irish conversion to Christianity is shown to be just skin-deep. This is one of the clearest signs of the author's disaffection with the Irish church.

This disaffection is partly expressed through the manipulation of various *topoi* of the voyage tale genre. In *Immram Maíle Dúin*, the hero's foster-brothers join the voyage, despite the druid's advice about the correct number of passengers. Here the author of the *immram* is particularly clever. In the *Nauigatio* and elsewhere the extra passengers are, by implication, a barrier to the will of God.[31] In this *immram* they ironically open the way to God's will and stymie the actions set in motion from Dubchluain. The latecomers' presence in the boat insures that Máel Dúin's search for revenge will fail, because they break the magical number of passengers prescribed by the druid. By breaching the taboo the passengers open up the possibility for ultimate salvation. The narrative expresses itself with forceful dramatic irony when two of Máel Dúin's companions declare as they approach the fort of his enemies:

> ... as diriuch don-fuc Dia 7 ro ghab Dia ar crannán remoinn. Tiagam 7 orgem an dun sa oro foillsigh Dia duinn ar naimdiu.[32] [... it is straight that God has brought us, and God was leading our boat before us. Let us go and destroy this fort since God has revealed our enemies to us.]

In fact, God has had nothing to do with the proceedings. It is Briccne, the highly dubious cleric-trickster, who revealed these enemies, and it is Nuca, the druid, who prepared Máel Dúin and his companions for the voyage. As the boat is suddenly swept out to sea, away from the fortress, Máel Dúin, unconsciously hits on the truth:

> Ba hand adbert Mael Duin, leicidh in noi ana tost cen imrum 7 an leth bus ail do Dia a brith, beraigh.[33] [Máel Dúin said: 'leave the boat at rest, without rowing, and wherever it should please God to bring it, let him bring it'.]

Máel Dúin, at this stage, is not aware of the full significance of what he is saying and he immediately blames his foster-brothers for breaking the druid's prohibition concerning the number of voyagers. Yet, for the audience it is an important marker and introduces one of the central ideas of the tale: individuals should hand themselves over to God's providence as opposed to seeking human-inspired revenge. The phrase *cen imrum* 'without rowing' is almost certainly a conscious reference to the Irish idea that a man may be set adrift on the sea for committing a criminal offence. Thus, judgement is left to God.[34] The idea of setting adrift became a theme for representing submission to the will of God,[35] and *Immram Maíle Dúin* is in this tradition. Máel Dúin's offence is his obsession with *dígal* 'revenge'. God's judgement sees Máel Dúin encounter many islands and wonders on the ocean. The hero returns to the shores of Ireland only when he is converted from the ethic of revenge to one of forgiveness and trust in God.

Throughout his *immram*, the perfect life of pilgrim and penitent ascetics contrasts with the immorality of clerics such as Briccne and the barren land inhabited by the druid Nuca. The ascetics of *Immram Maíle Dúin* appear to be influenced by the figure of Paul the Hermit from the *Nauigatio*, a character who is indebted, in turn, to Coptic traditions of ascetic renunciation, perhaps via Jerome's Life of Paul.[36] Máel Dúin encounters three such on his journey. All three are clothed only by their hair like Paul the hermit.[37] The first two function as foreshadowings of the third, the hermit who originally came from Tory Island.[38] The resemblances between this hermit and Paul are obvious. Both are motivated to go on their journey by a voice from a grave; both set their boat adrift on the ocean and allow God's will to guide them to their island retreat; both are fed there by a friendly otter. Yet as men they are different. Paul the hermit is a perfect ascetic. The hermit from Tory, although living a life of spiritual perfection when Máel Dúin meets him, was a sinful man in the past. His sin was *taiscid* 'hoarding'.[39] Greed is an important motif in the narrative. One of Máel Dúin's foster-brothers is killed by a supernatural cat when he tries to steal a golden necklace that symbolises the temptations of worldly riches.[40] Moreover, the hermit not only hoarded, he also stole church property. His sin mirrors the more obvious destruction of church property caused by *díbergaig* and men like Máel Dúin's father. The hermit's tale gives the themes of greed, theft, and redemption an added depth. The hermit's previous life had been as a dishonest and thieving monastic cook, but he has been converted to religious life. This hermit sums up the narrative thrust of *Immram Maíle Dúin* when he tells the hero:

Asbert an senoir friusom iar sin: ricfaidh uile do for tír 7 an fer ro marb t'athairseo, a Máel Duin, fonngébaigh a ndun ar for cind 7 níro marbaigh, acht tabruidh dilghudh dó, fo bithin robar saersi Dia di morguasachtaib imdaib 7 basa fir bidhbuidh báis do chena.[41]

[After that the old man said to them: 'You will all reach your country and the man who killed your father, O Máel Dúin, you will find him in a fortress before you and do not kill him, but forgive him, for God has saved you from many great dangers, and you too are men deserving of death'.]

Only in this way can Máel Dúin end the cycle of *díberg* and death. The hermit reverses the action of Briccne, a cleric who has allowed feud to take precedence over Christian forgiveness. Máel Dúin takes the hermit's injunction to heart. Not long after leaving him the voyagers come to a fertile island and see a falcon 'like the falcons of Ireland'.[42] Only one more island awaits them, that of the killers of Máel Dúin's father. Máel Dúin overhears the leader of these men declare that he will welcome Máel Dúin. One link of the chain of violence is broken. *Dígal* 'revenge' is replaced by *dílgud* 'forgiveness'. Máel Dúin's potential enemies make the hero welcome and he responds in kind. The narrative ends when one of Máel Dúin's companions, Diurán, visits Armagh and places the fragment of a silver net, a memento of the voyage, on the altar of the church there.[43] The action is a fitting symbol of the right ordering that is possible in Irish society; moreover, it rounds off a tale that had begun with an improper visit by Máel Dúin's father to a church, resulting in rape; it acts as an effective foil to the actions of the failed cleric Briccne at the ruined church of Dubchluain.

Immram Maíle Dúin is a rich and complex narrative and my discussion of its treatment of the church in society is by no means exhaustive. This discussion leads on to the question of the tale's social context and what, if anything, can be learned of its author. Its first editor, the great Whitley Stokes, remarked that the author must have been a layman, for otherwise he would not have criticised the church so trenchantly.[44] The criticism is certainly trenchant, but this does not prove lay authorship. In fact, the author was almost certainly a cleric. The reference in *Immram Maíle Dúin* to the *Aeneid*, for example, strongly points to a basic schooling in Latin, something that was available in a monastic environment.

There are further pointers. During the eighth and ninth centuries the Céli Dé sought to reinvigorate the religious standards of the Irish church. Reformist circles were particularly strong in the southern half of Ireland.[45] The church attacked in *Immram Maíle Dúin* is the older church, which is portrayed as lacking in moral authority, and this older church was a focus for Céle Dé criticism.[46] The hermit from Tory's description of his former church presents a picture of worldly wealth that contrasts with his life as an ascetic. The asceticism of the various hermits on the islands is praised unreservedly. The hermit from Tory, rather than Briccne, is the mirror of the perfect man of God. The author of *Immram Maíle Dúin* suggests that asceticism is one of the important characteristics of the ideal church, and this is consonant with the Céle Dé philosophy. On the other hand, *peregrinatio* or overseas pilgrimage was criticised by the Céli Dé. The text implicitly praises Máel Dúin as a type of temporary *peregrinus* and the hermit from Tory as a permanent one. This implies that while the author of *Immram Maíle Dúin* was heavily influenced by the Céli Dé, he did not necessarily buy the whole package.

Some consideration must also be given to the audience of this text, a consideration that might cast more light on the author. *Immram Maíle Dúin*, like the *Nauigatio*, explores the idea of communities, what form they should take, and how they should function. The hero is an aristocrat who is literally at sea in a world suffering violent upheaval. The *immram*'s communities are both secular and religious. The church of Armagh and the court of the Eóganacht king at Cashel are the two centres of stability in the text. Francis John Byrne has argued that the tale may refer to events in the eighth century, when the Eóganacht kings were reasonably strong.[47] This does not convincingly match the state of social disorder depicted in the tale. Munster in the second half of the ninth and early tenth centuries better fits the setting of this tale. Lawlessness and general instability seem to have followed in the wake of Viking incursions – a lawlessness exacerbated by the Eóganacht kings' failure in dealing with the simultaneous threats of the Vikings, the breakaway kingdom of Osraige and the ambitions of the Uí Néill. The text conveys a powerful image of a disintegrating society at ecclesiastical and secular levels. The inhabitants of one of the islands that Máel Dúin visits react with terror to the approach of the voyagers' boat.[48] The incident may be an exaggerated image of the disorganised state of Eóganacht Munster and its openness to Viking raids. Moreover, the idea that the raiders who killed Máel Dúin's father came from across the sea makes sense in Viking Age Ireland. The *Immram* suggests that a conversion to greater asceticism in the church, perhaps on a Céle Dé model, a willingness to forgive old enemies and unite against the forces of social disorder, and an adherence to the authority of a paradigmatic royal court provide the answer. The elitism of these suggestions is underlined by the fact that the only non-elite person specifically referred to in the narrative, an *aithech* 'rent-paying peasant' is described as both dead and a sinner.[49] Unfortunately for the Eóganacht kings, for whom this text is arguably a piece of special pleading, chaos and decline continued, until they were supplanted.

Throughout this essay I have continually referred to the author of *Immram Maíle Dúin*. This is not to deny the multiplicity of narrative and performance, which lies behind any medieval Irish tale. *Immram Maíle Dúin*, for example, refers to two conflicting traditions regarding the number of the voyagers.[50] Yet, it seems to me that *Immram Maíle Dúin* is the unified composition of a single individual. Stylistically, it is unremarkable and does not attain the literary merit of either the *Nauigatio* or sections of *Immram Brain*. Oskamp has concluded that *Immram Maíle Dúin* 'is a literary text, and not the written form of an oral tradition, transmitted for ages and ages'.[51] This is largely true. The author of the text has drawn on other *written* tales in his composition. It is this use of previous tales that elevates the quality of the narrative.

This quality is best seen in the tale's thematic sophistication. Its author uses the voyage tale genre to express his concerns about the church and its relations with lay society and the implicit participation of churchmen in lay violence. Through the adventures of Máel Dúin, a hero conceived in violence, he casts a critical eye on his contemporaries. The church of *Immram Maíle Dúin* may dominate Ireland but it is in urgent need of improvement. Máel Dúin's fateful voyage leads him to renounce violent values in favour of faith and forgiveness. Yet these values are easier to find amid the dangers of the ocean rather than in the named and known landscape of Ireland and its churches.

NOTES

This essay is a shorter version of a substantially longer piece that is planned for future publication.

1   There is a huge primary literature concerned with the naming of places in Irish. The best example is the genre of short anecdotes dedicated to explaining placenames, *dindshenchas*. For numerous instances see E. Gwynn (ed.), *The metrical dindshenchas* IV, (Dublin, 1924).

2   A remarkable number of place names contain ecclesiastical elements. *Cell* 'Kil', signifying a church is very common. For examples see E. Hogan, *Onomasticon Goedelicum locorum et tribuum Hiberniae et Scotiae* (Dublin, 1910), pp. 172–215.

3   A useful, if somewhat dated, study of classical geography is J. O. Thomson, *History of ancient geography* (New, York 1965); the reception of this classical tradition by medieval Christianity is studied in detail by N. Lozovsky, *'The Earth is our book': geographical knowledge in the Latin West ca.400–1000* (Michigan, 2000); a good example of Irish knowledge of these traditions is found in the work of Dicuill, *Dicuili Liber de Mensura Orbis Terrae*, J. J. Tierney (ed.) (Dublin, 1967), esp. I § 2.

4   *Dicuili Liber*, Tierney (ed.) (1967).

5   Ibid., VII §§ 11–13; for a re-edition of VII §§6–15 see D. Howlett, 'Dicuill on the islands of the north', *Peritia* XIII (1999), 127–34.

6   The origins of the *immrama* are discussed by K. Hughes, 'On an Irish litany of pilgrim saints compiled *c*.800', *Analecta Bollandiana* LXXVII (1959), 305–31; K. Hughes, 'The changing theories and practice of Irish pilgrimage', *Journal of Ecclesiastical History* XI (1960), 143–51; W. F. Thrall, 'Clerical sea pilgrimages and the imrama', in *The Manly anniversary studies in language and literature* (Chicago, 1923), pp. 276–83, is a much earlier statement of the idea; a more recent exposition of the Christian nature of the *immrama* is D. N. Dumville, '*Echtrae* and *Immram*: some problems of definition', *Ériu* XXVII (1976), 73–94.

7   M. Esposito, 'An apocryphal "Book of Enoch and Elias" as a possible source of the *Navigatio Sancti Brendani*', *Celtica* V (1960), 192–206; Dumville, '*Echtrae* and *immram*', 79, has noted the influence of the *Visio Sancti Pauli*.

8   H. Zimmer, 'Keltische Beiträge II: Brendans Meerfahrt', *Zeitschrift für deutsches Altertum* XXXIII (1889), 328–38, suggested that the Irish *immrama* were directly dependent on the voyages in *Aeneid* III–V; this has been demolished by W. F. Thrall, 'Virgil's Aeneid and the Irish imrama: Zimmer's theory', *Modern Philology* XIV (1917–18), 449–74.

9   The priority of the *echtrai* is discussed by Dumville, '*Echtrae* and *immram*', 73–94.
10 *Vita Columbae*, I §6.
11 The text has been edited, somewhat unsatisfactorily, by Selmer, *Navigatio Sancti Brendani Abbatis from early Latin manuscripts*, C. Selmer (ed.) (Notre Dame, 1959); J. J. O'Meara, *The voyage of Saint Brendan: journey to the promised land* (1976), is an excellent translation.
12 Selmer 'Introduction', *Navigatio*, xxvii–xxix, argues for a tenth-century date and a continental origin in Lotharingia. However, there is significant divergence in the tenth-century copies of the text and J. Carney, 'Review of Selmer, *Navigatio*', *Medium Aevum* XXXII (1963), 37–44, suggests a date in the first half of the ninth century and an Irish origin; M. Esposito, 'L'édition de la "Nauigatio S. Brendani"', *Scriptorium* XV (1961), 288, also affirms a ninth-century date and an Irish provenance; I. Orlandi, *Navigatio Sancti Brendani: Introduzione* (Milan, 1968), pp. 72–3, 131–60, suggests that the tale dates from the second quarter of the ninth century and that it was written in Ireland; D. N. Dumville, 'Two approaches to the dating of "Navigatio Sancti Brendani"', *Studi Medievali* XXIX (1988), 95–9, uses an ingenious genealogical political argument, centring on the Eóganacht Locha Léin, to date the text back to eighth-century Ireland; S. Mac Mathúna, 'The structure and transmission of early Irish voyage literature', in H. L. C. Tristram (ed.), *Texte und Zeittiefe* (Tübingen, 1994), p. 315, n. 7, tentatively supports a continental origin.
13 A classic examination, *inter alia*, is Carney, 'Review', 37–44; the monastic allegory of the text has been explored by C. Bourgealt, 'The monastic archetype in the Navigatio of St Brendan', *Monastic Studies* XIV (1983), 109–21, and D. A. Bray, 'Allegory in the *Navigatio Sancti Brendani*', *Viator* XXVI (1995), 1–10; the most illuminating recent study is T. O'Loughlin, 'Distant islands: the topography of holiness in the *Nauigatio Sancti Brendani*', in *The medieval mystical tradition England, Ireland and Wales* (Woodbridge, 1999), pp. 1–20.
14 The prose tale occurs in two recensions. The most important editions are 'The Voyage of Mael Duin', W. Stokes (ed.) *Revue Celtique* IX (1888), 452–95; X (1889), 50–95, and by Oskamp 'Immram Curaig Máele Dúin', in H. P. A. Oskamp (ed.), *The voyage of Máel Dúin: A study in early Irish voyage literature followed by an edition of Immram curaig Máele Dúin from the Yellow Book of Lecan in Trinity College, Dublin* (Groningen, 1970), pp. 100–85. I shall adopt the following methodology: as both Stokes's and Oskamp's editions use the same section numbers, I shall simply note *Immram Maíle Dúin*, followed by the section number where appropriate. However, when I use direct quotation, I shall cite Oskamp's edition as *Immram Maíle Dúin* II, followed by section, page and line number, and the variants offered by Stokes under *Immram Maíle Dúin* I, followed by section and page number(s).
15 The tale is generally known in secondary sources by the shortened title *Immram Maíle Dúin*, and I shall be adopting this usage.
16 A. G. van Hamel, 'The text of *Immram curaig Maíldúin*', *Études Celtiques* III (1938), 1–20, discusses the manuscripts and dating of the tale.
17 Carney, 'Review', 41–3, made note, in particular, of the borrowings from the *Nauigatio* into *Immram Maíle Dúin*. However, his conclusion, that the latter is a poor imitation is deeply flawed; more recently T. O. Clancy, 'Subversion at sea: structure, style and intent in the *Immrama*', in J. M. Wooding (ed.), *The otherworld voyage in early Irish literature: an anthology of*

criticism (Dublin, 2000), esp. pp. 203–9, goes some way to considering the text as a work of literature in its own right..

18 F. J. Byrne, 'The Eóganacht Ninussa', *Éigse* IX (1958), 18–29. His identification of Eóganacht Ninussa is based partly on *Immram Maíle Dúin* itself.

19 *Immram Maíle Dúin* II, 100.19, declares that this is where Kildare is today. This statement appears to be a later addition.

20 Examples given by R. Sharpe, 'Hiberno-Latin *laicus*, Irish *láech* and the devil's men', *Ériu* XXX (1979), 75–92; one of the most cutting attacks on *díberg* in saga is surely E. Knott (ed), *Togail Bruidne Da Derga* (Dublin, 1975).

21 G. Henderson (ed.), *Fled Bricrend: the feast of Bricriu*, Irish Texts Society 2 (London, 1899). Examples of Bricriu's function can be seen in §6, §§8–25; the relationship of Briccne and Bricriu was briefly suggested by Stokes (ed.), 'Voyage of Mael Duin', 449; followed by Oskamp (ed.), *Voyage of Máel Dúin*, 51.

22 R. Thurneysen (ed.), *Scéla Mucce Meic Dathó*, Mediaeval and Modern Irish Series 4 (Dublin, 1935), §6, is an example of Briccne rather than Bricriu being used.

23 *Immram Maíle Dúin* II, 104.15–20. *Immram Maíle Dúin* I, 458, offers the reconstruction *athloiscthe* in place of *athloisce*.

24 There are numerous examples in Hogan, *Onomasticon*, pp. 253–71.

25 Hogan, *Onomasticon*, p. 371. The church could be identified with Dooglaun near Tulla County Clare or, perhaps, Dooghcloon near Loughrea in County Galway. Either would be within striking distance of Corcomroe, Máel Dúin's next destination.

26 T. M. Charles-Edwards, 'The pastoral role of the church in the early Irish laws', in J. Blair and R. Sharpe (eds), *Pastoral care before the parish*, Studies in the Early History of Britain (Leicester, 1992), esp. pp. 69–74; D. Ó Corráin, 'Irish vernacular law and the Old Testament', in P. Ní Chatháin and M. Richter (eds), *Irland und die Christenheit* (Stuttgart, 1987), p. 302.

27 Examined by M. Griffin-Wilson, 'Cluain agus cluanaire', in W. J. Mahon (ed.), *Proceedings of the Harvard Celtic Colloquium* IX (Harvard, 1990), pp. 31–42. She derives this *cluain* via the IE root *klep-, meaning to steal.

28 W. Stokes, (ed.), 'Agallamh na Senórach', in W. Stokes, E. Windisch (eds), *Irische Texte mit Übersetzungen und Wörterbuch* IV (Leipzig, 1900) p. 15, refers to the hero Caílte as the *cleasach cluanuide* 'devious trickster' of Cluain Cesáin. *Cluain* may be acting as a pun. J. Carey, 'Otherworlds and verbal worlds in Middle Irish narrative', *Proceedings of the Harvard Celtic Colloquium* IX (Cambridge, Mass, 1990), pp. 36–7, suggests that an otherwise unattested place name in *Tochmarc Becfhola*, Cluain Dá Chailech, is a wordplay meaning 'beguiling of the two cocks'.

29 Oskamp (ed.), *Voyage of Máel Dúin*, 52.

30 *Immram Maíle Dúin* II, §1, 108.11; *Immram Maíle Dúin* I, 462.

31 *Nauigatio*, §7, §24, §17.

32 *Immram Maíle Dúin* II, §1, 106.2–4. *Immram Maíle Dúin* I, §1, 462: 'As diriuch don-fuc Dia 7 roghab Dia ar crannán remoinn. Tiagam 7 orgem an dá dun sa, o rofoillsigh Dia duinn ar naimdiu indiph.'

33 *Immram Maíle Dúin* II, §1, 108.7–9; *Immram Maíle Dúin* I, 462: 'Ba hand adbert Mael Duin: Leicid in noi ina tost cen imrum, 7 an leth bus ail do Dia a brith, beraidh.'

34 M. E. Byrne, 'On the punishment of setting adrift', *Ériu* XI (1932), 97–102; F. Kelly, *A guide to Early Irish law* (Dublin, 1988), pp. 219–21, summarises the legal context; the earliest literary example is Patrick's treatment of Mac Cuill in Muirchú's *Vita S. Patricii*, in L. Bieler (ed.), *The Patrician texts from the Book of Armagh* (Dublin, 1979), pp. 102–6.

35 A famous historical example of this impulse is recorded in the *Anglo-Saxon Chronicle*, s.a. 891. This describes three Irishmen who reached Cornwall in a boat without oars and subsequently went to Alfred's court.

36 *Nauigatio*, §26; Jerome, *Vita Pauli*, *PL* 23, 17–28.

37 *Nauigatio*, §26, 'nihil aliud indumenti erat sibi iunctum exceptis pilis qui egrediebantur de suo corpore' [he had no other clothes on him except for the hair that grew from his own body]. Compare this with *Immram Maíle Dúin* II, §19, 138.50, *Immram Maíle Dúin* I, §19, 494: '7 a folt ba hedach do/ ba hetach dó' [and his hair was his clothing]; §30, 160.3/ §30, 72: '7 ro thuighestair a indfudh uile hé/ a fhindfudh uile hé' [and his hair clothed him completely]; §33, 168.56/ §33, 80: '7 se tuighthe o findfut giul a chuirp' [and he was clothed from the white hair of his body].

38 *Immram Maíle Dúin*, §33.

39 *Immram Maíle Dúin* II, §33, 168.8; *Immram Maíle Dúin* I, §33, 82.

40 *Immram Maíle Dúin*, §11; this is clearly influenced by *Nauigatio*, §§6–7.

41 *Immram Maíle Dúin* II, §33, 172.30–4; *Immram Maíle Dúin* I, §33, 90, suggests *fonngébaid* in place of *fonngébaigh* and *marbaid* for *marbaigh*.

42 *Immram Maíle Dúin* II, §34 176.32; *Immram Maíle Dúin* I, §34, 90.

43 *Immram Maíle Dúin* II, §34, 178.1–3; *Immram Maíle Dúin* I, §34, 94.

44 Stokes (ed.), 'Voyage of Máel Dúin', 447.

45 K. Hughes, 'The distribution of Irish scriptoria and centres of learning from 730–1111' in N. K. Chadwick (ed.), *Studies in the early British church* (Cambridge, 1958), p. 263; N. F. Chadwick, *The church in early Irish society* (London, 1966), p. 182; F. J. Byrne, 'Derrynavlan: the historical context', *Journal Royal Society of Antiquaries of Ireland* CX (1980), 121.

46 The Céle Dé attitude is summed up in the collection of documents collected in E. J. Gwynn and W. J. Purton (eds), 'The monastery of Tallaght', *Proceedings of the Royal Irish Academy* (C) XXIX (1911–12), 115–79. See especially §4, §26, for attacks on the old churches.

47 Byrne, 'Eóganacht Ninussa', 29–30, partially bases his argument on the identification of Máel Dúin's mother's church as Kildare but this identification is based on what is probably a later gloss. The fact that Máel Dúin was a common eighth-century name is neither here nor there; Zimmer, 'Keltische Beiträge II', 289–90, also argued for the eighth century.

48 *Immram Maíle Dúin*, §24.

49 *Immram Maíle Dúin*, §33.

50 *Immram Maíle Dúin* II, 104.29–30; *Immram Maíle Dúin* I, 458.

51 Oskamp (ed.), *Voyage of Máel Dúin*, 72.

CHAPTER 13

Medical men and learned societies in Ireland, 1680–1785

Eamon O'Flaherty

The organisation of intellectual inquiry in Ireland developed quite late in the seventeenth century. Robert Burrowes, a fellow of Trinity College, Dublin, wrote in 1785 offering an explanation of the problems which political instability had posed for the progress of learning and science since the Norman invasion of the twelfth century:

> The important changes which took place in the government upon the invasion by Henry II were not carried out with so little disturbance as to permit the nation to apply itself immediately to the peaceful employments of literary inquiry; nor could it reasonably be presumed that two classes of inhabitants entirely dissimilar in their education and habits, and afterwards widely separated by a difference in religion, should be readily prevailed on to lay aside their mutual enmity and unite in the pursuit of speculative science.[1]

Burrowes's remarks are particularly relevant to the difficulties of intellectual life in Ireland in the sixteenth and seventeenth centuries. There was little organised educational or intellectual activity outside Gaelic Ireland prior to the seventeenth century. Scholarly and intellectual traditions did exist among the native Irish and Old English communities in the sixteenth century, but the introduction of the new learning associated with the scientific revolution was largely a phenomenon associated with the New English civilisation which was to prove triumphant in the second half of the seventeenth century. The absence of a university before 1592 and of organised learned societies before the Restoration meant that intellectual life was increasingly dominated by the imperatives of the New English conquest of the country. There was considerable intellectual investment in the Counter-Reformation in the seventeenth century, including Catholic projects to establish a university in Ireland at various times between the 1580s and the 1640s, but institutions of learning in

Ireland itself were dominated by the New English. The considerable outpouring of theological, controversial and historical literature from exiled Catholic intellectuals and scholars in continental Europe during the seventeenth century indicated something of the energy and vitality of Catholic Ireland in the Counter-Reformation period, but the failure of Catholic efforts to resist the Protestant victory of the seventeenth century meant that this aspect of Irish intellectual history was to have negligible effect on the development of institutional learning in Ireland from the 1650s onwards. Catholic intellectual activity was heavily clerical, as its resources were largely controlled by the church and dedicated to a largely successful effort at maintaining a confessional literature hostile to the revolution which had created the Protestant state of the late seventeenth century.[2] The intellectual concerns of the confessional state in Ireland reflected the agenda of a conquest, which sought to reshape the country in political, religious and cultural terms. The development of formal medical education in Ireland was subject to the processes of reorganisation which transformed intellectual and scientific activity according to the imperatives of the new state. Medical men also formed an important part of the small group of intellectually active individuals who dominated learned societies in the century after 1680. Medicine also shared in the ambiguities of the confessional state in Ireland, where a Protestant state co-existed with a population which was confessionally divided.

As with the law, the practice of medicine in Ireland crossed confessional boundaries. Attempts to regulate both professions in the interest of confessional uniformity were carried out with varying degrees of enthusiasm and success and neither profession was ever confessionally homogeneous. Indeed, whereas restrictions on Catholics practising law were strengthened in the course of the eighteenth century, resulting in the disappearance of Catholics from the bar, the medical profession was never affected by the penal laws to the same degree. Much of this has to do with the fairly ramshackle nature of regulation of medicine in Ireland in the post-Restoration period. Whereas corporations such as the church and the law were much more tightly organised from the mid-sixteenth century onwards, medicine was not amenable to similar control. The reasons for this are not unique to Irish medicine in the seventeenth and eighteenth centuries. The wide spectrum of those who practised some form of healing defied easy regulation by any single body or even group of bodies throughout this period. The absence of any formal medical education in Ireland until the beginning of the eighteenth century and corporate rivalries between the institutions in the course of the century contributed to a situation where overall control and regulation were apparently impossible. In confessional terms, the gradual exclusion of Catholics from many areas of public life in the course of the first half of the eighteenth century had no counterpart in medicine. Although Catholics were excluded from positions in the Irish College of Physicians after 1692 and were, of course, excluded from the university, there is no evidence of any attempt to prevent them from practising medicine and by the end of the century Catholics were eligible for election to the king's professorships of medicine attached to the Royal College of Physicians. This was simply one aspect of a fluidity which marked all aspects of Irish medical organisation in the period.[3]

Although there was provision for a medical fellow in Trinity from its foundation, and a Chair of Physic from 1662, there is no evidence of formal medical education in Trinity before 1711.[4] Significantly for the development of the Dublin medical school in the course of the eighteenth century, the establishment of a physicians' society with its own president at Trinity Hall in 1654, connected to the university but governing itself, set the pattern for the development of two important institutions collaborating, and often competing, in the provision of medical education in eighteenth-century Dublin. The rivalry between the two bodies was an important factor in the slow progress made by the Dublin school in the first half of the century. John Stearne's society of physicians was given a royal charter in 1667 and again in 1692. The Royal College of Physicians in Ireland was the examining body for medical degrees in Trinity after 1692, while maintaining an increasingly independent identity of its own. The College of Physicians was also empowered to regulate physicians and to prevent unlicensed physicians from practising, but this latter task never seems to have been carried out. Both Trinity and the College of Physicians expanded their educational role in medicine in the early decades of the eighteenth century. In Trinity, in 1711, lectureships were established in natural philosophy, anatomy, botany and chemistry and an anatomy theatre was built. Shortly afterwards the College of Physicians received a potentially handsome endowment from the bequest of Sir Patrick Dun to establish a King's Professor of medicine attached to the college rather than to the university. Because of a delay in implementing Dun's bequest, the King's Professor became a reality only in the middle of the century, though the strength of the endowment permitted the number of professors to be increased to three by 1742.[5] The relationship between Trinity and the College of Physicians was difficult, however, and frequent demarcation disputes led to a state of cold war between the two institutions resulting in an outright rift in 1761, on the issue of granting a degree to Fielding Ould, an expert in midwifery who became master of Bartholomew Mosse's lying-in hospital.

Quite apart from these problems, limited resources also meant that Dublin could not offer a level of medical education comparable to that available elsewhere.[6] From the late seventeenth century, when a small number of Irish physicians, including Thomas Molyneux, took medical degrees at Leyden, Irish students joined the large numbers of English and Scottish students attending the Leyden medical school. The high point of this movement was during the reign of Hermann Boerhaave in the first third of the eighteenth century. One hundred and twenty-two Irish medical students matriculated at Leyden during the period 1701–38, including the majority of the leading Irish practitioners of the first half of the century. From the 1720s, the Edinburgh school, heavily influenced by Boerhaave's pupils, notably Alexander Munro and John Rutherford, became another important source for Irish physicians.[7] What is also striking in the context of intellectual activity in Ireland between 1650 and 1750 is the very high proportion of graduates of Leyden, and MDs in particular, reflecting not just Leyden's pre-eminence in the development of clinical studies but also its status as an outstanding centre of scholarship in Europe at this time. There was nothing in Dublin comparable to the clinical training at Leyden or Edinburgh prior to the School of Physic Acts of 1785 and 1800, when Dun's bequest was partially diverted into establishing a clinic for the Dublin medical school. This picture of minimal development of clinical studies in Ireland – with the Trinity lecturers providing largely preliminary teaching for students destined for education abroad – was further complicated by the vigour of the other branches of medicine, beyond the elite of physicians, in their search for status and recognition in the course of the century. The Dublin apothecaries, surgeons and midwifery specialists of the eighteenth century sought to establish greater control of their own branches of medical science and practice from mid-century onwards.[8]

The institutional ambiguities of the eighteenth century are often seen as a prelude to the corporate professionalisation of the nineteenth, the point at which the historiography of the Dublin medical school usually begins.[9] What James McGeachie has called the 'heroic phase' of the Dublin clinical school epitomised by Wilde, Graves, Corrigan and Stokes has tended to cast a shadow over the significance of the earlier period. Considered in itself, the more fluid situation of the eighteenth century facilitated an interesting relationship between medical men and public, scientific and intellectual activity in eighteenth-century Dublin, which often bore fruit in areas far removed from the development of clinical medicine. Partly owing to the influence of Leyden and Edinburgh and partly to specifically Irish developments in medical organisation, there was a substantial movement in medical science and in public medicine in eighteenth-century Ireland. Yet it is arguable that the contribution of Dublin medical intellectuals to organised scientific activity in the eighteenth century was not distinguished by a contribution to medical science or education so much as by a proportionally significant participation in public learned societies dedicated to scientific and public-spirited enterprises, which were of importance in the ideology of Protestant Ireland in the Restoration period and in the eighteenth century. K. T. Hoppen's conclusion that the activities of the Dublin Philosophical Society of the 1680s represented the work of the common scientist working steadily away in the rank and file of contemporary scientific inquiry, rather than producing anything of remarkable scientific value by contemporary standards, is even more true of Irish contributions to medical science in the period as a whole. Certainly individuals like Thomas Molyneux, Alan Mullen, Richard Helsham, Bryan Robinson, John Rutty and Sylvester O'Halloran produced substantial amounts of work in medical science in this period. None of them, however, did so in the context of a definable Irish medical school, reflecting the fact that the majority of them had received the major part of their education abroad.

As additional evidence of vitality, Dublin physicians were particularly active in establishing charitable hospitals in the course of the eighteenth century. Although the charitable hospitals established in the eighteenth century – Swift's, Mercer's, Dr Steeven's (1733), the Meath and the Charitable Infirmary (1718, later Jervis Street) – acted more typically as refuges for the sick and indigent rather than as centres for clinical teaching or medical development, some of the doctors associated with them were also prominent in the public intellectual life of eighteenth-century Dublin. Attached to Dr Steeven's Hospital in its early years were Robert Griffith, first King's Professor of medicine on Patrick Dun's foundation (although he received no salary and probably gave no lectures); Edward Worth, who collected one of the most important medical libraries of the century in Dublin; and William Stephens who was active both as physician to the hospital and as a founding member of the Dublin Society in 1731. Stephens, like Worth, was one of the many Leyden graduates who played such a dominant role in the Irish medical profession in the first half of the eighteenth century. The combination of philanthropic and professional service was also characteristic of David McBride who was involved in founding the Meath Hospital. McBride was also an example of the extent to which the regulation of physicians was very hard to achieve in the eighteenth century. Initially apprenticed to a surgeon, he received his formal medical education in Edinburgh and was an MD of Glasgow University.

Both surgeons and apothecaries in Dublin were attempting to break through the barriers which separated them from the physicians in the eighteenth century. In 1745 the apothecaries broke away from the Barber Surgeons' Guild and were incorporated as a guild in their own right. The new St Luke's Guild provided an early political platform for one of its members, Charles Lucas, who launched his campaign as a radical constitutional campaigner from the guild politics of Dublin Corporation in the 1740s. Lucas's exile, mainly in England, after the Dublin election of 1749 enabled him to acquire a medical degree, but he never incorporated this after his return to Ireland. Lucas did, however, use his return to Irish politics as member of parliament for Dublin after 1760 to press for the reform of the organisation of the

Apothecaries' Guild notably in the act which he sponsored in 1761 for tightening the regulation of apothecaries in Ireland. This process culminated after Lucas's death in 1791 with the establishment of Apothecaries' Hall by parliament, completing the divorce of the apothecaries from the barber surgeons.[10] A similar and even stronger impetus lay behind the push by the surgeons to establish their professional credentials in the face of resistance by the physicians. Sylvester O'Halloran, whose work on glaucoma is generally regarded as the most distinguished pieces of Irish medical literature of the century, made proposals for the improvement of surgical training in 1765, advocating the establishment of a surgeons' college in a work which simultaneously showed his interest in surgery, professionalisation and medical history.[11] The search for professional status through regulation was an important part of the drive for a college of surgeons in the last quarter of the eighteenth century, pioneered by William Dease and others. The non-denominational character of the College of Surgeons established by Dease and his associates indicated both the beginning of the end of the Irish confessional state in the late eighteenth century and also the fact that medicine had never easily fitted into any overall system of regulation after the Glorious Revolution.

The loose grip of institutions and the slow pace of development of the medical school form the background to the intellectual output of Irish physicians during the eighteenth century, which was characterised at first glance by a certain eclecticism, reflecting the importance of voluntary associations of educated lay and professional individuals rather than organised academic inquiry. In the absence of any societies specifically dedicated to the discussion of medical topics prior to the 1750s, Dublin physicians and surgeons played a prominent part in the succession of learned societies which operated from the 1680s onwards. The political context of the societies forms an important part of understanding their role in the ideological as well as purely intellectual history of Ireland in the long eighteenth century. The first of these, the Dublin Philosophical Society established by William Molyneux in 1683, was consciously modelled on the Royal Society in England.[12] Like his brother William, Samuel Molyneux, who completed his medical education at Leyden and was Professor of Physic at Trinity between 1711 and 1733, had extensive contacts with Locke, Boyle, Petty and other English virtuosi. Apart from emulating the Royal Society in London, explicit in Petty's first 'Advertisement' – 'that they chiefly apply themselves to the making of experiments' – the Dublin Philosophical Society's founders also had their inspiration in the Baconian and pansophist programme of Samuel Hartlib and his circle in England and Ireland in the 1640s and 1650s. As has been forcefully argued, the 'common scientists' of the Philosophical Society can also be seen as the heirs to the mid-seventeenth-century conquest, with its daring conceit of the New Science as a force to reanimate the kingdom of

Ireland and realise its potential.[13] Hartlib had been explicit about the need for a thorough revolution in Irish society which would be directed by a scientific programme whereby a movement, or even an invisible college, of Protestant scientists and landlords could realise the potential of the conquered island. The experimental philosophy of the society, as expounded in the descriptions of its aims by St George Ashe, was deliberately imitative of the model offered by the Royal Society in London. The record of medical participation in the Philosophical Society's activities was substantial in the years of its greatest activity prior to the Williamite war. The medical contribution was not confined to medicine, and the papers read to the society by physicians show a polymathic range of interests in some of the members. A thematic analysis of the papers read to the society in 1684 and 1685 indicates the preponderance of papers read on medical topics, with over a fifth of the contributions in 1684 and over a quarter in 1685 on medical topics.[14] Alan Mullen, one of the first medical graduates of Dublin (where the first MDs had been only awarded from the 1670s), was the most prolific contributor to the society's proceedings in the 1680s. Physicians and a single surgeon also made up about a quarter of the membership of the society. In addition to his papers to the society, Mullen had also published an account of his dissection of an elephant in Dublin in 1680 and in 1684 he was active in establishing a laboratory and herbal garden for the society. Mullen's interests were primarily medical and he performed a number of public demonstrations, complementing the contribution of the surgeon member Josias Patterson, who contributed accounts of anatomical dissections. On the other hand, Thomas Molyneux's contributions were extremely wide-ranging and encompassed the full extent of the society's understanding of scientific activity. When the society was revived in 1693 after the Glorious Revolution, Molyneux contributed papers on archaeology, on the geology of the Giant's Causeway – a topic to which he was to return on several occasions and which attracted considerable interest outside Ireland – as well as papers on surgery and disease. The death of William Molyneux in 1698, the year in which he published his most famous work of patriot constitutionalism, *The case of Ireland stated*, saw the society lapse again and a brief revival by Samuel Molyneux was cut short by his decision to reside in England.

The most interesting development during the lifetime of the Dublin Philosophical Society was the revival of the project for a natural history of Ireland, which had first been instigated in the 1650s by Hartlib and the Boate brothers, both Leyden-educated Dutch physicians. The text of *Ireland's naturall history*, written by Gerard Boate, has been seen as the blueprint for the reconstruction of Ireland by a new Protestant governing nation envisaged by Hartlib.[15] Natural history was therefore the science necessary to provide the information through which the island could be re-animated and made profitable in a way of which the Irish and Old English Catholics were incapable for cultural and moral reasons. Hartlib's project represented the high-point of Cromwellian expectation with regard to Ireland in the 1650s when some, including at times Oliver Cromwell himself, saw Ireland as a country of limitless potential, a tabula rasa on which great things might be accomplished.[16] Despite the appearance of Boate's text, the natural history project was unfinished and Hartlib sought successors in two mathematicians, Robert Wood, a member of the Cromwellian administration, and Miles Symner, Professor of Mathematics at Trinity in 1652–60 and 1675–86. The project was still incomplete in the 1680s when William Molyneux undertook to produce an atlas of Ireland with descriptions of the natural history of the different counties. Both Molyneux brothers were involved in the atlas project, though William played the leading role in collaboration with the Welsh antiquarian Edward Lhuyd. Unlike the earlier phase of the natural history project, the extreme antipathy to the native Irish was not quite as evident in Molyneux's plan, suggested by the collaboration of New English projectors with Gaelic contributors, including Teigue O'Roddy who contributed an account of Leitrim and the Connacht antiquarian Roderick O'Flaherty, whose *Chorographical description of Iar Connacht*, published in 1685, is the most extensive survivor of the Molyneux plan.[17] Contact between Lhuyd and Thomas Molyneux was revived in the late 1690s and Lhuyd toured Ireland in 1699. A printed questionnaire formed part of the central organisation of the project. The Molyneux natural history was unrealised, like its predecessor, but a similar project was to resurface in the successor societies of the 1730s. The ideological context of these projects had undergone a transformation in the forty years between Boate and the Molyneux brothers. The Hartlibian emphasis on a transformation effected by a new Protestant civilisation was present also in Molyneux's patriotism, but the ambiguities of Molyneux's position contrasted with that of the previous generation. Molyneux's patriotism occupied a position which defined the constitutional liberties of the Irish Protestants in Lockean terms, while also appealing to an ancient constitution which could define the Irish Protestants in a more inclusive historical context, which focused on the role of the Irish parliament as one element of a series of continuities straddling the great upheaval of the civil war.

The development of a patriot ideology in Ireland after 1690 was explicit in the founding of the Dublin Society in 1731. Here the emphasis on utility and improvement, already evident among Jacobites and Williamites in the 1690s, was taken up by a large volume of Irish economic writing in response to the economic crises of the late 1720s. The political unrest within the governing Protestant elite, centring on British assertions of political authority from the late 1690s, combined with the economic crisis of the late 1720s to produce a body of economic literature, which was primarily focused on the need to develop a practical economic patriotism based on the improvement of agriculture and manufacture. The criticism of absentees who drew pensions on the Irish establishment by Thomas Prior, founder of the society, was reinforced in the Dublin Society by a utilitarian programme of agricultural and industrial improvement.[18] Five of the fourteen present at the first meeting of the Dublin Society were physicians, including Thomas Molyneux, who formed a connection with the Philosophical Society, John Madden, father of Samuel 'Premium' Madden, who established the system of incentives and prizes which was the centre of the society's strategy for agricultural and industrial improvement, and William Stephens, probably the most active medical member, who made important contributions on tanning and beekeeping which were among the society's early publications. William Maple, who became registrar of the Society, was not a physician but had been employed as a chemical operator in Trinity. Francis Le Hunte embodied the combination of medicine and land as a physician who was twice president of the College of Physicians and also a landowner. In its constitution, adopted in December 1731, the Dublin Society continued the experimental commitment of its predecessor, but along lines which were almost entirely devoted to the goal of improvement. The medical contribution was found mainly in the application of scientific principles to the agricultural and industrial concerns of the society in its early decades. A further aspect of the medical role was the close relationship between the medical world and the teaching of natural sciences at Dublin university. In the small world of eighteenth-century Dublin, the overlap between science, medicine and agronomy was considerable. But the society also developed a number of different activities in its early decades, establishing drawing schools in the 1740s, which were to lay the basis of artistic and architectural education in Ireland and employing officers to conduct agricultural experiments and geological surveys – the basis for the schools of chemistry and mineralogy which took shape in the 1790s.[19]

The dominance of utilitarian industrial and agricultural concerns in the Dublin Society's programme in the middle of the eighteenth century reflected the philosophy of practical improvement, which was the key to its foundation. However, the related theme of survey and natural history, which had been present in learned organisations from the 1650s, re-emerged in a parallel society which was established in 1744, the Physico-Historical Society. The members of the Physico-Historical Society were largely drawn from the membership of the Dublin Society, but the new society was specifically dedicated to the revival of the natural history project: to promote enquiries into the ancient and present state of the counties of Ireland. The Physico-Historical Society's membership overlapped with that of the Dublin Society, but its goals were more specific: it defined itself, at its inaugural meeting on 14 April 1744, as 'a voluntary society for promoting an inquiry into the ancient and present state of the several counties of Ireland'.[20] The society was a deliberate attempt to continue Molyneux's unfinished project to compile a survey of the Irish counties. Regular meetings were held at the beginning of every month in the House of Lords committee room in the parliament house. From the outset, the project was dominated by Walter Harris, the lawyer antiquarian, John Rutty, a physician based in Dublin, and Charles Smith, an apothecary from Dungarvan. Harris, who had already published a collection of the work of Irish historians in 1736, was the dominant figure at the early stages of the society. Indeed Harris's preliminary work on County Down was published in 1740, four years before the inaugural meeting, as *A topographical and chorographical survey of the county of Down . . . intended as an essay towards a fuller description of the kingdom of Ireland than has hitherto appeared*. Harris promised 'to remove the gross misrepresentations of Giraldus Cambrensis' and he set forward an ambitious plan which was modified by the society in 1744. Initially the plan proposed by Harris and his unnamed collaborators envisaged a cumulative effort whereby a printed questionnaire would be circulated throughout the country. The resulting contributions were to be collected by a committee, and these would form the basis for the final work. A fuller version of the work on County Down appeared in 1744 under the authorship of Harris and Charles Smith prior to the inaugural meeting of the Society. The book was intended as a model on which to proceed to a systematic survey of the civil and natural histories of the Irish counties. The dedication to Sir Hans Sloan, a native of County Down, famous as a herbalist and author of a *Natural history of Jamaica*, signalled the importance of the scientific aspect of the project. The preface to the 1744 County Down volume indicated that the idea of soliciting contributions from around the country had proved to be of limited value. Many of those written to 'communicated with freedom and cheerfulness. Yet the deficiencies were so great that the society judged it necessary to send into the world a rude and primitive skeleton of one particular county in order to show their design.'[21] A botanist, probably Isaac Butler, was employed to travel to Down to make collections of plants which were then classified in Dublin by two physicians, John Rutty and Leonel Jenkins. Rutty also undertook a survey of the mineral waters of the county – an area in which he had already published a considerable amount – while Jenkins did much of the classification of birds for the volume. The society also decided to undertake a survey of historical manuscripts, including the collections in Marsh's Library and in Trinity, including the 1641 depositions and the surviving manuscripts of Molyneux's unfinished project from the 1690s. The Table of Queries appended to the 1744 volume was a systematic questionnaire to direct contributors to the history. The schematic nature of the questionnaire was a clear echo of the two earlier natural history projects. The range of geological and botanical, demographic and topographical questions set out a systematic programme of knowledge integrating the natural and civil elements of the programme.[22] Beginning with 'Air', which included weather, entries were to be arranged under fourteen principal headings, including water, earth, stones, plants, minerals, animals, people, particular customs, manufactures, buildings, antiquities and public charities. The combination of civil and natural history in this plan was heavily weighted towards the latter, and the sub-categories of topics on which contributions were invited also indicated a utilitarian concern with improvement and the exploitation of natural resources.

Impressive as this was in theory, in practice the work of the Physico-Historical Society reflected the interests and limitations of the small core of active members who effectively were the society. The proportion of medical men was high among the society's active members, the other strong element being made up by the clergy of the established church. Edward Barry, Professor of Physic at Trinity, was the active vice-president of the society during its existence. Most of the money voted by the society in the first two years of its existence was paid to Charles Smith for the work he was carrying out on County Waterford, to Isaac Butler for collecting botanical specimens and to John Rutty, and Thomas Hore, an apothecary, for work on the natural history of Dublin mainly reflecting Rutty's interests in botany and the analysis of mineral waters. In 1746, the year Smith's volume on Waterford was published by the society, there was a rather unseemly row between Smith and Harris on the profits of the Waterford volume. In June 1746 Smith complained that Harris was demanding half the profit of the Waterford volume for his trouble in collecting material on the antiquities of the county. Despite appeals from the other members Harris threatened to go to law if necessary, and the dispute was settled by a compromise whereby Harris was to be given 100 copies of the Waterford volume, half of which were to be bought from Smith by the society. It is perhaps not too fanciful to imagine the social gulf which separated Harris, a well-connected and distinguished scholar-lawyer and Smith, an apothecary from Dungarvan, contributing to the dispute. Apart from giving us an insight into the politics of collaborative scholarship, the dispute marked the beginning of a long decline in the fortunes of the society. The voluntary basis of the society's activities posed many practical difficulties, including a chronic shortage of money due to the small number of subscriptions and a marked fall-off in attendance at meetings. Smith continued to receive financial backing from the society, however, and Rutty and Harris both continued as active members after 1746, but the natural history project, as distinct from the society, virtually became a one-man operation after 1746 as Smith continued to add to his series of county studies. *The ancient and present state of Cork*, the largest of the series, was published in 1749 under the auspices of the society. The Physico-Historical

Society ceased to exist after 1752, but Smith continued his series of Munster county studies, publishing the Kerry volume in 1756, and he also prepared draft studies of Limerick, Clare and Tipperary which were never published. Although he was an apothecary, Smith's interests were increasingly topographical and historical in the later volumes of his county studies, as evinced by the shrinking proportion devoted to natural history – which had formed such a major element of the original plan – in the Cork and Kerry volumes. He acknowledged Rutty's help with the sections on botany, mineralogy and, of course, mineral waters, in the Cork volume, but even in the section on natural history, Smith was mainly concerned with economic improvement, including 'useful hints for erecting several arts and manufactures in this county [Cork], either neglected or ill-prosecuted therein'. Critical of absentees, he enthusiastically quoted some of Berkeley's proposals for domestic industry and discouragement of imports.[23] Smith was probably also influenced by Berkeley's economic thought in his support for a national bank in Ireland as a basis for national credit and a secure paper currency.[24]

Smith and Rutty continued to collaborate closely in the period up to Smith's death in 1762. In particular, Smith was keen to push the cause of organised learning in Ireland through his books and through the formation, in 1756, of another learned society, the Medico-Philosophical Society. In his introduction to the Kerry volume, published in 1756, Smith published a 'Discourse on learned societies', in which he lamented the fact that Ireland was the only kingdom in Europe 'so much wanting in public spirit, that it is incapable of keeping up a society of gentlemen, who may meet at proper intervals for such laudable purposes'. Anticipating Robert Burrowes's remarks nearly thirty years later, Smith argued that Irish history had never favoured the organisation of learning until the Restoration, singling out Petty's *Political anatomy of Ireland* for special praise among the 'tracts relating to the civil polity and improvement of the kingdom'. The present time, Smith argued, was especially propitious for setting up learned societies in Ireland: 'the blindness of former ages and the miseries of the past are vanished. Now mankind are generally grown weary of the reliques of antiquity and satiated with religious controversies, and now, not only are the eyes of men open, but their hands are ready and prepared to work.'[25] The year in which Smith published this manifesto was also the first year of operation of the new society, dominated by medical men, which began as a series of 'accidental meetings' of a group of gentlemen interested in 'medical, natural and philosophical inquiries'. The manuscript of the proceedings of the society shows the ambitious nature of the enterprise in that it was clearly intended as a volume of papers modelled on the Royal Society's *Philosophical Transactions*. John Rutty, in a paper on 'The present state of natural history in Ireland', showed a certain dissatisfaction with the reliance of Irish scientists on *Philosophical*

Transactions for publication of their work, especially given the publication there of adverse commentary on Irish science.[26] In his 'Preliminary discourse' to the Medical and Philosophical Memoirs, Smith continued his argument about the need for a greater organisation of learning, but was not particularly optimistic. Self-seeking, self-promotion, 'the low arts of party or faction' are inimical to the spirit of inquiry, while the leaders of society are taken up with 'aggrandizing their families and supporting luxury . . . even at the expense of all that is dear to the well-wisher of his country'. Despite these misgivings, the members of the new society proposed a fairly wide field for its activities, giving pride of place to medicine, natural history and natural philosophy, but also 'ethical and political subjects'. These latter conformed to the familiar pattern of patriotic ideals, improvements in trade and manufactures, methods for employing the poor and significantly, the preservation of the health of the poor, including the discouragement of excessive drinking, one of Rutty's hobby-horses.[27] Smith's patriotic agenda of placing country before party and marrying science and improvement was also accompanied by a more traditional suspicion of Catholics. In April 1757 he communicated an acerbic critique of Charles O'Conor's recently published *Maxims relevant to the present state of Ireland*, in which he rehearsed familiar arguments about the danger of Catholic civil principles to a free constitution.[28]

The active membership of the Medico-Philosophical Society was quite small and Smith and Rutty dominated the society in its early years. Rutty played a leading role in the Medico-Philosophical Society, contributing papers on a range of subjects which reflected his own wide interests. In 1756 he presented a catalogue of Irish medicinal herbs which formed part of his life work on *materia medica* and grew out of his membership of an otherwise unrecorded botanical society of the first half of the century. Rutty's statistical interests were also reflected in his papers on the Dublin and London mortality bills and a 'physico-political paper' in which he estimated the numbers of Roman Catholics and Protestants in Dublin. In the first year of the society's existence Rutty also contributed papers on electricity, inoculation, the diet of the poor and the Lisbon earthquake, among many others. In his paper defending Irish natural history of February 1757 he was full of praise for the Dublin Society – 'not only a noble specimen of patriotism but also of a true taste for natural history' – and called for the establishment of a natural history museum attached to the society which would further the cause of inland navigation and industrial development. By any standards, Rutty's output and range of interests were extraordinary. One of the many Leyden graduates who dominated Irish medicine in the first half of the eighteenth century, his work combined an interest in diet, water quality, population and mortality statistics and the mineral resources of the kingdom. He kept a continuous series of weather records for Dublin for most of his life and attempted a correlation of weather observations and public health statistics.[29] Commissioned to write the natural history of Dublin by the Physico-Historical Society, he continued to work on the subject for almost thirty years, eventually publishing the book in 1772 under the auspices of the Dublin Society. A Quaker, he was also the author of a continuation of Thomas Wight's history of the Irish Quakers, which he published in 1752. In fact Rutty combined his scientific and medical work with an increasing concern for the spiritual life, keeping a spiritual diary from 1753 until just before his death in 1774. Unfortunately the spiritual diary, though voluminous and covering every day of Rutty's life for a quarter of a century, gives very little specific information on his professional or scientific career. Rutty developed a concept of spiritual healing, amply described in his diary, which he thought was more important than the cure of disease. 'Physick is not the ultimate end: for very often diseases are moral benefits, not moral evils; whereas every degree of vice is evil.'[30] Rutty felt guilty about spending too much time on his practice and his scientific research, as he did about eating too much and sleeping late. He did, however, record a certain satisfaction with being associated with the founding of the Medico-Philosophical Society recording on 22 November 1756: 'A happy thought of presenting C.S. with an old manuscript which partly laid a foundation for a most useful and virtuous medical society in this land of indolence, blessed be the lord! For I never dreamt of the good consequences, I humbly hope, entailed on this seeming accident.'[31] The wide scope envisaged for the society by Smith and Rutty was not destined to last. In July 1758 the society considered a proposal by George Cleghorn that it limit its work to chemistry, anatomy and pharmacy.[32] Cleghorn (1716–89), born in Scotland, had been a military surgeon before settling in Ireland in 1749 and becoming university anatomist. Although Rutty continued to contribute on his usual wide range of subjects after Cleghorn's proposal, the papers read to the society were increasingly confined to medical topics, with a high proportion read by Cleghorn himself.

From the 1760s a big change is evident in the Dublin scientific scene with the expansion of the Dublin Society, which from 1761 received about £5000 per annum from the Irish parliament; this led to a series of large-scale developments, including the establishment of an implement museum at Hawkins Street in 1781 and the botanic gardens at Glasnevin in 1795, among many other projects. The medical contribution to the development of learned organisation in eighteenth-century Ireland was large, but it had not been confined to the area of medical science. The development of the system of charitable hospitals during the eighteenth century showed the importance of voluntarism at a period when the operation of charitable and philanthropic activities by the established church and the state were limited. In terms of political economy, the natural history project, associated with Petty and the

Boate brothers in the middle of the seventeenth century, remained a key focus of learned activity through the Dublin Philosophical Society and later the Physico-Historical and Medico-Philosophical societies. An Enlightenment idea of scientific activity directed to the ends of universal improvement was clearly visible in d'Alembert's philosophical preface to Diderot's *Encylopédie* of 1754[33] but the programme of the Dublin Society in 1731 and the two mid-century learned societies reveals the strength of the pragmatic and patriotic orientation of organised learning and science in Ireland by the middle of the eighteenth century. The greatly expanded role of the Royal Dublin Society from the 1760s onwards saw many of the ideals of the mid-century scientists acquire an institutional framework, while the politics of improvement still featured strongly in the rhetoric of Irish science at the founding of the Royal Irish Academy in 1785.[34]

Notes

1 Robert Burrowes, 'Preface', *Transactions of the Royal Irish Academy* I (1787), ix–x.

2 See Jane Ohlmeyer, 'For God, king or country? Political thought and culture in seventeenth-century Ireland' in Jane Ohlmeyer (ed.), *Political thought in seventeenth-century Ireland: kingdom or colony?* (Cambridge, 2000), pp. 3–14; Bernadette Cunningham, *The world of Geoffrey Keating: history, myth and religion in seventeenth-century Ireland* (Dublin, 2000), pp. 25–31.

3 John F. Fleetwood, *The history of medicine in Ireland* (Dublin, 1983), pp. 42–51; Eoin O'Brien and J. D. H. Widdess. 'The beginnings of medical science' in Eoin O'Brien, Anne Crookshank and Gordon Wolstenholme (eds), *A portrait of Irish medicine* (Dublin, 1984); James Kelly, 'The emergence of scientific and institutional medical practice in Ireland, 1650–1800' in Elizabeth Malcolm and Greta Jones (eds), *Medicine, disease and the state in Ireland, 1650–1940* (Cork, 1999), pp. 21–39.

4 D. A. Webb and R. B. McDowell, *Trinity College, Dublin, 1592–1952* (Cambridge, 1982), pp. 41–4.

5 J. D. H. Widdess, *A history of the Royal College of Physicians of Ireland, 1654–1963* (Edinburgh, 1963).

6 Fleetwood, *History of medicine*, pp. 42–50; O'Donel T. D Browne, *The Rotunda Hospital, 1745–1945* (Edinburgh, 1947); Robert Harrison, 'Medical education at the Rotunda Hospital, 1745–1995' in Alan Browne (ed.), *Masters, midwives and ladies-in-waiting: the Rotunda Hospital, 1745–1995* (Dublin, 1995), pp. 67–8.

7 E. Ashworth Underwood, 'The first and final phases of the Irish medical students at the University of Leyden' in Eoin O'Brien (ed.), *Essays in honour of J. D. H. Widdess* (Dublin, 1978), pp. 6–15; E. Ashworth Underwood, *Boerhaaves's men at Leyden* (Edinburgh, 1972).

8 J. C. McWalter, *History of the worshipful company of apothecaries of the city of Dublin* (Dublin, 1916).

9 On this historiography see James McGeachie, '"Normal development" in an "abnormal place": Sir William Wilde and the Irish school of medicine' in Malcolm and Jones, *Medicine, disease and the state*, pp. 85–90.

10 On Lucas and the apothecaries see Jacqueline Hill, *From patriots to unionists: Dublin civic politics and Irish Protestant patriotism, 1660-1840* (Oxford, 1997), pp. 84, 205; McWalter, *History of the worshipful company*.

11 J. D. H. Widdess, *An account of the schools of surgery in the Royal College of Surgeons, Dublin, 1789–1948* (Edinburgh, 1949), pp. 5–6; Fleetwood, *History of medicine*, pp. 106–7.

12 K. T. Hoppen, *The common scientist in the seventeenth century: the Dublin Philosophical Society, 1603–1708* (London 1970); J. G. Simms, *William Molyneux of Dublin, 1656–1698* (Dublin, 1982), pp. 34–46.

13 T. C. Barnard, 'Samuel Hartlib and the cult and culture of improvement in Ireland' in Mark Greengrass et al. (eds), *Samuel Hartlib and universal reformation* (Cambridge, 1994), pp. 281–95.

14 Hoppen, *The common scientist*, appendix D.

15 Patricia Coughlan, 'Natural history and historical nature: the project for a natural history of Ireland' in Greengrass et al., *Samuel Hartlib*, p. 307.

16 On Cromwell's ideas see John Morrill, 'Cromwell and Scotland and Ireland' in John Morrill (ed.), *Oliver Cromwell and the English revolution* (London, 1990), pp. 161–3.

17 See also Joep Leerssen, *Mere Irish and fíor-ghael*, 2nd edn (Cork, 1996), pp. 281–93.

18 Desmond J. Clarke, *Thomas Prior, 1681–1751, founder of the Royal Dublin Society* (Dublin, 1951), pp. 24–38.

19 Henry F. Berry, *A history of the Royal Dublin Society* (Dublin, 1915), pp. 1–34; Desmond J. Clarke, *Bibliography of the publications of the Royal Dublin Society from its foundation in 1731* TS, 2nd edn (Dublin 1953), nos 1–39; Terence De Vere White, *The story of the RDS* (Tralee, 1955), pp. 7–19. See also *Proceedings of the Royal Dublin Society* I (1764), passim.

20 RIA MS 24.E.28, 1: Physico-Historical Society minute book.

21 Walter Harris and Charles Smith, *Antient and present state of the county of Down* (Dublin, 1744), p. vii.

22 Ibid., pp. xiv–xviii.

23 Smith, *The antient and present state of the county and city of Cork*, 2nd edn, 2 vols (Dublin, 1750), II, pp. 231, 251–3.

24 Ibid., II, pp. xii–xiv.

25 Smith, *The antient and present state of the county of Kerry* (Dublin, 1756), pp. xiii–xvi.

26 RCPI MS: 'Proceedings of the Medical-Philosophical Society', I, 111–12: Rutty, 'The present state of natural history in Ireland', (3 Feb. 1757). I am grateful to Mr Robert Mills, librarian of the College for his assistance and for permission to reproduce part of the manuscript.

27 RCPI MS, 'Proceedings', I, 1–5: Smith, 'Preliminary discourse' (April 1756).

28 RCPI MS, 'Proceedings', I, 123–5.

29 See, for example, *An essay towards a natural and experimental and medicinal history of the mineral waters of Ireland* (Dublin, 1757); *Chronological history of the weather and seasons, and of the prevailing diseases in Dublin* (Dublin, 1770).

30 Rutty, *A spiritual diary and soliloquies* (London, 1776), 28 Feb. 1756, p. 89.

31 Ibid.

32 RCPI MS, 'Proceedings', I, 308: 'A proposal for furthering the intentions of the society by Mr Cleghorn' (6 July 1758).
33 Jean le Rond d'Alembert, *Discours préliminaire de l'Encyclopédie* (Paris, 1754).
34 Burrowes, 'Preface', pp. xi–xiii; R.B. McDowell, 'The main narrative' in T. Ó Raifeartaigh (ed.), *The Royal Irish Academy: a bicentennial history* (Dublin, 1985), pp. 1–22.

CHAPTER 14

'Precedent Covenants'

Daniel Maclise's *Marriage of Strongbow and Aoife* and the Writers of Irish History

John McCafferty

Despite the fame of Daniel Maclise's much reproduced painting, the marriage of Aoife and Strongbow is treated almost as an aside in twelfth-century accounts and in most subsequent histories of Ireland.[1] Most sources and commentators simply record the fact of the union as the *Annals of the four masters* do for 1170: 'Mac Murchada gave his daughter to Earl Strongbow for coming into his army'.[2] Giraldus Cambrensis is equally laconic: 'Dermot's daughter Eva was lawfully married to the Earl'.[3] Much more attention was devoted to the events depicted in the background and immediate foreground of the painting – the siege and massacre at Waterford.[4] The subsequent campaign culminating in the capture of Dublin, which is hinted at in the painting by the mounted knights, was also given lavish attention by both annalists and historians.

This is not surprising, given the very marginal nature of the nuptials. The marriage was not the moment when Strongbow and Mac Murchada forged their alliance. It was most definitely not the moment when Henry II acquired his title to Ireland and so was not the instant in which English rule commenced in Ireland. If the aim was to depict a vital moment in Irish history then there were plenty of dramatic moments to choose from: Henry II's receipt of the papal bull *Laudabiliter* or the Christmas of 1171, when Henry entertained the Irish kings who had submitted to him (later depicted by Vincent Waldré on the ceiling of Dublin Castle banqueting room), or perhaps the moment when Mac Murchada may have paid homage to Henry in Aquitaine, in the autumn of 1166.[5] Waterford could even have been retained as the backdrop for Henry II's arrival there on the feast of St Luke, 18 October 1171, the first king of England to set foot on the island.[6] This was not an obvious picture to offer as the turning point in twelfth-century Irish history. Indeed some historical sources, such as the *Annals of Ulster*, the *Annals of Tigernach* and later writers such as Charles O'Connor in the eighteenth century did not bother with any reference to the wedding itself at all.

Others, such as Richard Cox writing in 1689, dismiss it as a variant of 'the lewd lies and idle genealogies' with which Irish histories were said to be riddled.[7] In this analysis Strongbow and Aoife were imperfect human means by which the providential transfer of Ireland to English control was said to have been completed. Cox and others like him would have preferred to concentrate on the clean line of constitutional politics rather than on the seamy subject of marital alliances. William Herbert, a sixteenth-century commentator was quite frank about his disdain for anything that might have happened prior to the king's advent: 'I gladly pass', he snapped, 'over the events of earlier years'.[8] Most historians have agreed with Cox and Herbert and stayed quite happily with high politics or with the military history of 1169 and afterwards. Only the original deal between Mac Murchada and Strongbow, which gave rise to the marriage, has sparked a very intermittent and rather sterile debate about Gaelic Irish law.[9]

Daniel Maclise staked all on the very wedding passed over or rejected by virtually everybody else. The Fine Arts Commissioners who were responsible for the decoration of the new Palace of Westminster designated it as a subject in 1847 but, as he worked it up, he made that subject his own.[10] It does of course allow for comely maidens, for dying in the streets and of course his trademark 'harp that once . . .'. Whether he was dismayed or delighted by the subject matter, it is clear that he read assiduously for his composition paying as much attention to the historical sources as to archaeological sources, which manifest themselves in the jumble of weapons, jewels and carvings that fill up the foreground. Like everyone else before or since who came to address the events of 1169–72, Maclise was forced to be heavily dependent on two main written accounts. The first is Giraldus Cambrensis's *Expugnatio Hibernica* which was completed about the summer of 1189.[11] Here was an account which was close in time to the events and by a man who had visited Ireland in 1183–4 and again from 1185 to 1186. Giraldus, whose grandmother had been Henry I's mistress, knew Henry II and he knew and was related to many of those involved in the affairs of the 1170s as they were his cousins. The *Expugnatio* is a massive work which was fuelled in equal measure by his desire for advancement in the church and his need to explain incursion into Ireland as a morally justified design of divine providence. There is much to be said about this work, but perhaps its most arresting feature is the undisguised and unabashed promotion of his own family.

> Who are the men who penetrate the enemy's innermost strongholds?
> The FitzGeralds.
> Who are the men who protect their native land? The FitzGeralds.
> Who are the men the enemy fear? The FitzGeralds.
> Who are the men whom envy denigrates? The FitzGeralds.[12]

Because it is so well written and because there is virtually nothing else of length, Giraldus's book has been by far the most influential of all writings about this stage in Irish history. It was easily available to Maclise and, even if he did not read it in detail, all subsequent writers were saturated by the interpretation, the sequencing of events, and the attribution of motives offered in the *Expugnatio*. These later commentators did, of course, gloss Giraldus one way or another, which in turn opened up a range of choices for Maclise.

The second major contemporary source was the *Song of Dermot and the Earl*, which was composed around 1225. The putative narrator of this Old French poem is Maurice O'Regan, Mac Murchada's interpreter and agent. In this romantic swashbuckling *chanson de geste* all the players are most chivalrous. It is unlikely, however, that Maclise had either the French text or a translation to hand so he is most likely to have used an English prose translation made by George Carew in the early seventeenth century.[13] This was easily accessible as it was contained in Walter Harris's 1770 antiquarian compendium *Hibernica*. Carew's rendering obliterated the kinder, gentler Mac Murchada for whom Aoife was 'the thing in the world he most loved' and left a cold chancer who used her as a pawn in his great game: 'he would gyve hym his daughter to wife and with her the whole kingdom of Leinster for his inheritance'.[14]

The Irish annals have little to say about the marriage but are much more interesting on the consequences of that union. The most significant Irish language influences on the painting date not from the twelfth but from the seventeenth century – the *Annals of the Four Masters* and Seathrún Céitinn's *Foras Feasa ar Éirinn*. An English translation of *Foras Feasa* by Dermod O'Connor had been available since 1723.[15] Then in 1851 John O'Donovan's massive edition and translation of the annals became available.

It would be very easy to tear this painting apart as an only slightly restrained piece of fantasy, but asking whether it is historically accurate is asking the wrong question. Tearing strips off Maclise for perceived inaccuracy is a cheap and easy thrill, but coming to terms with his clever distillation of the medieval, early modern and eighteenth- and nineteenth-century accounts is a more complex task. As an artist he took up a marginal moment and made of it a demanding and ultimately enigmatic canvas. He did not pick up the bare facts alone. Instead he painted almost eight centuries of reflection on the invasion or incursion of 1169. Whether the viewer or historian likes this gigantic piece or not, it still haunts the Irish historical imagination.

Partial recovery of what we might call Maclise's historical method can be achieved through combining a reading of texts the artist could be reasonably supposed to have procured, through conscientious but not obsessive reading, along with relating those same texts as far as it is possible to the painting. Maclise probably gave as much weight to modern works, that is eighteenth- and nineteenth-century histories, as he did to editions of Giraldus and the *Song*. His near contemporaries were more vivid, more purple in prose, and indeed by the close of the 1700s the marriage began to average out at three or four lines in most accounts. Ferdinando Warner and Thomas Leland, the 'philosophical historians' as they liked to consider themselves, shuddered at the thought of nuptials in the wake of a dreadful massacre.[16] Since he had illustrated so much of Thomas Moore's work, Maclise is likely to have turned to him in the first instance. The brief but graphic description in the *History of Ireland* clearly set off a spark:

> the still reeking horrors, therefore, of the sacked and ruined city were made to give place to a scene of nuptial festivity, the marriage of Strongbow with the princess Eva, according to the promise pledged to that lord at Bristol was, in haste and confusion, celebrated. Immediately after the ceremony, the banners of the respective forces were displayed and the whole army were in full march for Dublin.[17]

All of that blood and iron is easily discovered in the painting. The depictions of the protagonists come straight from Giraldus:

> The earl's nature was as follows. He had reddish hair and freckles, grey eyes, a feminine face, a weak voice and a short neck, though in almost all other respects he was of a tall build.[18]

The fey and somewhat feminine Strongbow stands in contrast to the dishevelled, almost devilish, Mac Murchada:

> Diarmait was tall and well built, a brave and warlike man among his people, whose voice was hoarse as a result of constantly having been in the din of battle. He preferred to be feared by all rather than loved. He treated his nobles harshly and brought to prominence men of humble rank. He was inimical towards his own people and hated by others. 'All men's hands were against him, and he was hostile to all men'[19]

John Hooker added, in his 1587 English translation of the *Expugnatio*, that Mac Murchada 'was become so terryble that none durst styrre against him' after 'Waterford . . . was gotten'.[20]

Tracing the connections between the various written accounts and other history books and the painting, or even between the Victorian craze for things

Celtic and the painting, is a fairly limited exercise. The roots of the dramatic or even melodramatic tension in the work are to be found in its intense engagement with the moral and didactic concerns of earlier writers. Most commentators, whether they regarded the events of 1170 as redemptive or catastrophic, wrestled with two sets of connected questions. First, what right had Strongbow to be in Ireland, what right had Mac Murchada to invite him and reward him with Aoife? Second, what consequences flowed from the open coercion of the massacre and the more covert coercion of the wedding?

Despite Henry II having given Mac Murchada permission to recruit from amongst his subjects, Richard FitzGilbert de Clare or Strongbow was a man in political disfavour, a man who had backed the wrong side in the recent struggle for the English crown.[21] He was a man who had 'up to this time . . . a great name rather than great prospects, ancestral prestige rather than ability, and had succeeded to a name rather than to possessions'.[22] Accordingly Strongbow cautiously sought renewed permission from the monarch to go to Ireland and, as Edmund Campion wrote: 'the king half in derision bade him on in the name of God even as far as his feete could bear him'.[23] So from the very outset there was a certain ambiguity about Strongbow's actions as a man who was, as it were, on the very margins of the king's will: Henry II did later on, in fact, try to halt Strongbow.[24] This image of the earl is supported by most accounts, which like Giraldus and the Kilkenny annals place emphasis on him as a fortune hunter or even a fortune worshipper.[25] Nonetheless Campion still reminds the reader that Strongbow was descended from one of the 1066 conquerors.[26] His actions were therefore glossed from the twelfth century onwards as being highly personal and contingent but also part of a wider process of Norman Conquest. They were flawed and providential, venial and predestined at the same time.

Historians had similar doubts about the legitimacy of Mac Murchada's proceedings. He too, according to Charles O'Connor, was in disfavour with a national monarch in the shape of Ruaidhrí Ó Conchobair.[27] The question also arose as to whether making Strongbow joint heir was permissible under what was understood to be Gaelic law. This was a matter which had never troubled medieval or early modern writers, whether English or Irish in origin.[28] Towards the end of the eighteenth century, historians such as Leland were beginning to say as a matter of course that Mac Murchada was not entitled to make such dispositions.[29] It is possible to debate this question both on its own rather dubious merits and as a manifestation of an infatuation with what was called 'Celtic', but what is really of significance here is the certainty that the repeated assertion of sharp dealing would have affected Maclise's composition. In this view of events, Mac Murchada was operating in the margins of the laws. If he was not breaking them then he was fudging them which, as far as Maclise understood, was precisely the position of Strongbow in relation to Henry II.

1 Guinness advertisement of 1966 commemorating the nine hundredth anniversary of the battle of Hastings. This detail from scene 68 of the Bayeux Tapestry is accurate, apart from the witty addition of a glass of stout. (Diageo Ireland)

2   Daniel Maclise, *The Marriage of Strongbow and Aoife* c.1854 oil on canvas 309 x 505 cm. (Reproduction of this painting and the details in plates 3 and 4 courtesy of the National Gallery of Ireland)

3   Strongbow, the reluctant Aoife and her father, Diarmait Mac Murchada.

4   Strongbow's followers. Hervey de Montmorency is third from the left.

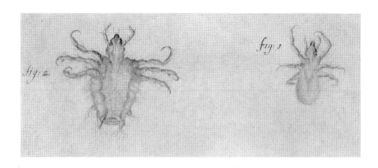

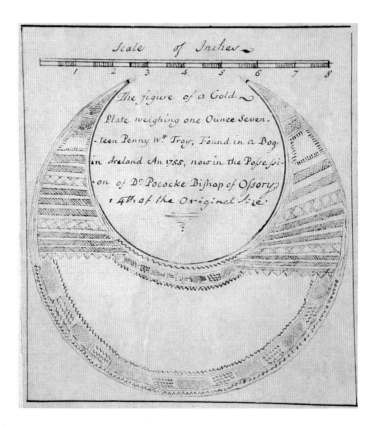

5 & 6 Microscopic drawings by Edward Barry and an anonymous archaeological drawing which together illustrate the wide range of activities of Irish learned societies of the mid-eighteenth century. (Royal College of Physicians of Ireland)

7   Eugène Delacroix, *Liberty Guiding the People* (1830). The most famous image of the mythology of revolution, including its principal elements: the barricade, the *gamin*, and an idealised Liberty who is identified with Marianne – the French woman who embodies the republic. (Musée du Louvre)

8   Dembour and Gangel, *February 1848*. A popular image of the mythologised barricade as the site of heroic combat. (Bibliothèque Nationale de France, Paris)

9   Barricades before the attack. Rue St Maur, 25 June 1848. The photograph illustrates Blanqui's comments about the irrationality of the barricade as a military tactic. (Bibliothèque des Musées de la Ville de Paris)

10   J. L. E. Meissonier, *The Barricade: Memory of Civil War* (1849). Violence is central to this image of the suppression of worker radicalism and betrayal of the revolutionary *peuple*. (Musée du Louvre)

11 & 12 Alfred Rethel, *The Dance of Death of the Year 1849*. Rethel's images of the suppression of the revolution in Dresden in 1849 caused a sensation in Paris, where they were seen as 'hiding in symbolic form a lively critique of contemporary events'. (Leipzig, 1849)

13 Soviet prisoner of war, Heidelager, Oerbke, 1941. The mistreatment of Soviet prisoners of war was not simply the result of circumstances on the Eastern front, but also of the decision, born out of racism, to ignore minimum standards required by international law. (Niedersächsische Landeszentrale für politische Bildung)

14 The *Wehrmacht* and genocide in Tarnopol. Photographs of German soldiers who were involved in massacres of civilians were at the centre of the first exhibition, and often shocked the public. At Tarnopol in the summer of 1941, the retreating Soviet forces started a pogrom. After the German occupation the murder of Jews continued. (Military History Archive, Prague)

15 'Not war in the conventional sense'. Photo of the second exhibition, Berlin, 2001–2. The second exhibition had large tracts of text to support its central thesis of the *Wehrmacht*'s involvement in war crimes. (Hamburg Institute for Social Research)

16   Paul Henry, *The Potato Diggers*. The idealised countryside, with tenant farmers in the foreground, corresponded to the official image of a rural nation, famously propounded by de Valera. (Reproduction courtesy of the National Gallery of Ireland)

17   Paul Henry, *In the West of Ireland*. Idyllic images of the Irish countryside, such as this, were employed by the state to encourage tourism, but government policy was often at odds with the values attached to nature and rusticity in official propaganda. (Reproduction courtesy of the National Gallery of Ireland)

18 Falconet's monument to Peter the Great in St Petersburg, often seen as a symbol of the northern capital. (Michael Laffan)

19 Zurab Tsereteli, Peter the Great, Moscow, a contrast to Falconet's classic image. (Michael Laffan)

20 The removal of the Dzerzhinsky monument, Moscow, August 1991, a high point of democratic euphoria. (*Moscow News*)

21 Dzerzhinsky in the Garden of Sculptures of the Era of Totalitarianism. (Michael Laffan)

22 Head of Lenin, Ulan Ude, still in place in 1996, exemplifying the limits of iconoclasm.

23 V. Klykov, Monument to Marshal Zhukov at the entrance to Red Square. This equestrian statue celebrating Russia's military exploits renews a traditional form in the post-Soviet era. (Michael Laffan)

24 Poklonnaya Gora, indicating the scale of the memorial.

25 Zurab Tsereteli, St George, Victory Monument.

26   The rebuilt Kazan Cathedral on Red Square. (Michael Laffan)

27   The rebuilt Cathedral of Christ the Saviour, the most famous
     example of historicism in modern Moscow.

28 St Sergei Radonezh blessing St Dmitri Donskoi on the eve of the battle of Kulikovo field. Haut relief on the external walls of the Cathedral of Christ the Saviour.

29 Popular shrine at the site of the Ipatiev House, Yekaterinburg, where the royal family was shot. This photograph was taken in 1996.

The solemnity of a wedding being blessed by a mitred and croziered bishop might then be taken as standing in contrast to the dubiousness of the two chief male characters. Giraldus very deliberately stressed that they were *lawfully* wedded. This is not a particularly surprising assertion given that the twelfth century was the very time that the canonists were attempting to formalise the church's position on marriage and also given the fact that the marriage customs of the Irish had been repeatedly criticised by English commentators throughout the period.[30] The reality was, and Maclise captures it well, that this union was the fulfilment of the clause of a treaty rather than a real nuptial. Even the apparent legal substance of the ceremony turns out to be quite brittle given the clear visual reference to lack of consent. Maclise's original cartoon brings this out even more explicitly by showing the bridesmaids holding martyr's palms.[31] Theologically the church considered freely given consent to be integral to the validity of the marriage and it was possible to procure an annulment on the grounds of deficient consent.[32] One annal even suggests that Aoife was already married so that this was a bigamous act.[33] Giraldus, and those who followed him, claimed that Mac Murchada had hawked Aoife about amongst potential allies until the widower Strongbow snapped her up.[34]

The actions of all of the key parties here are either legally defective or legally dubious. Above the law came moral considerations and here Maclise's reading would have led him to a pretty depraved lot. Even a very cursory trawl of the sources would have led the painter to the conclusion that Mac Murchada was a fiercely cruel character. For centuries, writer after writer had insisted that the king's viciousness had caused his own subjects and allies to desert him in his time of need.[35] Meredith Hanmer makes the Leinsterman frenzied and vengeful:

> For when 300 of the Ossory heads were throwne at his (MacMurrough's) feete (alas they had not offended) hee viewed them all, and finding one whom he knew, and mortally hated, he held him by the head and eares, and most brutishly with his teeth, bit the lips of the dead.[36]

All histories, including the relatively benign *Song*, claimed that Mac Murchada's famous abduction of Derbforgaill, which sparked off the chain of events that led to the recruitment of Strongbow, was driven by pure lust: 'Dermot MacMorroe, King of Leinster, halt and lecherous, vowed dishonestly to serve his lust on the beautiful Queen of Meath'.[37] So here was a man utterly impelled by lust – lust for power or sex. By the end of the eighteenth century, a very few voices began to claim that he was a gallant man but they tended to be drowned out by the longstanding claim that he was raddled, corrupt, morally diseased. More recently, it is worth observing in passing, historians have attempted to rehabilitate him as an innovative and 'modernising' king.[38] Although Strongbow has tended to get better press, he is still very far from being without moral taint in the eyes of some commentators. It is likely that Maclise's depiction of him standing on a cross was in part inspired by Seathrún Céitinn's *Foras Feasa Ar Éirinn* where he remarks that the warrior and his associates

> committed inexpressible outrages upon the natives, ravaged and destroyed churches and monasteries and expelled the clergy, regular and secular without distinction.[39]

The three central figures in the painting are the doomed and the cursed. The deaths of the two male powerbrokers are miserable and justifiably so in the eyes of the Four Masters. Strongbow, they record

> died in Dublin of an ulcer which had broken out in his foot through the miracles of SS Bridget and Columbkille, and of all the other saints whose churches had been destroyed by him. He saw, as he thought, St Bridget in the act of killing him.[40]

Mac Murchada fared no better:

> Diarmait Mac Murrough, king of Leinster, by whom Ireland was made a trembling sod – after having brought over the Saxons, after having done extensive injuries to the Irish, after plundering and burning many churches as Ceanannus, Cluain-Iraird etc. – died before the end of a year of an insufferable and unknown disease; for he became putrid while living, through the miracle of God, Columcille and Finnen, and the other saints of Ireland, whose churches he had profaned and burned some time before; and he died at Fearnamor, without a will, without penance, without the body of Christ, without unction as his evil deeds deserved.[41]

The marriage was itself luckless. Their one son, Gilbert, died young and was such a marginal figure that he was even airbrushed out of the sources which Maclise would have used. Aoife's daughter Isabel went on to marry William Marshal, with whom she had five sons and five daughters. Every single one of the male offspring died childless, which in turn led to the dismemberment of Strongbow's great lordship of Leinster.[42] Seathrún Céitinn was certain of the cause: 'divine vengeance ... fixed a mark of infamy upon the families of these plunderers so scarce a man of them left a son behind to enjoy the effects of their fathers' oppression'.[43] Generations of misfortune, then, followed from the fraught and coerced moment of the nuptials. Further misfortunes flowed for other children. The compact between Mac Murchada and Strongbow caused the high king, Ruairdhí Ó Conchobair, to execute Conchobar, Diarmait's son, as a punishment for violating earlier agreements.[44] Even Strongbow went on to kill his own son for cowardice in the field of battle.[45]

The death of the child depicted in the foreground of the canvas prefigures the deaths of the children of the three main actors. The wedding is celebrated in the midst of death and is also the harbinger of further deaths. It also stands between two other unions – one potential and one actual. A projected alliance between a daughter of Ruaidhrí Ó Conchobair and Mac Murchada's son never came to fruition, but one between a daughter of Ruaidhrí Ó Conchobair and Hugh de Lacy, a 'second wave' newcomer and conqueror of Meath, did take place.

The protagonists are framed by the vast depiction of the massacre at Waterford. This slaughter was, in fact, the second part of a storm of violence first unleashed at Dundolf or Baginbun: 'at the creek at Baginbun, Ireland was both lost and won'.[46] At that place, near the southern tip of the Hook peninsula, the men of Waterford had been defeated and Hervey de Montmorency, excoriated by Giraldus as cruel and amoral, had argued that seventy of the vanquished should be executed by being thrown over the cliff.[47] He is the third mounted knight on the left of the picture, looking drawn and agitated in contrast to grim purposefulness of the other knights. Maclise was well aware that this was the second major killing and all available accounts, whether medieval or modern, were most explicit about what Thomas Leland called the 'promiscuous carnage' of Waterford during which there was no ransom and no quarter given.[48] Meredith Hanmer, the seventeenth-century chronicler, and a very likely source for the artist, drew especial attention to the 'heaps of bodies' in the narrow streets of the city.[49] Almost every single source placed both the massacre and the wedding on 24 August, the feast of St Bartholomew, a date which had a lively resonance for the Protestant Maclise.[50]

Waterford was also a turning point. Giraldus stressed that the victory at Baginbun was quickly followed by the realisation that a great city would shortly be overcome and that from this: 'the English derived hope and comfort, their enemies fear and despair'.[51] It was also the place where, soon after, when the smoke and bodies were all gone, Henry II became the first king of England to set foot in Ireland. This blending of personal and national narratives is one of the most successful aspects of the canvas. Maclise excellently combines a stress on individual players with all of their individual decisions, individual failings and individual fortunes, all of which are to the fore in Giraldus and the *Song*, with the stress on national significance found in the *Annals of the Four Masters*, Seathrún Céitinn and the other seventeenth, eighteenth- and nineteenth-century historians. The high visual drama of this work is the exact counterpart of the subtitle of Cambrensis's *Expugnatio* – 'the book of prophetic history'.[52] For Giraldus, Strongbow's arrival fulfils prophecies of both Merlin and St Moling.[53] So while the human forms of Aoife, Diarmait and Strongbow occupy the centre of the viewer's attention, here they are actually caught up in forces much greater than themselves. At this very moment the wheel of fortune is turning rapidly, politics is prophecy fulfilled and strategy is also destiny. The knights are mounted, with banners displayed, and ready to move on Dublin, which will very shortly become the English royal capital and which was still so almost 700 years later in the 1840s.

It is worth adding here that this work, so clearly dependent on a reading of the written sources, appears to have first entered the scholarly narrative as a visual source in 1896 when Denis Murphy, who was editing the *Annals of Clonmacnoise*, directed readers of the entry for 1170 to 'a fine painting by Maclise in our National Gallery of the marriage of Strongbow and Eva'.[54]

What historical reading should be given to this gigantic nineteenth-century canvas? It has been interpreted variously as a nationalist or crypto-nationalist work.[55] It can also be given a unionist reading. It can even be argued that it is apolitical, romantic, a history painting in the grand style. This possible range of responses is very apt because what Daniel Maclise did succeed in capturing, above all, was the confusion, the stress, the nerves, the short-term thinking which had long-term consequences. For all the bloody spectacle and all the anatomy of coercion offered in the piece, the artist is also saying that there are no simple answers. He is saying that history is a mess: a complex mess, one not given to easy conclusions and glib analyses, one which demands hard thinking and hard study to penetrate. Because he makes this fundamental point about the past, Maclise deserves more credit than he has been given for his abilities as an historian or at least as a perceptive reader of the past. His representation in the *Marriage of Aoife and Strongbow*, of victory and defeat, of war and rumours of war, of sex and greed, which is neither gritty realism nor utterly fanciful allegory, encapsulates the obsessions and broodings of eight centuries of writing about Irish history. This is a canvas, then, which ends up saying as much about historians as it does about nineteenth-century history painting.

Notes

This is a version of a paper given at the Maclise symposium in the National Gallery of Ireland on 30 September 2000. I would like to thank Sighle Bhreathnach-Lynch for the invitation to speak on that occasion. 'Then according to the precedent covenants, Dermot gave his daughter Eva in marriage to Richard Strongbow', Meredith Hanmer's chronicle in James Ware (ed.), *Two histories of Ireland* (Dublin, 1633), p. 124.

1 Daniel Maclise, *The Marriage of Strongbow and Aoife*, c.1854, o\c (309 x 505 cm), National Gallery of Ireland, see plates 2–4.
2 John O'Donovan (ed.), *The annals of the kingdom of Ireland by the four masters*, 7 vols (Dublin, 1851), II, p. 1177 (*s.a.* 1170).

3   A. B. Scott and F. X. Martin (eds and trans.), *Expugnatio Hibernica: the conquest of Ireland by Giraldus Cambrensis* (Dublin, 1978), p. 67.
4   *Expugnatio Hibernica*, pp. 65–7.
5   For a discussion of this point, see Marie Therese Flanagan, *Irish society, Anglo-Norman settlers, Angevin kingship* (Oxford, 1989), chapters 2 and 3. See also *Expugnatio Hibernica*, pp. 27–31 and 95–7.
6   Henry landed at Crook on 17 October, stayed there overnight, and entered Waterford city the next day, *Expugnatio Hibernica*, p. 310.
7   Richard Cox, *Hibernia Anglicana* (London, 1689), p. 1.
8   Arthur Keaveney and John A. Madden (eds), *Croftus sive de Hibernia liber* (Dublin, 1992), p. 39.
9   For a review of this debate, see Flanagan, *Irish society*, pp. 80–105 and 112–36.
10 Nancy Weston, *Daniel Maclise: Irish artist in Victorian London* (Dublin, 2001), pp. 210–14.
11 *Expugnatio Hibernica*, pp. xxii–lxxviii. See also Robert Bartlett, *Gerald of Wales, 1146–1223* (Oxford, 1980).
12 *Expugnatio Hibernica*, pp. 169–71.
13 Walter Harris (ed.), *Hibernica*, 4 vols (Dublin 1747). Goddard Henry Orpen's edition and translation appeared after Maclise composed the painting as *The song of Dermot and the earl* (Oxford, 1892).
14 Orpen (ed.), *Song*, ll. 340–1; Harris, *Hibernica*, I, p. 13.
15 Dermod O'Connor (ed. and trans.), *The general history of Ireland . . . collected by the learned Jeoffry Keating* D.D. (Dublin, 1723). For an account of this translation and its reception, see Bernadette Cunningham, *The world of Geoffrey Keating* (Dublin, 2000), pp. 218–24.
16 Ferdinando Warner, *The history of Ireland*, 2 vols (Dublin, 1770), I, p. 260: 'he sent for his daughter and married her to the earl Strongbow according to his contract with all the solemnity that the place and the confusion of the time admitted of'. Thomas Leland, *The history of Ireland from the invasion of Henry II*, 3 vols (Dublin, 1773), I, p. 46: 'He [Diarmait] embraced his new associates and presented his daughter Eva to her intended spouse. When the clamour of war had been silenced, and the peace of the city re-established, he insisted, with an ostentation of good faith and gratitude that her marriage with Earl Strongbow should be immediately solemnized. Their hands being joined, and the nuptials celebrated, Dermod and his confederates proceed to settle their military operations, and leaving a garrison at Waterford bend their course towards Dublin.' For further background to the notion of producing a 'philosophical' history of Ireland, see W. D. Love, 'Charles O'Conor of Belnagare and Thomas Leland's "philosophical" history of Ireland' in *Irish Historical Studies* XIII, 49 (1962), 1-25.
17 Thomas Moore, *A history of Ireland*, 4 vols (London, 1835–46), II, p. 227.
18 *Expugnatio Hibernica*, pp. 86–7.
19 Ibid., pp. 40–1.
20 Liam Miller and Eileen Power (eds), *Holinshed's Irish chronicle* (Dublin, 1979), p. 162. This is a facsimile edition of the Irish part of Raphael Holinshed's *The first volume of the chronicles of England, Scotlande, and Irelande . . . until the year 1547*, 2nd ed. (London, 1587). That second edition was enlarged and extended by John Hooker *alias* Vowell. For a brief

account of the publishing history of this work, see Tony Sweeney, *Ireland and the printed word* (Dublin, 1997), pp. 334–5.

21 For the political background, see Marie Therese Flanagan, 'Strongbow, Henry II and Anglo-Norman intervention in Ireland' in J. Gillingham and J. C. Holt (eds), *War and government in the Middle Ages: essays in honour of J. O. Prestwich* (Woodbridge, 1984), pp. 62–77.

22 *Expugnatio Hibernica*, pp. 54–5.

23 Ware (ed.), *Two histories of Ireland*, p. 59.

24 *Expugnatio Hibernica*, p. 71; Orpen (ed.), *Song*, ll. 2198–2225.

25 *Expugnatio Hibernica*, p. 55; Richard Butler (ed.), *Annals of Ireland by Friar John Clyn* (Dublin, 1849), s.a 1170

26 Ware (ed.), *Two histories of Ireland*, p. 59.

27 Charles O'Connor, *Dissertations on the history of Ireland* (1766), p. 279: 'Dermod MacMurrough expelled by Roderic, king of Ireland, for enormous crimes of a public and private nature'.

28 Meredith Hanmer simply turned Giraldus's 'first-born daughter with the right of succession', *Expugnatio Hibernica*, p. 53 into 'his sole daughter and heire . . . and his whole interest in the kingdom of Leinster after his decease', Ware (ed.), *Two histories of Ireland*, p. 111. Edmund Campion opted for a similar translation: 'the delivery of his only daughter and heir unto marriage, and so the remainder of his kingdome', ibid., pp. 56–7.

29 Leland, *The history of Ireland*, I, 19: 'he engaged to give him his daughter Eva in marriage and make him heir to his kingdom; though sensible that he had no power to nominate his heir by the ancient usage and jurisdictions of his country'.

30 *Expugnatio Hibernica*, p. 99: 'Firstly it has been decreed that all the faithful throughout Ireland should repudiate cohabitation between those related by kinship or marriage, and should enter into and abide by lawful marriage contracts'. On this point see also Flanagan, *Irish society*, pp. 102–5; Art Cosgrove (ed.), *Marriage in Ireland* (Dublin, 1985) and, more generally, J. A. Brundage, 'Concubinage and marriage in medieval canon law' in V. L Bullough and J. A. Brundage (eds), *Sexual practices and the medieval church* (New York, 1982), pp. 118–28.

31 Watercolour on paper (51.2 x 80.2 cm), National Gallery of Ireland no. 6315.

32 William Lyndwood, *Provinciale* (Oxford, 1679), p. 271, (Lib. IV, tit. 2): 'Ubi non est consensus utriusque non est conjugium'. R. H. Helmholz, *Marriage litigation in medieval England* (Cambridge, 1974); M. M. Sheehan, 'Choice of marriage partner in the middle ages: the development and mode of application of a theory of marriage', *Medieval and Renaissance Studies*, N.S. 1 (1978), 1–33.

33 'MacCarthaigh's book' in Séamus Ó hInnse, *Miscellaneous Irish annals 1114–1437* (Dublin, 1947), p. 53, s.a. 1169: 'Richard, Earl of Striguil, came to Ireland with 200 knights and 1,000 archers to the assistance of MacMurrough on St Bartholomew's day. MacMurrough came with his knights to meet them, and gave his married daughter, Áine, to the Earl in consideration of his assisting him to conquer Ireland.'

34 *Expugnatio Hibernica*, p. 53: 'He [Diarmait] offered each of them in turn his first-born daughter with the right of succession to his kingdom'.

35 Ibid., p. 41; George Carew, 'A fragment of the history of Ireland by Maurice Regan' in Harris, *Hibernica* I, p. 12; Edmund Campion and Meredith Hanmer in Ware (ed.), *Two histories of Ireland*, pp. 55 and 110; O'Connor (ed. and trans.), *The general history of Ireland*, pp. 105–6; Leland, *The history of Ireland*, I, p. 17.

36 Ware (ed.), *Two histories of Ireland*, p. 114.

37 Edmund Campion in Ware (ed.), *Two histories of Ireland*, p. 55.

38 Leland, *The history of Ireland*, I, pp. 11–17. F. X. Martin, *No hero in the house: Diarmait Mac Murchada and the coming of the Normans to Ireland* (Dublin, 1975); Donnchadh Ó Corráin, 'Diarmait MacMurrough (1126–71) and the coming of the Anglo-French' in Ciaran Brady (ed.), *Worsted in the game: losers in Irish history* (Dublin, 1989), pp. 21–36.

39 O'Connor (ed. and trans.), *The general history of Ireland*, p. 116.

40 O'Donovan (ed.), *The annals of the kingdom of Ireland*, II, pp. 1182–3 (*s.a.* 1171).

41 Ibid. (*s.a.* 1176).

42 T. W. Moody, F.X. Martin and F.J. Byrne (eds), *A new history of Ireland* (Oxford, 1984), IX, p. 174.

43 O'Connor (ed. and trans.), *The general history of Ireland*, p. 116.

44 *Expugnatio Hibernica*, p. 69.

45 Ware (ed.), *Two histories of Ireland*, p. 158.

46 Ibid., p. 112.

47 *Expugnatio Hibernica*, pp. 61–5.

48 Leland, *The history of Ireland*, I, p. 45.

49 Ware (ed.), *Two histories of Ireland*, p. 124.

50 *Expugnatio Hibernica*, p. 65.

51 Ibid., p. 59.

52 Ibid., p. 25.

53 Ibid., p. 65.

54 Denis Murphy (ed.), *Annals of Clonmacnoise from the earliest period to AD 1408, translated into English by Conell Mageoghan, AD 1627* (Dublin, 1896), p. 208.

55 Pamela Berger, 'The historic, the sacred, the romantic: medieval texts into Irish watercolours' in Adele Dalsimer (ed.), *Visualizing Ireland: national identity and the pictorial tradition* (Boston and London, 1993), pp. 71–87; Fintan Cullen, *Visual politics: the representation of Ireland, 1750–1930* (Cork, 1997), pp. 47–9. Weston, *Daniel Maclise*, pp. 210–15.

CHAPTER 15

Newman's Dream Realised

Elgar, Gerontius and the Catholic Origins
of Modern Englishness

Richard Aldous

On 10 May 1941 the Royal Choral Society, England's premier choir, gathered at the magnificent Queen's Hall in London to perform Elgar's oratorio, *The Dream of Gerontius*. Its conductor, Dr Malcolm Sargent, later remembered that 'Hitler was doing his worst as far as London was concerned. We had no choral rehearsal until twelve o'clock that day, but we all knew every note of the work, and the emotional intensity of the situation made an inspired performance inevitable.'[1] London was by then enduring the heaviest period of the Blitz. One in six of its citizens had been made homeless. More than 20,000 had died in twelve months with an additional 25,000 wounded. Those who walked down Regent Street to the hall that afternoon were badly in need of uplift. An audience that each day contemplated mortality perhaps listened with particular empathy to the priest's prayer for Gerontius: 'By thy Spirit's gracious love, Save him in the day of doom.' Sargent later described how 'we all felt an uncertain foreboding for the future'.[2]

That night London suffered its worst bombing raid of the war. Winston Churchill had been prime minister a year to the day and the German bombers gave him an anniversary to remember: for five moonlit hours, they pounded the capital with incendiaries and high explosives; 1436 people were killed and 1792 injured. There were 2000 fires and 5000 houses were destroyed. Every mainline railway station was hit. Westminster Abbey suffered damage, as did the British Museum, the Law Courts, the Mint, the Mansion House and the Tower of London.[3] The debating chamber of the House of Commons was gutted.[4] Only hours after the *Gerontius* performance, an incendiary bomb lodged in the roof of the Queen's Hall sparked and exploded. The fire brigade attempted to douse flames with a fifty-foot hose but just as they got the blaze under control, water supplies ran out. German bombing had run London dry. The flames rekindled and within half an hour the roof was ablaze. With burning debris falling through to the auditorium, the Queen's Hall became an incinerator and burnt out in minutes. James Agate, drama critic for *The Sunday Times*, wrote in his diary the next day: 'Houses of Parliament hit, British Museum also; much more moved by the destruction, all but the wall, of Queen's Hall. This now presents the appearance of a Roman arena, and should be left as a memorial to Hitler.'[5] Malcolm Sargent made his own visit and wandered amidst the rubble. 'It is strangely fitting and became prophetic', he reflected:

> That the last music and poetry heard in that building was what is usually known as 'The Angel's Farewell'. The men's voices, as if speaking for a groaning and war-stricken humanity, murmured 'Bring us not, Lord, very low. Come back, O Lord, how long' whilst above them the voice of the Angel was singing 'Farewell, but not forever! Be brave and patient, swiftly shall pass this night of trial here, and I will come and wake thee on the morrow.' Then the whole chorus breathed 'Amen, Amen'. Within a few hours our beloved Queen's Hall met in very truth its night of trial.[6]

In 1941 Edward Elgar's *Dream of Gerontius* symbolised the stand of civilised values against the terrors of the Blitz. Yet it might have surprised Elgar that his intensely Roman Catholic work, heavily influenced by Richard Wagner, should have come to represent Englishness at such a moment of danger. *The Dream of Gerontius*, based on a poem of the same title by Cardinal Newman, had enjoyed a troubled existence during Elgar's own lifetime. It was never loved in the way of the composer's *Enigma Variations* or Cello Concerto and was more often the object of suspicion, even derision. The first performance, given at the Birmingham Festival on 3 October 1900, famously, was a disaster. Swinnerton Heap, the chosen chorus master, had died of pneumonia the previous spring and his septuagenarian replacement, W. C. Stockley, seemed unable to cope. When the German conductor, Hans Richter, arrived four days beforehand it was clear that the chorus did not know their parts. Worse, neither did Richter. His first sight of the music had come just ten days before performing it and, a notoriously slow learner, he spent the weekend before the concert 'pacing up and down his bedroom with the score on his mantelpiece' in a desperate attempt to master its difficulties.[7] On Saturday 29 September, at the only full rehearsal, Elgar launched a furious attack on the singers. 'I must record that things got very chaotic', wrote a chorus member afterwards, 'and everyone worked up to a high pitch and unfortunately E. E. more than anyone, naturally. He seemed desperate . . .'.[8] Hopes that Elgar may have entertained that a combination of bad temper and good luck might see his work through this performance were soon dashed. Rosa Burley, a family friend, attended the concert and later recalled:

Before the end of the *Kyrie* it was evident that the chorus did not know the parts they were trying to sing and as the music became more chromatic, they slipped hideously out of tune. It was appalling – far worse than one had thought possible. Those of us who knew the score and the lofty aims Edward had had in writing it suffered agonies as we thought of the misery it must be causing him and did not dare to look at him. . . . The whole thing was a nightmare.[9]

Elgar himself was inconsolable. He wrote to his friend August Jaeger – 'Nimrod' of the *Enigma Variations* – who had attended the performance:

I have worked hard for forty years and at the last Providence denies me a decent hearing of my work: so I submit – I always said God was against art and I still believe it. [A]ny thing obscene or trivial is blessed in this world and has a reward – I ask for no reward – only to live and hear my work. . . . I have allowed my heart to open once – it is now shut against every religious feeling and every soft, gentle impulse *for ever*.[10]

Elgar had to wait more than a year for *Gerontius* to be performed again in full and then in Germany rather than England. A German critic declared that 'not since the days of Liszt . . . has anything been created in the field of oratorio which can equal the grandeur and significance of this sacred cantata'.[11] When the work was repeated in Düsseldorf in 1902, Richard Strauss, Germany's leading composer, proposed a toast 'to the welfare and success of the first English Progressivist, Meister Edward Elgar'.[12] Yet at home the first London performance did not come until 1903. The fiasco of the premiere in 1900, according to his publishers, Novello, had ensured that 'unfortunately for us the work is a commercial failure' and thereafter was used to explain its unpopularity.[13] Disastrous as that first performance had been it only partially explains why a work considered 'the best of me'[14] by a composer acknowledged as the country's finest should have enjoyed such a troubled history. More significant was the work's explicit Catholicism.

'It stinks of incense', the Irish composer and former organist of Trinity College, University of Dublin, Charles Villiers Stanford is reputed to have said at the premiere of *Gerontius*. Suspicions about the work's overtly Catholic nature had surfaced even before it was written. The festival committee in Birmingham had expressed strong reservations about a setting of Newman's poem and agreed only when Elgar made it clear that it was *Gerontius* or nothing.[15] Stockley, the chorus master, was a nonconformist and made clear his own distaste at rehearsals. He allowed singers to make fun of the text. They reduced it to 'a poor joke, starting among some irresponsible young male choristers and spreading to the others'.[16] Stockley seemed content to let the work fail and, recalled one singer, 'so ruthlessly shortened rehearsals that sometimes [her] Wolverhampton party felt resentful at having taken the twelve miles' journey for so little result'.[17] Unease with the oratorio continued after the first performance. The dean of Gloucester refused to have it performed in his cathedral at the 1901 Three Choirs Festival (with which Elgar had been intimately involved since childhood). In 1902 Ivor Atkins, Elgar's friend and organist of Worcester cathedral, persuaded his own dean to allow a performance. Uproar followed as complaints flowed in about the invocations of Mary and references to purgatory sung in a Protestant cathedral. 'You know *Gerontius* is down for the Worcester Festival', Elgar wrote to Fr Richard Bellasis who had prepared the abridgement of Newman's poem:

> My clerical friends do not *mind* i.e. object to the subject and it passed committees without cavil. Now some objector has written to the Bishop and has stirred up strife: the Committee has drawn up a list of small omissions of words; if it is permitted to make such omissions the Bishop will sanction or countenance the performance.... The objectors will not have the litany of the Saints and sundry ejaculations.[18]

Newman's executors gave permission for cuts to be made and a pattern was established that would be replicated in cathedrals throughout the country. In 1920 a Catholic tenor, Gervase Elwes, denounced the dean of Worcester as 'bigoted, inartistic and idiotic' and refused to sing the role of Gerontius after being told 'that the name of the Mother of God should be excluded from the text'.[19] When Elgar died in 1934, the ban was still in operation. 'Let it further be noted that the Protestantism of England is complete and homogenous', commented the Catholic writer Hilaire Belloc as late as 1937 in *An essay on the nature of contemporary England*: 'There is in England less experience, political and social, of the opposing Catholic culture than in any other of the great Western nations.'[20]

Inherent dislike of *Gerontius*'s Catholicism was supplemented by the low status of Newman's reputation in the early decades of the twentieth century. Throughout its early life, Elgar's oratorio suffered because Newman had gone out of fashion and his life the subject of vicious academic dispute.[21] Henri Bremond, in *The mystery of Newman* (1907), brilliantly if unfairly characterised him as an alienated spirit, 'the solitary by choice' who 'by confining his universe to two beings, his Creator and himself, made forever that void at the very bottom of his heart'.[22] In 1918, Lytton Strachey published his iconoclastic portrait of nineteenth-century England, *Eminent Victorians*, in which Newman was held responsible for schism in the Church of England and shown to regret his conversion to Catholicism. 'If Newman had never lived, or if his father when the gig came round on the fatal morning, still undecided between the two Universities, had chanced to head in the direction of

Cambridge, who can doubt that the Oxford Movement would have flickered out its little flame unobserved in the Common Room of Oriel [College]?' Strachey asked.[23] The potency of inciting Newman's example was forcefully demonstrated in the parliamentary debates which scuppered the 1928 Prayer Book, portrayed by anti-Catholics as a Newmanesque attempt to subvert the Church of England.[24]

Anti-Catholicism had always been a feature of Elgar's life. 'Catholic, Catholic, quack, quack, quack, go to the Devil and never come back', Protestant boys had shouted outside his local church.[25] Worcester in the 1860s was a city dominated by its Anglican cathedral. 'It was then a quiet, somnolent old Cathedral city', remembered a contemporary of Elgar, 'a stronghold of the clergy and their wives'.[26] Elgar spent much of his childhood literally in the cathedral's shadow. His family's small house looked onto the north side of the cathedral where he 'played about among the tombs and in the Cloisters when I [could] scarcely walk'.[27] Yet while the cathedral dominated Worcester life, young Elgar inhabited a parallel world. He worshipped at St George's Church, built after Catholic Emancipation in 1829 to widespread dismay in the city. He was educated at Catholic schools and afterwards became a clerk in the offices of a Catholic lawyer. By his early twenties Elgar was regularly writing music for mass and was much talked about in the wider Catholic community. Yet excursions into Worcester society were often painful. In 1883 Elgar proposed to a local Protestant girl, Helen Weaver, but the engagement was broken off when her family expressed disapproval. Five years later he fell in love with another Protestant, Alice Roberts, from a prominent county family, and determined to marry her. Alice's family exerted every pressure without success to destroy the relationship. The couple married at Brompton Oratory in May 1899 with just a handful of guests present. Alice Elgar's family broke with her; in marrying a Catholic, she had excluded herself from Worcestershire's polite society. The couple moved to London where they lived in poverty but at least escaped notoriety.

The opprobrium that Alice Elgar brought on herself through the marriage came about because she had crossed a line; as an Anglican received into the Catholic Church she was a 'turncoat', a distinction shared with John Henry Newman. He had been the most charismatic Anglican priest and Oxford don of his generation. 'No don has ever captivated Oxford as John Henry Newman did', writes Noel Annan in *The dons*: 'For ten years or more every pronouncement he made, every direction toward which he seemed to be veering was scrutinised, interpreted and criticised and those luminous eyes scanned to see if they expressed praise or censure.'[28] As vicar of St Mary's university church from 1828, he had each Sunday the opportunity to influence some of the most promising minds in England. 'Who could resist the charm', asked the poet Matthew Arnold, 'of that spiritual apparition gliding in the dim afternoon light through the aisles of St Mary's, rising into the pulpit, and then in the most entrancing of voices, breaking the silence with words and thoughts – subtle, sweet, mournful?'[29] Newman's sermons might have been subtle, sweet, and mournful but they were also provocative, divisive and forceful. The bitterness and controversy that he stirred up in nineteenth-century Oxford polluted the university's air for generations.

Newman believed that the role of the university was to guide and purify the Anglican Church. The Church of England, he argued, was not Protestant but a Catholic Church purged of its Roman abuses. Its authority came as a body directly descended from the Twelve Apostles. This was the key tenet of the Oxford Movement, brought into being by John Keble but which found in Newman its great proselytising voice. His most notorious statement – *Tract 90* – was published in 1841 and claimed that the Thirty-Nine Articles of the Book of Common Prayer could be 'subscribed by those who aim at being Catholic in heart and doctrine'.[30] Oxford was outraged. College heads and bishops denounced him. Those who supported him found themselves blacklisted as candidates for livings and fellowships. Colleges even changed the time of hall dinner to prevent undergraduates from attending St Mary's. The man who had seemed to offer a *via media* between the crudity of evangelical Protestantism and the idolatry of Rome had turned out after all to be a papist wolf in Anglican clothing.[31] That it surprised no one when he finally 'poped' in 1845 did not stop the barrage of vitriol and condemnation. Many followed him into the Roman Catholic Church and were ostracised by their relations. His supporters who stayed in the Church of England felt betrayed and humiliated. Some of his closest friends – although not the saintly John Keble – refused ever again to speak to him. Of his own family just one sister would not break with him. The conversion of Newman had been a personal as well as a national tragedy.

Majority opinion in England had it that having betrayed his university and church, Newman had also been disloyal to his country. He was a man who enjoyed debate but the criticism that conversion had corrupted his Englishness bothered Newman for the rest of his life. In the mid-1870s, he clashed publicly on the subject with William Gladstone, perhaps the dominant politician of the age. For Gladstone, 'the church and people of England' were one and the same; to leave the Church of England was to abandon England itself.[32] In 1874, Gladstone argued that recent decrees about papal infallibility and the universal jurisdiction of the pope raised doubts about the loyalty of Roman Catholics to their country. 'No-one can become her [the Church of Rome] convert without renouncing his moral and mental freedom, and placing his civil loyalty and duty at the mercy of another', he wrote in *Contemporary Review* in October 1874.[33] No man, it seemed, could serve two masters, a view that underlay the Public Worship Regulation Act of the same year. Newman's riposte that papal infallibility was a question of doctrine, not personal conduct and would not increase Vatican influence over Catholic allegiances did little to undermine the credibility of Gladstone's central argument.[34]

Newman's most succinct statement on the challenge of being both Catholic and English came in February 1865 in a private letter to the editor of a Jesuit periodical, *Month*:

> I think that Protestants are accustomed to look on Catholics as being an un-English body, taking no interest in English questions, and indeed not being able to do so, useless and hostile to the nation, and mere instruments of a foreign power. . . . It seems to me that what is to be aimed at, is to lay a Catholic foundation of thought – and no foundation is above ground. And next, to lay it with Protestant bricks: I mean to use as far as possible, Protestant parties and schools in doing so, as St Paul at Athens appealed to the Altar of 'the Unknown God'.[35]

Newman was articulating the aim of a school of thought active at least since the turn of the century that sought to uncover the Catholic traditions of English society. This reflected a growing confidence inspired by the Catholic Revival. The historian John Lingard, for example, set himself the specific task of writing a history of England that would be acceptable to Protestants, whilst correcting the anti-Catholic bias of previous accounts such as those of David Hume and the Whig historians. Between 1819 and 1830 he wrote an eight-volume history that won guarded praise from Anglicans and was quickly accepted by Catholics as a standard reading of English history. An abridged version became a set text in English Catholic schools in 1854 and was still in use after the First World War (with a continuation by Hilaire Belloc).[36]

The Dream of Gerontius was Newman's own attempt to reintegrate Catholic tradition into English life. He later claimed to have composed it in just one night. 'On the 17th of January last it came into my head to write it', he told a friend on 11 October 1865: 'I really cannot tell how, and I wrote on till it was finished, on small bits of paper. And I could no more write anything else by willing it, than I could fly.'[37] Yet however quickly Newman wrote the poem, it was a long-considered and sophisticated attempt to lay 'Protestant bricks' on a 'Catholic foundation'.[38] That *Gerontius* is steeped in Catholic doctrine and liturgy is beyond doubt, yet so too is its evocation of an English tradition. Newman's eschatology tapped into the prevailing distaste of educated Victorians for a vision of the afterlife that involved hellfire and brimstone. Many found it impossible to reconcile a God of love with one who could also damn his children. 'I will call no Being good who is not what I mean when I apply that epithet to my fellow-creatures', wrote John Stuart Mill, 'and if such a Being can sentence me to Hell for not so calling Him, to Hell I will go'.[39] The most literal interpretation of everlasting punishment came from

Redemptorist Catholic priests who frequently offended English sensibilities. Priests like the appropriately named Fr Joseph Furniss recounted visions of hell in lurid detail:

> The little child is in the red-hot oven. Hear how it screams to come out; see how it turns and twists itself in the fire. . . . God was very good to this little child. Very likely God saw it would get worse and worse and never repent and so it would have been punished more severely in hell. So God in His mercy called it out of the world in early childhood.[40]

Prominent Broad Churchmen such as Charles Kingsley, A. P. Stanley, F. W. Farrar and F. D. Maurice queued up to denounce such teaching and were supported by leading poets including Coleridge and Arnold. Newman recognised Anglican distaste for sulphurous flames and in *The Dream of Gerontius* offered a more subtle vision of eternity with purgatory as a *via media* between an everlasting punishment and life with God. When Gerontius awakes after death it is not to the horrors of a fiery furnace but to 'A strange refreshment; for I feel in me an inexpressive lightness, and a sense of freedom, as I were at length myself, and ne'er had been before.'[41] Suffering is not completely absent – 'And the deep rest, so soothing and so sweet, hath something too of sternness and of pain', says Gerontius – but an Angel is there to assuage fear and 'has me fast within his ample palm'.[42] In this way, Newman offers a civilised vision of life after death based on English notions of fair play that is less about damnation and more akin to waiting for election to the Reform Club. Moreover, *Gerontius*'s elegant transition is expressed in a way that deliberately evokes the language of that most Protestant of poems, Milton's *Paradise lost*, and lends a comforting familiarity to Catholic teaching that might otherwise have seemed alien to Anglicans. Newman understood how far he was stretching a point, telling his friend Ambrose St John not to show *Gerontius* to anyone in Rome for fear that 'prosaic minds may find heresy'.[43]

The Dream of Gerontius captured a public mood and by the time of Newman's death in 1890 had been published in twenty-seven editions in England alone.[44] Alongside Tennyson's *In memoriam*, it was the most widely read and discussed meditation on death of the Victorian age. Its most famous admirer was General Charles 'Chinese' Gordon, whose death at Khartoum in January 1885 caused such public outrage that it precipitated the fall of a government. The general had been given a copy of *Gerontius* days before leaving for Egypt and the Sudan. As a High Anglican, Gordon personified Newman's target audience. Gordon's copy is closely annotated and the surname of the poem's dedicatee – John Joseph Gordon, a priest at Newman's Birmingham Oratory who died of tuberculosis – heavily circled. In the immediate aftermath of the general's death, he was elevated by public opinion to the status of hero, martyr and even saint. When it was reported that he had beforehand been reading *Gerontius*, admirers saw this as prophetic. Gordon's original of the poem was sent back to Newman at the Birmingham Oratory and the annotated text widely read by Anglicans and Catholics throughout England. One Catholic who owned the 'Gordon' edition of *The Dream of Gerontius* was Edward Elgar.[45]

The Dream of Gerontius had played a part in Elgar's life since early childhood. His pessimistic views about life stemmed partly from the early death of two brothers, both from scarlet fever. Elgar took the death in 1866 of his younger brother, Joseph, particularly badly and on the first anniversary was given a religious engraving by the local priest that he kept for the rest of his life. It showed the death of St Joseph and included words from *The Dream of Gerontius*, 'Jesus, Mary and Joseph, pray for me in my own agony'. Elgar first set words from *Gerontius* when he was the teenage organist at St George's church. When Alice's mother died suddenly in 1887, he gave his wife a copy of Newman's poem, as well as his own from which she copied General Gordon's markings. On their wedding day, Elgar's parish priest presented him with a specially bound copy of *Gerontius*. It was no surprise that the idea for a musical setting should have been 'soaking in my mind' for years.[46]

Elgar had a particular reason for being drawn to Newman's attempt to blend Catholic doctrine and English Protestant tradition. Although raised a Catholic, Elgar was the son of a religiously mixed marriage. His mother was a Catholic convert but his father remained a Protestant. William Elgar took up an appointment as organist at St George's church in 1846 but later came to regret it. In 1848 he married Ann Greening who thereafter came to church to hear him play. To his horror she became a Catholic. William detested 'the absurd superstition and play-house mummery of the Papist' but seemed powerless to stop his wife raising their children as Catholics.[47] 'Old man a regular terror as regards the Catholicity of his family', remembered one parishioner at St George's: 'used to threaten to shoot his daughters if caught going to confession'.[48] Growing up within a city dominated by the cathedral, in a household with a forceful and unhappy Protestant presence, ensured that Edward was sensitive to the mingling of traditions. That awareness was compounded by his marriage to an Anglican and generated in him a lifelong reflection on synthetic notions of Catholic and Protestant Englishness. In the 1890s, with the idea for *Gerontius* already incubating, Elgar also considered as a subject St Augustine's conversion of Britain to Christianity. 'I hope some day to do a great work – a sort of national thing that my fellow Englishmen might take to themselves and love – not a too modest ambition!' he wrote to Joseph Bennett, critic of the *Daily Telegraph* in 1898: 'I was going to write to *you* to ask if "S. Augustine" might form the basis of such a work, but some of my clerical friends seem to think that the squabbles about the early British church w[oul]d make the subject impossible without giving offence.'[49] This impression was confirmed by the committee of the Leeds Festival, which the previous year had commissioned a choral work from him but declined the offer of 'St Augustine' because it was 'too Catholic'.[50] 'I fear the work I proposed must not be done', he wearily concluded: '[I] thought of "St Augustine" as a central figure, but people seemed inclined to wrangle over him just now so I must let him rest.'[51] He turned without enthusiasm to the less complicated story of Caractacus, an English chieftain who lost a heroic battle against the Romans and was taken to Rome in AD 51 to be exhibited in triumph before Emperor Claudius. Yet Elgar's determination to write a great English, Catholic work remained and hopes transferred from Augustine to *Gerontius*. He remained afraid 'that the strong Catholic flavour of the poem and its insistence on the doctrine of purgatory would be prejudicial to success in a Protestant community', Rosa Burley later wrote: 'He told me that in fact Dvořák, who had planned a setting of the work for the 1888 [Birmingham] Festival, had been discouraged from making it for this very reason.'[52]

By 1900, Elgar had tangible evidence that his music could inspire and mirror national sentiment. Early in that year the relief of Mafeking from the Boer siege was greeted with ecstasy in Britain. To Elgar's satisfaction his patriotic cantata, *The Banner of St George*, was sung in celebration by choral societies throughout the land. The problem was how to achieve similar success with a more controversial Catholic subject. In the end, it was Newman's own example in *The Dream of Gerontius* that provided a paradigm for Elgar. Just as Newman had sought a *via media*, so the composer set *Gerontius* as an oratorio, the dominant English Protestant musical form.[53] Elgar's aim was to colonise oratorio for Catholicism. His publisher, A. J. Jaeger at Novello, captured the essence of the problem when he told Elgar bluntly that 'People will in Oratorios and Cantatas sing about Jews and Heathens, Gods and superstitions, but not, if they are English Protestants, about Mary and Joseph and Saints galore.'[54] Nevertheless Elgar was resolute: Newman's words would not be bowdlerised. 'As to the Catholic side, of course, it will frighten the low church party but the poem must on no account be touched!' he told Jaeger, 'sacrilege and not to be thought of: them as don't like it can be damned in their own way – not ours.'[55] The challenge was to take Newman's words and reinforce their English tradition through the music.

Elgar's *Dream of Gerontius* is in two parts; part one chronicles the death of Gerontius and part two follows the journey of his soul into the presence of God. Part one could hardly be more Catholic. At its heart is Gerontius's dying confession quoting directly from the Good Friday liturgy (*Sanctus fortis, sanctus Deus*) and ending with the priest's dismissal, *Proficiscere, anima christiana, de hoc mundo*.[56] To reinforce the Catholicity of the liturgy, Elgar used music sung at mass in churches throughout the country. He had written to Hubert Leicester, childhood friend and organist at St George's, Worcester, to ask for 'the old Blue cloth book . . . which used to be used at Church' and plundered its Gregorian settings.[57] This music from the liturgy was immediately apparent to Catholics in the audience at the premiere. Part two leaves a different impression. It is more dramatic than theological and engages directly with the Anglican tradition. The moment of communal affirmation – what Elgar called 'the Great Blaze'[58] – is a setting of 'Praise to the holiest in the height'. This had been included in the Anglican *Hymns ancient and modern* in 1868 and was among the most popular hymns in England. During composition, Elgar complained that 'every ass I meet says:- "I suppose" or "I hope you're going to keep to the *old A&M tune* for Praise to the Holiest!!!!!"'[59] He did not keep the favourite tune but did set the words as a magnificent chorus steeped in the English oratorio tradition, providing a familiarity that emphasised shared tradition and reconciliation. That a sceptical public with predominantly Anglican sensibilities remained largely unconvinced was a palpable blow to Elgar's morale. 'Blast the B[ritish] Public', he wrote in 1900: 'they have no souls, hearts or minds worth a thought'.[60]

Perhaps it was this attitude that caused the master of music at Peterborough Cathedral in 1912 to fling his score of *Gerontius* across the room at a young pupil. 'Sargent, this might appeal to you; I can't understand the fellow', he shouted.[61] 'I took it and looked at it in the train and my hair stood on end with excitement', Malcolm Sargent recalled more than fifty years later: 'I have loved *Gerontius* ever since.'[62] When he heard the work for the first time, he told a friend: 'I'm going to be a composer; I am going to be a second Elgar.'[63] In 1922, Henry Wood, England's leading conductor, had persuaded him that his future lay on the podium. Sargent conducted *Gerontius* for the first time in Leicester and, after the leader of the orchestra had written to Elgar praising his interpretation, he was invited to discuss the score with the composer himself in London. 'We spent the morning and the afternoon with *Gerontius*', Sargent later remembered, 'he playing the piano and singing, or tapping my shoulder while I played, going through every bar with the greatest care, pointing out to me every little difficulty in performance, or interrupting to recall some incident which occurred when he was composing it.'[64] That day began a relationship that lasted until the composer's death: 'From the first moment of our meeting we were obviously friends with an accepted mutual understanding', Sargent wrote.[65] Elgar even proposed him for membership of his club, The Beefsteak. Sargent championed Elgar's music during the 1920s and 1930s when it was deeply unfashionable. 'Many things have been written of Elgar's character', he once said, 'but to anyone who knew him or had eyes to see the real Elgar, both in his music and in himself, Elgar was a mystic.'[66] Eerily, given his lifelong relationship with the work, Sargent died on 3 October 1967, sixty-seven years to the day after the first performance of *Gerontius*.

The Dream of Gerontius remained a respected rather than loved work in England until the Second World War when its full national implications were revealed. That *Gerontius* was the last work sung in the celebrated Queen's Hall before it was bombed was pure chance but seemed to many more like fate. Its theme of death and renewal encapsulated the challenges of the Blitz and hopes for peace. Sargent was talking of more than just a concert hall when he said on the BBC shortly after its destruction: 'I look forward in complete confidence to the day when, in a new Queen's Hall, I can say with Gerontius, "But hark, a grand mysterious harmony: it floods me, like the deep and solemn sound of many waters." Once again I shall hear voices and instruments "utter aloud their grand responsive chant, Praise to the Holiest in the Height".'[67] It was for this reason that in April 1945, as Allied troops advanced towards Berlin, the British Council financed a first complete recording of *Gerontius* to distil the meaning of wartime experience.[68] '*The Dream of Gerontius* is perhaps the greatest work – and certainly one of the greatest – of what may be termed recent or modern British compositions', wrote Ernest Makower, chairman of the British Council Music Committee: 'It has a far wider recognition than any other work produced in the last fifty years on the continent.'[69] Heddle Nash, who had performed the role for Elgar and was undoubtedly its finest exponent, sang Gerontius.[70] The producer was Walter Legge, self-proclaimed 'pope of recording'.[71] Sargent had been hailed as the finest choral conductor in the world by Arturo Toscanini, publicly embracing him after a performance of *Gerontius* at the 1939 London Music Festival.[72] As a result the 1945 recording is amongst the best of any work in the twentieth century.[73] 'The greatness of Elgar is ours for all time', wrote Sargent immediately afterwards: 'May our performance and listening be worthy of our heritage'.[74] More than forty years after its conception, Elgar's *Dream of Gerontius* had finally become part of the fabric of English culture. As if to emphasise the point, Sargent inaugurated a tradition at the Royal Choral Society that saw *Gerontius* performed each Ash Wednesday. Elgar's Catholic oratorio thus joined two great Protestant devotional works, Handel's *Messiah* at Christmas and Bach's *St Matthew Passion* on Good Friday, as fixed points on the calendar of English religious observance.

The reason for this transformation of *Gerontius* from object of suspicion to national institution lay with Britain's wartime experience. Yet that success was more than a reflex response to a story about death and the hereafter by those whose lives were threatened each day. What resonated in *Gerontius* was the transition from an old to a new life. *Gerontius* begins with a dying man fearfully contemplating his time of trial before God. His personal suffering is at the forefront of the drama and presents an agonising vision of individual suffering. Despite a proliferation of priests and assistants, the death of Gerontius is a profoundly lonely experience. At the beginning of part two, Gerontius has already lost much of his individuality by becoming simply 'soul'. Freedom of action has been sacrificed to the angel. The end of the oratorio hears Gerontius as only one of a chorus of souls singing psalm 90, waiting in purgatory to go before the throne of God. His story is as much about salvation of the individual through the experience of the community as it is about death.

Gerontius offered a celebration of communal identity that matched the popular, self-perpetuating image of wartime society. Rationing, requisitioning of private property, evacuation of children and conscription heralded a fundamental shift away from personal freedom towards unprecedented state control over individual lives. Many welcomed this sacrifice of liberty to the community because it raised their quality of living, eradicated the worst symptoms of the 1930s depression, and gave them a clearly defined sense of their own important roles at a time of danger. There was much talk of a 'New Jerusalem' and, after 1940 when German invasion had been repelled, a flood of newspaper articles, books, films and, most famously, the Beveridge Report argued that it should be the central feature of the post-war world. The validation of this vision came with the Labour landslide at the 1945 general election.

The religious dimension to these expectations was made clear in William Temple's best-selling *Christianity and social order*. Published as a Penguin paperback in 1942, the year he became Archbishop of Canterbury, this taut and highly effective text offered a practical as well as theological vision of future society. Temple advocated a programme of social reform based on Christian values that included suggestions about housing, education, banking and working conditions. Running through the book was the theological dictum that Christianity was central to the social and economic order that conditioned everyday life. Between church doctrine and national politics, Temple argued, lay a series of 'middle axioms' – another *via media* – that might inform a vision of society emerging from war.[75] These were rooted in a Christian morality that was inclusive rather than strictly Anglican. Ecumenism 'is the great new fact of our era', said Temple at his enthronement in Canterbury.[76] Temple and George Bell, bishop of Chichester, who had been the other main contender for the see of Canterbury, led the way in expounding Christian unity and social reform.[77] Bell supplemented Temple's agenda with his own ideas on the arts as a vehicle for change and a bulwark against the degradation of society. The church, he argued, should work with musicians, artists and writers as agents of social change to offer a vision that would reflect the broader values of the Christianity.[78]

Ecumenism and the communal experience of war had diluted anti-Catholicism in England. Wars test critical solidarities such as family, love and nationality, often throwing loyalties that had happily coexisted into sharp conflict. Between 1939 and 1945, notions of Englishness were judged not so much by religion or class but more often by a simple question: 'will you stand and fight for your country, its values and traditions?' Elgar's *Dream of Gerontius* had been a conscious attempt to follow Newman's example of creating art with Protestant bricks on Catholic foundations and showed an overt desire to synthesise Catholicism and patriotism. That calculated identification with English traditions ensured that at a moment of national peril *The Dream of Gerontius* was a message in a musical language that could be heard and understood. The story of Gerontius resonated with those who had endured the struggle of war and yearned for a New Jerusalem. It might seem strange to us that Elgar, apparently so conservative in manner and politics, should anticipate the aspirations of the generation that overwhelmingly voted Labour in 1945. Yet Elgar was a step ahead. Above his signature on the final score, he inscribed words from *Sesame and lilies* by the nineteenth-century radical, John Ruskin, who died in 1900: 'This is the best of me; for the rest, I ate, and drank, and slept, loved and hated, like another; my life was as the vapour, and it is not; but *this* I saw and knew: this if anything of mine, is worth your memory.'[79]

Notes

This chapter began life as a conversation with Dr Simon Ball about Lord Annan's essay on Newman in *The dons: mentors, eccentrics and geniuses* (London, 1999). I am grateful to him and Professor Harry White for reading the first draft.

1 Robert Elkin, (foreword by Dr Malcolm Sargent), *Queen's Hall, 1893–1941* (London, 1944), p. 6.
2 Ibid., p. 8.
3 *Front line, 1940–41* quoted in Elkin, *Queen's Hall*, p. 128.
4 Peter Lewes, *A people's war* (London, 1986), p. 105.
5 Elkin, *Queen's Hall*, p. 129.
6 Ibid., p. 146.
7 Henry J. Wood, *My life in music* (London, 1946), p. 249.
8 Jerrold Northrop Moore, *Edward Elgar: a creative life* (Oxford, 1984), p. 330.
9 Rosa Burley and Frank C. Carruthers, *Edward Elgar: the record of a friendship* (London, 1972), p. 142.
10 Percy Young (ed.), *Letters to Nimrod: Edward Elgar to August Jaeger, 1897–1908* (London, 1965), pp. 109–10.
11 Geoffrey Hodgkins (ed.), *The best of me: a Gerontius centenary companion* (London, 1999), p. 195.

12 Ibid., p. 205.
13 Jerrold Northrop Moore (ed.), *Elgar and his publishers: letters of a creative life*, I *1885–1903* (Oxford, 1987), p. 249.
14 Ibid., p. 219.
15 Jerrold Northrop Moore (ed.), *Edward Elgar: letters of a lifetime* (Oxford, 1990), p. 84.
16 Burley, *Edward Elgar*, p. 140.
17 Ibid., p. 140.
18 Moore (ed.), *Elgar: letters of a lifetime*, p. 111
19 Percy Young, *Elgar, Newman and the Dream of Gerontius* (Aldershot, 1995), p. 133; this book examines Gerontius in the context of Roman Catholic music in England since the sixteenth century.
20 Hilaire Belloc, *An essay on the nature of contemporary England* (London, 1937), p. 9; Belloc was educated under Newman at the Oratory School, Birmingham.
21 See Sheridan Gilley, 'Wilfred Ward and his life of Newman', *Journal of Ecclesiastical History* XXIX, 2 (1978), 177–93.
22 Ibid., 177.
23 Lytton Strachey, *Eminent Victorians* (London, 1918) p. 23.
24 John Moorman, *A history of the Church in England*, 3rd edn (London, 1973), pp. 427–8.
25 Moore, *Edward Elgar*, p. 15.
26 Ibid., p. 18.
27 Jerrold Northrop Moore (ed.), *Edward Elgar: the Windflower letters* (Oxford, 1989), p. 140.
28 Noel Annan, *The dons*, p. 40.
29 Ibid., p. 40.
30 Ibid., p. 51.
31 For a discussion of *Tract 90* see, for example, David Nicholls and Fergus Kerr (eds), *John Henry Newman: Reason, rhetoric and romanticism* (Bristol, 1991), pp. 28–87.
32 Ibid, p. 139; 'I can no longer take the Communion in the Church of England', Archdeacon Henry Manning, future Catholic Archbishop of Westminster, had told his close friend, William Gladstone, at the altar rail when he converted to Rome: 'I rose up, and laying my hand on Mr Gladstone's shoulder, said "Come". It was the parting of the ways. Mr Gladstone remained and I went my way.' Strachey, *Eminent Victorians*, p. 54.
33 Nicholls and Kerr (eds), *John Henry Newman*, p. 135.
34 Ibid., p. 150.
35 Charles Stephen Dessain and Edward E. Kelly (eds), *The letters and diaries of John Henry Newman*, XXI *The Apologia: January 1864 to June 1865* (London, 1971), p. 423.
36 John Kenyon, *The history men* (London, 1983), pp. 86–9.
37 Quoted in Nicholls and Kerr (eds), *John Henry Newman*, p. 216.
38 Dessain and Kelly (eds), *The letters and diaries of John Henry Newman*, XXI, p. 423; for a textual analysis of *The Dream of Gerontius* see Elizabeth Jay's excellent essay, 'Newman's Mid-Victorian Dream', in Nicholls and Kerr (eds), *John Henry Newman*, pp. 214–32.
39 Quoted in David Newsome, *The Victorian world picture: perceptions and introspections in an age of change* (London, 1997), p. 199.

40 Quoted in Newsome, *The Victorian world picture*, p. 201
41 Full text of Newman's poem reprinted in Hodgkins (ed.), *The best of me*, p. 41ff.
42 Ibid.
43 Quoted in Nicholls and Kerr (eds), *John Henry Newman*, p. 221.
44 Young, *Elgar, Newman and the Dream of Gerontius*, p. 97.
45 For Gordon's annotated text see Hodgkins (ed.), *The best of me*, p. 41ff.
46 Moore, *Edward Elgar*, p. 290.
47 Ibid., p. 6.
48 Ibid., p. 17.
49 Moore (ed.), *Elgar: Letters of a lifetime*, p. 63.
50 Ibid., p. 61.
51 Ibid., p. 56.
52 Burley and Carruthers, *Edward Elgar*, p. 135.
53 Charles Rosen, *The romantic generation* (London, 1996), pp. 569–98.
54 Moore (ed.), *Elgar and his publishers*, I, p. 191.
55 Ibid., p. 190.
56 Moore, *Edward Elgar*, p. 297.
57 Moore (ed.), *Elgar: letters of a lifetime*, p. 56.
58 Moore (ed.), *Elgar and his publishers*, I, p. 184.
59 Ibid., p. 201.
60 Ibid.
61 Sargent Papers (private collection), annotated interview, 9 Aug. 1966.
62 Ibid.
63 Charles Reid, *Malcolm Sargent: a biography* (London, 1968), p. 106.
64 Theatre Museum (Covent Garden), Sargent Biographical File, 'Vitality in music' by Herbert Ashley.
65 Sargent Papers, 'Sir Edward's Land of Hope and Glory' by Sir Malcolm Sargent, unidentified newspaper clipping.
66 Theatre Museum (Covent Garden), Sargent Biographical File, 'Vitality in music' by Herbert Ashley.
67 Elkin, *Queen's Hall*, p. 146.
68 Re-released by Testament CD SBT 2025, *The Dream of Gerontius* (1993).
69 PRO, BW 2/178, Makower to Henn-Collins, 24 May 1943.
70 Author's interview with Nancy Evans, 10 July 1998.
71 Elisabeth Schwarzkopf, *On and off the record: a memoir of Walter Legge* (London, 1982), p. 107.
72 Author's interview with Sir William Glock, 15 Dec. 1997.
73 *Gramophone*, Dec. 1999, p.41; the recording is listed in the top seventy-five recordings of the century.
74 Sargent Papers, 'Sir Edward's Land of Hope and Glory'; West Yorkshire Archives (Kirklees), Huddersfield Choral Society, 1836–1986, KC200/1/1/12: Minute Book, 28 June 1946.
75 David L. Edwards, *Leaders of the Church of England, 1828–1944* (Oxford, 1971), pp. 321–8; many of Temple's suggestions found their way into the Butler Education Act (1944).

76 Moorman, *A history of the Church in England*, p. 452; Temple was instrumental in founding the British Council of Churches in 1942.

77 Bell's appointment to Canterbury after Temple's death in 1944 was blocked by the Prime Minister, Winston Churchill, who had been angered by the bishop's condemnation of the aerial bombing of Germany.

78 Edwards, *Leaders of the Church of England*, p. 337.

79 Moore (ed.), *Elgar and his publishers*, I, p. 219.

CHAPTER 16

'La Révolution Introuvable'

Raymond Aron, May 1968 and Symbolic Violence
in the French Revolutionary Tradition

David Kerr

At the end of April 1968, a local disciplinary problem at the Nanterre campus on the western fringe of Paris, through a combination of deft political manipulation and clumsy policing, precipitated a crisis in the French university system. Mass demonstrations by students in the capital on 6 May degenerated into widespread clashes between the student body and the Compagnies Républicaines de Sécurité (CRS). The violence recurred on the night of 10–11 May, when student rioters, with the sympathy and active support of the residents of the fifth and sixth arrondissements, barricaded themselves into the area of Paris they considered to be peculiarly theirs: the Latin Quarter. The perceived brutality of the forces of order gained the student protesters widespread sympathy. On 13 May, while the students occupied the Sorbonne, their call for a general strike was well received. In the following days, the stoppages spread across most sectors of the French economy. By 24 May, nine million workers were officially on strike. In the last week of May, the continuing violence on the streets of Paris, combined with the failure of the negotiated settlement between the government and the unions to win the backing of the rank and file across the country, appeared to be precipitating a political crisis. De Gaulle's television address of 24 May failed to reassure the public that the political leadership was capable of ending the economic paralysis. On the 28 May François Mitterrand proposed the creation of a provisional government to fill the political vacuum left by the vacillating President. A dispirited De Gaulle secretly flew to Baden-Baden on 29 May to consult General Massu on the attitude of the army. On his return, acting on the advice of his first minister Georges Pompidou, he deftly seized the political initiative by dissolving the National Assembly and announcing legislative elections for 23 and 30 June. This appeal to regular constitutional channels provided a democratic means of defusing the crisis. The militants who associated *élection* with *trahison* were stigmatised as extremists by a public that was already tiring of the disruption that permanent revolution brought to their daily lives. The workers gradually responded to the unions' and the Communist Party's call for a return to work. Increasingly isolated, the student movement collapsed after a final night of barricades and violence on 11 June. The Sorbonne was evacuated without difficulty five days later. The June elections sealed the end of the *mouvement de mai* in anti-climactic fashion by returning a reinforced Gaullist majority, leaving many disillusioned.[1]

Debate as to the nature and significance of the 'events' began in May 1968 itself and continues today. The extraordinary complexity of the crisis with its combination or coincidence of generational and class conflict, of reformism and utopian idealism, of demands for narrowly political liberties and for broader cultural (especially sexual) freedom, invited and invites conflicting interpretations.[2] In addition, the 'events' of 1968 have proved confusing in that they simultaneously contained novel forms of protest movement for an advanced capitalist or post-industrial society and anachronistic elements, references to an older tradition of popular protest. Participants and observers alike saw an analogy between the disturbances in Paris and the French revolutionary tradition. For example, Maurice Grimaud, prefect of police in May 1968, observing the clashes on the Place Maubert on 6 May, was struck by their disturbing familiarity to his mental image of nineteenth-century revolutions:

> A strange impression is coming over me . . . of a Paris instinctively recovering, in the little streets of the left bank, the reflexes it must often have had in the past, in July 1830 as in February 1848. Nothing is missing, neither the singing, nor the barricades, nor the fires, nor even the black flag . . . Yes indeed, it is the strong smell [of history] which our young people are breathing in with pleasure in the warm evenings of floréal 68.[3]

The students' construction of barricades from paving stones and felled trees (as well as cars and other heterogeneous and less traditional materials) was the factor which above all else both suggested the persistence of a collective memory of revolution and evoked a disquieting or exhilarating sense of historical *déjà vu*.

However, despite the re-emergence in the streets of Paris of the most potent symbol of the revolutionary tradition, the question of the relationship between the 'events' of May 1968 and earlier French revolutions was seldom seriously addressed in the aftermath of the crisis. Government ministers and the conservative press did immediately detect affinities between the irresponsible anarchism of May 1968 and the equally irresponsible anarchism of the

Paris Commune or the June Days of 1848. Study of the discourse of the French right in 1968 reveals the enduring structures of reactionary polemics in modern France. The repertoire of pejorative stereotypes of the activists and disobliging explanations of their motivations in 1968 shares with the reactionary discourse of the anti-Communards in the early 1870s both a vocabulary and a psychology. In 1968, as in 1871, the political and social aspirations of the *envergumènes* in revolt were submerged by scandalised rumours of foreign plots, sexual licence and material greed.[4] But if the intellectual tradition of counter-revolution in France was spontaneously evoked and revived in 1968, the same cannot be said of its counterpart and antagonist, the French revolutionary tradition. The French Left was singularly reluctant to draw analogies between the events in Paris in 1968 and the events in Paris in July 1830 or February 1848, for example. The leaders of the student movement identified themselves more readily with international communist revolution than with the native French tradition of revolutionary action, citing Régis Debray or Che Guevara on revolutionary tactics in preference to Auguste Blanqui. The spokesmen of the French Communist Party (PCF), needing to justify their objective alliance with de Gaulle for the preservation of the political and social status quo, were also unwilling to refer to the revolutions of the nineteenth century. Their conservative strategy during the crisis of May and June 1968 could be intellectually justified only by reference to a 'science' of revolution which could prove, through selective quotation from the works of the founders of Marxist-Leninism, that the conditions for revolution had not been met in 1968. The revolutionary agitation of the *groupuscules* could thus be dismissed as a romantic but irresponsible attempt to accelerate the historical process and the students' leaders branded as anarchist agitators by the communist establishment.[5] The conclusion of the official PCF argument thus ironically coincided with the Gaullist characterisation of the movement (although it was officially predicated upon the interests of the ultimate and indefinitely postponed revolution rather than on the visceral distaste for chaos in the streets of Paris which animated the openly reactionary elements in French society). While the self-proclaimed revolutionaries of 1968 considered their movement so profoundly radical that it could only be demeaned by nostalgic references to an antiquated tradition of republican or socialist – or even communist – agitation, republicans, socialists and communists all considered that their glorious revolutionary past could only be besmirched by association with the faintly ludicrous and ultimately unsuccessful agitation of May 1968.

The events of May 1968 offended by being carnivalesque and chaotic. The youthful impertinence of the student leaders and their sustained derision of familial, social and political authority made the historical recuperation of the crisis as difficult as the political recuperation of the movement.

The absence of quantifiable economic grievances sufficient to warrant such a dramatic response, the ill-defined ideology of the protest despite the untrammelled logorrhoea of the participants, and the symbolic nature of the exemplary acts employed by the students, all combined to mystify observers and discourage historical parallels.[6] The year 1968 was assimilated to previous revolutions only as a late, ludic, parody of past heroism. The students' use of revolutionary rhetoric and gestures was dismissed as superficial role-play and their movement as an empty simulacrum of revolution. The republican and socialist historiographical traditions differed in many respects as to the interpretation of successive revolutionary episodes since 1789. But over and above their scholarly and political quarrels as to the precise significance of revolution, and of each revolution, a consensus emerged that revolutions were (for the republican tradition), are and will be (for the socialist tradition) significant. Revolution had played a demonstrable, preponderant (if controversial) role in the fashioning of modern France and modern French identities. As a matter of national *amour-propre*, it was therefore necessary to treat the phenomenon of revolution with due seriousness. The reluctance to place the events of May–June 1968 within the context of French revolutions since 1789 can be attributed to the mistaken belief, common to both the Gaullists and the left, that in order to take revolution seriously one has to present revolutions as serious. Whether revolution was tamed and rendered intelligible to support a narrative of emerging national consciousness, or of increasing class consciousness or of modernisation, its chaotic elements, the contradictory mix of utopian, mystic and nostalgic aspirations of its actors, had to be marginalised. The high seriousness of posterity, no more than an indirect form of the 'vast condescension of posterity' lamented by Edward Thompson, imposed one reductivist historical paradigm or another on revolution. Taking the myth of revolution seriously too often implies a certain self-imposed deafness to the 'false notes' generated in the vast brouhaha that constitutes revolution as an historical phenomenon.

There is little to be learnt by an attempt to read May 1968 through a *grille de lecture* elaborated over the best part of two centuries by intellectuals and artists in France and across Europe. The events of 1968 cannot be easily or usefully integrated into a heroic tradition of revolution, be it French or international. If it is worthwhile reflecting on the relationship between 1968 and previous French revolutions, it is not to confirm that the events of May did not conform to the recognised vision of revolution, but to question the extent to which the mythology of revolution in France corresponds to the actual nature of French revolutions. In other words, to raise the possibility that the fact that May 1968 may only with difficulty be recognised as a revolution does not necessarily reflect unfavourably on the events of May (accused of failure to conform to an abstract model of revolution) but calls into question the definition of revolution (accused of being an abstract model which fails to conform to, or take adequate account of, the complex texture of the historical events which it classifies as revolutionary).

The fear of mutual contamination between revolution observed in 1968, with its unheroic aspects prominently displayed, and revolution remembered and celebrated – revolution in its Sunday best – can be seen in the controversy that surrounded the analysis of the events of May by Raymond Aron. A prominent sociologist and political scientist at the Sorbonne, critical of both left-wing orthodoxies and of Gaullism, Aron was an isolated figure in the French intellectual world and no stranger to controversy. On 29 May 1968 with his customary taste for provocation, he used his regular column in Le Figaro to comment on the escalation of the crisis in the French university system into a revolutionary crisis. Under the title 'Immuable et changeant', borrowed from his earlier study of the genesis of the Fifth Republic, he published a selection of quotations from Alexis de Tocqueville's *Souvenirs*, passages which related that jaundiced observer of French political life's response to the Revolution of February 1848. To these, Aron merely added a passage from Tocqueville's *L'ancien régime et la révolution*, a quotation from Ernest Renan's *La réforme intellectuale et morale* (written in the aftermath of the Paris Commune of 1871) and the hope that his readers' anxieties about the ongoing crisis would be allayed by a reminder of how authors 'without illusion and without repudiation' had come to terms with 'comparable periods'. The passages chosen illustrate the nineteenth-century conservatives' distaste for the intellectual poverty and role-play of nineteenth-century revolutionaries, the opportunism of revolution's eulogists among the intelligentsia, and the obstreperous but illiberal temperament of the French people. Aron's modest history lesson provoked an angry response, partly as a result of his implicit criticism of the student movement and its intellectual fellow-travellers (in particular his fellow sociologists), but chiefly because he had the temerity to break a taboo by casting an equally unsentimental eye on revolution both present and past.

In *La révolution introuvable, réflexions sur les événements de mai*, written in July and published in August 1968, Aron continued to explore the analogies between the events of May and earlier revolutions. The book's epigraph, two quotations from Proudhon's diaries from February 1848, 'On a fait une révolution sans idée' and 'La nation française est une nation de comédiens', encapsulate his ambition to place the crisis of 1968, warts and all, within a broader tradition of revolutionary activity. At various points in the work he drew explicit comparisons between the events of May and the Revolutions of 1830 and 1848, as well as the Paris Commune of 1871 and, less frequently, the wildcat strikes of June 1936.[7] Nevertheless, in *La révolution introuvable*, Aron's lucid irony was directed essentially towards recent events and he drew back from his earlier association of 1968 with 1848. In drawing a distinction between a *psychodrame*, the derogatory formula he used to characterise May 1968, and revolutions proper, he reintroduced and rehabilitated an implicit model of socio-political revolution to which the events of May 1968 failed to conform. May, he argued, had been a *psychodrame* rather than a revolution because the objective conditions necessary for a genuinely popular movement leading to an abrupt change of régime had not been in place. The militant student *groupuscules* had no popular support in the country; the PCF that did command a mass following among the working class had in effect supported the Gaullist status quo. There had therefore been no organisation both able and willing to exploit the situation, no alternative power to replace de Gaulle, with the result that the revolutionary rhetoric and posturing of the *enragés* had been no more than play-acting:

> The political situation was dominated by a limited and unwritten alliance between the Communist Party and the government. The Communist Party, as everyone knows, did not want big strikes and still less the politicisation of the general strike . . . As the Communist Party controlled the working masses and did not intend to stage an insurrection, a psychodrama was at issue. M. Sauvageot and M. Geismar [student leaders] acted and spoke like leaders of the Paris commune in 1789 or 1790, like the impromptu leaders of February 1848, in a totally different situation. Removing a president elected by universal suffrage and removing a king are not the same thing . . . This same Paris which, once again, almost made a revolution, later, as usual, voted conservative. All these people were imitating great precursors and revived revolutionary models inscribed on the collective unconscious. Psychodrama, rather than drama, for want of a revolutionary party, until the apparent disintegration of the powers inspired 'the great fear'. Psychodrama rather than drama because everything happened without physical violence. Nothing was more striking than the verbal delirium without human deaths.[8]

Fourteen years later, Aron's attitude to May 1968 had not evolved significantly. In his *Mémoires, cinquante ans de réflexion politique*, he defended his earlier position, stressing once again the theatrical nature of both the participants' behaviour and the reception that their performance received from the French public. May 1968 had begun as a transgressive inversion of the established order that had briefly charmed an easily amused public but which had lost all momentum as soon as the French people had abandoned its willing suspension of disbelief:

> This sudden diversion from daily tedium, the quasi-revolution, play-acted rather than made, inspire sympathy, even enthusiasm. The street scuffles which degenerate into riots, the clashes between demonstrators and a police force constantly accused of violence delight inveterate lovers of Punch and Judy shows, gluttons

for the gendarme's misfortunes; the merry escapade of the young people who go back to the 'demos' every evening refreshes the adults' hearts, as long as they don't discover that their car has been put out of action. The colourful crowd which peoples the lecture theatres and corridors of university buildings, the non-stop public meetings, the impromptu orators who scarcely consciously reproduce the gestures and speech of great precursors amuse and attract the curious . . . To the last days of liberty, good humour has the upper hand over the violence characteristic of these sorts of social explosion. None of all this is wholly serious. It's playacting, it's not totally 'for real'. Towards the end of the month, revulsion at the havoc gradually replaces fellow-feeling for these 'admirable young people': fear of a real revolution spoils the pleasure of the spectacle. [9]

Aron's distaste for the 'non-revolution'[10] of 1968 was based upon his assessment of the movement's ideological and strategic deficiencies. As the student leaders had no clear programme of reforms, their movement could only be negative, self-indulgent and destructive. Aron was of course aware that similarly unrepresentative minorities equally devoid of any constructive ideology had repeatedly managed to destroy régimes during the nineteenth century. Nevertheless, he refused to grant the events of 1968 even the scant respect he afforded the revolutionary movements of 1830, 1848 and 1871. His scorn for his students' amateur dramatics, even in comparison with the posturing of the nineteenth-century revolutionaries, was based on an unfavourable judgement of their seriousness of insurrectionary purpose. The yardstick he used to assess the sincerity of revolutionary intention was the extent of physical violence. The *soixante-huitards* had failed to embrace political violence with sufficient seriousness. The almost complete absence of fatalities during the disturbances of May and June 1968 is taken to indicate the underlying ludic quality of the events. Previous revolutions had manipulated violence for specific strategic ends: in 1968 the violence had, Aron argued, been merely symbolic. 'The nineteenth century revolutions killed few during the first phase', he conceded, 'but still there were deaths'. In 1968, in contrast, 'only the symbol of violence remains'.[11]

In support of this argument he contrasted the use of barricades in 1968 with their use in nineteenth-century insurrections. The barricades in the Latin Quarter in May 1968 had served no strategic purpose whatsoever in the fighting between the rioters and the forces of order, providing neither tactical offensive advantage nor adequate protection for their defenders. Rather than indicating a military challenge to the régime, they had been erected as a political challenge to the authorities:

The barricades had a symbolic character since they did not represent an effective means of defence against the police. In reality . . . the barricades belonged to a well-known technique, the technique of challenging the forces of order. The barricades ... put the government in a dilemma ... Either they left the students in control of the streets, creating the impression that the government had lost the ability to govern because the streets belonged to the insurgents, or else it unleashed the police against the students and, at least in the first phase, bourgeois opinion would rally to the insurgents, to the students against the CRS. [12]

Since the barricades of May 1968 had been no more than a gambit by means of which the responsibility for physical violence could be placed on the police, thus eliciting the sympathy of the respectable middle class opinion for the students, their presence did not indicate a genuine revolutionary continuity. On the contrary, the barricades of May were nostalgic, superficial references to a distinct and defunct historical tradition:

The revival of old techniques gives an impression of archaism, although the function of the techniques has changed. In the nineteenth century, barricades had some military efficacy. Today they play a role of sham military efficacy but keep or recover a psychological effect. Transition from a material to a symbolic effect. (Passage de l'efficacité matérielle à l'efficacité symbolique.)[13]

This shift from a military logic of barricade building, with a high incidence of physical violence, to a symbolic logic, with a concomitant 'délire verbal sans mort d'hommes', lies at the heart of Aron's ultimate refusal to place the events of May 1968 within the French revolutionary tradition. While his analysis of the economic and political circumstances of the spring of 1968, and of the isolation and unpopularity of the student militants, was sufficient for him to distinguish between May 1968 and what he considered to be broad-based popular revolutions such as the first French Revolution or the Russian Revolution of February 1917, it was the absence of death on the barricades which enabled him to distinguish 1968 from 1830, 1848 or 1871.

Aron's denial of the revolutionary credentials of the events of May on the grounds that the barricades built in 1968 were folkloric gestures more redolent with symbolic significance than serving any meaningful strategic function is, however, unduly dismissive. All the barricades built during successive revolutionary episodes in Paris from 1827 onwards could be classified in exactly the same terms.[14] From their first modern appearance in an insurrectionary episode in Paris, barricades were explicitly construed as being a historical revival of an unfamiliar phenomenon, unknown in Paris since the *journée des barricades* of 1573. The retrospective glorification of events in Paris in July 1830 in literary texts (both fictional and non-fictional) and the visual arts turned the barricade into the quintessential emblem of revolution. Every subsequent insurrectionary episode that featured barricades was condemned to being a conscious or unconscious (but generally deliberate) reference to the precedent of the July Revolution of 1830. The barricades of 1848 and 1871 were themselves folkloric gestures, less nostalgic than the barricades of 1968 perhaps, but equally derivative. Similarly, while it is undoubtedly true that the barricades erected on the boulevard Saint-Michel and in the streets surrounding the Sorbonne on the night of 10–11 May 1968 served no clear strategic purpose, the military effectiveness of the barricades erected in the French revolutions of the nineteenth century can be easily exaggerated. As in 1968, the barricades of 1830, 1848 and 1871 were erected haphazardly, more in an attempt to demarcate a zone of transgressive inversion of the status quo than in an attempt to facilitate the insurrectionary conquest of the city. Barricades were fundamentally theatrical, in nineteenth-century revolutions as in May 1968. They served as a ritual frame for political conflict and as such they functioned less as a precipitant of violence than to limit the loss of life by allowing violence to be staged as symbolic confrontation for legitimacy.[15]

Aron sought to demystify the students' barricades by exposing the mechanism by which they were used to project and channel a symbolic challenge to the authorities. His analysis of the structure of street politics in 1968 was acute and accurate, but the conclusion he drew – that the barricade in twentieth-century France was different in kind from the barricades of nineteenth-century France – is highly debatable. Aron's vision of a historical evolution from an *efficacité matérielle* (associated with high levels of physical violence and a genuine revolutionary impetus) to an *efficacité symbolique* (associated with low levels of physical violence, theatricality and insincerity) reveals a misunderstanding of the nature of nineteenth-century revolution. His desire to denigrate the events of May 1968 led him to ignore the lessons of Tocqueville and Proudhon (amongst others): that the successful Parisian revolutions of the nineteenth century had contained more symbolic violence than physical violence.

While it is true that revolutionary situations generally involve physical violence and attendant casualties (the single exception in modern French history being not 1968 but the successful and entirely bloodless revolution of September 1870), Aron's argument both overemphasises the centrality of physical violence to revolution and, more importantly, misconstrues the role which physical violence played in the unfolding of successive revolutions in modern French history. From the summer of 1789 the first revolution did of course contain episodes of mob violence and massacres of extreme cruelty. These brutal episodes set the tone for subsequent revolutionary mythology and posed awkward questions for revolutionary historiography. The storming of the Tuileries on the 10 August 1792, a full-scale offensive battle between the populace and the army, involving both artillery and cavalry, became the yardstick by which later insurrectionary comportment was judged. If revolutionary desire to overthrow the existing political order is held to manifest itself in the insurgents' ambition to kill or maim individual members of the counter-insurrectionary forces (be they regular troops, national guardsmen or policemen), the subsequent massacre of the Swiss guards amply testified to the seriousness of purpose of the *sans-culottes*. While violence is never entirely random, the popular excesses during the *grandes journées* of the first revolution were largely unco-ordinated. To the extent to which they displayed a pattern, it was a pattern of crowd behaviour that conformed to older, early modern forms of popular protest. Violence was an essential component and a defining characteristic of the first revolution, but the pattern of violence during the revolutionary decade 1789–99 did not become a model for subsequent revolutionary practice in France. The *terreur sauvage* and the surging crowds of the first revolution have haunted the imagination of conservatives and revolutionaries alike since 1789, but they remained an anomaly within the broader revolutionary tradition. The July Revolution of 1830 inaugurated a new insurrectionary practice, one in which physical violence was choreographed and to a considerable extent tamed in comparison with the unco-ordinated brutalities of the first revolution. The instrument through which physical violence was co-ordinated was the barricade. The barricade localised confrontation between the insurgents and the forces of order, allowed such confrontation to develop a theatrical aspect, and thus served to transpose violence from the physical to the symbolic sphere.

The image of barricades and insurrectionary warfare in the literary and iconographic traditions which evolved in the aftermath of the July Revolution gives a radically false impression of the strategies of revolution in nineteenth-century Paris. Barricades are presented as being a tactical ploy used by the insurgents as part of an aggressive, mobile plan of campaign to wrest control of the city. The barricade is presented above all as a space of armed confrontation between insurgents and the forces of order, a stage for scenes of heroism and military valour. Barricades did of course witness scenes of fighting in successive insurrectionary episodes of the nineteenth century, but their primary function was seldom strategic. Building barricades was indeed a curious, if not paradoxical, choice of strategy for revolutionaries whose ultimate objectives were to seize the spaces of political and symbolic power that would signify their control over the city and the country. For the barricade was a defensive position which isolated the insurgents from the forces of order and which replaced a mobile form of street warfare with a static form of confrontation. The strategic advantages of the barricade were that it offered some protection from both bullets and cavalry charges for the insurgents, while hampering troop movements and creating bottlenecks which enabled the insurgents to use the urban environment to their best advantage. Specifically, they could use sniper fire from surrounding buildings and throw furniture and other bulky objects down on the soldiers massed before the barricades in the narrow streets. These advantages were probably outweighed, however, by the strategic disadvantages of building barricades. First, the insurgents' movements were as hampered as the troops' by the presence of barricades – a point not lost on the student leaders in 1968, who advocated a more fluid form of street fighting.[16] In successful revolutions, the barricades had to be abandoned at a crucial stage to enable the insurgents to press forward and reach their main objectives (the Louvre, the Palais-Bourbon and, above all, the Hôtel de Ville). Secondly, the use of barricades encouraged the fragmentation of the insurrectionary forces and made the imposition of any common strategy almost impossible. The recourse to barricades and the means in which they were used reveal two essential points about the nature of nineteenth-century Parisian revolutions: the surprisingly low incidence and relative unimportance of physical violence and the crucial role of the Parisian national guard – acting as mediators between government and insurgents and judges of their relative claims to legitimacy – in determining the outcome of choreographed insurrections.

That the barricade was as much a stage for oratorical jousting as a space for physical confrontation was well known to theorists and practitioners of insurrectionary warfare. Even Auguste Blanqui, perhaps the most experienced urban guerrilla of the nineteenth century and the prophet of the insurrectionary putsch, was aware of the strategic deficiencies of the barricade and conscious that revolution was an art of political and moral persuasion rather than an art of military organisation. In 1868, after years of experience of revolutionary activity in Paris, he wrote a cogent critique of revolutionary tactics of street warfare.[17] Blanqui's analysis of the inadequacies of the insurgents' strategy in June 1848 is extraordinarily lucid. According to Blanqui, the quality which insurrectionary forces had most lacked in previous movements had been leadership. Insurgents were always by definition brave and devoted to their cause (they were often much more enthusiastic about fighting than their opponents), but they accepted no overall authority and followed no plan. Barricades, Blanqui wrote, were erected haphazardly by small groups of insurgents, who chose their position without considering the position of surrounding barricades or the overall objectives of the revolution. Very often they were constructed too close to one another. Sometimes a single street would be blocked by a succession of barricades.

> Five, ten, thirty, fifty men, recruited by chance, most of them unarmed, begin to overturn carts, lift and heap up paving stones to block the public road, sometimes in the middle of streets, more often at intersections. Many of these barriers would hardly present an obstacle to cavalry. In June more than 600 barricades were counted. About thirty at most on their own accounted for all the fighting in the battle. The others, nineteen out of twenty, did not burn a single cartridge cap.

Hence, those glorious bulletins which recounted with much fuss the removal of fifty barricades, where there wasn't a soul.[18]

During this time, other groups of insurgents raided isolated guardhouses, police stations and arms merchants in search of weapons, 'all this is done without concert or direction, but according to individual fantasy'. Meanwhile, the generals massed their troops at strategic points in preparation for the assault on the barricades that defended the centres of the insurrection. It was at this point, according to Blanqui, that the tactical naïveté of the insurgents became most apparent and most disastrous:

Absolutely no general command, hence, no direction; not even concerted action between the combatants. Each barricade has its particular, more or less numerous, but always isolated group . . . The insurgents do what they feel like: one goes off, another comes; they stay, they go, they come back as it pleases them. In the evening, they go off to bed . . . No one knows anything about what is happening elsewhere and no one cares either. Rumours circulate, sometimes discouraging, sometimes good. [The rebels] listen peacefully to canon-shot and fusillades, drinking at the bar of the tavern. As for coming to the aid of the positions under assault, no-one even considers it. 'Let every man defend his position and all will be well,' say the most reliable . . . While the insurgents smoke their pipes behind their heap of paving-stones, the enemy concentrates all his strength on one point, then on a second, a third, a fourth etc., and crushes the insurrection bit by bit, in this manner. The population is not bothered with frustrating this pleasant task. Each group awaits its turn philosophically and would not consider running to aid the neighbours. No! 'He defends his position, one mustn't abandon one's position.' And so they perish through absurdity.[19]

In these passages Blanqui's description of the insurgents sitting behind their barricades, quietly smoking pipes and drinking wine, listening to the distant sound of canon fire, and wandering off home in the evening, resembles Aron's description of the students in 1968 more than it resembles the heroic *image d'Epinal* of revolution.

A similar absurdity from a military point of view had marred all previous insurrections in Paris, according to Blanqui, leading him to draw a sobering conclusion: a Parisian insurrection, if it followed the same pattern, *'les vieux errements'*, no longer stood any chance of success. The Restoration government had collapsed in July 1830 because it had not believed an armed uprising possible. Popular enthusiasm alone had been sufficient to topple a government completely unprepared. Since 1830, however, government and the military had mastered the art of street warfare and 'soon recovered the natural superiority of art and discipline over inexperience and confusion'. Blanqui warned his followers not to be drawn into overconfidence by the success of the February 1848 uprising. The superior organisation of the armed forces gave them an invincible advantage, so long as the morale of troops and politicians held firm. However brave and however numerous the insurgents, a victorious insurrection, a revolution, could always be prevented by disciplined and motivated troops. This was as true for February 1848 ('If Louis-Philippe had defended himself seriously, the uniforms would have carried the day'),[20] as it was for 1868 when Blanqui penned his pessimistic prognosis of revolutionary prospects ('What would happen today? With the old techniques, the entire people would succumb if the troops held firm').[21]

In his preface to the 1895 edition of Marx's *Class struggles in France*, Engels also recognised the rhetorical aspect of revolutionary conflict. Discussing 'rebellion in the old style, street fighting with barricades, which decided the issue everywhere up to 1848', he warned would-be insurgents not to place too much hope in military organisation:

> Let us have no illusions about it: a real victory of an insurrection over the military in street fighting, a victory as between two armies, is one of the rarest exceptions. And the insurgents counted on it just as rarely. For them it was solely a question of making the troops yield to moral influences which, in a fight between the armies of two warring countries, do not come into play at all or do so to a much smaller extent.[22]

Even in the classic time of street fighting, therefore, barricades produced more of a moral than a material effect. They were a means of shaking the steadfastness of the military and of appealing to the civilian militias who arbitrated in the political competition between rival claims to legitimacy. If the insurgents' appeal via the barricades was heard, victory was assured; if not, defeat was inevitable.

> In Paris, in July 1830 and February 1848, as in most of the Spanish street fighting, a citizens' guard stood between the insurgents and the military. This guard either sided directly with the insurrection, or else by its lukewarm, indecisive attitude caused the troops likewise to vacillate, and supplied the insurrection with arms into the bargain. Where this citizens' guard opposed the insurrection from the outset, as in June 1848 in Paris, the insurrection was vanquished . . . But in all cases the fight was won because the troops failed to respond, because the commanding officers lost the faculty to decide or because their hands were tied.[23]

Similarly, Trotsky realised that the principal aim of any insurrection was to win over, rather than to destroy, the armed forces. The morale of the troops had to be sapped and their discipline broken either before or during an armed struggle if the insurgents were to stand a reasonable chance of overthrowing the established order. The most useful function of the barricade, he argued, was that it allowed insurgents to achieve sufficient physical proximity to the counter-insurrectionary forces so as to be able to cajole them effectively.[24]

Blanqui's analysis of the weakness of the technique of insurrection elaborated in Paris during the nineteenth century should not mask the fact that, despite its shortcomings in traditional strategic terms, it was an effective policy. For the crucial battle in the streets of Paris, even during periods of popular insurrection, was a political one. If, as Blanqui himself demonstrated, the morale of the counter-insurrectionary forces was all important as a determinant of the success or failure of insurrections, the real task of the insurgents was not to engage the troops in traditional warfare in the forlorn hope of defeating them and conquering the city militarily, but to create an atmosphere conducive to sapping the confidence of the government and its defenders. Insurgents and counter-insurgents strove to establish their moral authority over the city. In this political struggle, the barricade was a singularly successful tactic. The number and size of barricades were potent physical manifestations of the strength of revolutionary energy and their geographic spread across the city was indicative of the extent of support for the insurrection across the various classes of the Parisian population. Even if, as Blanqui argued, the majority of barricades saw no actual fighting and served no clear military purpose, they served to sow doubts in the minds of the national guards and the troops. The presence of barricades in the streets of Paris, after the founding example of 1830, marked a break in mundane time and served notice that history was being enacted. Through the act of constructing barricades, insurgents claimed a revolutionary legitimacy that sprang from the success of the July Revolution. Barricades proclaimed that *le peuple*, that ineffable but infallible and historic figure of revolutionary mythology, was present.[25] As such, they were a statement of intent. They obliged the forces of order, national guards and regular troops, to make a judgement as to whether, in storming the barricades, they were saving society from small bands of factious rebels (as in 1832 or 1834 or 1839 or 1871) or playing the role of unloved and unrewarded villains in a historical drama (as in 1830 or 1848). If the forces of order could be induced to accept the insurgents' self-definition, to accept the historical legitimacy of their movement, then resistance to the uprising melted away and insurrection became revolution.

Where Aron sought to locate the clearest evidence of historical discontinuity between 1968 and the French revolutionary tradition since 1830 – the use of barricades and the incidence of physical violence – there is instead considerable continuity. The students who, as Aron correctly observed, built barricades in Paris in 1968 to demarcate a zone of resistance and to challenge the guardians of public order to dislodge them, were acting in much the same fashion as the barricade builders of the nineteenth century. Aron both underestimated the extent of physical violence in May and June 1968 and misjudged the role which violence played in the French revolutionary tradition. In all the successful revolutions of the nineteenth century, violence remained highly stylised and was primarily symbolic. The bloodiest revolutionary episodes were those which failed, most notably of course the suppression of the Commune during the *la semaine sanglante* of May 1871, but also the June Days of 1848 or the insurrection of June 1832. Barricades were built as rhetorical gestures in a process of political communication; occasionally they became battlegrounds.

The greater incidence of violence of the nineteenth-century revolutions compared to 1968 corresponded to the technical limits of communication possible within the nineteenth-century city, limits which themselves favoured the Parisian assumption of the revolutionary initiative in 1830, 1848 and 1870. The almost complete absence of fatal casualties in 1968 does not so much indicate a lesser determination among the insurgents or the effects of a secular civilising process, as the changing media environment. In all the revolutions of the nineteenth century, violent exchanges had been far more efficacious as a means of generating martyrs for the insurrectionary cause than as a means of physically intimidating or eliminating the forces of order. It is worthwhile noting that almost all insurrectionary activity in the nineteenth century took place in the day. Had insurgents been primarily interested in taking control of stategically important spaces within Paris, they could have achieved this end most easily under cover of darkness. Revolution was not, however, simply about performing the correct gestures, it was about being seen to perform the correct gestures. Revolutionaries required an audience. The crowds of bystanders who surrounded the militants as the first barricades were erected were not simply impeding the reimposition of public order in the streets, they were performing an essential function as witnesses to the public flaunting of the political authorities. In this regard it is instructive to remember the insurrection orchestrated by Blanqui and Barbès in May 1839. Although their meticulous advance planning unravelled somewhat in the execution, the insurrection was undoubtedly the best organised of the nineteenth century. The insurgents achieved their stategic objectives swiftly, invading the Hôtel de Ville and proclaiming a revolutionary government before Louis-Philippe's authorities had time to react. The insurrection failed nevertheless, for Blanqui and Barbès had mistaken the nature of revolution, seeing it as a strategic-military operation rather than as a process of political communication. If the military were taken by surprise in May 1839, so was the public. The curtain fell, and the insurrection was swept aside, before Paris had had the opportunity to register that the performance had begun. In 1968, television, radio and electric street lighting allowed the students to dramatise their subversion and reach their intended audience while operating at night.

When urban revolution is recognised as a continuation of politics by other means (and other players) – a competition for *l'opinion bourgeoise* – as much as for military supremacy, the position of May 1968 within the revolutionary tradition becomes much more apparent. May 1968 did not live up to the heroic mythology of revolution, but in many aspects it did conform to a less exalted, less inspiring pattern of revolutionary behaviour. If May 1968 was festive in mood, so was the revolution of February 1848, and even the Commune began in an atmosphere of carnival. In May 1968 there was a gross disproportion between the lack of gravity of the initial stimulus and primary demand (a reform of the system of tertiary education whose necessity was widely recognised both within and without the university) and the amplitude of the means manipulated to achieve redress. The events of 1968 precipitated few immediate socio-political reforms, but generated a vague but general questioning of the political system and of 'consumer society'. As a formative moment in the lives of many, they contributed to forging the self-identity of a generation, *les soixante-huitards*. They were more important remembered than lived, generating exaggerated nostalgia in some and inflated terror in others. Their cultural resonance was finally much more significant than their political impact. Such characterisations, considered pejorative, are normally used to allege the negative specificity of the events of May 1968, their failure to conform to a revolutionary tradition. But all these criticisms could be applied with equal justification, if not perhaps to 1789, to the revolutions of 1830, 1848 and 1871.

Notes

1   For a convenient overview of the events, see M. Larkin, *France since the Popular Front* (Oxford, 1997), pp. 317–27.

2   For an introduction to the literature on 1968, see M. Winock, *La fièvre hexagonale. Les grandes crises politiques 1871–1968* (Paris, 1986); for greater detail see J.-P. Le Goff, *Mai 68, l'héritage impossible* (Paris, 2002).

3   M. Grimaud, *En mai fais ce qu'il te plaît* (Paris, 1977), pp. 115–16. A recent example of the voluminous literature on May 1968 by participants is J. Kristeva, *Revolt, she said* (Los Angeles, 2002), p. 15 for an explicit reference to the revolutionary tradition.

4   P. Lidsky, 'Permanence et fixité du langage pamphlétaire', postface to *Les écrivains contre la Commune*, 2nd edn (Paris, 1999).

5   The communist discourse on 1968 can be sampled in J. Duclos, *Anarchistes d'hier et d'aujourd'hui, comment le gauchisme fait le jeu de la réaction* (Paris, 1968); L. Salini, *Mai des prolétaires* (Paris, 1968); W. Rochet, *L'Avenir du Parti Communiste Français* (Paris, 1969).

6   For a long but typically obscure exposition of the theory of the *acte exemplaire*, see

Mouvement du 22 mars, *Ce n'est qu'un début, continuons le combat* (Paris, 1968), pp. 59–75.

7   R. Aron, *La révolution introuvable, réflexions sur les événements de mai* (Paris, 1968), pp. 28–9, 32–7, 40, 44, 64–7, 85–90, 110, 115, 134–5.

8   Ibid., pp. 33, 35.

9   R. Aron, *Mémoires, cinquante ans de réflexion politique* (Paris, 1983), p. 672–3.

10 Aron, *La révolution introuvable*, p. 88.

11 Ibid., pp. 35, 36. See also K. Reader, 'The symbolic violence of the May 1968 events in France' in R. Günther and J. Windebank (eds), *Violence and conflict in modern French culture* (Sheffield, 1994), pp. 57–65.

12 Aron, *La révolution introuvable*, p. 87.

13 Ibid., p. 88

14 The best scholarly treatment of the barricade as a political phenomenon can be found in the proceedings of the conference held at Paris 1 Panthéon Sorbonne in 1995, published as A. Corbin and J.-M. Mayeur (eds), *La barricade* (Paris, 1997). In her paper, '1919–1968 – Des barricades?', pp. 455–68, Danielle Tartakowsky notes her surprise that her analysis of the symbolic function of the barricades in 1968 did not differ greatly from the analysis of other participants studying the function and image of the barricade in the nineteenth century.

15 Reader, 'Symbolic violence', p. 61

16 See the student tract distributed on the 19 May 1968, reproduced in M. Sarrasin, J. Brune, J. Kader and M. Cazes, *Histoires de mai* (Choisy-le-Roi, 1978), pp. 68–72.

17 A. Blanqui, 'Instruction pour une prise d'armes' in *Textes choisis*, V. P. Volguine (ed.) (Paris, 1971), pp. 214–20.

18 Ibid., p. 215. The original reads 'dix-neuf ou vingt' but Blanqui's meaning is clear and this must be a mistransposition.

19 Ibid., pp. 215–17.

20 Ibid., p. 214.

21 Ibid., p. 218.

22 F. Engels, 'Introduction' in K. Marx, *The class struggles in France 1848 to 1850* (Moscow, 1979), p. 21.

23 Ibid., p. 22.

24 See the chapter entitled 'The art of insurrection' in L. Trotsky, *History of the Russian Revolution*, 3 vols (London, 1967), III, pp. 159–87.

25 See A. Pessin, *Le mythe du peuple et la société française du XIXe siècle* (Paris, 1992).

CHAPTER 17

Nature and Nationalism in Modern Ireland

Mary E. Daly

'Irish patriotism is pre-eminently patriotism of place: Armagh, the Glens of Antrim, the "four green fields" are inextricably interwoven with the national sentiment.'[1] When W. T. Cosgrave, president of the Executive Council of the Irish Free State, made the first live broadcast to Irish emigrants in the USA in 1931, on the eve of St Patrick's Day, his speech included long descriptions of some the most prominent features of the Irish landscape. He referred to

> the line of mountains fronting the Irish Sea as you look to the south from the Hill of Howth . . . the enchanting coast line from Dublin to Wexford with hills over ever-changing colour sloping down to the shore . . . the valleys of Glanasmole or Glencree, the lakes of Luggelaw, Lough Tay and Lough Dan . . . the murmur of the streams all through the Dublin and Wicklow Hills . . . the outlines of the thousands of little fields in the mountain glens, where your ancestors and mine laboured and had their homes.[2]

In 1925, the London, Midland and Scottish Railway Company reproduced two landscapes – *Connemara* and *A view of Lough Erne* – by the Irish painter, Paul Henry, as posters, and distributed them to travel agencies throughout Europe.[3] Bord Fáilte, the Irish tourist board, has also relied extensively on nature and scenery in its marketing campaigns for many decades.

Cosgrave's 1931 radio address deliberately set out to appeal to all Irish emigrants 'whatever be your creed in religion or politics' by including references to scenic locations in Northern Ireland, among them 'Antrim's glens and the valleys of Down'. In 1931, less than ten years after independence and partition, the Irish landscape appeared to offer uncontroversial images that would appeal to Unionists in Northern Ireland and to the rival nationalist sides in the 1922–3 civil war. The London, Midland and Scottish Railway

Company also attempted to use Henry's landscapes in a non-divisive manner by selecting one scene from the Irish Free State and one from Northern Ireland. Yet the Irish natural landscape has often proved to be a contentious matter. Although it includes many places that are memorable primarily by reason of their natural beauty, in other instances geography and topography carry more divisive and more contentious historical memories. In 1956, for example, when there was widespread public concern at the proposed sale of the Kenmare estate in County Kerry, a tract of over 8000 acres of land that included two of the three world-famous lakes of Killarney, one editorial in a local newspaper noted that the property had passed to the Kenmare family as a result of the 'brutal outlawry and ruthless confiscation meted out to the chief of Clan O'Donoghue'.[4] In the past the desire to preserve trees or open demesne parklands has often been in direct conflict with the demands of small farmers and labourers for land to be divided into smallholdings and the trees felled to make way for the plough. No part of Ireland suffered forced depopulation on the scale of the Scottish highlands, where crofters were removed in order to re-establish a wilderness which would be suitable for grouse, deer and other forms of sporting game,[5] though at Glenveagh, County Donegal, which became Ireland's second national park in 1975, a Scottish-born landlord evicted 244 tenants in 1861 following the murder of his land agent, leaving behind over 11,000 acres of barren land.[6] A report by the Office of Public Works, apparently unconscious of the irony, described the new national park as 'one of the last places in Ireland to be influenced by man'.[7]

Although Gaelic poetry and literature are replete with place names and references to the natural landscape, the Irish natural heritage did not feature prominently in the cultural nationalism that developed during the nineteenth and the early twentieth century, though in the 1840s Thomas Davis, one of the pioneering figures in Irish cultural nationalism, suggested that Irish travellers should tour Ireland first, before making a Grand Tour of the continent.[8] Cultural nationalists regarded the west of Ireland – the location of the country's most spectacular scenery – as Ireland's cultural heartland, but they were much more interested in the people than in the scenery or the flora and fauna. The Irish-speaking peasantry of the west of Ireland were regarded as the surviving representatives of the true Irish people: they were Gaelic-speaking, and had not yet been contaminated by an anglicised materialist culture.

Henry David Thoreau, the great American naturalist, rejected history because he believed that it was irreconcilable with nature.[9] In Ireland, history was paramount. Romanticism concentrated on rediscovering the country's rich archaeological heritage, the revival of the Irish language and the preservation of traditional sports such as hurling,[10] not on communing with nature. The comprehensive scientific survey of one of the western islands, Clare Island, which was carried out by the Royal Irish Academy during the years

1909–11[11] did not feature to any extent in the Irish nationalist discourse at that time. The Clare Island survey might have gained greater recognition if the chosen island had been Gaelic-speaking; it seems, however, that the survey team opted for Clare Island because the population spoke English and were consequently friendlier to outsiders. The Blasket Islands were seriously considered as an alternative,[12] and a survey of the Blasket Islands would undoubtedly have had a wider impact on public opinion. On the whole, Irish cultural nationalism valued places for their historic associations with Ireland's glorious past, such as Tara, the site of Ireland's pre-Christian high kings, the ruined monastic cities of Clonmacnoise and Glendalough, or sites that were linked with the struggle for national independence, such as Aughrim, the location of a late seventeenth-century battle, or Bodenstown, the burial-place of the late eighteenth-century Irish republican, Theobald Wolfe Tone. Unlike the United States, which relied heavily on natural wonders, such as Yosemite or Yellowstone Parks, as symbols of national greatness which could be presented as a new-world alternative to Europe's historical heritage,[13] Irish nationalism made little reference to nature, other than to reiterate that the country's manifest destiny was to remain as a rural, agrarian society, in direct contrast to an urban industrial Britain.[14]

Ireland was consequently slow to adopt measures to protect the natural landscape. The 1930 National Monuments Act, which updated earlier legislation passed by the Westminster parliament, provided for the preservation of places or items which were regarded as of national importance by reason of their historic interest, architectural tradition, artistic or archaeological interest. The earlier legislation had limited the definition of national monument to objects or properties dating from ancient or medieval times. Although the 1930 act extended this to include the eighteenth century and earlier, most speeches on the bill in the Dáil and Seanad referred to cromlechs, ogham stones, high crosses and ruined castles, not to later constructions.[15] Russborough House, a fine example of Irish Georgian architecture, was offered to the state in 1929, around the time that the National Monuments Bill was making its way through the Oireachtas. In 1930 an official in the Department of Finance, who was in favour of rejecting the offer, noted that:

> So far as the Minister has been able to gather neither Russborough House nor the family connected with it has ever been associated with any outstanding events or personalities in Irish history. Accordingly the interest which the place possesses is only its interest to connoisseurs of architecture, plus whatever interest it has as illustrating a certain phase of social life in Ireland. Opinions differ as to the aesthetic merits of the Georgian style of architecture, but, the period being relatively modern, good specimens of it are sufficiently numerous both in this country and in England to render State action to preserve this one superfluous.

He noted that 'there seems no point in an Irish Government preserving as a national monument a building not distinctively Irish'. Thus despite the inclusion of eighteenth-century buildings within the terms of the 1930 National Monuments Act, the requirement that they should be 'of national importance by reason of history, architectural tradition, artistic or archaeological interest' meant that few qualified. The official in the Department of Finance noted that 'it would require much special pleading to bring Russborough in any reasonable way within that definition'. He gave a list of places that met this standard: 'structures of pre-Christian antiquity at Newgrange, round towers, churches at Glendalough, the Rock of Cashel'.[16] All, coincidentally or otherwise, related to a pre-Norman Ireland. He ended by noting that if state funds were used to preserve eighteenth-century buildings, the cost of doing so might prejudice the preservation of 'real national monuments'. The Cabinet rejected the offer of Russborough House, which was subsequently purchased by a retired British army officer and horse-breeder.

Irish Georgian architecture was not regarded as 'distinctively Irish'. Although a similar charge could not be levelled against the natural landscape and the fauna and flora, they ranked very lowly in the national hierarchy, compared with the Irish language and Irish history. In 1922, a report on the national primary school curriculum compiled by the Irish National Teachers' Organisation, which was the largest teachers' trade union, recommended that nature study should be dropped as an obligatory subject in order to give more time for teaching the Irish language. This recommendation was implemented after 1934,[17] despite the fact that it was in direct conflict with another official objective of using the schools to promote agriculture and rural life. In 1943 de Valera made it known that he was not in favour of reintroducing rural science into the national school curriculum.[18]

The study of natural history in Ireland at the beginning of the twentieth century was dominated by members of Anglo-Irish ascendancy and the middle-class Protestant men and women who joined the Belfast Naturalists' Field Club and its Dublin equivalent.[19] There was little overlap in membership between the field clubs and the Gaelic League. It has been suggested that nature study provided a safe and uncontroversial outlet for men and women who wished to avoid taking sides on the question of nationalism or unionism. As Seán Lysaght has noted, a search through the eight hundred articles, books and reviews produced by Ireland's greatest natural scientist, Robert Lloyd Praeger, the director of the Clare Island survey – who was born in Belfast in 1865 of partly Dutch ancestry – reveals 'scarcely a reference to political events or cultural disputes'.[20] At a more practical level, the fact that very little biology and 'practically no field studies' were taught in Ireland during the early decades after independence meant that there was little intellectual momentum for the study and preservation of the natural heritage.²¹ This made it more difficult to devise an appropriate use for Ireland's first national park.

Yet the natural landscape has been shaped by history, and particularly by conquest and colonisation, and there is growing evidence that this was equally true of the natural landscape in other parts of the world.²² As English and Scottish settlement spread throughout Ireland, first in the twelfth and thirteenth centuries, and again following a period of retreat, in the sixteenth and seventeenth centuries, the surviving areas of wilderness and woodlands became the homes of the displaced native Irish, who might use these areas to launch occasional attacks on the new settlers. Indeed a religious map of Ulster mirrors the relief map, with Catholics more likely to be found on upland and mountainy land, and Protestants concentrated on the more fertile and more accessible plains. This Irish wilderness was gradually tamed. Trees were felled to meet Britain's insatiable demand for timber. Population increase and the growing demand for agricultural land led to families settling in more remote areas of the west. In 1600 one-eighth of Ireland was covered with forests; by 1800 this had fallen to one-fiftieth.²³ By the 1820s government-financed road schemes had opened up the remaining areas of wilderness, such as the Wicklow mountains – where the road was constructed in order to enable the military to flush out rebels after the 1798 rebellion – and remote western areas such as Connemara and west Cork.²⁴ Although Gaelic poets lamented the clearing of Irish woodlands as symbolising the end of a traditional culture and lifestyle, most notably in the poem Cill Cais,²⁵ a new Irish culture emerged, which was made possible only by the clearance of woodlands and population settlement on upland and marginal lands. Between the 1740s and the beginning of the Great Famine in 1845, the population of Ireland increased fourfold from 2 million to over 8 million. The highest rate of population increase occurred on the poorer land in the west, north-west and south-west of Ireland, which happened to be the areas with the most spectacularly wild scenery. This population expansion on mountains, hillsides, the edge of bogs, and other areas with low soil fertility was feasible only because the potato, which was introduced into Ireland in the seventeenth century, thrived in the damp climate of the west of Ireland, and on inferior soil. The 1841 Census of Population revealed that the greatest density of settlement was often found in such areas. In the mid-1840s, however, the potato, which had become the staple food of the population, was stricken by a blight, which destroyed the crop for five consecutive years and permanently reduced its yield. Between 1845 and 1851 approximately one million people died and one million emigrated.²⁶ The population of Ireland continued to decline after 1851, and by 1901 it stood at under 4.5 million, compared with a figure of 8.1 million in 1841. Uniquely in Europe, Ireland's population in the 1990s is significantly lower than in the 1840s. The loss in population was greatest in the counties along the western seaboard.

This population loss haunted succeeding generations of Irishmen and it contributed an important emotional dimension to Irish nationalism. Irish nationalists of the late nineteenth and early-twentieth centuries sought to restore the Irish population to at least its pre-famine level. Estimates of the desired population have ranged from the 1841 figure of 8 million upwards to 20, or even 45 million people. Furthermore, this population was to be settled as before the famine, on smallholdings that would be dominated by tillage farming, not in the cities.[27] It was widely believed that Irish people were unsuited to city life, despite the fact that Irish emigrants to the United States were much more likely to settle in cities than emigrants from other European countries such as Germany or Sweden.[28] In fact this idealised model of the life of an Irish peasant showed little respect for or knowledge of long-standing Irish traditions. From early times most of the Irish people have been cattle farmers, who engaged in an extensive, often semi-nomadic style of cattle ranching. During the summer months young men and women migrated with cows and perhaps pigs to higher land on hills or mountains, where they tended the herds and made butter. This style of agriculture was compatible with the survival of large tracts of semi-waste land, but not with a population of 8 million, the majority of them living off the land. The diffusion of the potato during the eighteenth century, and the introduction of extensive spade cultivation in the west and north of Ireland brought substantial changes to the Irish landscape. With the destruction of potato-based intensive farming during the famine, and the growing competition from grain imported from the United States during the second half of the nineteenth century, Irish agriculture reverted to its traditional emphasis on cattle raising, despite the fact that many nationalists deplored this trend. Cattle graziers were condemned as anti-social beings, whose interests were incompatible with national objectives. Britain was held responsible for most of the events that had contributed to the depopulation of the Irish countryside: the great famine, emigration, and the switch from tillage to cattle farming – the cattle were exported for fattening in Britain. Such attitudes coloured nationalist perceptions of the landscape. In *Rambles in Eirinn*, William Bulfin, an Irish nationalist, who ironically spent many years as an emigrant cattle rancher in Argentina, penned an extremely unsympathetic description of the plains of Counties Roscommon and east Galway, where the land was mainly used for grazing cattle and sheep. He described this area as 'the great ranch district beyond the Shannon':

> There are no woodlands, no groves, scarcely any trees at all. There is no agriculture – the fertile desert is uncultivated from end to end. Away from our feet to the crest of the far-off ridges the public road stretches in a straight line across the valley, between the stone walls, breast high, which separate it from the silent

fields on either side. On the broad pastures the flocks and herds are scattered, browsing the rich grass which grows over many a usurped hearth.

Bulfin assumed that his readers would react to this scene with anger: 'It is for the uptorn homes and the empty fields that you are angry'.[29] By contrast, he admired the landscape of the south-eastern county of Wexford. 'Between pasturage and meadowing there is more land under grass than crops, but the difference is not so marked as in the richest districts of the Midlands. I met no Wexford hilltop in my rambles from which I could not see cornfields and wide patches of green crops.'[30]

Thus the Irish land was viewed primarily in terms of its capacity to support an increased population. This attitude was at once both utilitarian and romantic. The romantic ideal is best summarised in a famous speech made in 1943 by Eamon de Valera, when he spoke of '[t]he Ireland which we have dreamed of . . . [as] a land whose countryside would be bright with cosy homesteads, whose fields and villages would be joyous with the sounds of industry, with the romping of sturdy children, the contests of athletic youth and the laughter of comely maidens'.[31] The manifesto of Fianna Fáil, Ireland's largest political party, included a commitment to establish as many families as practicable on the land.[32] By the late 1920s, when the Irish Land Commission had completed the process of transferring the remaining tenanted land from landlord ownership to peasant proprietors, it turned its attention to taking over unexploited land that was in the possession of landlords or graziers, and converting it into smallholdings. Over 120,000 hectares of parkland, which were acquired by the Land Commission, were either turned into small farms or covered with conifers.[33] One photograph in the Father Browne collection shows a former great house, surrounded by ploughed land. In 1932 an official account of the government's policy on land ownership described the efforts that were being undertaken to reclaim waste land in the west of Ireland for agricultural use, noting that this land included Ireland's most famous beauty spots and sporting grounds.[34] The enactment of the 1945 Arterial Drainage Act marked the beginning of a major programme of work on Irish rivers. By 1980 over 600,000 acres of land had been drained. In 1949 the first inter-party government announced a complementary programme of land drainage and improvement, which was known as the Land Project. This continued until the mid-1970s, when it was absorbed into the Farm Modernisation Scheme. By 1980 over 3 million acres had been drained under these programmes.[35] One scheme at Roundstone in Connemara involved the removal of large quantities of glacial rock.[36] Welsh agricultural scientists were recruited to advise on reclaiming upland, and Dutch experts drew up plans for extensive reclamation work on the estuaries and shoreline.[37] The original purpose behind these programmes was to create or at least preserve jobs in farming, and to raise agricultural output, but while these improvement and drainage schemes were being carried out thousands of acres were falling into disuse as farmers emigrated or elderly occupiers proved incapable of carrying out the necessary work.

Forestry was widely seen as offering another possible solution to the problem of rural employment. Between the seventeenth and the nineteenth centuries, most of the native woodlands were felled by the Anglo-Irish landlord class; those that survived, like the Killarney woods, did so because they were inaccessible. During the nineteenth century, however, landlords began to replant forests, a development that was not always welcomed by their tenants, who would have preferred the land to have been used to create smallholdings, however uneconomic they might have been. Under the Land acts that transferred ownership from landlord to tenant, landlords were free to retain the untenanted parts of their estates, which included wooded areas. Many opted to sell their entire estate, but before doing so they disposed of the remaining timber, and the 340,000 acres of woodland that existed in the 1880s had fallen by 1920 to approximately 130,000 acres.[38] By the early twentieth century forests were being seen as a natural resource, which could provide employment and enrich the nation,[39] while the Sinn Féin leader, Arthur Griffith, may have established a claim to be seen as a forerunner of the contemporary environmental movement, when he suggested that the Irish climate had deteriorated because of the deforestation of Ireland by the British.[40] Between 1919 and 1921 Dáil Éireann devoted considerable attention to developing forestry. The Wicklow landlord, Robert Barton, who was director (minister) of agriculture, appointed a separate forestry committee. Its main activity was organising Arbour Day on 1 November 1919.[41] Enormous numbers of evergreen and deciduous trees – horse chestnut, beech, elm, sycamore, willow, Norway spruce, larch and scotch pine – were dispatched to local railway stations for planting by schools, clergy and other interested parties By the following June it was estimated that 250,000–300,000 trees had been planted.[42] Every farmer was encouraged to plant sixteen trees, one for each of the men executed in 1916.[43] The encouragement given by the first Dáil to the planting of deciduous trees did not survive. After independence, economics not aesthetics became the main preoccupation and most state forests were planted with fast-growing conifers rather than traditional broadleaved trees. Many scenic vistas were obscured by these plantations. Moreover the continuing pressure to use all potentially agricultural land for farming meant that forests were relegated to the poorest soils, where only conifers could survive. By the late 1970s woods and plantations covered 5.2 per cent of the area of Ireland – the lowest percentage in Europe, but only 1.2 per cent of this land was covered by broadleaved woods.[44]

The word 'bog', an area of marshy and poorly drained soil, comes from an Irish word *bogach* which means 'soft ground'. This is one of the few Gaelic words that has come to be used as a term in natural science. Bogs covered seventeen per cent of land surface in the 1980s, the second highest percentage in western Europe.[45] Irish bogs have been regarded primarily as a source of fuel. With the disappearance of the woodlands, most rural homes were heated by turf or peat. The loss of turf rights was a major cause of concern to Irish peasantry, because it meant a serious loss of income, and it often gave rise to disputes between landlords and tenants.[46] As Ireland had little coal, efforts to become self-sufficient in energy depended on peat and hydro-electricity. A Turf Development Board was established in 1934 to harvest the nation's bogs, using the fuel to heat individual houses and to power electricity generating stations. By 1946 nearly half the total area of large midland raised-bogs, recorded in 1814, had been cut away,[47] and the remainder has been seriously depleted in the past fifty years. Boglands are an important ecosystem, which is rich in plant and animal life; the damp environment preserves important archaeological remains, including human remains and clothing, that would otherwise have been destroyed. The National Museum at Collins Barracks contains several examples of clothing that was retrieved from bogs. However, the idea of preserving even a small proportion of the surviving bogland has gathered momentum only since the 1970s. It has been led by outsiders, notably Dutch naturalists, who belatedly regretted the total depletion of boglands in the Netherlands.[48]

The robust and pragmatic attitude of the Irish farming class, who were the largest socio-economic group in Ireland immediately after independence, did little to encourage a protective attitude towards the natural environment. Living conditions were difficult for the majority of the rural population, and approximately one third of each generation emigrated to Britain or the United States. Land and other natural resources were viewed as sources of jobs or food. In *Tarry Flynn*, a quasi-autobiographical novel, Patrick Kavanagh, an Irish poet from a small-farming background, suggested that his farming neighbours regarded any expressions of wonder about nature as a sign of mental disorder. The fishing rights for salmon or trout on many Irish rivers continued to be owned by the descendants of Anglo-Irish landlords, with the result that popular opinion favoured poaching and the freedom to fish, rather than wildlife conservation. Some of the work carried out under the 1945 Arterial Drainage Act resulted in serious damage to fish stocks and wildlife.[49] Irish farmers saw themselves as victors in a long-standing struggle against an alien landlord class, and they were determined to hold firm to their hard-won property. In article 40 of the 1937 Constitution, the state undertook 'to vindicate the . . . property rights of every citizen'. Furthermore, an entire article relating to private property was included in the section dealing with fundamental rights, where the state acknowledged man's natural right 'to the private ownership of external goods' and guaranteed 'to pass no law attempting to abolish the right of private ownership or the general right to transfer, bequeath, and inherit property'.[50] These clauses would make it extremely difficult, perhaps even impossible, to control the ownership or use of farming land in the interests of environmental preservation, even if the political will to do this existed. When comprehensive physical planning legislation was belatedly enacted in 1963, the planning regulations did not apply to most farm buildings, to changes in land use for agricultural purposes or to any land that was owned by the state.[51]

The cumulative impact of an economic outlook that viewed the rural landscape in terms of its potential to provide employment, and a cultural nationalism that was based primarily on language and history, was the absence of any political demand until recent times for measures to protect the rural environment. Popular opinion preferred the government to spend money acquiring parkland for subdivision among smallholders, draining wetlands to provide additional land for farmers or their sons, and exploiting bogs in order to provide jobs. Elite opinion was not markedly different. In a radio lecture broadcast in 1948, which was designed to publicise the recent incorporation of An Taisce, Ireland's National Trust, Robert Lloyd Praeger, the distinguished naturalist and first president of An Taisce, remarked that

> Ireland, with its comparatively small population, its few great urban areas and its limited industry has not been much in danger of spoliation . . . all Ireland is in a sense a great national park already. We go almost everywhere we choose to go, and farmers or even gamekeepers seldom turn us off the land.

Although An Taisce suggested that national parks should be established in parts of Wicklow, Donegal and Connemara, it regarded the urban heritage, and the cutting of broadleaved trees as more urgent priorities.[52]

The Irish state established only one national park before the 1970s, the Bourn Vincent Memorial Park in Killarney, which was donated. By the mid-1940s, the only other properties that had been accepted by the Irish state were Iveagh House, a magnificent town house that had been owned by the Guinness family, which provided an appropriately formal setting for the Department of External Affairs, and the house and grounds at St Enda's, the school run by Patrick Pearse, the leader of the 1916 Rising. Other properties were rejected because they were not wanted, and their upkeep was seen as too costly.[53] When Russborough House, one of Ireland's finest Georgian mansions, was offered to the government in 1929 with its demesne lands, the parsimonious Department of Finance suggested that the value of the gift was 'a minus quantity'.[54]

Parsimony offers only a partial explanation for the failure to accept other properties. The Irish government could not envisage any valid use for a Georgian country mansion like Russborough House, and they were not disposed to open it to the public, because the heritage it reflected was not regarded as Irish. The history of Ireland's first national park suggests that they were equally incapable of imagining an appropriate use for a tract of the Irish countryside, except for agriculture and commercial forestry. The Bourn Vincent National Park at Killarney, County Kerry, which was created in 1932, contained sublime mountains, waterfalls, scenic lakes and a large area of Ireland's most important surviving broadleaf woodlands. The majestic scenery of Killarney has been internationally famous at least since the late eighteenth century, when an opportunistic artist produced a series of etchings and aquatints of the most spectacular local scenes.[55] By the mid-nineteenth century Killarney had a thriving tourist industry, which explains why it was automatically included on one of Ireland's first major rail networks, despite its remote location. The 13,000 acre Bourn Vincent National Park bordered all three of the famous Killarney lakes and it included the Torc waterfall. The park also contained plants that were rare or unknown in Britain and in central Europe, plants that were associated with Spain and with other Mediterranean countries.[56]

The park was given to the Irish nation by Arthur Vincent, an independent member of the Senate of the Irish Free State, who had been left a life interest in the estate by his wealthy American father-in-law, W. B. Bourn. Bourn had purchased the estate in 1910 from Lord Ardilaun, a member of the Guinness brewing family, who had in turn bought the estate from the Herbert family, who were its owners for many generations. Bourn and Vincent spent an estimated £110,000 improving the property, which was more than twice the purchase price of £50,000. Senator Vincent acknowledged that maintaining this property was 'going to be too big an undertaking for any private individual', and it appears that presenting it to the state may have helped to ease his tax liabilities. The property was first offered to the government in late July 1932; the cabinet approved the offer on 28 October, having seen a draft agreement. On 7 December, shortly before the Christmas recess, the Bourn Vincent Memorial Park Bill was introduced in Dáil Éireann and, very unusually, all stages of the legislation were passed in one day. The discussion consisted of little more than brief statements by both government and opposition, thanking the donor for his generous gift.[57] Neither the government files relating to the establishment of the park nor the Dáil debate discusses the function of a national park.

The subsequent history of the Bourn Vincent National Park confirms this lack of vision. The park was entrusted to the Commissioners of Public Works, who were responsible for the upkeep of all government property from prisons and courthouses to Dublin's Phoenix Park. The Commissioners were also responsible for arterial drainage. In addition to the 13,000 acre estate, the Commissioners took possession of Muckross House, a large nineteenth-century house, and a herd of Kerry cattle, a rare Irish breed that was native to this area.[58] The Commissioners of Public Works promptly transferred 1300 acres, one tenth of the estate, to the forestry section of the Department of Lands to be developed and exploited as a commercial forest and they made unsuccessful efforts to find a suitable tenant for the house. By 1936 additional lands had been let for grazing to local farmers; deer-stalking rights, woodcock shooting rights, and salmon fishing rights were also leased. The remaining land was described as mountainous and incapable of being developed either for forestry or for farming.[59] The only mention in the annual reports of the Commissioners of Public Works of any work to improve the estate concerned the opening of 'vistas' on a public road that bordered part of the park, in order to enable the public 'to get better views of the Lakes'.[60] The Commissioners of Public Works made many unsuccessful attempts to let Muckross House to a private tenant or as a hotel, but they refused to lease the house to An Óige, the Irish youth-hostelling association because 'the Commissioners would be unable to control young people of both sexes who might be expected to lodge there'. *The Irish Times* launched periodic attacks on the government for failing to make Muckross House available to the nation as intended by the donors.[61]

In 1945 the Board of Visitors of the National Museum, which had a statutory responsibility to report on all public museums, investigated the possibility of establishing a biological research station at Muckross House. The brief report, which was prepared by two of Ireland's leading academic botanists, appears to have been the first scientific evaluation of the ecology of the national park. Bailey Butler and Joseph Doyle, who were professors at University College Dublin, noted that the Bourn Vincent National Park was located in an area that was 'of intense interest' to European biologists, because it contained a number of unique animals and plants. No comprehensive scientific study of the flora and fauna had yet been carried out. They recommended conducting a natural history survey, which could form the basis for a comprehensive visitors' handbook (apparently none existed), with special attention being paid to the distribution and survival of the rare Lusitanian flora and fauna, and to a study of the surviving natural woodlands. In their opinion the Killarney lakes offered a promising location for a limnology (freshwater and lake biology) station. Although the file noted that the taoiseach, Eamon de Valera, had approved this report, no action followed.[62]

In 1953, Arthur Vincent, who had donated the estate, contacted the director of the Irish Arts Council, P. J. Little, who was a former Minister for Posts and Telegraphs in de Valera's cabinet, to express his concern about how the estate was being managed. Arthur Vincent complained that the forestry authorities were treating the section of the park under their control as a commercial forest; the remainder of the estate was being run as a sheep farm. He was also unhappy that Muckross House remained vacant. Vincent, who was apparently familiar with the American national parks, believed that 'if it were treated as a national park it would be possibly the finest and most beautiful park in the world'. He suggested that the house and the estate should become a centre for some international youth organisation, perhaps under the control of a religious organisation.

Patrick Little relayed these concerns to the government. The forestry division responded that it was satisfied that 'in the area a sylvicultural system is being, and will continue to be pursued whereby the amenities of the district and commercial forestry may both be served'. Commercial interests were not allowed to dominate the management of this land; the division was 'fully alive to their responsibility on the amenity and aesthetic aspects in a district which is so essentially and primarily a tourist centre and even if the Department were to relax on the reasonable preservation of those aspects the Killarney Tourist Association is very vigilant on the subject and not slow to raise its voice'. The forestry division reported that it had gone to considerable efforts to reassure the Killarney Tourist Association about its planting policy.[63] When the local tourist association objected to conifers being planted on the estate, the forestry division replied that 'if all the growth in Killarney consisted of hardwoods, without clumps of conifers through them with their various shades of green, the beauty of Killarney would not be at all as great as it is'. The Office of Public Works also reassured the taoiseach that the park was being satisfactorily managed for the enjoyment and recreation of the public; they claimed that tourists commented favourably on the blackface sheep and pedigree cattle that grazed in the park. However, P. J. Little expressed his 'very grave misgivings' at these efforts to exploit the park for grazing and forestry, while simultaneously claiming to preserve the scenery and meet the needs of tourists. He suggested that the management of the park should be transferred to the Irish Tourist Board 'with the sole objective of maintaining it as a famed place of beauty for tourists'.[64]

Although Little regarded commercial forestry and sheep and cattle grazing as incompatible with the running of a national park, he did not envisage any potential conflict between the needs of tourists and preserving the scenery. Over a long period during the twentieth century, the proponents of the national park movement in the United States were very much in favour of promoting tourism in the parks because it appeared to strengthen the case for establishing national parks.[65] In Ireland the link between tourism and a national park was also strong; it is doubtful whether the government would have accepted the gift of Muckross Park, if it had not been located in one of the country's prime tourist areas.

When Roland Bryce bequeathed Garnish Island, a small island close to the south-west coast, consisting mainly of a luxurious house and an exotic garden, to the Irish nation in 1954, the gift was viewed primarily as a tourist attraction, and was undoubtedly accepted for this reason.[66] Muckross Park and Garnish had both been open to the public for many years, while in private ownership. They were already proven tourist attractions, and the Glengariff tourist development association pressed the government to take Garnish into public ownership. Despite the fact that the Bourn Vincent National Park had been in existence for over twenty years, the civil service remained uncertain how Garnish Island should be managed. The solicitor attached to the Department of Finance did his utmost to prove that the bequest was void and should not be accepted, even hiring legal counsel to support his argument. Although the government rejected this advice, they were uncertain about what should be done with the property. Responsibility for Garnish Island was first given to the Department of Agriculture, despite the fact that they had no experience of managing such properties.[67] Control later passed to the Commissioners for Public Works.

The impression that the Irish government was a reluctant owner and manager of public lands, unless they were capable of being exploited for forestry or agricultural purposes, is confirmed by the official response to the proposed sale of the 8000 acre Kenmare estate at Killarney, which adjoined the Bourn Vincent Memorial National Park. In the past the earls of Kenmare and the Herbert family, the former owners of the Muckross Estate, had contested the ownership of the bed and soil of the three Killarney lakes and of the fishing rights. When the Kenmare estate was offered for sale in 1956 it might have appeared logical for the state to buy these lands and to attach them to the existing national park, particularly as the Kenmare lands contained most of the remaining important landmarks in the area, including Ross Castle. The earls of Kenmare had traditionally afforded the public generous access to the estate and this had continued under the ownership of Beatrice Grosvenor, a niece of the last Earl who offered the estate for sale in 1956. It was widely feared that a new owner would end this concession, which had no legal standing.

The campaign for the lands to be taken into public ownership attracted widespread support from predictable quarters such as An Taisce, the Irish Tourist Board and the Killarney Tourist Development Council, and, more surprisingly, from local newspapers throughout Ireland and from many local authorities, which were often hundreds of miles distant from Killarney. The extensive editorials in local newspapers suggest that Killarney was widely regarded as a site of national importance,[68] perhaps because many Irish couples visited it on their honeymoon and because of its international fame. Bing Crosby had recorded a popular song with the title 'How can you buy Killarney'. The proposed sale of the Kenmare estate seems to have prompted the first popular campaign in Ireland for the protection of the natural heritage. Many campaigners drew attention to the measures that existed in Britain and in Northern Ireland for protecting public parks.[69] The president of An Taisce, the physicist Felix Hackett, argued that the Bourn Vincent Park and the Kenmare estate 'form one great area of scenic beauty which requires to be under some such central control as is provided by the (British) National Park and Access to the Countryside Act 1949'. This act had been introduced at Westminster in response to pressure from the British National Trust. Several editorials in local newspapers suggested that the Irish government should establish a park similar to Tollymore Forest Park on the slopes of the Mountains of Mourne, which was opened to the public in 1930 by the Northern Ireland Ministry of Agriculture. It is interesting that Tollymore was more often cited as a possible blueprint than the adjoining Bourn Vincent Park. In private, the taoiseach, John A. Costello, admitted that 'it is essential that any purchaser of the property, whether alien or native, should not be at liberty to exploit one of our most famed scenic treasures to the national detriment'; nevertheless the government was unwilling to purchase the land. The Commissioners of Public Works expressed the opinion that the state should avoid acquiring the Kenmare estate if possible. They claimed that this opinion was based on their experience of administering the adjoining Bourn Vincent Park, but unfortunately they provide no further details, other than a reference to the high cost. Although the government expressed the hope that the Killarney Tourist Development Council or the local authority would buy the estate, it was widely known that they lacked the money to do so, and that the urban district council had no legal authority to borrow money for such a purpose. The government did not offer to provide even part of the cost. They acknowledged that if the property passed into private ownership, the constitutional rights of private ownership meant that the state would have little control over its future, and the existing planning laws offered no assistance. In the event the property was bought by an American businessman for £75,000, and the Irish Tourist Board, which played a much more active role than any department of state, succeeded in maintaining the existing rights to public access. The prospective owner gave a commitment to give all the undertakings which the existing owner would wish; he also undertook not to exploit the estate commercially.[70]

The sale of the Kenmare estate in 1956 coincided with a major crisis in the government finances, which resulted in severe cuts in public expenditure and tax increases.[71] Budgetary difficulties may account for the government's reluctance to purchase the Kenmare estate, though this was never stated, and the ambivalent, even hostile, attitude that successive governments displayed towards the adjoining Bourn Vincent National Park suggests that financial factors were not the only explanation. The evidence suggests that, if the estate had been bought by the state, it would have been a popular move.

The 1960s ushered in a period of economic expansion, which marked an end to the long period of population decline. Economic development put considerable pressure on the Irish urban environment; the Lemass government was actively encouraging British property companies to invest in central Dublin.[72] Consequently the major heritage campaigns of these years were concerned with protecting Dublin's Georgian buildings. With the growing importance of tourism, Muckross House finally found a useful role, as the site of a folk museum, but there was as yet no awareness of potential conflicts between tourism and protecting the natural environment. National parks continued to attract little attention. In 1969, when an Foras Forbartha (the National Institute for Physical Planning and Construction Research) published a report on *The protection of the national heritage*, which became a landmark document in the evolution of a national heritage policy, it explicitly excluded any general examination of scenic issues, arguing that this would raise 'questions of taste, of land use patterns and development pressures far wider than those involved in the conservation or historic or scientific values'. The sections relating to rural Ireland were concerned with preservation only for scientific reasons.[73] It was widely anticipated that Irish accession to the EEC in 1973 would result in a substantial expansion in Irish agricultural output, and any policy that appeared to threaten agricultural prosperity, such as extending national parks, would have been doomed to failure.

Circumstances have changed in recent years. Ireland is now a predominantly urban society. Since the late 1980s the Common Agricultural Policy of the European Union has imposed limits on the output of all the major commodities, such as milk, meat and grain, yet simultaneously EU structural programmes have subsidised farmers in disadvantaged areas to keep sheep and cattle, despite the resulting damage to the environment on western uplands.[74] In his speech introducing the second reading of Blascaod Mór National Historic Park Bill, 1989, the taoiseach, Charles Haughey, indicated that the Great Blasket merited national park status because the islands were 'majestic in their natural beauty and [are] a vivid reminder of a way of life now vanished but which many Irish people lived for countless generations'. The islands had become 'a place of pilgrimage' for many, and the legislation was designed both to protect the island, and to enable the Commissioners of Public Works to promote its use as a centre of culture, education, leisure and recreation.[75] There was no acknowledgement that these objectives might conflict. The management plan drawn up by the Office of Public Works in 1990 for the Killarney National Park – which now includes the former

Kenmare estate – begins by outlining the definition of a national park which was adopted in 1969 by the general assembly of the IUCN – 'to conserve natural plant and animal communities and scenic landscapes which are both extensive and of national importance', but it then expands the definition to include the conservation and protection of historic sites and aspects of cultural heritage. It also notes the importance of developing a 'mutually beneficial relationship' between a national park and the local community – a concept that was also raised in the debate on the legislation governing the Great Blasket National Park.[76] This suggests that utilitarian objectives, such as tourist development or boosting farm incomes, continue to outweigh the goals of preserving the natural environment, and that evidence of historical or cultural heritage are also needed to strengthen the case for preservation. Irish patriotism may be a patriotism of place, but it remains a place that is valued for its economic value or its history, not as an ahistorical, apolitical landscape.

Notes

1   W. K. Hancock, *Survey of British Commonwealth affairs*, I, *Problems of nationality 1918–1939* (Oxford, 1937), p. 381. The 'four green fields' is a widely used allegorical reference to Ireland's four provinces. It is found, for example, in W. B. Yeats's play, *Kathleen Ní Houlihan*.

2   National Archives Ireland, Department of an Taoiseach [hereafter, NAI DT]: files S 5111/7: speech broadcast over CBS radio stations 16 Mar. 1931.

3   S. B. Kennedy, *Irish art and modernism* (Belfast, 1991) p. 71.

4   NAI DT: s16047: the Kenmare estate; press-cutting from the *Waterford News*, 9 June 1956.

5   Eric Richards, *A History of the highland clearances: agrarian transformation and the evicitons 1746-1886* (London, 1982), pp. 239, 371.

6   W. E. Vaughan, *Sin, sheep and Scotsmen. John George Adair and the Derryveagh evictions, 1861* (Belfast, 1983), p. 11.

7   Office of Public Works, *Glenveagh Castle* (Dublin, 1993), p. 28.

8   John Wilson Foster, 'Nature and nation in the nineteenth century', in John Wilson Foster (ed.), *Nature in Ireland: a scientific and cultural history* (Dublin, 1997), p. 417.

9   Simon Schama, *Landscape and memory* (New York, 1995), p. 574. This book argues very much the contrary case.

10   Jeanne Sheehy, *The rediscovery of Ireland's past: the Celtic revival, 1800-1830* (London, 1980); John Hutchinson, *The dynamics of cultural nationalism: the Gaelic revival and the creation of the Irish nation state* (London, 1987).

11   Michael D. Guiry, 'No stone unturned. Robert Lloyd Praeger and the major surveys' in Foster (ed.), *Nature in Ireland*, pp. 299–307.

12   Timothy Collins, 'The Clare island survey of 1909–11: participants, papers and progress' in Criostóir Mac Carthaigh and Kevin Whelan (eds), *New survey of Clare island*, I, *History and cultural landscape* (Dublin, 2000), p. 6.

13 Alfred Runte, *National parks: the American experience* (Lincoln, Nebraska, 1987), pp. 11–32.

14 Mary E. Daly, 'Frugal comfort or lavish austerity? The economic desiderata of Irish nationalism', *Éire-Ireland* XXIX, 4 (winter 1994), 78–100.

15 Published Debates Dáil Éireann [hereafter PDDE] 24 Oct. 1929, cols 242–60; Published Debates Seanad Éireann [hereafter PDSE] 20 Nov.1929, cols 47–55.

16 NAI DT: S 5935: Russborough House.

17 Seán Lysaght, 'Contrasting natures: the issue of names', in Foster (ed.), *Nature in Ireland*, p. 441; D. H. Akenson, *A mirror to Kathleen's face: education in independent Ireland 1922–1960* (London, 1975).

18 P. L. Curran, 'The NUI and the provision of rural science teachers', in P. L. Curran (ed.), *Towards a history of agricultural science in Ireland* (Dublin, 1992), p. 181.

19 Collins, 'The Clare island survey of 1909–11' in Mac Carthaigh and Whelan (eds), *New survey of Clare island*, pp. 3–20.

20 Lysaght, 'Contrasting natures', p. 447.

21 Christopher Moriarty, 'Fish and fisheries' in Foster (ed.), *Nature in Ireland*, p. 295.

22 James Fairhead and Melia Leach, 'The nature lords', *Times Literary Supplement*, 5 May 2000, 3–4.

23 Eileen McCracken, *The Irish woods since Tudor times: distribution and exploitation* (Newton Abbot, 1971), p. 15.

24 J. H. Andrews, 'Road planning in Ireland before the railway age', *Irish Geography* V, 1 (1964), 17–41; T. W. Freeman, *Pre-famine Ireland: a study in human geography* (Manchester, 1956), pp. 110-13.

25 Sean Ó Tuama and Thomas Kinsella, *An Duanaire 1600–1900: poems of the dispossessed* (Dublin, 1981), pp. 328–31.

26 Mary E. Daly, *The famine in Ireland* (Dublin, 1986).

27 Daly, 'Frugal comfort or lavish austerity', 82-3; 86, 90.

28 David N. Doyle, 'The making of Irish-America, 1845–80' in W.E. Vaughan, *A new history of Ireland*, 5 vols (Oxford, 1996), VI, pp. 740–2.

29 William Bulfin, *Rambles in Eirinn* (Dublin, 1907), pp. 45–9.

30 Ibid., p. 259.

31 Maurice Moynihan (ed.), *Speeches and statements by Eamon de Valera, 1917–1973* (Dublin, 1980), p. 466.

32 Richard Dunphy, *The making of Fianna Fáil power in Ireland 1923–1948* (Oxford, 1995), p. 83.

33 Terence Reeves-Smyth, 'Demesnes', in F. H. A. Aalen, Kevin Whelan and Matthew Stout (eds), *Atlas of the Irish rural landscape* (Cork, 1997), p. 205.

34 A. F. Blair, 'The ownership of land' in *Saorstát Éireann: official handbook* (Dublin, 1932), pp. 113–14.

35 Richard Bruton and Frank J. Convery, *Land drainage policy in Ireland* (Dublin, 1982), pp. 6–22.

36 S14920A, Connemara Development Board.

37 NAI DT: S14477B.

38 Terence Reeves-Smyth, 'The natural history of demesnes' in Foster (ed.), *Nature in Ireland*, p. 556.

39 Charles Ernest Muriel, 'Forestry: its present position and future prospects in Ireland', *Journal of the Statistical and Social Inquiry Society of Ireland* XII (1909), 295.

40 Patrick Maume, *The long gestation: Irish nationalist life 1891–1918* (Dublin, 1999), p. 93. Griffiths claimed that deforestation was one of the factors responsible for the high rate of tuberculosis.

41 NAI Land Settlement Commission Archives. These have not yet been listed. My thanks to Caitríona Crowe for making them available.

42 Proceedings of Dáil Éireann, 17 Aug. 1921, p. 54.

43 Arthur Mitchell, *Revolutionary government in Ireland: Dáil Éireann, 1919–22* (Dublin, 1995), pp. 89–90.

44 'The rural environment' in David Cabot (ed.), *The state of the environment: a report prepared by the Minister for the Environment* (Dublin 1985), pp. 60–1.

45 G. J. Doyle, 'Conserving bogland' in John Blackwell and Frank Convery (eds), *Promise and performance: Irish environmental policies analysed* (Dublin, 1983), p. 191.

46 W. E. Vaughan, *Landlords and tenants in mid-Victorian Ireland* (Oxford, 1994), pp. 99–100.

47 John Feehan, 'Raised bogs', in Aalen et al., *Atlas*, p. 111.

48 Peter Foss and Catherine O'Connell, 'Bogland: study and utilization' in Foster (ed.), *Nature in Ireland*, pp. 195–6.

49 Bruton and Convery, *Land drainage policy in Ireland*, pp. 11–14.

50 Ronan Keane, 'Property in the constitution and in the courts' in Brian Farrell (ed.), *De Valera's constitution and ours* (Dublin, 1988), p. 137.

51 Mary E. Daly, *The buffer state: the historic roots of the Irish Department of the Environment* (Dublin, 1997), pp. 462–6.

52 Robert Lloyd Praeger, *Our National Trust*. A lecture broadcast on Radio Éireann, 10 Oct. 1948.

53 NAI DT: S9837: State Property Bill 1954.

54 NAI DT: S5935: Russborough House.

55 J. W. Foster, 'The topographical tradition in Anglo-Irish poetry', *Irish University Review* 4 (1974), 169–87.

56 Robert Lloyd Praeger, *The way that I went* (Dublin, 1937), pp. 360–4.

57 NAI DT: S6355A; PDDE, 7 Dec. 1932, cols 946–9.

58 NAI DT: S6355A.

59 On the 'worthless' lands argument as a prerequisite for the establishment of national parks in the United States, see Runte, *National parks*, pp. 67–8, 75–7.

60 Commissioners of Public Works, Reports for the year ending 31 March 1932, 1933, 1934, 1935 and 1936.

61 NAI DT: S6355B, Muckross House and Park.

62 NAI DT: S6355C.

63 NAI DT: S6355C.

64 NAI DT: S6355C

65 Runte, *National parks*, pp. 2–105.

66 NAI DT: S14977A, Garnish Island.

67 NAI DT: S14977B. The Department of Agriculture was given charge of Johnstown Caste, County Wexford, which was given to the nation in 1944 for use as an agricultural college. NAI DT: S16804, Agricultural Research in Ireland.
68 NAI DT: S16047A.
69 NAI DT: S16047A.
70 NAI DT: S16047A.
71 Kieran A. Kennedy and Brendan R. Dowling, *Economic growth in Ireland: the experience since 1947* (Dublin, 1975), pp. 220–1.
72 Daly, *The buffer state*, pp. 459–62.
73 An Foras Forbartha for the Minister for Local Government, *The protection of the national heritage* (Dublin, 1969).
74 Mary E. Daly, *The first department: a history of the Department of Agriculture 1900–2000* (Dublin, 2002), chapter 10.
75 PDDE, 24 May 1989, cols 1097–9.
76 Office of Public Works, *Killarney national park: management plan* (Dublin, 1990), p. 15.

CHAPTER 18

The *Wehrmacht* Exhibition and the Politics of History in Germany

William Mulligan

At the beginning of 1990, while Germans debated the modes and speed of unification, Günter Grass, Germany's foremost living novelist, warned '[W]hoever thinks about Germany now, must also consider Auschwitz.' It was a warning to his fellow-countrymen that a united Germany would have to deal with its past, and principally its Nazi past which had shaped not just Germany, but the fate of modern Europe. This warning was recalled in the spring of 2002 when Grass published his novella, *Im Krebsgang (Regression)*.[1] The publication of *Im Krebsgang* was a significant cultural event, not merely because it was Grass's first major work since he won the Nobel Prize for literature, but more importantly because of its subject. It told the story of the sinking of the *Wilhelm Gustloff* in January 1945 by a Soviet submarine and the deaths of 9000 Germans (including some military personnel, but mostly civilians), who were fleeing west to avoid the revenge which would be taken by the Red Army and the non-German local population who had suffered under Nazi occupation. In the words of one reader, Grass had broken his own 'taboo' by writing of the suffering of the German exiles from their settlements from eastern Europe (*die Vertriebene*).[2] Although the plight of the exiles had been an important theme in West German politics in the 1950s when integration projects had been supported by both the CDU and the SPD, it was sidelined from the 1960s onwards. It had become the preserve of the nationalistic right in the Federal Republic who used it as a means of relativising the crimes of the National Socialist regime.[3] Hence Grass's novella marked the re-emergence of German suffering in the war as an issue which was no longer restricted to the right wing of German politics.

During the 1990s the politics of history, or *Geschichtspolitik*, was transformed in the newly united democratic Germany. During that decade a series of political and public discussions took place, centred on the Nazi past.

German businesses compensated slave labourers, gold looted from Jewish victims was returned, and efforts to return art stolen during the war to its rightful owners were made. The debate on the Goldhagen thesis and the publication of Victor Klemperer's diaries added to the public debate. There were lengthy arguments about the Holocaust Memorial. Countless books and articles appeared on the Third Reich.[4] In short, as the temporal distance to the Nazi regime increased, its memorialised existence grew more central to the German historical consciousness. Elie Wiesel had continually pronounced that Germans had a moral responsibility to come to terms with their national past. On 27 January 2000, the anniversary of the day Auschwitz was discovered by the Red Army, Wolfgang Thierse, the SPD president of the *Bundestag*, felt able to respond to Wiesel (who was present in the *Bundestag*) that 'we in Germany are on the right path to accepting this message'. He continued: 'Finally I think of the openness, honesty and seriousness with which the past is debated here in the *Bundestag*. If it is true that the parliament is also a mirror of society, then we can take the debate over the controversial *Wehrmacht* exhibition as a sign that your message has been accepted, Herr Wiesel.'[5]

In fact the mild-mannered debate in the *Bundestag* was not characteristic of the polemics which accompanied the *Wehrmacht* exhibition on its tour around Germany and Austria between 1995 and the end of 1999. Produced by the Hamburg Institute of Social Research, a private institute funded by the wealthy tobacco heir, Jan Philipp Reemtsma, the *Wehrmacht* exhibition was the most controversial event in the politics of history in the 1990s. Its central thesis, that the *Wehrmacht*, in which 18 million German men had served, had willingly participated in a genocidal war and that its soldiers regularly committed war crimes, struck at one of the central myths of postwar West German society, namely that few people knew about Nazi crimes and that the army had fought an honourable fight, albeit for a criminal regime. The exhibition, composed of photographs of German soldiers committing atrocities, confronted veterans and their families, and therefore German society, with an image of the *Wehrmacht*'s role in the Second World War, which had been repressed in the collective memory.[6] An estimated 800,000 visited the exhibition and countless more were aware of it, as it dominated the German media in late 1996 and early 1997 when there were major political debates about it in Munich and Bremen, and again in late 1999 when Reemtsma withdrew the exhibition after its credibility had been called into question by the Polish historian, Bogdan Musial. However, it returned in Berlin in November 2001 in a different form, but with the same thesis, and at the time of writing, its only critics have been neo-Nazi groups.

The literature on the *Wehrmacht* exhibition is already extensive, with a number of source collections which gather material from the debates in Bremen and Munich. Although comprehensive, there remains significant documentation that is not included, primarily for reasons of space.⁷ These source collections, it should also be noted, were published by strong supporters of the exhibition though this does not diminish their usefulness. Supporters of the exhibition have also published a number of academic studies which examine the reception of the exhibition.⁸ However, they contained a range of different views about the success of the exhibition in dismantling the myth of the 'unsullied *Wehrmacht*'. Different methodologies, such as interviews, analyses of readers' letters and a study of interest groups, showed the variety of responses to the Nazi past, which cut across generational, gender and political lines.⁹ Since the end of the first exhibition in 1999, a lengthy article was published by Johannes Klotz, who had worked closely with the exhibition.¹⁰ Two major articles have been written on the evidence presented in the first exhibition, while a collection of articles has been published on the general theme of the exhibition.¹¹ However since these publications, the second form of the exhibition has opened which allows a new perspective on the debates surrounding the first exhibition. The uncontroversial reception of the new exhibition suggests that the legend of the 'unsullied *Wehrmacht*', which was the target of the first exhibition, has been laid to rest. The end of this myth, which was an important constitutive element of West German society, marked a change in the politics of history in the Federal Republic, although there will, in all likelihood, be further controversies about the Nazi past.

Coming to terms with the Nazi past has been a political necessity for the Berlin Republic. The politics which shaped the collective memory of the Bonn Republic was utterly changed by unification and the end of the Cold War. The myth of the 'unsullied *Wehrmacht*' had helped the reconstruction of West German society after the war. Guilt could be attributed to the Nazi leaders who were found guilty at Nuremberg and to specific creations of the National Socialist regime such as the Gestapo and the SS.¹² Soldiers simply followed orders and fought for their Fatherland in a desperate effort to protect their families from the barbarous Red Army. These same men then returned to rebuild a ruined nation after 1945. Questioning their past would have had unsettling consequences for West German society. Konrad Adenauer's foreign policy also depended on a selective reading of history which, on the one hand, recognised the deleterious consequences of Franco-German antagonism and, on the other, was motivated by a fierce anti-Communism. Memory after the war was often shaped by National Socialist propaganda, so that the Red Army was seen as an 'Asiatic threat' to European civilisation. The nature of the war on the Eastern front had to be downplayed as West German soldiers served with erstwhile enemies against the old Soviet foe. Hence the myth of the 'unsullied *Wehrmacht*' served a range of interests, from individual and collective biographies to the foreign policy aims of the Adenauer government.¹³

Even in the 1960s and 1970s, as work on the role of the *Wehrmacht* began to emerge from a generation too young to be implicated in the National Socialist regime, the myth of the 'unsullied *Wehrmacht*' remained entrenched in the collective historical consciousness. Events such as the Eichmann trial and the television series, *Holocaust*, only slightly widened the guilty circle. The belief remained that only relatively few in the Nazi elites were implicated in the atrocities of the Third Reich. In fact, it could be argued that the public debates on the Holocaust removed Auschwitz from its historical context of the Second World War. The gas chambers at Auschwitz were part of a much larger pattern of extermination which included mass shootings.[14] The focus on Auschwitz meant that the *Wehrmacht*'s role in genocide and war crimes went largely unnoticed by the public, despite the work of Hans Adolf Jacobsen on the Commissar order (which, in June 1941, ordered the immediate execution of captured Red Army commissars), Christian Streit on the treatment of Soviet prisoners of war and Manfred Messerschmidt on the *Wehrmacht*'s justice system.[15] The exhibition brought this knowledge into the public sphere.

In terms of the politics of history, the 1980s was dominated by the 'historians' dispute' when Ernst Nolte and Andreas Hillgruber argued that crimes of the Third Reich were a reaction to the Stalinist gulags and that historians should have empathy with *Wehrmacht* soldiers who died, protecting the Fatherland from the Red Army. These views were discredited. The singularity of Nazi crimes was stressed and it was pointed out that, as the *Wehrmacht* fought, it also enabled the Final Solution to continue.[16] Yet this did not mark a significant dent in the public acceptance of the myth of the 'unsullied *Wehrmacht*'.[17] The circle of perpetrators remained limited. If the *Wehrmacht* did enable Auschwitz to function, it was only indirectly. Soldiers were not actually running the gas chambers. Moreover the generation ruling the Federal Republic in the 1980s was too young to have been implicated in the crimes of the Third Reich. Helmut Kohl spoke in the Knesset of 'the fortune of the late birth' (*die Gnade der späten Geburt*). In the eyes of CDU dominated government and important right-wing historians, such as Michael Stürmer, the Federal Republic had to emerge from the shadow of the Nazi past. More positive chapters of German history could create a more positive national identity.[18]

The transformations which took place between 1989 and 1991 – the fall of the Berlin Wall, the unification of Germany and the end of the Cold War – created new conditions for the politics of history. In 1994 Heinrich August Winkler suggested that the left had used the division of Germany as an atonement for the Nazi past. Was, he asked, 'the absolute denial of state unity a half-conscious attempt to escape the most terrible chapter of German history once and for all, to dispose of it definitively – a more subtle attempt than everything conservative apologists have done in this direction, but also too comfortable to be convincing? If that is so, is the most difficult part of the effort to learn from history still to come for the Germans?'[19] In the same issue, Anne Marie le Gloannec argued: '[A]s a new democratic state, the Federal Republic offered more than a guarantee against the past; it provided in a sense, an escape from it.'[20] Barthold Witte, editor of the German quarterly *liberal*, contended that the failed *Machtpolitik* of the first half of the century 'are central experiences with deep and lasting effects on Germany and the Germans. . . . The German experiences of the first half of this century have proven to be more than past history and more than just a German affair.'[21] There was a broad consensus that history would have a fundamental role to play in the formation of a new German national identity. However, there was rather less consensus on what that history should be. Stefan Berger feared a revival of programmatic nationalistic histories which had been characteristic of Prussian historiography in the late nineteenth century, whereas others such as Hans Peter Schwarz, biographer of Adenauer, regretted the 'muted trumpets' with which historians greeted unification.[22]

The international environment changed with a number of consequences for the politics of history. The end of dictatorship in eastern Europe meant that archives were slowly opened up to historians. Both the exhibitions used a considerable number of sources from eastern European archives. However, this was largely an addition to the vast amounts of source material available in West German archives. The end of the Cold War meant that historians could look anew at the war on the eastern front without being accused of apologetics for Communist regimes. There was a new recognition in western Europe that the Second World War had been won and lost on the eastern front. The relatively heroic nature of the war in the west was superseded by grim accounts of the war in the east.[23]

Beyond the changed perspective there was also the matter of the new republic's relations with its eastern neighbours. A series of historical traumas which had been suppressed in eastern Europe re-emerged. The Nazi occupation, slave labour, and the deportation of Jews from their homes in eastern Europe to extermination camps came into the public sphere throughout central and eastern Europe. An exhibition which opened at the Sachsenhausen concentration camp in December 2001 showed that 12,000 out of 60,000 internees died during the period of Soviet occupation. The Russian government was outraged at what it saw as 'an attempt to whitewash the crimes of the Nazis'. The German government refused to mediate between victims of Soviet repression and the Russian government, noting that 'the suffering of the German NKVD victims was tragic, but it had its roots in the previous Nazi wrongs'.[24] Just before the exhibition opened in Munich, the German and Czech governments issued a declaration in which the Czech Republic regretted the expulsion of Germans in 1945, while the Federal Republic recognised that this was a result of Nazi aggression. Current relations were not to be affected by the past though representatives of 'exiles' were loath to accept this final settlement.[25] The end of the Cold War altered the role of the *Bundeswehr* in foreign policy. It had become part of international peacekeeping forces in the Balkans. The *Wehrmacht*'s record was used by advocates of military intervention and non-intervention. Hannes Heer, the historical director of the first exhibition, argued for intervention in the Balkans, while Walter Manoschek, also involved with the first exhibition and author of a book on the *Wehrmacht*'s role in the murder of Serbian Jews, was an opponent of such a policy. Although Reemtsma was opposed to the instrumentalisation of the exhibition in this way, events in the 1990s forced Germans to look at the Nazi past once again.[26]

The 1990s was a decade in which the Nazi past remained at the centre of the politics of history, despite the potential controversies of other pasts, such as the 1968 generation and most obviously the legacy of the German Democratic Republic.[27] Although historians had long known and written about the Commissar order and the mistreatment of millions of Soviet prisoners of war, it was the *Wehrmacht* exhibition which brought this knowledge into the public sphere. What happened in the 1990s was that cherished historical myths were undermined by accurate historical knowledge. The history of the *Wehrmacht* exhibition, in both its incarnations, showed the difficulty of this process. If the repression of historical knowledge is one of the marks of an authoritarian regime, then open acknowledgement and engagement with the past are marks of a liberal democracy.[28] While it would be unwise to claim that democracy in the Federal Republic depended on the success of the exhibition, its ups and downs did show how sensitive the German public were to credible archival evidence. Theo Sommer, in the weekly, *Die Zeit*, argued:

> [T]he more unambiguously we accept the past and the more openly we discuss it, then the more naturally we can stand upright in the ranks of nations a half century after Hitler's war. Seen in this way, the photographs in the Wehrmacht exhibition can make us free. To deny them on the other hand means that we will stumble blindly and ignorantly into the future with the silences which come from an ill-fated past.[29]

Acknowledging the past was the surest way to convince Germans and Europeans that the Federal Republic would not threaten international stability as the first united Germany had done.

The exhibition opened in 1995, the year of the fiftieth anniversary of the end of the war. The end of the war remained, in the words of Theodor Heuss, the first president of the Federal Republic, 'a tragic paradox'. The end of

Nazi rule and the terrors of the war were superseded by the occupation of Germany, mass rape and the expulsion of Germans from the east. Fifty years later this paradox had not been resolved and the roles of perpetrators and victims were as confused as they had been at the end of the war. Generational differences were evident in readers' letters. One reader, born in 1970, criticised the war generation for using German victims of Allied bombings and the deaths of two million ethnic Germans in eastern Europe as a subliminal 'corpse accounting' (*Aufrechnungsmasse*) for the victims of Nazi genocide and *Wehrmacht* crimes.[30] A reader born in 1930 responded, asking whether he was guilty for the occupation of the Rhineland in 1936 or for the continuance of the Nazi regime until 1945 because he had helped to gather the harvest in 1944. He criticised those who judge the war generation 'from the safe distance of time in their well-upholstered pads'.[31] When the exhibition opened in March 1995, therefore, it was seen in the context of a wave of *Vergangenheitsbewältigung*, or coming to terms with the past.

The exhibition was organised by the Hamburg Institute of Social Research, which was funded by Jan Philipp Reemtsma, whose father had made his fortune in the tobacco business and who had done business with Nazi leaders. The historical director of the first exhibition was Hannes Heer, born in 1941 and a former member of the (West) German Communist Party. The background of both men would be used by opponents of exhibition. Reemtsma continually claimed that they did not expect the exhibition to generate the polemics it did. Originally the exhibition was part of a larger project 'Civilisation and barbarism: in the face of our century', which would look at the violent tendencies of modernity by examining the last 200 days of the Second World War, from the discovery of Auschwitz to the dropping of atom bombs on Hiroshima and Nagasaki.[32] The first exhibition was dominated by photographs, and this raised problematic questions about their validity as historical evidence. However, the original plan was to have substantially more text, as the second one had. Museum experts warned the institute that that this conception would be 'too burdened with text, with pictures which would be too small and not sufficiently shocking. Nobody would visit such an exhibition.'[33] The nature of the presentation was one of the major shortcomings of the first exhibition with unattributed sources and the separation of the photographs from the text.

Moreover the fact that the institute accepted the advice of experts on museum exhibitions calls into question Reemtsma's assertion that he and Heer did not intend to provoke a major public reaction. After all, an exhibition is supposed to provoke, to challenge accepted views by presenting new knowledge. They might not have expected the intensity of the debate, especially in Munich. Yet to a certain extent, once they put it on display, the exhibition was no longer their exhibition but part of the German public's historical consciousness. The word 'taboo' was often used by the organisers, signifying the scale of the myth which they hoped to challenge. Any challenge to a society's taboos arouses controversy. Reemtsma commented that the reaction to the exhibition showed the 'underestimated impact of the war a half century later'.[34] In an interview in 1999 he predicted that the taboo of the *Wehrmacht*'s role in war crimes had been broken, but that others would emerge.[35] Although the thesis of the first exhibition was sound, the presentation was aimed at the emotions.

The emotional response which it could generate was evident in Karl-Heinz Janßen's review in *Die Zeit* in March 1995, just after it opened: 'from all the walls, from all the corners [the exhibition] screams MURDER.' In the visitors' book someone had written, 'Dad, where were you?', which was a reformulation of the 1968 generation's question, 'Dad, what did you do in the War?' Janssen concluded on this theme: '[O]ur fathers and grandfathers, you knew what happened, or you could have known. Now it is time to remember.'[36] Wolfram Wette, of the Military History Research Bureau and one of the most controversial historians in Germany, praised the exhibition for showing a 'more dismal picture of the conduct of war in the east.' The depiction of the Sixth Army as being responsible for atrocities carried out in Kiev and the massacre at Babi Yar was emblematic of the changed perception of the *Wehrmacht*. Previously the Sixth Army had been associated with heroic defeat at Stalingrad. Now the reason why they were fighting at Stalingrad was presented to the public – they were waging a 'war of destruction', to borrow the phrase of the exhibition. Wette concluded:

> [T]he more historical research concerns itself with the Wehrmacht's conduct of war, the more dismal the picture becomes. However it remains an indispensable requirement to differentiate between the various levels of responsibility within a military structure to which almost twenty million men belonged between 1939 and 1945. The simple German solider, who was forced to serve against his will and knew about or even became involved in the crimes, cannot be simply equated with the generals and their assistants. These carry an incomparably higher level of responsibility for the war of destruction. It was they who issued orders based on blind racism and which opened the way to the murder of civilians and prisoners of war.[37]

In this one article Wette pointed to two possible reactions to the exhibition which would later diverge into opposing camps. Firstly, he noted how the myth of the 'unsullied *Wehrmacht*' was being eroded by historical research which was the basis of the exhibition's thesis. Secondly, he suggested that there should have been a more differentiated account of the involvement in atrocities. Future critics of the exhibition would argue that it was too generalised and use this criticism to undermine the basic thesis that the

Wehrmacht as an institution had become involved in the criminal conduct of the war.

At the same time, some readers' letters showed the reactions of opponents of the exhibition. Unlike the Goldhagen debate which was dominated by historians, the controversy over the *Wehrmacht* exhibition saw historians retreat into the shadows, emerging to powerful effect only at the end of the debate. One letter disputed Wette's claim that the Sixth Army was responsible for Babi Yar, and cited the book by a leading Holocaust historian, Wolfgang Benz, *Legende, Lügen, Vorurteile*.[38] In fact the Sixth Army supported and made the massacre at Babi Yar possible.[39] Nevertheless debating the evidence was rare amongst the opponents of the exhibition, at least until the work of Musial and Ungváry. Another strategy was to attack institutions and people. One reader argued that the Military History Research Bureau had long tried to defame the *Wehrmacht*, and therefore its publications were prejudiced. The exhibition was merely trying to revoke the judgement of the Nuremberg tribunal which had not prosecuted the *Wehrmacht*'s supreme command. The letter concluded: '[T]he aim is clear: once again the current generation should be infected with the idea that their fathers and grandfathers, if not criminals themselves, were deeply involved in criminal units. As a consequence of this they would have to adhere to deeply impacting feelings of guilt until the end of their lives.'[40] These letters anticipated some of the later criticisms. They focused on Wette's article, but later the Military History Research Bureau and the exhibition were seen as part of a broad coalition who wanted to denigrate the honourable struggle of the *Wehrmacht*. The second letter writer avoided the evidence and chose to question motives, and he also pointed to the legacy of the Nuremberg trials which was seen partly as a declaration of the innocence of the *Wehrmacht* and partly as an Allied attempt to destroy the moral fabric of the German nation.

Until late 1996 the exhibition managed to tour Germany with relatively little controversy. In Stuttgart there were successful efforts to change the location away from the *Landtag* and instead it took place in the DGB-Haus.[41] During 1995 and 1996 *Vergangenheitsbewältigung* focused on the fiftieth anniversary of the end of the war in May 1995 and then on the Goldhagen thesis, which was published in German in August 1996, though the first reviews appeared on the basis of the English edition.[42] At first glance both the exhibition and the Goldhagen thesis appeared to deliver similarly damning verdicts of collective guilt – the eliminationist anti-Semitism of the Germans explained the Shoah and the participation of eighteen million Germans in a military apparatus responsible for the deaths of millions of prisoners of war and civilians reinforced the criminality of the German nation. However, there were important differences.[43] For a start anti-Semitism was an inadequate explanation for the murder of millions of civilians and prisoners of war. Goldhagen's thesis still concentrated on the relatively small group of people who had been guarding concentration camps, as well as the *Einstazgruppen* which were part of the SS. The circle of perpetrators was widening, but not to eighteen million. Goldhagen also soothed contemporary German pride by congratulating them on the way in which they recognised their role in the Holocaust. Germany was now a normal western country with an open historical record, a model for other states. The exhibition, on the other hand, portrayed the suppression of the past with the implication that Germany had not yet come to terms with the Nazi past. Where Goldhagen drew a line under that past, the exhibition seemed to threaten a renewed and awkward confrontation with precious myths.

As the Goldhagen debate faded away in late 1996, the *Wehrmacht* exhibition moved to centre stage when the Bremen Senate debated whether the exhibition could be held in the *Rathaus* (parliament building). Bremen, one of the German *Länder*, had an SPD–CDU coalition and neither the SPD mayor, Henning Scherf, nor the CDU chairman, Bernd Neumann, was willing to see the collapse of the coalition over the location of an exhibition. On the other hand, both parties wanted to shore up political support. The right had long sought to normalise German history, an effort which the left opposed by stressing the Nazi past. In the words of one observer, historical truth was 'what served the political interests of the SPD and CDU and their power in the Great Coalition'.[44] The debate in Bremen combined municipal pride, the identity of the parties, and their views of German history. During the debates in 1996 and 1997 opponents appealed to old myths, questioned the motives of the organisers and posed as defenders of national honour and generational cohesion. Political supporters, on the other hand, developed arguments based on the democratic imperative of knowing the historical 'truth' and the national interest of recognising past crimes.

In both Bremen and Munich it was parties of the right which initially raised the issue of the venue of the exhibition, only to see it rebound in their face. It would have been far more politically astute to allow the exhibition to go ahead. Political debate heightened the profile of the exhibition, which until then had been the subject of some minor sniping by veteran groups and elements on the radical right. But in the middle of October 1996 the leader of the CDU party in the senate, Ronald Mike Neumeyer, accused the exhibition of being defamatory and announced that it should not be held in the *Rathaus*. There was even an attempt to schedule the renovation of the *Rathaus* so as to clash with the exhibition.[45] In November, just before the debate in the *Rathaus*, the split between the coalition parties became clear. The CDU decided to take an unequivocal stand against an exhibition which it condemned as 'demagogic and unscientific', though it failed to take issue with specific evidence presented either in the photographs or in the accompanying catalogue. It predicted that the exhibition would lead to a split in the Bremen population, a reference to generational differences.[46]

The failure to engage with the evidence and historiography on the *Wehrmacht* led the CDU, and later the CSU, into treacherous terrain. Their arguments, which were directed at the organisers and style of the exhibition, were utterly unconvincing. The adoption of a moral stance on the exhibition by posing as the defenders of the war generation against unscrupulous left-wing agitators left the two right-wing parties vulnerable to accusations of sharing the same historical consciousness as the neo-Nazis. This was clearly overstating the position of the CDU but it was valuable political capital for the SPD which could move into the centre ground on the politics of memory. One SPD senator stressed that there could be 'no solidarity between democrats and murderers', and that it was the 'duty to show the younger generation how out of nihilism, racism and national darkness a ruling system could be erected for the extermination of opponents of all types, including whole ethnic groups'.[47] In an open letter signed by several members of the Greens, the Citizens' Union and the SPD the use of the *Rathaus* for the exhibition became a moral and democratic imperative: '[N]early all German men served in the *Wehrmacht* during the Second World War. Precisely because of this the discussion is an opportunity for the whole society which has its place in the centre of the city.' The CDU was merely continuing its 'tradition of suppressing the past'. There was 'no truth about the Nazi past which did not hurt somebody', but the painful engagement had to take place.[48]

The lines had been drawn. The CDU entered the lists as the defender of national honour against a one-sided and biased presentation of the *Wehrmacht*'s role in the war. The SPD and Greens adopted the position of champions of the historical 'truth', and, by implication, the moral guardians of democracy against the coalition of the CDU and the radical right which was based on deliberate ignorance of history. While the SPD and Greens adopted a moral posture, the Hamburg Institute for Social Research reiterated the academic quality of the thesis which made research 'known to a broad public beyond the circle of experts'. Reemtsma dismissed the objections of the CDU which 'without knowing it itself has the problem that it is supported by extremely precarious material. There are libellous texts about this exhibition from the extreme right of the spectrum.'[49] When the cabinet failed to resolve the deadlock about the location the senate held a debate.[50]

The debate in the Bremen senate lacked some of the more bizarre arguments of the debate in the Munich *Stadtrat* (city council), which did so much to undermine the credibility of the opponents of the exhibition. The debate focused on two issues: the presentation of the exhibition's thesis and the consequences of that thesis for the politics of history. The CDU speaker, Neumeyer, outlined five related objections. Firstly the exhibition failed to offer any context for the actions of the soldiers who were young men and who faced terrible punishment if they refused to participate in the murder of civilians. (There is no evidence of any punishment for refusal to participate in war crimes.[51]) It failed to recognise the contribution of the officer corps to the German resistance, and it therefore offered an undifferentiated examination of the *Wehrmacht* in the war. Thirdly it was an attack on the generation 'which in spite of the millions of individual sufferings built up this democratic Federal Republic, based on the rule of law'. Hence the exhibition became an attack on the present German state. Linked to this was the fourth argument, which warned of the generational splits that would be caused by the exhibition. Finally the exhibition became an attack on the *Bundeswehr* because, according to Neumeyer, the message of the exhibition was that all soldiers were murderers. While conceding that the exhibition should take place in Bremen, he did not believe that it belonged in the *Rathaus*: '[T]he *Rathaus* is the *Rathaus* of all the citizens. One should not bring the divisions of society into this *Rathaus*, and the *Rathaus* should certainly not tolerate a half-truth.'[52]

Ranged against these criticisms, speakers from the Greens and SPD inverted the significance of the location of the *Rathaus*. Horst Isola (SPD) argued that the exhibition had become the central topic of political discussion in Bremen, and precisely because of this 'the work of memory should be at the centre of our society and not at the edge and parliaments are at the centre of our political life'. Where the CDU's strategy of *Vergangenheitsbewältigung* depended on the suppression of uncomfortable historical issues, Isola argued that Germany could emerge from the past and earn the respect of her neighbours only by engaging with the past.[53] Whereas the right sought to promote the legitimacy of Germany as a major European power by constructing a relatively positive national historical narrative, the left sought to secure Germany's international reputation by acknowledging the scale of Nazi crimes. Kuhn, of the Greens, took issue with the argument that the exhibition was one-sided: '[I]n the past year in the *Rathaus* we had an exhibition on the resistance which also dealt with the resistance within the military. . . . Only a small percentage of the officer corps, at most two or three per cent, could have identified with what was shown in that exhibition.'[54] The suppression of what happened on the eastern front was one of the foundation stones of West German society. Another was the elevation of the men of the July plot to heroic status as symbolic of a good Germany by Adenauer in the 1950s.[55] The exhibition, by inverting the image of the *Wehrmacht* in contemporary German society, threatened the CDU more than the other parties.

The debate in Bremen ended in a compromise as befitted a *Land* with a coalition government. The *Wehrmacht* exhibition went ahead in the *Rathaus* but the exhibition on military resistance, entitled 'Revolt of the conscience', was scheduled for a second appearance. The exhibition did not appear in Bremen until July, by which stage the Munich debate had taken place. There were more controversies in Bremen as Reemtsma threatened to sue Neumann for claiming that the photographs had been falsified.[56] Perhaps the most salient points made in the Bremen debate were by historians. Professor Hans-Ulrich Thamer of Münster suggested that the exhibition failed to relate the 'mentalities' of the soldiers to the crimes. Professor Wolfgang Benz, who had noted that the exhibition could not meet the standards expected in a scholarly book, still praised it for provoking thought, 'and that is important because it is one of the tasks of a cultured nation to remember'.[57] This debate, which had taken place on 26 February 1997, was completely overshadowed by events in Munich. Until historians managed to transmit their research to the public, the myth of the 'unsullied *Wehrmacht*' would continue. The decision of Arnulf Baring, an historian of West German foreign policy, to cancel an appearance at a CSU rally in Munich owing to the heated political temperatures, showed the reluctance of historians to guide the debate, and perhaps their inability to do so when polemics were more important than knowledge and argument.[58]

The debate in the Bremen *Rathaus* had demonstrated the weakness of the arguments against the general thesis, if not the presentation of the exhibition. This weakness was accentuated by the methods of argument used in the Munich debate. In Munich the political situation was very different. The *Land* government was formed by the CSU party under Edmund Stoiber, but the exhibition was scheduled to be held in the *Rathaus* and the decision lay with the city council which was dominated by the SPD and led by Christian Ude. There were no immediate political gains or losses to be made and the arguments were less circumspect, especially by the coalition of right-wing opponents. Peter Gauweiler, leader of the Munich CDU, and Manfred Brunner, former member of the FDP and leader of the right-wing *Bund freier Bürger* (BfB), unintentionally lent the exhibition publicity and credibility with their speeches and articles between December 1996 and February 1997.

Mobilisation against the exhibition began in September 1996 when the BfB proposed a comparative exhibition on German and Soviet prisoners of war.[59] However, until the debate, the Bavarian press was more interested in the accords between Germany and the Czech Republic which dealt with the historical legacy of the war.[60] The intensity of the debate in Munich was partly due to the presence of Sudeten German expellees, which gave the contours of memory a sharper edge in Bavaria than in Bremen. As in Bremen the opponents failed to contest the evidence, yet proceeded to contest the thesis by relativising Nazi crimes and making personal attacks on the organisers. The SPD and the Greens were able to portray themselves as defenders of the truth and accuse the CSU of making neo-Nazi history 'socially acceptable'.

On 11 December 1996, in the city council, Brunner opened the debate by disputing the value of the photographs as evidence. He then went on to argue that if Germans could not decide on whether the *Wehrmacht* committed crimes, then the debate could be adjudicated by former enemies. He quoted from Marshal Zhukov's memoirs that the German soldier was 'tenacious' and 'disciplined'. Opponents frequently quoted François Mitterrand's 1995 speech which exculpated the soldiers of the *Wehrmacht* from Nazi crimes. This was proof of the 'greatness' of the *Wehrmacht* which was linked with its tragedy. This was a selective choice of foreign opinion, and doubtless civilian survivors in the former eastern bloc would have given a very different answer, as indeed would the vast majority of the historical profession. This reliance on dubious sources, and on political statements rather than historical evidence, was one of the features of the opposition to the exhibition. Brunner also revived the early post-war myths, citing Adenauer's assertion in the *Bundestag* on 6 May 1951 that the number of people involved in crimes was so low that no damage had been done to the *Wehrmacht*'s reputation. He claimed that the *Bundeswehr* would be damaged because soldiers currently serving would fear that their deeds would be misrepresented in fifty years time, omitting to mention that the regimes which the *Bundeswehr* and *Wehrmacht* served were very different.[61]

The most bizarre parts of his argument involved an attack on the motivations of Reemtsma and Heer, and what he called the 'red-green generation'. He suggested that Reemtsma was indulging in his own act of suppression: '[I]f Mr Reemtsma means that the family got its money, which he inherited, from close connections with the Nazis, then he can draw the necessary consequences from this, rather than disparaging the memory of the dead. For that I have no sympathy.'[62] The inference that Reemtsma had gone to all the effort of helping to organise the exhibition as an exercise in personal catharsis required a stretch of the imagination, as did Brunner's speculations on the motives of the SPD and the Greens:

> the Red–Green generation of politicians distinguishes itself in wishing to escape the tribunal by becoming the tribunal themselves. And it is a very interesting thought that we have today a political generation, mainly in the SPD and the Greens, which knows exactly that it should be put in front of a tribunal – the mass murder of unborn life is just one example I will name here.[63]

The crude equivalence of abortion and Nazi crimes bore no relevance to the thesis of the exhibition.

The difficulty for the CSU was that it opposed the exhibition, and therefore laid itself open to belonging in the same camp as the extreme BfB. Hans Podiuk's speech was relatively restrained though his use of a right-wing pamphleteer, Rüdiger Proske, as an expert on the history of the *Wehrmacht*, showed how few reliable historians were willing to condemn the thesis of the exhibition.[64] He retold the story of a seventy-five-year-old woman, married three months before the outbreak of the war, who now saw her husband's reputation defamed (he had died in 1942). This was a clever variation on the theme of generational division. It gave the *Wehrmacht* soldiers who, in the scheme of opponents of the exhibition, were merely doing their duty and defending their Fatherland, a personality which might evoke sympathy. The inclusion of members of the military resistance as perpetrators was 'the limit', in Podiuk's view. He then went on to call for a more differentiated history of the *Wehrmacht*.[65]

The SPD and Greens took full advantage of the awkward association in this matter of the CSU with the BfB. Councillor Sabina Csampai (Green Party) accused the CSU and BfB of damaging 'the reputation of the city of Munich', and Brunner of making 'National Socialism socially acceptable'. The association of historical 'truth', democracy and the left was underlined. She claimed that the Red–Green generation had brought 'democracy and liberalness into this state', a novel interpretation of the origins of the Federal Republic. Now this same group was supporting the 'exhibition, which is trying to pave the way for truth'.[66] Councillor Dietmar Keese (SPD) wondered why the CSU was so fearful of the exhibition's message: '[O]bviously they are considering those who do not want a debate, even today. However, that is not a point of view which will bring our democracy forward.'[67] The CSU was anti-democratic according to the SPD and Greens, not only because of its association in this debate with the radical right, but also because it opposed the historical 'truth'. The CSU would become more vulnerable to these accusations when neo-Nazi marches accompanied the opening of the exhibition in Munich.

During the debate in the city council it was clear that the CSU was split over the exhibition, and as some of its members made more extreme (and ridiculous) statements, this split grew. Franz Forchheimer, on the liberal wing of the CSU, was one of the few city councillors who had actually seen the exhibition. While he thought that it could be improved, he believed 'it is valuable because it begins a necessary debate. It must be made sufficiently clear that people in the *Wehrmacht* committed crimes. Naturally there were also many who committed none.'[68] Meanwhile Peter Gauweiler, in what many saw as an attempt to raise his profile in a city where he had lost one mayoral election, wrote an article in the CSU paper, *Bayern-Kurier* in which he suggested that Reemtsma should organise an exhibition on the deaths caused by tobacco. In the same article he claimed that the left was less interested in history than in 'intensifying the punishment of Nuremberg on Germany and conducting a campaign of moral destruction against the German people'. (The exhibition's title used the same term *Vernichtungskrieg*.)[69]

Gauweiler's comments dominated the media in the days before the opening of the exhibition on 24 February. The CSU was now split. Stoiber, the Bavarian minister president and Theo Waigel, the federal finance minister, kept their counsel, though the former criticised the exhibition as a generalisation. The general secretary of the CSU, Bernd Protzner, was also unforthcoming about Gauweiler's comments, but maintained that the party 'had always cut itself off from the extreme right wing of the political spectrum'.[70] Podiuk defended Gauweiler after a meeting of CSU councillors, and condemned the 'left-Green private institute', and the 'communist industrialist heir' who sponsored the exhibition. At the same time Forchheimer, and Thonheiser, who had clashed with Gauweiler on the Goldhagen thesis, refused to attend a ceremony to lay a wreath at the tomb of the unknown soldier in Munich. The timing of the ceremony, which had been promoted by Gauweiler, had been purposely chosen to clash with the opening ceremony for the exhibition at Munich University.[71] On the evening of 24 February 1997, two rival interpretations of the history of the *Wehrmacht* were dramatised.

Early on Monday evening Gauweiler laid a wreath at the tomb in front of a crowd of people. Rainer Stephan of the left-leaning *Süddeutsche Zeitung* described it:

> [I]t is a haunting scene from the underworld which the observer at the edge of the ceremony finally catches. Shoulder to shoulder they are standing there, the old and the young comrades, the Munich CSU city councillors, the young women and men of the Young Union in their cashmere pullovers, the students from the duelling corps and members of the Bundeswehr in their uniform. Naturally the Bundeswehr soldiers are not allowed to attend a political meeting in their uniforms; but they are allowed to attend a wreath-laying ceremony.[72]

A biased and sarcastic account, it nevertheless showed the solemn reaffirmation, in the eyes of the CSU and supporters, of the honour of the *Wehrmacht*. A simple ceremony which had been carried out innumerable times was now instrumentalised in the context of a political debate. Honouring the fallen of the war became a means of challenging the thesis of the exhibition. The implication was that if the thesis of the exhibition was correct then the mourning ritual of nation since 1945 had been false.

Meanwhile Ude was articulating his version of the politics of history at the Audimax Hall at the university when he went out of his way to greet Forchheimer and Dr Löbl, head of the Munich *Bundeswehr* school. The distinction between right and left over the exhibition was no longer absolute, although it remained important. At first he stressed that the exhibition was not supposed to be a tribunal on a whole generation. This was to misunderstand the pedagogical purpose of it. While it asserted that the *Wehrmacht* was a criminal institution, it did not mean that all eighteen million soldiers were *ipso facto* criminalised. Guilt was personal, but responsibility for the past was collective. Nor was it anti-military. The *Bundeswehr* was the complete opposite to the *Wehrmacht*, a defensive, democratic army. He defended the choice of the *Rathaus*, in the same way as the Bremen SPD: '[I]n a democracy the parliament is the site of controversial discussions, and such an important theme [as this exhibition presents] cannot be dealt with in concealed shame.'[73] Whereas the CDU in Bremen had argued that division could not be brought into the *Rathaus*, the SPD had embraced this particular historical controversy.

Ude noted the significance of the exhibition and the debate for the politics of history in the united Germany:

> [M]ore than fifty years after the end of the Second World War we should be able to look these historical facts in the eye, even if they are uncomfortable for some. We must ensure that past injustice is recognised as such, and not suppressed, hidden or relativised in order to do justice to the victims, and also to those who bore no guilt. Only when there are no taboos or varnishing in dealing with the truth will we be free from the suspicion of only wanting to see the wrongs of others; only then can we call the persecution of the Sudeten Germans and other German ethnic minorities an injustice, the destruction of German cities as inhumane without arousing the impression that we only want to count up the bodies and continue the spiral of mutual accusation which has caused so much disaster in this century.[74]

It might be argued that Ude was engaging in relativisation at this point, but in fact he had restored the chronology of victimhood, where German victims were ultimately caused by German aggression. It was this recognition of cause and effect that was becoming the new consensual politics of history in the Federal Republic.

There was still significant opposition to the exhibition, but it was diminishing because of its dangerous political associations and more importantly the weakness of the argument. The Bavarian culture minister, Hans Zehetmair of the CSU who was responsible for education at all levels in the *Land*, was careful to distance the government from the exhibition's opening at the university. In a statement which served to subvert meaning, and to confuse cause and effect, the Culture Ministry claimed:

> [N]obody seriously disputes the necessity of an honest, academic and differentiated debate about the history of the Third Reich. The question of the role and responsibility of the Wehrmacht also belongs to this. However, in view of the debate of the last few weeks, it must be said that judgements which affect and discriminate against millions of participants in the war insult a large part of the older generation,

lead to new differences and create new breeding ground for those who want to live in the past.[75]

In an interview on the day after the exhibition opened, Zehetmair admitted that he had only seen the catalogue, but that it was 'superficial and one-sided'. While he would not prevent schools from visiting it, he believed 'it was not worth recommending'.[76] The *Münchner Merkur* reported that four classes had seen the exhibition within the first two days, and 200 did so by the end of the exhibition.[77] The message from the Bavarian government was that the exhibition was 'bad history' since it tried to educate a new generation about the Nazi past, but it did not appear to impede teachers, nor the university, from making their own decisions.

Gauweiler's cause was not helped by a further dramatisation of the opposing views of history when a neo-Nazi demonstration planned for 1 March against the exhibition provoked a counter-demonstration of trade unionists, the SPD and the Greens. The neo-Nazi demonstration was allowed to proceed on two conditions. Firstly that there were no Hitler salutes, and secondly that they were not to enter Geschwister Scholl Platz, near the university, which had been named after the White Rose resistance siblings executed by the Nazis.[78] The neo-Nazi march was blocked by a counter-demonstration at Munich's Marienplatz. The *Münchner Abendzeitung* triumphantly entitled its story 'New Germany': '[T]he great majority of Munchners do not want to hear Peter Gauweiler's radical right-wing tirades. The man is finished in political terms in this city – hopefully. Thousands of citizens took part [in the counter-demonstration] on Saturday. . . . That was good for the city, a hopeful sign.'[79] In fact Gauweiler was re-elected head of the Munich CSU in July 1997, but Ude's majority in the mayoral elections in 2001 increased.[80] The general reaction to the demonstration and Gauweiler showed how much the opposition to the exhibition had damaged the myth of the 'unsullied *Wehrmacht*'. The conservative *Frankfurter Allgemeine Zeitung*, which blamed the 'self-hatred' of Germans on the Goldhagen book and the exhibition, considered the behaviour of the CSU 'astonishing'.[81]

However, in 1999 it seemed as though the organisers of exhibition had celebrated too soon. Since events in Munich in 1997 the exhibition had survived bomb attacks and demonstrations. It had also been the subject of a largely innocuous debate in the *Bundestag*.[82] Then in October 1999 a Polish historian, Bogdan Musial, and an Hungarian historian, Krisztián Ungváry, published articles in important academic journals which did what none of the previous critics had tried, and questioned the actual evidence put forth in support of the thesis.[83] The publications of Musial and Ungváry marked the return of the historians to the fray. Just as the myth of the 'unsullied *Wehrmacht*' had been vulnerable to the historical evidence, now the thesis and credibility of the exhibition came into question. Critics had always mentioned the photographs but without being able to point to any significant errors. Their sense that this was the weakest point of the exhibition was correct. What was visually stimulating was academically tenuous. The public success of shocking pictures would also lead to the collapse of the first exhibition.

Musial had informed the Hamburg Institute for Social Research of his findings in December 1997, but the following February Bernd Boll, a researcher at the institute and author of several articles on the *Wehrmacht*, investigated and refuted Musial's claims about the murder of Jews at Zloczów. Musial, on the basis of research into Soviet mass shootings of Poles in 1941, had asserted that the photographs were of corpses killed by the retreating NKVD, and that they were wrongly attributed as victims of the *Wehrmacht*. Then in January 1999 a few articles appeared, suggesting that some of the photographs were false.[84] In March 1999 the institute issued a press declaration stating that no photographs would be withdrawn, and accused Musial of unprofessional behaviour and of 'starting a media offensive'. Musial's planned and then cancelled appearance on the same platform as the totally discredited Rüdiger Proske was used to discredit his actual research.[85] The exhibition's organisers now resorted to the same mode of argument as their opponents by attempting to discredit research on the basis of association and politics. None the less in July, Reemtsma admitted that the photographs which had shown the victims at Zloczów had been removed since they were the victims of the NKVD. He went on to say: '[N]o exhibition in this country has been as closely observed and controlled; but only in our case have mistakes, which can happen anywhere, or even suspected errors on the basis of questionable sources, had whole newspaper articles written as a result.'[86] Having overcome the earlier opposition, the organisers now appeared irritated with what turned out to be valid criticism.

Musial first looked at the photographs, and then at the general thesis. He pointed out that some of the photographs showed exhumed bodies. Therefore if *Wehrmacht* soldiers had carried out these murders they would have had to kill, bury and then exhume the bodies before photographing them. Moreover, the pattern of *Wehrmacht* shootings showed that soldiers forced the victims to dig deep graves in an effort to disguise the atrocities. Some of the photographs showed shallow graves. What these represented, argued Musial, were the victims of the NKVD who had retreated rapidly in the face of German advances in the summer of 1941. These victims were then photographed for German propaganda purposes.[87] He criticised the poor quality of the catalogue which did not give precise sources, and estimated that nine were definitely incorrectly attributed, and a further twenty-two were dubious. Out of 1433 photographs this was a small amount. However, he claimed that 'the consequences for the exhibition are much graver than this quantitative relationship at first suggests'.[88] He pointed out that many of the photographs did not show actual crimes, while the ones he had discovered were falsely attributed had a far greater impact because they showed clear crimes. His findings called the status of other photographs into question.

Musial's final argument was more problematic but it went to the core of the thesis of the exhibition. Parts of the *Wehrmacht* were involved in crimes, but research had not shown how much. Therefore it was unwise to speak of the *Wehrmacht* as a 'whole organisation' which was undoubtedly under the control of the political, and by extension the military, leadership. In 'more concrete terms' almost 18 million people were in the *Wehrmacht* and research had not yet shown who was involved in the actual crimes.[89] The logic of this was of course a complete atomisation of this history of the *Wehrmacht*, examining the record of every single soldier. Armies do function in this manner. The criticisms did not amount to a reincarnation of the legend of the 'unsullied *Wehrmacht*', as Ungváry pointed out: 'I am one of the critics of the exhibition but I must disappoint its opponents. Even the flaws in the presentation of the photographs does not prove the view of the 'unsullied *Wehrmacht*'. However, he disputed the thesis of the exhibition that the *Wehrmacht* participated in all the crimes. Not even Hitler wanted to kill all Slavs, rather he wanted to enslave them. The *Wehrmacht* was not the second pillar of the regime alongside the party: Hitler had his SS. Finally the exhibition had underestimated the reality of the partisan war which was not simply an excuse to conduct genocide.[90] Musial and Ungváry had moved from criticism of the evidence to criticism of the thesis.

At first the Hamburg Institute for Social Research maintained that the exhibition would not have to be completely reworked. In late October after the appearance of the articles, Hannes Heer told *Der Spiegel* that the photographs would be checked, whilst dismissing Ungváry's assertion that ten per cent of the photographs were false as 'an old extreme right calculation'. Heer maintained that the thesis of *Wehrmacht* involvement in war crimes was correct.[91] However, two weeks later Reemtsma decided to withdraw the exhibition in order to protect the credibility of the overall thesis: '[T]he exhibition and the Institute were rapidly losing credibility, and there was a danger that the criticism of detail would render the basic thesis of the exhibition lacking in credibility.' It was further evidence of the 'sensitivity to truth in our society'.[92] Initially a three-month moratorium prevented the exhibition from going to New York. A commission of historians, including Omer Bartov, Reinhard Rürup and Manfred Messerschmidt, was put in place to examine the evidence.[93]

While the end of the exhibition was a major media event, politicians who had been involved in previous debates appeared to shy away from the topic. The impact on public opinion was difficult to measure. Michael Wolffsohn of the Munich *Bundeswehr* University feared that the 'innumerable mistakes of the exhibition will serve as a justification for those living in the past who do not want to admit the crimes of the *Wehrmacht*'.[94] Musial, in a different tone, claimed that in the 'first few years nobody believed the critics; by the end of 1999 everyone believed the critics'.[95] Horst Möller, the head of the Institute for Contemporary History in Munich, was the most senior figure in the German historical profession to argue that the *Wehrmacht* as a whole was not involved in war crimes.[96] Norbert Frei, a leading authority on *Vergangenheitsbewältigung* in the early Federal Republic, was more confident that nobody disputed the 'core thesis' of the exhibition.[97] The report of the Historians' Commission published in 2000 pointed to a number of flaws. Firstly the use of photographs in the exhibition had been dubious. Secondly the exhibition was too generalised, and more differentiation was necessary. The commission cleared Heer of manipulating the photographs. Moreover it confirmed the basic thesis of the first exhibition that the *Wehrmacht* had been involved in war crimes. It then urged the institute, in the light of public interest in the topic, to put on a second exhibition which would take these criticisms into account. The report of the commission was a clear defeat for the opponents of the exhibition.[98]

Attacks on the second exhibition have come only from the extreme right, which dismissed the changes as 'cosmetic'. The exhibition remained the work of a 'self-important moneybags', and a 'dyed in the wool Communist and manic anti-German'.[99] They also organised a protest march.[100] Reemtsma was unwilling to say whether the second exhibition had turned the Nazi past into history. He believed that this process would take 100 years so that the proverbial three generations could pass.[101] Volker Ullrich of *Die Zeit* was equally circumspect:

> [T]he new exhibition will not set off long suppressed emotions which had been aroused [by the first one]. And this is not just because its precise, analytical style offers any hardly room for attack, but because the basic thesis has been largely accepted in the meantime. Whether, as some suspect, this rings in a new phase in the German politics of history, in which a consensus forming narrative replaces the furious controversies about the Nazi past, remains to be seen.[102]

Michael Jeismann, a cultural historian, was more confident that the second exhibition 'marks a moment in which the National Socialist past loses its direct, biographical virulence and becomes a consensus history'.[103] Eckhard Fuhr saw it as a triumph for the historical profession. The information transmitted by the exhibition 'had long been researched. Due to the first *Wehrmacht* exhibition five years ago it led to a great debate between the generations and the political camps. With the new exhibition academe reclaims primacy in the politics of the past (*Vergangenheitspolitik*). It has a good chance of having the final word.'[104]

These prognoses were published within days of the exhibition opening. Yet at the time of writing the only attacks on the exhibition have come from the extreme right which is certain to frighten off potential political opponents of the exhibition. The second exhibition is, as one reviewer put it, a 'clinic of history'.[105] The thesis of the second exhibition remains the same: the *Wehrmacht* and the National Socialist leadership agreed that the rules of war would not apply in Operation Barbarossa, and that this led to a genocidal war of extermination which was a 'radical break with the concept of the norms of civilisation'.[106] The presentation of the evidence was the significant difference between the two exhibitions. Photographs, while retained on a smaller scale, were overshadowed by a mass of texts, containing letters, memoranda and orders which supported the thesis. There were eyewitness accounts of atrocities to which one could listen. Sources were attributed. It was more of a scholarly thesis on walls than an exhibition, and it may not have been feasible had the first exhibition not generated such debate. There could be no doubt that the thesis was supported by the evidence.

Reemtsma's caution about the historicisation of the Nazi past is justified. The equally intense *Historikerstreit* of the 1980s evidently did not mark an end to the public debate on the Nazi past. If the French Revolution can still arouse passions in France (and indeed elsewhere), then the Nazi era, which serves in many respects as a the founding myth of the Federal Republic, will remain the central theme in the politics of history. Ian Kershaw believes that a century must pass before Hitler is history. Neighbours will not allow Germany to forget its destructive past.[107] However, the debate over the *Wehrmacht* represents a hugely significant milestone towards the historicisation of the Third Reich. While the number of victims of Nazism had long been accepted, now the focus has turned towards the perpetrators. This has been much more difficult for German society to accept. Evidently nowhere near all Germans were war criminals. Some ordinary Germans (and citizens of other nations) were, and the acceptance of this has been the major contribution of the exhibition and the surrounding debate to the politics of history. By recognising their own role as perpetrators, Germans can now raise the question of their victim status without relativising the Nazi past. Whether other states and nations are as prepared to confront their own past is another matter. Returning to the opening remarks, the publication of Grass's books marked a shift in the politics of history. Up to then the fate of the expellees had been merely reported. In 2002 the mainstream media began to pursue the issue of its own volition.[108]

The other important element in the debate on the exhibition has been the role of historical knowledge, or 'truth' as its political supporters often called it. The fluctuations in the fortunes of the exhibition were dependent on the credibility of its evidence. Appeals to old myths of the 'unsullied *Wehrmacht*' by opponents only served to highlight the weakness of their arguments. Musial's and Ungváry's contributions destroyed the first exhibition. However, it also led to a paradigmatic shift in the presentation of a history exhibition. The second one was source driven and appealed to reason. This was instrumental in disarming potential critics. This also marks an important step in the politics of history in Germany because the public will not accept historical knowledge and understanding which is based on myths and anecdotal tales.

Notes

1   'Das tausendmalige Sterben', *Der Spiegel* 6 (2002).

2   See the readers' letters in *Der Spiegel* 8 (2002).

3   Robert Moeller, 'War stories: the search for a usable past in the Federal Republic of Germany', *American Historical Review* CI, 4 (1996), 1008–48.

4   Robert Shandley (ed.), *Unwilling Germans? The Goldhagen debate* (Minneapolis, 1998); Michael S. Cullen (ed.), *Das Holocaust-Mahnmal. Dokumentation einer Debatte* (Zurich, 1999); Ulrike Winkler (ed.), *Stiften gehen. NS-Zwangsarbeit und Entschädigungsdebatte* (Cologne, 2000).

5   Wolfgang Thierse speech to the *Bundestag*, 27 Jan. 2000.

6   Hamburg Institute for Social Research, *The German army and genocide. Crimes against war prisoners, Jews and other civilians, 1939–1944* (New York, 1999); this is the English language version of the original catalogue.

7   Helmut Donat, Arn Strohmeyer (eds), *Befreiung der Wehrmacht. Dokumentation der Auseinandersetzung über die Ausstellung 'Vernichtungskrieg. Verbrechen der Wehrmacht 1941 bis 1944' in Bremen, 1996/7* (Bremen, 1997) (hereafter *Befreiung*); Landeshauptstadt München, Kulturreferat (ed.), *Bilanz einer Ausstellung. Dokumentation der Kontroverse um die Ausstellung 'Vernichtungskrieg. Verbrechen der Wehrmacht 1941 bis 1944' in München, Galerie im Rathaus, 25.2 bis 6.4.97* (Munich, 1998).

8   Michael T. Greven and Oliver von Wrochem (eds), *Der Krieg in der Nachkriegszeit. Der zweite Weltkrieg in Politik und Gesellschaft der Bundesrepublik* (Opladen, 2000); Hamburger Institut für Sozialforschung (ed.), *Eine Ausstellung und ihrer Folgen. Zur Rezeption der Ausstellung 'Vernichtungskrieg. Verbrechen der Wehrmacht 1941 bis 1944* (Hamburg, 1999); Hamburger Institut für Sozialforschung (ed.), *Besuch einer Ausstellung. Die Ausstellung 'Vernichtungskrieg. Verbrechen der Wehrmacht 1941 bis 1944' in Interview und Gespräch* (Hamburg, 1998); Hannes Heer, 'The difficulty of ending a war: reactions to the exhibition "War of extermination: crimes of the Wehrmacht 1941 to 1944"', *History Workshop Journal* LXVI (1998), 187–203.

9   See the contributions of Klaus Latzel, 'Soldatenverbände gegen die Ausstellung 'Vernichtungskrieg'. Der lange Schatten des letzten Wehrmachtsberichts', in Greven, Wrochem (eds), *Krieg in der Nachkriegszeit*, pp. 325–36; Johannes Klotz, 'Die Rezeption der Ausstellung 'Vernichtungskrieg' in Leserbriefen', in ibid., pp. 307–22; and Ilka Quindeau, 'Erinnerung und Abwehr. Widersprüchliche Befunde zur Rezeption der Ausstellung "Vernichtungskrieg"', in ibid., 291–305.

10 Johannes Klotz, 'Die Ausstellung "Vernichtungskrieg. Verbrechen der Wehrmacht 1941 bis 1944". Zwischen Geschichtswissenschaft und Geschichtspolitik', in Detlef Bald, Johannes Klotz and Wolfram Wette (eds), *Mythos Wehrmacht. Nachkriegsdebatten und Traditionspflege* (Berlin, 2001), pp. 116-73.

11 Bogdan Musial, 'Bilder einer Ausstellung. Kritische Anmerkungen zur Wanderausstellung "Vernichtungskrieg - Verbrechen der Wehrmacht 1941 bis 1944"', *Vierteljahrshefte für Zeitgeschichte* XLVII, 4 (1999), 563-91; Krisztián Ungváry, 'Echte Bilder - Problematische Aussagen. Eine quantitative und qualitative Analyse des Bildmaterials der Ausstellung "Vernichtungskrieg - Verbrechen der Wehrmacht 1941 bis 1944"', *Geschichte in Wissenschaft und Unterricht* (1999), 584-95; Rolf-Dieter Müller and Hans Erich Volkmann (eds), *Die Wehrmacht. Mythos und Realität* (Munich, 1999).

12 See for example Robert Gellately, *The Gestapo and German society: Enforcing racial policy, 1933-1945* (Oxford, 1990).

13 Omer Bartov, *Hitler's army: soldiers, Nazis, and war in the Third Reich* (Oxford, 1992), pp. 8-11.

14 An excellent example can be found in Christopher Browning, *The path to genocide: essays on launching the Final Solution* (Cambridge, 1992), pp. 169-83.

15 Klaus Naumann, '"Wieso erst jetzt?" oder die Macht der Nemesis. Der geschichtspolitische Ort der Ausstellung', in *Eine Ausstellung und ihre Folgen*, pp. 274-6.

16 For the various contributions see *Historikerstreit. Die Dokumentation um die Einzigartigkeit der national-sozialistischen Judenvernichtung* (Munich, 1987); more broadly see Charles Maier, *The unmasterable past: history, holocaust and German national identity* (Cambridge, MA, 1988).

17 The German term is 'die saubere Wehrmacht'.

18 On the politics of history in the Federal Republic see Edgar Wolfrum, *Geschichtspolitik in der Bundesrepublik Deutschland. Der Weg zur bundesrepublikanischer Erinnerung 1948-1990* (Darmstadt, 1999), pp. 333-43.

19 Heinrich August Winkler, 'Rebuilding a nation: the Germans before and after unification', *Daedalus* (1994), 119.

20 Anne Marie le Gloannec, 'On German identity', *Daedalus* (1994), 138.

21 Barthold Witte, 'Two catastrophes, two causes and how the Germans dealt with them', *Daedalus* (1994), 249.

22 Stefan Berger, 'Historians and nation-building in Germany after reunification', *Past and Present* 148 (1995), 187-222; for the Schwarz quote, 208.

23 See the immensely popular Anthony Beevor, *Stalingrad* (London, 1998).

24 See the reports 'Atrocity museum angers Russians', *Observer*, 23 Dec. 2001, and 'Verhaften und Vergessen', *Der Spiegel* 3 (2002).

25 'Prag bedauert Vertreibung der Sudetendeustch', *Süddeutsche Zeitung*, 10 Dec. 1996.

26 'Die Wehrmacht war keine Mörderbande', *Frankfurter Allgemeine Zeitung*, 27 Nov. 2001; Walter Manoschek, *'Serbien ist judenfrei.' Militärische Besatzungspolitik und Judenvernichtung in Serbien 1941/2* (Munich, 1994).

27 See the special edition of *Geschichte und Gesellschaft*, Ingrid Gilcher-Holtey (ed.), *1968 - vom Ereignis zum Gegenstand der Geschichtswissenschaft* (Göttingen, 2000); for a review of the first

wave of publications on the GDR, see Christoph Kleßmann, Martin Sabrow, 'Contemporary history in Germany after 1989', *Contemporary European History* VI, 2 (1997), 219–43.

28 See for example Jeffrey Herf on the politics of memory in the German Democratic Republic, *Divided memory: The Nazi past in the two Germanys* (Cambridge MA, 1997), pp. 2, 69–200.

29 Theo Sommer, 'Nur Hinsehen macht frei', *Die Zeit*, 28 Feb. 1997.

30 'Leserbriefe', *Frankfurter Allgemeine Zeitung*, 6 Apr. 1995. For a systematic survey of letters relating to the exhibition, see Klotz, 'Die Rezeption der Ausstellung "Vernichtungskrieg"', in Greven, Wrochem, *Der Krieg in der Nachkriegszeit*, pp. 307–23.

31 'Leserbriefe', *Frankfurter Allgemeine Zeitung*, 12 Apr. 1995.

32 Jan Philipp Reemtsma, 'Was man plant, und was daraus wird. Gedenken über ein prognostisches Versagen', in Greven, Wrochem (eds), *Der Krieg in der Nachkriegszeit*, pp. 273–4.

33 'Die Wucht der Bilder', *Der Spiegel* 29 (1999).

34 Reemtsma, 'Was man plant', p. 281.

35 'Die Wucht der Bilder', *Der Spiegel* 29 (1999).

36 Karl-Heinz Janßen, 'Als Soldaten Mörder wurden', *Die Zeit*, 17 Mar. 1995.

37 Wolfram Wette, 'Die Legende von der sauberen Wehrmacht. Eine Hamburger Ausstellung zeichnet ein düsteres Bild von der Kriegführung im Osten', *Frankfurter Allgemeine Zeitung*, 6 Apr. 1995.

38 'Leserbriefe', *Frankfurter Allgemeine Zeitung*, 18 Apr. 1995.

39 Klaus Jochen Arnold, 'Die Eroberung und Behandlung der Stadt Kiev durch die Wehrmacht im September 1941: zur Radikalisierung der Besatzungspolitik', *Militärgeschichtliche Mitteilungen* 58 (1999), 23–63; also Brendan Simms, 'Walther von Reichenau: der politische General' in Ronald Smelser and Enrico Syring (eds), *Die Militärelite des Dritten Reiches* (Frankfurt, 1998), p. 439.

40 'Leserbriefe', *Frankfurter Allgemeine Zeitung*, 18 Apr. 1995.

41 Helmut Donat, Arn Strohmeyer (eds), *Befreiung der Wehrmacht. Dokumentation der Auseinandersetzung über die Ausstellung 'Vernichtungskrieg. Verbrechen der Wehrmacht 1941 bis 1944' in Bremen, 1996/7* (Bremen, 1997), pp. 134–5.

42 Shandley, *Unwilling Germans?* pp. 5–6.

43 Angelika Königseder, 'Streitkulturen und Gefühlslügen. Die Goldhagen-Debatte und der Streit um die Wehrmachtausstellung' in Johannes Heil, Rainer Erb (eds), *Geschichtswissenschaft und Öffentlichkeit. Der Streit um Daniel J. Goldhagen* (Frankfurt, 1998), pp. 295–309.

44 Arn Strohmeyer, 'Die Auseinandersetzung um die Wehrmachtausstellung in Bremen – ein Lehrbeispiel der unrühmlichen Art' in *Befreiung*, p. 35.

45 Wigbert Gerling, 'Große List – und trotzdem Tüchen', *Weser-Kurier/Bremer Nachrichten*, 18 Oct. 1996 in *Befreiung*, pp. 107–8.

46 'So lange die Front hielt, gab es KZs', *taz Bremen*, 12 Nov. 1996 in *Befreiung*, p. 120.

47 Ibid.

48 'Die Wehrmachtausstellung gehört ins Rathaus. Offener Brief von Bremer Bürgerinnen und Bürgern', *taz Bremen*, 12 Nov. 1996 in *Befreiung*, pp. 122–3.

49 'Lore Kleinert im Gespräch mit Jan Philipp Reemtsma', Radio Bremen II, 12 Nov. 1996 in *Befreiung*, pp. 124–6.

50 Axel Schuller, 'Senat tritt mit zwei Rednern auf', *Weser-Kurier/Bremer Nachrichten*, 12 Nov. 1996 in *Befreiung*, p. 127.
51 Browning, *Path to genocide*, p. 174.
52 For the text of Neumeyer's speech see *Befreiung*, pp. 132–5.
53 Ibid., p. 142.
54 Ibid., p. 147.
55 David Clay Large, '"A beacon in the darkness": the anti-Nazi resistance legacy in West German politics', *Journal of Modern History* 64 supplement (1992), S 176–8.
56 *Befreiung*, pp. 161–3.
57 Ibid., pp. 212–15.
58 Frank Müller, 'Verbrechen der Wehrmacht', *Süddeutsche Zeitung*, 15 Feb. 1997.
59 Landeshauptstadt München, Kulturreferat (ed.), *Bilanz einer Ausstellung. Dokumentation der Kontroverse um die Ausstellung 'Vernichtungskrieg. Verbrechen der Wehrmacht 1941 bis 1944' in München, Galerie im Rathaus, 25.2 bis 6.4.97* (Munich, 1998) p. 59; this comprehensive collection contains some of the central contributions in the press, the debate in the city council, readers' letters, extracts from the visitors' book, and the report of the exhibition guides (hereafter *Bilanz*).
60 In the *Süddeutsche Zeitung* on the day of the debate there was an article reporting from Prague and an interview with Franz Neubauer, a leading representative of the Sudeten Germans, but no article on the forthcoming debate; on 13 Dec., there was a short description by Frank Müller, 'Brunner, der Unbelehrbare'.
61 *Bilanz*, pp. 63–71.
62 Ibid., pp. 74–5.
63 Ibid., p. 69.
64 Rüdiger Proske, *Wider den Mißbrauch der Geschichte deutscher Soldaten zu politischen Zwecken. Eine Streitschrift* (Mainz, 1996).
65 Bilanz, pp. 76–82.
66 Ibid., pp. 84–7.
67 Ibid., pp. 95.
68 'Das war ein Vernichtungskrieg', *Nürnberger Nachrichten*, 19 Feb. 1997 in *Bilanz*, p. 118.
69 'Gauweiler: ich nehme nichts zurück', *Süddeutsche Zeitung*, 21 Feb. 1997.
70 'Stoiber lehnt Aussage zu Gauweiler ab', *Süddeutsche Zeitung*, 25 Feb. 1997.
71 'CSU-Stadtrat knöpft sich Gauweiler vor', *Süddeutsche Zeitung*, 20 Feb. 1997.
72 'Wenn alle nach der Ehre fragen', *Süddeutsche Zeitung*, 26 Feb. 1997.
73 *Bilanz*, pp. 22–33, contains the text of the speech.
74 *Bilanz*, p. 31.
75 *Süddeutsche Zeitung*, 15 Feb. 1997, statement by the Bavarian Culture Ministry.
76 'Nicht empfehlenswert', *Süddeutsche Zeitung*, 25 Feb. 1997 in *Bilanz*, pp. 136–7.
77 *Bilanz*, pp. 15, 138.
78 'Die Welt schaut auf München', *Abendzeitung München*, 1 Mar. 1997 in *Bilanz*, p. 148.
79 'Neues Deutschland', *Abendzeitung München*, 3 Mar. 1997 in *Bilanz*, pp. 159–60.
80 'Gauweiler zum Münchner CSU-Vorsitzender gewählt', *Frankfurter Allgemeine Zeitung*, 11 July 1997.

81 See Renate Schosteck, 'Martern der Geschichte', *Frankfurter Allgemeine Zeitung*, 3 Mar. 1997; Roswin Finkenzeller, 'Die Ausstellung taucht nichts, ebenso wie ihre Kritiker' in ibid.

82 Omer Bartov, 'Germany's unforgettable war: the twisted road from Berlin to Moscow and back', *Diplomatic History* xxv, 3 (2001), 419; Peter Schneider, 'Der Bundestag wolle beschließen. Zur Debatte über die Ausstellung "Vernichtungskrieg – Verbrechen der Wehrmacht 1941 bis 1944"' in *Eine Ausstellung und ihrer Folgen*, pp. 112–22.

83 Musial, 'Bilder einer Ausstellung'; Ungváry, 'Echte Bilder'.

84 'Leichen im Obstgarten', *Der Spiegel* 3 (1999); 'Die falschen Fotos zum richtigen Thema', *Berliner Morgenpost*, 25 Jan. 1999.

85 Hamburger Institut für Sozialforschung, Pressemitteilung, 'Hamburger Institut für Sozialforschung wird zur Zeit keine Fotos aus der Ausstellung 'Vernichtungskrieg. Verbrechen der Wehrmacht 1941 bis 1944' herausnehmen', 26 Mar. 1999, available on the h-net website at (http://www2.h.msu.edu/~german/ discuss/ others/wehrmacht.htm#his).

86 'Die Wucht der Bilder', *Der Spiegel* 29 (1999).

87 Musial, 'Bilder einer Ausstellung', 563–4.

88 Ibid., 589.

89 Ibid., 590.

90 Krisztián Ungváry, 'Reemtsmas Legenden', *Frankfurter Allgemeine Zeitung*, 5 Nov. 1999.

91 'Wir nehmen Vorwürfe ernst', *Der Spiegel* 43 (1999).

92 Reemtsma, 'Was man plant', pp. 288–9.

93 'Die Wehrmachtausstellung wird vorerst nicht mehr gezeigt', *Frankfurter Allgemeine Zeitung*, 5 Nov. 1999.

94 'Wehrmachtsausstellung in der Historikerkritik', *Der Spiegel* 45 (1999).

95 Quoted in Reemtsma, 'Was man plant', p. 288.

96 Bartov, 'Germany's unforgettable war', 422.

97 Norbert Frei, 'Faktor 1000', *Frankfurter Allgemeine Zeitung*, 2 Nov. 1999.

98 Klotz, 'Zwischen Geschichtswissenschaft und Geschictspolitik', pp. 163–6.

99 NPD Pressemitteilung, 28 Nov. 2001.

100 'Ausschreitungen bei NPD-Demo', *Süddeutsche Zeitung*, 1 Dec. 2001.

101 'Die Wehrmacht war keine Mörderverbände', *Frankfurter Allgemeine Zeitung*, 27 Nov. 2001.

102 Volker Ullrich, 'Von strenger Sachlichkeit', *Die Zeit*, 16 Dec. 2001.

103 Michael Jeismann, 'Das Ende der Wiedergänger', *taz*, 29 Nov. 2001.

104 Eckhard Fuhr, 'Ganz in Weiß', *Die Welt*, 29 Nov. 2001.

105 Herbert Seifert, 'Rückkehr der Texte', *Neue Zürcher Zeitung*, 29 Nov. 2001.

106 This was written on the first stand after the entrance; from the author's notes.

107 *Spiegel* special, *Die Gegenwart der Vergangenheit. Die Spiegel-Serie über den langen Schatten des Dritten Reiches* (2001) 8, 13.

108 See for instance the four part series in *Der Spiegel* 13–16 (2002) on the expulsion of German minorities.

CHAPTER 19

The City as Symbol

Architecture and Ideology in Post-Soviet Moscow

Judith Devlin

> Moscow is more than the capital of the Soviet state. Moscow is an idea,
> embracing all our culture in its entire national movement.
>
> A. N. Tolstoy.

In August 2000, two events symbolised the renaissance of the Russian Idea in the post-soviet Russia: the canonisation of Tsar Nicholas II and the dedication of the rebuilt Cathedral of Christ the Saviour in Moscow. These were not isolated developments. A similar inspiration informed President Putin's version of the Russian Idea for the year 2000 (and President Yeltsin's earlier quest for this grail) while the general refashioning of the capital in the 1990s reflected the new regime's cult of historicism. What these developments signalled was the end of Russia's latest bout of *zapadnichestvo*, of the attempted westernisation that culminated in the 1991 'revolution' and was shattered in the ruins of the White House in October 1993 and of Grozny in December 1994. Between 1989 and 1993, the language of Russian nationalism was a marginal phenomenon, confined to the wilder fringes of political life, if forcefully articulated by part of the cultural establishment. The political authorities, however, spoke the language of liberalisation, democratisation, market reform – even if this rhetoric rapidly lost conviction in the political and economic crisis that developed after 1991. By the end of the decade, with the election of Vladimir Putin as president, the state was committed to the elaboration of a new theory of 'official nationality' – in many ways indebted to its precursor in pre-revolutionary Russia. This official nationalism was not spontaneous but the deliberate creation of powerful interest groups that sought legitimacy and authority by appealing to popular disenchantment with reform and 'westernising' reformers, and it points to the re-emergence of a widely preached myth of Russia at the end of the twentieth century.

The new official nationalism was reflected most graphically in the changing aspect of the Russian capital, Moscow. By 2000, central Moscow was strikingly different from the Soviet capital of the mid-1980s: its historic streets restored, renamed, lined with expensive restaurants, luxury shops and dotted with new monuments, it exuded an air of affluence in striking contrast to the provinces, where abject poverty and reminders of the Soviet past were everywhere on view. The contrast between capital and country, at the end of the century, was as great as under the *ancien régime* and the impression created by the city was misleading. Nonetheless, the new aspect of Moscow was not fortuitous. Just as Lewis Mumford argued that the baroque city should be seen as an expression of the power, ambition and values of the absolute ruler,[1] so contemporary Moscow can be read as a political statement by Russia's new rulers, and the reinvention of the urban landscape of Moscow has attracted the attention of several scholars.[2] In a similar vein, this essay asks what past the authorities have chosen to commemorate and celebrate? What values have they sought to communicate? What sources of legitimation have been invoked and how have they been reflected in the city's architecture and the rituals of public life that they enclose? Finally, what does this reinvention of public space suggest about the new political order in Russia?

THE RUSSIAN IDEA

The myth of Russia as a unique civilisation, alien, even hostile to Europe, first elaborated in late medieval and early modern Russia, was reinvented in the nineteenth century. Espoused by the throne as a bulwark against democracy and revolution, it existed also in a subversive, revolutionary variant – parodied by Dostoevsky in *The demons* (1872) – and was reflected in the literary myth of Petersburg. The theory of 'official nationality', as it has become known, was propounded by Nicholas I's education minister, Count S. S. Uvarov, in the 1830s: summarised in the famous triad 'Orthodoxy, autocracy and nationality', it suggested that the three pillars of Russia were autocracy ('the main condition of the political condition of Russia' according to Uvarov), Orthodoxy ('a Russian, devoted to his fatherland, will agree as little to the loss of a single dogma of our Orthodoxy as to the theft of a single pearl from the Tsar's crown') and popular patriotism (*narodnost'*).[3] Little more, as Riasanovsky observes, than a propaganda device, official nationality attempted to exploit the nationalism which had emerged among the educated classes, in the wake of the Napoleonic invasion,[4] in order to strengthen a dynasty whose moral authority had been challenged and eroded by the Decembrist revolt of 1825. Voluble apologists of obscurantist and repressive autocracy abounded in the nineteenth century – the most fatal of whom was arguably the tutor of the last tsar and chief procurator of the Holy Synod until 1905, Konstantin Pobedonostsev, who inculcated in his charge a deep aversion to democracy.

Official nationality, which amounted to the state ideology of late Tsarist Russia, suggested that Russia, embodying alternative principles, would save Europe from the allure of revolution. As the poet and diplomat Fedor Tyutchev put it in 1848: 'For a long time now, only two forces have existed in Europe – revolution and Russia. . . . On the outcome of [this] struggle . . . will depend for many centuries to come the entire political and religious future of humanity'. The reason for this antithesis lay in the nature of Russian culture. Russia was distinguished from the West by virtue of its religious culture, by its spirit of self-sacrifice and humility:

> 'Russia', insisted Tyutchev, 'is above all a Christian empire. The Russian people is Christian not only because of the Orthodoxy of its beliefs . . . It is Christian because of that capacity for renunciation and sacrifice which serves as the foundation of its moral order.'[5]

The idea that Russian spirituality was destined to save Europe from the ills of modernity – rationalism (derived from the earlier heresy of Roman Catholicism), individualism, consumerism and democracy – was popular also outside official circles. It was cultivated among generations of romantic conservatives, including Dostoevsky, who, in his panegyric to Pushkin on 8 June 1880, proclaimed that Orthodox Russia was destined to 'say the last word' to humanity – that is to usher in a new phase in the history of civilisation (based on the reconciliation of East and West, Russia and Europe, 'in accordance with the gospel of Christ').[6] Other jaundiced critics of contemporary Europe conceived of Russia as returning to its aesthetically refined Byzantine roots (this from the writer and diplomat, Konstantin Leontiev, long rusticated in a remote Balkan posting) or a resurgent Russia, conquering the inimical, but fortunately decadent West (as the ex-army officer Danilevsky imagined).[7] The populist revolutionaries turned this vision on its head: Russia would represent not a conservative utopia, hierarchical and Orthodox, antithetical to the liberal and democratic ideals of the imagined Europe, but a revolutionary utopia, egalitarian and socialist, based on the native peasant commune equally inimical to European models of progress. 'We do not consider ourselves legal executors of your past', Alexander Herzen wrote in his 1851 *Letter to Jules Michelet*. 'Russia will never be Protestant. Russia will never be *juste milieu*. Russia will never stage a revolution with the sole aim of ridding herself of Tsar Nicholas only to replace him by a multitude of Tsar-deputies, Tsar-tribunals, Tsar-policemen, Tsar-laws.'[8] These competing visions of Russia's destiny and the 'Russian Idea' shared a number of features: hostility to the political culture of the contemporary West – its legalism, representative institutions and the debilitating luxuries of capitalism. Left and right in nineteenth-century Russia were at least united by the disfavour with which most regarded Europe: what divided them was the future of Russia.

The Russian intelligentsia, with its myth of national identity, was also inhabited by a sense of the provisional character of the existing order. Nowhere was this more clearly expressed than in the so-called 'myth of Petersburg'. Petersburg was the symbol *par excellence* of the imperial regime. Created *ex-nihilo* on the marshes of the north-western extremity of the bi-continental empire by the will of the first unequivocally westernising tsar, Peter's city was unrepresentative of the country whose capital it became towards the end of his reign. A city constructed to reflect the European ambitions and imperial glory of Russia's eighteenth-century rulers, its situation, the imposing symmetry of its layout, the elaborate court rituals of its social life, were experienced as alienating and understood as an image of the voluntarism and artificiality of the world it enclosed.

This view of the city dated back at least to Pushkin's *Bronze horseman* (1833). In Pushkin's poem, the city comes to life: the Bronze Horseman (Falconet's famous statue of the city's founder, Peter the Great) (plate 18) pursues and finally kills the hero, the modest clerk Yevgeny. Yevgeny has been driven demented by the death of his fiancée in the 1824 floods and thus, ultimately, by the conception and spirit of the city. For Pushkin, the city – elegant, neo-classical, rational in its planning and proportions, European – is unable to contain the elemental forces it presumes to master. It thus symbolised the Russian monarchy and its ethos: European, westernising, fundamentally at odds with the Asiatic country and culture it tried to control. For many nineteenth-century Russian intellectuals, this conflict was summarised in the polarities of artificial/elemental; rational/irrational and emotional; individualistic and atomised/communal and whole; Europe and the West/ Russia. For them, Petersburg was not just the capital of Tsarism but the symbol of its flawed attempt to change the heart and essence of Russia. This was a theme that recurred in nineteenth-century Russian literature. In Gogol's *Overcoat* (1842), the central character, the clerk Akaky Akakievich, is killed by the chill of the city's winter and the coldness and indifference of the high official of the regime, on whom, as a ghost, he wreaks his revenge. Dostoevsky, in *Notes from the underground* (1864), called Petersburg 'the most abstract and premeditated city in the whole world', depicting it as a breeding ground for the revolutionaries and rationalising individualists, who exemplified the pathology of modern life.

Andrei Bely, in his novel *Petersburg*, which first appeared in book form in 1916, took up this view of the city as the ultimate rational (thus European) city ('Nevsky Prospekt is rectilineal . . . because it is a European prospect'),[9] slyly protesting, not as a slavophile (or Russian romantic nationalist) but as a symbolist, for whom intuition, the apprehension of cosmic forces, was the ultimate key to truth. Bely's novel unfolds between 30 September and 9 October 1905 – at the height of the revolution which nearly toppled the dynasty, in a dry run of 1917. The plot concerns a terrorist attack on a high official, Apollon Apollonovich Ableukhov. Throughout the novel, a bomb is at issue and begins to tick in chapter five. The bomb threatens not only the life of the official (a man who symbolises the stultifying, European regime), but also the life of the regime he represents. We understand this city and its marionette-like characters to be trapped in a web of artifice, a *machine infernale*, which stands at odds with the more vital world beyond its confines:

> A shiver ran down Apollon Apollonovich's spine [. . .] The landscape of the country actually frightened him. Beyond the snows, beyond the ice, and beyond the jagged line of the forest, the blizzard would come up. Out there, by a stupid accident, he had nearly frozen to death [. . .] From there, an icy hand beckoned. Measureless immensity flew on: the Empire of Russia.[10]

The Bronze Horseman, the statue of Peter, symbolises the division in the novel between the two Russias, the native elemental and the artifical, European Russia of the imperial elite. The threat to this culture posed by the plot on the official's life coincides with the 1905 revolution, which as a theme is developed at length. Not that Bely admired the conspirators, or the *ancien régime* and its secret policemen: he poked fun at all of them, parodying Dostoevsky. Russia was doomed, he suggested, less on account of politics as on account of its culture.

Like many Russian, and indeed European, intellectuals of the time, Bely was concerned with escaping from the tyranny not only of the Romanovs but of modern European culture and its mechanistic reductive worldview: hence, contemporary Russians' cult of primitivism – exemplified by Stravinsky's *Rite of Spring*, Goncharova and Larionov's art, Mayakovsky's futurism. It was to lead one school of Russian writers (the so-called Scythians, including Bely's fellow-symbolist, the poet Alexander Blok) and of *émigré* scholars (the Eurasians) to welcome the revolution as Russia's chance to shake off the warped European legacy of the imperial past and to reinvent Russian society, harmonising the radically new with her rediscovered primitive Asiatic character. (As Blok put it in his famous poem *Scythians*, written in January 1918, 'For we are Scythians, we are Asians [. . .]'). Bely echoed these sentiments when he wrote: 'As for Petersburg, it will sink. . . . Great will be the strife . . . The yellow hordes of Asians will set forth from their age-old abodes and encrimson the fields of Europe in oceans of blood. There will be, o yes, there will – Tsushima! . . . Kulikovo Field, I await you.'[11] This was not so much an instance of the Yellow Peril, of imperialist Europe's ignorance and fear of a world it underestimated and misunderstood, but metaphorical language. For Bely, like Blok, was haunted by the sense of the otherness of the real Russia and the foreignness of the capital and the regime it symbolised and glorified; hence, his emphasis on the vulnerability of the city he evoked.

If Petersburg was a symbol of the futility and vulnerability of tsarist Russia, Moscow had its own place in Russian cultural tradition. The myth of Moscow as the Third Rome, elaborated after the fall of Constantinople, enabled the rapidly expanding Muscovite state of the fifteenth and sixteenth centuries to justify its ambitions. Rome and Constantinople had fallen, but Moscow would succeed them and, offering refuge to the true faith, would become the centre of a new, righteous and universal dispensation. The eclipse of Muscovy and the rise of imperial Russia and its capital Petersburg ensured that Moscow, in the later eighteenth and nineteenth centuries, became a symbol of Russian tradition for the opponents of westernisation. In the twentieth century, with the early Soviet regime's rejection of decadent Europe and the rise of Stalin's 'socialism in one country', Moscow became not so much a symbol of national tradition as, once again, of a universal eschatology, promising a reign of justice that the Soviet Union alone embodied in the present. From the Third Rome to the First City of Socialism, Moscow was thus proposed to the spectator as the symbol of the character and achievements of Russia.[12] Hence, it is no surprise that the post-Soviet regime should attempt to reinvent Moscow, to present the city as a reflection of the ideas it purports to represent.

THE NEW RUSSIA: ICONOCLASM

One of the earliest gestures of rejection of the Soviet past was the place name changes adopted at the end of the Soviet era. These embraced cities (such as Leningrad, which reverted to St Petersburg following a referendum in June 1991, and Sverdlovsk, which became Yekaterinburg) as well as towns and streets all over Russia. Many changes in fact predated the collapse of Party and Soviet power in August 1991.

The issue arose, in the first place, because Russia had undergone so many toponymic changes since 1917. If the towns and cities of tsarist Russia had been conceived as monuments to the glory of Russian monarchy and empire, the Bolsheviks had been no less concerned to reclaim these spaces for the revolution.[13] Streets, institutions, towns and cities named after the royal family and tsarist rulers were now called after Lenin (as when the village of Romanovo became Lenino) or fatidic moments and symbols of revolutionary history (such as the urban centres of Krasnodar, Pervomaiskoe and, an incongruous testament to the Soviets' veneration of industrial development, Antrasit!). The major campaigns of toponymic changes followed victory in the civil war, in 1922, and stalinist consolidation, in 1934-6, by which time about fifty per cent of the USSR's settlements had been renamed for ideological purposes.[14] The Khrushchev years launched a new round of historical and toponymic revision, most famously erasing all commemoration of Stalin (with Stalingrad becoming Volgograd, Stalinabad/Dushanbe, Molotov/Perm).[15] The later Brezhnev years renewed the Party leadership's taste for glorifying itself, with towns being named after Suslov, Brezhnev, Andropov and Chernenko. However, in what was ultimately to become a much more sweeping exercise, these changes were reversed, between 1987 and 1989, by the new Party leadership under Gorbachev, which was anxious to mark its rejection of Brezhnevite conservatism, vanity and corruption.

In the new circumstances of reform, however, the Party was to lose control of this exercise and of public memory, as reflected in place names. Under *glasnost'*, as tentative attempts to re-evaluate twentieth-century Russian history got under way, the recovery of historical memory and culture became one of the principal means through which the later Soviet regime sought to retrieve its legitimacy. The intelligentsia, encouraged by this new-found interest in the national cultural heritage, suggested further name changes. The Soviet Cultural Fund and Moscow City Council in 1988-89 established commissions on toponyms and a conference, held in 1989, demanded twenty-five city name changes throughout the Soviet Union. Many of these changes implied the rejection of the revolutionary myths of the Soviet regime in favour of pre-revolutionary tradition.[16]

This trend was exemplified by the fate of the Moscow metro, a prestige project of the early 1930s, whose famous underground palaces were designed to glorify the stalinist regime, its values and myths.[17] Originally, the stations had been named to reflect the new Soviet pantheon (a hybrid of putative pre-Soviet revolutionaries and martyrs of Tsarism and the proletarian and political heroes of the Lenin and Stalin revolutions). Now Stalin's metro was no longer to be honoured in the toponymy of central Moscow and its central stations were rebaptised. The first moves in this direction came in the early *glasnost'* years: in 1986, Metrostroevskaya (Metro Builders' Street) reverted to the historical Ostozhenka (from the haystacks in the seventeenth-century royal meadows there) and Kirovskaya station (named after the Leningrad Party leader assassinated in 1934) became Chistye prudy ('Clean Ponds'). In eschewing the name of Kirov, the metro station was historicised by attributing to it the pre-revolutionary, pre-stalinist toponym of the corresponding street surface. If the underground were now pseudo-historical, the surface remained, at this point, sovietised and the street names remained as yet unchanged.

Implicitly, in these moves, however, Stalinism was rejected as the lineage of the late Soviet state in favour of the Muscovite past. This awkward and implausible reinvention of identity proceeded unevenly, at many levels, in the late 1980s: in historical, literary and political debate, in art shows and publishing, and it ultimately escaped the Party's control. More changes to the metro followed in 1990, when Democratic Russia won control of Moscow city council: Kalininskaya station (named after Stalin's head of state) and Gorkovskaya (after the supposed father of socialist realism and leading literary luminary of the early stalinist regime) were renamed and Ploshchad' Nogina (after an early Bolshevik leader of Moscow) became Kitai gorod (not, in fact, China Town, but a reference to the hurdles of the city walls). The reinvention of the metro resumed in 1992. Thus Prospekt Marksa (Marx) and Dzerzhinskaya were rebaptised in line with the restored toponyms of the street surface; Lenino became Tsaritsyno.[18] Ostensibly, this was a case of restoring historical names and significance to the urban landscape: in reality, it appears to have been more concerned with the ascription of new, albeit pseudo-historical values to a significant segment of the public space (as when the original stalinist names were historicised).

Even before the Soviet regime collapsed in August 1991, Moscow City Council inaugurated a series of toponymic changes, in which not only stalinist leaders and heroes (Kirov, Kalinin, Pavlik Morozov) and early Soviet leaders (Sverdlov and Dzerzhinsky) but the revolution itself, its hallowed dates and values, its founders and inspirers (Marx and Lenin) were renounced in favour of historical tradition and memory, interrupted by the Bolshevik revolution. The first significant wave of street-name changes was introduced on 5 November 1990, when Moscow city council renamed six central squares and twenty main streets. Thus the Fiftieth Anniversary of the Revolution Square (so baptised in 1967) once again became the Manezh (Riding School); Dzerzhinsky Square reverted to the Lubyanka; Kolkhozhnaya (Collective Farm) Square to Sukharevskaya. Streets that recovered their historic names included Prospekt Marksa which reverted to Mokhovaya (Mossy Street), Okhotny ryad (Hunters' Row) and Teatral'ny pro'ezd (Theatre Passage). October 25th Street (renamed in 1935 to celebrate the Bolshcvik revolution, according to the pre-1918 calendar) became Nikolskaya. Kirovskaya (named in honour of Stalin's assassinated rival, Sergei Kirov) reverted to the traditional Myasnitskaya (Butchers' Street). Gorky Street returned to Tverskaya. Pavlik Morozov Lane (a name adopted in 1939 to honour the Komsomol child martyr who denounced his father as a kulak to the Secret Police during collectivisation) retrieved its historic name of Novovagankovskii; while Atheist Lane (Bezbozhii pereulok) was restyled Protopopovskii (after a nineteenth-century merchant).[19] The significance was clear: the entire revolutionary past (not just its stalinist deviations) was jettisoned.

The City as Symbol

By 1994, within the recently established historic zone of the city centre, 120 streets had been renamed, reverting to their pre-revolutionary, generally Muscovite era, names. Post-Soviet Moscow presented itself, as far as the toponymy of the city centre was concerned, as a city untouched by the revolution and its values: it appeared to be suffering from amnesia. In the grim districts that sprawled beyond the historic centre, the Soviet city and its place names remained largely untouched. But these areas drew little attention and few resources from the country's leadership, which interested itself in the political and administrative centre, where it lived and worked, and which it persisted in seeing as a symbol of the regime.

Having come to power proclaiming the illegitimacy of the old order, the new authorities naturally were concerned with extirpating its symbols. However, they did not choose to commemorate their own seizure of power with monuments to new heroes or in the street names of the city centre. There were few such renamings, one example being the change in 1993 from Novokirovskii to Prospekt Akademika Sakharova (after the human rights activist and leader of the embryonic democratic movement in late Soviet Russia).[20] The reversion to historical names was the preferred option, although this was almost as ideologically inspired as the Bolsheviks' name changes: in Moscow, it enabled the regime to claim the legacy of the Muscovite past, whose Russianness (unlike that of the Russian democrats) was not in dispute. Moscow had emerged from obscurity to lead the Russian defeat of the Tatars, establish Russian statehood and military might and embody a unique religious culture. It held none of the ambiguities of Petersburg, with its associations with westernisation and the controversial rule of the later Romanovs.

Iconoclasm was an early, but short-lived, impulse. Until the end of 1993, the new authorities presented themselves as democrats, opposed to the Soviet legacy (as their toponymic changes suggested), and the years between the failed coup in August 1991 and the December 1993 elections marked the *apogée* of their always ambivalent iconoclasm. Even in this period, however, historicism – rather than innovation – was characteristic of the new regime.

Even before the fall of the Soviet regime, *glasnost*'s revelations, the relaxing of draconian public order regulations and growing nationalism in the periphery combined to provoke, in 1989–90, a wave of popular vandalism and iconoclasm against Soviet monuments, and especially those dedicated to Lenin. The Soviet authorities were naturally anxious to restrain these demonstrations of alienation from the regime and of disrespect for its quasi-sacred symbols. Gorbachev was provoked to affirm that:

> The CPSU resolutely opposes the desecration of monuments to Lenin, of symbols of our statehood and our country's culture, of the graves of fighting men who fought in the defence of the Fatherland.[21]

The corresponding presidential decree, issued on 13 October 1990, confirmed the virtually sacred significance of monuments to Lenin, the Revolution and the Second World War banned any further alterations to or demolition of them and demanded increased penalties for such offences.[22] The USSR Congress of Peoples' Deputies responded by adopting a draft law on the subject in June 1991 that provided for a ten-year prison sentence for repeat offenders.[23] The Congress well understood the symbolic significance of the demolition of these monuments to the centralised Soviet state, but its attempts to check the tendency were unavailing. The defeat of the coup, two months later, unleashed a new wave of popular iconoclasm.

The new city authorities were cautious, rather than enthusiastic, in their endorsement of this impulse. On 22 August, when it became apparent that the coup had failed, thousands of Muscovites gathered at symbolic city sites: from the White House, seat of the democratically elected RSFSR Parliament and epicentre of the apparently democratic revolution, they proceeded to Red Square, the heart of Soviet Russia and on to the nearby Central Committee building on Staraya Ploshchad' and the Lubyanka (and KGB headquarters), where the 1958 statue to Felix Dzerzhinsky (head of the Cheka) was surrounded by a crowd of about 50,000. The iconoclasm even of this famous episode, however, is open to question. The demonstrations in the centre of the city were not wholly spontaneous but to some extent marshalled and choreographed by the political victors, as photographs of the flag-carrying crowds suggest. Furthermore, the culmination of the proceedings – the dismantling of Dzerzhinsky's statue – was not the unequivocal result of a popular uprising, like the storming of the Bastille: it was the city authorities who removed the statue, to the cheers of the crowds (plate 20). According to Timothy Colton, the authorities reluctantly intervened to achieve what the crowds could not, because of the statue's weight. For John Murray, not even the crowds were intent on toppling the statue: in his observation, the mood was more festive than revolutionary or iconoclastic. Incontestably, however, the crowd swarmed around this symbol of the *ancien régime*, celebrating the demise of the old order and affirming the inversion of its values. More carnival than classic revolution, perhaps, this moment furnished one of the most enduring images of the end of the Soviet regime.[24]

Other statues to Soviet leaders and heroes were removed by the authorities that same week: Sverdlov (from the front of the Bolshoi Theatre), Kalinin and Pavlik Morozov. They were placed – and were to be joined by many others – in the Garden of Sculptures of the Era of Totalitarianism, which opened in the grounds of the Tretyakov Gallery's modern hall on 31 August (plate 21). These were the tip of the iceberg. The capital, in 1980, included 130 memorials to Lenin alone, including thirty statues and busts.[25] Enormous monuments continued to be realised after that: such as that by Lev Kerbel on

October Square, erected in 1986.[26] The issue of what to do with them became an embarrassment for the authorities. There were calls to remove them all, but the City Council's commission on the issue decided to remove (and preserve) most, while leaving some in position: seven of the sixty-eight large statues of Lenin were left untouched, as were nineteen out of forty-eight statues of major Soviet figures.[27] These included Lev Kerbel's 1986 monument to Lenin and his statue of Marx on Theatre Square. (Kerbel was a leading monumental sculptor from the 1960s, but this may not be the only reason his works were left in place: Soviet sculptors were paid by weight, and his Lenin was rumoured to be too heavy to move.) Practicality, as well ambivalence about the destruction of the symbols of the Soviet past, seems to have informed this caution. In much of Russia, many Soviet era statues remain in place and the political complexion of a city may be read from its monuments (plate 22). The Red Belt and Volga region are still dotted with Lenins.[28]

The Lenin mausoleum

The new authorities' ambivalent attitude to the Soviet legacy is well illustrated by their response to their biggest embarrassment: Lenin's corpse, embalmed on Red Square, and the single most significant symbol and shrine of the Soviet regime. A quasi-religious cult developed around the body of the dead leader, whose sanctity and immortality were proclaimed by the propaganda machine, and whose mausoleum became the spiritual centre of the regime and of its key rituals.[29] Soldiers marching to the defence of Moscow, in November 1941, paraded past the mausoleum, from whose balustrade the stalinist leadership reviewed them; here the victory parade was held in May 1945, as were all the regime's significant festivals, principally the May Day and Revolution Day parades. A site of mass pilgrimage in the 1920s and 1930s and, especially after Stalin's death, it was also a shrine where rites of passage in private life were marked: school leavers paid their respects on their last day in school, couples visited after their wedding (although the grave of the unknown soldier became a popular substitute in late Soviet Russia). By 1976, 77 million people were alleged to have visited it.[30]

Assiduously cultivated as a sacred place, the mausoleum was embedded in official mythologies and it was hard suddenly to dislodge Lenin's social prestige, especially since *glasnost'* had not extended to the discussion of the historical record of this secular saint. Several years after the end of the Soviet regime, the writer Vasily Aksenov believed that 'a very large majority of the people [. . .] are still convinced that the holiest thing in the country rests in the mausoleum in Red Square'.[31] If opinion polls in the capital did not support his view, voting patterns in the provinces, indicating widespread support for the revived Communist Party (the KPRF), pointed to the persistence of old values. The first attempts to raise the question of the body and what to do with it had none the less been made, amid sharp controversy, in the heady days of the spring and summer of 1989. As the first quasi-democratic parliament in Soviet history since 1918 met in Moscow, the writer Yuri Kariakin, in reverential tones, suggested that Lenin should be buried with his mother in SPB, as he had wished: 'The mausoleum, with Lenin's body – it's not Lenin's mausoleum, it's still Stalin's mausoleum.' Tanks rumbling past disturbed the body. 'Scientists and artists sculpt that face – it's a nightmare. To create an impression when there's nothing there [. . .] Let the body rest where he, Lenin, wanted it to be.'[32] It was thus in terms of proper reverence for the dead, for a man who merited respect, rather than on grounds of hostility to the man's record, legacy and role in the symbolic arsenal of the Soviet state that Kariakin proposed change. None the less, his suggestion was greeted as an attack on the regime's core values, as sacrilegious and destructive, as the response of the conservative deputy, A. A. Sokolov, indicated:

> Today's attacks on the Party are aimed . . . at undermining trust in the Party and its agencies, at breaking its links with the people. . . . Some blasphemous words . . . have been said here about the Lenin mausoleum and the memory of Vladimir Ilyich.[33]

The proposal to bury Lenin was too controversial for the wily Yeltsin to embrace in 1990, and he reportedly declared against removing him from the mausoleum.[34]

The popular mood in the capital was changing, however, as two attempts to vandalise the monument, in the spring and early summer of 1991, suggested.[35] After the coup, opinion polls showed that Muscovites favoured the burial of the Soviet leader, and while support for this idea fluctuated and declined in the 1990s, it still remained the majority view. In September 1991, 68 per cent favoured burial, with 25.5 per cent opposed to it: these figures had hardly changed by October 1993; in April 1995, 47 per cent were in favour and 37 per cent opposed; in June 1997, 54 per cent supported the idea and 32 per cent were against it.[36]

How did the post-Soviet authorities respond? In view of their proclaimed allegiances and of popular preferences, one might have expected the rapid ejection of Lenin from Red Square. But he is still there, if no longer the object of an official cult. What had happened in the 1990s? Why had he not been removed and buried? *Ab initio*, the new authorities treated the body cautiously. In January 1992, at the beginning of the economic reforms, funding for maintaining the Lenin's body was cut. The previously pampered scientists at the mausoleum worked *gratis* (continuing to visit the body twice weekly and doing major repairs every eighteen months). Later, they were assisted by money from the Fund for the Defence of the Memory of Lenin, established in February 1993 by *Pravda* to protect the mausoleum and Central Lenin Museum. These resources proved inadequate and, by 1997, the state contributed only 20 per cent of the mausoleum's budget. Mayor Luzhkov responded to this quandary by allowing the staff set up a ritual service, to handle embalming and luxury 'death' services for the *nouveaux riches* (at prices allegedly ranging from $1500 to $10,000).[37]

Finance was only one aspect of this decline, which started slowly and proceeded cautiously. Not until the autumn of 1993, and the reduction of the parliamentary opposition with the bombardment of the White House at the start of October, did Yeltsin and the authorities feel sufficiently emboldened to attack this central Soviet symbol. The rituals through which the state honoured the body were maintained until late October 1993, when Post No. One (the guard of honour) was transferred from the mausoleum to the Grave of the Unknown Soldier. Yuri Luzhkov, who had taken over from Gavriil Popov as mayor of Moscow in 1991, simultaneously submitted for the president's signature a draft decree providing for the reburial of Lenin in St Petersburg and of some of the other 400 ashes in the Kremlin Wall, but Yeltsin prevaricated. It was announced that a decision would be taken within six months, but nothing more was done.[38] In the interval the democratic parties, associated with the government, had been resoundingly defeated in the December 1993 Duma elections by the revived communist party (the KPRF) and the rabidly nationalist Zhirinovsky. The powers no longer had the confidence to remove this symbol of a Soviet past that the electorate was apparently reluctant to jettison in its entirety. In 1995, however, with parliamentary elections due in December and presidential elections approaching the following year and with the communist leader, Gennady Zyuganov, emerging as the front runner, it was deemed opportune to dislodge some of the Leninist memorabilia and symbols in the Kremlin. Lenin's memorial flat in the Kremlin was removed to Leninskie Gorki in April 1995 and, in August, the Kremlin statues to Lenin were banished. However, the mausoleum remained open to summer visitors, although the elaborate ritual, which had emphasised honour rather than curiosity, had been somewhat relaxed.

On winning the Presidency again in the summer of 1996, Yeltsin, once he had recovered from his heart attacks and illnesses, emerged in March 1997 to announce that a referendum would be held to decide the issue and pronounced in favour of reburial in St Petersburg. KPRF deputies in the Duma responded with a law banning any further modification of Red Square and extremists retaliated with threats to and attacks on the new monuments to Peter the Great and to Tsar Nicholas II.[39] No referendum was called and the question was quietly dropped until the eve of the next round of parliamentary and presidential elections in 1999 and 2000. In May 1999, the patriarch of the Russian Orthodox Church called for the burial of all revolutionary figures, including Lenin, in an appropriate site elsewhere, objecting that it was inappropriate to hold rock concerts in what was effectively a graveyard. This declaration reflected the church's growing power and self-confidence under the new regime: however, Aleksii was careful not to denounce Lenin and his record, mentioning instead the possibility of a pantheon. His remarks were deliberately ambiguous and could be understood either as an attack on the Soviet past and its symbols or as an affirmation of proper religious concern for reverence for the dead. In fact, he had little to fear from the KPRF, which had largely reinvented itself as a nationalist party and whose leader courted the Russian Orthodox Church. The communists naturally maintained their opposition to the burial of Lenin, with Gennady Seleznev, the Duma chairman, suggesting that it would be divisive and lacking respect for the people's reverence for this 'relic'. Yeltsin agreed that Lenin should be buried:

> The only question is when. It's a serious problem. The Lenin Mausoleum is an historical symbol of our past. But I agree with Patriarch Aleksii II of All Rus' that it isn't human, it isn't Christian to put on display the body of a person who died a long time ago.

Equivocating to the end, he instead considered referring the issue to a commission.[40]

Hence, while the communists consistently maintained their opposition to reburial, the new powers were hesitant to commit themselves. Little changed in the rationale of those who tentatively suggested burial: Kariakin's arguments in 1989 were essentially repeated by Yeltsin in 1999, except that he was able to shelter behind the moral authority of the Orthodox Church. None of the authorities challenged Lenin's iconic status or evoked his contemptuous attitude to democracy or, indeed, human life, in discussing his removal from Red Square. Instead, by the late 1990s, the past he represented was no longer to be rejected unequivocally or wiped from memory, but to be accepted, to some degree, as part of national tradition. As to whether this period of history was to be deplored, to be built on or overcome, was a question that – in this instance – the authorities sidestepped. Like the communist opposition, the regime leaders were preoccupied with national reconciliation and unity. President Putin's pronouncement on the question, in the summer of 2001, illustrates this:

> When I see that the overwhelming majority of the population want this [Lenin's removal from the mausoleum and burial], then it can become a subject of discussion. Until I see this, it will not be considered.[41]

The City as Symbol

Unsurprisingly, the former KGB officer was reluctant to attack this ultimate symbol of the Soviet past and the mausoleum remained open to visitors. By the end of the 1990s, the hostility and rejection of the revolutionary heritage, characteristic of the start of the decade, was a thing of the past. Stalinism might be rejected but Soviet history as a whole was not.

MONUMENTS AND MEMORY

Russia's new rulers, however, no longer drew their legitimacy from the Soviet past. Once the mausoleum was sidelined, a new repertoire of symbols and rituals was required to honour and display the body politic, to represent its values and establish its moral authority. How did the new regime proceed to rearrange the capital, with this task in mind? What new monuments did it erect?

Whereas the Bolsheviks immediately set about reclaiming public space, investing it with new symbolism and meaning, initially tolerating a radically innovative style, as well as inventing a pantheon of heroes and heroines, at least some of whom were modern and new, and while Lenin attached importance to this campaign of 'monumental propaganda' for the new regime, no equivalent impulse was discernible among Russia's rulers in the early 1990s. Yeltsin was certainly not a Lenin, nor was he surrounded by an artistic and intellectual elite of comparable talent to that within the ambit of the early Soviet leaders. More fundamentally, however, Russia's new rulers reinvented themselves, in their quest to hold power. Initially seen as reformers and democrats, they were soon enmired in a power struggle that produced political deadlock and squandered their political capital. Democratic ideals evaporated in the political and economic chaos, as was demonstrated by the elections of December 1993, and the regime that emerged from this trial was presidential, semi-autocratic, more democratic in appearance than in essence, more interested in the traditions of Russian statehood and nationalism than in democratic theory as a source of legitimacy. The regime also became increasingly hesitant to jettison the entire symbolic legacy of the Soviet past, which continued to hold a nostalgic appeal for many Russians.

The trend in the new monumentalism illustrates this. One of the few monuments to the Terror in fact predated the 'revolution' and like most of the subsequent memorials on this subject was not the result of a state commission. A rock from the first Soviet labour camp on the Solovetsky Islands was carried to Moscow and, on 30 October 1990, placed in a small square off the Lubyanka, in memory of the millions of victims of the gulag. It was seen, at the time, as a 'sign of our enlightenment, an act of repentance and a pledge that the past will never be repeated'.[42] A break with the Soviet past was also evident in early post-Soviet monuments. The three young men who died during the street fighting in August 1991 were given, as martyrs of the revolution, a state funeral presided over by the patriarch of the Russian Orthodox Church, Aleksii II. A memorial was erected to them at their graves in Vaganskoe cemetery in August 1992, but a cross erected to their memory in Revolution Square, according to the writer Aksenov, was broken by extreme communists and not restored. These and a trolleybus, damaged in attacks on the parliament and parked outside the former Central Museum of the Revolution, were the only significant memorials to August 1991. Strikingly, as Elizabeth Grey has pointed out, the new regime was not anxious to memorialise itself and its origins.[43] Even the White House, symbol of democratic resistance to the coup, lost both its political and its symbolic significance in the mythology of the new regime, when it was bombarded by Yeltsin in October 1993. It had become a symbol of opposition to the new regime and the ruin stood as a sign of the hopes and illusions of 1991. The parliament was moved to Stalin's hulking Gosplan building, opposite the Kremlin, where the president's offices were located and which now became the symbolic centre of the new presidential order. Legitimacy had reverted, as Grey observed, to the traditional locus of power.[44] The irony of a democratic government being located in a medieval fortress – itself a symbol of autocracy – did not escape Russia's intellectuals, as the architect Mikhail Khazanov remarked: 'I do not know a city where a democratic government would continue to be based in a medieval fortress'. Mikhail Yampolsky has argued that the Kremlin was conserved in the nineteenth and early twentieth centuries as a conscious gesture of rejection of modernity by Russia's tsars and as a symbol of hostility to Europe by both Russia's traditional and modern rulers.[45] The siting of the presidential offices in the Kremlin indicated the sources of legitimacy to which the new rulers wished to lay claim and illustrated their sense of their place in Russian history: it suggested that they saw themselves not as representing a break with Russian traditions of charismatic and authoritarian rule, as one might have expected, but as heirs to it. As President Putin put it, on his inauguration in the Kremlin, on 7 May 2000:

> The Kremlin, a place which is sacred for our people . . . is the heart of our national memory. Our country's history has been shaped here, inside the Kremlin walls, over centuries. And we do not have the right to be heedless of our past.
>
> We must not forget anything. We must know our history, . . . draw lessons from it and always remember those who created the Russian state, championed its dignity and made it a great powerful state. We shall preserve that memory and we shall preserve that tradition through the ages.[46]

Increasingly, public monuments reflected the growing interest in the Muscovite past, in pre-Petrine, religious Russia, unsullied by western influences. This trend reflected the growing public disenchantment with westernisation and what were felt to be its dubious benefits (pauperisation of much of the population, the collapse of statehood, rising crime and mortality rates). Whereas the opening to the West inaugurated by Gorbachev was broadly welcomed and a mania for all things American and disparagement of all things Russian had swept the capital at the end of the 1980s and start of the 1990s, the public mood had changed, and politicians no longer found it opportune to urge the need to join the wider world, as Alexander Yakovlev had done at the Party congress in 1990.

Key elements of Muscovite tradition – Orthodoxy, autocracy and military might and valour – were celebrated in many of the public monuments of the 1990s. The main perpetrators of the new style were Vyacheslav Klykov, a sculptor associated in the late 1980s with an apparently officious branch of the radical nationalist movement, *Pamyat'*, and Zurab Tsereteli, a monumental artist who received his first commission in the 1960s and who was close to the mayor, Yuri Luzhkov. Klykov was responsible for a new statue to the apostles of Russia and symbols of Russian culture and Orthodoxy since the development of Russian pan-slavism in the early 1860s, SS Cyril and Methodius. Erected in 1992 in the presence of the patriarch, the statue's inauguration and location pointed to the developing fashion for nationalism and the emerging place in public life of the Russian Orthodox Church.[47] Two big commissions executed by Klykov in the mid-1990s, which expressed the ideals of monarchy and militarism, included a statue to Tsar Nicholas II, who was still at that stage a political embarrassment to the regime. The statue was, in consequence, erected in a village outside Moscow, where it was later to be destroyed by communist extremists, who objected to proposals to eject Lenin from Red Square. More prominent was his statue to Marshal Zhukov at the entrance to Red Square, which was unveiled in front of the president, mayor and patriarch in May 1995, during the celebrations of the fiftieth anniversary of victory in the Second World War (plate 23). A traditional equestrian statue, it represents Zhukov on his famous white charger, reviewing the victory parade in 1945, while references to the recently rediscovered image of the warrior-saint George the Triumphant (or Dragonslayer) are contained on the base.[48] Yeltsin had approved the proposed monument to Zhukov in January 1994 as a 'symbol of Russian patriotism and valour', apt to 'replace the Lenin mausoleum and tombs of other Soviet leaders'. The writer Yuri Burtin commented tartly that:

> The real historical concrete Zhukov is not needed by the ideology. A stone idol is needed, to replace the worn-out forms of previous idols. . . . The statist-military outlook is seeking props, which are incompatible with the spiritual content of the Fatherland war. And it needs, naturally, new means of graphic agitation.[49]

Zurab Tsereteli was the most controversial artist in 1990s Russia. His 95 metre-high Peter the Great, in Roman attire, perched on the rigging of a galleon (or a pile of galleons) and topped by an aircraft warning light, was erected on the banks of the Moskva river, in honour of the city's 850th anniversary celebrations in 1997 (plate 19). The choice of Peter the Great was out of keeping with the mayor's preferred architectural style and with the traditions of the city, but perhaps reflected the aspiring president's quasi-monarchical and westernising ambitions. (Luzhkov's westernism was confined mainly to the economic sphere, to the realisation of a Dickensian capitalism and guaranteed access for the elite to the banks, assets and pleasures of the West.) But more than the monarchical symbolism, it was the tastelessness of this monument to kitsch that excited Moscow's intellectuals, who, in 1997, in vain attempted to hold a referendum proposing the demolition of Tsereteli's many monuments. Protestors observed that commissions and town planning under the new regime were neither more open nor more democratic than under the Soviets.[50]

Despite his predeliction for historicist kitsch, Luzhkov did not entirely abjure Soviet tradition: the city, he claimed in an interview about his preparations for Moscow's 850th jubilee in 1997, had its plan of 'monumental propaganda'. Moscow was far behind European cities in its monumental architecture, despite the greater richness of its culture. Continuing the Soviet tradition of co-opting cultural figures, Luzhkov chose to commemorate mostly artists who fell foul of the Soviet authorities: by 1995, statues to Vysotsky and Yesenin had been erected in the city centre and sixty more sites were being considered for statues to, inter alia, Tsvetaeva, Rakhmaninov and Meyerhold, as well as less contested figures. The mayor warned, however, against understanding this project as an attempt to ape Europe: it was intended to celebrate Russian culture.[51] A new official nationalism clearly informed these ventures.

Poklonnaya Gora

The chief exception to the dominant Muscovite style was the memorial constructed in the early 1990s to commemorate the Great Patriotic War and celebrate victory over Hitler, where, exceptionally, Soviet history and monumental style were deployed to celebrate nation and army. It was completed at a particularly difficult time for Yeltsin and his associates. No sooner had the political opposition been reduced and its power base, the parliament, emasculated by the December 1993 constitution, than the short-lived recovery which ensued was sacrificed to the ill-prepared, incompetently pursued and deeply unpopular war in Chechnya that was launched in December 1994. The war revealed all the shortcomings of the regime: its scant respect for legality and democratic procedure, its corruption, inefficiency and irresponsibility. As conscripts died and the impotence of the once formidable army

The City as Symbol

was exposed, it became all the more urgent to find an ideal other than discredited democracy and a cause other than the present regime and its war, to celebrate. The fiftieth anniversary of victory, which fell in May 1995, could not have been better timed: it afforded the regime a ready-made myth of national unity and self-sacrifice, of military valour and triumph in adversity to propose to its hard-pressed citizenry. Instead of the abject spectacle of the present, the public were invited to contemplate past glories and to celebrate Russian military tradition. The fact that the war had furnished the later Soviet regime with its most assiduously cultivated and effective legitimising myth (much of the truth about the war being suppressed until the end of the 1980s and even beyond)[52] was an asset, rather than discouragingly inappropriate: it was simply borrowed by the new regime.

The serendipity of the myth had not in fact been fully appreciated when the *glasnost'* era controversy over the planned Victory memorial was resolved by the new authorities (the mayor of Moscow and the ministers of culture and defence) in April 1992. Under Gorbachev, conservationists had objected to the monumentalism of the original plans, which were wholly insensitive to both the site and the subject.[53] The new authorities simply adopted the original plans, making some minor adjustments, and rapidly realised them. The symbolism of the completed memorial, which opened in May 1995, while Soviet in inspiration, was primarily a monument to the glory of the nation, its army and its military traditions and achievements, and as such suited the new regime.

The memorial included 44,000 square metres of exhibition space, four museums and a park (plate 24). From the entrance near the Borodino Arch (destroyed in 1936 and restored in 1968), a central alley (with five terraces, corresponding to the five years of the war, lined with fifteen fountains representing the fifteen USSR republics) led to the central square and museum area. To the left of the alley stood one of the new elements in the plan: the Orthodox chapel of St George the Triumphant (Dragonslayer), retrieved as a symbol of Moscow in the 1990s and a symbol of Russian military tradition. In the middle of the central Square of Victors rose another Tsereteli monument, in the form of an obelisk representing a giant Russian bayonet, 141.8 metres high (symbolising the 1418 days the war lasted), and crowned by the pagan goddess of war, Nika, and two angels. At its foot, a smaller statue depicted St George, dispatching the dragon of fascism (plate 25). The entrance to the museum was dedicated to the traditions of the Russian army: banners of the 1812 and Second World War armies were displayed, along with portraits and busts of Soviet and tsarist generals (such as Kutuzov). Under the cupola of the Hall of Glory, the names of 11,717 heroes of the Soviet Union and twenty-two heroes of the Russian Federation were inscribed on tablets, those of 'hero-cities' of the Soviet Union on the wall; a bronze figure of a Warrior-Victor stood in the middle of the hall. The Hall of Memory contained books recording the names of approximately 19.5 million victims of the war (an ongoing project) and Lev Kerbel's white marble *pietà* of a mother grieving over a dead soldier. There was a museum of military hardware, and much space was given to huge dioramas by the Soviet-era Grekov War Artists' Studio, mythologising key moments of the war – the defence of Moscow, the siege of Leningrad, the victory at Stalingrad and the storming of Berlin.[54] Unmentioned in this memorial were the needless loss of civilian life at the start of the war and of soldiers' lives throughout, the great brutality of the high command, the NKVD's shooting of civilians as they retreated and again during Soviet advance and the privileges of the elite during the siege of Leningrad, while Stalin was presented in generally positive terms. The pathos of the monument was thus highly selective and it embodied a Soviet reading of history.

In its ostentation, heroic symbolism and quasi-modern idiom, the style of the monument was Soviet. The religious symbols and the Orthodox church were later accretions. The intention in 1995 was to add a mosque (to symbolise the brotherhood of the peoples and Russia's Eurasian character), but a synagogue was vetoed on the grounds that it would infringe on a holy, national site. The patriarch held a requiem in the church for victims of the war, as part of the Victory anniversary ceremonies, testifying to the Russian Orthodox Church's growing importance in state ritual and symbolism. Tsereteli's monument was also new: the original design envisaged diminutive soldiers carrying a vast banner inscribed with Lenin's profile. The new monument was more ambiguous, as few people realised who Nika was or why she was represented. Otherwise, the monument reiterated the Soviet myth of the war: as a war of national unity, patriotism and willing self-sacrifice for the defence of the Motherland.[55]

Lest the public miss its significance, the point was hammered home in the speeches at the opening ceremony (which was attended by Yeltsin, the patriarch, Luzhkov, CIS and foreign leaders) and during the elaborate Victory celebrations. The memory of victory, according to the prime minister, Viktor Chernomyrdin, was impervious to time and a source of pride and joy. The enemy had been unable to break the spirit of the people in their desire to fight for the freedom and independence of the Motherland. The friendship of the peoples and their cooperation had helped them through the war and would help Russia now. The memorial was a symbol of this inclusive national memory and would remind future generations of victory, self-denial, honour and glory. It would honour those, thanks to whom the Russian Motherland continued to exist.[56]

The defence minister, Pavel Grachev, encouraged by the revival of military ceremonial and celebration, suggested that the monument was destined to become a 'holy place for all Russians [*rossiyan*]'. He recognised the role of allied aid in the victory but assigned the decisive role to 'our great people', their 'love of the Fatherland', and the 'unity of the whole country'. Victory Day (May) was now 'the most holy date in the biography of the Fatherland' and a 'day of spiritual cleansing and unification'.

> The Great Victory is our common sacred thing [svyatynya] and common glory, ... the indivisible achievement of all the brother peoples [of the USSR] ... The peoples of the former Union were and remain brothers. ... We must remain supports for each other today too ...

The Victory should be a powerful source of unity for all Russian society: 'May Victory Day always remain a symbol of our national unity'.[57]

Ritual commemoration of the war thus assumed something of the style and significance of a religious rite, by virtue not only of the language used in elevating it to sacred status, but in the symbolic meaning attached to it. Official discourse about the War was not a historical narrative, describing past events, but an affirmation of the continued vitality and relevance of this 'immortal' episode in the present, of the regenerative and inspirational powers for contemporary Russian society of the ideals it represented: courage and self-sacrifice (martyrdom), patriotism and devotion to the Fatherland (belief), national unity and common purpose. The mythology would be recalled and enacted each year, as before 1991, in the rituals of 9 May, and permanently displayed at the shrine of Poklonnaya Gora. In short, the rites of memory, in relation to the war, enabled the nation to undergo spiritual purification and renewal, according to the official version. Many of these themes and meanings would be read into subsequent monuments to the nation, with national repentance and purification, national unity, endurance and self-sacrifice, belief in past and future glory of the nation as standard elements in the canonical interpretation of their significance.

Not that this account went unchallenged. Yuri Burtin, who had lived through the war, noted that:

> The new symbols ... bear absolutely no relation to the Great Patriotic War, not so much because its soldiers had never heard of St George or the pagan Nika. The question here is not about form but about content.

Nika would be a more appropriate symbol for a Nazi monument, he observed caustically. The war had been fought not for glory, but for survival: it remained in popular memory as an appalling tragedy, a bitter time, whereas the 'new symbols made that war a justification for war as such'.[58] Despite these reservations, the official line on the war remains that defined in 1995.[59] President Putin's speech in the Kremlin on 7 May 2000 illustrates this:

> There are dates which are unaffected by time, distance or even political change. One such holy day for us is 9 May . . . Victory Day . . . unites and reconciles everybody in Russia. . . . It is the glorious history of our mother country which becomes the most important thing.

The following day, Tsereteli announced that a bronze bust to Stalin, and other wartime leaders, was to be erected at Poklonnaya Gora, and a plaque to Stalin and other recipients of the Order of Victory would be unveiled, in the president's presence, at the Kremlin on 9 May.[60]

RESTORATION AND HISTORICISM

If the new authorities placed renewed emphasis on nationalism and militarism in their emerging mythology, they also infused it with new religious and historical references. From the outset, they had been anxious to present themselves as successors to pre-revolutionary history – not only through the return of street names, but even in the nomenclature of the new institutions after 1993. The parliament created by the December 1993 constitution called itself the Duma, and was styled the Fifth Duma (following the fourth, which had been superseded in February 1917).

Much of the new architecture was also retrospective. Central Moscow, in the 1990s, witnessed a wave of restorations that attempted to undo Stalin's destruction of the monuments of old Moscow in the 1930s. The significance of the gesture (the rejection of Stalinism, as the essence of revolutionary socialism) was obvious. Many of the major reconstructions were religious, giving the Russian Orthodox Church new ritual and symbolic prominence in post-Soviet Moscow. Among the principal restorations was that of the Kazan Cathedral of the Mother of God on Red Square, which had been blown up in 1936 (plate 26). Built in 1630, the cathedral had accommodated the famous Kazan Icon of the Mother of God, which had been taken into battle by the national army of Minin and Pozharsky in 1612, in a campaign that was to put an end to the Time of Troubles (as the early 1990s were also often called in the press) and expel the Polish invader. It was here that Kutuzov was blessed before Borodino. It was thus a site of national and historic, as well as of religious, significance and was a symbol of patriotic resistance to foreign invaders. The decision to rebuild it was taken by Mayor Popov in 1990, when the new foundation stone was laid. The rebuilt church was rededicated by Patriarch Aleksii II, on 4 November 1993, in the presence of Yeltsin and Luzhkov, and the Vladimir Icon of the Mother of God and Rublev's Trinity icons were to be returned to it. The event was a 'big celebration for all who love Russia', commented *Pravda*, now newly enthused by religious nationalism.[61]

In the autumn of 1993, Luzhkov proposed for Yeltsin's signature a draft decree 'On the Restoration of the Historical Image of Red Square'. 'What particular period is meant?' wondered the commandant of the threatened Lenin mausoleum, observing that in the reign of Ivan III there had been fifteen churches and graveyards there.[62] The accretion of contradictory symbols made the issue politically controversial and any solution arbitrary. It was none the less decided to proceed with a return to the Muscovite style, favoured under the last tsars as an image of autocracy, in the area of the Kremlin. The Red Staircase of the Faceted Palace in the Kremlin, which had been pulled down in 1933, was restored in 1994. The draft decree also proposed replacing the Kremlin towers' red stars with double-headed eagles (a minor, February 1917 modification of tsarist symbolism)[63] and restoring the Resurrection Gates, which until 1931 had stood at the entrance to Red Square and enclosed the Chapel of the Icon of the Iberian Mother of God. Both projects were realised in 1995, despite Yeltsin's failure to sign the decree.

What inspired these moves? At one level, the post-Soviet regime was interested in forging a new nationalist mythology with which to legitimise itself, especially since its record of government and authority was so contested. Architecture, monuments and ceremonial were striking expressions of this mythology, which increasingly drew on Russian state tradition. This involved allowing the Russian Orthodox Church something of its previous place in pre-revolutionary Russia in the sites and ceremonials of power. Services had already been resumed in the Uspensky Cathedral of the Kremlin in the late autumn of 1989 and in St Basil's in October 1990, while churches had been returned to the Russian Orthodox Church all over Russia since the Millennium of the Baptism of Rus' in 1988. The church was to play an increasingly important role in the political symbolism of the new Russia. By the mid-1990s, this was already evident. On the consecration of the chapel in the Resurrection Gates, in October 1995, Prime Minister Chernomyrdin declared that the Russian Orthodox Church 'was taking its rightful place in the life of society by making its own unique contribution to the cause of creating a great, powerful and beautiful Russia, proud of its past and looking confidently to the future'.[64]

Yuri Luzhkov played a key role in these developments. As mayor since 1991, he exercised great power, not only over the city administration, but also over its economic life, where little could happen without his approval. Given that most of Russia's wealth was concentrated in Moscow, he had enormous resources at his command. By 1996, when he was triumphantly confirmed in office, he was not only a staunch ally of Yeltsin but also openly ambitious to succeed him. Among the means he hoped to use to achieve this was a programme of public works that would transform the image of the capital. These projects were trumpeted in publications and mass media controlled by

Luzhkov.[65] The message the transformed city was to communicate was encapsulated by a journalist, who noted the predominantly historicist character of Moscow architecture:

> On Moscow's squares and streets an 'ideology in pure form' is being proclaimed. . . . Before our eyes a conception of the city is emerging, where architectural forms do not merely speak, but 'shout' about the rebirth of historical Russia with its traditional tastes.[66]

Hence, Luzhkov's personal ambitions coincided with the regime's requirements, which is what enabled him to proceed. The city was to be a monument to a new national ideology, to proclaim the resurrection of state and nation that had overcome the Revolution and Stalin's destructive reign, returned to its historic and religious roots, and revived under its new charismatic leaders. Meant to embody a myth, the city (or its historic centre) was also to be a monument to its chief architect – Luzhkov. As one architect sardonically commented, the mayor was determined to create a 'new Moscow style', which owed more to the prevailing tastes in *obkom banyas* and money-making than to aesthetics.[67]

The Cathedral of Christ the Saviour

The most striking illustration of these impulses was the rebuilding of the Cathedral of Christ the Saviour, an enterprise that provoked much controversy and study (plate 27).[68] The significance of the original monument was controversial and ambiguous. Originally conceived as a pantheon to the heroes of the Great Patriotic War against Napoleon and sanctioned by Alexander I in 1812, the project ground to a halt in 1827 amid allegations of corruption and waste. Reconceived by the father of the new Russian style, Konstantin Ton, at the behest of Nicholas I, building resumed in 1839 and was completed only in 1881, in the reign of the arch-conservative Alexander III. The new building eschewed Vitberg's neo-classicism for a reinvented Russian medievalism, and the cathedral, the largest in Russia and chief church of the Russian Orthodox Church, was now seen as a monument to Nicholas's ideology of official nationality. It celebrated the pillars of tsarist Russia: church, autocracy and army. The point was emphasised when a statue to Alexander III, representing him as crowned monarch, was erected outside it for the tercentenary of the Romanov dynasty, in 1912. The myth had it that the common people had paid for it through donations (as officially it was a monument to the nation, its patriotism and military prowess) but it was in fact funded largely by the state, at enormous cost.[69]

Not surprisingly, the church was a prime candidate for destruction under the Bolsheviks, who attacked it as 'the ideological fortress of the accursed old world'. Eisenstein symbolised the advent of revolution, in the opening sequences of his myth-making film *October* (1927), by showing the destruction of the statue to Alexander III.[70] (Later in the movie, he represents the Kerensky–Kornilov counter-revolution by reversing these sequences, thus reassembling the statue.) Not until 1931, however, was the destruction of the cathedral itself to proceed, on Stalin's command. It was demolished only after three explosions and its marble was used, inter alia, to decorate Stalin's new metro stations. In its place, Stalin planned a grandiose Palace of Soviets that, in the winning design by Boris Iofan, approved in 1934, was to be topped by a ninety metre, 6000-ton statue of Lenin. (This Lenin was deliberately to be taller than the Statue of Liberty, just as the 416 metre palace was intended to outstrip the 408 metre Empire State building, erected in what Timothy Colton calls the Gomorrah of capitalism, New York, in May 1931.) In the event, war overtook the project and the palace was never erected. Instead, an open-air heated swimming pool was opened on the site in 1960.[71] Critics of communism delighted in this symbolism, seeing it as 'a black hole in [Russians'] historical memory, in [our] human conscience, in the topography of power' that should be filled with 'a visible symbol of the Nation's Greatness', according to the writer Vladimir Sidorov. A school history textbook, published in 1993, asked: 'Is it not striking that in the very same place where the builders of the Palace of Soviets showed themselves to be powerless, Russian masters, a hundred years before had been able to erect what was then the biggest cathedral in Moscow?'[72] The new regime would be happy to respond with an act of creativity and power.

The idea of rebuilding the cathedral was first raised by the nationalist intelligentsia in September 1989, as a means of national recovery and moral recovery and as a tribute to Russia's past military glory. The campaign was led by the nationalist writer Vladimir Soloukhin, who imagined that the project would be funded mainly by popular donation.[73] It remained the forlorn cause of a handful of conservative nationalists, despite being sanctioned by Yeltsin in 1992, until the autumn of 1994, when it was taken up by Luzhkov.[74] It fitted admirably into his purposes, enabling him to pose as a 'creator' (in contrast to the destroyer, Stalin, and – though the point was not made explicitly – those destructive radical democrats who had wrecked Russia in the early 1990s); as a nationalist, as a *gosudarstvennik-derzhavnik*, one of the long line of Russian state-builders. The symbolic content of Ton's building was not out of keeping with his own style and instincts.

Organising the president's support, establishing a public oversight committee presided over by the patriarch (this was to be another 'sacred' enterprise) and including some well-known nationalist intellectuals, arranging tax concessions (not unlike money-laundering facilities) for business sponsors' (de facto compulsory) contributions, Luzhkov pushed the project through at almost stalinist tempi.[75] The foundation stone was laid to coincide with Orthodox Christmas 1995, following a religious service in a Kremlin cathedral, a religious procession and a ceremonial blessing by Aleksii II. Executed as a miracle of speed and efficiency, the project was completed in time for the celebrations of Moscow's 850th anniversary in September 1997, when it was solemnly inaugurated at a church service attended by the political powers. The interior décor (managed by Tsereteli) was finished in summer 2000. Supposedly funded by public subscription, in fact the cathedral was estimated to have cost the state and city of Moscow *c*.$400 million, at a time when miserly pensions, teachers' and doctors' salaries were paid months in arrears, when conscripts and soldiers in the army endured hunger and privation, when the majority of Russian churches were falling down and the physical infrastructure in much of the country was falling apart.[76] Unsurprisingly, the project was criticised on financial grounds and also as an inauthentic restoration and inappropriate to the new Russia.[77] The church was arguably another example of *potemshchina*, exemplifying the gap between appearance and reality in Russian history.

The recreated cathedral, on the banks of the Moskva opposite the Kremlin, resembled a gigantic medieval Russian church: it was a sort of Slavic Vatican (than which the original had been intended, predictably, to be bigger). Secular power lay across the river, spiritual power was on the right bank. The new building was to become the liturgical and ceremonial centre of Russian Orthodoxy and, apart from the vast main church, it included ample accommodation for the Russian Orthodox Church's administrative services: an extra, basement floor was added to the original designs, to include a 1250-seat conference centre (for church councils), offices for the Holy Synod, car parking for 600 cars, as well as a chapel and a museum of modern ecclesiastical art (where the style was set by followers of Ilya Glazunov).[78] The new cathedral reiterated the glorification of the military victory of 1812 (over the West) and added to this references to the victory of 1945. Heroes' names were inscribed on the walls, while frescoes and outer sculptures depicted prefigurations, drawn from Russian and Biblical history, of these military feats, in which Russian leaders and the Russian people, inspired and blessed by the Russian Orthodox Church, defeated the (implicitly infidel) foreign invader. Thus, a painting within depicted the warrior-saint Prince Dmitri Donskoi being blessed by the monk St Sergei Radonezh, before the famous battle of Kulikovo field, outside Moscow, when medieval Russia inflicted a decisive defeat on the Tatars in 1380. The same scene was repeated on the exterior walls in bronze (plate 28). Another *haut relief* showed St Dionisii 'blessing Prince Pozharsky and the Citizen Minin to liberate Moscow from the Polish invaders [*sic*]'. Biblical scenes were subject to a narrow historical and nationalist reading: thus, Abraham's return from victorious battle and greeting by Melchisidech were intended to remind the viewer 'of the return of Alexander I after the victory over Napoleon being met by the allies as a liberator [sic]'.[79] The cathedral was thus a monument to militant nationalism, in which religion, if not subordinated to state and nation, elevated nation and state to equivalent status with it.

It clearly affirmed the power of the church and its importance in the topography and new rituals of power. In its location, the cathedral symbolised the union of church and state. The sculptor V. P. Mokrousov had already observed in the late 1980s that its site

> is a holy place, like the belly-button of Russia. The heart is the Kremlin, right beside it was the spiritual, cultural centre, the centre of warlike glory, of defence of the Fatherland, of our beauty, Orthodoxy. This role was played by the Cathedral of Christ the Saviour.[80]

This point was reiterated some years later by the chief architect, M. Posokhin. 'The Cathedral of Christ the Saviour is the spiritual centre of the country: here will be the main Orthodox cathedral, then the Kremlin – the heart of the capital, the residence of the President.'[81] The location was not accidental: now, it also permitted the integration of religious ritual into the new state ceremonial. Isabelle de Keghel points out that the authorities lost no time in including the cathedral into state occasions, even before the famous 850th jubilee of Moscow.

The rebuilt church was the product of a new charismatic authoritarianism, which, in the mid-1990s during the first Chechen war, preferred a myth of national participation in the reconstruction of the country to any real popular control over policy. The authorities' rhetoric emphasised that this monument was dedicated to the power and glory of church and state, to military prowess of the nation, to the new Russian Idea.[82] When the state adopted the project in the autumn of 1994, Yeltsin blessed what he called this mission, which would help Russians in the existing difficult times of destruction, creation and moral cleansing (from Soviet sins). Russia needed the cathedral: it would lead Russians to national agreement and a new, less sinful life of goodness.[83] This quasi-religious language became mandatory for all official interventions on the subject: the enterprise was no mere secular one, but a sort of sacred rite, through which Russians would find redemption and salvation. If a civic religion deploys the sacred for secular purposes, here we see the process in reverse: the secular pursuit of power and glory (as in the myth of the national war) was sacralised and, it was hoped, disguised as a vital rite of passage in the nation's progress towards its destiny of grandeur, prosperity, moral purification and ultimate vindication.

Yeltsin's emphasis on the cathedral as a means of national repentance and moral recovery, of renewed creativity after the long years of revolutionary destructiveness, was a theme taken up in all other interventions on the subject. The patriarch's first pronouncements on the project treated it as an act of penance and took the form of a prayer and admonishment. Prefacing his remarks with the sign of the cross, he observed that whereas the destruction of this symbol of nationhood and Russian 'warlike glory' had been a general sin, its recreation was a 'holy deed', which alone could wash away the earlier transgression. He hoped that '[t]he recreation of the cathedral, which was a symbol of Moscow, will unite us all in one impulse of creation rather than destruction. In this, our repentance and unity and agreement will be expressed'. The project would be a healing one and the rebuilding of the cathedral would stand as a metaphor for the rebuilding of Russian nationhood, its unity and strength.[84] While Aleksii liked to see the fate of the church as symbolising the fate both of the Russian Orthodox Church and of the Russian people, he also stressed, in an address in the cathedral at Easter 1997, that it was 'symbol of the greatness of Russian [*rossiiskoi*] State power'. Not only would the nation recover through its reconstruction, so would the state: 'The recreation of this church is a symbol of the resurrection of *Rus'*, a sign of hope in better times for the peoples ... who are returning to God'.[85] The function of the resurrected cathedral was thus multiple: religious and moral, national and patriotic, but, above all, it was a religious act of salvation for the nation. This interpretation was to be reiterated in the church's subsequent pronouncements.[86]

Luzhkov gave the clearest expression to the cathedral's multiple meanings in a speech at the laying of the foundation stone on 7 January 1995. The original monument had symbolised the Russian people's patriotism; once destroyed by Stalin, it became 'a symbol of the sorrow, loss, destruction and lack of spirituality into which our country sank for many years'. Recreated, it would be

> a symbol of repentance ...; a symbol of the unity of the Russian people, a symbol of pacification and organisation of the Russian Land [*Zemlii Russkoi*], a symbol of the power and prosperity of a great power, recreated by us together with the Church, ... a symbol of hope, of the finding [*obretenie*] and creation which await our country.

It would remind Russians that a great state was created not only by feats of arms, but also by prayer to God, confidence and action to rebuild the Russian land.[87] This, the listener/reader was to understand, was just what the mayor could offer, as the rebuilding of the cathedral would show.

The rites that developed around the building and opening of the cathedral thus helped to establish and enact the new state mythology, with its sacralisation of national destiny. In the project, the new union of church and state – formally separate, but in practice propping each other up – was manifest. The Russian Orthodox Church, despite proclaiming its belated independence from the state, in fact worked closely with the new regime and the army, especially from 1994, attempting to boost its flagging morale and to furnish it with the patriotic-military education formerly dispensed by the CPSU.[88] Thus Ton's recreated monument again became a symbol of a new theory of official nationality, based on the alliance of church, state and mythologised nation, which held more than echoes of the old autocratic political culture. Critics indeed pointed to the incongruity of its symbolism: 'But to build a monument to the Nicholaevian epoch today? It would be hard to conceive a stranger occupation for a country building democracy', commented one journalist. Another noted the religious language and ritual deployed in relation to it by national politicians: they referred glibly to 'national repentance' and 'national holy shrines' in relation to this essentially secular, political exercise.[89] But the cathedral has become a key site in the new political spectacle, as well as a popular tourist site and a shrine in which the new popular religiosity of Russians may be observed.

RITUAL AND CEREMONIAL

Attempts to invent a new calendar of state ritual in the early 1990s were unsuccessful: Soviet festivities had lost their ideological underpinning, although some were retained and new meanings ascribed to them.[90] However, the new state's fatidic calendar went largely unnoticed and uncelebrated by ordinary people.[91] By the latter half of the 1990s, religious holidays – as before the revolution – supplied many of the main public festivals: statesmen went to church and were blessed by churchmen, religious slogans draped the streets at Christmas and Easter where once communist banners had hung. The patriarch's messages were broadcast on the national media at Christmas, Easter and other holy days, while civic ceremonies – such as the celebration of Victory Day and the state burial of the last Tsar, when requiems were sung in all Russian churches – were increasingly accompanied by religious rites.[92] To add to their threadbare legitimacy, Russian politicians in the 1990s became assiduous churchgoers. The patriarch has been present at the inauguration of Russian presidents since 1991: in March 2000, this imposing ritual (in the Kremlin, where the tsars had come to be crowned) included a visit by the new incumbent to the Cathedral of the Annunciation (the Russian Tsars' private church), where the patriarch conducted a service to mark his assumption of office.[93] The church in turn received great tax and trade concessions and large grants of money and assets from the state.[94]

The new state's lack of conviction and clear sense of identity, which state ceremonial and symbolism suggested, were illustrated also by the fate of the national anthem. In 1990, the Soviet anthem was replaced by an air from Glinka's 1836 opera *Ivan Susanin* (as it was again called under Stalin, who took exception to the title that Nicholas I imposed in the work: *A life for the Tsar*). This work, about a peasant who, during the Time of Troubles, sacrifices his life to save the first Romanov tsar by deceiving the invading Poles, was taken as a statement of Russian musical nationalism.[95] The new authorities could not agree on accompanying words and Glinka's air was finally replaced, by President Putin, in March 2001, with the old stalinist 1944 anthem (and a new Great Russian nationalist text, written as before by Sergei Mikhalkov).[96] In December 2000, President Putin justified this proposal (which included the simultaneous adoption of the tricolour and the double-headed eagle as state flag and emblem respectively) by referring to the achievements of the tsarist and Soviet past and of previous generations of Russians. There had long been controversy over the state symbols because people were

> ideologising these state symbols to the maximum degree. They are associating them with the grim aspects of the history of our country. But there have always been such periods ... What do we do then with the achievements of Russian culture?
>
> As for the Soviet period of our country, can we honestly say that it left us with nothing to remember except the Stalin-era camps and the repressions? What do we do, then, with Dunayevsky, Sholokov and Shostakovich.... And what about our victory in the spring of 1945?

People should put conflict over competing views of history behind them, Putin implied, and unite instead around the inspiring narrative of the nation's achievements which he proposed to enshrine in state ritual as in architecture. Innovation and historical revision were equated with disreputable amnesia:

> Our history has already seen a period in which we rewrote everything from scratch. We could go the same route today: we could rewrite our flag, our national anthem, our state seal. But then there would be no question that we would deserve to be called 'Ivans Who Claim No Memory of their Origins' [a term used by the tsarist police, usually translated as 'of unknown ancestry'].

This approach was not uncontested, but the intelligentsia was more isolated in its scepticism and protests than a decade earlier. History and memory, so sharply debated in the late eighties and early nineties, generated less controversy by the turn of the millennium. The cellist Rostropovich was among a group of intellectuals who objected to the new/old anthem, however, arguing, on 5 December 2000, that the attempt to fuse Soviet and tsarist history into a single legacy, on which modern Russia could draw, was misguided:

The melody is one of the most vivid symbols of our bygone era. No new lyrics can erase the words glorifying Lenin and Stalin that have become permanently attached to Alexandrov's music.

We would like to remind those who have forgotten that, before Stalin chose that melody for the national anthem, it was the anthem of the Bolshevik party! ... The head of state should recognise that millions of his fellow citizens ... will never respect an anthem that ... insults the memory of the victims of Soviet repression. Precisely because we can remember, we are convinced that the history of Russia will always be merely sutured to the history of the USSR.

Zurab Tsereteli and fifteen other cultural figures supported the president, however, suggesting that '[b]y putting together three symbols from different eras, the president is reasserting the continuity of all of Russian history. This historical compromise could provide a basis for strengthening the civic harmony we need so badly today.'[97] Official artists thus supported the powers in their attempts to create an official nationalism that celebrated the national past, tsarist and Soviet. Innovative symbolism was thus eschewed in favour of a myth of national unity and recovery.

This trend was observable also in the reiterated attempts, after 1996, to elaborate a new Russian Idea as the new state ideology.[98] As a literary-philosophical exercise, this did not succeed (not for want of any number of recycled nationalist creeds in 1990s Russia), largely because it was hard to construct a coherent and plausible account of the hybrid ideology that the state embraced and embodied in its restored capital.[99]

A clearer indication that the new Russia was looking backwards and inwards for legitimation and ideas was the furnished by the fate of those other problematic dead bodies: those of the royal family. Exhumed in 1991, to Yeltsin's embarrassment (as he had been responsible for demolishing the house in Sverdlovsk where they had been shot, in 1977 on the orders of the KGB, which did not stop the site becoming a shrine in the 1990s) (plate 29), the question of what to do with the remains was evaded by the authorities for years. Afraid of burying Lenin, they were no less afraid of burying the last tsar and his family. If it were to be done, where should it take place? (The mayors of Moscow, St Petersburg and Yekaterinburg vigorously disputed possession in the mid-1990s.)[100] How should it be done? Did burial perhaps suggest that the tsar was a martyr or as legitimate a ruler as the current authorities, some of whom were implicated in obliterating all memory of him? But was the pre-revolutionary order not also useful to invoke?

Initially, the new political leaders prevaricated and established a commission on the authenticity of the bones (as, in 1993, did the Russian Orthodox Church, for which the remains were an even greater embarrassment, as they threatened to intensify the divisions between conservatives and reformers in the church and precipitate the loss of further believers to the rival Russian Orthodox Church Abroad).[101] Finally, in January 1998, the bones were declared authentic and Yeltsin decreed that they should be buried on 17 July, on the eightieth anniversary of the royal family's death, with full honours according to the traditional rites of monarchical burial, and interred in the traditional resting place of Russia's tsars in the SS Peter and Paul Cathedral in St Petersburg.[102]

The state burial was understood by an Orthodox priest writing in *Russkaya mysl'* as 'a symbolic act of universal significance, signifying the end of "Soviet Russia" and the restoration of the historic succession of Russian statehood' and 'an act of repentance for Soviet crimes'. For Prince Nikolai Romanov, it meant that 'we are burying a part of our common history, the bloodiest part. It is behind us now'. Instead, 'the history of a new Russia, reconciled with the past will commence [. . .]'. For Yeltsin, who decided to attend only at the last moment, it was also a matter of Russia's collectively putting the past behind it, of overcoming the legacy of the revolution, but it was only one act in this process of repentance, healing and reconstruction which had begun in 1991: 'It is a symbol of the unity of our people, of atonement of shared guilt. . . . We must end the century, which for Russia has been a century of blood and lawlessness, in repentance and reconciliation'.[103] Once again, the years of controversy were ended by an elaborate ritual, in which the new state, in the shape above all of Yeltsin, enacted repentance and national unity in a piece of spectacular political theatre.

The Russian Orthodox Church officiated at the funeral, despite denying the authenticity of the remains. This did not prevent it from attempting to resolve this problem, two years later, in August 2000, by canonising the tsar and his family as passion-bearers and victims of the revolution, who had borne their sufferings and death with humility. They were, however, treated as simple Russians, not as rulers, and were canonised among the 1090 martyrs of Russia's twentieth century proclaimed by the millennial council of the church.[104] The basis on which the tsar and his family were canonised had been a matter of prolonged debate within the church: liberals objected to his unedifying record both as a man and as a ruler; they also feared that canonising him as a royal martyr (like SS Boris and Gleb) would endorse the principle of monarchical rule. While conservatives were supportive of these political connotations of canonisation, they wanted to elucidate whether the royal family had been victims of a Jewish-Masonic ritual murder. Church authorities hesitated and conducted prolonged and inconclusive researches into the authenticity of the remains and the suitability of the royal family for this distinction. Popular support for canonisation in the lower levels of the church grew and the patriarchate received many letters and demands for canonisation; thousands of miracles, cures and instances of weeping and bleeding icons of

Nicholas and his family were reported. It being no longer possible to prevaricate, the final solution was a political compromise, which satisfied popular pressure without causing too much political controversy.[105]

This rehabilitation of the tsar, in the reconstructed and solemnly rededicated Cathedral of Christ the Saviour, appeared to proclaim to the world how far Russia had travelled since 1991. The symbols of Russia's religious and monarchical tradition were re-enthroned. This was far from suggesting that the new Russia saw itself as the liberal democratic state that people had imagined a decade earlier; the history and values now reclaimed were those of authoritarian and charismatic rule, based not on popular sovereignty but on church, army and national myth.

CONCLUSION

This approach reflected a change in public attitudes over the decade: opinion polls indicated declining support for liberal democracy and growing hostility to the West.[106] Not only the people but also the political elite were increasingly disenchanted with the West and its supposed cultural-political attributes and policies. The post-Soviet regime emerged in Russia in the mid-nineties in the form of a hierarchical state, with an atrophied civil society, limited press freedom, a weak judiciary, a quasi-official church and excessive powers vested with the Presidency and the new elite. By 1997, Russia bore some resemblances to the corporatist state and this complexion was reflected in the adoption of more nationalist attitudes by the political elite. This trend was accelerated by a series of crises in relations with the West: NATO's westward expansion in 1998 and the collapse of the ruble in August 1998; NATO's military intervention in Kosovo in the spring of 1999. The Kosovo precedent, which emboldened the Russian authorities to resume the Chechen war in the autumn of 1999 – a war whose popularity ensured Putin's election as president the following March – demonstrated the sea-change in Russian popular attitudes since 1994.

Contenders to replace Yeltsin as president were careful to cultivate a 'patriotic' image, emphasising their readiness to defend Russia and her interests against western attempts to dominate her. Not only the ex-premier Yevgeny Primakov and his belated ally Luzhkov, but also the rapidly promoted Vladimir Putin, premier since August 1999, were anxious to depict themselves as free from western influences and connections, as defenders of law and order (as opposed to the corruption and chaos of the Yeltsin years), as men able to revive Russia's great power status.[107] Hence, their links with the old regime, and in the case of Primakov and Putin with the KGB, were no impediment to their popularity and rising fortunes. When Boris Yeltsin resigned, on 31 December 1999, on the eve of the new millennium, and handed over to the until recently almost unknown Vladimir Putin, the era of revolutionary upheaval seemed to have drawn to a close. As Russia set out on its new millennium, with a new president (from a familiar old firm), its political symbolism and myths suggested that the legacy of the Soviet and tsarist past – their nationalism, militarism and cult of the strong state and ruler – had not been banished as dramatically as it had seemed in August 1991, when Dzerzhinsky's statue was toppled and a new era of freedom, openness and democracy was celebrated. It seemed an ironic commentary on the fate of those hopes that, on 16 Seotember 2002 only a handful of people turned out to demonstrate against Mayor Luzhkov's proposal, made two days earlier, of restoring Dzerzhinsky to his pedestal outside the Lubyanka, a muted echo of the crowds who had celebrated his removal.[108]

Notes

I would like to thank John Murray, of Trinity College, Dublin, for reading a draft of this paper and making several helpful comments on it, and Michael Laffan, of UCD, for apposite illustrations.

1   L. Mumford, *The city in history* (London, 1966), p. 429.

2   See K. Smith, 'An old cathedral for a new Russia: symbolic politics of the reconstituted church of Christ the Saviour', *Religion, State and Society* xxv, 2 (1997), 163–75; Elizabeth Grey, 'Signposts to the past: reinventing political symbols, Moscow 1985–1995' (PhD thesis, University of Cambridge, 1998), to whom I am grateful for kind permission to consult her work; I. de Keghel, 'Die moskauer Erlöserkathedrale als Konstrukt nationaler Identität', *Osteuropa* 2 (1999), 145–59; John Murray, *Politics and place-names: changing names in the late Soviet period* (Birmingham, c.2000).

3   See N. Riasanovsky, *Nicholas I and official nationality* (Berkeley and Los Angeles, 1959), pp. 74–5.

4   On this, see A. Koyré, *La philosophie et le sentiment national en Russie* (Paris, 1929).

5   F. Tyutchev, 'Russia and revolution' (1848) quoted in Riasanovsky, *Nicholas I and official nationality* (1959), p. 123.

6   F. Dostoevsky, *Dnevnik pisatelya* (St Petersburg, 1999), p. 507.

7   K. Leontiev, 'Vizantizm i slavyanstvo' and 'Chem i kak liberalizm nam vreden?' in *Zapiski otshel'nika*, rev. edn (Moscow, 1992). For a survey of these views, see H. Kohn, *Pan-slavism: its history and ideology* (Notre Dame, 1953); J. Lavrin, *Russia, Slavdom and the western world* (London, 1969); M. Petrovich, *Russian pan-slavism* (New York, 1956); E. Thaden, *Conservative nationalism in nineteenth century Russia* (Seattle, 1964); A. Walicki, *The slavophile controversy* (Oxford, 1975).

8   A. Herzen, 'Letter to Jules Michelet' in A. Herzen, *From the other shore* (Oxford, 1979), pp. 199–200.

9   A. Bely, *Petersburg*, trans R. Maguire and J. Malmstad (London, 1978), pp. 2, 10–11: 'All of Petersburg is an infinity of the prospect raised to the nth degree. Beyond Petersburg, there is

nothing'. For similar comments on the geometry of the urban landscape and absolutism, see Mumford, *The city* (1966), pp. 421-5, 442-7.

10 Bely, *Petersburg*, pp. 52-3.

11 Ibid., p. 65.

12 See for example, Dimitri Stremooukhoff, 'Moscow the Third Rome: sources of the doctrine' in M. Cherniavsky (ed.), *The structure of Russian history: interpretive essays* (New York, 1970), pp. 108-25; M. Cherniavsky, *Tsar and people: studies in Russian myths* (New York, 1969), pp. 36-9; Sidney Monas, 'Petersburg and Moscow as cultural symbols' in T. G. Stavrou (ed.), *Art and architecture in nineteenth century Russia* (Bloomington Indiana, 1983), pp. 26-39; K. G. Isupov (ed.), *Moskva-Peterburg: pro et contra: dialog kul'tur v istorii natsional'nogo samosoznaniya: antologiya* (St Petersburg, 2000); A. Blum, 'Changer la ville, changer l'homme' in C. Gousseff (ed.), *Moscou 1918-1941: de l'homme nouveau au bonheur totalitaire* (Paris, 1993), pp. 73-92; C. Gousseff, 'Requiem pour le temple' in ibid., pp. 131-45.

13 See J. van Geldern, *Bolshevik festivals 1917-1920* (London and Berkeley, 1993), pp. 43-6, 82-5. For Lenin's April 1918 Decree on Monumental Art, see V. I. Lenin, *On literature and art* (Moscow, 1970), pp. 222-3 and A. Lunacharsky, 'Lenin and the arts' in ibid., pp. 256-60. C. Lodder, 'Lenin's plan for monumental propaganda' in M. Cullerne Bown and B. Taylor (eds), *Art of the Soviets* (Manchester, 1993), pp. 16-32.

14 A. Room, *Placenames of Russia and the former Soviet Union* (Jefferson NC, London, 1996), p. 8. Between 1923 and 1936, twelve Party decrees and resolutions were issued, changing 233 toponyms to names based on Lenin, a further seventy-three based on Ulyanov and forty-one on Ilyich. L. Ryazanova-Clarke and T. Wade, *The Russian language today* (London and New York, 1999), pp. 283-6. Timothy Colton, *Moscow, governing the Soviet metropolis* (Camb. Mass., 1995), p. 267.

15 Ryazanova-Clarke and Wade, *Russian language today* (1999), p. 289.

16 Murray, *Politics and place-names* (2000), pp. 5-33 for the development of the toponymic movement in late Soviet Russia. Ryazanova-Clarke and Wade, *Russian language today*, pp. 290-1; Grey, 'Signposts', pp. 41-4. By 1992, sixty-three cities had reverted to their historical names. For a nationalist intervention (on the renaming of the monastic site of Zagorsk), see 'Radi dukhovnogo ozdorovleniya', *Literaturnaya Rossiya*, 11 Nov. 1989.

17 J. Bouvard, 'Les palais souterrains du métropolitain' in C. Gousseff (ed.), *Moscou 1918-1941* (1993), pp. 93-129; Colton, *Moscow*, pp. 255-7. For a contemporary stalinist exegesis of the metro's significance, see A. Kosarev (ed.), *Istoriya metro imeni L.M. Kagaonovicha: kak my stroili metro* (Moscow, 1935). For a study that concentrates on the politics and economics of the project, see Dietmar Neutatz, *Die Moskauer Metro: von den ersten Plänen bis zur Grossbaustelle des Stalinismus* (Cologne, Weimar and Vienna, 2001).

18 Ryazanova-Clarke and Wade, *Russian language today*, p. 295.

19 V. Reshetnikov, 'Old Moscow to be rehabilitated', *Current Digest of the Soviet Press* LXII, 44 (1990), 29. Ryazanova-Clarke and Wade, *Russian language today*, pp. 294-6.

20 Ryazonova-Clarke and Wade, *Russian language today*, pp. 296-7; Colton, *Moscow* (1995), p. 734. There was significant opposition to the proposal to rename a street after Sakharov even within Moscow City Council's Renaming Commission. I am grateful to John Murray for this observation.

21 Gorbachev addressing the October 1990 CPSU Plenum, in *Current Digest of the Soviet Press* XLII, 41 (1990), 4.
22 'Decree of the president . . . on the Desecration of Monuments', *Current Digest of the Soviet Press* XLII, 41 (1990), 25–6.
23 *Current Digest of the Soviet Press* XLIII, 23 (1991), 14.
24 For images and commentaries, see *Ogonek* 36–7 (1991). My thanks to John Murray for his eye-witness impressions of this event. For a retrospective account, see Colton, *Moscow* (1995), pp. 656–7. For an interpretation of this iconic moment, see M. Yampolsky, 'In the shadow of monuments: notes on iconoclasm and time' in N. Condee (ed.), *Soviet hieroglyphics: visual culture in late Soviet Russia* (Bloomington, Indiana, 1995), pp. 105–7. Attempts to replace Dzerzhinsky with a cross were allegedly frustrated by the authorities.
25 Colton, *Moscow*, p. 365. Two hundred and fifty-nine Lenin statues still survive, 'Klub glavnikh redaktorov', Kul'tura t.v., 26 Nov. 2002.
26 M. Yampolsky, 'In the shadow of monuments', in Condee (ed.), *Soviet hieroglyphics*, p. 96.
27 Colton, *Moscow*, p. 734.
28 See V. Aksenov, *Moskovskie novosti* (hereafter *MN*), 13–19 Nov. 1997, 1, 4.
29 See N. Tumarkin, *Lenin lives! The Lenin cult in Soviet Russia* (Cambridge, Mass., 1983).
30 See Christel Lane, *The rites of rulers: ritual in industrial society – the Soviet case* (Cambridge, 1981), pp. 210–12.
31 Aksenov, *MN*, 13–19 Nov. 1997, 4. Murray, *Placenames* (2000), p. 136 cites a poll of 1996, which suggested that many Russians saw Lenin as the second greatest leader after Peter the Great.
32 Yu. Kariakin, *Current Digest of the Soviet Press* XLI, 28 (1989), 17.
33 A. A. Sokolov, *Current Digest of the Soviet Press* XLI, 29 (1989), 18.
34 N. Krivomazov, *Current Digest of the Soviet Press* XLIII, 44 (1991), 18.
35 Murray, *Placenames*, pp. 164–5 lists sixteen assaults on Lenin monuments between 1990 and 1991.
36 Grey, 'Signposts', p. 59, n.121, K. Verdery, *The political lives of dead bodies: reburial and post-socialist change* (NY, 1999), p. 44. Colton, *Moscow* (1995), p. 906, n. 119.
37 N. Gervorkyan, *MN*, 22 Oct. 1993, 15. I. Zbarsky and S Hutchinson, *Lenin's embalmers* (London, 1998), pp. 195–6.
38 Gervorkyan, *MN*, 22 Oct. 1993, 15. *MN*, 22 Oct. 1993, 1.
39 Zbarsky and Hutchinson, *Lenin's embalmers*, pp. 205–6. Grey, 'Signposts', p. 60. Verdery, *The political lives of dead bodies*, pp. 12–13, 131–2, n. 28. V. Voloshina, *MN*, 3–9 Apr. 1997, 3.
40 'Patriarch', *Current Digest of the Post-Soviet Press* LI, 21 (1999), 11. 'Seleznev', *BBC Summary of World Broadcasts*, SU/3550B/4 (15) 2 June 1999. 'I won't be running', *Current Digest of Post-Soviet Press* LI, 27 (1999), 11.
41 *Nezavisimaya gazeta*, 17 July 2001, 1.
42 G. Batsanova, *Current Digest of the Soviet Press* XLII, 44 (1990), 30. This was also the spirit in which it was laid, in the observation of the author. One of the few subsequent monuments to the gulag, by Ernest Neizvestny, was opened in Magadan in 1995. See A. Tolstoy, *Itogi*, 18 June 1996, 74.
43 V. Bykov, *MN*, 1–18 Sept. 1991, 2. Aksenov, *MN*, 13–19 Nov. 1997, 4. Grey, 'Signposts', pp. 78–80.

44 Grey, 'Signposts', p. 81. M. Urban, 'Remythologising the Russian state', *Europe-Asia Studies* L, 6 (1998), 982–3, notes this revalorisation of space and points also to the conversion of the Manezh, site of the great democratic demonstrations in 1990–1, into a shopping mall.

45 Khazanov interviewed by A. Kyrlezhev, *Russkaya mysl'*, 16–22 July 1998, 19. Yampolsky, 'In the shadow of monuments', in Condee (ed.), *Soviet hieroglyphics*, p. 97.

46 *BBC Summary of World Broadcasts*, SU/3834 B/1, (3), 8 May 2000.

47 Grey, 'Signposts', p. 52.

48 *Rossiiskaya gazeta* (hereafter *RG*), 11 May 1995, 1 for description. For criticisms of the aesthetics of the Zhukov statue, see Chegodaeva, *MN*, 28 May–4 June 1995, 19. Grey, 'Signposts', p. 72, points out that the Zhukov statue represents a rejection of Soviet iconography and a return to Russian national style. For further analyses see Tolstoy, *Itogi*, 18 June 1996, 74; W. Slater, 'Russia's imagined history: visions of the Soviet past and the new "Russian Idea"', *Journal of Communist Studies and Transition Politics* XIV, 4 (Dec. 1998), 81–3.

49 Grey, 'Signposts', pp. 70–1. Y. Burtin, *MN*, 11–18 June 1995, 19.

50 'On the verge of a referendum', *MN*, 27 Feb.–5 Mar. 1997, 15. Monuments to which objections were raised included Peter the Great, his Tragedy of the Peoples at Poklonnaya gora and Children's Fairytales in the Manezh shopping complex, of which he was the chief designer. See too Hearst, *The Guardian*, 5 July 2001, 16.

51 Y. Luzhkov, *Nashe nasledie* 35–6 (1995), 10. Tolstoy, *Itogi*, 18 June 1996, 74.

52 See N. Tumarkin, *The living and the dead: the rise and fall of the cult of World War II in Russia* (NY, 1994), pp. 127–8, 134–44, 175–81, 209–11. Lane, *Rites of rulers*, pp. 140-9. Lane, 'From ideology to political tradition: recent developments in Soviet beliefs and rituals in the "patriotic tradition"' in C. Arvidson and L. Blomqvist (eds), *Symbols of power: the esthetics of political legitimation in the Soviet Union and Eastern Europe* (Stockholm, 1987), pp. 87–96. S. Creuzberger, '"Ich war in einem völlig anderen Krieg". Die sowjetische und russische Historiographie über den "Grossen Vaterländischen Krieg"', *Osteuropa* 5 (1998), 505–9, 517–18.

53 For the pre-history of the monument, the objections to it and attempts to redesign it, see Tumarkin, *The living and the dead*, pp. 216-20; M. Chegodaeva, *MN*, 11–18 June 1995, 19; Ye. Lisanov, *Krasnaya zvezda*, 7 May 1995.

54 Lisanov, *Krasnaya zvezda*, 7 May 1995. 'Prazdnik', *RG*, 11 May 1995, 3.

55 Another memorial to the War was opened at the Kursk battlefield on 3 May 1995. Here too the theme of the unity of the people of the former USSR in a great national effort was emphasised by the leaders present: Deputy Prime Minister Oleg Soskovets (associated with the Party of War), the Belarusian leader Lukashenko, the former Politburo member Nikolai Ryzhkov and Patriarch Aleksii II. The memorial consisted of a museum; the new church of SS Peter and Paul, dedicated by the patriarch; and a Victory memorial by Vyacheslav Klykov at the battlefield. The latter was a fifty-metre high bell-tower topped by the Kursk Madonna, with reliefs on its sides, representing 'heroic episodes from Russian history and spirituality' (St George, Zhukov, the Holy Trinity, tanks and cannons). It was intended to remind people that victory was due not so much to military hardware as to 'the people's historic experience, its spirituality,' according to its creator. The complex was again remarkable for its fusion of traditional religious, national and Soviet iconography, and as an indication of the Russian Orthodox Church's increasing integration into the new

state ceremonial and symbolism. Ralph della Cava, when he visited the site, noted that it had become a centre of pilgrimage. Lisanov, *Krasnaya zvezda*, 5 May 1995; 'Geroizm' *RG*, 5 May 1995, 1; R. della Cava, 'Reviving Orthodoxy in Russia', *Cahiers du monde russe* XXXVIII, 3 (July–Sept., 1997), 394 n. 35, 410.

56 Chernomyrdin, *RG*, 11 May 1995, 2. See *RG*, 8 May 1995, 1–2 for Yeltsin's Victory Day speech, which was more revisionist in tone, although it also presented the War as a national (rather than, as previously, a regime) achievement.

57 'Prazdnik', *RG*, 11 May 1995, 3.

58 Burtin, *MN*, 11–18 June 1995, 19. See also Chegodaeva, *MN*, 11–18 June 1995, 19.

59 See for example *RG*, 6 May 2000, pp. 1, 4–5.

60 *BBC Summary of World Broadcasts*, SU/3835 B/2 (3, 4) 9 May 2000. Stalin's bust and plaque now stand in the entrance with those other historic generals including Zhukov and Kutuzov.

61 R. Armeyev, *Current Digest of the Soviet Press* XLII, 44 (1990), 29. Ye. Mikhailova and Paradin, *Pravda*, 5 Nov. 1993, 1.

62 *MN*, 22 Oct. 1993, 1. Gevorkyan, *MN*, 22 Oct. 1993, 15.

63 See R. Stites, 'The origins of Soviet ritual style: symbol and festival in the Russian revolution' in Arvidson and Blomqvist, *Symbols of power*, p. 28. The parallels between February 1917 and 1991 in the paucity, conservatism and nature of ceremonial and symbolic change is striking.

64 Cited in Grey, 'Signposts', p. 51.

65 See Luzhkov interview in V.P. Yenisherlov, 'Moskva na puti k yubileyu', *Nashe nasledie* 35-6 (1996), 5–8, where he endorses much of the Soviet contribution to Moscow's architecture but deplores stalinist demolitions and outlines his own architectural plans for the 850th anniversary of Moscow. Luzhkov, *My deti tvoi, Moskva* (Moscow, 1996) a glossy version of his autobiography produced for the 1996 mayoral elections, contains not only nostalgic references to his modest Soviet childhood and the War years, but also many pictures of his public works in Moscow, both restorations and new buildings. For the presidential campaign in 2000, the supporting literature was less narrowly focussed. V. Milyutenko, *Mer v kepke* (Moscow, 1999) was a cheap format mass edition, which included long sections on his public works (designed to show Luzhkov as a competent *khozyain*, the master who runs a tight ship. I. Bortsov, *Luzhkov* (Rostov-on-the-Don, 1999) stressed his character as a religious, nationalist and state-builder, keen on good links with the provinces.

66 D. Shvidkovsky, *Itogi*, 18 June 1986, 75.

67 Kyrlezhev, *Russkaya Mysl'*, 16–22 July 1998, 18–19.

68 For two detailed, perceptive accounts, see K. Smith, 'An old cathedral for a new Russia', *Religion, State and Society* XXV, 2 (1997), 163–75; Isabelle de Keghel, 'Die moskauer Erlöserskathedrale als Konstrukt nationaler Identität', *Osteuropa* 2 (1999), 145–59.

69 'Khram Khrista Spasitelya', *Voenno-istoricheskii zhurnal* 8 (1990), 26–31; 'Khram Khrista Spasitelya', *Voenno-istoricheskii zhurnal* 1 (1991), 89, 92. A. Ivanov, 'Taina chertol'skogo urochishcha', *Nauka i zhizn'* 1 (1989), 67–9. For Ton, and his place in the cultural history of mid-nineteenth century Russia, see T. A. Slavina, *Konstantin Ton* (Moscow, 1989), pp. 86–93; 112–23 for his work on the cathedral.

70 See Richard Taylor, *October* (London, 2002), pp. 18–21. Taylor observes that Eisenstein used a papier-maché reproduction of the statue, which had already been destroyed.

71 Gropius and Le Corbusier were among those who submitted designs for the Palace: V. Paperny, *Kul'tura dva* (Ann Arbor, 1985), pp. 22–3; L. Smirnov, 'Sotsialisticheskaya utopiya kak arkhitekturnaya real'nost'', *Nashe nasledie* 35-6 (1995), 203–5; Colton, *Moscow*, pp. 260, 262, 264; Helen Rappaport, *Joseph Stalin: a biographical companion* (Santa Barbara and Oxford, 1999), p. 201. See too C. Gousseff, 'Requiem pour le temple' in C. Gousseff (ed.), *Moscou, 1918–1941* (1993), pp. 130–45, who sheds interesting light of the cathedral's role in the 1920s.

72 Texts reproduced by I. de Keghel, 'Ein "Nationalheiligtum" wird wieder entdekt', *Osteuropa* 2 (1999) A72, A76–7.

73 'Fond', *Literaturnaya Rossiya*, 29 Sept. 1989, 11. The language of their appeal was quasi-religious. Borisov, 'Tsentr sobornosti', *Literaturnaya Rossiya*, 29 Sept. 1989, 11. 'Pod klyuch?', *Literaturnaya Rossiya*, 22 Sept. 1989, 11. V. Soloukhin, *Literaturnaya Rossiya*, 2 February 1990, 8, who stressed that the rebuilt church should retain its original significance as a memorial to the 1812 war. Smith. 'Old cathedral', *Religion, State and Society* xxv, 2 (1997), 167–8.

74 B. Sporov, 'Vossozdanie' in M. S. Mostovsky (ed.), *Khram Khrista Spasitelya* (Moscow, 1996), pp. 218–21. This is a useful collection of official statements about the project. Korneshov, *RG*, 17 May 1994, 7.

75 'Etapy stroitel'stva', *Yuny khudozhnik* 6 (1996), 26; M. Ryazantsev, 'I sovtvorim plody dostoinye pokayaniya', *Nashe nasledie* 35-6 (1995), 222–5; M. Deich, 'Khram Khrista ili pamyatnik meru?', *Ogonek* 48–9 (1994), 10.

76 See the declarations of S. G. Semanenko, deputy director of the Fund for Financial Support for the Reconstruction of the Cathedral of Christ the Saviour, in Semanenko, 'Shchedrost' dushi', *Yuny khudozhnik* 6 (1996), 27; Ryazantsev, *Nashe nasledie* 35-6 (1995), 225; Smith, 'Old cathedral', 169; S. Varshavchik, 'Chto khram gryadusshchii nam gotovit?', *Ogonek* 45 (1995), 29; Deich, *Ogonek*, 48–9 (1994), 10; Loshchits, *Liternaturnaya Rossiya*, 24 Nov. 1989, 21. Chegodaeva, *MN*, 20 Aug. 1989; Gromov, *RG*, 10 Jan. 1995.

77 S. Smolkin, *RG*, 15 Oct. 1994, 3. A. Bossart, 'Teatr vremen Luzhkova i Sinoda', *Stolitsa*, 8 Jan. 1995, 11. P. Palamarchuk, *Literaturnaya Rossiya*, 25 Aug. 1989, 6.

78 M. Posokhin and A. M. Denisov, 'Vtoroe rozhdenie khrama', *Yuny khudozhnik* 6 (1996), 24–5. Varshavchik, *Ogonek* 45 (1995), 29.

79 L. V. Shirshov and I. V. Novik, *Khram Khrista Spasitelya: vossozdanoe skul'pturnoe i zhivopisnoe ubranstvo* (Moscow, 1999), pp. 25, 28, 40.

80 Sporov, 'Vossozdanie' in Mostovsky (ed.), *Khram Khrista Spasitelya* (1996), p. 215.

81 Posokhin and Denisov, 'Vtoroe rozhdenie khrama', *Yuny khudozhnik* 6 (1996), 22. I. de Keghel, *Osteuropa*, 2 (1999), 156.

82 De Keghel notes this significance, I. de Keghel, *Osteuropa* 2 (1999), 147, 156. Another critic observed that the cathedral had been intended by Alexander I as a monument to the Divine People, by Nicholas I as a monument to himself, while in the 1990s, it became a symbol not just of 'the Russia we have lost' but also of nostalgia for superpower status and imperial ambitions, M. Pozdnyaev, 'Khram Khrista Spasitelya', *Novoe vremya* 36 (1994), 37.

83 Yeltsin, 'Obrashchenie', *RG*, 7 Sept. 1994.

84 Speech of 7 September 1994 reproduced in Sporov, 'Vossozdanie' in Mostovsky (ed.), *Khram Khrista Spasitelya* (1996), pp. 209–12. The oversight committee's initial address of

7 September 1994 on the topic was, like the patriarch's speech, sprinkled with Biblical quotations and couched in something between the style of an episcopal missive and a tsarist *ukaz*. It also presented the project in terms of universal moral cleansing, repentance for the blood spilt in Soviet times, and called on Russians to take 'the road to the church', ibid., p. 213. The tone was maintained by Luzhkov, on this occasion, and by Yeltsin, the following year, when decreeing tax breaks for the sponsors, ibid., pp. 214, 247–8.

85 Aleksii II (Ridiger), patriarch of all Russia, 'Nyne k nemu vozvrashchaemsya', *Yuny khudozhnik* 6 (1996), 2.

86 'Slovo [. . .] Patriarkha', *Zhurnal Moskovskoi Patriarkhii* 6 (1997), 19 for his speech at the Easter service in the cathedral. 'Slovo Patriarkha', *Zhurnal Moskovskoi Patriarkhii* 10 (1997), 25–6 for his speech on 3 September 1997 opening of the cathedral. 'Bol'shoi khorovoi sobor', ibid., p. 31, for comments on the jubilee concert held there on 6 September 1997, which again stresses that the cathedral is a symbol of Faith, Fatherland and National Unity.

87 Speech reproduced in Sporov, 'Vossozdanie' in Mostovsky (ed.), *Khram Khrista Spasitelya* (1996) pp. 244–5. For echoes of this official line see Ryazantsev, *Nashe nasledie* 35–6 (1995), 225; Z. Tsereteli, 'V rusle drevnikh traditsii', *Yuny khudozhnik* 6 (1996), 27, 42; Shidkovsky, *Itogi*, 18 June 1996, 75.

88 See G. Seide, 'Orthodoxie, Staatsmacht und Armee', *Osteuropa* 10 (1996), 1013–15, 1019. N. Gvozdev, 'The new Party card?', *Problems of Post-Communism*, XLVII, 6 (Nov.–Dec. 2000), 29–38, who argues that Orthodoxy is set to become the new ideology and civil religion of post-Soviet Russia. For further evidence of close church-state relations, especially with the military, see R. della Cava, *Cahiers du monde russe* XXXVIII, 3 (July–Sep. 1997), 394–5, 397–8.

89 Smolkin, *RG*, 15 Oct. 1994. Gromov, *RG*, 10 Jan. 1995.

90 'RF: politics', *Current Digest of the Post-Soviet Press* XLIX, 45 (1997), 13 for divergent public attitudes to the renamed celebrations of 7 November.

91 May Day, 7 November and 8 March (International Women's Day) were retained. 12 June 1990 was proclaimed Russian Independence Day in 1992, but it was controversial in the political class and most people were unaware of its existence. Grey, 'Signposts', pp. 95–6, 116. 22 August was designated State Flag Day in 1994 but also failed to catch on, M. Kushtapin and N. Paklin, *RG*, 22 Aug. 1997.

92 Della Cava, *Cahiers du monde russe* XXXVIII, 3 (July–Sept. 1997), 92–3. Gvozdev, *Problems of Post-Communism* XLVII, 6 (Nov.–Dec. 2000), 36 cites the journalist Yekaterina Viktorova as observing that Easter had replaced May Day as a source of public drama and meaning.

93 For the inauguration ceremony, see 'Prezidentskii salyut', *RG*, 6 May 2000, 1. Bychkov, *Moskovskii komsomolets*, 16 Aug. 2000.

94 N. Davis, 'Tribulations, trials and troubles for the Russian Orthodox Church', *Religion in Eastern Europe* XX, 6 (December 2000), 39–42, for the church's murky financial privileges.

95 Musicologists do not agree, however, with this traditional Russian reception of the work. See David Brown, 'Mikhail Glinka', in *The new Grove Russian masters*, 3 vols (London, 1986), I, pp. 9-12; John Warrack, 'Russian opera' in R. Leach and V. Borovsky (eds), *A history of the Russian theatre* (Cambridge, 1999), pp. 203–4.

96 *Vedomosti Federal'nogo Sobraniya Rossiiskoi Federatsii*, 9 (242), 21 Mar. 2001, 52–3.

97 'Putin picks Soviet anthem, stirs discord', *Current Digest of the Post-Soviet Press* XXII, 49 (3 Jan. 2001), 1–4; Soboleva, *Rossiskaya gosudarstvennaya simbolika* (Moscow, 2002), pp. 187–8.

98 Yeltsin called for a Russian Idea to unite the nation and inspire its rebirth in July 1986 and appointed Georgii Satarov to head a commission on the subject. They were to come up with a proposal for the end of the millennium. Instead, Satarov judged a competition launched by the government newspaper, *RG*, on the subject. 'Kto my, kuda idem', *RG*, 30 July 1996. M. Urban, 'Remythologising the Russian state', *Europe-Asia Studies* 1, 6 (1998), 969. First prize went to a local deputy in Saratov, who argued that incompatibility with the West was the first principle of Russianness, with collectivism, 'non-marketness', love of faith, nation and *derzhavnost'* as other fundamental charcteristics, G. Sudakov, *RG*, 17 Sept. 1996, p. 4. Satarov produced no more than an analysis of this debate, Satarov (ed.), *Rossiya v poiskakh idei. Analyz pressy* (Moscow, 1997).

99 For analyses of the rise of a new official nationalism, see: Christiane Uhlig, 'Nationale Identitätskonstruktionen für ein postsowjetisches Russland,' *Osteuropa* 12 (1997), 1191–206, who sees the revival of nationalism in intellectual and political circles as a response to the failure of modernisation; Gerhard Simon, 'Auf der Suche nach der "Idee für Russland"', *Osteuropa* 12 (1997), 1167–89, who suggests that a new patriotic consensus (which defined Russia as a great power whose interests and culture diverged from the West) had emerged by the mid-1990s; Dmitri Shlapentokh, 'Eurasianism, past and present', *Communist and Post-Communist Studies* XXX, 2 (1997), 129–51, who sees post-Soviet Russia as evolving along nationalist and authoritarian lines and drawing ideological inspiration from the Eurasianism of the emigrés of the 1920s; V. Tolz, 'Forging the nation: national identity and nation-building in post-communist Russia', *Europe-Asia Studies*, l, 6 (1998), 993–1022, who, by contrast with Shlapentokh, sees the Yeltsin regime as attempting to promote ideas of civic nationhood, although increasingly influenced by the nationalist ideas of the opposition; Urban, 'Remythologising the Russian state', 985 notes the similarity of the ideas of the communist-patriots, democrats and 'state scribes' on the national idea; E. Shiraev and V. Zubok, *Anti-Americanism from Stalin to Putin* (NY, 2000), traces the rise of this phenomenon in the 1990s and the influence of neo-conservative nationalism on Russian foreign policy.

100 'Controversy over the Tsar's remains', *Current Digest of the Post-Soviet Press* XLIX, 45 (1997), 13; ibid., XLIX, 46 (1997), 9, 23.

101 I. Sviridov, *Russkaya mysl'*, 5–11 March 1998, 1, 19; I. Ilovaiskaya, *Russkaya mysl'*, 23–29 July 1998, 19; M. Meilakh, *Russkaya mysl'*, 23–29 July 1998, 17; 'state funeral', *Current Digest of the Post-Soviet Press* L, 29 (1998) 4; L. Aron, *Boris Yeltsin: a revolutionary life* (London, 2000), pp. 111–13.

102 I. Sviridov, *Russkaya mysl'*, 5–11 Mar. 1998, 1, 19; 'Pogrebenie', *Russkaya mysl'*, 23–29 July 1998, 18; 'State funeral', *Current Digest of the Post-Soviet Press* L, 29 (1998), 1–5; *Current Digest of the Post-Soviet Press* L, 28 (1998), 8; Aron, *Boris Yeltsin* (2000), p. 683.

103 Yeltsin cited in 'State funeral', *Current Digest of the Post-Soviet Press* L, 29 (1998), 4. Nikolai Romanov cited in ibid., 1, 5. Sviridov, *Russkaya mysl'*, 5–11 March 1998, 19.

104 'Press conference on results of Jubilee Bishops' Council', 17 Aug. 2000, www.russian-orthodox-church.org.ru. 'Russian Orthodox Church canonises last Tsar', *BBC Summary of World Broadcasts*, SU/3920 B/1, (1), 16 Aug. 2000; 'Council canonises Tsar', *Current Digest of*

Post-Soviet Press LIII, 33 (2000), 42–3; W. Slater, 'A modern-day saint? Metropolitan Ioann and the post-Soviet Russian Orthodox Church', *Religion, State and Society* XXVIII, 4 (2000), 313–14; Davis, *Religion in Eastern Europe*, XX, 6 (Dec. 2000), 42–3; D. Pospelovsky, *Russkaya mysl'*, 13 Feb. 1997, 4.

105 'Doklad predsedatelya kommissii Svyatogo Synoda po kanonizatsii', *Zhurnal Moskovskoi Patriarkhii* 6 (1997), 26–8.'Patriarch sees canonisation', *BBC Summary of World Broadcasts*, SU/3920 B/2 (6), 15 Apr. 2000; 'Church canonises Tsar', *Current Digest of Post-Soviet Press* LIII 33 (2000), 8; Davis, *Religion in Eastern Europe* XX, 6 (Dec. 2000), 42–3; Kyrlezhev, 'Yubileiny arkiepeisky sobor', *Russkaya mysl'*, 31 Aug.–6 Sep. 2000, 1, 20–1; G. Stricker, 'Zar Nikolaj II', *Osteuropa* 11 (2000), 1187–96.

106 Fifty per cent of Russians in 1995 and 55 per cent in 1999 believed Western democracy to be incompatible with Russia's traditions (while 28–30 per cent disagreed). In November 1999, 41 per cent believed the West wanted Russia to be a third-world state and 38 per cent that it wanted to destroy Russia as an independent state. Shiraev and Zubok, *Anti-Americanism* (2000), pp. 71–1, citing VTsIOM and ROMIR polls. For an important study of public opinion, see M. Wyman, *Public opinion in post-communist Russia* (L., NY, 1997).

107 For Putin's nationalism see: 'Russia at the turn of the millennium' in N. Gevorkyan, N. Timakova and A. Koleshikov (eds), *First person: an astonishingly frank self-portrait of Russia's President Vladimir Putin* (London, 2000), pp. 209–19, where he stresses the importance of the Russian Idea, based on patriotism, the greatness of Russia, statism, social solidarity (i.e. *narodnost', derzhavnost', sobornost'*). *BBC Summary of World Broadcasts* SU/3865 B/1 (1) 13 June 2000; ibid., SU/3888 B/1 (1), 10 July 2000, a carefully crafted call for a strong state to defend civic, economic and political freedoms; ibid., SU/3893 B/1 (1). For analyses, see E. Schneider, *Putins Aufsteig zur Macht* (Berichte des Bundesinstituts für ostwissenschaftliche und internationale Studien, 29/2000); S. Mendelson, 'The Putin path: civil liberties and human rights in retreat', *Problems of Post-Communism* LXVII, 5 (Sept.–Oct. 2000), 3–12; Amy Knight, 'The enduring legacy of the KGB in Russian politics', *Problems of post-communism* LXVII, 4 (July–Aug. 2000), 3–15; 'Putin, Russia languish in a semi-Soviet limbo', *Current Digest of the Post-Soviet Press* LII, 33 (2000), 11, 24.

108 O. Latsis, *Novye izvestiya*, 29 June 2000, 1, 4. M.-P. Subtil, *Le Monde*, 18 Sept. 2002, 1. N. Davydova, *MN*, 17–23 Sept. 2002, 7.

Index

Aberdeen, Lord, 186
Abingdon chronicle, 18
Acallam na Senórach, 244
Acheson, Dean, 199, 201–2
Adams, Gerry, 212
Adenauer, Konrad, 338, 340, 347, 349
Adomnán, abbot of Iona, 240
Adrian IV, Pope, 68, 108
Aeneid, 240, 241, 247
Æthelwig, abbot of Evesham, 19, 23
agriculture, 319, 331
    beef trade, 146
    cattle graziers, 321–2
    and environment, 324–5
    experimental, 261
Agriculture, Department of, 223, 329
Aiken, Frank, 194
Aleksii II, patriarch, 375–6, 378, 384, 388, 390
Alexander I, tsar, 386, 389
Alexander III, pope, 63, 64, 69
Alexander III, tsar, 386, 387
America, British, *see also* United States
    emigration to, 137, 138–44
    immigration laws, 134–5, 136–8
    Irish-born elites, 132–49, 155–75
    penal laws, 134–6, 144
    trade with, 145–7
    and Ulster, 133–4, 148
American National Biography (Garraty), 159–60, 161, 163
American Revolution, 136, 147, 148, 157
    Irish officers and, 166
anglicisation, 88–9, 133
Anglo-American alliance
    Carter initiative, 207–10
    effects of First World War, 186–90
    effects of Second World War, 191–8
    influence of Ireland, 185–213
    post-Cold War, 211–13
Anglo-Irish Agreement, 1985, 209, 210
Anglo-Irish Economic Committee, 224–5, 228–9
Anglo-Irish Free Trade Area Agreement, 1965, 224–5, 228, 231
Anglo-Irish Treaty, 1921, 190, 193

Anglo-Norman Conquest, 1169, historiography of, 25–32
Anglo-Saxons, 12–13, 15–16, 27
Annals of Clonmacnoise, 278
Annals of the Four Masters, 270, 272, 276, 277
Annals of Tigernach, 271
Annals of Ulster, 271
anti-Semitism, 344–5
Antrim, County, 100, 165
Arbour Day, 323
architecture
    Moscow, 364, 384–91
    preservation of, 318–19, 331
Ardfert and Aghadoe, diocese of, 82, 85
Ardilaun, Lord, 326
Armagh, 247, 248
army, *see* military service
Arnold, Matthew, 286–7, 289
Aron, Raymond, 310
    analysis of mouvement de mai, 303–7
    on use of barricades, 312–13
Arterial Drainage Act, 1945, 322, 324
Arts Council, Irish, 327–8
Asquith, H. H., 186–7
Attlee, Clement, 198, 201–2, 203
Aughrim, battle of, 134, 318
Augustine, St, 290–1
Auschwitz, 336, 337, 339, 342
Austria, 64, 88, 203, 337
    Irish colleges in Hausmacht, 100
    and Italy, 63, 65
    positions of Irish, 98–9

Babi Yar, massacre of, 343, 344
Bach, J. S., 293
Baginbun, Anglo-Norman landing at, 25, 277
Balfour, Arthur, 187, 190
Baltimore, Md, 147–8, 166, 167, 174
Bannockburn, battle of, 38, 40, 42, 44, 47
Bantry Bay, County Cork, 189
Barcelona, Treaty of, 1529, 109
Barons' wars, The (Drayton), 50
barricades
    in *mouvement de mai*, 305–7
    in Paris revolutions, 306–10

Index

Barton, Robert, 323
Becket, Thomas, archbishop of Canterbury, 42
  holy oil of, 47
Belfast Naturalists' Field Club, 319
Belfast News-Letter, 141, 147
Belloc, Hilaire, 285, 288
Bely, Andrei, 366–8
Benz, Wolfgang, 344, 348
Berehaven, County Cork, 189, 193
Berkeley, Bishop George, 264
Berkeley Castle, 41, 48
Berlin, 382
  fall of Wall, 55, 211, 339
  Wehrmacht exhibition, 337
Bertolini, Francesco, 66–7
Beveridge Report, 294
Birmingham Festival, 283, 284–5, 291
Birmingham Oratory, 289, 290
Blanqui, Auguste, 301, 309–11, 313
Blascaod Mór National Historic Park Bill, 1989, 331
Blasket Islands, 318
Blok, Alexander, 367, 368
Boate, Gerard, 259–60
Boate brothers, 259, 267
Bohemia, 85, 88, 99
Boniface IX, pope, 49
Bord Fáilte, *see* Irish Tourist Board
Bordeaux, 87, 102
borough charters, reform of, 124, 126
Bossi, Umberto, 56, 70
Boston, 137, 148, 172
botanic gardens, Glasnevin, 266
Boundary Commission, 191
Bourn Vincent Memorial Park, Killarney, 325–7, 329, 330, 331
Bower, Walter, 44, 45
Bowes, John, lord chancellor, 135–6
Boyd, Wesley, 226, 227
Boyne, battle of the, 127, 134
Brabant, Margaret, duchess of, 47
Braganza, Joao de, king of Portugal, 97
Braudel, Fernand, 155, 175
Brecht, Bertolt, 52
Bremen, 352
  Wehrmacht exhibition, 337, 345–8
Brendan, St, voyage of, 240
Bridlington Priory, 42
Britain, *see also* Anglo-American alliance
  and America, 132, 158
  and EEC/EU, 185
    applications, 221–33
    associate membership possible, 227–33
  emigration to, 324
  first British Empire, 132, 136

Brown, George, 225–7
Brown, R. A., 12–13, 14, 15–16, 16, 17, 21
Brown brothers, 166, 167
Bruce, Edward, 43
Bruce, Robert, 46
Brunner, Manfred, 348, 349
Brut chronicle, 40–1, 42
Buckingham, duke of, 50
Bulfin, William, 321–2
Bulkeley, Richard, 164, 165
Bund freier Bürger (BfB), 348, 349–50
Burgundy, duchy of, 102, 109
Burgundy, duke of, 98, 102
Burke, Edmund, 135
Burley, Rosa, 283–4, 291
Burren, County Clare, 244–5
Burrowes, Robert, 253, 264
Burton, Philip, 204–5
Bush, President George, 211, 212
Bush, President George W., 213
Butler, Isaac, 262, 263
Butler, Sir Theobald (Toby), 127
Byrne, Francis John, 31, 248

Callaghan, James, 209
Calvinism, 80, 85, 88
Cambrai, Treaty of, 1529, 109, 110
Campion, Edmund, 274
Canada, 135
  compared with United States, 157–8
  elite-to-population ratio, 162–3
  industrial development, 166–7
  Irish elites in, 155–75
    education, 172–3, 174
    industry, 166–7, 173
    journalism, 169–70, 173
    law, 171
    politics, 167–9, 173
  Irish emigration to, 159
  population, 158
Cantù, Cesare, 63, 64
Carascevo, Hungary, 79–80
Carey, Governor Hugh, 207
Carleton, Guy, 164–5
Carleton, Thomas, 164, 165
Carlyle, Thomas, 15–16
Carmelites, 44, 50
Carolina, 139, 141, 144, 148
carroccio, 57, 60, 65
Carson, Sir Edward, 188, 190
Carter, President Jimmy, 207–10
Cary, Henry, Viscount Falkland, 50
Casement, Sir Roger, 187
Cashel, County Tipperary, 248, 319
Catelyn, Sir Nathaniel, 118

Index

Cathedral of Christ the Saviour, Moscow, 363, 395
   rebuilding of, 386–91
Catherine of Aragon, 103, 104, 105, 107
Catholic Church, 365, *see also* Counter-Reformation
   ascendancy attitude to, 259–60, 265
   in Canada, 165, 174
   Casement trial, 187
   church building, 84
   and disloyalty, 287–8
   in *Dream of Gerontius*, 284–6, 291–2
   and English historiography, 288
   and *Laudabiliter*, 108
   medical education, 254–5
   in North America, 134–6, 159
     education, 172–3
   in Northern Ireland, 198, 204–5
   social reformers, 156
   in 17th c. Hungary, 79–81
Catholic Revival, 288
CDU, Germany, 336, 339
   and *Wehrmacht* exhibition, 345–8, 352
Céitinn, Seathrún, 272, 276, 277
Central Intelligence Agency (CIA), 199, 203
Chamberlain, Austen, 189
Chamberlain, Neville, 192, 193
charitable hospitals, 257
Charitable Infirmary, Dublin, 257
Charles I, king of England, 50
Charles II, king of England, 128
Charles II, king of Spain, 101
Charles III, king of Spain, 97
Charles the Bold, duke of Burgundy, 98, 102
Charles V, emperor, 98–9
   Treaty of Dingle, 102–11
Chechnya, war in, 380–1, 389, 395
Christian Democrats (DC), Italy, 55
Christianity, early
   in *Voyage of Máel Dúin*, 243–4, 245, 246–7, 248
Church of England
   and Catholicism, 288–9
   and Newman, 286–7
Church of Ireland, 143, 175
   and Counter-Reformation, 83, 84
   evangelisation, 84
   Irish in Canada, 163–4
   membership of learned societies, 263
   Ulster plantation, 133
Churchill, Sir Winston, 193, 194, 198, 232, 282
Churchill, Sir Winston (1680), 50
Civil War, American, 157, 170, 172
   Irish officers, 173
Civil War, English, 133, 260

Clare, County, 98, 264
Clare Island, survey of, 317–18, 319
Clarendon, second earl of, 119–20, 121
   on Nagle, 122–3
Clement VII, pope, 107, 108, 109
Clinton, President Bill, 211–13
Clonmacnoise, County Offaly, 244, 318
Cobh (Queenstown), County Cork, 189, 193
Cold War, 185, 207, 212, 338
   end of, 339, 340, 341
   Ireland and Anglo-American alliance, 198–207
College of Physicians, Irish, 255, 261
College of Surgeons, 258
Commendatio lamentabilis (John of London), 37
commission of grace, 121–2
Commissioners of Public Works, 326–7, 329, 330, 331
Common Agricultural Policy, 331
Commonwealth, British, 119, 185, 198
   Ireland leaves, 200
Communist Party, France (PCF), 300, 301, 304
Communist Party, Germany, 342
Communist Party, Russia, 373–4, 375
Como, 59, 63, 69
Compagnies Républicaines de Sécurité (CRS), 299, 306
Connemara, County Galway, 320, 322
Conry, Florence, archbishop of Tuam, 101
conscription crisis, 1918, 188–9
Conservative Party, 190, 209–10
   and Clinton, 211–12
Constance, treaty of, 1183, 58–9, 61, 67
   'liberties' recognised, 69
Constitution of Ireland, 1937, 324–5
Convict Act, Pennsylvania, 1722, 138
Cork, 146, 165, 169
Cork, County, 119, 126, 127, 320
   emigration from, 147
   Smith survey, 264
Cornwallis, Lord, 164
Cosgrave, W. T., 316
Costello, John A., 198, 200, 222, 232, 330
Council of Europe, 222
Council of Ministers, 224, 226
Counter-Reformation, Irish, 78–91, 100
   clergy unmolested, 85
   continental education, 82–3
   episcopate, 86, 90
   intellectual development, 253–4
   receptivity to preachers, 89–90
   role of continental-educated clergy, 85–8
   role of Irish colleges, 100
Coventry letter, 123–4, 126
Craxi, Bettino, 55

Cremona, 58, 59, 63, 69
Cromwell, Oliver, 84, 260
Crosby, Bing, 330
Crowland Abbey, 20
CSU, Germany
    and *Wehrmacht* exhibition, 346, 348–53
cultural nationalism, 317, 318, 325
Czech Republic, 340–1

Dáil Éireann, 228, 318, 323, 326
d'Alembert, Jean le Rond, 267
D'Alton, Revd E. A., 27–8, 30
d'Avaux, comte, 126, 127
Davies, Sir John, 118, 133
Davis, Thomas, 317
Davy, Adam, 46, 47
D'Azeglio, Massimo, 65
de Bonis, Marino, SJ, 78–81, 82, 83, 84, 87, 89
de Clare, Elizabeth and Margaret, 42
de Clare, Richard FitzGilbert, *see* Strongbow
de Courcy, John, 28
de Gaulle, General Charles, 98, 225
    attitude to EEC enlargement, 224, 227–8, 229–30
    May 1968, 299, 301
    second veto, 229, 230
de la More, Sir Thomas, 41
de Lacy, Hugh, 277
de Lacy, Walter, 23
de Montmorency, Hervey, 277
de Neueby, Richard, 45
de Sourdis, Cardinal, 87
de Tynwelle, Thomas, 45
de Valence, Aymer, earl of Pembroke, 51
de Valera, Eamon, 192, 232, 319, 322, 327
    neutrality, 193, 194–8
    US visit, 199
Dease, Ellen, 173, 174–5
Debray, Régis, 301
Democratic Party, USA, 156, 167–8, 188
Denmark, 200, 203
Derry, 140, 142, 194, 204
    Bloody Sunday, 206
Devoy, John, 170
Dictionary of American Biography (Johnson and Malone), 159–60, 161, 163
Dictionary of Canadian Biography, 159–60, 161–2
Dingle, County Kerry, 105
Dingle, Treaty of, 1529
    negotiations, 102–10
    significance of, 110–11
Dominicans, 44, 45, 47, 48, 50
Domville, Sir William, 124
Donegal, County, 97, 143

Donlon, Seán, 207–10
Dostoevsky, F. M., 364, 365, 366, 367
Down, County, 262–3
Downing Street Declaration, 211
Dream of Gerontius (Elgar), 282–95
    Catholicism in, 284–6, 291–2
    first performance, 283–5
    popularity in wartime, 293–5
    structure of, 291–2, 293–4
Duane, William J., 167, 169
Dublin, 32, 139, 146, 164, 166, 169, 170, 174, 278
    Anglo-Norman capture of, 270
    borough reform, 124
    conservation of, 331
    emigration from, 147
    museum, 266
    natural history of, 263, 266
    religious divisions, 265
    weather records, 265–6
Dublin Castle, 122, 189
    and Nagle, 120, 121
    plantations, 133
Dublin Corporation, 257
Dublin medical school, 255, 256
Dublin Philosophical Society, 257, 258–9, 261, 267
Dublin Society, 257, 260–1, 265, 266, 267
    expansion, 266–7
Dun, Sir Patrick, 255, 256, 257
Duty Act, 1730, 138
Dvořák, A., 291
Dzerzhinsky, Felix, 370, 372, 396

Easter Rising, 1916, 186–7, 323, 325
Eden, Anthony, 193, 194, 232
Edinburgh school of medicine, 256, 257
education
    nature study, 319
    in North America, 172–3, 174, 175
Edward I, king of England, 37–8, 48, 50
Edward II, king of England
    contemporary criticism of, 39–44
    cult of sainthood, 46–9
    death of, 41, 47, 52
    historiography of, 37–52
    impostors, 45
    prophecies, 46–7
    sexuality of, 49–50, 51, 52
    tomb of, 48
Edward II (band), 52
Edward III, king of England, 38, 39, 41, 48, 50
Edward the Confessor, king, 21–2, 39, 46
Eichmann trial, 339
Eisenstein, S. M., 387

Elgar, Edward
   Dream of Gerontius, 282–95
Ellis, Havelock, 51
Ely chronicle, 18–19
emigration, 316, 324
   American restrictions, 136–8
   changing attitudes to, 144–5
   emigrants' letters, 141, 142, 143
   Great Famine, 320
   Irish in America, 137, 138–44
      Irish-born elites, 155–75
      urban, 321
   later emigrants blocked, 168–9
   promotion of, 139, 140–4
Engels, F., 311
England, *see also* Britain
   alliance with France, 103, 107, 109
   continental colleges for, 100
   Counter-Reformation, 86
   and Desmond, 102, 105, 107
   free trade, 158–9
Enlightenment, 61, 267
environment, protection of, 175, 318–19, 323, 331–2
Eóganacht Ninussa, 241–2, 248
Europe, Irish integration with, 97–111
European Commission, 224, 227
European Economic Community (EEC), 331
   and Anglo-Irish relations, 224–7
   associate membership, 227–32
   British applications and Ireland, 221–33
   Irish approach to, 222–4
European Free Trade Association (EFTA), 232
European Union (EU), 97, 185, 331
Evesham Abbey, 11, 13, 24
   writ of military summons, 19–21
evictions, 317
Exclusion Crisis, 1680, 50
Expugnatio Hibernica (Giraldus Cambrensis), 271–2, 273, 275, 277
External Affairs, Department of, 195, 198, 205, 223, 325

Federal Bureau of Investigation (FBI), 212
Fenianism, 170
Ferdinand II, emperor, 100
Ferdinand VI, king of Spain, 97
Fernández, Don Gonzalo
   Desmond negotiations, 103–7
feudalism
   and Irish nationalism, 30–1
   and military service, 12–18, 23–4
   and modernisation, 31
Fianna Fáil, 229, 322

Finance, Department of, 222–3, 318–19, 325, 329
Fine Arts Commissioners, 271
First World War
   Anglo-American alliance, 186–90
FitzGerald, Garret, 207, 210
FitzGerald, James, 9th earl of Desmond, 102
FitzGerald, James, 11th earl of Desmond, 97
   assassination, 110
   status of, 108
   Treaty of Dingle, 102–11
FitzGerald, Maurice, 10th earl of Desmond, 102
FitzGerald, Thomas FitzThomas, 108, 110
FitzGerald family (Geraldines), 272
   diplomacy with Spain, 102–11
Five dreams of Edward II (Davy), 46
Flanders, 99, 109, 110
Fled Bricrend, 243
Flores historiarum, 38, 39
Foras Feasa ar Éirinn (Céitinn), 272, 276, 277
Foras Forbartha, An, 331
Forchheimer, Franz, 350, 351
Foreign Affairs, Department of, 208, 210
Foreign Office, UK, 194, 202, 206, 209
forestry, 323, 327, 328
Forza Italia, 55
'Four Horsemen', USA, 207, 208
Framework for Agreement, NI, 211
France, 38, 39, 46, 49, 97, 98, 135, 187, *see also mouvement de mai*; Paris Commune
   attitude to Irish EEC entry, 228, 229–30
   defeated by Italy, 109
   England allied with, 103, 107, 109
   feudalism, 17
   Geraldine links, 102
   German occupation, 193
   Irish colleges, 87
   and Italy, 63
   military service, 22
   revolutionary movements, 303, 313
      1870, 307
      July Days, 1830, 303, 305, 307, 308, 310, 312, 314
      June Days, 1848, 301, 303, 305, 307, 313, 314
         Blanqui's description, 309–11
      May 1968 and symbolic violence, 299–314
   and Treaty of Dingle, 110
Francis I, king of France, 102, 109
Franciscans, 40, 43, 100
Franz-Josef, emperor, 98
Frederick I, Barbarossa, emperor, 56, 58, 59–60, 62, 63, 64, 66–7
   strengthening royal powers, 69–70

Index

Frederick II, emperor, 69
French Revolution, 1789, 62, 156, 306, 314, 357
  links with May 1968, 300
  violence of, 307–8
Fuhr, Eckhard, 356–7
fyrd, institution of, 21–2

Gaelic Ireland
  in arts, 274
  education, 253
  law, 271
  and Reformation, 88–9, 89
  Spanish links, 101
Gaelic League, 319
Galway, County, 105, 127, 321–2
Garnish Island, 329
Garraty, John, see *American National Biography*
Garrett, George, 198, 200–1, 202
Gascony, 37, 38, 45, 46, 49
Gauweiler, Peter, 350–1
Gaveston, Piers, 41, 44, 49–50, 52
General Agreement on Tariffs and Trade (GATT), 228
Genoa, 59, 107, 109
geography
  atlas survey, 260
  early medieval, 239–40
geological surveys, 261
Germany, 189, 321
  de Valera's condolences to, 197
  emigration to Canada, 174
  and Italy, 63, 68
  politics of history, 336–58
  Reformation, 84, 85, 88–9
  unification of, 211, 339
  Wehrmacht exhibition, 336–58, 337–8
Gesta Edwardi de Carnarvon, 41–2, 49
Gestapo, 338
Ghinucci, bishop of Worcester, 107
Giant's Causeway, 259
Gilchrist, Andrew, 225, 229
Giraldus Cambrensis, 262, 270, 277
  Expugnatio Hibernica, 271–2, 273, 275, 277
Gladstone, William E., 15, 287
Glazunov, Ilya, 388
Glendalough, County Wicklow, 318, 319
Glenveagh, County Donegal, 317
Glinka, M. I., 392
Glorious Revolution, 134
Gloucester, earl of, 42, 44
Gloucester Abbey, 48
Gloucester Cathedral, 285
Goldhagen thesis, 337, 344–5, 351, 353
Gorbachev, president, 369, 371, 379, 381
Gordon, General Charles 'Chinese', 289–90

Government of Ireland Act, 1920, 190
Grachev, Pavel, 382–3
Grandes chroniques, 38
Grass, Günter, 336, 357
Gray, David, 193–4
Great Blasket National Park, 332
Great Famine, 320
Green, Alice Stopford, 30
Green Party, 346, 347, 348, 350, 353
Gregory IX, pope, 69
Grekov War Artists' Studio, 382
Grey, Lord Edward, 189–90
Griffith, Arthur, 323
Guimera, Augustin, 99
Guinness family, 325, 326

Hackett, Felix, 330
Halifax, N.S., 164, 166, 167
Hamburg Institute for Social Research, 337, 342, 346, 354, 355
Handel, G. F., 293
Hanmer, Meredith, 275, 277
Habsburg monarchy
  role of Irish, 99–102
  Treaty of Dingle, 102–11
Harold II, king, 22
Harris, Walter, 262, 272
Hartlib, Samuel, 258–9, 260
Hastings, battle of, 14–15, 22, 23, 25
Haughey, Charles, 25, 227, 229, 331
Haverkamp, Alfred, 67
Heath, Edward, 233
Heer, Hannes, 341, 342, 349, 355, 356
Henry, Paul, 316–17
Henry I, king of England, 19, 20, 24, 25, 271
Henry II, king of England, 24, 42, 46, 108, 253, 270, 271, 277
  and Strongbow, 274
Henry III, king of England, 39
Henry III, king of France, 49
Henry VIII, king of England, 52, 109
  Desmond alliance against, 102, 103, 104–5, 107, 110
  raises Ireland to kingdom status, 110
  recognises FitzThomas-FitzGerald, 110
  seen as schismatic, 108
Hereford, bishop of, 47
Hereford Cathedral, 20
Herly, Maurice, dean of Ardfert, 106
Higden, Ranulf, 39–40, 42, 47, 49
Hillery, Patrick, 205–7
Hincks, Francis, 165, 169
Hiroshima, 342
Histoire des républiques italiennes (Sismondi), 62–3

410

Index

Historiae Catholicae Iberniae compendium
    (O'Sullivan Beare), 89
historiography
    Anglo-Norman Conquest (Ireland), 25–32
    Catholic, 288
    Edward II, 37–52
    French revolutionary tradition, 302
    Lombard league, 60–5
        20th c., 67–70
    Norman Conquest (England), 12–25
    post-war Germany, 336–58
Hitler, Adolf, 197, 355, 357, 380
Holcot, Robert, 45, 48
Holinshed, Raphael, 49–50
Holy Land, 46, 47
Home Rule, 185, 190
homosexuality
    Casement, 187
    Edward II, 49–50, 51, 52
Hooker, John, 273
Howard, Sir Robert, 50
Hubert, Sir Francis, 50
Hull, Cordell, 192
Hume, David, 288
Hume, John, 207
Hungary, 82, 83, 84, 87, 89
    Irish in, 99
    Jesuit mission, 78–81
hunger-strikes, 1981, 209
Hurd, Douglas, 211, 221
Huxley, Aldous, 11
Hymns ancient and modern, 292

Iceland, 200, 239
iconoclasm, Russian, 368–73
Im Krebsgang (Grass), 336
Immram Brain mac Febail, 241, 248
Immram Curaig Maíle Dúin, see *Voyage of Máel Dúin, The*
immrama, 239–40
Innocent III, pope, 68
Innocent IV, pope, 69
Inter-Party government, 1948, 198, 322
Irish colleges abroad, 90, 99–100
    graduates of, 87–8
    role of, 100
Irish Convention, 188
Irish Free State, 191, 316, 317
Irish Land Commission, 322
Irish language, 317, 318, 319
Irish Republican Army (IRA), 208, 209, 211
Irish Servant Act, Pennsylvania, 1729, 138
Irish Times, The, 226, 227, 231–2, 327
Irish Tourist Board (Bord Fáilte), 328, 329, 330
Isabella, queen consort, 37, 39, 45

Isabella II, queen of Spain, 97
Italy, 48, 52, 102, 103, 109, 203
    clerics in Kenmare, 81–2
    Lombard League, 55–70
    national anthem, 65
    nationalism, 62–7
    unification of, 56, 66–7

Jackson, Andrew, 167
James I, king of Scotland, 45
James II, king of England, 50, 119, 123, 125, 135
    exile, 125–8
Jesuit order, 78–9, 119, 288
    in America, 135, 136
    missions, 84, 87
Jews
    deportations, 340
    Holocaust, 337, 345
    post-war reparations, 337
John of Bridlington, 42
John of London, 37, 38
John of Powderham, 45
John XXII, pope, 47, 48
Johnson, Job, 139, 140, 142, 143
Johnson, President Lyndon, 204
Johnson, Sir William, 164

Kavanagh, Patrick, 324
Keble, John, 287
Kenilworth Castle, 43
Kenmare, County Kerry, 82, 317, 332
    sale of estate, 329–31
Kennedy, President John Fitzgerald, 204
Kennedy, Senator Edward, 207, 209
Kerbel, Lev, 372–3, 382
Kerens, Richard, 167, 173
Khartoum, battle of, 289–90
Kildare–Geraldine rebellion, 1534-5, 110
Kilkenny, 174
    annals, 274
Killarney, County Kerry, 317, 323
    Kenmare estate, 329–31
    national park, 325–7, 331–2
Killarney Tourist Association, 328
Killarney Tourist Development Council, 329, 330
King, William, bishop of Derry, 118, 119
Kingsley, Charles, 289
Kinsella, Thomas, 170
Klykov, Vyacheslav, 379
knight service, see military service
Knights Hospitaller of St John, 103
Kohl, Helmut, 339
Kremlin, 378, 385, 391
Kutuzov, M. I., 384

Index

Labour Party, UK, 213, 294
Lalor, Alice, 174, 175
Lancaster, Thomas, earl of, 41, 44, 45, 47, 51
   cult of, 47, 49
land ownership, 141, 324–5
   Free State ideals, 321–2
   Restoration acts
      changes sought, 121–6
      repealed, 126
      Tyrconnell plans, 121–4
      Williamite settlement, 134, 141
Land Project, 322
land reclamation, 322–3
Landriano, battle of, 109
Lanercost Friary, 40, 43
Langton, Walter, bishop of Coventry and Lichfield, 37–8
language, role in Counter-Reformation, 80, 84–5
Laudabiliter (papal bull), 108
le Baker, Geoffrey, 41, 47, 48
Leake, Treaty of, 1318, 45
learned societies, 1680–1785, 253–67
Ledwidge, Bernard, 228
Lee, Edward, 105, 107
Leeds Festival, 291
legal profession, regulation of, 253
Legge, Walter, 293
Legnano, battle of, 56, 61, 63
   commemorations of, 65–7
   700th anniversary, 65, 67
Leland, Thomas, 273, 274, 277
Lemass, Seán, 222–3, 224
Lend Lease, 193
Lenin, V. I., 368–9, 370, 377, 379, 382, 393
   mausoleum of, 373–7, 385
   monuments, 371–3, 387
Leningrad, 368, 382
Leyden medical school, 255–6, 257, 265
Liber de mensura orbis terrae (Dicuill), 239
Lillis, Michael, 207–8
Limerick, 97, 143, 146
   siege of, 127
Linen Act, 1705, 145
linen industry, 145–6
Lloyd George, David, 186–7, 188, 190
Locke, John, 258, 260
Lodi, 59, 63, 69
Logan, James, 136, 139, 140
Lombard league, 55–70
   in literature and art, 64–6
   medieval sources, 57, 58–61
   modern version, 68–70
   myths, 61–5
   20th c. writings, 67–70

London, 133
   Blitz, 282–3, 293
Longford, Lord, 123
Loreto, Sisters of, 173, 174–5
Lorraine, duchy of, 97
Lothian, Lord, 193
Louis XIV, king, 126, 127
Lovett, Albert, 1–4, 5–7, 155, 175
Lucas, Charles, 257–8
Lutheranism, 85, 88–9
Luzhkov, Yuri, 375, 379, 380, 382, 395, 396
   architectural restoration, 384–6
   cathedral rebuilding, 387–8, 390
Lynch, Jack, 206, 207
   and EEC entry, 228
   associate membership, 229–32
   British co-operation, 224, 225–7
Lysaght, Seán, 319

Maastricht Treaty, 97
Mac Murchada, Conchobar, 276, 277
mac Murchada, Diarmuid, 270–1
Macaulay, T. B., 98
MacBride, Seán, 198, 200–1, 201–2
   US defence treaty, 203–4
McCann, Hugh, 205, 225, 228, 230
MacCarthy, Major-General Justin, 121
MacCarthys of Muskerry, 89, 108
McGregor, Revd James, 148
Maclise, Daniel
   Marriage of Strongbow and Aoife, 270–8
Macmillan, Harold, 204
MacNeill, Eoin, 30–1
Madden, Samuel 'Premium', 261
Máel Dúin, *see Voyage of Máel Dúin, The*
Mafeking, relief of, 291
Maffey, John (Lord Rugby), 194, 195–6, 197, 198
Maguire, Archbishop Dominic, 121
Major, John, 211, 212
Malachy, Fr, OFM, 43
Mamiani, Terenzio, 64–5
Maritime provinces, 158, 169, 174
Marlborough, duke of, 50
Marlowe, Christopher, 50, 51, 52
Marriage of Strongbow and Aoife, The (Maclise), 270–8
Marshall, George C., 198–9
Marshall Plan, 199, 222
Marsh's Library, Dublin, 262
Marx, Karl, 311, 370, 373
Mary I, queen of England, 110
Maryland, 135, 144, 148
   advertisement for, 139

412

Catholics in, 136
emigration to, 147–8
immigration law, 134, 137–8
Massachusetts, 134, 135, 137, 148
medical education, 254–8
continental, 255–6
and learned societies, 254, 256, 258–67
Medico-Philosophical Society, 264–6, 266, 267
Merlin, prophecies of, 41, 42, 277
Mervyn, Sir Audley, 118, 128
Messerschmidt, Manfred, 339, 355
Milan, 58, 59, 60, 62–3, 65, 69
duchy of, 102
Military History Research Bureau, Germany, 343, 344
military service, 12, 27–8
Irish in Europe, 98–9
role in feudalism, 12–18, 17–18, 23–4
sources for, 18–21
system of, 21–5
Mill, John Stuart, 288
Millar, Frederick Hoyer, 199–200
Milton, John, 289
Mitterand, François, 299, 349
Molyneux, Samuel, 258, 259
Molyneux, Thomas, 255, 257, 259, 261
Molyneux, William, 258, 259, 260, 262
Monnet, Jean, 232
Montreal, 166, 172
Moore, Thomas, 273
Moscow, 393
architectural restoration, 384–91
architecture and ideology, 363–96
cathedral of Christ the Saviour, 363, 386–91, 395,
Lenin mausoleum, 373–7
monuments, 371–3, 379–80
placename changes, 369–71
Poklonnaya Gora, 380–4
Mourne, Mountains of, 330
mouvement de mai
Aron's analysis of, 303–7
media environment, 313–14
use of barricades, 305–7
Moynihan, Pat, 207
Muckross House, 327–9, 331
Munich
Wehrmacht exhibition, 337, 340, 342, 346–7, 348–53
Munster
county studies, 264
emigration from, 146–7
plantation, 132, 133
Musial, Bogdan, 337, 344, 353–5, 356, 358

Naas, County Kildare, 174
Nagle, James, 119, 126
Nagle, Sir Richard
attorney general, 124, 126
career of, 118–28
Coventry letter, 123–4, 126
in exile, 127–8
military adviser, 126–7
political involvement, 119–20
Speaker of parliament, 126
and William of Orange, 125–6
Napoleon Bonaparte, 62, 364, 386, 389
national monuments, 318–19
National Monuments Act, 1930, 318–19
National Museum, Dublin, 324, 327
National Park and Access to the Countryside Act, 1949, UK, 330
national parks, 320, 325–7, 331
National Security Council (NSC), 199, 204, 209, 212
National Trust, 325
nationalism
and emigration, 321
and feudalism, 30–1
in Italy, 62–7
and landscape, 316–32
and Lombard league, 68–70
in modern Ireland, 316–32
in North America, 174
in Russia, 363–8
natural history, 265, 266, 327
learned societies, 261–5
nature
and nationalism, 316–32
nature study, 259–60, 266–7, 319–20
Nauigatio Sancti Brendani Abbatis, 240, 241, 245, 246, 248
Navigation Acts, 136, 138, 145
neo-guelphism, 63–4
Neumann, Bernd, 345, 348
Neumeyer, Ronald Mike, 345, 346–7
neutrality, 193, 222
US response to, 192, 193–8
New England, 135, 136, 139, 148
New English, 108, 119
scientific learning, 253–4
New Ireland Forum, 209, 210
New York, 136, 142, 148, 156, 164, 167, 186, 355, 387
education, 172
emigration to, 138, 147, 148
industrial development, 166
linen imports, 145
penal laws, 134–5

Index

New York, *cont.*
   servants' laws, 139–40
   Twin Towers attack, 9.11.01, 213
Newfoundland, 136, 147, 162, 169, 172
Newgrange, County Louth, 319
Newman, John H., cardinal
   Dream of Gerontius, 283, 285–90
Nicholas I, tsar, 364, 365, 386, 392
Nicholas II, tsar, 375
   canonisation, 363
   monument, 379
   reburial, 394–5
Nicholas of Wisbech, 47
Nixon, Richard, 204–5, 206, 207
Nolte, Ernst, 339
NORAID, 208
Norman Conquest, 1066, historiography of, 12–25
North Atlantic Treaty Organisation (NATO), 198, 222, 395
   approach to Ireland, 199–201
   Ireland refuses invitation, 203–4
   in NI, 200–1, 203, 211
Northern Ireland, 185, 186, 191, 330
   and Anglo-American alliance, 204–13
   attitude of US State Department, 204–7
   Carter initiative, 207–10
   Catholics in, 198
   landscape, 316
   and NATO, 200–1, 203, 211
   US naval bases, 194
   US troops in, 194
Norway, 84, 86, 193, 200, 203
Nova Scotia, 135, 163, 164, 165
Nugent, chief justice, 125
Nugent, Honora, 119
Nugent, John, 170
Nugent, Thomas, 124
Nuremberg Tribunal, 338, 344

Ó Bruadair, Dáibhidh, 124
Ó Conchobair, Ruaidhrí, 274, 276, 277
Ó Corráin, Donnchadh, 31
Ó hEideáin, Seán, 205
O'Brien, Conor Cruise, 126
O'Callaghan, Edmund Bailey, 156
O'Connell, Malachy, 82
O'Connell, Maurice, 82
O'Connell, Richard, 82–3
O'Connor, Charles, 271, 274
O'Donnell, Red Hugh, 110
Office of Public Works, 317, 328, 331–2
O'Flaherty, Roderick, 260
O'Halloran, Sylvester, 257, 258
Óige, An, 327

O'Kelly, Seán T., 197
Old English, 108, 119, 253, 260
   Counter-Reformation, 88–9
O'Neill, Hugh, 88, 110
O'Neill, Tip, 204–5, 207, 208, 209, 210
Ontario, 158, 162, 164, 174
   education, 172, 173, 174–5
   press, 169
Operation Barbarossa, 357
Orange order, 165, 169, 188
Ordinances, 1311, 51
Organisation for European Economic Co-operation, 222, 223
Orleton, Adam, bishop of Winchester, 43
Ormond, duke of, 123
O'Roddy, Teigue, 260
Orpen, Goddard Henry, 25, 27, 30
Ossory, diocese of, 83–4
O'Sullivan Beare, Count Dermot, 99
O'Sullivan Beare, Philip, 89
O'Sullivan Beare family, 105
Otto, bishop of Freising, 59, 61, 69
Oxford Movement, 286–7, 287
Oxford University, 40, 42, 44, 45
   Edward II's foundations, 50

Padania, 56, 70
Page, Walter H., 187, 188
Pamyat', 379
papacy, 110
   Avignon, 48
   Desmond appeal to, 108
   Edward II prophecy, 46
   imperial alliance, 103
   league of Cognac, 107
   and Lombard league, 68, 69
   role in Italy, 63–4
Paris
   mouvement de mai, 1968, 299–314
   peace conference, 1919, 189
   use of barricades, 306–10
Paris Commune, 1871, 301, 303, 305, 307, 314
   use of violence, 313
Paris, Matthew, 19, 38
Parke, Robert, 142, 143
parliament, Irish, 11, 126, 260, 266
   lawyers in, 118
   Nagle as Speaker, 126
   and Restoration land acts, 124–6
   Tyrconnell plans, 121–4
partition (of Ireland)
   and NATO, 200–1
   US attitude to, 191–2, 195, 198, 199
Paul IV, pope, 110
Paul the Hermit, 246

Index

Pavia, 59, 63, 69
Pearse, Patrick, 325
penal laws, 134–6, 139, 144
   medical education, 254–5
Penn, William, 136, 139
Pennsylvania, 135, 144, 148, 167
   Convict Act, 138
   emigration encouraged, 140, 142
   servants' protection, 139–40
Peter the Great, 366, 367, 375, 380
Peterborough Cathedral, 292
Petersburg, St, 363, 366–8, 394
Petty, Sir William, 123, 124, 258, 264, 266
Philadelphia, 147, 148, 156, 167, 174
   Catholics in, 136
   emigration to, 147
   industrial development, 166
   linen imports, 145, 146
Philip II, king of Spain, 100, 110
Philip III, king of Spain, 100, 101, 110
Philip IV, king of France, 37
Philip IV, king of Spain, 99
Philip the Good, duke of Burgundy, 98
Philip V, king of Spain, 110–11
Philippa, queen consort, 48
Physico-Historical Society, 261–4, 267
Pius IX, pope, 64
plantations, 132–4
Plowden, Francis, 127
Podiuk, Hans, 349–50, 351
Poem on the evil times of Edward II, 44
politics
   of German history, 336–58
   Irish in North America, 167–9
Polychronicon (Higden), 39–40, 42, 47
Pompidou, Georges, 299
Pontida, congress of, 60–1, 70
   oaths of, 63, 65
population decline, 320, 321–2
Porter, Sir Charles, lord chancellor, 121, 122
Praeger, Robert Lloyd, 319, 325
Presbyterians, 188
   emigration from Ulster, 148–9
   emigration to North America, 140, 143–4, 159, 172
   Ulster plantation, 133–4
Propaganda Fide, 81–2
Proske, Rüdiger, 350, 354
Protestants, in Ireland
   ascendancy established, 134
   difficulties, 88–9
   economic literature, 260–1
   natural history project, 259–60
   and scientific learning, 254, 256–7, 258–9, 319
   and Tyrconnell viceroyalty, 124

Protestants, in North America, 167, 172–3
Proudhon, P. P., 303, 307
public service
   in Canada, 164–5
   Irish in USA, 165–6
Public Worship Regulation Act, 1874, 287
Putin, President Vladimir, 363, 378, 383–4
   and Lenin mausoleum, 376–7
   national anthem, 392–3
   succeeds Yeltsin, 395–6

Quakers, 135, 142, 144, 266
Quebec, 162, 163, 164–5, 166, 169
   disunionist, 174
   education, 172
Quebec Act, 164
Queen's Hall, London, 282–3, 293
Queenstown (Cobh), County Cork, 189, 193

Reagan, President Ronald, 209–10
rebellion
   1534–5, 110
   1641, 83
Red Army, 338, 348
   Commissar order, 339, 341
Reemtsma, Jan Philipp, 337, 341, 342–3, 346, 348, 349, 354, 357
   second exhibition, 356
   withdraws exhibition, 355
Reformation, 78, 108
   in Ireland, 83–5, 88–9
Republic of Ireland
   declared, 200
   and EEC application, 221–33
      associate membership possible, 227–33
   inauguration of, 202
Republic of Ireland Act, 1948, 185, 198, 200
Republican Party, USA, 156, 167, 211
republicanism, Italy, 62–7
Restoration, 119
   land acts, 121–4, 124–6
   land acts repealed, 126
revolutionary tradition, French
   definitions of revolution, 302–3
   links with 1968, 300–14
   media environment, 313–14
   role of barricades, 308–10
   role of troops, 311–12
   role of violence, 313
Reynolds, Walter, archbishop of Canterbury, 42–3
Rice, Sir Stephen, 124, 125
Richard II, king of England, 48–9, 50
Richardson, H. G., 18, 20
Richter, Hans, 283

Ringstead, Thomas, bishop of Bangor, 48
Robert, king of Scotland, 38
Robert of Newington, 42
Robert of Reading, 39
Roberts, Alice, 286, 290
Robinson, William Erigena, 170
Rogers, William, US Secretary of State, 205–7
Romanov, Prince Nikolai, 394
romanticism, 317, 322
Rome, 86, 108
    Irish colleges, 87
    and Lombard league, 69
Roosevelt, Eleanor, 193, 198
Roosevelt, President Franklin D., 161, 192, 193, 196, 197, 199
    on Irish neutrality, 194
Roosevelt, President Theodore, 185
Roscommon, County, 140, 321–2
Round, John Horace, 25, 27, 28
    historiography of Norman Conquest, 12–18
    sources used by, 18–21
Royal Choral Society, 282, 293
Royal College of Physicians, 255
Royal Dublin Society, 267
Royal Irish Academy, 267, 317–18
Royal Society, 258
    journal, 264–5
Ruskin, John, 295
Russborough House, 318–19, 325, 326
Russell, Peter, 164, 165
Russia, *see also* Moscow
    architectural restoration, 384–91
    hostility to West, 365–6
    iconoclasm, 368–73
    Lenin mausoleum, 373–7
    monumentalism, 377–84
    national anthem, 392–3
    reburial of royal family, 393–4
    Revolution, 1917, 306
    ritual and ceremonial, 391–5
    'Russian Idea', 364–8
Russian Orthodox Church, 375–6, 379, 382, 384, 385
    reburial of royal family, 393–4
Rutty, John, 257, 262, 263, 264, 265–6

Sachsenhausen concentration camp, 340
St Albans Abbey, 48
    chronicle of, 38, 49
St Enda's School, 325
St George's Church, Worcester, 286, 290, 292
St Giacomo Maggiore, monastery of, 60–1
St Mary's university church, Oxford, 286–7
St Peter's Abbey, Gloucester, 39
St Werburgh's Abbey, Chester, 39–40

Sargent, Dr Malcolm, 282, 283, 292–3
Schumann, Robert, 232
Scotichronicon (Bower), 44, 45
Scotland, 37, 38, 46, 84, 86, 157, 317
    continental colleges for, 100
    defeat of Edward II, 38, 40, 42
    emigrants, 161, 174
    in Ireland, 133–4, 156
    itinerant preachers, 43
Seanad Éireann, 318
Second World War, 194, 222, 372
    effects of, 294
    German historiography, 336–58
    Ireland and Anglo-American alliance, 191–8
    London blitz, 282–3, 293
    Russian commemorations, 379, 380–4
Seitz, Raymond, 211, 212
Settlement and Explanation, acts of, 121–4
Seven Years' War, 146, 163
Sforza, Francesco, duke of Milan, 109
Sheridan, Thomas, 124, 125, 127
Sinn Féin, 186, 211, 323
    Adams US visa, 212
    German plot, 189
Sismondi, J.-C. L. S. de, 62–3
slavery, 23, 141, 168
    America, 147
    wartime Germany, 337, 340
Smith, Charles, 262, 263–4, 265
Smith, Jean Kennedy, 212
Smith, Sir Thomas, 132
Smuts, Jan Christian, 193
Snelling, Sir Arthur, 228–9
Social Democratic and Labour Party (SDLP), 207
Socialist Party (PSI), Italy, 55
Soderberg, Nancy, 212
Soloukhin, Vladimir, 387
Solovetsky Islands, 377
Sommer, Theo, 341
Song of Dermot and the Earl, 272, 273, 275, 277
Sorbonne, University of, 303, 307
    occupation of, 299, 300
Southwell, Sir Robert, 123
Soviet Union, 203, *see also* Russia
    collapse of, 185
    place names, 368–70
    post-war German attitudes to, 338, 339, 340
Spain, 88, 136, 155, 198, 203
    Irish citizenship rights, 100–1, 102
    Irish colleges, 86, 87, 100
    Irish links, 101
    Irish privileges in, 110–11
    positions of Irish in, 97, 98–9
    Treaty of Dingle, 102–11

Index

SPD, Germany, 336, 337
   and *Wehrmacht* exhibition, 345–8, 348–50, 352–3
Spring-Rice, Cecil, 186, 187–8
SS, 338, 345, 355
Stalin, Joseph, 369–70, 374, 378, 387, 390, 392, 393
   monument, 384
Stalingrad, battle of, 343, 382
Stamford Bridge, battle of, 22
Stanford, Charles Villiers, 284
State Department, US, 197–8, 212
   attitude to neutrality, 192, 196–7
   attitude to partition, 192, 199
   'British School', 199–203
   legation in Republic, 202
   NATO invitation, 200–1
   and NI, 204–7, 209
Statute of York, 1322, 51
Stenton, Frank Merry, 12, 16, 17
Stephen, king, 23–4
Stephens, William, 257, 261
Stockley, W. C., 283, 284–5
Stoiber, Edmund, 348, 351
Strachey, Lytton, 285–6
Stratford, John, archbishop of Canterbury, 41
Stratford, John, bishop of London, 43
Strauss, Richard, 284
Strongbow
   alliance with Murchada, 270–1
   death of, 276
Stubbs, Bishop William, 18, 51
Sunderland, earl of, 120, 121, 123, 124
Surrender and Regrant, 88
Sweden, 203, 321
Sydney, Viscount, 127
Synge, Edward, archbishop of Tuam, 133, 134

Taisce, An, 325, 329, 330
Talbot, George, 140
Talbot, John, 169
Talbot, Richard, earl of Tyrconnell, *see* Tyrconnell, earl of
tangentopoli, 55–6
Tara, County Meath, 318
taxation
   cess, 88, 89
   and military levies, 23–4
Temple, Sir John, 122
Temple, William, archbishop of Canterbury, 294
Tennyson, Alfred Lord, 289
Thatcher, Margaret, 209–10
Thomas of Otterbourne, 40
Thompson, Edward, 302

Thompson, R. Ellis, 167, 170
Thomson, George, 233
Thoreau, Henry David, 317
Tipperary, County, 119, 264
Tochmarc Becfhola, 244
Tocqueville, Alexis de, 173, 175, 307
   Souvenirs, 303
Toleration Act, Maryland, 1649, 135
Tollymore Forest Park, 330
Ton, Konstantin, 386, 391
Toronto, 166, 167, 172
Tory Island, 242, 246
Toscanini, Arturo, 293
tourism, 328–9
Tout, T. F., 51
Tranchell, Peter, 52
Transportation Act, 1717, 137, 138
Treaty of Rome, 222, 228
Treaty ports, 193, 194
Trinity College, Dublin, 87, 253, 260, 261, 263, 284
   historiography, 28
   medical education, 255, 256, 258
   Ulster plantation, 133
Trotsky, Leon, 311–12
Truman, President Harry, 196–8, 199, 204
Tsereteli, Zurab, 379, 380, 381, 382, 384, 388, 393
Turkey, 84, 87, 89, 103, 198
   in Hungary, 78–81
   threatens Vienna, 109
Tyrconnell, earl of, 126, 127
   and Nagle, 120–4
   viceroy, 124–5

Ude, Christian, 348, 351–2, 353
Ulster, 166
   devolved parliament, 1920, 190
   emigration from, 146, 147, 148–9
   plantation, 133–4
   Presbyterian emigration encouraged, 140, 143–4
   religious distribution, 320
Ungváry, Krisztián, 344, 353–4, 355, 358
Unionists, 186–7, 188, 316
   parliamentary influence, 209
United Nations, 196, 205, 206
United States of America, 158, 316
   compared with Canada, 157–8
   emigration to, 160–1, 321, 324
   enters First World War, 189
   enters Second World War, 194
   industrial development, 166–7, 173
   Ireland and the Anglo-American alliance, 185–213

United States of America, *cont.*
   and Irish attitude to NATO, 203-3
   Irish elites in, 165-6
      education, 172-3, 174
      industry, 166-7, 173
      journalism, 169-70, 173
      law, 170-1
      politics, 167-9, 173
   national parks, 328
   nature and nationalism, 318
Urban IV, pope, 69
Urban VI, pope, 49
urbanisation, 89, 331
   Anglo-Norman, 28-30

Valladolid, 105, 107
Vance, Cyrus, 208
Venetian Republic, 102, 107
Verdi, Giuseppe, 65-6
Verses of Gildas, 46, 47
Vikings, 26, 32, 248
Vincent, Arthur, 325, 327-8
Vita Columbae (Adomnán), 240
Vita Edwardi secundi, 41, 43
Vita et mors Edwardi secundi, 41
Vitalis, Orderic, 18, 19
Voyage of Mael Duin, The, 239-49
   audience, 248
   author, 247-9
   Christian communities, 243-4, 245, 246-7
   framing tale, 242-3
   hermit, 242, 246-7

Wagner, Richard, 283
Wales, 37, 43, 84
Walker, Patrick Gordon, 201
Walsh, Thomas, archbishop of Cashel, 85
Walshe, Joe, 195, 196
Walsingham, Thomas, 49
Warnock, William, 204
Waterford, 32, 146, 169
   siege of, 270, 273, 277
Waterford, County, 119, 263
Wehrmacht exhibition, 337-8, 340
   myth of *Wehrmacht*, 339-40
   opening of, 341-2
   photographs discredited, 354-5
   reactions to, 342-4
   second, 356-7
   withdrawn, 355-6
West, Richard, lord chancellor, 137
West Indies, 136, 137, 146
Western European Union, 225-6
Westminster Abbey, 38-9
Wette, Wolfram, 343, 344
Wexford, County, 27, 189, 322
Whiddy Island, 189
Whitaker, T. K., 222-3, 224, 227, 228-9, 231
'Wild Geese', 98-9
Wilde, Sir William, 256
Willcocks, Joseph, 165, 169
William, king of Scotland, 18-19
William III, of Orange, king of England, 126, 127, 135
William of Pagula, 44
William Rufus, king of England, 24
William the Conqueror, 13, 24, 27
   Evesham writ, 19-21
Wilson, Harold
   and associate EEC membership, 228-33
   EEC application, 221-2, 224, 225-7
Wilson, President Woodrow, 187-8, 189
Winchelsey, Robert, archbishop of Canterbury, 42
Winkler, Heinrich August, 339-40
Wolfe Tone, Theobald, 318
Wolffsohn, Michael, 355-6
Wolsey, Thomas, cardinal, 105, 107, 110
Wood, Henry, 292
Worcester Cathedral, 285, 286
Wulfstan, Bishop, 23
Wyndham, Thomas, 141

Yekaterinburg, 368, 393
Yeltsin, President Boris, 363, 374-9, 382
   architectural restoration, 384-5
   cathedral rebuilding, 387, 389-90
   decline of power, 380-1
   reburial of royal family, 393-4
   resignation, 395-6

Zehetmair, Hans, 352-3
Złoczów murders, 354-5